Major Problems in the History
of the American South

MAJOR PROBLEMS IN AMERICAN HISTORY SERIES

GENERAL EDITOR
THOMAS G. PATERSON

Major Problems
in the History
of the American South
Volume II: The New South

DOCUMENTS AND ESSAYS

EDITED BY
PAUL D. ESCOTT
WAKE FOREST UNIVERSITY

DAVID R. GOLDFIELD
UNIVERSITY OF NORTH CAROLINA, CHARLOTTE

D. C. HEATH AND COMPANY
Lexington, Massachusetts   Toronto

For Lauren and David
and
Eleanor and Erik

Cover: *Saturday Morning* by J. Kelly Fitzpatrick
Montgomery Museum of Fine Arts

Published simultaneously in Canada.

Printed in the United States of America.

International Standard Book Number: 0-669-19924-9

Library of Congress Catalog Card Number: 89-85075

10 9 8 7 6 5 4 3 2 1

Preface

Historian David M. Potter has written that the South has been "a kind of Sphinx on the American land." Nothing in the two volumes of *Major Problems in the History of the American South* will challenge that description of a great American enigma. We hope, though, that readers will become more enlightened by these volumes' documents and essays as they search to know what the South was and is. If nothing else, southern history and southern historiography teach humility. The South, less a geographical region than a state of mind, is a fickle place, and writers have grasped it about as well as they might a greased pig. But for all who have endeavored to unlock its essence, the fun has been in the hunt and in the insights that come from what English professor Fred Hobson has called "the southern rage to explain." The selections in this book, like those in the other volumes of D. C. Heath's Major Problems in American History Series, are intended to interest readers in that quest to explain.

In this second volume, we begin the hunt by offering a small sampling of what others—with no agreement, of course—have described as distinctive about the South. In subsequent chapters, we take the reader on a basically chronological tour through southern history from the dislocations of Reconstruction to the soaring towers and sprawling shopping malls of the Sunbelt South. We have selected documents that evoke the atmosphere of the times as well as inform readers of the major issues that southerners have confronted. In choosing the essays, we have attempted to strike a balance between the classic literature and the exciting scholarship on the South published during the past decade. We have avoided any particular ideological bent and have tried to present both sides of a story—a difficult task, because most southern stories have too many sides to count. Most of all, we want readers to reach their own conclusions about the major interpretive problems in southern history. Chapter introductions, as well as headnotes to the documents and essays, help set the questions in historical and interpretive perspective. Since so much fine work has focused on the South (as the lists of books and articles for further reading at the end of each chapter attest), it is inevitable that we have omitted someone's favorite essay or document. We will be happy to redress grievances in future editions. Please let us know your preferences.

Numerous friends and colleagues contributed to the two volumes. Early on, we polled some southern historians on the essays and documents that they believed ought to appear here. Their replies were helpful and heartening. We particularly want to note the insights of Edward L. Ayers, Paul H. Bergeron, David L. Carlton, Michael B. Chesson, Janet L. Coryell, Mary A. DeCredico, John Duffy, Raymond Gavins, Jack Temple Kirby,

William Link, Melton McLaurin, James Tice Moore, Theda Perdue, Lawrence N. Powell, James M. Russell, Edward M. Steel, Jr., Thad Tate, William Bruce Wheeler, and Jon Wiener. Detailed and extremely helpful written reviews of draft tables of contents were provided by Edward L. Ayers, F. N. Boney, Robert F. Martin, Mary Beth Norton, Lawrence N. Powell, Howard N. Rabinowitz, and Terry L. Seip. Becky Bell of the Country Music Foundation, David E. Alsobrook of the Jimmy Carter Library, Cheryl Roberts of the Urban Institute at the University of North Carolina, Charlotte, and the staffs at Atlanta mayor Andrew Young's office and the Lyndon B. Johnson Library in Austin, Texas, were especially helpful in gathering documents for us. Barbara Lisenby and her interlibrary loan staff at the University of North Carolina, Charlotte, and Carrie Thomas of the Z. Smith Reynolds Library at Wake Forest University relentlessly tracked down both primary-source documents and essays. Finally, we were fortunate to work with a professional and congenial group at D. C. Heath, particularly Sylvia Mallory, James Miller, Cathy Labresh Brooks, and Margaret Roll. Thomas G. Paterson, the editor of the Major Problems in American History Series, provided timely assistance and encouragement.

As in all of our work, the patience and support of our families have been most important. We dedicate this book to our children, who are enjoying the benefits of growing up in the South.

P. E.

D. G.

Contents

CHAPTER 3
Myths and Realities of the New South
Page 70

CHAPTER 4
Land and Labor in the New South
Page 102

CHAPTER 5
Populism
Page 129

C H A P T E R 6
Segregation and Disfranchisement
Page 161

C H A P T E R 7
Progressivism
Page 204

CHAPTER 8
The Religious South
Page 277

CHAPTER 9
New Realism in Southern Culture
Page 322

CHAPTER 10
The New Deal
Page 378

CHAPTER 11
The South and the Second World War
Page 412

C H A P T E R 14
Race and Politics in the Recent South
Page 608

C H A P T E R 15
An Enduring Culture?
Page 652

CHAPTER
1

What Is the South?

Historian Michael O'Brien noted that "no man's South is the same as another's." Although there is general agreement that the South is (or at least was, at some time) distinctive from other parts of the United States, there is no consensus on either the nature or the duration of that difference. Definitions of the South have stressed everything from the obvious (for example, climate and white supremacy) to the obscure (the line below which grits replace hash browns).

Part of the problem is that there are many Souths. The folks who lived in the South Carolina lowcountry were very different in terms of ethnicity, accent, ideology, occupation, religion, music, and language from the people of the southern Appalachians. There are distinctions within states—lowcountry versus upcountry, piedmont versus coastal plain, and delta versus piney woods. These disparities have led some to contend that the South is more a state of mind than a geography.

Yet some thing or things draw these disparate areas together, and observers since the first settlements have tried to identify what, in fact, constitutes "the South." The task is more than a mere intellectual exercise. As with the study of any ethnic group, distinction helps to define identity. And the study of the South has helped to define our national identity as well. The South has often served as a counterpoint, both good and bad, to the rest of the country. In learning what is special about the South and how it became that way, we are learning about our national culture as well.

✠ ESSAYS

W. J. Cash's *The Mind of the South* is among the most eloquent and forceful statements of a southern identity, though the Charlotte journalist's emphasis on the continuity of southern history has provoked sharp responses from some historians, among them Yale University's C. Vann Woodward. The first two essays present Cash's and Woodward's differing views. Defining southern distinctiveness is a major academic industry and in fact, as Wake Forest historian David L. Smiley notes in the next essay, has become a distinctive element in itself. Assuming the South's difference, the obvious question is, "Different from what?" Sheldon Hackney, historian and president of the University of Pennsyl-

1

vania, demonstrates in the last essay that the North had a significant hand in creating a distinctive South, and the South often functioned as a mirror image of the rest of the nation.

The Continuity of Southern History

W. J. CASH

There exists among us by ordinary—both North and South—a profound conviction that the South is another land, sharply differentiated from the rest of the American nation, and exhibiting within itself a remarkable homogeneity.

As to what its singularity may consist in, there is, of course, much conflict of opinion, and especially between Northerner and Southerner. But that it is different and that it is solid—on these things nearly everybody is agreed. Now and then, to be sure, there have arisen people, usually journalists or professors, to tell us that it is all a figment of the imagination, that the South really exists only as a geographical division of the United States and is distinguishable from New England or the Middle West only by such matters as the greater heat and the presence of a larger body of Negroes. Nobody, however, has ever taken them seriously. And rightly.

For the popular conviction is indubitably accurate: the South is, in Allen Tate's phrase, "Uncle Sam's other province." And when Carl Carmer said of Alabama that "The Congo is not more different from Massachusetts or Kansas or California," he fashioned a hyperbole which is applicable in one measure or another to the entire section.

This is not to suggest that the land does not display an enormous diversity within its borders. Anyone may see that it does simply by riding along any of the great new motor roads which spread across it—through brisk towns with tall white buildings in Nebraska Gothic; through smart suburbs, with their faces newly washed; through industrial and Negro slums, medieval in dirt and squalor and wretchedness, in all but redeeming beauty; past sleepy old hamlets and wide fields and black men singing their sad songs in the cotton, past log cabin and high grave houses, past hill and swamp and plain. . . . The distance from Charleston to Birmingham is in some respects measurable only in sidereal terms, as is the distance from the Great Smokies to Lake Pontchartrain. And Howard Odum has demonstrated that the economic and social difference between the Southeastern and Southwestern states is so great and growing that they have begun to deserve to be treated, for many purposes, as separate regions.

Nevertheless, if it can be said there are many Souths, the fact remains that there is also one South. That is to say, it is easy to trace throughout the region (roughly delimited by the boundaries of the former Confederate States of America, but shading over into some of the border states, notably Kentucky, also) a fairly definite mental pattern, associated with a fairly definite social pattern—a complex of established relationships and habits of thought, sentiments, prejudices, standards and values, and associations of ideas, which, if it is not common strictly to every group of white people in the South, is still common in one appreciable measure or another, and in some part or another, to all but relatively negligible ones.

It is no product of Cloud-Cuckoo-Town, of course, but proceeds from the common American heritage, and many of its elements are readily recognizable as being simply variations on the primary American theme. To imagine it existing outside this continent would be quite impossible. But for all that, the peculiar history of the South has so greatly modified it from the general American norm that, when viewed as a whole, it decisively justifies the notion that the country is—not quite a nation within a nation, but the next thing to it.

To understand it, it is necessary to know the story of its development. And the best way to begin that story, I think, is by disabusing our minds of two correlated legends—those of the Old and the New Souths.

What the Old South of the legend in its classical form was like is more or less familiar to everyone. It was a sort of stage piece out of the eighteenth century, wherein gesturing gentlemen moved soft-spokenly against a background of rose gardens and dueling grounds, through always gallant deeds, and lovely ladies, in farthingales, never for a moment lost that exquisite remoteness which has been the dream of all men and the possession of none. Its social pattern was manorial, its civilization that of the Cavalier, its ruling class an aristocracy coextensive with the planter group—men often entitled to quarter the royal arms of St. George and St. Andrew on their shields, and in every case descended from the old gentlefolk who for many centuries had made up the ruling classes of Europe.

They dwelt in large and stately mansions, preferably white and with columns and Grecian entablature. Their estates were feudal baronies, their slaves quite too numerous ever to be counted, and their social life a thing of Old World splendor and delicacy. What had really happened here, indeed, was that the gentlemanly idea, driven from England by Cromwell, had taken refuge in the South and fashioned for itself a world to its heart's desire: a world singularly polished and mellow and poised, wholly dominated by ideals of honor and chivalry and *noblesse*—all those sentiments and values and habits of action which used to be, especially in Walter Scott, invariably assigned to the gentleman born and the Cavalier.

Beneath these was a vague race lumped together indiscriminately as the poor whites—very often, in fact, as the "white-trash." These people belonged in the main to a physically inferior type, having sprung for the most part from the convict servants, redemptioners, and debtors of old Virginia and Georgia, with a sprinkling of the most unsuccessful sort of European peasants and farm laborers and the dregs of the European town slums. And so, of course, the gulf between them and the master classes was impassable, and their ideas and feelings did not enter into the make-up of the prevailing Southern civilization.

But in the legend of the New South the Old South is supposed to have been destroyed by the Civil War and the thirty years that followed it, to have been swept both socially and mentally into the limbo of things that were and are not, to give place to a society which has been rapidly and increasingly industrialized and modernized both in body and in mind— which now, indeed, save for a few quaint survivals and gentle sentimentalities and a few shocking and inexplicable brutalities such as lynching, is almost as industrialized and modernized in its outlook as the North. Such an idea is obviously inconsistent with the general assumption of the South's great difference, but paradox is the essence of popular thinking, and millions—even in the South itself—placidly believe in both notions.

These legends, however, bear little relation to reality. There was an Old South, to be sure, but it was another thing than this. And there is a New South. Industrialization and commercialization have greatly modified the land, including its ideology. . . . Nevertheless, the extent of the change and of the break between the Old South that was and the South of our time has been vastly exaggerated. The South, one might say, is a tree with many age rings, with its limbs and trunk bent and twisted by all the winds of the years, but with its tap root in the Old South. Or, better still, it is like one of those churches one sees in England. The facade and towers, the windows and clerestory, all the exterior and superstructure are late Gothic of one sort or another, but look into its nave, its aisles, and its choir and you find the old mighty Norman arches of the twelfth century. And if you look into its crypt, you may even find stones cut by Saxon, brick made by Roman hands.

The mind of the section, that is, is continuous with the past. And its primary form is determined not nearly so much by industry as by the purely agricultural conditions of that past. So far from being modernized, in many ways it has actually always marched away, as to this day it continues to do, from the present toward the past.

The Discontinuity of Southern History

C. VANN WOODWARD

Among the major monuments of broken continuity in the South are slavery and secession, independence and defeat, emancipation and military occupation, reconstruction and redemption. Southerners, unlike other Americans, repeatedly felt the solid ground of continuity give way under their feet. An old order of slave society solidly supported by constitution, state, church and the authority of law and learning and cherished by a majority of the people collapsed, perished and disappeared. So did the short-lived experiment in national independence. So also the short-lived experiment in Radical Reconstruction. The succeeding order of Redeemers, the New South, lasted longer, but it too seems destined for the dump heap of history.

Perhaps it was because Cash wrote toward the end of the longest and

American Counterpoint: Slavery and Racism in the North-South Dialogue by C. Vann Woodward. Copyright © 1964, 1966, 1968, 1969, 1970, 1971 by C. Vann Woodward. Reprinted by permission of Oxford University Press, Inc.

most stable of these successive orders, the one that lasted from 1877 to the 1950's, that he acquired his conviction of stability and unchanging continuity. At any rate, he was fully persuaded that "the mind of the section . . . is continuous with the past," and that the South has "always marched away, as to this day it continues to do, from the present toward the past." Just as he guardedly conceded diversity in advancing the thesis of unity, so he admits the existence of change in maintaining the thesis of continuity, change from which even the elusive Southern "mind" did not "come off scot-free." But it was the sort of change the French have in mind in saying, *"Plus ça change, plus c'est la même chose."* Tidewater tobacco, up-country cotton, rampaging frontier, flush times in Alabama and Mississippi, slavery, secession, defeat, abolition, Reconstruction, New South, industrial revolution—*toujours la même chose!* Even the Yankee victory that "had smashed the Southern world" was "almost entirely illusory," since "it had left the essential Southern mind and will . . . entirely unshaken. Rather . . . it had operated enormously to fortify and confirm that mind and will." As for Reconstruction, again, "so far from having reconstructed the Southern mind in the large and in its essential character, it was still this Yankee's fate to have strengthened it almost beyond reckoning, and to have made it one of the most solidly established, one of the least reconstructible ever developed."

The continuity upon which Cash is most insistent is the one he sees between the Old South and the New South. He early announces his intention of "disabusing our minds of two correlated legends—those of the Old and New South." He promises in Rankean terms to tell us "exactly what the Old South was really like." He concedes that there was a New South as well. "Nevertheless, the extent of the change and of the break between the Old South that was and the New South of our time has been vastly exaggerated." The common denominator, the homogenizing touchstone is his "basic Southerner" or "the man at the center." He is described as "an exceedingly simple fellow," most likely a hillbilly from the backcountry, but fundamentally he is a petit bourgeois always on the make, yet ever bemused by his vision of becoming, imitating, or at least serving the planter aristocrat. Cash's crude Irish parvenu is pictured as the prototype of the planter aristocrat. Cash is confused about these aristocrats, mainly I think because he is confused about the nature and history of aristocracy. He admires their "beautiful courtesy and dignity and gesturing grace," but deplores their "grotesque exaggeration" and their "pomposity" and suspects that the genuine article should have been genteel. He grudgingly acknowledges their existence, but denies the legitimacy of their pretenses— all save those of a few negligible Virginians. He seems to be saying that they were all bourgeois, that therefore the Old South was bourgeois too, and therefore essentially indistinguishable from the New South. New and Old alike were spellbound by the spurious myth of aristocracy. This and the paradoxical fact that those parvenu aristocrats actually took charge, were a real ruling class, and the continuity of their rule spelled the continuity of the New South with the Old.

The masses came out of the ordeal of Civil War with "a deep affection

for these captains, a profound trust in them,'' a belief in the right "of the
master class to ordain and command.'' And according to Cash, the old
rulers continued to ordain and command right on through the collapse of
the old order and the building of the new. He detects no change of guard
at Redemption. So long as the industrialists and financiers who stepped
into the shoes of the old rulers gave the Proto-Dorian password and adopted
the old uniforms and gestures, he salutes them as the genuine article. In
fact they were rather an improvement, for they represent "a striking extension of the so-called paternalism of the Old South: its passage in some
fashion toward becoming a genuine paternalism." Cash enthusiastically
embraces the thesis of Broadus Mitchell's "celebrated monograph" that
the cotton-mill campaign was "a mighty folk movement," a philanthropic
crusade of inspired paternalists. The textile-mill captains were "such men
as belonged more or less distinctively within the limits of the old ruling
class, the progeny of the plantation." Indeed they were responsible for
"the bringing over of the plantation into industry," the company town.
Even "the worst labor sweaters" were "full of the ancient Southern love
for the splendid gesture," fulfilling "an essential part of the Southern paternalistic tradition that it was an essential duty of the upper classes to
look after the moral welfare of these people."

To the cotton mills the neopaternalists add the public schools for the
common whites and thus "mightily reaffirm the Proto-Dorian bond." The
common poverty acted as a leveler (back to the Unity thesis) and brought
"a very great increase in the social solidarity of the South," a "marked
mitigation of the haughtiness" of the old captains, now "less boldly pa-
tronizing," and "a suppression of class feeling that went beyond anything
that even the Old South had known." The common white felt "the hand
on the shoulder . . . the jests, the rallying, the stories . . . the confiding
reminders of the Proto-Dorian bond of white men." That, according to
Cash, was what did in the Populist revolt and the strikes of the lint-head
mill hands as well. For from the heart of the masses came "a wide, diffuse
gratefulness pouring out upon the cotton-mill baron; upon the old captains,
upon all the captains and preachers of Progress; upon the ruling class as
a whole for having embraced the doctrine and brought these things about."

Of course Cash professes not to be taken in by Progress like the red-
necks and the lint-heads. He realizes that Progress and Success had their
prices and he sets them down scrupulously in the debit column of his ledger.
"Few people can ever have been confronted with a crueler dilemma" than
the old planter turned supply merchant to his former huntin' and fishin'
companion as sharecropper: "The old monotonous pellagra-and-rickets-
breeding diet had at least been abundant? Strip it rigidly to fatback, mo-
lasses, and cornbread, dole it out with an ever stingier hand . . . blind your
eyes to peaked faces, seal up your ears to hungry whines. . . ." And that
sunbonnet, straw-hat proletariat of the paternalistic mill villages? By the
turn of the century they had become "a pretty distinct physical type . . .
a dead white skin, a sunken chest, and stooping shoulders. . . . Chinless
faces, microcephalic foreheads, rabbit teeth, goggling dead-fish eyes, rickety

limbs, and stunted bodies. . . . The women were characteristically stringy-haired and limp of breast at twenty, and shrunken hags at thirty or forty." Something admittedly was happening to the captains, too, what with "men of generally coarser kind coming steadily to the front." And in "all the elaborate built-up pattern of leisure and hedonistic drift; all the slow, cool, gracious and graceful gesturing of movement," there was a sad falling off, a decay of the ideal. "And along with it, the vague largeness of outlook which was so essentially a part of the same aristocratic complex; the magnanimity . . ."

Admitting all that, "But when the whole of this debit score of Progress is taken into account, we still inevitably come back to the fact that its total effect was as I have said." *Plus ça change!* "Here in a word, was triumph for the Southern will . . . an enormous renewal of confidence in the general Southern way." In [Henry W.] Grady's rhetoric, "Progress stood quite accurately for a sort of new charge at Gettysburg." To be sure, Southern Babbitts eventually appeared, but even they were "Tartarin, not Tartuffe . . . simpler, more naïve, less analytical than their compatriots in Babbittry at the North. . . . They go about making money . . . as boys go about stealing apples . . . in the high-hearted sense of being embarked upon capital sport." Yet, like the planter turned supply merchant or captain of industry, "they looked at you with level and proud gaze. The hallmark of their breed was identical with that of the masters of the Old South—a tremendous complacency." And Rotary, "sign-manual of the Yankee spirit"? Granting "an unfortunate decline in the dignity of the Southern manner," it was but "the grafting of Yankee backslapping upon the normal Southern geniality. . . . I am myself," Cash wrote, "indeed perpetually astonished to recall that Rotary was not invented in the South." And does one detect "strange notes—Yankee notes—in all this talk about the biggest factory, about bank clearings and car loadings and millions"? Strange? Not for Jack Cash. "But does anybody," he actually asked, "fail to hear once more the native accent of William L. Yancey and Barnwell Rhett, to glimpse again the waving plume of, say, Wade Hampton?"

How could he? How could any historian? He sometimes reminds one of those who scribble facetious graffiti on Roman ruins. He betrays a want of feeling for the seriousness of human strivings, for the tragic theme in history. Looking back from mid-twentieth century over the absurd sky-scrapers and wrecked-car bone piles set in the red-clay hills, how could he seriously say that the South believed it "was succeeding in creating a world which, if it was not made altogether in the image of that old world, half-remembered and half-dreamed, shimmering there forever behind the fateful smoke of Sumter's guns, was yet sufficiently of a piece with it in essentials to be acceptable." A great slave society, by far the largest and richest of those that had existed in the New World since the sixteenth century, had grown up and miraculously flourished in the heart of a thor-oughly bourgeois and partly puritanical republic. It had renounced its bour-geois origins and elaborated and painfully rationalized its institutional, legal, metaphysical, and religious defenses. It had produced leaders of skill, ingenuity, and strength who, unlike those of other slave societies, invested their honor and their lives, and not merely part of their capital, in that society. When the crisis came, they, unlike the others, chose to fight. It proved to be the death struggle of a society, which went down in ruins. And yet here is a historian who tells us that nothing essential changed. The ancient "mind," temperament, the aristocratic spirit, parvenu though he called it—call it what you will, *panache* perhaps—was perfectly preserved in a mythic amber. And so the present is continuous with the past, the ancient manifest in the new order, in Grady, Babbitt, Rotary, whatever, *c'est la même chose.*

I am afraid that Cash was taken in by the very myth he sought to explode—by the fancy-dress charade the New South put on in the cast-off finery of the old order, the cult of the Lost Cause, the Plantation Legend and the rest. The new actors threw themselves into the old roles with spirit and conviction and put on what was for some a convincing performance. But Cash himself, even though he sometimes took the Snopeses for the Sartorises, plainly saw how they betrayed to the core and essence every tenet of the old code. "And yet," he can write,

> And yet—as regards the Southern mind, which is our theme, how essentially superficial and unrevolutionary remain the obvious changes; how certainly do these obvious changes take place within the ancient framework, and even sometimes contribute to the positive strengthening of the ancient pattern.
>
> Look close at this scene as it stands in 1914. There is an atmosphere here, an air, shining from every word and deed. And the key to this atmosphere . . . is that familiar word without which it would be impossible to tell the story of the Old South, that familiar word "extravagant."
>
> [Then, after a reference to the new skyscrapers in the clay hills:]
>
> Softly; do you not hear behind that the gallop of Jeb Stuart's cavalrymen?

The answer is "No"! Not one ghostly echo of a gallop. And neither did Jack Cash. He only thought he did when he was bemused.

After some years in the profession, one has seen reputations of historians rise and fall. The books of Ulrich Phillips and later Frank Owsley began to collect dust on the shelves, and one thinks of Beard and Parrington. In America, historians, like politicians, are out as soon as they are down. There is no comfortable back bench, no House of Lords for them. It is a wasteful and rather brutal practice, unworthy of what Cash would agree are our best Southern traditions. I hope this will not happen to Cash. The man really had something to say, which is more than most, and he said it with passion and conviction and with style. Essentially what he had to say is something every historian eventually finds himself trying to say (always risking exaggeration) at some stage about every great historical subject. And that is that in spite of the revolution—any revolution—the English remain English, the French remain French, the Russians remain Russian, the Chinese remain Chinese—call them Elizabethans or Cromwellians, Royalists or Jacobeans, Czarists or Communists, Mandarins or Maoists.

That was really what Cash, at his best, was saying about Southerners, and he said it better than anybody ever has—only he rather overdid the thing. But in that he was merely illustrating once more that ancient Southern trait that he summed up in the word "extravagant." And, for that matter, his critic, poured in the same mold, may have unintentionally added another illustration of the same trait. If so, Jack Cash would have been the first to understand and not the last to forgive. Peace to his troubled spirit.

Quest for a Central Theme

DAVID L. SMILEY

In the history of Southern history in America the central theme has been the quest for the central theme. Local and state historians, students of regionalism and sectionalism, along with authors of American history surveys, have agreed in accepting the hypothesis that there is an American South and that it has had, historically, a unifying focus at its center. Furthermore, it has become customary among many historians to emphasize sectionalism as a key factor in American political history and to seek the causes for the apparent division of national patriotism. The man in the street, though his views may be hazy or overemotional, is confident that there are distinctive social and political patterns, perhaps traceable to a unique agricultural base, which combine to make the regions below the Potomac a recognizable entity, and most Americans at one time or another have engaged in the pursuit of a central theme in Southern history.

In its broadest sense the attempt to generalize regional folkways into an American South is part of the search for a national identity. Since the days of Noah Webster's early crusade for American English orthography and usage and Ralph Waldo Emerson's 1837 appeal for an American culture—Oliver Wendell Holmes called it "our intellectual Declaration of Independence"—Americans have earnestly sought to define the elusive qualities of their civilization and have squirmed uncomfortably when critics such as Harriet Martineau or Charles Dickens ridiculed their efforts. There are interesting parallels between the national response to Dickens' *American Notes* and the Southern umbrage at the publication of Fanny Kemble's *Georgia Journal*. Still, the search for a national identity went on, and alongside it, as if in overt denial of a homogeneous national character, the search for Southern distinctiveness continued.

The reasons for the dichotomy in the national personality are complex and often obscure. At the same time that it served the purposes of American patriotism to sound a bold trumpet for a native civilization, it was politically advantageous to assent to the proposition that that civilization contained two "nations," opposites in fundamental aspects. The subsequent defeat

David L. Smiley, "The Quest for the Central Theme in Southern History." Reprinted with permission from *The South Atlantic Quarterly*, Vol. 71:3 (Summer 1972), pp. 307–325. Copyright 1972 by Duke University Press.

of one "nation" by the other had the effect, on both sides, of inspiring each to glamorize its superior civilization and to denigrate that of the other as alien, un-American, and lacking in enduring and essential values. Especially was this activity prevalent among Southerners, where it took the form of reverence for the Lost Cause and allegiance to the cult of the Old South. In paying homage to a mythical past they were but acting out a characteristic common to peoples defeated by material or military force, i.e., the tendency to emphasize the superiority of less tangible qualities which their civilization allegedly produced in great quantity. This happened in the post–Civil War South at a thousand veterans' campfires, in political orations on days set aside to the memory of the dead, and in graduation addresses replete with scholarly appurtenances, and soon the emphasis began to appear in presumably objective histories and biographies of the Confederacy and its leaders.

In these expressions, down to the latest Rebel yell or defiant wave of the Confederate battle flag, there was the axiomatic acceptance of the belief that there was in fact an American South and that it possessed clearly defined traits which set it apart from the rest of the nation. In some instances, notably in the rhetoric of ambitious politicians and regional promoters, these assumptions conveyed overtones of immediate advantage to the author. A widely accepted central theme or distinguishing characteristic of the American South, for example, might affect a person's vote for or against a party, a personality, or a platform. On other occasions it might encourage or discourage decisions concerning the migration of industries and the choice of sites for capital investments, or the transfer of individual talents to sunnier climes or a more favorable labor situation.

At the same time, other statements of the central theme emerged from the labors of those committed to the highest obligations of scholarship: to sift the evidence and to generalize its meaning into an idea whose purpose is to enlarge understanding and to stimulate additional study and thought. In each case the motivation, though vastly different in purpose and effect, remains confused and unclear, and a study of the themes and forces which have attracted scholarly attention is significant in illuminating the problems and clarifying the objectives of the broader quest for national identity.

Basically and historically the effort to express the essence of the American South in a central theme has turned upon two related streams of thought. One has been to emphasize the causal effects of environment, while the other has put uppermost the development of certain acquired characteristics of the people called Southern. The work of the scholar Ulrich B. Phillips well illustrates the dual thrust of the endeavor. The South, he declared in a famous article, was a section dominated by racial conflict. It was "a land with a unity despite its diversity, with a people having common joys and common sorrows, and, above all, as to the white folk a people with a common resolve indomitably maintained—that it shall be and remain a white man's country." The "cardinal test of a Southerner and the central theme of Southern history," he said, was the desire to preserve the supremacy of the white race.

A few months after the article appeared, however, Phillips published

Life and Labor in the Old South, in which he defined the South in terms of environmental causation. "Let us begin by discussing the weather," he wrote, "for that has been the chief agency in making the South distinctive." Behind the central theme of white supremacy Phillips could now discern a determinative meteorological pattern. Climate encouraged the production of staple crops, he declared, and staple crops promoted the plantation as the most efficient institution for their cultivation; the plantation's demand for large quantities of cheap labor led to slave importations; the presence of large numbers of Africans resulted in turn in a continuing race problem and the effort to maintain white supremacy. The acquired characteristic of racism now became a "house that Jack built" upon the foundation of a causative weather pattern.

Although critics have eroded much of Phillips' work, searchers for the central theme continued to follow the twin trails that he blazed. Generally they have undertaken to document either the theme of a dominant pattern of life or they have looked beyond the characteristic itself to seek geographical, meteorological, or psychological determinants of the significant traits. Sometimes a student has combined all of these in a single sentence. "The South," wrote Wendell H. Stephenson, "is a geographical location, a group of factors that differentiated the region and its inhabitants from other sections of the United States, and a state of mind to which these factors gave rise."

Thus, in one way or another, seekers for the central theme in Southern history have illustrated Phillips' observations that the South was either the home of a peculiar behavior pattern—all but universally present among people who considered themselves Southern and all but universally absent elsewhere in the land (the inheritance theory)—or a place where men's lives were molded by impersonal forces of climate or geography (the environmental view).

Perhaps the earliest assumption among those in quest of the central theme has been that the South is the product of a dictatorial environment. Phillips himself spoke of climate, in the form of heavy rainfall and an overheated sun, as causative factors in Southern life. Deluges eroded the topsoil, packed plowed lands, and ran off in floods, he said, and these rains conditioned the soils of the South. The sun was "bakingly hot"; it parched vegetation and enervated Europeans. Clarence Cason agreed that the South was a hot land. It was that part of the United States where the mercury reached 90 degrees in the shade at least one hundred afternoons a year. According to the climate theory, the tyrant sun slowed life to a languid crawl, impelled men to choose the shaded sides of streets, and induced cooks to concoct gastronomical delights to tempt heat-jaded appetites. It also dictated an emphasis upon staple crops, and as a consequence influenced the labor system of the South. Cason related with approval the Mississippi proverb that "only mules and black men can face the sun in July" in support of the comforting philosophy that only dark-skinned menials, presumably equipped by an all-wise Creator to endure the heat, should perform physical labor.

The idea that the central theme of Southern history may be found in the environment, in a causal relationship between a tropical climate and a peculiar way of life, has been a persistent one. In 1778 Judge William Henry Drayton told the South Carolina Assembly that "from the nature of the climate, soil and produce of the several states, a northern and southern interest naturally and unavoidably arise," and this view found ready acceptance. In his *Notes on Virginia* Thomas Jefferson remarked that "in a warm climate, no man will labor for himself who can make another labor for him." For this reason, he said, "of the proprietors of slaves a very small proportion indeed are ever seen to labor." Not only did the sun dictate a Southern interest and an aversion to toil; it also purified the Anglo-Saxon blood lines. In 1852 a newspaper editor pointed out that South Carolina lay in the same latitude as Greece and Rome, which was a "pretty good latitude for a 'breed of noble men.'" Six years later an observer commented that the "gentleman and lady of England and France, born to command, were especially fitted for their God given mission of uplifting and Christianizing the Negroes because they were softened and refined under our Southern sky." These views continued into the present century. Hamilton J. Eckenrode declared that in the warm climate of the American South a superior Nordic race became "tropicized" and thus improved in quality, and Francis B. Simkins also defined the South as the result of an adjustment of Anglo-Saxon peoples to a subtropical climate. He went on to deplore the modern preference for sun-tanned women and architectural styles that broke with the ante-bellum tradition, and—perhaps with tongue in cheek—he regarded all admiration for Southern temperatures as a form of Yankee carpetbaggery. "Because of the tyranny of books and magazines imported from strange climates," he said, Southerners had lost their fear of the sun, and in so doing had denied their birthright. They were "prompted to construct artificial lakes, treeless lawns, and low-roofed houses without porches or blinds."

Such is the environmental view—the causal effects of climate upon Southern folkways—and its inaccuracies are manifest. There is no unity in Southern climate, for the section includes startling variations in pattern and is wholly temperate rather than tropical in nature. William A. Foran pointed out that it was climate of opinion rather than climate in fact that influenced the configurations of life and thought among Europeans inhabiting the Southern regions of North America. "The Great South of 1860," Foran said, "began at Mason's and Dixon's line, just twenty-five miles south of the Liberty Bell on Independence Square, and ranged on through fifteen degrees of latitude." It encompassed almost every type of North American climate, "from pleasantly-tempered Virginia and magnolia-scented Charleston to the arctic blizzards of Texas. . . . Can historians speak glibly of a southern climate, much less of a tropical one," he asked, "of a land whose rainfall varies from zero to seventy inches a year?"

But the important question concerns the causal relationship between high temperatures and a distinctive life style. Even if there were a demonstrable meteorological unity to Southern weather, that would not of itself determine a particular social order, an agricultural pattern, or a way of life. That it did so in fact is the basic assumption of the advocates of the environmental theory. Yet climate neither forecast nor foreordained a staple crop-slave labor-race segregation cycle such as Phillips and others have described. Edgar T. Thompson explicitly rejected the Phillips thesis. "The plantation was not to be accounted for by climate," he said; the climate-plantation-slavery syndrome was instead a defense mechanism. "A theory which makes the plantation depend upon something outside the processes of human interaction, that is, a theory which makes the plantation depend upon a fixed and static something like climate," he declared, "is a theory which operates to justify an existing social order and the vested interests connected with that order."

Whatever forces produced the plantation—perhaps a complex combination of the English manorial tradition and the immediate need for a social unit that could provide a measure of economic independence and military defense—it has existed in low-country regions of the South as an important institution. Many seekers for the central theme have considered it, therefore, as the distinctive characteristic of Southern life. First used to describe a group of "planted" colonists, the word came to mean a system of farming with tenants, indentured servants, peons, or slaves working under the direction of proprietors who owned great estates and who used their wealth and social position to play active roles in their communities' affairs. As a close-knit social and political group, the planters exerted an influence that was indeed often predominant. In some regions they were able to define their interests as those of the entire population, and their way of life as typical of the whole. With the enthusiastic co-operation of nostalgic novelists, poets, song composers, and advertising agents, the plantation and its gentlemen of distinction became the epitome of the Southern ideal. For a generation prior to the Civil War its proponents were able to impose the "plantation platform" of opposition to national banks, internal improvements at federal government expense, and tariffs of protection upon the policies of the general government. At the same time, opponents of the Jeffersonian agricultural Arcadia and the Calhounian logic of dominant particularism came to view the plantation as the symbol of all that was evil or amiss about America. It represented wealth amassed by exploiting an immoral labor system, disunionist and antinationalistic sentiments, support for policies that tied the whole country to a humiliating economic colonialism, and political power resting upon a snobbish and superficial aristocracy. For these reasons, enemies of the plantation regarded it as "un-American." Still, it served as a definition of the South. The plantation system was an ancient one; in varying forms it antedated the rise of chattel slavery, and after emancipation it persisted in fact and fancy as a distinctive entity. It was also fairly well distributed over the coastal plains and river valleys, regions earliest settled and seat of preponderant voting strength, and it extended into a roughly similar topography as settlement advanced into the Southwest. The plantation pattern of production was therefore general enough to serve as an archetype, however superficial, of a recognizable Southern society.

The great estate, with its paternalistic Massa and Missus, and the values it allegedly conserved, has provided much of the romantic Southern tradition. "The plantation," said Sheldon Van Auken, "is central to any understanding of the South." Since before there were white men in New England, he declared, it has been the most significant aspect of a South differentiated by it from the rest of the nation. More than other forms of economic and social organization the plantation provided security to laborers and a satisfying way of life to its operators. It set the standards for the entire South, Van Auken concluded, and it has remained the ideal image of the South. Earlier, Francis P. Gaines studied the plantation as a Southern tradition and declared that "the supremacy of the great estate in the thinking of the South cannot be successfully challenged."

But despite the plantation's exalted place in tradition, at no time was it the typical pattern of life in the Southern regions. It was a hothouse flower that could not hold its own in the low country and could not survive the cooler breezes of the uplands. Many students, including both Gaines and Van Auken, pointed out that the plantation did not penetrate into the hilly regions where yeoman farmers predominated and where a different way of life prevailed; except for isolated regions in the Virginia tidewater and the South Carolina low country, it did not monopolize life anywhere. The Owsleys have demonstrated that the plantation was not typical even of the Alabama black belt and was becoming less important in the decade of the 1850's. And according to Avery Craven, by 1860 Virginia and Maryland had "come largely to the small farm and the small farmer." The governor of Virginia reported that the state was no longer characterized by the "large plantation system," but had developed into an agriculture of "smaller horticultural and arboricultural farming." . . .

The plantation was, presumably, the home of other significant factors in the Southern image—the planter and his code of honor, and the institution of slavery—and students turned to these as central characteristics. As Avery Craven put it, "Only two factors seem to have contributed to the making of anything Southern—an old-world country-gentleman ideal and the presence of negroes in large numbers." The small minority of well-to-do planters lived in conscious imitation of the old English squires, stocking their homes with books and musical instruments, importing furnishings and clothing, and providing tutors for their children. In their personal relationships the more refined among them practiced a gallant chivalry. "When you institute a comparison between the men of the North and the South, does it not result in favor of those of the South?" a speaker in the Kentucky constitutional convention of 1849 asked. "Has not the South acquired for itself a character for frankness, generosity, high-toned honor, and chivalry which is unknown in the North?"

This was the country-gentleman ideal as a characteristic of the South. Though many planters ignored the demands of the code, in theory it set Cavalier Southerner apart from Roundhead Yankee. It provided a theme for the Southern Agrarians, who saw in it a conservative civilization which had, in the words of John Crowe Ransom, come "to terms with nature." Living "materially along the inherited line of least resistance," the planters sought "to put the surplus of energy into the free life of the mind." But to emphasize the country-gentleman as the typical inhabitant of the Southern regions, and to pretend that he alone possessed a code of disinterested obligation to public service or polite manners, ignored a host of other types equally Southern and overlooked commendable contributions to statecraft made by men who lived in other quadrants of the country.

Much more common as a unifying factor was another by-product of the plantation system of production, slavery and the Negro. Thomas P. Govan declared that the South was that part of the United States in which slavery continued for sixty years after it was abandoned elsewhere, but was in all other respects similar to the rest of the country. The only important sectional conflict in America, he said, arose from the fact that Negroes were held as slaves; emancipation eliminated the single Southern distinctive and removed the cause of its desire to be independent. The subsequent insistence upon white supremacy, Govan contended, merely meant that Southerners acted like other men of European origins when they confronted large numbers of people of differing ethnic types. To define the South as the land of white supremacy, he concluded, overlooked the very real racism among non-Southern Americans and incorrectly suggested that only Southerners were capable of bigotry and intolerance. Yet Charles S. Sydnor cited the presence of the Negro as the most popular of the monocausationist theories explaining the differences between Southerners and other Americans.

The plantation also fostered a rural environment with its strange mixture of the polished and the primitive, and some students have defined the South in terms of its folkways. Andrew N. Lytle stated the central theme as a "backwoods progression" of an agrarian Arcadia, and others of the Agrarian School have emphasized the essential "South-ness" of a slowed pace of life, enjoyment of living, and leisure for contemplation and meditation. John Hope Franklin saw a different product of a rural South. It was a land of violence whose peoples possessed a "penchant for militancy which at times assumed excessive proportions." The Southern reputation for pugnacity, he added, "did not always command respect, nor even serious consideration; but it came to be identified as an important ingredient of Southern civilization."

Another critique of the Agrarian School came from David Potter. Declaring that the agrarian formula fitted the South remarkably badly, he defined the section as a place where older folkways persisted. "The culture of the folk survived in the South long after it succumbed to the onslaught of urban-industrial culture elsewhere," he said. "It was an aspect of this culture that the relations between the land and the people remained more direct and more primal in the South than in other parts of the country." In addition, relationships of people to one another "imparted a distinctive texture as well as a distinctive tempo to their lives." Americans regarded the South with a kind of nostalgia, he noted; its basis was not an ideal utopian society that never existed, but a "yearning of men in a mass culture for the life of a folk culture which really did exist."

Thus the climate and its alleged offspring, the plantation, the planter, the staple crop, and the Negro, all set in a rural scene surrounded by primitive folkways, have provided students with the ingredients for a central theme. Another avenue into the character of the Southern regions has been to pursue the second of Phillips' hypotheses and to describe the South on the basis of social patterns. Charles S. Sydnor suggested both the problem and the possibilities. Southern historians, he pointed out, studied a region which had no definite boundaries and therefore faced the prior necessity of delimiting their subject. In doing so, they pioneered in the study of social history. They considered the distinctive traits of the people called Southern and then sought "to discover the geographical incidence of these characteristics." Thus the student of the South "was driven from the problem of area back to the prior problem of essence," Sydnor declared; "his initial task was to discover what the Old South was. From the nature of the case he was compelled to be a social historian."

Elaborating upon his own analysis, in another article Sydnor listed some distinctively Southern culture patterns. Among them he described an inherited way of life modeled after that of the English gentry, slavery, malaria, hookworm, lynching, farm tenancy, the advocacy of states' rights, mockingbirds, and a unique attitude toward law and order. Following Sydnor's suggestions, other South-seekers offered additional criteria: the South is the place where people celebrate Christmas but not the Fourth of July with fireworks; it is where cooks add salt pork to the extended boiling of green vegetables; it is the domain of hominy grits; it is the land of one-party politics, one-horse plowing, and one-crop agriculture. Charles F. Lane declared that "the preference for the mule as a draft animal is one of the least-considered traits characterizing Southern culture" and proposed a map showing the mule population of the country as a way of marking boundaries around the South.

Other observers defined the South as the center of Protestant evangelical fundamentalism. Edwin McNeill Poteat declared that "the South is religiously solid" in much the same way that it was, to him, politically solid. To most Southerners heresy remained heresy, he said, and "they still in the main submit readily to demagogy in the pulpit, and enjoy the thrill of denominational competition." The religious South exhibited a "more homogeneous quality than any other section," Poteat concluded. There was some agreement with this idea. "The distinctiveness of the Old South," said Francis B. Simkins, "is perhaps best illustrated by its religion. Historic Protestantism was reduced to the consistencies of the Southern environment without sacrificing inherent fundamentals." Charles W. Ramsdell noted that religious fundamentalism was a Southern characteristic, and pointed out its effects in the reaction to the biological discoveries of the evolution of species, the effort to prohibit the manufacture and sale of beverage alcohol by constitutional amendment, and the resurgence of the Ku Klux Klan.

Another proposal in the quest for cultural distinctives held that the South was a collection of "settlement characteristics." The geographer Wilbur Zelinsky catalogued these traits as the pattern in which men house themselves. "In the course of field observations of house types, urban morphology, farmsteads, and other settlement characteristics," he said, "I have discovered a constellation of traits that are apparently co-terminous with the South and function collectively as a regional label." Some of the traits he emphasized were houses placed well back from the street and from each other, low or nonexistent curbings, sidewalk arcades in front of town shops, a central location for courthouses in county seats, a large number of rural nonfarm homes, a lack of "spatial pattern" to farm buildings, and a high rate of building abandonment. "The observer can be reasonably certain that he is within the Southern culture area when the bulk of these traits recur with great frequency," Zelinsky concluded, "and particularly when they are assembled into one or another of the regional house types."

Related to the description of the South as a land of rather slovenly dwelling patterns is David Bertelson's idea that the distinguishing characteristic of Southerners is laziness. By his definition, however, they were afflicted not with a lack of energy but with a dearth of social unity. Southerners sought individual rather than social goals and were motivated by a desire for private gain, he said. They were prototypes of the "robber barons" who sought wealth without social responsibility, and were so thoroughly committed to economic motivation that the relatively un-self-seeking abolitionists baffled them. To Bertelson the South was an individualistic, chaotic economy in an America whose other inhabitants held some idea of community purpose, and this gave Southerners a sense of apartness and led both to the formation and to the failure of the Confederacy. Before and during the war, he said, the idea that labor meant liberty for private gain destroyed all efforts to create community and strengthened the view of outsiders that Southerners were lazy.

A similar view was that of Earl E. Thorpe, who also argued that freedom was a chief characteristic of Southerners. To Thorpe, however, its emphasis was upon sexual license. Easy access to black females who "desperately wanted displays of recognition and affection" meant that there was less repression in the South than elsewhere, and freedom led to romanticism, hedonism, and pugnacity. The Southern white male, confronting the criticism of a more inhibited outside world, became militant in the defense of his society and his frequently deceived womenfolk. Thorpe thus described a Freudian South lying just below the land of Id, a harem of sexual freedom rather than a place of economic individualism.

Another recent proposal, offered by C. Vann Woodward, held that the only distinguishing feature that may survive the social revolution of the post-1945 era is the memory of the Southern past. "The collective experience of the Southern people," he said, has made the South "the most distinctive region of the country." It was an experience that repudiated the most cherished aspects of the American self-image, for it was a record of poverty in a land of plenty, pessimism and frustration among a people wedded to optimism and unending success, and guilt complexes in a naively innocent America. Indeed, Woodward comes close to saying that the central theme of Southern history is Southern history. However helpful the idea may be in interpreting the dreary years after Appomattox, it ignores the peculiarities and events that caused such an aberrant history in the first place.

Another currently popular thesis, also based upon the harsh unpleasantness that surrounds much of Southern existence, contends that the Southerner is more inclined to romanticism than are other Americans. The Southerner is distinguished by his preference for fantasy and myth. "The quality that makes him unique among Americans," said T. Harry Williams, is his ability to conjure up "mind-pictures of his world or of the larger world around him—images that he wants to believe, that are real to him, and that he will insist others accept." George B. Tindall suggested the possibility that "we shall encounter the central theme of Southern history at last on the new frontier of mythology," and he listed some of the myths about the South that have at one time or another gained support: the Pro-Slavery South, the Confederate South, the Demagogic South, the States' Rights South, the Lazy South, and the Booster South. "There are few areas of the modern world," he declared, "that have bred a regional mythology so potent, so profuse and diverse, even so paradoxical, as the American South." Here again the searcher finds the results of an allegedly distinctive South, one of the inheritance family of character traits, but provides little illumination as to its cause.

The effort to locate the South by defining it as a single characteristic produced still another statement of the central theme. Outlined by Avery Craven and Frank L. Owsley and amplified by others, it argued that the South was the product of attacks from without. In this view the South was a state of mind, a conscious minority reacting to criticism by forging a unity as a defense mechanism. Opposition drew people together in defense of their peculiarities when their natural course would have been to fight among themselves. It began, according to Craven, with the tariff controversy in the 1820's and it became full grown in the abolition crusade.

Frank L. Owsley further developed the theme that the South came into being only when it became the victim of outside attack. "There was very little defense or justification of slavery until the commencement of a vigorous abolitionist assault from the North," he said. But "the attack upon slavery and the South resulted in the development of a philosophical defense of slavery. . . . So violent and dangerous did this new crusade appear to Southerners that a revolution in Southern thought immediately took place." Owsley declared that attacks upon the South had continued since the Civil War, but these merely succeeded in making the section more united than before. Charles W. Ramsdell, B. B. Kendrick, and A. B. Moore, along with others, defended the "outside attack" thesis, while Frank E. Vandiver emphasized an "offensive-defensive" pattern of Southern response to external criticism. Implicit in this argument is the assumption that a united South began as a Yankee invention.

The contention that the idea of a South grew out of external attacks produced its corollary—that the South was the result of a conscious effort to create a sense of unity among a diverse population with conflicting interests. In the effort, Southern leaders used all available arguments— climate, race, soil, staple-crop similarities, the agrarian philosophy with its country-gentleman ideal and the plantation as a romantic tradition, and slavery as a positive good. Some of them dramatized, if they did not actually invent, attacks from without as aids to their campaign for sectional unity. "If there is a central theme," said Robert S. Cotterill, "it is the rise of Southern nationalism." The study of the emergence of a divergent nationalism attracted many scholars. The South "was an emotion," Avery Craven wrote, "produced by an assumption on the part of outsiders of a unity there which did not exist, by propaganda within which emphasized likenesses rather than differences and created a unity of fear where none other existed."

In the conscious effort to create a South, every hint of attack from outside the section came as a godsend. William Lloyd Garrison and his abolition newspaper might well have passed unnoticed had not Southern publicists called attention to him by putting a price upon his head. Critics of the Southern system such as Elijah P. Lovejoy in Illinois and Cassius M. Clay in Kentucky found themselves the objects of violent mob resistance. In 1859 Edmund Ruffin, an energetic Southern unifier, expressed gratitude for the John Brown raid upon Harpers Ferry because of its beneficial effects upon "the sluggish blood of the South," and he took it upon himself to send samples of Brown's pikes to the governors of the slave states lest they forgot. After the war, Reconstruction again called forth a movement for white unity in the face of political and economic coercion— new attacks from without—and into the twentieth century there appeared leaders willing to evoke memories of the past as weapons against proposed changes in existing social or educational arrangements.

The flaw in the hypothesis of a movement to unify a people in the face of real or imaginary attacks from without has two aspects. First, as with all devil theories of historical motivation, it assumes almost magical powers of clairvoyance among promoters of the movement; and second, what it describes are but activities common to politicians practicing their profession wherever found, not uniquely Southern behavior at all. It was not surprising that Southern leaders should appeal for unanimity in support of their programs and candidacies; indeed, it would require explanation had any not done so. And that they could have foreseen the consequences of their conduct places a severe strain upon credulity.

From this confusing and sometimes contradictory survey of central themes in Southern history and life the suspicion emerges that the American South defies either location or analysis. It appears to be in fact an enigma challenging comprehension, "a kind of Sphinx on the American land." Its geographical boundaries are imprecise at best, and the characteristics of its population resist valid generalization. To say this is not to say that the South does not exist; it is to suggest that it exists only as a controlling idea or belief upon which men acted, risked, and died. The idea of the South is real; it is one of the most important ideas in American history, and that gives it significance.

The South idea has played a fundamental role in national development. In the early days of the Republic, as part of the debate between Thomas Jefferson and Alexander Hamilton which formed the basis of the first party divisions under the Constitution, the idea of a South contributed to the definition of public policy. As the internal dispute became more heated, it entered into the compromises that Americans made over the admission of Missouri, in the tariff settlement in 1833, and in the agreements of 1850. The idea appeared in party platforms and in the selection of candidates, and in 1860 it was an essential element in the division within the Democratic party.

The idea of a South produced an internal civil war whose outcome established the American nation. That result might have occurred in the absence of civil war, and also without the South idea, temporarily expressed as a Confederacy of states hostile to national union. But as it happened, the emergence of American nationality depended upon the idea of a South that posed a challenge to national citizenship and solidarity. In the postwar settlement—the constitutional amendments comprised in the peace treaty between the sections—the idea of the South profoundly affected the nature of the re-established Union upon national and pluralistic foundations. Later, when war emotions had cooled and industrial production expanded, it was the idea of the South that influenced the form and the content of the reactionary compromises of 1877. In the twentieth century the idea of a South re-emerged as men debated the meaning of national citizenship and the civil liberties the nation owed its citizens.

The American South is therefore not a place or a thing; it is not a collection of folkways or cultural distinctives. It is an idea. Those of whatever persuasion or tradition who believe themselves to be Southern are indeed Southern, and the South exists wherever Southerners form the predominant portion of the population. The study of the idea of Southness is thus a part of intellectual history, or, because it is an exercise in faith, it belongs among the academic offerings in the department of religion.

Perhaps a more fruitful question for students of the American South would be, not *what* the South is or has been, but *why* the idea of the South began, and *how* it came to be accepted as axiomatic among Americans. Whose interests were served when people spoke and thought of the South as an entity? How did the agents of the opinion-forming and opinion-disseminating institutions transmit the idea that allegiance to a section should transcend loyalty to the nation? What have been the effects upon American history of the belief in the idea of a South? Answers to these questions will go far to remove the study of the South from the realm of classifying and cataloguing to the tasks of probing causes and effects and the weighing of motivations. These are the true functions of the historian.

The South as a Counterculture

SHELDON HACKNEY

All around us extraordinary crises threaten to intrude into the serenity of our daily lives, and we are aware as seldom before of the striking disjunction between the personal and the public realms. At this time, when the habits of mind formed by our national historical experiences with individualism, affluence, progressive growth and military victory seem to be interfering with our ability to face up to the problems of racial justice, poverty, environmental despoliation and war, we should ask how our regional heritage speaks to our present needs. As the nation's largest and oldest counterculture, the South has much to teach us.

This, no doubt, seems a bizarre assertion to those familiar with the making of the contemporary counterculture. Much of the impetus for the cultural rebellion of youth lately has come from the assault of the civil rights movement on the South in the 1960s, so it would be a supreme irony if there were strong resemblances between the culture of the South and the culture created by young Americans seeking alternative values.

As analyzed sympathetically by Theodore Roszak in *The Making of a Counter Culture*, today's counterculture is at bottom a revolt against the dehumanizing effect of scientific and technological values, and against the bureaucratic society whose very efficiency depends upon desensitizing people to individual needs and differences. Artificial barriers that separate people, be they psychological, institutional, or social, say the current rebels, have to be torn down. In contrast to the ideal of material progress through rational analysis, the counterculture focuses on the quality of life and the need for individuals to have more power over the decisions that affect their lives.

The revolt against authoritarianism in favor of the New Left's ideal of participatory democracy has become more generally a revolt against authority of any kind. Only personal experience can serve as the basis of belief, a precept that should be appreciated by Southern Protestants who trace their form of worship back to the frontier. . . .

. . . In simplistic terms, it is a matter of the heart versus the head. There is a widespread feeling that the life of reason has failed us because so many barbarities are perpetrated in its name and so many evils exist within its sight. The technocratic rationalism of the war in Vietnam is the thing that lends it a special horror.

Furthermore, so the argument goes, technocracy and bureaucracy stultify spontaneity and thus make individual authenticity impossible. In contrast to the innovative thinkers of the late nineteenth and early twentieth centuries, such as Sigmund Freud, who were interested in the nonrational in order to control it better, we are confronted with Normal O. Brown, who argues that civilization's discontents will remain unless currently repressed instinctual drives are released from control by the superego. At the risk of putting the matter even more simplistically, the counterculture is a protest against the commercialization of life.

What are we to make of all this from our special vantage point in the South? I begin with history, because I accept as truth what Jack Burden says in Robert Penn Warren's novel, *All the King's Men*: "If you could not accept the past and its burden there was no future, for without one there cannot be the other, and . . . if you could accept the past you might hope for the future, for only out of the past can you make the future."

The key to the Southern past is that Southerners are Americans who have taken on an additional identity through conflict with the North. The process differentiating the South from the American non-South in the early nineteenth century was based on divergent economic interests growing from differing labor systems, and depending in part upon the Southern context of a sparse, occupationally homogeneous population and the lack of an urban middle class. With that beginning, the Southern sense of separateness has been constructed of many layers of defensiveness, particularism, isolation, guilt, defeat and the reactions to changes initiated from without: abolitionism, the Civil War, Reconstruction, poverty, depressions, industrialization and lately the civil rights movement. Through all this, white Southerners learned to see themselves as an oppressed minority with a giant sense of grievance, an identity they share with blacks, although for different reasons.

The counterattack of the Southern press against the hypocrisy and self-righteousness of the North during the Second Reconstruction is but another activation of this traditional defensive mentality. The same siege mentality can be seen subtly at work among historians and others who attribute the slow pace of modernization in the South to the region's colonial status and the imperial domination of Northern economic interests. Furthermore, the sense of persecution can be seen influencing the literature of the region. When Quentin Compson in *Absalom! Absalom!* comes to call on Rosa Coldfield before going off to Harvard, he is reminded, as he must have been a thousand times before, of the Yankee's persecution of the South. "So," says Rosa Coldfield, "I don't imagine you will ever come back here and settle down as a country lawyer in a little town like Jefferson since Northern people have already seen to it that there is little left in the South for a young man."

Nevertheless, Southerners are Americans, and in a real sense the need to be different was forced upon them by circumstances and by outsiders. The resulting approach-avoidance relationship of South to North explains why one finds in the South the coexistence of hyper-Americanism and cultural peculiarity.

The "approach" side of this curious psychological transaction can be seen best since the Civil War in the New South movement, beautifully dissected by Paul Gaston in *The New South Creed*, one of whose messages is that a conquered people frequently will imitate its conquerors. The chief tenet of the New South crusade is that industrialization is the way to secular salvation, and its optimistic dogma has from the first been that the South is destined to be the most prosperous place on earth, a new Eden. The bearers of these glad tidings were not only wise men out of the North, but local prophets as well, of whom Henry Grady was the most renowned in the nineteenth century. Today's champions of the New South tend to be the more institutional, hungry utilities and state industrial development offices, but the message is the same: The South is the land of milk and honey, or at least of water and electricity, and one can move into this land of low taxes and docile labor with little of the difficulty experienced by the children of Israel.

Southerners, when operating on the "avoidance" side of the American mirror, traditionally have had to define themselves in opposition to a presumed American norm, and in that sense at least, the South is a real counterculture. When the South was first created, the North was becoming the special carrier of Yankee commercial culture with its stress upon hard work, thrift and the cash basis of value. The mythical Southern planter, created in novels as an alternative to the emerging Yankee, was therefore a noneconomic man, the result of the South's need for a myth that would distinguish it from, and make it morally superior to, the North. . . .

The planters of the legend, explains William R. Taylor in *Cavalier and Yankee*, were exemplars of noncompetitiveness. They were generous, loving, gentle, noble and true to their word. Rather than the instinctive nobility of the unspoiled savage, however, the planter had the benefits of a benign and salubrious country life and rigorous training in a civilized code. But it was not the code of the Yankee. The legendary planter was free of personal ambition, particularly of the material sort, and his natural impulses were disciplined, not by calculation of gain, but by his concern for family and racial traditions, by rigid standards of decorum and a complicated code of personal honor. That our fictive hero was also weak, improvident, indolent and ineffectual betrays a flaw of disbelief on the part of his creators and explains why (Oh, confounder of women's liberation) Scarlet O'Hara always ended up running Tara. Southern writers shared more than they realized of the mainstream cultural values of the nation.

Northern writers, conversely, played an important part in the creation of the plantation legend, but for reasons differing from those of their Southern brothers. Faced with severe social dislocations growing out of geographic mobility, industrialization, immigration and urbanization, some Northerners began to fear the erosion of the old republican style of life characterized by simplicity and prudence. In growing numbers during the decades before the Civil War, such men began to focus their discontent on the planter and the slave system upon which he depended, as the primary threat to the Puritan virtues upon which the republic was founded. At the same time, many other Northerners were becoming painfully aware that the helter-skelter process of social mobility in America could not monitor the conditions under which men competed, and thus could not guarantee the moral worth of the men who succeeded. The image of the Yankee as an acquisitive, grasping, uncultivated and amoral man was not acceptable to many sensitive Northerners. Some reacted by imputing to the Yankee a transcending social virtue. They argued in effect that the ascetic, single-minded, materialistic and opportunistic Yankee benefited society by making a profit. Others, however, helped to create the planter or the Southern gentleman as the counterpoint to the Yankee. The Southern gentleman was made to possess all of the virtues that the Yankee lacked. He had honor and integrity, indifference to money questions and business, a decorous concern for the amenities of life and a high sense of social responsibility. In the age of democratic expansion, anxious men sought an antidemocratic Good Society and they found it in the mythical, static, Southern plantation.

Southern intellectuals responded obligingly by spending an enormous amount of energy romantically constructing Biblical or feudal or classical Greek alternatives to the liberal capitalism of the nation at large. John C. Calhoun, to an extent, and George Fitzhugh, more fundamentally, attacked the dehumanization inherent in the wage slavery of free enterprise. According to Fitzhugh in his books, *Sociology for the South or The Failure of Free Society* and *Cannibals All: or, Slaves Without Masters*, free competition was only legalized exploitation. It was merely freedom for the strong to oppress the weak. Anticipating Herbert Marcuse, one of the political philosophers of the New Left, Fitzhugh pointed out that not only was physical wretchedness the result of this war of all against all, but psychological wretchedness as well. For under capitalism one man's success was marked by another man's failure; fortunes shifted rapidly, and the result was that the human personality was marked by insecurity, anxiety and unhappiness. To complete his rejection of Jefferson, Fitzhugh advocated strong and positive action by the government to build up industries and cities in the South. Rejecting the doctrine of progress and the principle of equality, Fitzhugh held that only within the framework of absolute dependence and superiority could genuine reciprocal affection exist between human beings. A society seeking solutions in fantasy could scarcely get further away from the American consensus.

After the Civil War, the mutual symbolic interaction of North and South continued under the new conditions. While the myth of the New South was being created in a great rush of popular fervor, the myth of the Old South was simultaneously being created, packaged and marketed in the North and the South. Reflecting this divided mind of the South, Joel Chandler Harris recorded his Uncle Remus stories at the same desk where he wrote for the *Atlanta Constitution* editorials infused with New South boosterism. Harris, George Washington Cable, Thomas Nelson Page, Mary Noailles Murfree and their fellow writers in the 1880s established the primacy of Southern themes in American letters. Archaic romance and local color stories appealed to Northern audiences facing the reality of rapid social change in their daily lives. Southern sensibilities called for pathos balanced with the theme of sectional reconciliation. Through it all ran an intense sense of place and awareness of the past-in-the-present that are trademarks of Southern literature. The stock Southern character, for Northern as well as Southern writers, was still the embodiment of noncommercial nobility, the counterpoint to the shrewd but crude robber baron who ruled the Gilded Age.

The Agrarians, a group of Southern intellectuals centered at Vanderbilt University in the 1920s and 1930s, did not perpetuate this cavalier myth, but they were nonetheless engaged in the old Southern sport of defining an alternative to the national consensus. As their manifesto, *I'll Take My Stand*, put it in 1930, "All the articles bear in the same sense upon the book's title-subject: all tend to support a southern way of life against what may be called the American way; and all as much as agree that the best terms in which to represent the distinction are contained in the phrase, Agrarian versus Industrial." It was a frontal assault on the principles of Northern and modern civilization, a continuing comparison between the disordered present and the heroic past, which has always been the currency of groups disturbed by change.

The Agrarians, echoing George Fitzhugh, denied the virtue of machine-produced wealth and decried the brutalization of man and the philistinization of society that inevitably resulted from an industrial order. As humanists, they insisted that labor, the largest item in human life, should be enjoyed. This was impossible under industrialism. The art and culture they held most valuable was that which grew out of natural folk ways of doing, living and thinking. All else was superficial. Present day devotees of the *Whole Earth Catalog*, organic gardening and the handicraft industry would find this pretty heavy stuff.

More abstractly, the Agrarians placed the relationship of man to nature close to the center of their philosophy. They believed that "there is possible no deep sense of beauty, human heroism of conduct, and no sublimity of religion, which is not informed by the humble sense of man's precarious position in the universe." In other words, "there is more in the land than there is in the man," or, as John Crowe Ransom put it, "Nature wears out man before man can wear out nature. . . . It seems wiser to be moderate in our expectations of nature, and respectful; and out of so simple a thing as respect for the physical earth and its teeming life, comes a primary joy, which is an inexhaustible source of arts and religions and philosophies." The thing that differentiates these romantic conservatives most clearly from their descendants among today's youthful counterculturists is that the Agrarians linked community with continuity. They thought that "tradition is not simply a fact, but a fact that must be constantly defended." Nevertheless, paradoxical as it might seem, there is a large area of agreement between the culture of the South as understood by the Agrarians and the contemporary counterculture.

Like all paradoxes, the similarity between the culture of the South and the counterculture has its limitations. The world view of Southern Protestantism, which dominates the mind of the region, makes a virtue out of suffering in a way members of the counterculture would not understand or accept, even though the emphasis upon redemption through a personal conversion experience might find some resonance among young Americans seeking instant salvation along various secular and spiritual paths. Just as the counterculture is unthinkable in a country lacking the affluence provided by the work ethic in league with technocracy, Southern culture would not long survive apart from the rationalism whose hegemony it was created to challenge. The problems of human survival are not going to be solved by consulting the *I Ching* or Tarot cards.

Even so, at the present, when ten times more college students take courses in astrology than in astrophysics, when middle Americans, numbered by their lives as members of endless audiences, are in search of affective relationships, the South has much to offer. To an increasingly fragmented world the South offers an integrated view of life. There is no such thing as being "in fashion" now; styles in clothes and in most areas of life are too various and are multiplying too rapidly for a single standard to exist even for a short time. Contemporary art runs a gamut from the Wyeths to Helen Frankenthaler, and style has become a collective noun. Such currently popular writers as Donald Barthelme and Jerzy Kosinski render life into brilliant snippets of experience that coagulate without melding. Compare this to the vision of William Faulkner in which past, present and future are linked together; in which individuals don't merely rub up against each other in fleeting encounters but are enmeshed in each other's lives; in which individual lives over long periods of time are bound together by their connection to place. There is a wholeness to life in the South, even in its harsh and ugly aspects, and this is a useful antidote to a world in which increasing individuality means increasing isolation.

The price of wholeness is finitude. Freedom and the power to act are circumscribed when one is tied to a community. Rather than something that a counterculture must construct in the future after all the restraints of organized society have been cast off, community for Southerners is a set of conditions and obligations to be fulfilled through courage and honor. Strangely enough, Southerners, both white and black, do not feel alienated from themselves even though they feel alienated from the national sources of economic and political power.

It may also seen strange to find illegal defiance of national authority coexisting so comfortably in the South with superpatriotism, but that is a consequence of the dual identity of Southerners, and grows out of their double history. As C. Vann Woodward points out in *The Burden of Southern History*, the South's experiences with defeat, poverty and guilt have set it apart from the nation. In contrast to the national belief that problems have solutions, Southerners harbor the countervailing suspicion that there are limits to human power.

There is a salutary humanistic lesson in discovering the vine of fate entangling Southern history. Whether that vine is wisteria or kudzu may vary according to ideological taste, but the message that there are areas of life not susceptible to rational control or bureaucratic manipulation strikes a resonant note. As a perceptive journalist observed of a group of irate town fathers in Mississippi who had just been struck by another federal court edict, "Of course, they are not really surprised because, being Southerners and therefore fatalistic, they live always half expecting disaster." . . .

Southern history forces us to be aware not only of complexity, but also of defeat and failure. It would be wrong to reject or oppose the improvement in social welfare that will come from the intrusion of the machine into the garden, but we should oppose the Icarian notion that change comes without costs, and that the South will be immune from history. Only through such a constant realization do we have a chance to industrialize and humanize at the same time, to walk the thin line between defeatism and morally obtuse boosterism.

In striving to live with our past without being oppressed by it, the proper stance is one of ambivalent judgment, an ironic distance between oneself and his history that energizes rather than immobilizes. The modern man facing his existential predicament might well be guided by the lesson contained in the following Hasidic legend recorded by Elie Wiesel in his book, *Souls on Fire:*

> One of the Just Men came to Sodom, determined to save its inhabitants from sin and punishment. Night and day he walked the streets and markets preaching against greed and theft, falsehood and indifference. In the beginning, people listened and smiled ironically. Then they stopped listening: he no longer even amused them. The killers went on killing, the wise kept silent, as if there were no Just Man in their midst.
>
> One day a child, moved by compassion for the unfortunate preacher, approached him with these words. "Poor stranger. You shout, you expend yourself body and soul; don't you see that it is hopeless?"
>
> "Yes, I see," answered the Just Man.
>
> "Then why do you go on?"
>
> "I'll tell you why. In the beginning I thought I could change man. Today, I know I cannot. If I still shout today, if I still scream, it is to prevent man from ultimately changing me."

⚓ *F U R T H E R   R E A D I N G*

David Bertelson, *The Lazy South* (1967)

James Branch Cabell, *Let Me Lie* (1947)

F. Garvin Davenport, *Myth and Southern History* (1970)

Carl N. Degler, *Place over Time: The Continuity of Southern Distinctiveness* (1977)
———, "Thesis, Antithesis, Synthesis: The South, the North, and the Nation," *Journal of Southern History* 53 (1987), 3–18

John Hope Franklin, *The Militant South* (1956)
———, "The Great Confrontation and the Problem of Change," *Journal of Southern History* 38 (1972), 3–20

Wilson Gee, "The Distinctiveness of Southern Culture," *South Atlantic Quarterly* 37 (1939), 119–29

Patrick Gerster and Nicholas Cords, eds., *Myths and Southern History* (1974)

C. Hugh Holman, *The Immoderate Past: The Southern Writer and History* (1977)

Lewis M. Killian, *White Southerners* (1970)

Florence King, *Southern Ladies and Gentlemen* (1975)

Jack Temple Kirby, *Media-Made Dixie* (1978)

A. Cash Koeniger, "Climate and Southern Distinctiveness," *Journal of Southern History* 54 (1988), 21–44

Sharon McKern, *Redneck Mothers, Good Ol' Girls, and Other Southern Belles* (1979)

Grady McWhiney, *Southerners and Other Americans* (1973)

Bill C. Malone, *Southern Music/American Music* (1979)

U. B. Phillips, "The Central Theme of Southern History," *American Historical Review* 34 (1928), 30–43

David M. Potter, "The Enigma of the South," *Yale Review* 51 (1961), 142–51

Francis Butler Simkins, *The Everlasting South* (1963)

William R. Taylor, *Cavalier and Yankee* (1961)

Frank E. Vandiver, ed., *The Idea of the South: Pursuit of a Central Theme* (1964)

Alice Walker, "The Black Writer and the Southern Experience," *New South* 25 (1970), 23–26

C. Vann Woodward, *The Burden of Southern History* (1961)

Howard Zinn, *The Southern Mystique* (1964)

CHAPTER
2

Reconstruction

At one time, historians echoed the assessment of Reconstruction prevailing among white southerners: that Reconstruction had been a disastrous episode in which unscrupulous northern carpetbaggers, aided by traitorous scalawags and unqualified blacks, wrested power in southern governments and inaugurated an orgy of corruption, robbery, and misrule. But the civil-rights movement and new historical research since 1960 has led to a complete revision of this once-standard interpretation. While noting the importance of many white southerners' opposition to racial and other changes, revisionist studies have presented a much more factual assessment of the personnel and policies of Reconstruction. The twists and turns of policymaking in Washington, from Andrew Johnson's first and apparently harsh plan to the adoption of so-called Radical Reconstruction, are now better understood, and more objective attention has been given to the actions and character of Republicans—white and black—in the South.

What exactly did Reconstruction policies require? What consideration was given to land reform or land redistribution? What kind of competition prevailed between Democrats (or Conservatives) and Republicans in the South? What policies did Republican governments follow? And what impact did the Ku Klux Klan and other terrorist organizations have on Reconstruction? This chapter explores these probing questions.

DOCUMENTS

Andrew Johnson's proclamations, reprinted as the first document, described the first plan of Reconstruction, which he implemented and then partially abandoned during 1865. His Amnesty Proclamation applied to the entire South; separate proclamations for reestablishing governments in each state followed the model of the North Carolina Proclamation. Although portions of the Amnesty Proclamation suggest that Johnson intended to remove prominent slaveholders from power, the President issued wholesale pardons to leading Confederates, even those who had violated his proclamations and sought office without a pardon. Alarmed by the return of Confederate leaders to power and upset by state laws that restricted southern blacks' liberty—the Black Codes—the northern Congress stepped in. Congress's involvement in Reconstruction is summarized in the

proposed Fourteenth Amendment, which Johnson's white governments in the
southern states rejected, and then in the Military Reconstruction Act of 1867—
the second and third documents, respectively. Certain "Radical" Republicans
urged stronger measures that were not taken. Thaddeus Stevens, a leading Radical
in the House, was the principal, but one of the few, advocates of land confiscation
and redistribution. Note the features in his proposal, outlined in the
fourth document, that are designed to make it appealing to the many who disapproved
of it. The fifth document contains excerpts from the *Raleigh* (North Carolina)
Sentinel that reveal how quickly southern opponents of Congress's measures
began to construct the legend of Reconstruction misrule. As these excerpts
show, Southern Conservatives or Democrats also typically blamed all violence
on the Republicans; their views are revealed in the sixth and seventh documents.
To many southern whites, the granting of the right to vote to black people was
simply intolerable, as shown in document eight. The ninth document reprints instructions
to South Carolina's Red Shirts, armed supporters of Democratic gubernatorial
candidate Wade Hampton. These instructions make clear that white
Democrats were determined to regain control of the government at any price.
The final selection comprises cartoons by Thomas Nast for *Harper's Weekly* that
comment graphically on the issues of Reconstruction.

Andrew Johnson Begins Reconstruction, 1865

Amnesty Proclamation

. . . To the end that the authority of the Government of the United States
may be restored and that peace, order, and freedom may be established,
I, Andrew Johnson, President of the United States, do proclaim and declare
that I hereby grant to all persons who have, directly or indirectly, participated
in the existing rebellion, except as hereinafter excepted, amnesty
and pardon, with restoration of all rights of property, except as to slaves,
. . . but upon the condition, nevertheless, that every such person shall take
and subscribe the following oath (or affirmation) and thenceforward keep
and maintain said oath inviolate, . . . to wit:

I, ———, do solemnly swear (or affirm), in presence of Almighty God,
that I will henceforth faithfully support, protect, and defend the Constitution
of the United States and the Union of the States thereunder, and that I
will in like manner abide by and faithfully support all laws and proclamations
which have been made during the existing rebellion with reference to the
emancipation of slaves. So help me God.

The following classes of persons are excepted from the benefits of this
proclamation:

First. All who are or shall have been pretended civil or diplomatic
officers or otherwise domestic or foreign agents of the pretended Confederate
government.

Second. All who left judicial stations under the United States to aid
the rebellion.

Third. All who shall have been military or naval officers of said pretended
Confederate government above the rank of colonel in the army or
lieutenant in the navy.

Fourth. All who left seats in the Congress of the United States to aid the rebellion.

Fifth. All who resigned or tendered resignations of their commissions in the Army or Navy of the United States to evade duty in resisting the rebellion.

Sixth. All who have engaged in any way in treating otherwise than lawfully as prisoners of war persons found in the United States service as officers, soldiers, seamen, or in other capacities. . . .

Eighth. All military and naval officers in the rebel service who were educated by the Government in the Military Academy at West Point or the United States Naval Academy.

Ninth. All persons who held the pretended offices of governors of States in insurrection against the United States. . . .

Thirteenth. All persons who have voluntarily participated in said rebellion and the estimated value of whose taxable property is over $20,000. . . .

Provided, That special application may be made to the President for pardon by any person belonging to the excepted classes, and such clemency will be liberally extended as may be consistent with the facts of the case and the peace and dignity of the United States.

North Carolina Proclamation

. . . Whereas the rebellion which has been waged by a portion of the people of the United States against the properly constituted authorities of the Government thereof in the most violent and revolting form, but whose organized and armed forces have now been almost entirely overcome, has in its revolutionary progress deprived the people of the State of North Carolina of all civil government; and

Whereas it becomes necessary and proper to carry out and enforce the obligations of the United States to the people of North Carolina in securing them in the enjoyment of a republican form of government:

Now, therefore, in obedience to the high and solemn duties imposed upon me by the Constitution of the United States and for the purpose of enabling the loyal people of said State to organize a State government whereby justice may be established, domestic tranquillity insured, and loyal citizens protected in all their rights of life, liberty, and property, I, Andrew Johnson, President of the United States and Commander in Chief of the Army and Navy of the United States, do hereby appoint William W. Holden provisional governor of the State of North Carolina, whose duty it shall be, at the earliest practicable period, to prescribe such rules and regulations as may be necessary and proper for convening a convention composed of delegates to be chosen by that portion of the people of said State who are loyal to the United States, and no others, for the purpose of altering or amending the constitution thereof, and with authority to exercise within the limits of said State all the powers necessary and proper to enable such loyal people of the State of North Carolina to restore said State to its constitutional relations to the Federal Government and to present such a republican form of State government as will entitle the State to the guaranty of the United States therefor and its people to protection by the United States against invasion, insurrection, and domestic violence: *Provided,* That in any election that may be hereafter held for choosing delegates to any State convention as aforesaid no person shall be qualified as an elector or shall be eligible as a member of such convention unless he shall have previously taken and subscribed the oath of amnesty as set forth in the President's proclamation of May 29, A.D. 1865, and is a voter qualified as prescribed by the constitution and laws of the State of North Carolina in force immediately before the 20th day of May, A.D. 1861, the date of the so-called ordinance of secession; and the said convention, when convened, or the legislature that may be thereafter assembled, will prescribe the qualification of electors and the eligibility of persons to hold office under the constitution and laws of the State—a power the people of the several States composing the Federal Union have rightfully exercised from the origin of the Government to the present time.

And I do hereby direct—

First. That the military commander of the department and all officers and persons in the military and naval service aid and assist the said provisional governor in carrying into effect this proclamation. . . .

Second. That the Secretary of State proceed to put in force all laws of the United States the administration whereof belongs to the State Department applicable to the geographical limits aforesaid.

Third. That the Secretary of the Treasury proceed to nominate for appointment assessors of taxes and collectors of customs and internal revenue and such other officers of the Treasury Department as are authorized by law and put in execution the revenue laws of the United States within the geographical limits aforesaid. . . .

Fourth. That the Postmaster-General proceed to establish post-offices and post routes and put into execution the postal laws of the United States within the said State. . . .

Fifth. That the district judge for the judicial district in which North Carolina is included proceed to hold courts within said State in accordance with the provisions of the act of Congress. . . .

Sixth. That the Secretary of the Navy take possession of all public property belonging to the Navy Department within said geographical limits and put in operation all acts of Congress in relation to naval affairs having application to the said State.

Seventh. That the Secretary of the Interior put in force the laws relating to the Interior Department applicable to the geographical limits aforesaid.

Congress Proposes the Fourteenth Amendment, 1866

Sec. 1. All persons born or naturalized in the United States, and subject to the jurisdiction thereof, are citizens of the United States and of the State wherein they reside. No State shall make or enforce any law which shall abridge the privileges or immunities of citizens of the United States; nor shall any State deprive any person of life, liberty or property, without due process of law, nor deny to any person within its jurisdiction the equal protection of the laws.

Sec. 2. Representatives shall be apportioned among the several States according to their respective numbers, counting the whole number of persons in each State, excluding Indians not taxed. But when the right to vote at any election for the choice of electors for President and Vice President of the United States, representatives in Congress, the executive and judicial officers of a State, or the members of the Legislature thereof, is denied to any of the male inhabitants of such State, being twenty-one years of age, and citizens of the United States, or in any way abridged, except for participation in rebellion or other crime, the basis of representation therein shall be reduced in the proportion which the number of such male citizens shall bear to the whole number of male citizens twenty-one years of age in said State.

Sec. 3. No Person shall be Senator or Representative in Congress, or elector of President or Vice President, or hold any office, civil or military, under the United States, or under any State, who, having previously taken an oath as a member of Congress, or as an officer of the United States, or as a member of any State Legislature, or as an executive or judicial officer of any State, to support the Constitution of the United States, shall have engaged in insurrection or rebellion against the same, or given aid or comfort to the enemies thereof. But Congress may, by a vote of two-thirds of each House, remove such disability.

Sec. 4. The validity of the public debt of the United States, authorized by law, including debts incurred for payment of pensions and bounties for services in suppressing insurrection or rebellion, shall not be questioned. But neither the United States nor any State shall assume or pay any debt or obligation incurred in aid of insurrection or rebellion against the United States or any claim for the loss or emancipation of any slave; but all such debts, obligations, and claims shall be held illegal and void.

Sec. 5. The Congress shall have power to enforce, by appropriate legislation, the provisions of this article.

The Military Reconstruction Act, 1867

Whereas no legal State governments or adequate protection for life or property now exists in the rebel States of Virginia, North Carolina, South Carolina, Georgia, Mississippi, Alabama, Louisiana, Florida, Texas, and Arkansas; and whereas it is necessary that peace and good order should be enforced in said States until loyalty and republican State governments can be legally established: Therefore

Be it enacted, . . . That said rebel States shall be divided into military districts and made subject to the military authority of the United States . . .

Sec. 2. . . . It shall be the duty of the President to assign to the command of each of said districts an officer of the army, not below the rank of brigadier general, and to detail a sufficient military force to enable such officer to perform his duties and enforce his authority within the district to which he is assigned.

Sec. 3. . . . It shall be the duty of each officer assigned as aforesaid to protect all persons in their rights of person and property, to suppress insurrection, disorder, and violence, and to punish, or cause to be punished, all disturbers of the public peace and criminals, and to this end he may allow local civil tribunals to take jurisdiction of and to try offenders, or, when in his judgment it may be necessary for the trial of offenders, he shall have power to organize military commissions or tribunals for that purpose; and all interference under color of State authority with the exercise of military authority under this act shall be null and void. . . .

Sec. 5. . . . When the people of any one of said rebel States shall have formed a constitution of government in conformity with the Constitution of the United States in all respects, framed by a convention of delegates elected by the male citizens of said State twenty-one years old and upward, of whatever race, color, or previous condition, . . . and when such constitution shall provide that the elective franchise shall be enjoyed by all such persons as have the qualifications herein stated for electors of delegates, and when such constitution shall be ratified by a majority of the persons voting on the question of ratification who are qualified as electors of delegates, and when such constitution shall have been submitted to Congress for examination and approval, and Congress shall have approved the same, and when said State, by a vote of its legislature elected under said constitution, shall have adopted the amendment to the Constitution of the United States, proposed by the thirty-ninth Congress, and known as article fourteen, and when said article shall have become a part of the Constitution of the United States, said State shall be declared entitled to representation in Congress, and senators and representatives shall be admitted therefrom on their taking oaths prescribed by law, and then and thereafter the preceding sections of this act shall be inoperative in said State: *Provided,* That no person excluded from the privilege of holding office by said proposed amendment to the Constitution of the United States shall be eligible to election as a member of the convention to frame a constitution for any of said rebel States, nor shall any such person vote for members of such convention.

Sec. 6. . . . Until the people of said rebel States shall be by law admitted to representation in the Congress of the United States, any civil governments which may exist therein shall be deemed provisional only, and in all respects subject to the paramount authority of the United States at any time to abolish, modify or control, or supersede the same; and in all elections to any office under such provisional governments all persons shall be entitled to vote, and none others, who are entitled to vote under the provisions of the fifth section of this act; and no person shall be eligible to any office under any such provisional governments who would be disqualified from holding office under the provisions of the third article of said constitutional amendment.

Thaddeus Stevens Advocates the Redistribution of Land, 1865

Reformation *must* be effected; the foundation of their institutions, both political, municipal and social *must* be broken up and *relaid,* or all our blood and treasure have been spent in vain. This can only be done by treating and holding them as a conquered people. Then all things which we can desire to do, follow with logical and legitimate authority. As conquered territory Congress would have full power to legislate for them; for the territories are not under the Constitution except so far as the express power to govern them is given to Congress. They would be held in a territorial condition until they are fit to form State Constitutions, republican in fact not in form only, and ask admission into the Union as new States. If Congress approve of their Constitutions, and think they have done works meet for repentance they would be admitted as new States. If their Constitutions are not approved of, they would be sent back, until they have become wise enough so to purge their old laws as to eradicate every despotic and revolutionary principle—until they shall have learned to venerate the Declaration of Independence. . . .

We propose to confiscate all the estate of every rebel belligerent whose estate was worth $10,000, or whose land exceeded two hundred acres in quantity. Policy if not justice would require that the poor, the ignorant, and the coerced should be forgiven. They followed the example and teachings of their wealthy and intelligent neighbors. The rebellion would never have originated with them. Fortunately those who would thus escape form a large majority of the people, though possessing but a small portion of the wealth. The proportion of those exempt compared with the punished would be I believe about nine tenths.

There are about six millions of freemen in the South. The number of acres of land is 465,000,000. Of this those who own above two hundred acres each, number about 70,000 persons, holding in the aggregate (together with the States) about 394,000,000 acres, leaving for all the others below 200 each about 71,000,000 of acres. By thus forfeiting the estates of the leading rebels, the Government would have 394,000,000 of acres beside their town property, and yet nine tenths of the people would remain untouched. Divide this land into convenient farms. Give if you please forty acres to each adult male freed man. Suppose there are one million of them. That would require 40,000,000 of acres, which deducted from 394,000,000 leaves three hundred and fifty-four millions of acres for sale. Divide it into suitable farms and sell it to the highest bidders. I think it, including town property, would average at least ten dollars per acre. That would produce $3,540,000,000,—Three billions, five hundred and forty millions of dollars.

Let that be applied as follows to wit:

1. Invest $300,000,000 in six per cent. government bonds, and add the interest semi-annually to the pensions of those who have become entitled by this villainous war.

2. Appropriate $200,000,000 to pay the damages done to loyal men North and South by the rebellion.
3. Pay the residue being $3,040,000,000 towards the payment of the National debt.

What loyal man can object to this? Look around you, and everywhere behold your neighbors, some with an arm, some with a leg, some with an eye carried away by rebel bullets. Others horribly mutilated in every form. And yet numerous others wearing the weeds which mark the death of those on whom they leaned for support. Contemplate these monuments of rebel perfidy, and of patriotic suffering, and then say if too much is asked for our valiant soldiers.

Look again, and see loyal men reduced to poverty by the confiscations by the Confederate States, and by the rebel States—see Union men robbed of their property, and their dwellings laid in ashes by rebel raiders, and say if too much is asked for them. But above all, let us inquire whether imperative duty to the present generation and to posterity does not command us to compel the wicked enemy to pay the expenses of this unjust war. In ordinary transactions he who raises a false clamor and prosecutes an unfounded suit, is adjudged to pay the costs on his defeat. We have seen that, by the law of nations, the vanquished in an unjust war must pay the expenses.

Our war debt is estimated at from three to four billions of dollars. In my judgment, when all is funded and the pensions capitalized, it will reach more than four billions.

The interest at 6 per cent only, (now much more)	$240,000,000
. . . .	120,000,000
For some years the extraordinary expenses of our army	
and navy will be	110,000,000
	$470,000,000

Four hundred and seventy millions to be raised by taxation—our present heavy taxes will not in ordinary years, produce but little more than half that sum. Can our people bear double their present taxation? He who unnecessarily causes it will be accursed from generation to generation. It is fashionable to belittle our public debt, lest the people should become alarmed, and political parties should suffer. I have never found it wise to deceive the people. They can always be trusted with the truth. Capitalists will not be effected for they can not be deceived. Confide in the people, and you will avoid repudiation. Deceive them, and lead them into false measures, and you may produce it.

We pity the poor Englishmen whose national debt and burdensome taxation we have heard deplored from our childhood. The debt of Great Britain is just about as much as ours, ($4,000,000,000) four billions. But in effect it is but half as large,—it bears but three per cent interest. The current year the Chancellor of the Exchequer tells us, the interest was $131,806,990, ours, when all shall be funded, will be nearly double.

The plan we have proposed would pay at least three fourths of our debt. The balance could be managed with our present taxation. And yet to think that even that is to be perpetual is sickening. If it is to be doubled, as it must be, if "restoration" instead of "reconstruction" is to prevail, would to God the authors of it could see themselves as an execrating public and posterity will see them. . . .

But, it is said, by those who have more sympathy with rebel wives and children than for the widows and orphans of loyal men, that this stripping the rebels of their estates and driving them to exile or to honest labor would be harsh and severe upon innocent women and children. It may be so; but that is the result of the necessary laws of war. But it is revolutionary, say they. This plan would, no doubt, work a radical reorganization in southern institutions, habits and manners. It is intended to revolutionize their principles and feelings. This may startle feeble minds and shake weak nerves. So do all great improvements in the political and moral world. It requires a heavy impetus to drive forward a sluggish people. When it was first proposed to free the slaves, and arm the blacks, did not half the nation tremble? The prim conservatives, the snobs, and the male waiting maids in Congress, were in hysterics.

The whole fabric of southern society *must* be changed, and never can it be done if this opportunity is lost. Without this, this Government can never be, as it never has been, a true republic. Heretofore, it had more the features of aristocracy than of democracy.—The Southern States have been despotisms, not governments of the people. It is impossible that any practical equality of rights can exist where a few thousand men monopolize the whole landed property. The larger the number of small proprietors the more safe and stable the government. As the landed interest must govern, the more it is subdivided and held by independent owners, the better. What would be the condition of the State of New York if it were not for her independent yeomanry? She would be overwhelmed and demoralized by the Jews, Milesians and vagabonds of licentious cities. How can republican institutions, free schools, free churches, free social intercourse exist in a mingled community of nabobs and serfs; of the owners of twenty thousand acre manors with lordly palaces, and the occupants of narrow huts inhabited by "low white trash?"—If the south is ever to be made a safe republic let her lands be cultivated by the toil of the owners or the free labor of intelligent citizens. This must be done even though it drive her nobility into exile. If they go, all the better.

It will be hard to persuade the owner of ten thousand acres of land, who drives a coach and four, that he is not degraded by sitting at the same table, or in the same pew, with the embrowned and hard-handed farmer who has himself cultivated his own thriving homestead of 150 acres. This subdivision of the lands will yield ten bales of cotton to one that is made now, and he who produced it will own it and *feel himself a man.*

It is far easier and more beneficial to exile 70,000 proud, bloated and defiant rebels, than to expatriate four millions of laborers, native to the soil and loyal to the Government. This latter scheme was a favorite plan of the Blairs with which they had for awhile inoculated our late sainted President. But, a single experiment, made him discard it and its advisers. Since I have mentioned the Blairs, I may say a word more of those persistent apologists of the South. For, when the virus of Slavery has once entered the veins of the slaveholder, no subsequent effort seems capable of wholly eradicating it. They are a family of considerable power, some merit, of admirable audacity, and execrable selfishness; with impetuous alacrity they seize the White House, and hold possession of it, as in the late Administration, until shaken off by the overpowering force of public indignation. Their pernicious course had well nigh defeated the reelection of Abraham Lincoln; and if it should prevail with the present Administration, pure and patriotic as President Johnson is admitted to be, it will render him the most unpopular Executive—save one—that ever occupied the Presidential chair. But there is no fear of that. He will soon say, as Mr. Lincoln did: "YOUR TIME HAS COME!"

This remodeling the institutions, and reforming the rooted habits of a proud aristocracy, is undoubtedly a formidable task; requiring the broad mind of enlarged statesmanship, and the firm nerve of the hero. But will not this mighty occasion produce—will not the God of Liberty and order give us such men? Will not a Romulus, a Lycurgus, a Charlemagne, a Washington arise, whose expansive views will found a free empire, to endure till time shall be no more?

This doctrine of restoration shocks me.—We have a duty to perform which our fathers were incapable of, which will be required at our hands by God and our Country. When our ancestors found a "more perfect Union" necessary, they found it impossible to agree upon a Constitution without tolerating, nay guaranteeing Slavery. They were obliged to acquiesce, trusting to time to work a speedy cure, in which they were disappointed. *They* had some excuse, some justification. But we can have none if we do not thoroughly eradicate Slavery and render it forever impossible in this republic. The Slave power made war upon the nation. They declared the "more perfect Union" dissolved. Solemnly declared themselves a foreign nation, alien to this republic; for four years were in fact what they claimed to be, We accepted the war which they tendered and treated them as a government capable of making war. We have conquered them, and as a conquered enemy we can give them laws; can abolish all their municipal institutions and form new ones. If we do not make those institutions fit to last through generations of free men, a heavy curse will be on us. Our glorious, but tainted republic has been born to new life through bloody, agonizing pains. But this frightful "Restoration" has thrown it into "cold obstruction, and to death." If the rebel states have never been out of the Union, any attempt to reform their State institutions either by Congress or the President, is rank usurpation.

A Southern Newspaper Denounces Reconstruction, 1869

That the State has been cursed and almost ruined by a class of "carpet bag" vultures from the North, aided by degenerate and too often corrupt natives, is patent to anybody who opens his eyes. We have not been slow to tell the people of the villianies that have been perpetrated and are yet being perpetrated, day and night, by the present State government, at the expense and injury of the people, black and white. We intend to continue to do so regardless of cost or consequences.

Our firm conviction is that the people will not tolerate these villainies a great while longer; the day of reckoning cometh, and it will be terrible. The "carpet bagger" race will then hurry off to some other field of spoils and laugh at the calamity of their dupes and co-workers in iniquity; but the *native* culprit must answer at the bar of public opinion, and in many cases at the bar of the Court for high crimes. We tell the native scalawags that the day is not far distant, when the thin vail that now hides their crimes from public gaze will be withdrawn, and they will be exposed to the scorn and indignation of an outraged people. Yes, and that small class of our people who claim to be good and true men, who, for the sake of a little gain, have *secretly* colluded with the bad wretches who have plundered and impoverished the people without mercy, they, too, will be exposed. Yes, we repeat, the day will be mercilessly exposed. And such perpetration or crime will thenceforth be a *stench* in the nostrils of all decent men, white and black. Everybody will bate them, mock and hiss at them as they pass by. The Penitentiary fraud will be exposed, the Railroad frauds will be exposed; it will yet be known how much money was used to corrupt the members of the Legislature, who used it, who paid it, and where it came from; it will yet be known how many warrants have been made on the Treasury not authorized by law. We have the best of reasons for saying that the passage of the Railroad acts cost the State tens and hundreds of thousands of dollars. The people will yet ferret out those who so recklessly and criminally spent the treasure of the people. Yes, gentlemen, the day of reckoning will come. Mark what we say! Let every man watch how he connects himself even innocently with those who have so outraged the State and the people.

Southern Conservatives' View of Violence, 1869

Gov. Holden seems much exercised about the recent murders in Jones county, and it is proper he should be.

When a negro who offered brute violence to a respectable lady of Alamance was chastised, and the men who chastised him appeared with sheets over their heads at the house of Mr. Badham and Colonel Albright to scare them out of the Leagues, the Governor sent up his militia for their protection.

When the Governor's "beloved" son Joseph William, Speaker of the House, accompanied by the Governor's friends who hold office in the Capitol, made an attack upon the Editor of the SENTINEL, armed with pistols, clubs, and bowie knives, the Governor applauded their murderous attempt in a public speech to five hundred negroes who crowded in and about the City Hall. When the Governor and his son left the Hall the negroes left huzzahing for Joe.

When three barns were recently burnt in Orange, in which were consumed grain, forage and horses, the Governor sent out no militia or even detectives. This burning was no doubt done by men who belonged to the Governor's secret oath bound association of which he is the head centre.

The Foscue family of Jones county were murdered by League men; a whole family was put to death, Colonel Nethercutt, of Jones, was murdered in his own house in the night time and no doubt by members of their diabolical Leagues, organized throughout the State by the Governor himself.

Old Mr. Briley, of Pitt, was most inhumanly murdered by a carpet-bag Leaguer and three negroes belonging to the League.

In Wilson county a negro was beaten with 300 stripes by Leaguers for voting the Democratic ticket. Judge Thomas, signer of the ordinance of secession and League Judge, refused to allow the negro's counsel to prove that this outrage was committed by order of the League. Notwithstanding, the Leaguers were convicted and sentenced to jail, and the Governor, being President of the League, pardoned the perpetrators of this outrage. No wonder that murder, assassination, and all manner of lawlessness are on the increase.

The Constitution, the law and the Courts are disregarded by the Executive himself. He rescued a prisoner from the hands of the Marshal in defiance of law, and in contempt of the Supreme Court.

The Governor, as head of a secret political club, has trampled on all subordination and broken or borne down the unarmed laws of the State. He has uselessly called in a lawless militia to execute the civil law; nor did he desist from such lawless calls until his own militia murdered and cut each other's throats.

This state of things, though most extraordinary, for this country and this State, is not to be wondered at. It is all the workings, doings and proceedings of secret oathbound political clubs and societies. Where there is two there will be murder, arson, burglary and all manner of attrocious crimes.

We tell the Governor that his Leagues are the secret cause of all the troubles, tumults, barn burnings and assassinations which have occurred in this once quiet land of law and order. Things cannot remain much longer in their present confusion and disorder. The murders and burnings will go on between the two secret political clubs until the whole people will be hurried into the rage of civil discord, revenge and violence.

It is time,—high time that the Executive should dissolve his Leagues and quit his rings.

Congressional Testimony on the Ku Klux Klan, 1871

General John B. Gordon on the Loyal Leagues and the Origin of the Ku Klux Klan

The instinct of self-protection prompted that organization; the sense of insecurity and danger, particularly in those neighborhoods were the negro population largely predominated. The reasons which led to this organization were three or four. The first and main reason was the organization of the Union League, as they called it, about which we knew nothing more than this: that the negroes would desert the plantations, and go off at night in large numbers; and on being asked where they had been, would reply, sometimes, "We have been to the muster;" sometimes, "We have been to the lodge;" sometimes, "We have been to the meeting." These things were observed for a great length of time. We knew that the "carpet-baggers," as the people of Georgia called these men who came from a distance and had no interest at all with us; who were unknown to us entirely; who from all we could learn about them did not have any very exalted position at their homes—these men were organizing the colored people. We knew that beyond all question. We knew of certain instances where great crime had been committed; where overseers had been driven from plantations, and the negroes had asserted their right to hold the property for their own benefit. Apprehension took possession of the entire public mind of the State. Men were in many instances afraid to go away from their homes and leave their wives and children for fear of outrage. Rapes were already being committed in the country. There was this general organization of the black race on the one hand, and an entire disorganization of the white race on the other hand. . . . It was therefore necessary, in order to protect our families from outrage and preserve our own lives, to have something that we could regard as a brotherhood—a combination of the best men of the country, to act purely in self-defense. . . .

Ben Hill on the Klan

Question. You have not studied this organization?

Answer. I have only investigated a few cases for the purpose of ascertaining who were the guilty offenders. One reason for investigating the few cases was upon the attempt to reconstruct Georgia some time ago, and these Ku-Klux outrages were made to bear very, very heavily against even Union parties [who opposed returning Georgia to military rule]. I wanted to know if that was the case, and if so, I wanted the people to put down the Ku-Klux. In the second place, I arrived at the conclusion that a great many of these outrages were committed by gentlemen who wanted a reconstruction of the State, and committed those outrages to give an excuse for it. I have always thought that two or three of the most outrageous murders committed in the State were really committed by persons of the same political faith of the parties slain.

Question. And committed for the political effect they would have?

Answer. I think so. And a great many of us who have really wanted to be reconstructed have been between fires.

Question. Will you have the kindness to state to what cases you last referred, where persons were killed by their friends?

Answer. I think Ashburn [a Republican] was killed by his own political friends.

Question. So as to have the benefit of the political capital that could be made out of it?

Answer: I do not think the motive for killing Ashburn was altogether that; I think there was a personal grudge, or jealousy on the part of some of his political friends. And though my mind is not positive, I am inclined to believe that this fellow Adkins was killed expressly for political capital by his own friends. I was positive about that at one time, but I am not so positive about it now.

Question. Killed by his own friends?

Answer. Yes, sir; though I think it likely some of the others were in it also. I may be wrong, but that was the conclusion to which I arrived. . . .

Question. So far as I have observed your papers, (and I have examined them both before I came into the State and since, I mean the democratic papers,) two lines of thought on this subject seem to run along through them; one is to deny the existence of this organization, and the other is to discountenance with unmeasured abuse every effort to punish such offenses, and even to inquire and ascertain whether in fact they exist. . . . Why is that?

Answer. I am unable to give you a very satisfactory reason. I think myself that the great body of our people are really anxious to put down anything of this sort, the great body of our people of the best class, almost without exception. There are a very few, however, who, as you have stated, have denied unconditionally the existence of such things at all, even in the local and sporadic form I have mentioned, for I do not myself believe that they have existed in any other form. I think they have discountenanced the effort of some people to investigate them, first, because they professed to believe that they did not exist; second, because I think a great many of them have honestly been actuated by a simple desire to pander to what was considered sectional prejudice on this subject. I think we have a class of people in our State, and democrats, too, who are willing to use this occasion, as a great many politicians use all occasions to make themselves popular, by simply pandering to what they consider the sectional prejudices of the hour. I think some have been extreme and ultra in denouncing all pretense of lawlessness, merely for the purpose of making political capital for themselves individually.

Question. Take the case of an honest man, desirous to do justice and to know the truth, who reads nothing but the democratic papers in Georgia, would he believe that there had been any of these outrages and enormities committed from anything he would see in those papers, published as matters of information or for the purpose of denouncing them and rebuking them?

Answer. Heretofore, I believe, that if a man was shut up to the information derived from the democratic press of Georgia, he would have believed that there was no such thing; but I believe now the thing would be different. A great many of our papers are awakening to the fact that there is such a thing as I say, local and temporary in its character. I have believed, myself, for a long time, that there have been these local organizations, and I believe they have been . . . not political in their character. Some few have been political, no doubt; I think that in some cases democrats have availed themselves of the public sentiment for the purpose of exterminating a radical; and I believe some colored people have organized for plunder and robbery. But I believe there have been some cases where men have been made victims by their own political friends for party purposes and ends. I think democrats have been guilty; that plunderers and robbers have been guilty; and I believe that radicals have been guilty for the purpose of making [political] capital.

Question. Can you state any particulars you may have heard in reference to the attack on Ware?

Answer. Yes, sir; I can state what I heard. A body of about twenty-five or thirty disguised men went one night and met him upon the road. (I think this was the case of Jourdan Ware.) I am not certain that they went to his house. I believe they met him on the road, somewhere or other, and demanded of him his arms and his watch. I believe he gave up his arms, and they shot him upon his refusal to surrender the watch, and he died a day or two afterward.

Question. Did you ever hear that there was any accusation of his having done anything wrong?

Answer. No, sir; I think not, except I believe I did hear that there was some complaint of his impudence, or something of that sort.

Question. We hear from a great many witnesses about the "impudence" of negroes. What is considered in your section of the country "impudence" on the part of a negro?

Answer. Well, it is considered impudence for a negro not to be polite to a white man—not to pull off his hat and bow and scrape to a white man, as was always done formerly.

Question. Do the white people generally expect or require now that kind of submissive deportment on the part of the negroes that they did while the negroes were slaves?

Answer. I do not think they do as a general thing; a great many do.

Question. Are there many white people who do require it?

Answer. Yes, sir; I think there are a great many who do require it, and are not satisfied unless the negroes do it.

Question. Suppose that a negro man has been working for a white man, and they have some difference or dispute in relation to wages, will your people generally allow a negro man to stand up and assert his rights in the same way and in the same language which they would allow to a white man without objection?

Answer. O, no sir, that is not expected at all.

Question. If the colored man does stand up and assert his rights in language which would be considered pardonable and allowable in a white man, that is considered "impudence" in a negro?

Answer. Yes, sir; gross impudence.

Question. Is that species of "impudence" on the part of the negro considered a sufficient excuse by many of your people for chastising a negro, or "dealing with him?"

Answer. Well, some think so. . . .

Question. In your judgment, from what you have seen and heard, is there something of a political character about this organization?

Answer. I think it is entirely political.

Question. What makes you think so?

Answer. Because the parties who are maltreated by these men are generally republicans. I have never known a democrat to be assaulted. . . .

Question. Give the committee your judgment in relation to the object with which this organization has been gotten up. What do its members intend to attain by it?

Answer. Well, sir, my opinion is that the first object of the institution of the Ku-Klux, or these disguised bands, was to cripple any effect that might be produced by Loyal Leagues. That is my opinion—that this organization was an offset to the Loyal Leagues.

Question. But the Ku-Klux organization kept on increasing after the Loyal Leagues were disbanded?

Answer. Yes, sir.

Question. What, in your opinion, is the object of keeping up the Ku-Klux organization and operating it as they do? What do they intend to produce or effect by it?

Answer. My opinion is, that the purpose was to break down the reconstruction acts; that they were dissatisfied with negro suffrage and the reconstruction measures and everybody that was in favor of them.

Question. Do you think this organization was intended to neutralize the votes of the negroes after suffrage had been extended to them?

Answer. Yes, sir, I think so.

Question. How? By intimidating them?

Answer. Any way. Yes, sir, by intimidation.

Question. Making them afraid to exercise the right of suffrage?

Answer. Yes, sir.

Question. Do you believe that the organization and its operations have, in fact, produced that effect?

Answer. I think they have to some extent.

Question. What is the state of feeling which has been produced among the colored people by this armed, disguised organization, and the acts they have committed?

Answer. Well, in my section of the country, the colored people, generally, are afraid now, and have been for some time, to turn out at an election. They are afraid to say much, or to have anything to do with public affairs. I own a plantation on Coosa River, upon which I have, perhaps, about 40 negroes, and some of them have been pretty badly alarmed, afraid to say much. Some have lain out in the woods, afraid to stay at home.

White Conservatives Petition Congress, 1868

It is well known by all who have knowledge on the subject, that while the negroes of the South may be more intelligent and of better morals than those of the same race in any other part of the world where they exist in equal density, yet they are in the main, ignorant generally, wholly unacquainted with the principles of free Governments, improvident, disinclined to work, credulous yet suspicious, dishonest, untruthful, incapable of self-restraint, and easily impelled by want or incited by false and specious counsels, into folly and crime. Exceptions, of course, there are; chiefly among those who have been reared as servants in our domestic circles, and in our cities. But the general character of our colored population is such as we have described. . . .

Are these the people in whom should be vested the high governmental functions of establishing institutions and enacting and enforcing laws to prevent crime, protect property, preserve peace and order in society, and promote industry, enterprise and civilization in Alabama, and the power and honor of the United States? Without property, without industry, without any regard for reputation, without control over their own caprices and strong passions, and without fear of punishment under laws, by courts and through juries which are created by and composed of themselves, or of those whom they elect, how can it be otherwise than that they will bring, to the great injury of themselves as well as of us and our children, blight, crime, ruin and barbarism on this fair land? . . .

Continue over us, if you will do so, your own rule by the sword. Send down among us, honorable and upright men of your own people, of the race to which you and we belong: and ungracious, contrary to wise policy and the institutions of the country, and tyrannous as it will be, no hand will be raised among us to resist by force their authority. But do not, we implore you, abdicate your own rule over us, by transferring us to the blighting, brutalizing and unnatural dominion of an alien and inferior race: a race which has never shown sufficient administrative capacity for the good government of even the tribes into which it has always been broken up in its native seats; and which in all ages, has itself furnished slaves for all the other races of the earth.

Instructions to Red Shirts in South Carolina, 1876

1. That every Democrat in the Townships must be put upon the Roll of the Democratic Clubs. . . .

2. That a Roster must be made of every white and of every Negro in the Townships and returned immediately to the County Executive Committee.

3. That the Democratic Military Clubs are to be armed with rifles and pistols and such other arms as they may command. They are to be divided into two companies, one of the old men, the other of the young men; an experienced captain or commander to be placed over each of them. . . .

12. Every Democrat must feel honor bound to control the vote of at least one Negro, by intimidation, purchase, keeping him away or as each individual may determine, how he may best accomplish it.

13. We must attend every Radical meeting that we hear of whether they meet at night or in the day time. Democrats must go in as large numbers as they can get together, and well armed, behave at first with great courtesy and assure the ignorant Negroes that you mean them no harm and so soon as their leaders or speakers begin to speak and make false statements of facts, tell them then and there to their faces, that they are liars, thieves and rascals, and are only trying to mislead the ignorant Negroes and if you get a chance get upon the platform and address the Negroes.

14. In speeches to Negroes you must remember that argument has no effect upon them: they can only be influenced by their fears, superstitions and cupidity. Do not attempt to flatter and persuade them. . . . Treat them so as to show them, you are the superior race, and that their natural position is that of subordination to the white man. . . .

16. Never threaten a man individually. If he deserves to be threatened, the necessities of the times require that he should die. . . .

29. Every club must be uniformed in a red shirt and they must be sure and wear it upon all public meetings and particularly on the day of election.

30. Secrecy should shroud all of our transactions. Let not your left hand know what your right hand does.

Thomas Nast Views Reconstruction, 1865, 1874

"Worse Than Slavery"

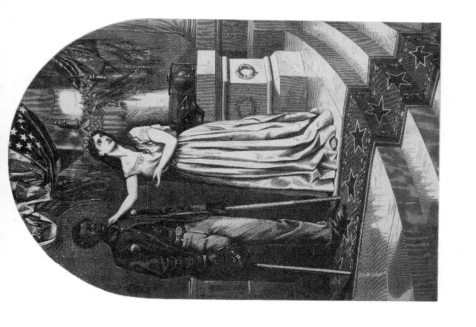

Columbia.—"Shall I Trust These Men,

And Not This Man?"

47

⚓ E S S A Y S

Historian William C. Harris of North Carolina State University has reexamined both the actions and the motives of the much-maligned carpetbaggers. Although some northerners in the Reconstruction South were corrupt or scoundrels, Harris shows in the first essay that most of those called carpetbaggers had quite different, and often laudable, motives. Their chief crime was to challenge traditional racial, political, and social arrangements in the region. In the second selection, Eric Foner, professor of history at Columbia University, has delineated with care the role that blacks played in Reconstruction and the importance of the Ku Klux Klan. Historian J. Mills Thornton of the University of Michigan focuses in the third essay on fiscal and tax policies of the Republican administrations in the South. His findings show that the cost of Republican programs damaged the party's political prospects, particularly its ability to appeal to small white farmers.

Carpetbaggers in Reality

WILLIAM C. HARRIS

The tainted reputation of the carpetbagger during the post–Civil War period is undergoing a remarkable revision. Viewed for decades as the chief of villains in the melodrama known as Radical Reconstruction, the carpetbagger, or northerner who went south after the war and engaged in politics, has attracted during the last few years a number of defenders among historians of the postwar era. The image that now emerges, though far from exculpating them for their failures and abuses of power, represents carpetbaggers as basically decent individuals who in most cases entered the South seeking the main chance through commercial and planting endeavors rather than through political activity. Many became insolvent as a result of the disastrous agricultural failure of 1866, and some of the less enterprising abandoned the region at this time, returning to the North to inveigh against the inhospitable South. Only after the passage of the military Reconstruction Acts of 1867, enfranchising blacks and temporarily disfranchising the former leadership class in the South, did many of the remaining northerners become involved in the politics of their adopted states. Regarded as liberators by the freedmen, the influence of these newcomers among the new citizens virtually ensured their rapid rise to positions of state and local leadership in the young Republican organizations of the region.

In office, the performance of the carpetbaggers was mixed in the opinion of present-day historians. While some were extravagant and corrupt, others, like Governors Adelbert Ames of Mississippi and Daniel Henry Chamberlain of South Carolina, "were economy-minded and strictly honest." Even those who pursued material gain through political power often did so in

From "The Creed of the Carpetbaggers" by William C. Harris, *Journal of Southern History* XL (May 1974), pp. 199–224. Copyright © 1974 by the Southern Historical Association. Reprinted by permission of the Managing Editor.

collaboration with acquisitive southern Democrats. Of course, the carpet-baggers disturbed race relations in the South: to have done otherwise would have been an abject abandonment of the freedmen to the devices of un-sympathetic southern whites. But carpetbaggers, revisionist historians find, did not incite blacks to violence against their former masters; in fact, they frequently took the position of their conservative neighbors on inflammatory racial issues, notably the question of social integration.

These revisionist perspectives are both provocative and suggestive. However, they are views derived from limited research. The revisionist generalization, for example, that carpetbaggers were a variegated lot is based upon vignettes of a handful of the more prominent northerners, not upon grass-roots studies of the motives, policies, and activities of a rela-tively large number. Additional research, testing, and refining of hypotheses concerning this class of politicians is needed. Data should be sought to reveal in full measure the experience and character of carpetbagger lead-ership in southern Reconstruction.

This essay suggests the utility of such basic research. The focus is upon a single aspect of the story of the carpetbaggers—their objectives and ideals in participating in the politics of postwar Mississippi. . . .

The politically active carpetbag class in Mississippi was never very numerous, probably at no time exceeding two hundred men and never including the majority of the postwar northern settlers in the state. Most of the newcomers from above the Ohio were of the farmer class and, either because of their fear of ostracism by local whites or their hostility to the advanced doctrines of Negro rights, shunned affiliation with the Republican party. On the other hand, carpetbaggers, or those northerners who joined and labored for the Republican party, generally were the most affluent and best educated of the northern immigrants in the state. And these men frequently accumulated considerable property in Mississippi before entering politics. Such elite qualities were especially true of carpetbaggers whose influence was statewide, but evidence exists that a number of relatively obscure members of this political class, those who organized and led local Republican clubs and Union Leagues, often serving in county and town offices, were also men of means and some erudition.

Carpetbagger ideology in Mississippi was a product of the intense re-publican idealism that swept the North during the Civil War era, finding its most profound expression in the minds of young, educated officers in the Union army. Generally men of some mobility even before the war, the northerners who came to the state after the conflict had never felt the constraints of provincial ties usually characteristic of life in a single com-munity. To an impressive extent their allegiance was to the stirring national ideals produced by the sectional conflict and the subsequent northern com-mitment to freedom; their vision was broad and optimistic, with a belief in progress through the revitalized republican institutions of the Founding Fathers.

The principal goal of the carpetbaggers was the eradication of the ves-tiges of slavery and rebellion which they believed still existed in the South.

They sought to replace these baneful anachronisms with the progressive spirit of Union and freedom. These were broad and ambiguous concepts, but northerners in Mississippi thought they knew their precise meaning and the requirements for fulfilling them. In their view, slavery and secession were coexistent if not synonymous; similarly, Union and freedom were paired. The slavery-secession syndrome, according to these agents of a new order for the state, had not only caused the internecine war but had also been the reason for the destitution, economic inefficiency, ignorance, intolerance, and violence they found to a deplorable extent in the postwar South. "The effects of the [slave] institution upon the character of its devotees," a leading carpetbagger observed after living in the state for two years, "are a thousandfold more appalling than the most vivid imagination ever dreamed. What slavery failed to touch has been wrecked by secession and treason. The social, business, religious, and political history of the south will show more bad faith, deception, and treachery in a single State [there] than in all the States of the north together." Not until the "hydra-headed monster" of secession had been completely expelled could the South and Mississippi hope to be regenerated and become like the progressive states of the North.

Secession and rebellion had become institutionalized in the Democratic party, carpetbaggers believed, and it followed that the national agency for the redemption of the South should be the Republican party. Triumphant in the war against Democratic copperheads and secessionists, the Republican party must ensure in Reconstruction that Union sacrifices had not been made in vain. Specifically, the South should be reconstructed along lines that would guarantee loyalty to the Union, bona fide freedom for blacks, and tolerance of the opinions of all. Despite the intensity of their views, most carpetbaggers in Mississippi would probably not have agreed with [Governor] Adelbert Ames that Reconstruction was merely an extension of the Civil War and that their purpose in the state was "Mission with a large M," but most of them accepted the necessity of certain changes in the South designed to preserve the fruits of the national victory. . . .

Once in power, carpetbaggers, who proved to be the predominant element in the Republican administrations from 1870 to 1876, set about to implement the progressive features of the new constitution. Shunning a conception of themselves as revolutionary agents or as ultra-Radicals, these northerners were nonetheless convinced that certain reforms were essential before Mississippi could advance into the mainstream of American life. After five years of peace the state still suffered from lawlessness, violence, ignorance, and intolerance of the rights of those who disagreed with the white majority. These vestiges of the blighted past, they believed, must be stamped out before the spirit of progress and equality could take permanent root in the state.

In the minds of the reformers the most important prescription for the retrogressive ills of Mississippi society was a comprehensive system of public schools for both races. Even the shadowy Ku Klux Klan owed its existence to the ignorance of the masses, according to carpetbagger Amos Lovering, a former Indiana judge. Such lawless activities as those practiced by the Klan, he declared, could only be permanently suppressed through the power of "universal education in morals and mind." Charles W. Clarke, the thirty-year-old native of Vermont who drafted the public-school article in the constitution, asserted that education was "the energizing agent of modern civilization" and a necessity for the continuance of republican government and institutions. Furthermore, Clarke and others of his class believed that education was the answer to the race problem in southern society. Enlighten the white masses and their prejudices against Negroes would fade away, they argued; at the same time schooling for the blacks would elevate them to a position in society nearly equal to whites, and their irresponsible behavior in freedom would inevitably cease. In the Republican press, on the campaign stump, and in the legislature, carpetbaggers trumpeted the virtues of public education. Much of their rhetoric was simply promotional, but the emphasis and zeal with which they pursued educational reform suggest strongly the faith of these northerners in its remedial and progressive qualities.

On the question of mixed schools most carpetbaggers preferred to remain silent or ambiguous, hoping to avoid a commitment to equality for blacks that would arouse the prejudices of the bulk of white Republicans, incite conservatives to violent opposition, and inevitably destroy the infant school system. Some, like their southern white neighbors, were simply antagonistic to any social mixing of the races, although they generally were able to keep their racism subdued for political, if for no other, reasons. A few northerners such as Clarke, Henry R. Pease, the state superintendent of education, and Albert T. Morgan probably favored the principle of integration, but they shied away from public statements suggesting that they questioned the dual arrangement established by the legislature of 1870. The only white Republican in Mississippi during Reconstruction to advocate publicly the integration of the public schools was a scalawag and a former slaveholder, Robert W. Flournoy.

After only one year's experience with the free school system, Superintendent Pease reported outstanding progress, including a remarkable improvement in white attitudes toward public education, despite the burning of several Negro schools by the Klan. But difficulties developed as the financial costs of the system proved greater than anticipated, and the goodwill of whites toward it declined. As a result Pease and his associates turned to the federal government for aid. Writing in the state educational journal, Hiram T. Fisher asserted: "It is the utmost folly to talk about establishing free schools permanently in the South without national aid. . . . The little that has been done [already] . . . far surpasses anything that the friends of education can or will do in the South for the next twenty years if they are compelled to rely solely upon their own resources." Congress, he declared, must act before it was too late to save free schools in the financially depressed region. Although viewed as radical and unconstitutional in most quarters, the demand for federal aid received the strong support both of Mississippi carpetbaggers of Radical tendencies and those of the moderate persuasion as well.

To effectuate these demands for national aid, carpetbag congressman Legrand Winfield Perce of Natchez on January 15, 1872, introduced in the House of Representatives a bill to apply the annual proceeds from the sale of federal lands to education in the states. Even though the measure did not single out the South for special treatment, the amended version of the bill had this effect, since it provided that the distribution of the funds during the first ten years would be based on the proportion of illiterates in the population of each state, a category in which the southern states clearly led the nation. The first federal-assistance bill for public school to be given serious consideration by Congress, the far-reaching Perce proposal passed the House but failed in the Senate. . . .

Though never achieving the society of virtue and enlightenment that the educational program was supposed to produce, the carpetbag principle of free schools did not die in Mississippi when the Republican political edifice collapsed. The conservative Redeemers of the late 1870s and the 1880s, despite their public resolves to purge the state of carpetbag innovations and to economize in state expenditures, found it desirable to maintain the semblance of the comprehensive system of public education that their bitter enemies had established during Reconstruction.

Even though public education was the cornerstone of the carpetbaggers' reform program, they realized somewhat vaguely that other measures were also required to transform Mississippi into a progressive commonwealth. Perhaps most carpetbaggers, especially those of moderate leanings, believed that the adoption of the Fifteenth Amendment and the establishment of Republican civil rule in the state made further legislation guranteeing fundamental rights unnecessary. The ferociousness of Ku Klux Klan attacks in 1870 and 1871 and the continuation of general lawlessness, however, convinced many that additional laws, either state or federal, along with a vigorous enforcement, were essential to the security of the new order. In the United States Senate during the zenith of Klan activity in the South, Adelbert Ames, who was always suspicious of the intentions and behavior of southern whites, led the effort to reawaken Republicans in Mississippi, and especially blacks, to the dangers posed by the resurgence of the "Ku Klux Democracy." At the same time, encouraged by his Radical colleagues in Mississippi, the young, idealistic native of New England urged Congress to apply the full power of the army to end the spreading political violence in the South.

Moderate carpetbaggers, on the other hand, sought frantically to prevent this, believing, as so many of their brethren in the North did, that "The ready resort to the military is one of the most dangerous precedents which we can establish as a party." In an effort to prevent federal intervention, Governor Alcorn and his associates, including carpetbaggers, secured the passage of a state Ku Klux Klan law, legislated against the carrying of concealed weapons, and organized the militia. When these measures failed, many moderate carpetbaggers abandoned their reservations and supported the federal Klan law of 1871, designed to put down terror societies in the South.

Northerners in Mississippi were even more reluctant to accept the necessity for further legislation protecting the rights of blacks. During the early, exuberant days of the new order they seemed genuinely to believe that the ballot for blacks and universal education for whites would lead to an end of racial hostility and prejudice in the state. Many carpetbaggers obviously held racial attitudes similar to those of native whites, but it is also clear that an impressive number of them viewed black inferiority as only temporary, and they believed that Negroes would soon come up to or approach closely the standards set by whites. At any rate, most northerners in the state interpreted black capacity in a far more sympathetic light than did their white neighbors.

In the beginning carpetbaggers especially objected to proposals advanced by a handful of Negro leaders in the legislature to guarantee the rights of freedmen in public places. Believing that the Constitution already required the equal treatment of blacks on railroads and steamboats, even the Radical state senator Albert T. Morgan, who married a mulatto schoolteacher, at this time denounced as premature and politically disastrous any measure that would go beyond this right in the direction of social equality. Reflecting the position of those northerners with strong racial prejudices, the carpetbag editor of the Vicksburg *Times and Republican* minced no words in castigating lawmakers who proposed such schemes, especially the state civil rights bill of 1872, which resembled Charles Sumner's national measure. Holding views amazingly similar to those of southern conservatives during the age of segregation, this editor announced that Radical legislators in Jackson should "recognize the fact that the pathway of the colored man through life shall not be higher and shall not be lower than the pathway of the white race, but that it shall be seperate [*sic*] and distinct, and yet be equal. The two races can not be hurled together into an indiscriminate mass without the consent of both. . . . We know that it [the civil rights bill] is repugnant to the feelings of both races; we know that both races look upon such attempts with horror, as foreboding the destruction of both." Nonetheless, after some reflection many moderate carpetbaggers, as well as Radicals, came to support the bill, and in 1873 it became law.

Probably more representative of carpetbag opinion on the treatment of blacks in public was the position of Governor Ridgely C. Powers, generally a moderate in politics, who signed the civil rights bill in 1873. Addressing the state Senate in 1870, he explained that he could "see some reason for refusing to ride in the same car or steamboat, or for declining to sit in the same assembly with drunkards, gamblers, robbers and murderers, but to refuse to come into such proximity with men because they happened to bear a different complexion from my own, would be to acknowledge a mean prejudice, unworthy of an age of intelligence. . . . The time, I apprehend, has past for estimating a man by the color of his skin rather than by the qualities of his heart, or the strength of his intellect." . . .

. . . As might be expected, carpetbaggers were caught up in the mania for railroad construction, although most of them probably did not view such internal improvements as the *sine qua non* for economic rehabilitation and progress that conservatives did. On one occasion the editor of the Jackson *Mississippi Pilot* had to reassure his readers that, regardless of its concern with other issues, the Republican leadership in the state had no intention of slighting Mississippi railroads. As "the great civilizer of nations," railroads, carpetbaggers asserted, should receive the financial support of all levels of government—federal, state, county, and community. Such aid would be repaid in many ways: lands would appreciate in value, economic activity would be stimulated, new enterprises would arise, tax revenues would increase, and a large number of immigrants would be attracted to Mississippi. The Vicksburg *Times and Republican* confidently claimed that the railroads "will certainly bring prosperity and population" to the state.

Although equally as interested as the old citizens in promoting internal improvements, leading carpetbaggers warned against haphazardly conceived railroad projects. Unlike overanxious conservative leaders during the Johnsonian period, they urged legislative planning for the construction of roads that would serve the general interests of the state. As Stafford of the Jackson *Mississippi Pilot* put it, railroads should be constructed for the benefit of Mississippi and her people "without regard to section, locality, race, color, or previous condition." The provision in the constitution against extending the state's credit to aid private corporations, Stafford and others of his class believed, should be no barrier; they fully expected the legislature to evade the clause by providing direct assistance to the railroads. When the chips were down, transplanted northerners, as much as their conservative associates in railroad development, abandoned their good intentions and succumbed to local influences and interests in supporting the construction of roads that would benefit only their own communities or districts.

Black Activism and the Ku Klux Klan

ERIC FONER

In 1867, politics emerged as the principal focus of black aspirations. In that *annus mirabilis*, the impending demise of the structure of civil authority opened the door for political mobilization to sweep across the black belt. Itinerant lecturers, black and white, brought the Republican message into the heart of the rural South. A black Baptist minister calling himself Professor J. W. Toer journeyed through parts of Georgia and Florida with a "magic lantern" exhibiting "the progress of reconstruction. . . . He has a scene, which he calls 'before the proclamation,' another 'after the proclamation' and then '22nd Regt. U. S. C[olored] T[roops] Duncan's Brigade'."

Voting registrars instructed freedmen in American history and government and "the individual benefits of citizenship." In Monroe County, Alabama, where no black political meeting had occurred before 1867, freedmen crowded around the speaker shouting, "God bless you," "Bless God for this." Throughout the South, planters complained of blacks neglecting their labor. Once a week during the summer of 1867, "the negroes from the entire county" quit work and flocked to Waco, Texas, for political rallies. In Alabama, "they stop at any time and go off to Greensboro" for the same purpose. On August 1, Richmond's tobacco factories were forced to close because so many black laborers attended the Republican state convention.

So great was the enthusiasm that, as one ex-slave minister later wrote, "Politics got in our midst and our revival or religious work for a while began to wane." The offices of the black-controlled St. Landry (Louisiana) *Progress*, where several hundred freedmen gathered each Sunday to hear the weekly issue read aloud, temporarily displaced the church as a community meeting place. More typically, the church, and indeed every other black institution, became politicized. Every AME [African Methodist Episcopal] preacher in Georgia was said to be actively engaged in Republican organizing, and political materials were read aloud at "churches, societies, leagues, clubs, balls, picnics, and all other gatherings." One plantation manager summed up the situation: "You never saw a people more excited on the subject of politics than are the negroes of the south. They are perfectly wild."

The meteoric rise of the Union League reflected and channeled this political mobilization. Having originated as a middle-class patriotic club in the Civil War North, the league now emerged as the political voice of impoverished freedmen. Even before 1867, local Union Leagues had sprung up among blacks in some parts of the South, and the order had spread rapidly during and after the war among Unionist whites in the Southern hill country. Now, as freedmen poured into the league, "the negro question" disrupted some upcountry branches, leading many white members to withdraw altogether or retreat into segregated branches. Many local leagues, however, achieved a remarkable degree of interracial harmony. In North Carolina, one racially mixed league composed of freedmen, white Unionists, and Confederate Army deserters, met "in old fields, or in some out of the way house, and elect candidates to be received into their body."

By the end of 1867, it seemed, virtually every black voter in the South had enrolled in the Union League or some equivalent local political organization. Although the league's national leadership urged that meetings be held in "a commodious and pleasant room," this often proved impossible; branches convened in black churches, schools, and homes, and also, when necessary, in woods or fields. Usually, a Bible, a copy of the Declaration of Independence, and an anvil or some other emblem of labor lay on a table, a minister opened the meeting with a prayer, new members took an initiation oath, and pledges followed to uphold the Republican party and the principle of equal rights, and "to stick to one another." Armed black sentinels—"a thing unheard of in South Carolina history," according to one alarmed white—guarded many meetings. Indeed, informal self-defense organizations sprang up around the leagues, and reports of blacks drilling with weapons, sometimes under men with self-appointed "military titles," aroused considerable white apprehension.

The leagues' main function, however, was political education. "We just went there," explained an illiterate North Carolina black member, "and we talked a little; made speeches on one question and another." Republican newspapers were read aloud, issues of the day debated, candidates nominated for office, and banners with slogans like "Colored Troops Fought Nobly" prepared for rallies, parades, and barbecues. One racially mixed North Carolina league on various occasions discussed the organization of a July 4 celebration, cooperation with the Heroes of America (itself experiencing a revival among wartime Unionists in 1867), and questions like disenfranchisement, debtor relief, and public education likely to arise at the state's constitutional convention. A York County, South Carolina, league "frequently read and discussed" the Black Code, a reminder of injustices in the days of Presidential Reconstruction.

The detailed minute book of the Union League of Maryville, Tennessee, a mountain community with a long-standing antislavery tradition, offers a rare glimpse of the league's inner workings. It records frequent discussions of such issues as the national debt and the impeachment of President Johnson, as well as broader questions: "Is the education of the Female as important as that of the male?" "Should students pay corporation tax?" "Should East Tennessee be a separate state?" Although composed largely of white loyalists—mainly small farmers, agricultural laborers, and town businessmen, many of them Union Army veterans—and located in a county only one-tenth black, the Maryville league chose a number of black officers, called upon Tennessee to send at least one black to Congress, and in 1868 nominated a black justice of the peace and four black city commissioners, all of whom won election.

The local leagues' multifaceted activities, however, far transcended electoral politics. Often growing out of the institutions blacks had created in 1865 and 1866, they promoted the building of schools and churches and collected funds "to see to the sick." League members drafted petitions protesting the exclusion of blacks from local juries and demanding the arrest of white criminals. In one instance, in Bullock County, Alabama, they organized their own "negro government" with a code of laws, sheriff, and courts. (The army imprisoned its leader, former slave George Shorter.)

This hothouse atmosphere of political mobilization made possible a vast expansion of the black political leadership (mostly, it will be recalled, freeborn urban mulattoes) that had emerged between 1864 and 1867. Some, like the Charleston free blacks who fanned out into the black belt spreading Republican doctrine and organizing Union Leagues, did have years of political activism behind them. Others were among the more than eighty "colored itinerant lecturers" financed by the Republican Congressional Committee—men like William U. Saunders, a Baltimore barber and Union

Army veteran, James Lynch, who left the editorship of the *Christian Recorder* to organize Republican meetings in Mississippi, and even James H. Jones, former "body servant" of Jefferson Davis. Of the black speakers who crisscrossed the South in 1867 and 1868, Lynch was widely regarded as the greatest orator. "Fluent and graceful, he stirred the audience as no other man did or could do," and his eloquence held gatherings of 3,000 freedmen or more spellbound for hours at a time.

Not a few of the blacks who plunged into politics in 1867 had been born or raised in the North. Even in South Carolina, with its well-established native leadership, Northern blacks assumed a conspicuous role. One white participant in the state's first Republican convention, "astonished" by "the amount of intelligence and ability shown by the colored men," singled out Ohio-born William N. Viney, a young veteran (he was twenty-five in 1867) who had purchased land in the low country and, after the passage of the Reconstruction Act, organized political meetings throughout the region at his own expense. Many Northern blacks, like Viney, had come south with the army; others had served with the Freedmen's Bureau, or as teachers and ministers employed by black churches and Northern missionary societies. Still others were black veterans of the Northern antislavery crusade, fugitive slaves returning home, or the children of well-to-do Southern free blacks who had been sent north for the education (often at Oberlin College) and economic opportunities denied them at home. Reconstruction was one of the few times in American history that the South offered black men of talent and ambition not only the prospect of serving their race, but greater possibilities for personal advancement than existed in the North. And as long as it survived, the southward migration continued. As late as 1875, twenty-two year old D. B. Colton came to South Carolina from Ohio and promptly won a position as election manager. As a consequence, Northern black communities were drained of men of political ambition and of lawyers and other professionals. Having known discrimination in the North—Jonathan C. Gibbs had been "refused admittance to eighteen colleges" before finding a place at Dartmouth—black migrants carried with them a determination that Reconstruction must sweep away racial distinctions in every aspect of American life.

Even more remarkable than the prominence of Northern blacks was the rapid emergence of indigenous leadership in the black belt. Here, where few free blacks had lived before the war, and political mobilization had proceeded extremely unevenly before 1867, local leaders tended to be ex-slaves of modest circumstances who had never before "had the privilege" of expressing political opinions "in public." Many were teachers, preachers, or individuals who possessed other skills of use to the community. Former slave Thomas Allen, a Union League organizer who would soon win election to the Georgia legislature, was a propertyless Baptist preacher, shoemaker, and farmer. But what established him as a leader was literacy: "In my county the colored people came to me for instructions, and I gave them the best instructions I could. I took the New York Tribune and other papers, and in that way I found out a great deal, and I told them whatever

I thought was right.'' In occupation, the largest number of local activists appear to have been artisans. Comprising 5 percent or less of the rural black population, artisans were men whose skill and independence set them apart from ordinary laborers, but who remained deeply embedded in the life of the freedmen's community. Many had already established their prominence as slaves, like Emanuel Fortune, whose son, editor T. Thomas Fortune, later recalled: ''It was natural for [him] to take the leadership in any independent movement of the Negroes. During and before the Civil War he had commanded his time as a tanner and expert shoe and bootmaker. In such life as the slaves were allowed and in church work, he took the leader's part.'' The Union League catapulted others into positions of importance. James T. Alston, an Alabama shoemaker and musician and the former slave of Confederate Gen. Cullen A. Battle, had ''a stronger influence over the minds of the colored men in Macon county'' than any other individual, a standing he attributed to the commission he received in 1867 to organize a local Union League.

And there were other men, respected for personal qualities—good sense, oratorical ability, having served in the army, or, like South Carolina Republican organizer Alfred Wright, being ''an active person in my principles.'' Calvin Rogers, a Florida black constable, was described by another freedman as ''a thorough-going man; he was a stump speaker, and tried to excite the colored people to do the right thing. . . . He would work for a man and make him pay him.'' Such attributes seemed more important in 1867 than education or political experience. ''You can teach me the law,'' wrote one black Texan, ''but you cannot [teach] me what justice is.'' Nor, in a region that erected nearly insuperable barriers against black achievement, did high social status appear necessary for political distinction. ''All colored people of this country understand,'' a black writer later noted, ''that what a man does, is no indication of what he is.''

In Union Leagues, Republican gatherings, and impromptu local meetings, ordinary blacks in 1867 and 1868 staked their claim to equal citizenship in the American republic. Like Northern blacks schooled in the Great Tradition of protest, and the urban freemen who had dominated the state conventions of 1865 and 1866, former slaves identified themselves with the heritage of the Declaration of Independence, and insisted America live up to its professed ideals. In insistent language far removed from the conciliatory tones of 1865, an Alabama convention affirmed its understanding of equal citizenship:

> We claim exactly *the same rights, privileges and immunities as are enjoyed by white men*—we ask nothing more and will be content with nothing less. . . . The law no longer knows white nor black, but simply men, and consequently we are entitled to ride in public conveyances, hold office, sit on juries and do everything else which we have in the past been prevented from doing solely on the ground of color. . . .

Violence . . . had been endemic in large parts of the South since 1865. But the advent of Radical Reconstruction stimulated its further expansion.

By 1870, the Ku Klux Klan and kindred organizations like the Knights of the White Camelia and the White Brotherhood had become deeply entrenched in nearly every Southern state. One should not think of the Klan, even in its heyday, as possessing a well-organized structure or clearly defined regional leadership. Acts of violence were generally committed by local groups on their own initiative. But the unity of purpose and common tactics of these local organizations makes it possible to generalize about their goals and impact, and the challenge they posed to the survival of Reconstruction. In effect, the Klan was a military force serving the interests of the Democratic party, the planter class, and all those who desired the restoration of white supremacy. Its purposes were political, but political in the broadest sense, for it sought to affect power relations, both public and private, throughout Southern society. It aimed to reverse the interlocking changes sweeping over the South during Reconstruction: to destroy the Republican party's infrastructure, undermine the Reconstruction state, reestablish control of the black labor force, and restore racial subordination in every aspect of Southern life. . . .

By and large, Klan activity was concentrated in Piedmont counties where blacks comprised a minority or small majority of the population and the two parties were evenly divided. But no simple formula can explain the pattern of terror that engulfed parts of the South while leaving others relatively unscathed. Georgia's Klan was most active in a cluster of black belt and Piedmont cotton counties east and southeast of Atlanta, and in a group of white-majority counties in the northwestern part of the state. Unknown in the overwhelmingly black South Carolina and Georgia low-country, the organization flourished in the western Alabama plantation belt. Scattered across the South lay counties particularly notorious for rampant brutality. Carpetbagger Judge Albion W. Tourgée counted twelve murders, nine rapes, fourteen cases of arson, and over 700 beatings (including the whipping of a woman 103 years of age) in his judicial district in North Carolina's central Piedmont. An even more extensive "reign of terror" engulfed Jackson, a plantation county in Florida's panhandle. "That is where Satan has his seat," remarked a black clergyman; all told over 150 persons were killed, among them black leaders and Jewish merchant Samuel Fleischman, resented for his Republican views and reputation for dealing fairly with black customers.

Nowhere did the Klan become more deeply entrenched than in a group of Piedmont South Carolina counties where medium-sized farms predominated and the races were about equal in number. An outbreak of terror followed the October 1870 elections, in which Republicans retained a tenuous hold on power in the region. Possibly the most massive Klan action anywhere in the South was the January 1871 assault on the Union county jail by 500 masked men, which resulted in the lynching of eight black prisoners. Hundreds of Republicans were whipped and saw their farm property destroyed in Spartanburg, a largely white county with a Democratic majority. Here, the victims included a considerable number of scalawags and wartime Unionists, among them Dr. John Winsmith, a member of "the old land aristocracy of the place" wounded by Klansmen in March 1871. In York County, nearly the entire white male population joined the Klan, and committed at least eleven murders and hundreds of whippings; by February 1871 thousands of blacks had taken to the woods each night to avoid assault. The victims included a black militia leader, found hanging from a tree in March with a note pinned to his breast, "Jim Williams on his big muster," and Elias Hill, a self-educated black teacher, minister, and "leader amongst his people." Even by the standards of the postwar South, the whipping of Hill was barbaric: A dwarflike cripple with limbs "drawn up and withered away with pain," he had mistakenly believed "my pitiful condition would save me." Hill had already been organizing local blacks to leave the region in search of the "peaceful living, free schools, and rich land" denied them in York County. Not long after his beating, together with some sixty black families, he set sail for Liberia.

Contemporary Democrats, echoed by subsequent scholars, often attributed the Klan's sadistic campaign of terror to the fears and prejudices of poorer whites. (More elevated Southerners, one historian contends, could never have committed these "horrible crimes.") The evidence, however, will not sustain such an interpretation. It is true that in some upcountry counties, the Klan drove blacks from land desired by impoverished white farmers and occasionally attacked planters who employed freedmen instead of white tenants. Sometimes, violence exacerbated local labor shortages by causing freedmen to flee the area, leading planters to seek an end to Klan activities. Usually, however, the Klan crossed class lines. If ordinary farmers and laborers constituted the bulk of the membership, and energetic "young bloods" were more likely to conduct midnight raids than middle-aged planters and lawyers, "respectable citizens" chose the targets and often participated in the brutality.

Klansmen generally wore disguises—a typical costume consisted of a long, flowing white robe and hood, capped by horns—and sometimes claimed to be ghosts of Confederate soldiers so, as they claimed, to frighten superstitious blacks. Few freedmen took such nonsense seriously. "Old man, we are just from hell and on our way back," a group of Klansmen told one ex-slave. "If I had been there," he replied, "I would not want to go back." Victims, moreover, frequently recognized their assailants. "Dick Hinds had on a disguise," remarked an Alabama freedmen who saw his son brutally "cut to pieces with a knife." "I knew him. Me and him was raised together." And often, unmasked men committed the violence. The group that attacked the home of Mississippi scalawag Robert Flournoy, whose newspaper had denounced the Klan as "a body of midnight prowlers, robbers, and assassins," included both poor men and property holders, "as respectable as anybody we had there." Among his sixty-five Klan assailants, Abram Colby identified men "not worth the bread they eat," but also some of the "first-class men in our town," including a lawyer and a physician.

Personal experience led blacks to blame the South's "aristocratic classes" for violence and with good reason, for the Klan's leadership included planters, merchants, lawyers, and even ministers. "The most respectable citizens are engaged in it," reported a Georgia Freedmen's Bureau agent, "if there can be any respectability about such people." Editors Josiah Turner of the Raleigh *Sentinel*, Ryland Randolph of the Tuscaloosa *Monitor* (who years later recalled administering whippings "in the regular *ante bellum style*"), and Isaac W. Avery of the Atlanta *Constitution* were prominent Klansmen, along with John B. Gordon, Georgia's Democratic candidate for governor in 1868. When the Knights of the White Camelia initiated Samuel Chester in Arkansas, the pastor of his church administered the oath and the participants included Presbyterian deacons and elders "and every important member of the community." In Jackson County, Florida, the "general ring-leader of badness . . . the generalissimo of Ku-Klux" was a wealthy merchant; elsewhere in the black belt, planters seem to have controlled the organization. Even in the upcountry, "the very best citizens" directed the violence. "Young men of the respectable farming class" composed the Klan's rank and file in western North Carolina, but its leaders were more substantial—former legislator Plato Durham, attorney Leroy McAfee (whose nephew, Thomas Dixon, later garbed the violence in romantic mythology in his novel *The Clansman*), and editor Randolph A. Shotwell. As the Rutherford *Star* remarked, the Klan was "not a gang of *poor trash*, as the leading Democrats would have us believe, but men of property . . . respectable citizens." . . .

. . . Violence had a profound effect on Reconstruction politics. For the Klan devastated the Republican organization in many local communities. By 1871, the party in numerous locales was "scattered and beaten and run out." "They have no leaders up there—no leaders," a freedman lamented of Union County, South Carolina. No party, North or South, commented Adelbert Ames, could see hundreds of its "best and most reliable workers" murdered and still "retain its vigor." Indeed, the black community was more vulnerable to the destruction of its political infrastructure by violence than the white. Local leaders played such a variety of roles in schools, churches, and fraternal organizations that the killing or exiling of one man affected many institutions at once. And for a largely illiterate constituency, in which political information circulated orally rather than through newspapers or pamphlets, local leaders were bridges to the larger world of politics, indispensable sources of political intelligence and guidance. Republican officials, black and white, epitomized the revolution that seemed to have put the bottom rail on top. Their murder or exile inevitably had a demoralizing impact upon their communities.

The violence of 1869–71 etched the Klan permanently in the folk memory of the black community. "What cullud person dat can't 'membahs dem, if he lived dat day?" an elderly Texas freedman asked six decades later. The issue of protection transcended all divisions within the black community, uniting rich and poor, free and freed, in calls for drastic governmental action to restore order. To blacks, indeed, the violence seemed an irrefutable denial of the white South's much-trumpeted claims to superior morality and higher civilization. "Pray tell me," asked Robert B. Elliott, "who is the barbarian here?"

More immediately, violence underscored yet again the "abnormal" quality of Reconstruction politics. Before the war, Democrats and Whigs had combated fiercely throughout the South, but neither party, as Virginia Radical James Hunnicutt pointed out, advised its supporters "to drive out, to starve and to perish" its political opponents. Corrupt election procedures, political chicanery, and even extralegal attempts to oust the opposition party from office were hardly unknown in the North, but not pervasive political violence. "I never knew such things in Maine," commented an Alabama carpetbagger. "Republicans and Democrats were tolerated there." Democracy, it has been said, functions best when politics does not directly mirror deep social division, and each side can accept the victory of the other because both share many values and defeat does not imply "a fatal surrender of . . . vital interests." This was the situation in the North, where, an Alabama Republican observed, "it matters not who is elected." But too much was at stake in Reconstruction for "normal politics" to prevail. As one scalawag pointed out, while Northern political contests focused on "finances, individual capacity, and the like, our contest here is for life, for the right to earn our bread . . . for a decent and respectful consideration as human beings and members of society."

Most of all, violence raised in its starkest form the question of legitimacy that haunted the Reconstruction state. Reconstruction, concluded Klan victim Dr. John Winsmith, ought to begin over again: "I consider a government which does not protect its citizens an utter failure." Indeed, as a former Confederate officer shrewdly observed, it was precisely the Klan's objective "to defy the reconstructed State Governments, to treat them with contempt, and show that they have no real existence." The effective exercise of power, of course, can command respect if not spontaneous loyalty. But only in a few instances had Republican governments found the will to exert this kind of force. Only through "decided action," wrote an Alabama scalawag, could "the state . . . protect its citizens and vindicate its own authority and *right to be*." Yet while their opponents acted as if conducting a revolution, Republicans typically sought stability through conciliation.

Tax Policy and the Failure of Radical Reconstruction

J. MILLS THORNTON III

One of the most pernicious difficulties afflicting the historiography of Reconstruction is that few historians of Reconstruction have done much research on the antebellum period that preceded it. White Southern voters who judged Reconstruction policies at the polls viewed those policies from the perspective of a lifetime's experience with their state government; history did not begin for them in 1867. But too many historians approach Reconstruction as the carpetbaggers at the time did: devoid of any thorough knowledge of what the earlier policies of Southern governments had been, relying instead on a few facts and hostile legends. This absence of an accurate conception of the antebellum context is arguably a principal reason that the carpetbaggers were so markedly unsuccessful in their efforts to hold the allegiance of native white voters. And it is the principal reason, I believe, that recent historians have so misunderstood the factors underlying white small farmers' desertion of the Republican cause.

In his first book [*Tom Watson: Agrarian Rebel*], published more than forty years ago, Professor C. Vann Woodward laid much stress upon the necessity of appreciating the connections between antebellum political assumptions and postbellum discontent among white small farmers. He sought to show that the lines of descent in Southern history join antebellum policies and the attitudes of the Populists. But that lesson has still not been learned. Recent historians of Reconstruction, displaying little sensitivity to the world view of nineteenth-century Southern small farmers, have therefore been unable to offer any compelling explanation for small farmers' behavior during the decade. Small farmers' increasing distrust of the Republicans, and their eventual cooperation with the Redeemer Democrats in overthrowing Reconstruction, have been attributed simply to racism.

I would certainly not wish to question the power of racial antipathies in shaping the course of Southern history. Racism cannot serve, however, as an all-purpose explanation for small farmers' electoral behavior. Another essential concern of the work of Professor Woodward has been his effort to demonstrate that lower-middle- and lower-class whites have often been willing to rise above their racial attitudes when presented, as in Populism, with a political or economic movement that offered real hope of ameliorating their hard lot. As depicted in much of the recent historiography, Republicanism ought to have been just such a movement. Republicans, we are told, established or greatly increased support of public schools. They aided the building of railroads into the hill counties. They looked with favor on a wide variety of eleemosynary institutions. If white small farmers were not wholly averse to cooperating with blacks in the Populist effort to make the government the defender of the masses, one must wonder why their racism had so inhibited such cooperation only fifteen years earlier.

The answer, of course, is that Republicanism was not at all like Populism. One important difference between them, I should admit, reinforces the notion that racism was at the root of small-farmer behavior: the Populists did not take nearly so strong a stand in favor of legal guarantees of equal rights for blacks. But the Populist experience seems to me to indicate that small farmers might even have tolerated on practical political grounds the passage of state and federal civil-rights acts, if the Republican party had otherwise been vigorously espousing policies that promised small farmers important benefits. Far from promising them benefits, however, Republican policies may actually have seemed to be inimical to their interests. Many poorer whites did indeed support the Republicans early in Reconstruction, even though doing so meant working with blacks and Yankees. But the fiscal policies that the Republicans implemented, once in power, drove, I think, white small farmers into the arms of the Redeemers. And the final irony of this process is that many Republicans, particularly those who were carpetbaggers, never really comprehended why the small farmers were so hostile to these policies.

The explanation I would offer for the white small farmers' perception of Republican fiscal policies turns upon an understanding of the fiscal policies that they replaced. The principal source of tax revenue in all of the Lower South states during most of the antebellum period was the tax on slaves. The slave tax constituted some 60 percent of the total receipts in South Carolina and 30 to 40 percent in the others. The substantial revenues from this source allowed the states to hold their land taxes at quite low levels. Even toward the end of the antebellum period, when the land tax rose somewhat to meet greatly increased expenditures, it generally remained under two mills on the dollar. In addition, the states levied a variety of specific taxes on luxuries and capital. Only the modest land tax and a small poll tax—a levy of from 25 cents to one dollar on white males between twenty-one and forty-five—were broad-based taxes. The result of this tax structure was in large measure to exempt poorer whites from direct taxation. It would appear that the wealthiest third of the citizenry in the Lower South paid at least two-thirds of its taxes.

The abolition of slavery brought dramatic changes to the Southern tax structure, as to all areas of Southern life. Reconstruction legislators turned to the land tax to make up for the loss of the slave tax; the land tax produced some two-thirds, and in a few cases an even larger proportion, of the state revenues during the decade. At the same time, disbursements rose far above those of antebellum levels. The greater reliance on the land tax and the increase in disbursements together forced extraordinary increases in the millage rates. In Mississippi, for instance, the tax rose from 1.6 mills near the end of the antebellum years, to 9 mills in 1871 and $12\frac{1}{2}$ mills in 1873. Alabama taxed at a rate of 2 mills in 1860 and $7\frac{1}{2}$ mills in 1870. In Louisiana the millage rate was 2.9 in 1860, but $20\frac{1}{2}$ in 1872, and $14\frac{1}{2}$ in 1874. In Florida the millage rate went from $1\frac{2}{3}$ mills in 1860 to 7 mills in 1870 and 13 mills in 1874. These rates reflect only state taxes, of course. In Florida in 1874 the counties assessed an additional $11\frac{1}{2}$ mills, for a total rate of $24\frac{1}{2}$ mills. These large new taxes fell on every property owner. For the first time in Southern history the burden of taxation came home to the small farmer. Largely exempted from taxation throughout the antebellum years, he was suddenly called upon to support a very active government.

It might be said, of course, that in return for this new contribution the small farmer received much in disbursements for social-service programs. But such a contention would, I believe, misrepresent the small farmer's own perspective. Because the citizenry to be served had been virtually doubled by the emancipation of the slaves, and because the inflation of prices caused by the war required, until the panic of 1873, the expenditure of more money in order to purchase the same amount of goods and services, so that disbursements for many programs were apparently but not really larger, white small farmers had in many cases in the antebellum period actually received benefits equal to or greater than those they received during Reconstruction, and for a great deal less in taxes. Recent historiography, for instance, has emphasized Republican generosity to the public-school systems in the South. However, public-school expenditures per eligible child, measured in constant dollars, remained about the same in one state, rose in two, but still only to quite modest levels, and actually declined in two others. I need hardly add that the freedmen, because they owned very little property, paid directly only a small proportion of the taxes: 2.3 percent of the property-tax receipts and 7.4 percent of the total tax receipts in Georgia in 1874, when they composed some 46 percent of the population. As the white small farmer could well have seen his situation, therefore, he was paying far more in taxes, but his contribution was in considerable measure state-enforced altruism; he was getting back little more in services than he had received earlier. . . .

It does not seem to me that the recent historiography of Reconstruction has shown a sufficient awareness of just how large the receipts and disbursements of the Southern state governments during the decade were, in comparison with the figures from preceding and following years. They dwarfed the totals from the 1850s, though the 1850s had been a period of massive expansion in governmental activity in most of the Lower South states. . . . I do not, of course, mean to endorse the assumption . . . that the size of the figures is prima facie evidence of wastefulness. On the contrary, I believe that the heart of the Republicans' political dilemma . . . is that the vast social needs of a devastated region peopled with millions of destitute citizens, black and white, clearly justified the states in undertaking expenditures on a scale equal to the problem. Indeed, one can make a persuasive argument that the expenditures, far from being excessive, were insufficient. But such an argument looks at the matter from the perspective of an administrator seeking to deal with the demands of a difficult situation. The reality of democracy demands that the politician look at matters from the perspective of the voter as well, and the two perspectives are by no means always congruent. In the case of Reconstruction, however great the social needs apparent from the capital may have been, it would not have been irrational for the white small farmer to have felt himself overtaxed and underserved by Republican policies. In the present section, I shall attempt to suggest what may have been his viewpoint on what was happening to him, as opposed to the viewpoint of his governors, which dominates the current secondary literature.

In the first place, it is necessary to underscore . . . that taxes increased rapidly in this decade. . . . I need not belabor this point further; it in any case is generally acknowledged. Far less often recognized is the apparent shift in tax incidence which accompanied the abolition of slavery. Slaves had, of course, been a very large part of the total wealth in the antebellum South. One index to their value is that in nine of the fifteen slave states in 1860, according to the federal census of that year, the assessed value of personal property exceeded that of real estate, whereas this situation obtained in only three of the nineteen free states. Slaves were a form of property whose ownership was concentrated almost exclusively in the hands of wealthier citizens. And slaves were an obvious and readily assessable asset. The slave tax had therefore been chiefly responsible for the progressive features of the antebellum tax structure.

After the abolition of slavery, only intangible personal property—stocks, bonds, notes, money at interest—remained as a form of property whose ownership was essentially limited to the wealthy. A property tax on intangibles is, however, notoriously easy to evade, and intangibles did not constitute a substantial part of Southern wealth in any case. Nor is the property tax a very effective method of taxing a business corporation. The Reconstruction statutes insisted that capital and the property of corporations had to be taxed, of course. But receipts from these sources were never very large, perhaps 15 percent of the totals. An additional 15 percent came from other personalty, including wagons, farming implements, furniture, and livestock. The poll tax usually contributed another 5 to 10 percent. It was not the taxes from these sources, however, that really sustained the rapidly expanding Reconstruction governments. Sixty percent or more of this burden fell on a single object of taxation—land.

In the antebellum period, the land tax had seldom exceeded a third of the tax receipts. The presence of the slave tax had allowed legislators to keep land-tax rates low. Just as governmental activity and the consequent need for revenue soared to levels unexampled in peacetime, however, the states faced a newly, and markedly, constricted tax base. It was the decision of Republican legislators to let the land tax alone bear the burden formerly divided between the land and slave taxes.

Of course the value of real estate in the South during this unsettled period had declined markedly from the late 1850s, returning to the levels of the early 1850s. Therefore, the fact that tax rates increased by four to eight times does not imply that actual taxes rose so much. Still, the increase in taxes was steep enough. The following [data] illustrate the taxes due on a 160-acre farm in Alabama and Mississippi in various years, assuming that the farm was worth the average assessed value per acre in the year. In Alabama, though the value per acre had declined by a third between 1860 and 1870, the tax on the farm had multiplied by almost two and a half times, and the average tax in the Reconstruction years was double the level of 1860. In Mississippi, the tax in 1871 was three and a half times what it had been in 1857, and in 1873 it was almost five times the figure for 1857, though in 1873 the value of the farm was almost 40 percent less than in 1857.

It might be argued, on the other hand, that the actual tax, in dollar terms, was still a modest one. But such a contention misunderstands the situation of a small farmer operating on the edge of the cash economy. For him these taxes were indeed significant, because his cash income was so small. We may form a rough estimate of what the cash income of the owner of a 160-acre farm was in these two states. The federal censuses of 1860 and 1870 inform us that approximately two-thirds of the farm was unimproved acreage; let us assume that our farmer has 60 of his 160 acres in cultivation. Perhaps two-thirds of the improved acreage was given over to the growth of food crops for use by the farmer's family. On the remaining 20 acres, he might plant cotton to be marketed for cash. During Reconstruction, and we may assume also during the 1850s, the average yield of cotton was a bit less than four-tenths of a bale per acre. Thus our farmer marketed some eight bales. In the marketing years 1855–56 to 1860–61, the weighted average of ordinary-grade cotton sold at New Orleans was 8.445 cents a pound. In the marketing years 1870–71 to 1875–76, the comparable figure was 12.9 cents a pound. These figures, after we deduct 5 percent for factorage fees and transportation costs, produce a cash income for the farmer of about $257 a year in the late 1850s and about $392 a year in the early 1870s. The latter amount is, incidentally, less than 18 percent greater than the former one in constant dollar terms, because of the postwar inflation of prices. If these estimates are reasonable, then the state land tax alone represented 1 percent or more of the farmer's total cash income in Alabama during the Reconstruction years, except for the brief period in 1871–72 when the Democrats regained power. And it was some $1\frac{1}{2}$ to 2 percent of his income in Mississippi during the period. The Alabama percentage is nearly double that for 1855 and 50 percent above that for 1860. The Mississippi percentage in 1873 is more than treble that for 1857.

To the state land tax must be added the county and school-district land taxes, the personalty tax on livestock, farm implements, and similar possessions, and the poll tax, which in Alabama was $1.50, and in Mississippi was $2.00 in 1870 but $1.00 in 1873. It is not at all unreasonable, therefore, to estimate that our owner of a 160-acre farm paid some 2 to 4 percent of his total cash income to the tax collector during Reconstruction. And when we reflect that a considerable part of the farmer's cash income necessarily went to pay the immediate expenses of his farming operation—to pay for seed, supplies, and, very probably, interest on his debts—then it becomes apparent that the taxes would have been an even larger percentage of his discretionary income. If a fourth of his cash income remained after the payment of unavoidable farming expenses, he would have paid some 8 to 10 percent or more of that remainder in taxes. Taxation at this level would most certainly not have been inconsequential for the small farmer. Nor are we reduced to mere speculation about its effect, in Mississippi at least. We need only note that by the spring of 1871, that state was reporting nearly 3,330,000 acres—14 percent of its entire taxable acreage—as having been forfeited to the government for nonpayment of taxes.

The abolition of slavery, then, because it moved so much of the burden of taxation to land, apparently brought about in the Lower South a marked shift in tax incidence downward in the social scale. At the same time, rapidly rising tax rates brought taxes to a level at which they became genuinely onerous to the small farmer. But, it might be said, if the small farmer was paying large taxes for the first time, he was also receiving substantial governmental services for the first time. Though at first glance this position looks very plausible, it does not, I think, accurately depict the small farmer's situation as he may well have perceived it. . . .

. . . Whites paid almost all of the direct taxes both before and after the Civil War. In the antebellum period the only blacks who were taxpayers were, of course, the handful of free Negroes. But even after the war, the freedmen owned virtually no property, and therefore for all practical purposes they were subject directly only to the poll tax. Beginning in 1874 Georgia reported tax receipts segregated by race. The returns for 1874 indicate that blacks, who made up some 46 percent of the population in that year, paid only 2.3 percent of the property taxes. The addition of the poll taxes brings the black percentage of the total tax receipts to 7.4. Indeed, it was precisely the ability of the poll tax to extract a contribution from the propertyless that made it seem to Southern legislators—during Reconstruction, as before and afterward—the ideal tax for the support of the public schools. It was the one tax paid by a significant minority—and just after emancipation probably the majority—of the parents whose children used the schools. This attitude among the legislators is connected with the view general among white voters that they were being taxed to provide services to nontaxpayers. Now, this attitude was in part a misconception. Blacks who were renters or sharecroppers contributed to tax receipts indirectly by providing a part of the income out of which the white property owner paid the tax on the farm. But however unfair the attitude was, it was certainly real. After redemption, indeed, it produced a vigorous campaign throughout the South to expend on black schools only those school taxes actually paid by black citizens. . . .

. . . While the number of taxpayers remained essentially constant after emancipation, the number of citizens needing state services was doubled at a stroke. Disbursements expressed in aggregate terms seem quite small in the antebellum era and much larger during Reconstruction. But the reality is almost the reverse. Because the citizenry was half as large before the Civil War, disbursements per citizen actually declined during Reconstruction. Republicans were well aware of this distinction; it was their standard reply to Democratic charges of profligate waste. But we must note that it was the Democratic charge rather than the Republican reply which appears to have struck home with the white small farmer. As I have said, the Republican argument looked at the problem from the point of view of the administrators, of those in charge of the government. It was necessary for expenditures to expand rapidly even to maintain services at their former levels, they said, because prices were higher and because twice as many people had to be served. But such an explanation, however cogent it was in fact, would probably have seemed to the white farmer only an elaborate rationalization for a gross injustice. . . . The reality for the white farmer was a sharp increase in taxes and a decline in services. From this perspective, it was quite natural that the notion that the large new taxes were going into the pockets of corrupt officials—bolstered as the notion was by a number of cases of genuine corruption among the Republicans—was convincing. And even if it had not been, the simple fact of high taxes and small returns, produced by dividing the tax receipts between hard-pressed whites and "nontaxpaying" blacks, would probably have been damning enough.

⚓ *F U R T H E R   R E A D I N G*

Michael Les Benedict, *A Compromise of Principle* (1974)
Carol R. Bleser, *The Promised Land* (1969)
Orville Vernon Burton, *In My Father's House Are Many Mansions* (1985)
Dan T. Carter, *When the War Was Over* (1985)
Richard N. Current, *Those Terrible Carpetbaggers* (1988)
Edmund L. Drago, *Black Politicians and Reconstruction in Georgia* (1982)
W. E. B. Du Bois, *Black Reconstruction* (1935)
Paul D. Escott, *Many Excellent People* (1985)
W. McKee Evans, *Ballots and Fence Rails* (1966)
Roger A. Fischer, *The Segregation Struggle in Louisiana, 1862–1877* (1974)
Eric Foner, *Reconstruction* (1988)
William Gillette, *Retreat from Reconstruction, 1869–1879* (1979)
William C. Harris, *Day of the Carpetbagger* (1979)
James Haskins, *Pinckney Benton Stewart Pinchback* (1973)
Thomas Holt, *Black over White* (1977)
Elizabeth Jacoway, *Yankee Missionaries in the South* (1979)
Jacqueline Jones, *Soldiers of Light and Love* (1985)
J. Morgan Kousser and James M. McPherson, eds., *Region, Race, and Reconstruction* (1982)
Peggy Lamson, *The Glorious Failure* (1973) —
Edward Magdol, *A Right to the Land* (1977)
Robert C. Morris, *Reading, 'Riting, and Reconstruction* (1981)
Elizabeth Studley Nathans, *Losing the Peace* (1968)
Otto H. Olsen, *Carpetbagger's Crusade* (1965)
———, ed., *Reconstruction and Redemption in the South* (1980)
Claude F. Oubre, *Forty Acres and a Mule* (1978)
Joseph H. Parks, *Joseph E. Brown of Georgia* (1976)
Lillian A. Pereyra, *James Lusk Alcorn* (1966)
Michael Perman, *Reunion Without Compromise* (1973) —
———, *The Road to Redemption* (1984)
Lawrence N. Powell, *New Masters* (1980)
Howard N. Rabinowitz, ed., *Southern Black Leaders in Reconstruction* (1964) —
George C. Rable, *But There Was No Peace* (1984)
James Roark, *Masters Without Slaves* (1977)
Kenneth M. Stampp, *The Era of Reconstruction, 1865–1877* (1965) —
Mark W. Summers, *Railroads, Reconstruction, and the Gospel of Prosperity* (1984) —
Emma Lou Thornbrough, ed., *Black Reconstructionists* (1972)
Albion W. Tourgee, *A Fool's Errand* (1879)
Allen W. Trelease, *White Terror* (1971) —
Okon E. Uya, *From Slavery to Public Service* (1971)
Charles Vincent, *Black Legislators in Louisiana During Reconstruction* (1976)
Vernon L. Wharton, *The Negro in Mississippi, 1865–1890* (1947)
Sarah Woolfolk Wiggins, *The Scalawag in Alabama Politics, 1865–1881* (1977)
Joel Williamson, *After Slavery* (1966)

Myths and Realities of the New South

Following Reconstruction a vision appeared of a new south invigorated by industry and economic progress. Advocates of the New South urged southerners to change some of their traditional ways and imitate the victorious Yankees in habits of thrift, labor, and industry. By this means the South could learn from its defeat in the Civil War and strengthen itself for the future.

By 1900 notable changes had occurred. A southern textile industry had developed far beyond its antebellum roots, railroads had extended their lines throughout the region, and other industries were flourishing, such as tobacco manufacturing in Virginia and the Carolinas and iron and steel production in Birmingham, Alabama. Small farmers throughout the South had entered the market economy and were raising cash crops such as cotton and tobacco. Although the role of merchants, manufacturers, and factory workers in the economy remained small, it was growing.

What did advocates of the New South hope to accomplish? Who led this movement, and what were their motives? How much change occurred, and who did not benefit? Finally, how different was the New South from the Old? These are key questions that historians are asking as they assess the New South period.

✝ DOCUMENTS

Two of the foremost exponents of the New South vision were Atlanta newspaper editor Henry W. Grady and Carolinas industrialist Daniel Augustus Tompkins. Both often spoke before northern audiences, boasting of the South's progress and defending its policies. The excerpts from their speeches and writings in the first two selections cover some of their major ideas and suggest the tone of New South exhortations. The notion that enthusiasm for textile development grew into a public-spirited, community movement was enshrined in the early historical writings of Broadus Michell; the third document, from his book *The Rise of Cot-*

ton Mills in the South, describes the "cotton mill campaign." Hopes for industrial prosperity animated Warren C. Coleman, a black entrepreneur. In the fourth document, he calls on others of his race to support his plans for a cotton mill run by blacks. Not all comments on the New South were enthusiastic, however. When asked about their conditions by a North Carolina state agency, the Bureau of Labor Statistics, mill workers identified many areas of dissatisfaction, noted in the fifth selection. Finally, small farmers and farm laborers increasingly found themselves left out of any New South prosperity, as their comments to the North Carolina bureau plainly show in the last document.

Speeches by Henry W. Grady on the New South, 1886, 1889

From Speech Before Boston's Bay State Club, 1889

I attended a funeral once in Pickens county in my State. . . . This funeral was peculiarly sad. It was a poor "one gallus" fellow, whose breeches struck him under the armpits and hit him at the other end about the knee—he didn't believe in *decollete* clothes. They buried him in the midst of a marble quarry: they cut through solid marble to make his grave; and yet a little tombstone they put above him was from Vermont. They buried him in the heart of a pine forest, and yet the pine coffin was imported from Cincinnati. They buried him within touch of an iron mine, and yet the nails in his coffin and the iron in the shovel that dug his grave were imported from Pittsburg. They buried him by the side of the best sheep-grazing country on the earth, and yet the wool in the coffin bands and the coffin bands themselves were brought from the North. The South didn't furnish a thing on earth for that funeral but the corpse and the hole in the ground. There they put him away and the clods rattled down on his coffin, and they buried him in a New York coat and a Boston pair of shoes and a pair of breeches from Chicago and a shirt from Cincinnati, leaving him nothing to carry into the next world with him to remind him of the country in which he lived, and for which he fought for four years, but the chill of blood in his veins and the marrow in his bones.

Now we have improved on that. We have got the biggest marble-cutting establishment on earth within a hundred yards of that grave. We have got a half-dozen woolen mills right around it, and iron mines, and iron furnaces, and iron factories. We are coming to meet you. We are going to take a noble revenge, as my friend, Mr. Carnegie, said last night, by invading every inch of your territory with iron, as you invaded ours twenty-nine years ago.

From Grady's Speech, "The New South," Delivered to the New England Club in New York, 1886

We have established thrift in city and country. We have fallen in love with work. We have restored comfort to homes from which culture and elegance

From Joel Chandler Harris, *Life of Henry W. Grady*, Cassell Publishing Company, 1890.

never departed. We have let economy take root and spread among us as rank as the crabgrass which sprung from Sherman's cavalry camps, until we are ready to lay odds on the Georgia Yankee as he manufactures relics of the battlefield in a one-story shanty and squeezes pure olive oil out of his cotton seed, against any down-easter that ever swapped wooden nutmegs for flannel sausage in the valleys of Vermont. Above all, we know that we have achieved in these "piping times of peace" a fuller independence for the South than that which our fathers sought to win in the forum by their eloquence or compel in the field by their swords.

It is a rare privilege, sir, to have had part, however humble, in this work. Never was nobler duty confided to human hands than the uplifting and upbuilding of the prostrate and bleeding South—misguided, perhaps, but beautiful in her suffering, and honest, brave and generous always. In the record of her social, industrial and political illustration we await with confidence the verdict of the world.

But what of the negro? Have we solved the problem he presents or progressed in honor and equity toward solution? Let the record speak to the point. No section shows a more prosperous laboring population than the negroes of the South, none in fuller sympathy with the employing and land-owning class. He shares our school fund, has the fullest protection of our laws and the friendship of our people. Self-interest, as well as honor, demand that he should have this. Our future, our very existence depend upon our working out this problem in full and exact justice. We understand that when Lincoln signed the emancipation proclamation, your victory was assured, for he then committed you to the cause of human liberty, against which the arms of man cannot prevail—while those of our statesmen who trusted to make slavery the corner-stone of the Confederacy doomed us to defeat as far as they could, committing us to a cause that reason could not defend or the sword maintain in sight of advancing civilization.

Had Mr. Toombs said, which he did not say, "that he would call the roll of his slaves at the foot of Bunker Hill," he would have been foolish, for he might have known that whenever slavery became entangled in war it must perish, and that the chattel in human flesh ended forever in New England when your fathers—not to be blamed for parting with what didn't pay—sold their slaves to our fathers—not to be praised for knowing a paying thing when they saw it. The relations of the southern people with the negro are close and cordial. We remember with what fidelity for four years he guarded our defenseless women and children, whose husbands and fathers were fighting against his freedom. To his eternal credit be it said that whenever he struck a blow for his own liberty he fought in open battle, and when at last he raised his black and humble hands that the shackles might be struck off, those hands were innocent of wrong against his helpless charges, and worthy to be taken in loving grasp by every man who honors loyalty and devotion. Ruffians have maltreated him, rascals have misled him, philanthropists established a bank for him, but the South, with the North, protests against injustice to this simple and sincere people. To liberty and enfranchisement is as far as law can carry the negro. The rest must be left to conscience and common sense. It must be left to those among whom his lot is cast, with whom he is indissolubly connected, and whose prosperity depends upon their possessing his intelligent sympathy and confidence. Faith has been kept with him, in spite of calumnious assertions to the contrary by those who assume to speak for us or by frank opponents. Faith will be kept with him in the future, if the South holds her reason and integrity.

But have we kept faith with you? In the fullest sense, yes. When Lee surrendered—I don't say when Johnson surrendered, because I understand he still alludes to the time when he met General Sherman last as the time when he determined to abandon any further prosecution of the struggle—when Lee surrendered, I say, and Johnson quit, the South became, and has since been, loyal to this Union. We fought hard enough to know that we were whipped, and in perfect frankness accept as final the arbitrament of the sword to which we had appealed. The South found her jewel in the toad's head of defeat. The shackles that had held her in narrow limitations fell forever when the shackles of the negro slave were broken. Under the old régime the negroes were slaves to the South; the South was a slave to the system. The old plantation, with its simple police regulations and feudal habit, was the only type possible under slavery. Thus was gathered in the hands of a splendid and chivalric oligarchy the substance that should have been diffused among the people, as the rich blood, under certain artificial conditions, is gathered at the heart, filling that with affluent rapture but leaving the body chill and colorless.

The old South rested everything on slavery and agriculture, unconscious that these could neither give nor maintain healthy growth. The new South presents a perfect democracy, the oligarchs leading in the popular movement—a social system compact and closely knitted, less splendid on the surface, but stronger at the core—a hundred farms for every plantation, fifty homes for every palace—and a diversified industry that meets the complex need of this complex age.

The new South is enamored of her new work. Her soul is stirred with the breath of a new life. The light of a grander day is falling fair on her face. She is thrilling with the consciousness of growing power and prosperity. As she stands upright, full-statured and equal among the people of the earth, breathing the keen air and looking out upon the expanded horizon, she understands that her emancipation came because through the inscrutable wisdom of God her honest purpose was crossed, and her brave armies were beaten.

D. A. Tompkins on the New South, c. 1900

First Speech Excerpt

When I left South Carolina to go North, I thought I was leaving a country which had never had any important manufactures. Later, when I was in the middle of industrial life in the North, I conceived the idea of writing

From George Taylor Winston, *a Builder of the New South*, Doubleday, Page & Company, 1920.

an industrial history of the United States. To my amazement I found that the agricultural South, from which I had come in a spirit of industrial despair, was the cradle of manufactures in the United States.

The industrial development of the South was as much advanced a hundred years ago as that of any other part of the Union. The census of 1810 shows that the manufactured products of Virginia, the Carolinas, and Georgia exceeded in variety and value those of all the New England States taken together. There were more homespun cotton manufactures in Virginia, South Carolina, and Georgia than in the thirteen other states and territories; more flax in Virginia than in any other state. Prior to 1812 Southern manufactures were in the line of household arts. These manufactures were generalized and dispersed, not localized and integrated; the aggregate was considerable.

In the Piedmont region of the Carolinas many charcoal blast furnaces were in operation a century ago. Cotton mills now operated by water power are on sites which were formerly occupied by Catlin forges, rolling mills, cotton factories, and other manufacturing plants. At these forges and rolling mills were made bars, nails, plowshares, and other products. One product was a special metal for rifle barrels. There were notable gunmakers in the Piedmont region in the time of these forges and rolling mills; and they required an extra good quality of metal for their rifles. These gun-makers supplied to the home people and to the frontiersmen of Tennessee and Kentucky most of the rifles which played such a part in frontier life, and were such a factor in the early development of American civilization. I have seen a copy of a contract in accordance with which the entire machinery equipment for a cotton mill was constructed in a machine shop at Lincolnton, N.C., in 1813.

When the Union was formed and a nation was organized, the order of the states in population and wealth was, Virginia first, Pennsylvania second, North Carolina third. In enterprise and development the South surpassed all other parts of the Union. The institution of slavery changed the relative position of North and South, the institution of slavery—not the negro— but the institution. The negro has never been in the way of industrial progress as much as the Indian was originally. But the institution of slavery had a tremendous adverse influence; and this would have been the same if the slaves had been white instead of colored.

The Southern States prospered before slavery became the dominant influence. The prosperity before that time was a prosperity of manufactures, commerce, and agriculture. As slavery grew in importance and influence, manufactures and commerce declined. The invention of the cotton gin emphasized the importance and profit of cotton culture with slave labor. The South became a country exclusively devoted to the production of staple crops: tobacco, rice, cotton, and sugar—all with slave labor. The free white mechanics were driven to the Northwest. My own grandfather owned and operated a carriage factory, which, for lack of white mechanics, he finally abandoned in favor of cotton production with negro slave labor.

Those who advocated slavery were interested in the extension of the system to the Southwest. The system founded upon agriculture with slave labor alone necessarily fell. From the time that slavery became the dominant influence the South made very little progress. From 1830 to 1860 South Carolina and North Carolina practically stood still; then wealth fell into the hands of fewer people, general development ceased, resources were neglected, migration was large and constant both to the central Northwest by white laborers and to the Southwest by slave owners with their slaves. As far as the character of the people and the resources of the country were concerned, the industrial progress of the Piedmont Carolinas should have been parallel with that of Pennsylvania.

Second Speech Excerpt

The South is in a state of change. A condition of civilization which grew upon the basis of the institution of slavery is dying and fading away. A condition of civilization based upon the new conditions imposed by the results of the late war has commenced to grow, and its growth is healthy and vigorous.

There are tenacious people of fine education who are living in the dying conditions of ante-bellum life, some by obstinate preference, some of necessity. These constitute the Old South. They are, as a rule, growing poorer day by day, and will continue to grow poorer, until the most tenacious of them pass out of life; and with them will go the system to which they persist in adhering.

The people who have adapted themselves to the new conditions imposed by the results of the Civil War constitute what we are beginning to hear called the New South. They have divorced from their minds the idea that for a Southern man there is no occupation but raising cotton with negro labor, and that free negro labor constitutes a curse to a country.

The New South finds within the South unlimited raw material from which products required by the whole world may be produced. The New South finds that the conditions which surround these vast resources in raw material are such that only energy and good judgment are required to produce many articles of commerce cheaper and better in the South than can be done in any other country in the world.

The New South is of healthy growth. It is already a young giant. It is absorbing the assets of the old, and adding to them at the same time by turning the raw material of the country, heretofore mostly untouched, into products from the sale of which come handsome profits.

In the Piedmont region of North and South Carolina cotton factories are springing up quietly but with a rapidity equalled nowhere in the United States in any industry, except by that of iron-making in Alabama and Tennessee.

While the opportunities of an iron maker in the South are excellent, it may admit of argument whether there are not many places in Pennsylvania or Ohio where they are as good, or better; but the superior advantages enjoyed by a cotton spinner operating in the South are conspicuous. Much cotton is now being spun in the South which comes direct from the field to a gin which is part of the equipment of the factory. This cotton is free from innumerable little losses to which cotton shipped to the New England states, or abroad, is liable, in the way of sampling, cost of freight, damage by careless handling in the mud, and otherwise, at railway stations, etc. The profits of Southern mills are evidence of these advantages.

The only difficulty experienced so far in the development of the industry of cotton spinning in the South has been the lack of experience of proprietors and operatives. By the energy of enterprising men, this difficulty is being rapidly overcome. The late E. M. Holt, of Alamance County, N. C., was a pioneer. He was eminently successful in his efforts to operate machinery for spinning and weaving cotton. His sons seem to have inherited his energy and his enterprise, and each of them is largely interested in factories that have been established either by their father or themselves.

In the same county Messrs. Scott, Donnell & Scott have demonstrated that a small factory may be as successful as a large one if it is handled with the same care and judgment. The junior member of the firm, Mr. John Scott, has taken hold of the work of the factory in a manner and with a success that make him a worthy example to other young Southerners whose businesses furnish neither sufficient occupation nor profit to satisfy them. He is neither afraid to work nor to be seen working.

All along the Piedmont belt there are men who have attained to such success as entitles them to distinction. . . .

Atlanta is full of enterprises and enterprising men, and the growth of that city is a fair example of the results of Southern raw material and Southern labor combined. Here, too, the diversity of enterprise is marked. Here it is possible to contract for the products of cotton or cottonseed. Here are the headquarters of marble companies supplying marble as fine as the Italian stone. Granite is supplied for paving the streets of cities to the north and west. Here are manufactured cotton gins, steam engines, and various machines used in the preparation of cotton for the market. In Macon, J. F. Hanson is the successful manager of two splendidly equipped cotton factories; and at Columbus there are the Eagle and Phoenix Mills, than which none in Massachusetts has been more successful.

In Alabama, O. O. Nelson, of Montgomery, and George O. Baker, of Selma, have been foremost in the development of the new industry of crushing cottonseed for its products. And in connection with the growth of the iron interest the names of Doctor Caldwell of Birmingham, and A. H. Moses of Sheffield, are more than well known in connection with the growth of two cities and the marvellous multiplication of the original dollars invested by the corporations of which they are the heads. Both these gentlemen undertook the management of the affairs of the companies they now represent at a time when prospects did not look bright, and when the stock of the respective companies was not particularly marketable. Under their management the properties they control have increased in value more than any other properties in the United States have ever been known to do before. While these places stand conspicuous for their growth from almost nothing to marvellous wealth, other places have grown also, and other men in lesser degrees have done excellent work in Chattanooga, Anniston, South Pittsburg, etc., etc.

With all this improvement and marvellous progress how is it that we now and then see in a well-written public journal that the South is growing poorer? It is because the editor lives amongst people who have not yet consented to give up antebellum ways and ideas.

Third Speech Excerpt

The factories in North Carolina now manufacture about 300,000 bales of cotton into cloth and yarn a year. For this work there are employed in round numbers 30,000 operatives. This work is done with about one million spindles. It must be understood, of course, that I speak in figures that are even and somewhat approximate, but that are near enough the exact figures to illustrate this argument with reasonable accuracy.

In order to manufacture the entire cotton crop of the South into plain white and coarse colored goods there would be required something like 30,000,000 spindles and 1,000,000 operatives. The population of the Southern States may be reckoned at 20,000,000. Does anybody doubt that out of this 20,000,000 there is idle time enough wasted, even by those who would be willing to work, to furnish 1,000,000 good operatives in cotton factories? Go into any ordinary cotton market town where no cotton factories have as yet been built, and at any time from 7 A.M. to 10 P.M. count the people who are loafing, and the number found would more than make up the quota of people for its share of the workers necessary to manufacture the cotton crop. This loafing habit; this superabundance of people who are capable of working but who are loafing in the country and in towns where there are no factories, is conspicuous by comparison with the town where manufacturing enterprises have been established. By the same comparison the dilapidation of the houses is conspicuous; the poverty of the farmers in the adjacent country and the wretched condition of the roads are more than conspicuous.

Happily these old conditions are passing away. In many sections they have already passed away. The people of the South are naturally enterprising and resourceful. In the early days of the republic the south was the manufacturing end of the union. The first steamship ever to cross the ocean went out of Savannah. The South Carolina railway, when it was building, was the greatest engineering enterprise of the world. According to the United States census of 1810, the manufactured products of Virginia, the Carolinas, and Georgia, exceeded in value and variety those of the entire New England States. This is mentioned in no disparagement of New England but rather to show that our forefathers were men of enterprise and that they had confidence to venture on their own judgment. They never waited for somebody to come from somewhere and develop their resources for them. If they thought a cotton factory or a railroad would be a good thing they built it. The only mistake they made was in thinking that the colored brother as a slave was a good thing. The growth of slavery dried up a well-developed manufacturing tendency in the South.

Now slavery is gone, the last vestige of that anarchy that succeeded the Civil War is also now gone. Wherever the people have recovered something of the confidence of their forefathers in enterprise they have prospered beyond their own expectations or hopes. . . .

For more than a quarter of a century the political and social conditions in the South have been very unfavorable for the development of material interests. The generation that is now passing away has withstood a test of Anglo-Saxon civilization—fighting against the strong prejudices of other people of their own blood living at a distance, and against semi-barbaric influences at home that were supported and urged on by those prejudices. This contest is well nigh over. It is no wonder that during its progress so little advance was made in material prosperity; but it is a wonder that the production of cotton has kept ahead of that of other advancing cotton-growing countries. This result alone, together with the saving of civilization and the preservation of the social status of the South, shows the ability of the people of the South to carry to the maximum limit the white man's burden. In the same time Egypt and India, both under English control, have been pushing forward in the production of cotton, becoming our serious competitors.

For the coming generation the way to prosperity is wide open and plain. The passing generation has won the fight against anarchy and left to their children a heritage more valuable than any riches. It is now simply a question of redemption from poverty. To do this we must combine farming and manufacturing. The factories will require operatives, who in turn must have foodstuffs, which will make a market for the farmer's supplies. Cotton can then be made cheap, because diversified crops, which can be sold for cash, will bring in a supplemental income. Indeed the time may come when cotton will be the surplus crop instead of being, as now, the main crop.

It is my firm belief that in the near future no community can afford to be without its cotton factory, its cottonseed oil mill, and its fertilizer works.

The Myth of the "Cotton Mill Campaign," 1921

Notices of ceremonies held when a mill commenced operation convey sometimes touchingly the pride of a community in the plant and the public character of the enterprise. Townspeople were like children with a very precious new toy; newspapers described the arrangement of the machinery in the factory with the keenest interest.

The potency of associative effort, so marked in Southern cotton mill building in this period, overcame timidity that might have been prompted by a frank and individual canvass of attending economic facilities. "The mill at Albemarle, North Carolina, had its origin in the desire of the Efirds to have a mill at the town. Whether there existed real advantages or not, the people would make it appear that there were advantages for that par-ticular location. Many mills were located at places where there was the

From Broadus Mitchell, *The Rise of Cotton Mills in the South, 1921,* pp. 129–132, 134–135. Used by permission of The Johns Hopkins University Press.

spirit for them, rather than where they would be, economically, most successful.'' A Marylander knowing the industry thoroughly said there was little community interest in his State, but that ''down South the community interest was very strong. Every little town wanted a mill. If it couldn't get a big one, it would take a small one; if not a sheeting, then a spinning mill.''

''A good deal of patriotism developed,'' said a not impressionable mill man, ''and every town would vie with others in building mills. Some people took stock and sold it at a discount when it was apparent that the mill would be operated. They were willing to give so much to secure the mill for the town.'' There is no stronger indication of the different spirit characterizing the building of mills in the eighties as contrasted with earlier periods than the fact that after 1880 many plants were located within the corporate limits of towns and cities. In the earlier enterprises community spirit had not counted, and even the mills of the seventies, such as Piedmont, were taken to the water powers. Eager discussion as to the comparative advantages of water and steam power marked this transition. From being an excuse for the town, the cotton mill came to be erected to invigorate a place that was languishing. It has been said that at least half the South Carolina mills were community enterprises. Later, when the commercial spirit was more pronounced, factories were built just outside the corporation to escape town taxes.

In the case of some investors with whom assistance to the town was an indirect motive, the creation of a payroll, putting more money in circulation, was the causal stimulus. An editorial recommended the Charleston Manufacturing Company ''as a means of enlarging the common income. . . . The employment given to hundreds of persons . . . will increase the value of house-property at once. They who earn nothing can't spend much. It was calculated last year that every $228 invested in cotton manufactures in South Carolina supported one person. . . . It is evident that the building of half-a-dozen cotton factories would revolutionize Charleston. Two or three million dollars additional poured annually into the pockets of the shopkeepers . . . would make them think that the commercial millennium had come.

To give employment to the necessitous masses of poor whites, for the sake of the people themselves, was an object animating the minds of many mill builders. One does not have to go outside the ranks of cotton manufacturers to find denials of this, but a study of the facts shows how frequent and normal was the philanthropic incentive. . . .

No undertaking was born more emphatically in the impulse to furnish work than the Salisbury Cotton Mills. All the circumstances of the founding of this factory were singularly in keeping with the philanthropic prompting. The town of Salisbury, North Carolina, in 1887 had done nothing to recover from the war. It was full of saloons, wretched, unkempt. It happened that an evangelistic campaign was conducted; Mr. Pearson, remembered as a lean, intense Tennesseean, preached powerfully. A tabernacle was erected for the meeting, which lasted a month and, being undenominational, drew from the whole town and countryside. The evangelist declared that the great morality in Salisbury was to go to work, and that corruption, idleness and misery could not be dispelled until the poor people were given an opportunity to become productive. The establishment of a cotton mill would be the most Christian act his hearers could perform. "He gave Salisbury a moral dredging which made the people feel their responsibilities as they had not before, and made them do something for these folks. There had been little talk of manufacturing before Pearson came; there had been some tobacco factories in the town, but they had failed. The Salisbury Cotton Mills grew out of a moral movement to help the lower classes, largely inspired by this campaign. Without the moral issue, the financial interest would have come out in the long run, but the moral considerations brought the matter to a focus."

A Black Entrepreneur Builds a Cotton Mill, 1896

Please allow me to call the attention of the public to the fact that a movement is on foot to erect a cotton mill at Concord to be operated by colored labor. The colored citizens of the United States have had no opportunity to utilize their talents along this line. Since North Carolina has fairly and justly won for herself in the Centennial at the World Fair at Chicago and at the Atlanta Exposition the honored name of being "the foremost of the States," she will further evidence the fact if she is the first to have a cotton mill to be operated principally by the colored people. We are proud of the spirit and energy of the white people in encouraging and assisting the enterprise and will our colored people not catch the spark of the new industrial life and take advantage of this unprecedented opportunity to engage in the enterprise that will prove to the world our ability as operatives in the mills thereby solving the great problem "can the Negroes be employed in cotton mills to any advantage"? And now that the opportunity is before us, experience alone will determine the question and it behooves us to better ourselves and do something, and as one man . . . [make] the effort that is to win for us a name and place us before the world as industrious and enterprising citizens.

Don't think for a moment that this desireable and enviable position can be obtained by merely a few of our people, but on the other hand, it will require the united effort of the race. Then when the people of the white race who are our friends clearly see that we are surely coming, they will "come over into Macedonia and help us." The enterprise will be just what we make of it. There is nothing to gain but everything to lose by allowing the enterprise to prove a failure.

In case of a failure, it will be due to mere neglect. If it proves a success, it will be to the honor and glory of the race. If racial weakness is set forth, it will only strengthen the sentiment already expressed about us. We can see the finger of Providence directing our cause, for we believe that God helps only those who help themselves. If we show no desire to succeed in this, and in all the enterprises designed for the industrial and financial development of the race, then it can be proven that our Liberty is a failure. We cannot afford to be idle or lukewarm in this matter. There is too much connected with it that would not let our conscience rest if we did not make the effort to carry out the plan. Can there be any among us who do not wish to see the moral, intellectual, religious and industrial character of our people elevated to a higher and broader plan[e] of civilization and true usefulness? There is no middle ground. We are either going forward or backward. The watchword is onward and upward, and if we ever expect to attain the heights of industrial usefulness, we must fall in line and march shoulder to shoulder in one solid phalanx along the road that leads to fortune and fame.

When we grasp the opportunities offered for the betterment of our condition, we are performing the great task which will at last determine our future position in the ranks of the great nations of the world. The markets of Madagascar, Zanzibar and other tropical regions where there are millions of inhabitants are open for all goods that can be produced in the mills.

Let us not be discouraged but move onward with the enterprise, with that spirit and determination that makes all things possible for those who strive in real earnest.

Mill Workers' Comments on the New South, 1887, 1889

1887

Superintendent Cotton Mill—Ten hours are enough for a day's work, where children are worked from twelve years old and up, and I think the mills of this section are willing to it, if all would adopt it. I think there should be a law making all run 60 hours per week, and compelling parents to send their children to school. I work 11½ hours per day, at $75 per month. Have four in family and one at school. Live in my own house.

Employee—There are about 225 to 250 hands engaged at different classes of work in this mill, about 100 of them children—many of them very small children, under 12 years of age. Wages are about as good here as at any mill in the State and I think better than at many of them, the only trouble about wages is that they are not paid in cash—trade checks are issued with which employees are expected to buy what they need at the company's store, which is not right. The same system is practised I am told, at the most of the cotton mills in the State, but that does not make it right and just. The tobacco factories in this town pay the cash every week. Any man who has ever tried it knows there is a great difference in buying with cash. This, with the long hours required for a day's work, (12 hours) is the only cause for complaint; the officers are kind and close attention to work and sobriety and morality is required of all who work here.

Employee—I work in the cotton mills. They employ men, women and children—many children who are too small to work, they should be at school; the parents are more to blame than are the mill-owners. The hands in the mills in this section are doing very well, and if they only received their pay weekly in cash instead of "trade checks," and store accounts they would not complain if they were paid in cash and were allowed to buy for cash where they pleased, it would be much better. Ten hours are enough for a day's work. I believe the mills here would be willing to it if there was a law making all conform to it. I believe compulsory education would be a benefit too.

Employee—This mill runs day and night. The day hands commence work at 6 o'clock in the morning and run tell 7 o'clock at night. They stop at 12 o'clock for dinner and ring the bell at 12:30 o'clock. I contend that the hands are in actual motion 13 hours per day. The trade check system is used here, and is not as good as cash, at this place nor any other place. If the hands trade their checks to any other firm, and they present them for cash, this firm demands a discount of 10 per cent. The best trade check used in this county is not worth over 75 per cent. Some of the checks used in this county are almost worthless. This long-hour system is destroying the health of all the young women who work in the mills. The employment of children in the mills at low wages keeps a great many men out of employment. Our Legislature should do something in regard the long-hour system and trade checks, and compel employers to pay cash for labor; then, you see, competition in trade would take place, and we could save some of our earnings, which would enable us to have night schools and improve our condition much in the way of education.

1889

Employee—There is room for big improvement for the good of operatives in cotton-mills. Twelve hours per day is too long to keep operatives at work, especially women and children. The check system ought to be stopped. A girl works for fifty cents per day, has three in family to support, gets a check each day for work, and buys her supplies from the company's store. When the four weeks are ended she has no checks and will get no cash. Just so long as they give checks and pay once a month, they will keep us on the grind-stone, and we cannot get justice or give it, in this condition. The day is coming when mill-owners will find out that if they give their hands good houses to live in, pay them cash, and teach them how to live and take care of their earned money, both parties will prosper and grow fat.

Employee—I work in a cotton-mill and am paid once a week in "trade checks," but the company I work for will cash them any time. I think that twelve hours a day is too long for any one to work in a mill. Nine hours is long enough for any one to work in the dust and lint of a factory. I think that the Legislature ought to pass a law making eight or nine hours a day's work in work-shops, mines and factories, and also a law to prevent the employment of children under fourteen years of age therein. The wages at the factories are about the same they were three years ago, but the cost of living has decreased about five per cent.

Tenants and Farmers Assess the New South, 1887–1889

Extracts from Letters to the Bureau on Various Subjects
from Tenants and Farm Laborers in the Different Counties
of the State

1887

A. R.—There is general depression and hard times and almost broken spirits among the tenant farmers. There are many things that contribute somewhat to this bad state of things but the one great cause is the outrageous per cent. charged for supplies bought on credit; it is sapping the life of North Carolina.

F. M. S.—The poor cannot clothe their children decently enough for a school room because of the exorbitant rate of interest they are charged for supplies; they are obliged to pay whatever the merchants charge. This is a most pressing evil and should be stopped by law or it will soon swallow us body and soul.

T. D. H.—Some think they pay only 25 or 30 per cent. for what they buy on crop liens, but if they will figure it out, they will see it is 100 to 200 per cent. per annum on the amount they buy over cash prices. There would be an over supply of labor if they would work. Negroes with some education will not work on the farm if they can help it. They have a keener desire for education than the whites and attend school much better.

W. J. M.—I think the present depressed condition of the farming interest is largely due to the mortgage system in buying supplies. There is no chance for improvement where this system is in operation.

J. M. B.—There is no man and no county that can long exist on 50 per cent. charged on everything eaten by farmers; unless a remedy is found the county will be ruined very soon.

O. E.—There ought to be a law passed forbidding any man planting more than ten acres in cotton to the horse.

J. S. M.—The condition of the farmers is bad and will get no better until we adopt some system and unite in our efforts to better ourselves and stop looking to others to help us; we must depend upon ourselves. When we become united we can get all the legislation we need; not till then.

J. L. H.—Merchants require a mortgage on whatever property tenant has, besides the crop. They are more strict this year than ever before. There were many that could not pay out last year. Tenants pay an advance of at least 25 per cent. on the average.

J. H. R.—The system of buying on time and using guano has broken up many farmers, and has driven so many to the towns to seek employment that wages have been greatly reduced. If this state of things continues it will soon put all the land in the hands of a few men and ruin all classes.

F. W. R.—Attendance at school ought to be enforced by law; the schools are now usually taught in winter when the child of the poor man is poorly clad and hence unable to attend; in summer they must work, and so they do not attend school. This should not be so—we must get out of this condition or we shall go backward as a people and State.

S. A. H.—Many whites do not send their children to school for want of proper clothes. The people are in a bad condition and most of their lands are mortgaged, in most cases too irredeemably. I see no hope for the county to get better unless the government comes to their help and lends them money at 1 per cent. to redeem their land and gives them twenty years to pay out. Wages have decreased on farms owing I believe to the tariff.

S. S.—We farmers work very hard, but get in no better condition. Evidently there is something wrong. The towns flourish, while in the country, where the producing element is, the people get worse off. We do not mind the work—were raised to it—but would like to get something for it.

W. H. B.—The mortgage system is working its deadly way into this county, and making sad havoc where its tempting offers are once entered into. Alas! one never gets out from its magic embrace until he dies out or is sold out. I wish this ruinous law could be repealed, and with it the homestead law, which is the father of the mortgage system.

L. P.—The trouble in this county is the awful time prices that we have to pay the merchants, not less than 50 per cent. The price of labor is low and it should be higher, but the farmer can't afford to pay even present prices, because the high per cent. keeps him down. The homestead law should be repealed and then the lien law and the high time prices would have to go.

P. H. H.—The poor tenant and farm laborers and in many cases land-owners, are in a bad condition, mostly on account of the heavy per cent. charged by merchants for supplies.

J. E. D.—Labor is down; so is the farmer. The merchant is the prosperous man now. Half of the farms are mortgaged to the commission merchants, who charge 50 per cent. above cash prices. Half of the farmers of this county are bound to merchants by the mortgage system.

1889

Remarks.—In my opinion, the greatest evil with the farmers here is, that the land-owners will rent their lands and hire their teams to tenants, and furnish provisions; the consequence is, the tenant gets so far in debt to the landlord that, before the crop is laid by, the tenant gets dissatisfied and fails to work the crop as it ought to be, and, therefore, raises bad crops and the land is left in bad condition. If the landlord would hire the labor, his land would be in better condition and labor would be better also.

Remarks.—The year in this section was not favorable to farming.

Spring late. The heavy rain-fall in June and July injured the general crop badly, particularly cotton. The sweet-potato crop not good—too much rain. Had a killing frost on the nights of October 5 and 6, which did considerable damage.

Remarks.—I will name a few evils the farmer has to contend with, viz: The price of everything produced by the farmer is fixed by the merchant, or purchaser, as well as everything bought by the farmer, and high rates for transportation on railroads. The first evil mentioned can be overcome by the farmers paying cash for what they purchase, and cooperation. The second should be overcome by proper legislation—a Railroad Commission Bill.

Remarks.—The mortgage system, with the consequent high prices exacted for supplies, and the one-crop (cotton) system hangs like an incubus about this people and have well-nigh ruined them financially. The system of working the public roads now in vogue with us is very unsatisfactory with us, not to say unjust. Capital or property and labor should both be taxed to keep up the public highways. My idea would be to value an ablebodied man, with nothing but his head, say at $500 or $1,000 each, as the exigencies of the case might demand, and then require every $500 or $1,000 worth of capital or property to contribute a like amount, either in labor or its equivalent in money. I have given this matter much thought and this strikes me as the most equitable and feasible plan. Our public school system in this part of the State is very inefficient.

Remarks.—Time was in this vicinity nearly every farmer not only supported himself and family from the products of the farm, but had something to spare as well. That time has passed away, I fear, forever. Then very little cotton was raised, and the farmers looked well to grain crops, horses, cattle, hogs and sheep. There was not much opulence, but much of substantial independence. Now, instead of being a year before, they are a year, at least behind, and, toil as they may, too many of them at the close of the year, when the books are opened, find the balance-sheet against them, "though every nerve was strained." The mortgage system, which hangs like a pall of death over many an honest, hard-working man, will ruin any business interest in this country. No farmer can borrow money, or buy on crop-time, at an advance of from thirty to fifty per cent. No farmer can farm successfully without some money; the present rates offered him amounts to prohibition. I cannot, in the brief space allowed, recount many of the ills now affecting us, or make any suggestion in palliation of them. To be brief, farmers are very much dispirited at the outlook, while they have worked harder for the last two years than at any time within my knowledge.

⚓ *E S S A Y S*

C. Vann Woodward, a history professor emeritus from Yale University, began the scholarly reevaluation of this period with his impressive book *Origins of the New South*. In the first selection, Woodward examines the growth of textiles, the New South's leading industry, and comments provocatively about the influence of industry on southern values. In the second essay, Paul M. Gaston of the University of Virginia describes the men who led the New South movement and the various goals they urged the region to attain. Not all of these goals became reality, a fact that has caused some historians to consider how different the New and Old South were. In the final essay, Laurence Shore, who received his Ph.D. from the Johns Hopkins University, questions whether the leadership and ideology of the post-Reconstruction South were in fact new.

The Rise of Southern Industry

C. VANN WOODWARD

The dramatic elements in the rise of the Southern cotton mill gave the movement something of the character of a "crusade." The successful competition with New England, the South's old political rival, the popular slogan, "bring the factories to the fields," and the organized publicity that attended every advance, have combined to enshrine the cotton mill in a somewhat exalted place in Southern history. Burdened with emotional significance, the mill has been made a symbol of the New South, its origins, and its promise of salvation. Facts that embarrass this interpretation of cotton-mill history have been somewhat neglected.

Rising in the Old Order, the cotton mills of the South showed a rather remarkable tenacity and even prosperity in the troubled decades that followed secession. Of the three leading cotton-manufacturing states of the South, North Carolina doubled the value of her output between 1860 and 1880, Georgia tripled her ante-bellum record, and South Carolina quadrupled hers. These gains continued right through the supposedly blighting years of Reconstruction. The case of a large Augusta mill was by no means unique. Running some 30,000 spindles and 1,000 looms, this mill paid cash dividends averaging 14.5 per cent a year during the seventeen years following 1865 and laid aside a surplus of about $350,000. These and other facts call into serious question the tradition of dating the beginning of the cotton-mill development of the South from 1880.

In the eighties the rate of cotton-mill expansion was simply accelerated, but it was accelerated to a speed never attained in earlier years, a pace vastly exceeding the rate of growth outside the South. In his report on the cotton-textile industry in the Census of 1890, Edward Stanwood wrote that "the extraordinary rate of growth in the south" during the eighties was "the most important" aspect of the period. In 1900 he was even more emphatic, saying that "The growth of the industry in the South is the one great fact in its history during the past ten years." The number of mills in the South mounted from 161 in 1880 to 239 in 1890, and to 400 in 1900—an increase of 48.4 per cent in the eighties and 67.4 in the nineties. This, as compared with a national increase of 19.7 and 7.5 per cent in the two

Reprinted by permission of Louisiana State University Press from *Origins of the New South, 1877–1913* by C. Vann Woodward, pp. 131–135, 153–155. Copyright © 1971 by Louisiana State University Press and The Littlefield Fund for Southern History, University of Texas.

decades, and an apparent decrease in New England. A great number of the new mills, moreover, were equipped with more up-to-date machinery than the mills of the old textile regions. The first factory operated entirely by electricity was located in the South, and many improvements first found their way into the country through that region. The increase in the number of mills reveals only a fraction of the expansion. In the four leading states of North and South Carolina, Georgia, and Alabama—in which virtually all the increase took place—the average number of spindles per mill increased from 3,553 in 1880 to 10,651 in 1900. In total number of spindles the same states rose from 422,807 in 1880 to 1,195,256 in 1890, a gain of 182.7 per cent; and in the next decade the total mounted to 3,791,654 or an additional increase of 217 per cent in the nineties. Between 1880 and 1900 the total number of operatives in all Southern mills rose from 16,741 to 97,559; the number of bales consumed, from 182,349 to 1,479,006; the capital invested, from $17,375,897 to $124,596,874. Not untypical of the relative rate of expansion was the increase in capital invested in cotton manufactures, which, between 1890 and 1900 amounted to 131.4 per cent in the South as compared with 12.1 per cent in New England.

Both the historians and the promoters of the cotton-mill campaign have held that the movement was motivated by "moral incitement" and became "a form of civic piety" in the South. While the incentives common to most industrialization were admittedly present, "the moral considerations brought the matter to a focus." The cotton-mill executives were "thinking for the whole people." The extent of this motivation should be carefully explored, but it is well to point out first that in the early years of the movement, according to the census report of 1900, "the return upon investment in Southern cotton mills has greatly exceeded that upon factories in the North." In 1882 an average of 22 per cent profit was received on investments in Southern mills, under good and bad management—and there was much of the latter. There were failures as well as successes among the new mills. But profits of 30 to 75 per cent were not unheard of in those years.

As important as these inducements undoubtedly were, they cannot account for the public zeal that, in the Carolinas, Georgia, and Alabama, converted an economic development into a civic crusade inspired with a vision of social salvation. Not only did this process occur in cities like Charleston, Atlanta, and Charlotte, with their efficient chambers of commerce, big newspapers, and Northern visitors and settlers, but even more typically in isolated Piedmont towns. Old market villages of a few hundred citizens that had drowsed from one Saturday to the next since the eighteenth century, were suddenly aflame with the mill fever and "a passion for rehabilitation." Stock was often subscribed in small holdings. Among the professions from which early mill executives were called, Broadus Mitchell lists lawyers, bankers, farmers, merchants, teachers, preachers, doctors, and public officials. City dailies and country weeklies devoted columns to the crusade and itinerant evangelists added the theme to their repertoire. With a headlong zeal not uncharacteristic of the region in war as in peace, the Southeast embraced the cotton mill. "Even machinery was wrapped with idealism and devotion," according to one account.

Much was made by mill promoters of the philanthropic motive of giving "employment to the necessitous masses of poor whites." Undoubtedly this motive was sincere in some cases. Its force, however, is somewhat diminished by evidence submitted by the promoters themselves. Francis W. Dawson of Charleston, one of the most forceful propagandists for cotton mills, wrote in 1880 that employment in the mills subjects the poor whites "to elevating social influences, encourages them to seek education, and improves them in every conceivable respect." In the same editorial he stated that in South Carolina there were at that time "2,296 operatives, upon whom 7,913 persons are dependent for support. The amount paid out in wages monthly is $38,034." The average worker and dependent thus enjoyed an income of a little over twelve cents a day. In the same article Dawson estimated that the profits of these factories "ranged from 18 to $25\frac{1}{2}$ per cent a year . . . under the most unfavorable circumstances." The profit motive did not necessarily preclude the philanthropic motive, but it does seem to have outweighed it in some instances.

The question of the relative proportion of Southern and Northern capital in the Southern cotton mills is hedged with difficulties. Acknowledging the importance of Northern investment in Georgia and in areas of other states, authorities are in substantial agreement that after the seventies and before the depression years of the nineties, when Northern capital moved southward in quantities, the initiative lay with the South, and the chief source of capital was local. One writer finds "no evidence of any cotton mill established in North Carolina by Northern interests before 1895." This could not be said of any other mill state. A widespread practice was to raise only part of the required capital locally and then issue a large percentage of the stock of a new mill to Northern textile machinery and commission firms. Dependence upon these absentee firms, which often charged exorbitant rates of interest and employed injurious marketing practices, resulted in milking off a sizable proportion of profits. . . .

Within the little islands of industrialism scattered through the region, including the old towns as well as the new, was rising a new middle-class society. It drew some recruits from the old planter class, but in spirit as well as in outer aspect it was essentially new, strikingly resembling the same class in Midwestern and Northeastern cities. Richmond, former capital of the Confederacy, observed the social revolution within its walls with complacency: "We find a new race of rich people have been gradually springing up among us, who owe their wealth to successful trade and especially to manufactures. . . . [They] are taking the leading place not only in our political and financial affairs, but are pressing to the front for social recognition. . . . 'The almighty dollar' is fast becoming a power here, and he who commands the most money holds the strongest hand. We no longer contemn the filthy lucre. . . . They may be parvenuish, and want something of the polish which is the heritage of birth or only acquired by many generations of refining influences; but these are trifling matters. . . . Our provincial characteristics are fast disappearing, and we are not only advancing towards metropolitan development, but are losing our petty, narrow prejudices and becoming truly cosmopolitan. . . . We are not longer a village but a city.''

The *Industrial South* asked in the title of an editorial, ''Shall We Dethrone Our Idols?'' and answered with a thumping affirmative. It seems that ''the founders of our American system . . . forgot to consider that the American public was to be peculiarly a community of business men, and that what it would most need was the practical wisdom of business men in the administration of its affairs. And so from the beginning the places of trust and honor were filled by warriors and orators.'' The inference was plain: ''Beyond all question we have been on the wrong tack and should take a new departure.'' With Virginia leading the way, this heedless iconoclasm swept the South. ''If proselytism be the supreme joy of mankind,'' declared Henry Watterson in 1877, ''New England must be pre-eminently happy, for the ambition of the South is to out-Yankee the Yankee.'' There were even breaches in that irreducible citadel of Southernism—Mississippi. ''We are in favor,'' announced a Vicksburg paper to a hushed Delta, ''of the South, from the Potomac to the Rio Grande, being thoroughly and permanently Yankeeized.''

The facts of the record would not seem to warrant the contention that ''whereas in England many from the middle class became captains of industry, here [in the South] the characteristic leadership proceeded from the aristocracy.'' According to this interpretation, the English industrialists were ''small men who struck it lucky,'' whereas the Southern mill men were ''gentlemen.'' A study of the background of 254 industrialists in the South of this period reveals that ''about eighty per cent came of nonslave-owning parentage.'' Out of a total of 300 studied only 13 per cent were of Northern birth. Professor John Spencer Bassett, the historian, who took a peculiar delight in the rise of the new and the decline of the old ruling class, wrote that ''The rise of the middle class has been the most notable thing connected with the white population of the South since the war. . . . Everywhere trade and manufacturing is almost entirely in the hands of men who are sprung from the non-planter class, and . . . the professions seem to be going the same way.'' As for the old planters, a decadent class, Bassett thought, ''They have rarely held their own with others, and most frequently they have been in the upper ranks of those who serve rather than those who direct business. . . . But the captains of industry . . . are men who were never connected with the planter class.'' A shrewd New England observer corroborated the Southerner's view when he wrote in 1890: ''now, like a mighty apparition across the southern horizon, has arisen this hope or portent of the South,—the Third Estate,—to challenge the authority of the old ruling class.'' He advised his section against ''exclusive observation of the old conflict of races'' in the South. ''For the coming decade, the place to watch the South is in this movement of the rising

Third Estate. What it demands and what it can achieve in political, social, and industrial affairs . . . on these things will depend the fate of this important section of our country for years to come.''

Mark Twain on a Southern junket in the eighties was brought face to face with these men of the New South: ''Brisk men, energetic of movement and speech; the dollar their god, how to get it their religion.'' Somewhat awkwardly, but with great show of self-assurance, this new man adjusted to his shoulders the mantle of leadership that had descended from the planter. Some considerable alteration was found necessary: less pride and more ''push,'' for example. Punctilio was sacrificed to the exigencies of ''bustle,'' and arrogance was found to be impracticable in the pursuit of the main chance.

Up and down the ranks of society the professions began to cut their garments to the new pattern. . . .

For the ambitious if backward Southerner there were manuals of instruction in the new morals and manners. One, for example, entitled *The Law of Success*, appeared in 1885 under the imprint of the Southern Methodist Publishing House. The Southern author adduced his maxims empirically ''from the crystallized experiences of twelve hundred successful men,'' for the most part Southerners who were ''all self-made.'' His rules, ''in harmony with all moral obligations,'' were primarily laid down for ''success in private business.'' But they were also the assured ''means by which to accomplish any purpose,'' including those of ''artists, authors, bankers, dentists, editors.'' The reader was instructed in ''selecting a wife with a view to making his life a success,'' and in ''the commercial value of the Ten Commandments and a righteous life.'' The theory was advanced that ''even social calls and visiting the club-room may prove paying investments of one's time.'' Allegedly an educator himself, the author evidently kept up with the ''trend'' and perhaps was a little in advance. ''The educator of the future,'' he wrote, ''will teach his pupils what will pay best. He will teach them the art of thinking, which, for the purpose at hand, I may define to be the art of turning one's brains into money. He will not teach dead languages, obsolete formulas, and bric-a-brac sciences . . . which are never used in the ordinary transactions of the forum, the office, the shop, or the farm.'' Th proof, again, was empirical: ''The richest man in Arkansas never had any schooling whatever.''

Well might Bishop Atticus G. Haygood ask, ''Does History record an example in any race or age, where a people of strong character went so far in fifteen years as the Southern people—a race of Anglo-Saxon blood—have gone since 1865 in the modification of opinions, in the change of sentiments that had been, through generations, firmly fixed in all their thinking and feeling? The change in the opinions and sentiments of the Southern people since 1865 is one of the most wonderful facts of history.''

Perhaps the most curious aspect of the revolution in values, manners, and institutions that was daily leveling those distinctive traits that [E. L.] Godkin [editor of the *Nation*] believed set the South as far apart from the North as Ireland was the romanticism that accompanied and partially obscured the process. For along with the glittering vision of a "metropolitan" and industrial South to come there developed a cult of archaism, a nostalgic vision of the past. One of the most significant inventions of the New South was the "Old South"—a new idea in the eighties, and a legend of incalculable potentialities.

The first step was the Lost Cause itself. In 1880, in the earlier and more abject stage of the Great Recantation, [Henry] Watterson's paper could say blandly that "The 'bonny blue flag' is the symbol of nothing to the present generation of Southern men. . . . The Southern Confederacy went down forever fifteen years ago. Its issues and ensigns went down with it." An exaggeration, to be sure, but such a statement, even a suggestion of it, ten years later would have been well-nigh unthinkable. By that time the official position on the progress of the Lost Cause was typified by the editor who declared simply, "It is not lost! On earth it may be lost forever. But might never did make right." The deeper the involvements in commitments to the New Order, the louder the protests of loyalty to the Old.

Spokesmen for the New South

PAUL M. GASTON

The principal spokesmen for the emerging New South movement, with but one notable exception, were all born in the 1850's. Too young to serve in the war, they passed through childhood and adolescence under its influence and reached maturity during the Reconstruction era. Thus their formative years coincided with the period of their region's greatest failure. Quite naturally, the perspective which this experience gave them sharpened their criticisms of the Old South and led them to look to the North in their search for those variables which accounted for Southern poverty in a land of plenty.

Henry Woodfin Grady, the most famous of the New South spokesmen, was born in Athens, Georgia, in 1850. The Athens of Grady's youth was the trading center for surrounding farms and plantations and Grady's father was a prominent local merchant, co-owner of the firm of Nicholson and Grady, a notable mercantile establishment in the community. On the eve of the Civil War the elder Grady sold his share in the firm, invested heavily in real estate, and retained half-ownership in the store building, a gas works, and a saw mill. It was an evironment admirably suited for the future New South prophet. Commercial in its essence, young Grady's world was built on bustle, energy, and shrewdness, and he experienced none of the genteel leisure allegedly characteristic of the planter class which had led his region into war.

In the wake of the havoc wrought by the war, Grady secured a college education at the University of Georgia, followed by a year of postgraduate study at the University of Virginia. When he left Virginia he began the career in journalism that was to be his life work. During the 1870's he was associated with several Georgia newspapers and served as Georgia correspondent for a number of Northern papers, beginning with the New York *Herald* in 1876. It was also in 1876 that he joined the staff of the Atlanta *Constitution*, the journal that he would mold into the major organ of the New South movement. Four years later, on the strength of a $20,000 vote of confidence from Cyrus W. Field, he bought a quarter-share in the *Constitution*. From then until his death in 1889 he preached the gospel of the New South in editorial columns and in frequent public addresses in both the South and the North. When he died, the nation's press hailed him as the most effective leader of the New South movement and the New York *Times* declared that he was both the symbol and the creator of the dynamic spirit in the South.

Born a year after Grady, in 1851, Daniel Augustus Tompkins had roots in the plantation South. One of his grandfathers, a first cousin of John C. Calhoun, lived in a "fine country home," while the other, who had been a captain during the Revolutionary War, owned a North Carolina plantation. His father was a wealthy South Carolina planter, owning two thousand acres of land and forty slaves. The war, and Tompkins's restless spirit, severed his connection with the plantation, and he rapidly began to plan a career as publicist and industrialist.

After undergraduate training at the South Carolina College, Tompkins studied in the Rensselaer Polytechnic Institute at Troy, New York, and worked later as a machinist at the Bessemer Steel Works in Troy and then with the Bethlehem Iron Works in Pennsylvania. While employed by Bethlehem Iron he traveled to Germany to take part in the construction of an iron plant there. He was in Missouri next, with the Crystal Plate Glass Works and Crystal Railway Company, but he moved to Charlotte, North Carolina, in 1882, where he was to make his reputation as a promoter and exemplar of the New South creed. As an industrialist he quickly rose to prominence as the principal proprietor and president of three large cotton mills, director of eight others, and stockholder in many more. In addition to his conspicuous role in the cotton-mill industry, and as the father of the cottonseed oil industry, he became a chief publicist of the New South movement as owner of three newspapers—of which the Charlotte *Observer* was the most influential—author of innumerable pamphlets, contributor to manufacturing journals, and popular after-dinner speaker.

The longest-lived of all the New South prophets, and a man who was still writing fervent New South editorials during the administration of Herbert Hoover, was Richard Hathaway Edmonds. Born on a Virginia farm in 1857, Edmonds later claimed that his boyhood experience there had exercised a direct influence upon his mature thinking. The farm was small, he recalled, and there was too little money for hired help to free the youngster from heavy labors. "I worked, and worked hard," he said, "and it was in my opinion the best experience which I ever had, and it has influenced my life for good ever since." It was from this experience, Edmonds believed, that he derived the "gospel of work" that was to form a central part of his later teachings. In fact, Edmonds was probably captured by his own later propaganda and consequently exaggerated the significance of his boyhood labors. His uncle recalled Edmonds as a fragile youth on whom even the slightest amount of work would have made a profound impression. Later in life the uncle observed that Edmonds was "totally unable to drive a nail," and in the uncle's opinion Edmonds's program derived from his keen and inquiring mind rather than from his farm experience.

In 1871 the Edmonds family moved to Baltimore, where the future New South spokesman was to distinguish himself. During the next decade he pondered the economic problems of the South, traveled widely in the region, and concluded that the depressing poverty of a people living in a land richly endowed in natural resources was the greatest scandal of his day. Determined to reorient what he considered the misguided economic policies of the region, he wrote that the South's basic problem was its lack of industries and cities; the way to create them, he believed, was to organize an informed and effective movement of enlightenment. He rejected politics as the least hopeful approach and put his faith in journalism. The journal that he founded, the *Manufacturers' Record*, began its career in 1881 and soon was widely recognized as the leading industrial periodical of the South. Edmonds turned it into a missionary journal, and its pages fairly bristled with glowing descriptions of the industrial future of the region. . . .

As they grew up in, and pondered, the depressed state of the South in the postwar years—and as the burgeoning wealth of the North was incessantly thrust before them as evidence of their backwardness—the New South prophets were early persuaded that their plight was not the result of the war itself (as so many Southerners believed) but that it was a natural consequence of those conditions which had led to defeat in the first place. The essential lesson which they learned and then translated into the first plank of the New South program was that wealth and power in the modern world flowed from machines and factories, not from unprocessed fields of white cotton. To make the region rich, then—to bring into existence the opulent South—they became in the first place proponents of industrialism and urbanism.

In an ironic sense, they welcomed the desolation and poverty that confronted them, for it created inescapably the necessity of rebuilding the Southern economy; and, in rebuilding, they would persuade the region to reconsider its ancient prejudices and redirect its energies into new paths. Edwin Lawrence Godkin, assessing the chances of the program from his perspective as editor of *The Nation*, wrote in 1880 that the conversion of the South to the "industrial stage of social progress" would not be a more difficult task than that which the abolitionists had undertaken, ultimately with success. For one thing, Godkin pointed out, there was in the new situation a large body of indigenous opinion sympathetic to the conversion. But Godkin recognized that there would be difficulties in prying the Southern mind from its agricultural precepts. Among the New South advocates themselves there was also a keen awareness of the weight of tradition that would be against them, and as late as 1900, when their ideology had captured large segments of the population, Tompkins sadly acknowledged that "long training as an agricultural people has brought to us a certain abiding degree of prejudice against manufactures and commerce."

To dislodge this "prejudice" and to enlist public spirit and funds in their program, the spokesmen of the New Order knew that more was required of them than a positive program of regeneration. Before they could feel secure in advancing the industrial argument, they had to elaborate a damning critique of the institutions of the Old South. It was not enough, they reasoned, that the old system had been wrecked; it had to be so thoroughly discredited that no one would wish to revive it, in however altered a form. . . .

. . . [Their] essential message was [that] slavery and a spirit of anti-industrialism and anti-urbanism had been responsible for the South's great failure; the New South must root out all remnants of that heritage.

Assailing the errors of the past and denouncing their perpetuation in the present, the New South spokesmen turned confidently to the positive aspects of their blueprint for an opulent South. The commanding feature of their plan, of course, was the design for an industrial society. But the South in the 1880's continued to be overwhelmingly rural and agrarian, and it required no great insight to see that a program for the reconstruction of the Southern economy could not neglect agriculture. Despite their passion to erect an industrial utopia, then, the New South spokesmen also drafted a program for a renovated agricultural system infused with the values of business enterprise. Moreover, the vital connection between a sound farm economy and dynamic industrial growth was quickly perceived and assiduously worked out. The spirit of [Alexander] Hamilton and [Henry] Clay was much alive in Edmonds when he wrote that a "harmonious relationship between industry and agriculture would make the South, with its vast natural resources and human power, 'the garden spot of the world.'"

Sidney Lanier, the pre-eminent poet of the region, was especially hopeful about the future of Southern agriculture. In a famous essay entitled "The New South," published in *Scribner's Monthly* in 1880, he acknowledged and saluted the revolutionary changes which he believed had taken place since the war. The New South which he saw emerging was characterized by political, social, moral, and aesthetic developments that augured well for the future of the region. But, most important of all, he believed, "The New South means small farming." As he interpreted the statistics of land tenure, Lanier concluded that plantations were giving way to farms and staple-crop agriculture to diversified pursuits. An economic democracy in the countryside was in the making.

In "Corn," one of his better poems, Lanier turned his views into a meter-making argument for the new agriculture. The farmer whose life he depicts is driven to ruin by his persistent dependence on cotton. The soil becomes depleted and the farmer impoverished; escape from this vicious circumstance can be found only by migrating, and so he leaves the South, finding a new home in the West. Thus, the tyranny of cotton drives the sturdy men out of the region, depleting not only the land but the human resources as well. To diversify the crops and divide the land, Lanier implies, would solve the problems of the farmer and of the region.

Cotton's dominion was the great *bête blanche* of the New South spokesman and its tyranny occupied a central position in their economic and promotional writings. Edmonds filled column after column in the *Manufacturers' Record* with blasts at "the all-cotton curse" and Grady railed against the "all-cotton plan" with dependable regularity in his editorials and elsewhere. "It is time for an agricultural revolution," Grady announced in one editorial. "When we once decide that southern lands are fit for something else besides cotton, and then go to work in earnest to multiply and diversify our products and industries, independence and wealth will be the certain reward of our intelligent and industrious farmers." Cotton's tyranny, according to the New South view, was all-pervasive. For the region as a whole it retarded economic growth and thus per capita income by frustrating industrial development. It put the farmer at the mercy of a capricious international market and tied him to a credit system that drove him deeper into debt each year. With a lien on his crop and a mortgage on his home he failed to realize that much of the profits from the cotton crop went out of the region, never to return, and it never occurred to him to grow crops which might be marketed locally; or, if it did, he lacked either the knowledge or the credit, or both, to undertake new systems.

To break this unhappy syndrome, the New South spokesmen early became advocates of agricultural diversification. Over and over again the farmer was told to cut his cotton acreage in half and plant the other half in smaller crops. The possibilities for agricultural diversification were without limit, or so it must have appeared to readers of Grady's optimistic essays on the variety of crops suitable for Southern agriculture. . . .

. . . The task of promoting the South to outsiders was one that every small chamber of commerce undertook, each vying with the other for success. Pamphlets, articles, brochures, and books by the hundreds were sent out across the land to tell non-Southerners where they should come to make their fortunes. M. B. Hillyard's *The New South*, a book full of optimistic statistics, was published by Edmonds and, at his direction and expense, copies were placed in hotel reading rooms, public libraries, and on board passenger ships plying the seven seas. The inquiring reader would find a volume "richly bound in the finest Russian leather, with gilt edge and gilt title." Individual cities were often singled out for special attention in the promotional campaign, as in the case of Anniston, Alabama, Edmonds invited Kelley to do an article on this "model city of the South," declaring that it "would be read over the country, and would be worth many thousands and tens of thousands of dollars." Kelley was happy to oblige, and "Anniston: A Romance of the New South" appeared in the 1887 columns of the *Record*.

Another favored device frequently used to advertise the promise of the South was the industrial and agricultural exposition. New South spokesmen reacted with pleasure to Atlanta's International Cotton Exposition in 1881, and the October 5 issue of the *Constitution* was a special, record-breaking thirty-two page edition celebrating its opening. The next month Grady wrote that the South had never previously had such an opportunity to make its advantages known. As the exposition device caught on, national attention focused on it and the leading periodicals published friendly descriptions. A correspondent for the *Century Magazine* reviewed the New Orleans exposition of 1885 in a two-piece article and concluded that everyone could now plainly see that "there are vast and inviting fields to the south of us waiting to be conquered for our industries and our commerce." Impressed by the region's rapid recovery from the ravages of war, this correspondent believed that the South stood "in the portal of a great industrial development. Two years later, Grady pronounced the Piedmont Exposition a great success, explaining that "within its commodious exposition halls are to be found the raw materials side by side with the finished products, all the result of the energy and enterprise of the new south." Energy, enterprise—and opportunity: these were the charming allurements the expositions were designed to reveal to the prospective investor in the South's future.

Old South Leaders in the New South

LAURENCE SHORE

A long-standing interpretation of the postbellum South posits the war's destruction of the antebellum ruling elite. The eminent historian C. Vann Woodward acknowledged that a few postbellum leaders—Joseph Brown, for example—had been leaders of the "old type." But because he believed that a massive change had to occur within an old-type leader to enable him to become a postbellum leader, Woodward found only a few Joseph Browns. Identities are not merely masks to be exchanged at will, Woodward suggested. Antebellum Southern identity was so different from the capitalistic ethic that Henry Grady preached that it was inconceivable to the author of *Origins of the New South* that many antebellum leaders could assume a "New South" identity.

But antebellum leaders had not rejected key values associated with a capitalistic ethic. Rather, need to justify slavery had resulted in their peculiar twist on the national capitalistic persuasion. Massive changes therefore were not necessary. Experienced ideologists and politicians reasserted their influence in the two decades following emancipation precisely because they were well equipped to make the changes that were necessary.

"Words are powers," a writer for *De Bow's Review* commented in 1868. "They are frequently evidences of accomplished change, or agencies in the production of change. They reveal, or they determine, an altered

From *Southern Capitalists: The Ideological Leadership of an Elite, 1832–1885*, by Laurence Shore. © 1986 The University of North Carolina Press. Reprinted by permission.

habit of thought." The key point here is that postbellum ideologists altered their own and strove to alter other Southerners' habit of thought; they did not have to invent or steal a completely new, alien way of thinking. As William Burwell, editor of *De Bow's Review*, noted in 1870, antebellum "statesmen were ready to acknowledge the value of commercial intercourse and industrial progress," but "there was apprehension that the labor and local systems of the South might be endangered by their introduction."

Now that the apprehension was gone, and with the new reality of Southern Republicans promising economic progress, many proslavery ideologists readily modified their message. Emancipation, they now declared, did not equal disaster, but a new opportunity to correct the old system's errors. Not surprisingly, 1850s proslavery reformers of the William Gregg type were especially fitted to lead reorientation. Men such as Steadman of Tennessee and Georgia and James M. Wesson of Mississippi could easily draw from their antebellum message of industrial development, diversified agriculture, and strengthened respect for the mechanical arts. They stood as obvious examples that the New South had roots in the Old South in economic ideology as well as in ideologists. . . .

One may argue that it is all very well to demonstrate reemergence of cultural ideologists throughout the postbellum era—familiar names in journals and experienced voices at agricultural fairs—but what about antebellum roots of Southern political leaders after Congressional Reconstruction? The presence of old leaders in 1865–66 helped push Congress to formulate and pass the 1867 acts that demolished the Johnson program of restoration. Although Congressional Reconstruction did not engender radical economic or social change, it did remove from power (and disfranchise) the bulk of the antebellum and Confederate ruling elite. Republican political ascendancy was established throughout the South for a number of years, varying by state. C. Vann Woodward has concluded that "the old rulers were discredited along with the Lost Cause, disfranchised as a class and frequently dispossessed as individuals."

If old leaders had failed to regain the positions of governor, United States senator, and United States representative following overthrow of Republican rule in the 1870s, it would be pointless to contend that old leaders continued to direct the shaping of Southern ideology, no matter how many postbellum writers had antebellum ties. After all, ideological direction is founded in political power. Access to power entails access to means of communication that shape the public mind.

But consideration of the Redeemer period only strengthens the thesis that the people who spoke for the postbellum South had also spoken for the antebellum South. Indeed, even many ardent secessionists who stayed quiet during Presidential Reconstruction won positions of political dominance in the 1870s and 1880s.

In Georgia, Redeemer Democrats generally had long experience in the exercise of power. Alfred H. Colquitt's 1876 gubernatorial triumph marked the resumption of political power of someone who had in every sense belonged to the Southern elite. Colquitt came from a wealthy planter family and had served as a United States congressman (1853–55), antebellum Georgia legislator, and Confederate army commander. Moreover, during Republican rule he became president of the State Agricultural Society (1870) and remained in that post until his 1876 election victory. Colquitt was not, however, the first Democrat to succeed a Republican governor in Georgia. Charles M. Smith occupied the governor's office from 1872–77, and though his old-order credentials were not as impressive as Colquitt's, Smith had served in the Confederate Congress. He had also grown up on a plantation. The two governors who succeeded Colquitt were Alexander Stephens (1882–83) and Henry G. McDaniel (1883–86). Stephens requires no identification. McDaniel had been a delegate to Georgia's secession convention.

Of Georgia's six Democratic United States senators from 1875–87, four had held important political offices before the war—Benjamin Hill, Colquitt, Joseph Brown (secessionist and former Republican), and Thomas M. Norwood. M. Pope Barrow, a "new man," served only as a one-year replacement following Hill's death. John Brown Gordon had previously held no political office, but he was a famous Confederate general and was as closely linked to the Confederacy as Alexander Stephens.

From 1873–87 Georgia elected twenty-four Democrats to the United States House of Representatives. Thirteen had antebellum experience as elected officials. Alexander Stephens led each delegation from 1873 to 1882, when he was elected governor. Benjamin Hill (antebellum legislator, secession convention delegate, and Confederate senator) served a term in Congress before entering the Senate. If one were to calculate the number of terms that old leaders served from 1873–87, instead of the number of old leaders elected, the appearance of restoration would grow still sharper.

Numbers and influence do not, of course, necessarily match. For example, in a group of seven leaders, six may be new but one, an old leader, may dominate the group. Or six may be old, but the lone new person may dominate. However difficult it may be to assess influence, one must sometimes go beyond mere numbers to identify the "first among equals."

In Georgia politics in the 1870s and 1880s, who were the first among equals, in the eyes of astute contemporaries? In this state, at least, the problem of assessing influence is simple. Five men unquestionably stood above the rest: Alexander Stephens, Benjamin Hill, and the "Georgia Triumvirate"—Colquitt, Joseph Brown, and John Brown Gordon. All five, as I have already shown, had been influential leaders before and/or during the war. Moreover, even though Robert Toombs, one of the state's most powerful politicians before and during the war, did not hold office after 1865, he remained an important figure in Georgia politics and dominated the state constitutional convention in 1877. Toombs had been a rabid secessionist.

Alabama's Redeemer leaders, like Georgia's, had held places among the antebellum ruling elite. From 1870–86 Alabama elected four Democratic governors, three of whom—George Houston, Robert B. Lindsay, and Edward A. O'Neal—had intimate antebellum ties. Houston sat in the state legislature as early as 1832, and served in the United States House from

1847–61 (excluding the 1849–51 term). Lindsay was a state legislator in the 1850s and married into one of northern Alabama's wealthiest planter families. O'Neal was also a northern Alabama planter and had been one of the most ardent and effective secessionist leaders in that section.

In the United States Senate, the evidence of restoration in Alabama is overwhelming. John T. Morgan . . . was a secessionist and Confederate brigadier general who had stayed out of politics during Presidential Reconstruction because of his secessionist past. But he always believed that he would regain political prominence. He would simply have to bide his time. In 1877 Morgan's time came. He stayed. For the next thirty years John Morgan was a United States senator. From 1879–97 he had only three different senatorial colleagues: George Houston, Luke Pryor (also as antebellum officeholder), and James L. Pugh. Pugh, moreover, was really Morgan's only partner, as the combined tenure of Houston (who died in 1879) and Pryor was less than a year.

Pugh, like Morgan, was no stranger to leadership. In the antebellum era he had been a United States representative and an advocate of secession. During the war he sat in both Confederate Congresses. His presidency of the state Democratic convention in 1874 testified to his continuing influence and foreshadowed his senatorial triumph.

A case for new men could possibly be made if one considers Alabama's congressmen from 1877–85. Only a handful had prewar legislative or editorial credentials. Although many had lawyer/planter backgrounds that were hardly "bourgeois" (in the terminology of historians such as Woodward and Eugene Genovese), the majority clearly had not been old-order leaders. But the presence of "graybeards" in the governor's mansion and the Senate chamber—Houston (born 1811), O'Neal (born 1818), Pugh (born 1820), Morgan (born 1824)—seems to be of greater weight in determining the locus of power in post-Republican Alabama politics.

In Mississippi the locus of Redeemer power is easily determined. As in Georgia, a triumvirate of antebellum/Confederate leaders dominated Mississippi politics: L. Q. C. Lamar, James Z. George, and Edward C. Walthall were Mississippi's post-Reconstruction Democratic senators and party directors (Lamar was also a congressman from 1873–77). In addition, Mississippi's congressional delegations had a strong antebellum cast. Of the state's nine Democratic representatives from 1875–85, six had antebellum leadership credentials. Among these six were Ethelbert Barksdale (pre- and postwar editor of the *Jackson Clarion*, Confederate congressman, and avid supporter of Jefferson Davis) and Otho R. Singleton, longtime antebellum United States congressman and state legislator, secessionist, and Confederate congressman.

It has been argued that the postbellum predominance of men such as Lamar and George represents a break with antebellum leadership because Lamar and George wielded more power in the 1870s and 1880s than they had in the 1850s. But this is strange reasoning. Although one must concede that Lamar and George enjoyed greater postbellum influence, one must also note their close association with antebellum Mississippi's most powerful politicians (e.g., Davis, A. G. Brown, Jacob Thompson), their rising influence under the nurturing wing of antebellum elders, their firm espousal of various proslavery arguments, their advocacy of secession, their important roles in the secession convention, and public recognition of their position as leaders of and spokesmen for antebellum and Confederate Mississippi.

Surely, then, the point to stress is continuity in personnel across the chasm of war and Reconstruction, even as one acknowledges that some antebellum leaders did not successfully cross the chasm. Here a counterfactual perspective elucidates the point: had there been no war, had the slave South continued to exist into the 1870s and 1880s, who would have been Mississippi's most influential leaders during this period? The only reasonable answer is Lamar and George, the same men who supposedly represent a break with the old order.

In speaking of continuity across the war, one must take care not to delimit too narrowly antebellum identities of those who continued as leaders. Sharp-cut classifications have misled students of Southern history. It may be tempting to characterize the South's Redeemer leaders as men with antebellum Whig party loyalties whose affection for diverse business dealings was restrained by the region's plantation agriculture orientation. But the Whig label turns out to be ill fitting. Moreover, as the historian W. J. Cooper, Jr. reminds us, the very enterprise of attempting to distinguish between Southern Whigs and Democrats on the overriding issue in the antebellum South—slavery—is fruitless. We must be satisfied with "proslavery leaders" as a description of antebellum identity of Redeemer politicians. This broad classification has the virtue of allowing us to capture the fact of greatest significance: the elected leaders and shapers of public opinion in the postbellum South's free-labor world had played similar roles in the antebellum South's slave-labor world. . . .

I am not arguing that a tightly knit antebellum ruling elite remained in power to become a tightly knit postbellum ruling elite. There never was a tightly knit elite, antebellum or postbellum. But the most influential political leaders and shapers of public opinion in the postbellum period, 1865–85, had held similar positions before and during the war. In that earlier period, the *sine qua non* of leadership was ability to justify and to protect slave labor. A large, heterogeneous group of wealthy planters and their lawyer and journalist allies undertook this task. Neither defeat in war, nor emancipation, nor Presidential Reconstruction, nor Congressional Reconstruction, prevented a significant portion of this large group from continuing to exercise power.

As John Morgan of Alabama had indicated, secession turned out to be an ineffectual policy for slavery's protection. But it was not necessarily a foolish policy. Moreover, for the antebellum ruling elite it was not a suicidal policy. A few individuals, most notably Edmund Ruffin, were unwilling to face a free-labor world. But so many more not only faced the new order but directed it. When men such as L. Q. C. Lamar, Joseph Brown, Zebulon Vance, and Wade Hampton adapted to new conditions and cultivated relationships with large corporations, this did not reflect merely a nominal connection to the old planter regime. Rather, this indicated that a planter/lawyer, proslavery background had been excellent preparation for success in economic and political leadership in free-labor society. In the new politics, as in the new economics, ruling whites continued to rule.

⚓ *F U R T H E R   R E A D I N G*

Dwight B. Billings, Jr., *Planters and the Making of a "New South"* (1979)
Orville V. Burton and Robert C. McMath, eds., *Toward a New South?* (1982)
David L. Carlton, *Mill and Town in South Carolina, 1880–1920* (1982)
John Milton Cooper, Jr., *Walter Hines Page* (1977)
Paul D. Escott, *Many Excellent People* (1985)
Walter J. Fraser, Jr., and Winfred B. Moore, Jr., eds., *From Old South to New* (1981)
Paul M. Gaston, *The New South Creed* (1973)
Steven Hahn, *The Roots of Southern Populism* (1983)
Melton A. McLaurin, *The Knights of Labor in the South* (1978)
———, *Paternalism and Protest* (1971)
Broadus Mitchell, *The Rise of Cotton Mills in the South* (1921)
Sydney Nathans, *The Quest for Progress* (1983)
Gail W. O'Brien, *The Legal Fraternity and the Making of a New South Community, 1848–1882* (1986)
Crandall A. Shifflett, *Patronage and Poverty in the Tobacco South* (1982)
Laurence Shore, *Southern Capitalists* (1986)
John F. Stover, *The Railroads of the South, 1865–1900* (1955)
Nannie M. Tilley, *The Bright-Tobacco Industry, 1860–1929* (1948)
Peter Wallenstein, *From Slave South to New South* (1987)
Michael Wayne, *The Reshaping of Plantation Society* (1983)
Jonathan M. Wiener, *Social Origins of the New South* (1978)
C. Vann Woodward, *Origins of the New South* (1951)

CHAPTER
4

Land and Labor in the
New South

The future of the New South was not to be determined by industry alone. As the mounting protests of farmers made clear, the region's progress depended heavily on developments in agriculture, that sector of the economy in which most people—whites and blacks—worked. After Reconstruction it became increasingly clear that a distinctive system of labor—one based on sharecropping and the crop lien—had arisen in southern agriculture and that the results were tragically disappointing both for many workers and for the South as a whole.

All scholars agree that one fundamental, underlying reason for poor returns in agriculture was a worldwide decline in cotton prices. Demand was growing much more slowly than between 1800 and 1860, and the South's booming production led only to depressed prices. Then why did the South maintain its heavy reliance on cotton? The answer lies in the sharecropping and furnishing systems, which locked farmers and farm workers into the production of a crop whose price was falling.

What was sharecropping, and how did it develop? What role did merchants, landowners, and laborers—black and white—play in the sharecropping system? How did race affect it? Did it benefit sharecroppers or lead to abuses of them? Historians and economists have scrutinized these questions as part of their pursuit of larger issues: How did sharecropping affect the South's overall economic system? How did the region's economy differ from the North's economy? Why did the South become so poor and backward?

⚓ D O C U M E N T S

The first document is a contract executed in January 1886 between a sharecropper and a landowner in North Carolina; it is typical of innumerable contracts made in the South in the last decades of the nineteenth century and well into the twentieth. The second document is an agricultural lien, or "crop lien," which gave assurance to the landowner that his expenses in "furnishing" the cropper with food and supplies during 1876 would be repaid. The crop lien customarily accompanied any sharecropping agreement. (This document also pledged the cropper's real and personal property, if necessary, to repay the man who furnished him.) In the third document, Nate Shaw, a black sharecropper, describes some of his experiences with the sharecropping system. His account reveals both the workings of the system and its special dangers for a black man, due to pervasive racism. The last document provides a differing but not entirely incompatible view of sharecropping by William Alexander Percy, a white man who in the 1930s became the head of a large landowning family in Mississippi.

A Sharecropping Contract, 1886

This contract made and entered into between A. T. Mial of one part and Fenner Powell of the other part both of the County of Wake and State of North Carolina—

Witnesseth—That the Said Fenner Powell hath bargined and agreed with the Said Mial to work as a cropper for the year 1886 on Said Mial's land on the land now occupied by Said Powell on the west Side of Poplar Creek and a point on the east Side of Said Creek and both South and North of the Mial road, leading to Raleigh, That the Said Fenner Powell agrees to work faithfully and dilligently without any unnecessary loss of time, to do all manner of work on Said farm as may be directed by Said Mial, And to be respectful in manners and deportment to Said Mial. And the Said Mial agrees on his part to furnish mule and feed for the same and all plantation tools and Seed to plant the crop free of charge, and to give the Said Powell One half of all crops raised and housed by Said Powell on Said land except the cotton seed. The Said Mial agrees to advance as provisions to Said Powell fifty pound of bacon and two sacks of meal pr month and occationally Some flour to be paid out of his the Said Powell's part of the crop or from any other advance that may be made to Said Powell by Said Mial. As witness our hands and seals this the 16th day of January A.D. 1886

Witness   *A. T. Mial* [signed]   [Seal]

                                                      his
W. S. Mial [signed]   *Fenner* ✗ *Powell*   [Seal]
                                                     mark

A Crop Lien, 1876*

No. 123.—Lien Bond secured by Real and Personal Property.

STATE OF NORTH CAROLINA,

Wake County.

Articles of Agreement, Between *Alonzo T. Mial* of said County and State, of the first part, and *A. Robert Medlin* of the County and State aforesaid,

---

* A lien bond between A. Robert Medlin and Alonzo T. Mial; 1876. All italicized words were handwritten in the original. (*Source:* Alonzo T. and Millard Mial Papers, North Carolina Department of Archives and History.)

of the second part, to secure an Agricultural Lien according to an Act of General Assembly of North Carolina, entitled ''An Act to secure advances for Agricultural purposes'':

Whereas, the said *A. R. Medlin* being engaged in the cultivation of the soil, and being without the necessary means to cultivate his crop, *The Said A. T. Mial* ~~have~~ has agreed to furnish goods and supplies to the said *A. R. Medlin* to an amount not to exceed *One Hundred and fifty* Dollars, to enable him to cultivate and harvest his crops for the year 1876.

And in consideration thereof, the said *A. R. Medlin* doth hereby give and convey to the said *A. T. Mial* a LIEN upon all of his crops grown in said County in said year, on the lands described as follows: *The land of A. R. Medlin adjoining the lands of Nelson D. Pain Samuel Bunch & others.*

And further, in Consideration thereof, the said *A. R. Medlin* for One Dollar in hand paid, the receipt of which is hereby acknowledged, have bargained and sold, and by these presents do bargain, sell and convey unto the said *A. T. Mial his* heirs and assigns forever, the following described Real and Personal Property to-wit: *All of his Stock horses, Cattle Sheep and Hogs—Carts and Wagons House hold and kitchen furnishings.* To Have and to Hold the above described premises, together with the appurtenances thereof, and the above described personal property, to the said *A. T. Mial his* heirs and assigns.

The above to be null and void should the amount found to be due on account of said advancements be discharged on or before the *1st* day of *November* 1876: otherwise the said *A. T. Mial his* executors, administrators or assigns, are hereby authorized and empowered to seize the crops and Personal Property aforesaid, and sell the same, together with the above Real Estate, for cash, after first advertising the same for fifteen days, and the proceeds thereof apply to the discharge of this Lein, together with the cost and expenses of making such sale, and the surplus to be paid to the said *A. R. Medlin*, or his legal representatives.

IN WITNESS WHEREOF, The said parties have hereunto set their hands and seals this *29th* day of *February*, 1876.

his

A. Robert ✗ *Medlin* , [seal]
mark

Witness: *L. D. Goodloe* [signed]

A. T. Mial [signed], [seal]

Nate Shaw's Story (c. 1910), 1971

I didn't make two good bales of cotton the first year I stayed with Mr. Curtis. Sorry land, scarce fertilizer, Mr. Curtis not puttin out, riskin much on me and I a workin little old fool, too. I knowed how to plow—catch the mule out the lot, white man's mule, bridle him, go out there and set my plow the way I wanted—I knowed how to do it. Bout a bale and a half was what I made.

The second year he went out there and rented some piney wood land from Mr. Lemuel Tucker, sixteen acres bout a half mile from his plantation and he put me on it. Well, it was kind of thin but it was a king over Mr. Curtis's land. I worked it all in cotton; what little corn I had I planted on Mr. Curtis's place. Well, I made six pretty good bales of cotton out there for Mr. Curtis and myself. When I got done gatherin, wound up, by havin to buy a little stuff from Mr. Curtis at the start, in 1907—it sort of pulled the blinds over my eyes. It took all them six bales of cotton to pay Mr. Curtis. In the place of prosperin I was on a standstill. Second year I was married it took all I made on Mr. Tucker's place, by Mr. Curtis havin rented it from Mr. Tucker for me, to pay up 1908's debts and also 1907's debts—as I say, by me buyin a right smart to start me off to housekeepin, cleaned me. I had not a dollar left out of the cotton. And also, Mr. Curtis come in just before I moved off his place—I was determined to pay him and leave him straight; in fact, I reckon I just had to do it because he'd a requested it of me, movin from his place, clean up and leave myself clear of him.

Mr. Curtis had Mr. Buck Thompson to furnish me groceries. Mr. Curtis knowed all of what Mr. Thompson was lettin me have; kept a book on me. See, he was standin for everything Mr. Thompson gived me; he paid Mr. Thompson and I paid him—the deal worked that way—out of my crop. So he made somethin off my grocery bill besides gettin half my crop when the time come.

Took part of my corn to pay him. He come to my crib, him and Mr. Calvin Culpepper come together to my crib and got my corn, so much of it. And what I had he got the best of it, to finish payin him on top of them six bales of cotton.

Then I moved to Mr. Gus Ames', 1908. Mr. Ames' land was a little better than Mr. Curtis's, but it was poor. Worked his pet land hisself and whatever he made off me, why, that was a bounty for him. I didn't make enough there to help me.

Hannah was dissatisfied at it, too. We talked it over and our talk was this: we knew that we weren't accumulatin nothin, but the farmin affairs was my business, I had to stand up to em as a man. And she didn't worry me bout how we was doin—she knowed it weren't my fault. We was just both dissatisfied. So, we taken it under consideration and went on and she was stickin right with me. She didn't work my heart out in the deal. I wanted to work in a way to please her and satisfy her. She had a book learnin, she was checkin with me at every stand. She was valuable to me and I knowed it. And I was eager to get in a position where I could take care of her and our children better than my daddy taken care of his wives and children.

Mr. Curtis and Mr. Ames both, they'd show me my land I had to work and furnish me—far as fertilize to work that crop, they'd furnish me what *they* wanted to; didn't leave it up to me. That's what hurt—they'd furnish me the amount of fertilize they wanted regardless to what I wanted. I quickly seed, startin off with Mr. Curtis in 1907, it weren't goin to be enough. First year I worked for him and the last year too he didn't allow me to use over twenty-two hundred pounds of guano—it come in two-hundred-pound sacks then—that's all he'd back me up for all the land I worked, cotton and corn. It was enough to start with but not enough to do any more. Really, I oughta been usin twice that amount. Told him, too, but he said, "Well, at the present time and system, Nate, you can't risk too much."

I knowed I oughta used more fertilize to make a better crop—if you puts nothin in you gets nothin, all the way through. It's nonsense what they gived me—Mr. Curtis and Mr. Ames, too—but I was a poor colored man, young man too, and I had to go by their orders. It wasn't that I was ignorant of what I had to do, just, "Can't take too much risk, can't take too much risk." Now if you got anything that's profitable to you and you want to keep it and prosper with that thing, whatever it is, however you look for your profit—say it's a animal; you're due to look for your profit by treatin him right, givin him plenty to eat so he'll grow and look like somethin. Or if you fertilize your crop right, if you go out there and work a row of cotton—that's evidence of proof—I have, in my farmin, missed fertilizen a row and it stayed under, too. Them other rows growed up over it and produced more. If you don't put down the fertilize that crop aint goin to prosper. But you had to do what the white man said, livin here in this country. And if you made enough to pay him, that was all he cared for; just make enough to pay him what you owed him and anything he made over that, why, he was collectin on his risk. In my condition, and the way I see it for everybody, if you don't make enough to have some left you aint done nothin, except givin the other fellow your labor. That crop out there goin to prosper enough for him to get his and get what I owe him; he's makin his profit but he aint goin to let me rise. If he'd treat me right and treat my crop right, I'd make more and he'd get more—and a heap of times he'd get it all! That white man gettin all he lookin for, all he put out in the spring, gettin it all back in the fall. But what am I gettin for my labor? I aint gettin nothin. I learnt that right quick: it's easy to understand if a man will look at it. . . .

Now it's right for me to pay you for usin what's yours—your land, stock, plow tools, fertilize. But how much should I pay? The answer ought to be closely seeked. How much is a man due to pay out? Half his crop? A third part of his crop? And how much is he due to keep for hisself? You got a right to your part—rent; and I got a right to mine. But who's the man ought to decide how much? The one that owns the property or the one that works it? . . .

If you want to sell your cotton at once, you take it to the market, carry it to the Apafalya cotton market and they'll sample it. Cotton buyin man cuts a slug in the side of your bale, reaches in there and pulls the first of it out the way and get him a handful, just clawin in there. He'll look over that sample, grade that cotton—that's his job. What kind of grade do it make? You don't know until he tells you. If it's short staple, the devil, your price is cut on that cotton. Color matters too, and the way it was ginned—some gins cuts up the cotton, ruins the staple.

They had names for the cotton grades—grade this, or grade that or grade the other. Didn't do no good to argue with the man if you didn't agree with the grade. Thing for you to do if he graded your cotton, examined it and gived you a low bid, take it to the next man.

Much of it is a humbug just like everything else, this gradin business. Some of em don't pay you what that cotton's worth a pound. They want long staple, clean cotton: the cleaner and the prettier it is and the nearer it comes to the specification of the staple they lookin for, the more they'll offer you. Generally, it's a top limit to that price and that's what they call the price cotton is bringin that year. If it's forty-cent cotton or six-cent cotton, it don't depend much on *your* cotton. It's a market price and it's set before you ever try to sell your cotton, and it's set probably before you gin your cotton and before you gather it or grow it or even plant your seed.

You take that cotton and carry it around to the cotton buyers. You might walk in that market buildin to a certain cotton buyer and he'll take your sample and look it over, look it over, give it a pull or two and he just might if he's very anxious for cotton, offer you a good price for it. But if he's in no hurry to buy your cotton and he gives you a price you don't like you can go to another buyer.

Heap of em buyin that cotton to speculate; he got plenty of money, wants to make more money, he buyin that cotton for himself and he don't care what company buys it from him. Maybe he might be buyin for a speculatin company, a company what does business in speculation. Or he might be buyin for a company that uses that cotton. Or if he can handle the matter, he buys for two companies.

Niggers' cotton didn't class like a white man's cotton with a heap of em. Used to be, when I was dealin with them folks in Apafalya, some of em you could have called em crooks if you wanted to; they acted in a way to bear that name, definitely. Give a white man more for his cotton than they do you.

I've had white men to meet me on the streets with a cotton sample in my hand, say, "Hello, Nate, you sellin cotton today?" White men, farmers like myself, private men; some of em was poor white men.

I'd tell em, "Yes, sir, I'm tryin. I can't look like get what my cotton's worth."

"What you been offered?"

"Well, Mr. So-and-so—"

"O, I see here such-and-such a one offered you so-and-so-and-so—"

Heap of times the scaper that I offered to sell him my cotton had a knack of puttin his bid on the paper that the cotton was wrapped up in. I didn't want him to do that. The next man would see how much this one bid me and he wouldn't go above it.

And so, I'd have my cotton weighed and I'd go up and down the street with my sample. Meet a white man, farmin man like myself, on the street; he'd see what I been offered for my sample—the buyer's marks would be on the wrapper—or I'd tell him. And he'd take that sample, unwrap it, look at it; he'd say, "Nate, I can beat you with your own cotton, I can get more for it than that."

Aint that enough to put your boots on! The same sample. He'd say, "Let me take your sample and go around in your place. I can beat what they offered you."

Take that cotton and go right to the man that had his bid on it and he'd raise it; right behind where I was, had been, and get a better bid on it. I've gived a white man my sample right there on the streets of Apafalya; he'd go off and come back. Sometime he'd say, "Well, Nate, I helped you a little on it but I couldn't help you much."

And sometime he'd get a good raise on it with another fellow out yonder. He'd bring my sample back to me with a bid on it. "Well, Nate, I knowed I could help you on that cotton."

That was happenin all through my farmin years: from the time I stayed on the Curtis place, and when I moved to the Ames place and when I lived with Mr. Reeve, and when I moved down on Sitimachas Creek with Mr. Tucker, and when I lived up there at Two Forks on the Stark place, and when I moved down on the Pollard place and stayed there nine years. Colored man's cotton weren't worth as much as a white man's cotton less'n it come to the buyer in the white man's hands. But the colored man's labor—that was worth more to the white man than the labor of his own color because it cost him less and he got just as much for his money. . . .

I come up to my house one day—I was out checkin on my fences— and my wife told me there was a card in the mailbox tellin me to come to the bank in Apafalya and sign papers on my place. I said, "If I go, any way I go, you goin with me." See, she had book learnin and she could read and write. So I told her, "Well, we'll go to Apafalya this evenin, right after dark."

She was right down with me. Sometimes she'd say, "Darlin, you know what's best to do. But you can't decide *what* to do until you knows every side of the proposition. And bein that you can't read and write, it's profitable for us all for you to make me your partner."

I told her, one day, and many a time, "I'm married to you. And I think my best business should be in your hands. If anybody knows the ins and outs of it, you the one to know. But so far as workin in the field, I aint never had a high opinion of that and I intend to always be that way. Your business is at the house, mine's out in the field."

She was a girl that her mother would put all her business in her hands— her mother couldn't read and write. You could drop any sort of paper in front of Hannah and she could pick it up and read it like a top. She was pretty far advanced in education. She wasn't a graduate but she understood anything and could talk it off, too. She was, in a way of speakin, the *eyes* and I was the mouthpiece.

So, when I went there to sign them papers, I told her, "You goin with me."

I wanted her to read them papers to me; I knowed they weren't goin to do it. All I had to do was sign, but I wanted to know what I was signin.

Watson had taken over the place from the federal government and it was him I had to sign with. My wife and I jumped in the car and went right on to Apafalya. Got there and walked in—weren't nobody there in the bank but Mr. Grace and Mr. Watson. O good God, the doors flew right open and I broke out; I couldn't help it, I got red hot. I was signin—called it signin papers on that place. I knowed what I was signin before I signed; that's what brought the devil up.

"Hi, hello, Nate."

"Hello, Nate."

"How do you do, Mr. Watson, Mr. Grace."

Said, "Well, you come here to sign your papers, didn't you?"

I said, "Yes sirs, that's why I'm here."

Pushed it through the window for me to sign. My wife was standin right there and I just handed it to her. That's when I found out the devil was in the concern; that kept crossin my mind all the time and that kept me, to a great extent, from signin any notes at all with Watson.

Hannah turned away, stepped off a step or two, whipped that paper right over in a jiffy. She come back with it and touched me on my arm. I listened to her. She said, "Darlin, that paper covers everything you got: your mules, wagon, all your tools and your cows and hogs and everything you got's on that paper."

Good God, when she told me that I hollered. I just pushed the paper back to em through the bars. I said, "I won't sign that paper, noway under the sun it could be fixed like it is."

I'd expected to come there that night and sign papers on the land—Watson knowed what I had—not reach out and take my mules, my wagon, my hogs, my cows, on that paper. And if I'd a signed it like they was preparin me to do, I could have lost it all. Just be late payin on the land and they would take everything I had. I had sense enough through my wife to see what they was tryin to do to me. Woooooooooo, I meant to buck it.

I said, "Aint that land sufficient to stand for itself and not none of my personal property on it? I can't carry it nowhere."

Tried to saddle everything I had. Right there I burst like a butterbean in the sun. I wouldn't sign that note for Jesus Christ. I just stuck that paper back through them bars—I knowed the type of him. I felt a fire in my heart; told my wife, "Let's go."

If I couldn't do better I was goin to move away from there. Soon as I told my wife, "Let's go," and got nearly to the door, "Come back, come back, Nate, we can change the paper; come back, come back, we can change it."

I just say now I was a fool—I went back. They changed that paper to suit me and I signed it. It just spoke for the land then. So I signed to buy the place from Mr. Watson and if I couldn't make the payments all they could do was take it back. . . .

And I killed all the meat we could use until I killed meat again—from winter to winter. I had a white man walk through my yard—two of em, Mr. Albert Clay and Mr. Craven. I don't know Mr. Craven's given name but that was Mr. Clay's brother-in-law. Come through my yard one Saturday evenin and I had killed three big hogs, me and my little boys, and had em stretched out over the yard after I cut em up.

They walked up to my back yard on the north side of the house—that old house I was livin in was built east and west—and they come up from towards my barn. I was surprised in a way but I didn't let it worry me, people go where they want to and walk anywhere they want to. Mr. Albert Clay and Mr. Craven come up from towards my barn. My barn set west of the house and back behind the barn was my pasture. Well, they come right up cross the back yard—that yard was covered with meat from three big hogs I'd just killed and had the meat put out; it was all of nine hundred pounds of meat. They looked there in that yard and stools, boxes, tables, benches, and everything had planks across em and them planks was lined with meat, just killed and cut out. Dressed, gutted, and cut open but not fully cut up, layin out, ready for salt.

Mr. Craven made a big moderation. "Where'd you get all this meat, Shaw? What are you goin to do with all this meat?"

It was all over the yard, coverin everything in sight. Three great big hogs weighed over three hundred pounds apiece. Had more meat there than you could shake a stick at.

"That's more meat than ever I seed any nigger—" that's the way he said it—"I aint never seed that much meat that no one nigger owned it."

They looked hard, didn't stop lookin. After a while they crept on out of there, still stretchin their eyes at that meat. They didn't like to see a nigger with too much; they didn't like it one bit.

William Alexander Percy Views Sharecropping, 1941

I have no love of the land and few, if any, pioneer virtues, but when Trail Lake became mine after Father's death, I must confess I was proud of it. I could reach it in three quarters of an hour. It was a model place: well drained, crossed by concrete roads, with good screened houses, a modern gin, artesian-well water, a high state of cultivation, a Negro school, a foolish number of churches, abundant crops, gardens and peach trees, quantities

From *Lanterns on the Levee* by William Alexander Percy. Copyright 1941 by Alfred A. Knopf, Inc. and renewed 1969 by LeRoy Pratt Percy. Reprinted by permission of Alfred A. Knopf, Inc.

of hogs, chickens, and cows, and all the mules and tractors and equipment any place that size needed.

Father had operated it under the same contract that Fafar used on the Percy Place. The Negroes seemed to like it and I certainly did. I happen to believe that profit-sharing is the most moral system under which human beings can work together and I am convinced that if it were accepted in principle by capital and labor, our industrial troubles would largely cease. So on Trail Lake I continue to be partners with the sons of ex-slaves and to share fifty-fifty with them as my grandfather and Father had done.

In 1936 a young man with a passion for facts roved in from the University of North Carolina and asked to be allowed to inspect Trail Lake for the summer. He was Mr. Raymond McClinton, one of Doctor Odum's boys, and the result of his sojourn was a thesis entitled "A Social-Economic Analysis of a Mississippi Delta Plantation." That's coming pretty stout if you spend much of your time trying to forget facts and are stone-deaf to statistics. But some of his findings were of interest even to me, largely I suspect because they illustrated how Fafar's partnership-contract works in the modern world. In 1936, the year Mr. McClinton chose for his study, the crop was fair, the price average (about twelve cents), and the taxes higher than usual. Now for some of his facts:

Trail Lake has a net acreage of 3,343.12 acres of which 1,833.66 are planted in cotton, 50.59 are given to pasture, 52.44 to gardens, and the rest to corn and hay. The place is worked by 149 families of Negroes (589 individuals) and in 1936 yielded 1,542 bales of cotton. One hundred and twenty-four of the families work under Fafar's old contract, and twenty-five, who own their stock and equipment, under a similar contract which differs from the other only in giving three-fourths instead of one-half of the yield to the tenant. The plantation paid in taxes of all kinds $20,459.99, a bit better than $6.00 per acre; in payrolls for plantation work $12,584.66— nearly $4.00 an acre. These payrolls went to the Negroes on the place. The 124 families without stock of their own made a gross average income of $491.90 and a net average income of $437.64. I have lost Mr. McClinton's calculation of how many days of work a plantation worker puts in per year, but my own calculation is a maximum of 150 days. There is nothing to do from ginning time, about October the first, to planting time, about March the fifteenth, and nothing to do on rainy days, of which we have many.

These figures, as I read them, show that during an average year the 124 families working on Trail Lake for 150 days make each $437.64 clear, besides having free water and fuel, free garden plot and pasturage, a monthly credit for six months to cover food and clothing, a credit for doctor's bills and medicine, and a house to live in. The Negroes who receive this cash and these benefits are simple unskilled laborers. I wonder what other unskilled labor for so little receives so much. Plantations do not close down during the year and there's no firing, because partners can't fire one another. Our plantation system seems to me to offer as humane, just, self-respecting, and cheerful a method of earning a living as human beings are likely to devise. I watch the limber-jointed, oily-black, well-fed, decently clothed peasants on Trail Lake and feel sorry for the telephone girls, the clerks in chain stores, the office help, the unskilled laborers everywhere—not only for their poor and fixed wage but for their slave routine, their joyless habits of work, and their insecurity.

Even with a place like Trail Lake, it's hard to make money farming. Although I kept myself helpfully obscure during the first years of my plantation-ownership, retaining the same excellent employees and following Father's practices, I began losing money almost at once, and in two years (they were depression years for everybody, I must confess) I had lost over a hundred thousand dollars and Trail Lake was mortgaged to the hilt. For the next four or five years I was in such a stew and lather getting that mortgage reduced and taxes paid, I lost track of goings-on in the outside world and missed the first tide of talk about share-croppers. Those hundred and twenty-four families of mine with $437.64 in their jeans worked "on the shares" and called themselves "croppers," but I wasn't familiar with the term "share-croppers." As used by the press, it suggested to me no Delta group and I assumed vaguely that share-croppers must be of some perverse bucolic genus that probably originated in Georgia and throve in Oklahoma. But one day I read that the President of the United States had excoriated bitterly and sorrowfully "the infamous sharecropper system." I asked a Washington friend of mine in what locality that system of farming prevailed. He knocked the breath out of me by answering: "On Trail Lake." I woke to the discovery that in pseudo-intellectual circles from Moscow to Santa Monica the Improvers-of-the-world had found something new in the South to shudder over. Twenty years ago it had been peonage. In the dark days when the collapse of the slave-trade had almost bankrupted good old New England, it had been slavery. Now it was the poor share-croppers—share-croppers over the whole South, but especially in the Delta. That very partnership of Fafar's which had seemed to me so just and practical now was being denounced as avaricious and slick—it was Mr. Roosevelt's "infamous system." We who had operated our plantations under it since carpetbag days were taunted now with being little better than slave-drivers by the carpetbaggers' progeny and kin. Obviously we are given to depravity down here: the South just won't do. In spite of prayers and advice from the "holier-than-thou's" it's always hell-bent for some deviltry or other. At this moment there's another of those great moral daybreaks on, and its east is Washington. In the glow I realize that Fafar and Mur, Father and I suffered from moral astigmatism—for all I know, from complete moral blindness: we were infamous and didn't even suspect it. Well, well, well. That makes a Southerner feel pretty bad, I reckon.

Notwithstanding an adage to the contrary, truth, as I've observed it, is one of the least resilient of herbs. Crushed to earth, it stays crushed; once down, it keeps down, flatter than anything except an oat field after a wind-storm. The truth about share-croppers has been told and retold, but, being neither melodramatic nor evidential of Southern turpitude, it isn't believed. I am not a well-informed person, but I know the truth about share-cropping and . . . I have told enough for earnest seekers to infer what it is; I have not done this, however, in the naïve hope that my words will do the slightest good or change the views of a single reader; my reason is other and quite unworthy: there's a low malicious pleasure in telling the truth where you know it won't be believed. Though rightly considered a bore and a pest in the best Trojan circles, Cassandra, no doubt, had her fun, but, at that, not nearly so much as the Knights of the Bleeding Heart who in politics and literature years from now will still be finding it fetching and inexpensive to do some of their most poignant public heart-bleeding over the poor downtrodden share-croppers of the deep South.

Share-cropping is one of the best systems ever devised to give security and a chance for profit to the simple and the unskilled. It has but one drawback—it must be administered by human beings to whom it offers an unusual opportunity to rob without detection or punishment. The failure is not in the system itself, but in not living up to the contractual obligations of the system—the failure is in human nature. The Negro is no more on an equality with the white man in plantation matters than in any other dealings between the two. The white planter may charge an exorbitant rate of interest, he may allow the share-cropper less than the market price received for his cotton, he may cheat him in a thousand different ways, and the Negro's redress is merely theoretical. If the white planter happens to be a crook, the share-cropper system on that plantation is bad for Negroes, as any other system would be. They are prey for the dishonest and temptation for the honest. If the Delta planters were mostly cheats, the results of the share-cropper system would be as grievous as reported. But, strange as it may seem to the sainted East, we have quite a sprinkling of decent folk down our way.

Property is a form of power. Some people regard it as an opportunity for profit, some as a trust; in the former it breeds hubris, in the latter, noblesse oblige. The landed gentry of Fafar's time were of an ancient lineage and in a sober God-fearing tradition. Today many have thought to acquire membership in that older caste by acquiring land, naked land, without those ancestral hereditaments of virtue which change dirt into a way of life. On the plantation where there is stealing from the Negro you will generally find the owner to be a little fellow operating, as the saying goes, "on a shoe-string," or a nouveau riche, or a landlord on the make, tempted to take more than his share because of the mortgage that makes his title and his morals insecure. These, in their pathetic ambition to imitate what they do not understand, acquire power and use it for profit; for them the share-cropper system affords a golden opportunity rarely passed up.

Two courses of action would be effective against unworthy landlords: the Negroes could and should boycott such landlords, quietly and absolutely; the government could and should deny government benefits to the landlord who will not put the terms of his contract in writing, who will not carry out those terms and who will not permit the government to prove by its own inspection that they have been carried out. In place of these suggested remedies, I can only recommend changing human nature. All we need anywhere in any age is character: from that everything follows.

✧ E S S A Y S

In the first essay historian Jonathan Wiener of the University of California, Irvine, explores the relationship between class structure and economic development in the South. After examining class conflict and the plantation system during the early years of Reconstruction, Wiener argues that the South's labor system was essentially different from that of the North, a fact that made "postwar Southern capitalism qualitatively different from the Northern pattern." Harold Woodman, professor of history at Purdue University, differs from Wiener in some respects; he sees a capitalistic society emerging, although it is one "arising on the ruins of a premodern slave society." In the second selection, Woodman argues for the importance of the recasting of class structure and its effects on three groups of southerners: former slaves, former slaveowners, and yeoman farmers. In the final selection, two economic historians, Roger L. Ransom of the University of California, Riverside, and Richard Sutch of the University of California, Berkeley, analyze the causes of the South's backwardness. Although their research identified several important economic causes, they emphasize the pervasive effects of racism in southern society.

Bound Labor in Southern Agriculture

JONATHAN M. WIENER

[Economic historians Joseph D.] Reid, [Stephen J.] DeCanio, and [Robert] Higgs have seen decentralized family sharecropping as the most rational organization of agriculture, not only for blacks but also for white planters. The social history of the immediate postwar period, however, indicates that the planters reached different conclusions about what constituted economic rationality. They believed that the most profitable course was to maintain the plantation as a centralized unit of production. By using supervised gang laborers who were paid wages and incorporated into the organizational structure of the antebellum plantation, the planters hoped to preserve economies of scale and centralized management. Engerman has argued that this program was fully comprehensible as an effort to maintain the method and social organization of production developed over sixty years; his study of land values and of output per worker indicates that "the planters were correct in the attempts to return to gang labor."

Jonathan M. Wiener, "Class Structure and Economic Development in the American South, 1865–1955," *American Historical Review*, October, 1979, pp. 973–976, 978–983. Copyright © 1979 by Jonathan M. Wiener. Reprinted by permission of the author.

The three cliometricians have exaggerated the extent to which landlords freely competed for tenants. Planters organized to limit the free market in labor and to force freedmen to work on plantation gangs, sought to enlist the Freedmen's Bureau in the same effort, and worked in the state legislatures to establish repressive laws. Some turned to terror—to the Ku Klux Klan—to force blacks to labor in plantation gangs. Planters throughout the South in the years immediately following the war organized to limit competition among themselves. At a typical meeting in the fall of 1867, planters in Sumter County, Alabama, unanimously resolved that "concert of action" was "indispensable" in hiring labor. Thus, all would offer the same terms to the freedmen, and none would "employ any laborer discharged for violation of contracts." Other planters held similar meetings in places like Sumter, South Carolina, and Amite County, Mississippi, followed by statewide meetings of planter representatives. The report of the Freedmen's Bureau in 1866 complained of the planters' "community of action," and the Joint Congressional Committee on Reconstruction heard evidence on the same phenomenon. As one planter explained the strategy to John Trowbridge in 1866, "The nigger is going to be made a serf, sure as you live. It won't need any law for that. Planters will have an understanding among themselves: 'You won't hire my niggers, and I won't hire yours,' then what's left for them? They're attached to the soil, and we're as much their masters as ever." Planters went beyond these informal organizations and used state power to enforce the interests of their class and prevent those individualists among them who desired to engage in market economics. "Enticement" acts passed in every Southern state immediately after the war made it a crime to "hire away, or induce to leave the service of another," any laborer "by offering higher wages or in any other way whatsoever." The criminal defined by this law was not the black who left his plantation, but the planter who sought a free market in labor.

Reid, DeCanio, and Higgs have also exaggerated the extent to which blacks were free to move. Louisiana law, for instance, made it a crime to "feed, harbor, or secrete any person who leaves his or her employer," and enticement laws in most states provided that farm laborers hired away by better offers could be forcibly returned to the original employers. Vagrancy acts were even more extreme efforts to control the mobility of labor. The definition of vagrancy usually included "stubborn servants . . . , a laborer or servant who loiters away his time, or refuses to comply with any contract . . . without just cause." Planters could thus enlist local courts in keeping "their" laborers on their plantations.

The planters' bitter opposition to the presence of the Freedmen's Bureau did not stop them from seeking to enlist the bureau's agents in an effort to tie blacks to the land. Planters put intense and calculated social pressure on the Union representatives in their midst. As early as 1864, a War Department report warned that officials in charge of the freedmen were "received into the houses of the planters and treated with a certain consideration," so that, under the "influences" that the planters brought to bear, officials often ("without becoming fully conscious of it") became "the employers' instrument of great injustice and ill-treatment toward . . . colored laborers." A black-belt newspaper explained in 1866 that Union officials who were "gentlemen" were "received into the best families . . . on probation" but those who kept "company with Negroes . . . could not get into society." When the Freedmen's Bureau opened an office in the Alabama black belt, "the white people . . . determined to win their good will," according to Walter L. Fleming. "There were 'stag' dinners and feasts, and the eternal friendship of the officers, with a few exceptions, was won." Fleming gave more credit to the persuasive power of stag dinners with planters than the feasts probably deserved, but he was undoubtedly correct in describing the planters' intentions as well as the effect of their efforts: some agents of the Freedmen's Bureau helped planters get freedmen to work on terms agreed to by planter organizations and often sided with planters in disputes with freedmen.

Finally, some planters restricted blacks' freedom to move by resorting to terror. Historians concerned with the politics of Reconstruction have overlooked the extent to which the Klan in the black belt was an instrument of the planter class for the control of labor. Planters played a major role in organizing and directing Klan activities there; and Klan terror contributed to the repression of black labor, primarily by threatening those who contemplated emigration. As early as 1866, masked bands "punished Negroes whose landlords had complained of them." According to the Congressional testimony of one planter, when blacks "got together once to emigrate . . . , disguised men went to them and told them that if they undertook it they would be killed," in order to keep "the country from being deprived of their labor." In the words of a black belt lawyer, the Klan was "intended principally for the negroes who failed to work." And Allen W. Trelease has shown that the Klan pursued blacks who "violat[ed] . . . labor contracts by running away."

Despite the planters' use of informal organization, formal law, the Freedmen's Bureau, and the Klan, they failed to preserve the plantation as a centralized unit cultivated by gangs of wage laborers. To understand this failure, it is necessary to look beyond the abstract logic of the market and focus on the relatively concrete process of class conflict between planters and freedmen. Rational as the planters' effort was, preservation of the centralized plantation confronted an insurmountable obstacle: the freedmen's refusal to agree to it. Their widespread resistance to working for wages in gangs, which appears in the sources as a "shortage of labor," played a crucial role in the reorganization of agriculture after the war. Such shortages were reported throughout the plantation South in the immediate postwar years. Robert Somers, who visited the South in 1871 and wrote a book about his experiences, titled his chapter on the Alabama black belt "Despair of the Planters for Labor." Reports by the Freedmen's Bureau and the Boston textile firm of Loring and Atkinson concurred. The freedmen's idea of a rational system of production differed from that of the planters; the blacks hungered for land. Eugene Genovese has quoted a plantation mistress's description of a typical situation at the war's end: "our most trusted servant . . . claims the plantation as his own." The Joint Congressional Committee on Reconstruction noted the freedmen's fierce "passion . . . to own land," and the Montgomery *Advertiser* agreed that blacks were "ravenous for land." The freedmen made their claim on the basis of a kind of labor theory of value; as a "Colored Convention" proclaimed in Montgomery in May 1867, "the property" that the planters held was "nearly all earned by the sweat of our brows, not theirs." And an exslave wrote in 1864, "we wants land—dis bery land dat is rich wid de sweat ob we face and de blood ob we back."

By creating a "shortage of labor," the freedmen defeated the planters' efforts to preserve the plantation as a single, large-scale unit worked by gangs. Increasingly in 1867 and 1868, planters divided their plantations into small plots and assigned each to a single family. In establishing decentralized family sharecropping as the prevailing organization of cotton production after the war, the planters made a major concession to the freedmen and their resistance to the slavelike gang system. The Selma *Southern Argus*, one of the most articulate and insightful voices of the planter class, admitted this explicitly: sharecropping was "an unwilling concession to the freedman's desire to become a proprietor . . . , not a voluntary association from similarity of aims and interests." Thus, class conflict shaped the form of the postwar plantation more than did purely economic forces operating according to the logic of the free market. . . .

. . . The North's economy depended on the market mechanism to allocate "free" labor; capitalists competed for labor and laborers were free, at least in theory, to move in response to better offers. This was the "classic capitalist" route to industrial society. Until the Great Depression of the 1930s, planters in the postwar South used more directly coercive methods of labor allocation and control. These restrictions on the South's labor market distinguished the planter from the Northern bourgeois, turned the sharecropper into a kind of "bound" laborer, and made the development of postwar Southern capitalism qualitatively different from the Northern pattern.

To argue that Northern agricultural laborers enjoyed freedoms denied to their Southern counterparts is not to say that the capitalist development of the North eliminated exploitation, oppression, or poverty. But their characteristic forms were different in kind from those under which Southern sharecroppers labored. The typical laborer in the "bonanza" wheat farms of the Northern plains was a migrant wage worker who was oppressed not by peonage but by seasonal unemployment and the need to travel great distances over the course of the year. The terms of disparagement for these workers—"tramps," "bums," "riffraff"—precisely described their mobility, their absence of ties to the land. In other areas of the North, agricultural laborers worked primarily as "hired hands" on family farms and received wages by the month or, during the harvest season, by the day. Farm labor took other forms in the truck gardens of the East and on the great farms of California's central valley. Studies of tenancy in the Midwest contain no evidence that debt peonage was widespread. Northern farm laborers were "forced to be free," the fate of labor wherever agriculture develops in classic capitalist fashion.

The most important institution in the South's system of bound labor was debt peonage. Pete Daniel's work on this central element in postwar Southern history is indispensable. Tenants began each season unable to finance the year's crop and had to seek credit from their landlords or the local merchants, who required that the tenant remain until the debt was paid, however many seasons that took. Hard-working tenants could be made to stay by exaggerating their indebtedness through dishonest book-keeping; undesirable ones could be ordered to move on, with their debts transferred to a new landlord. The movement of tenants among landlords preserved the system's repressive nature as long as the debt moved with the tenant, as typically it did. Movement alone does not, therefore, disprove the existence of debt peonage. Its extent is difficult to measure precisely; no doubt it varied along with economic cycles. Most contemporaries and historians describe it as a characteristic feature of cotton agriculture in the postwar South, and one study has found that 80 percent of the sharecroppers in Alabama had an indebtedness of more than one year's standing.

Debt peonage was not limited to sharecroppers; nor were they nec- essarily more exploited and oppressed by the labor-repressive system than were cash renters, usually regarded as one step up the socioeconomic ladder. During the 1890s, when cotton prices reached their low point for the century, renting replaced sharecropping at an astonishing rate. Higgs, for one, has taken this shift to rental labor as a sign of progress, "a response to the growth in the number of experienced black farmers to whom landlords were willing to grant such contracts." An alternative interpretation is more plausible: the economic collapse during that decade made it more profitable for landlords to collect rent instead of a share of the cotton crop from their tenants. Landlords, therefore, responded to the depression by forcing their tenants to assume the full extent of the risk, a risk in which the planters had previously shared. Landlords could still require tenants to obtain credit from them, thereby earning interest and tying their renters to the land by debt peonage until another season, when cotton might become profitable once again; then renters could be turned back into sharecroppers.

The actions of the planter class during the Mississippi River flood of 1927 are revealing. High water covered fifty miles on each side of the channel, submerging the delta plantation district and driving four hundred thousand black tenants from their homes. The planters believed, according to William Alexander Percy, one of their leaders, that "the dispersal of our labor was a longer evil . . . than a flood." They insisted that laborers not be permitted to leave the region so that the tenants could be returned to the plantations when the waters receded. The Red Cross and the National Guard operated refugee camps and helped the planters by acceding to their demand that the camps be "closed"—fenced and locked—so that the blacks could not get out and labor recruiters from other areas could not get in. The governor of Mississippi himself denounced labor recruiters who offered employment elsewhere to victims of the flood. Planters argued that, since labor contracts had already been signed for the 1927 season and since advances had been made to tenants, blacks had to go back and work after the flood, even though it became clear that the waters would not recede quickly enough to permit any planting. The Red Cross distributed emergency supplies not to the blacks inside the locked camps but to the local planters, some of whom billed their tenants after passing on the supplies, creating further indebtedness. The NAACP [National Association for the Advancement of Colored People] denounced the "peonage" practiced in refugee "concentration camps," but the planters succeeded in preventing blacks from leaving the region and in tightening the bonds that tied the tenants to their landlords.

The regional apparatus of involuntary servitude that prevailed between Reconstruction and World War II extended well beyond debt peonage; it also consisted of five different kinds of laws, all of which worked to restrict the free market in labor: enticement statutes, which made it a crime for one planter to hire laborers employed by another; emigrant agent laws, which severely restricted the activities of out-of-state labor recruiters; contract enforcement statutes, which made it a criminal offense for tenants to break contracts with landlords; vagrancy statutes, drawn broadly enough to permit landlords to enlist the aid of local courts to keep laborers at work; and the criminal surety system, backed up by the system of convict labor, which permitted convicts to serve their sentences laboring for private employers. Enticement acts were revived in eight out of ten Southern states after Reconstruction and survived with amendments into the mid-twentieth century. An Alabama statute from 1920 outlawed even attempted enticement. Like the enticement laws, emigrant agent acts were intended to control competition among white employers rather than to punish workers who moved. They sought to prevent the activities of out-of-state labor recruiters by levying prohibitive license fees. In the Carolinas, the license cost one thousand dollars per county, with a penalty for unlicensed recruiting of up to five thousand dollars or two years in prison. Six states of the Deep South passed such laws between 1877 and 1912, and three more did so between 1916 and 1929.

Other laws limited the freedom of laborers to move. Vagrancy acts forced workers to sign labor contracts. Penalties and apparently enforcement as well increased between 1890 and 1910 in response to the rise of agrarian insurgency. Georgia's law of 1895 provided for a fine of one thousand dollars or six to twelve months on the chain gang for those found without employment. The vagrancy acts permitted sheriffs to function as labor recruiters for planters, rounding up "vagrants" at times of labor shortage. Additional laws upheld labor contracts. Late in the nineteenth century six states passed "contract enforcement" and "false pretenses" statutes, which held that a worker's unjustified failure to work constituted "*prima facie* evidence of the intent to injure or defraud the employer."

An Alabama law of 1903 did not permit the defendant to rebut testimony about his intentions. Under "criminal surety" laws, employers were permitted to pay the fines of individuals convicted under contract enforcement or vagrancy proceedings; the convict had to work for that employer until his earnings repaid the fine. Thus a laborer whose work displeased his landlord could not only be convicted of a crime but also be compelled by the court to labor for the same employer. The alternative for convicts was the chain gang, and almost anything was preferable to its brutality. A distinctly Southern institution, it was reserved primarily for convicts who refused to sign criminal surety contracts or who were unable to get any landlord to pay their fine and hire them.

Thus, the Southern states established a net of laws to limit the mobility of labor. Vagrancy acts forced workers to sign labor contracts; contract enforcement and false pretenses laws prevented them from leaving. If they left nevertheless, the criminal surety system could return them to the employer, who was backed by the threat of the chain gang. Enticement and emigrant agent statutes prevented another employer from seeking their labor. In the North a laborer whose work displeased his employer could be fired; in the South he could be convicted of a criminal offense. This web of restrictive legislation distinguished the South's labor system from that of the classically capitalist North.

How successful were these laws? It is difficult to tell. William Cohen has suggested that one measure is the extent of their litigation in higher courts, an expensive and time-consuming practice—undertaken, presumably, only if enforcement were of great importance. The Alabama criminal surety law came before the state supreme court at least sixteen times between 1883 and 1914, and the Georgia contract enforcement law was litigated in appellate courts on eighty different occasions between 1903 and 1921. These cases suggest fairly extensive reliance on the law to repress labor, for those argued in the appellate courts were only the tip of the iceberg. The mere threat of prosecution usually sufficed to bring about the desired result; and, since only a handful of sharecroppers had the resources to appeal a conviction, planters, sheriffs, and local judges had virtually a free hand. Informal practice extended the law; extralegal and illegal acts were often undertaken to accomplish the same ends. In September 1901 local officials in the Mississippi black belt rounded up "idlers and vagrants" and drove them "into the cotton fields," where the farmers were "crying for labor." In February 1904 police in Newton, Georgia, made "wholesale arrests of idle Negroes . . . to scare them back to the farms from which they emanated." In 1908 the steamer *America* docked at a Natchez wharf, seeking to recruit black laborers. White businessmen established a local committee, whose methods according to one Southern reporter were "so emphatic that the negroes concluded to abandon their idea of leaving."

Legal and illegal efforts to restrict the mobility of labor in the South did not, of course, completely succeed; they only made it difficult. But the planter class did not require that every laborer be tied to his landlord, only that most, too frightened to leave, remain in order to preserve the low-wage, labor-intensive system of production. The most resourceful, energetic, and determined were always able to escape from their landlords and from the region, and more did so each year—but not because the planters made no effort to stop them. The typical departure occurred under cover of darkness, with family and neighbors sworn to secrecy. Large-scale black migrations from the South took place only twice between Reconstruction and the Depression: the "Kansas Fever" exodus of 1879–80 [a large migration of blacks to Kansas and other midwestern states] and the migration during World War I. Aside from these two movements, the migration rate from Southern states was significantly lower than that from other areas of the country, another measure of the success of repressive law and regional practice.

A New Plantation System

HAROLD D. WOODMAN

The transition from slavery to freedom deserves far more attention than it has been given by any of the new historians. Wartime destruction of life and property, the disruption of banking and commerce, and the uncertainties incident to the aftermath of war are important problems, but they must be seen in the context of an even more important problem: economic Reconstruction required that former slaves learn to be free workers and that former masters learn to be employers.

This simple point may appear obvious, but its significance, in my opinion, is profound. When former masters claimed that the blacks would not work except under compulsion and that blacks were unreliable and irresponsible and paid little attention to meeting their contractual obligations, they were obviously expressing their racist views. But they were doing more. They were acknowledging that they lacked the experience and the knowledge necessary to deal with free labor. The Black Codes and the extralegal intimidation and violence reflected the same thing as did plans to find new labor. When former masters considered replacing blacks with imported Chinese coolies, a form of labor they believed would be servile, docile, and easily controlled, they were acknowledging that this was the only kind of labor they knew how to handle.

This inability to deal with free labor was compounded by another related problem: implicit in employer-employee relationships in a capitalistic society is the notion of equality between the contracting parties. This was

From "Sequel to Slavery" by Harold D. Woodman, *Journal of Southern History* XLIII, No. 4 (November 1977). Copyright © 1977 by the Southern Historical Association. Reprinted by permission of the Managing Editor.

not a matter of concern merely to the philosophically minded, but a practical problem which planters faced and could not accept.

Most historians have noted the short-lived attempt to pay cash wages to freedmen immediately following emancipation. Less noted and seldom appreciated was a concurrent and longer-lasting procedure of paying share wages to the freedmen. This is often confused with sharecropping, but in fact, at least in the early postwar years, it was quite different. To the landowner share wages provided a way to pay wages without the need to have cash on hand. Moreover, since payment would not be made until a crop was harvested it would help to keep workers at work through the entire season. The planters expected that the laborers would work much as they did under slavery. Indeed, plantations using this form of wage payment had overseers and other supervisory personnel much as they had before the war. I suspect that it was mainly this kind of wage payment that the authors of the Black Codes had in mind when they drafted that restrictive and racist legislation.

To former slaves share wages encouraged vastly different expectations. In their eyes payment in the form of a share of the crop made them partners in the enterprise. As partners they felt that they should have a say in the way the plantation was run and should be free to order their lives and work in a manner that they felt best—just as the planter did. Among other things, this meant the right to arrange their own working hours and work pace and the right to withdraw their wives and children from the fields. Where the planters saw (or expected) a servile labor force continuing to work just as they had in the old days, the freedmen saw (or expected) a partnership which implied equality.

In short, what was happening in the early days after emancipation was a struggle between former masters trying to resurrect the old system as they knew it and former slaves trying to give some real meaning to their freedom. Therefore, the idea of contracting to work for wages (money or shares) had two different meanings for the contracting parties. Emancipation had ended the master-slave relationship, but it did not destroy the ideological legacy of slavery. Planters and freedmen alike lacked the experience, the discipline, the understanding, and the ideology necessary to create an employer-employee relationship.

At the same time the masses of the white population who never owned slaves were also undergoing a momentous process of social change for which they had little experience. Hill-country whites, who had been largely self-sufficient yeomen, were being transformed into commercial farmers. Like the former slaves they borrowed from local merchants to whom they gave crop liens, but they also secured their loans with mortgages on their lands. In the process, many lost their lands and came to occupy a status little different from that of the blacks. As with the planters and freedmen the prewar experience and ideology left the hill-country whites ill-prepared for the new world into which they were thrust.

If this much be granted, or at least be taken as a working hypothesis, then I suggest that we might profitably look at the period 1870 to 1900 as a time marked by the making of a working class from former slaves (and formerly self-sufficient whites) and the making of a bourgeois employer class from former slaveowners. From this perspective the various forms of tenant farming that evolved during this period—thirds and fourths, halves, standing rent, and cash rent—can be seen not only as market responses or the actions of risk takers and risk averters but also as part of the emergence of new classes and new class relationships.

We know that the general trend during this period was an increase in tenancy and in the long run an increase in sharecropping at the expense of other forms of tenure arrangements. But there was enormous variation from place to place and from time to time, and this variation deserves fuller investigation and explanation.

I would suggest that an underlying tendency amidst the variation was the movement of most blacks and many whites to the status of wage laborers, even though the census figures seem to indicate otherwise. It was not until 1920 that the census distinguished share tenants from sharecroppers. Yet by 1900 the Department of Agriculture was already making the distinction in their reports, as were the state legislatures and the courts in the law.

The Department of Agriculture reports maintained that the croppers were really wage workers under the same kind and degree of supervision and control as ordinary hired wage workers; their pay was half of the crops produced on a specified piece of land. They were not tenants who paid a portion of what they produced as rent. The difference was important, and the law made the difference precise: a share tenant was obliged to pay an agreed-upon portion of his production to the landlord; the remainder was his to dispose of as he wished (subject, of course, to merchants' or other liens). The cropper, however, had no right to dispose of "his half." All he had was a laborer's lien against the landowner to the extent of the value of his half. Here was, in short, another "peculiar institution," a special southern form of wage laborer. Share wages had returned once again, but now any idea that such an arrangement implied a partnership was gone and forgotten.

The net result of these changes was the resurrection of the plantation, not the antebellum plantation and not a plantation on the Central American model but rather one on the model of a large-scale, thoroughly capitalistic farm. At the same time it was uniquely southern, affected by the legacy of slavery, racism, and the peculiarities of southern culture and politics. Low incomes earned by black and white farmers in labor-intensive agriculture provided limited stimulus for economic development. A working class sharply divided by racial antagonisms failed to cooperate either in unions or in lasting political alliances to bring reforms. By the turn of the century Jim Crow legislation further divided the races, and disenfranchisement laws prevented political activity by virtually all the black and large sections of the poor white population. Planter capitalists, along with merchants and textile and other manufacturers enjoyed a kind of unfettered capitalism—to borrow a phrase Stanley M. Elkins used in a very different context. The majority of the population—and hence the South as a whole—remained poor. The New South was not that envisioned by Henry W. Grady and his followers; nor was it the South envisioned or hoped for by the blacks and their allies. Nevertheless, it was new. The racist legacy of slavery, important as it was, should not obscure the truly revolutionary change that emancipation brought to the South.

Thus, the New South might best be seen as an evolving bourgeois society in which a capitalistic social structure was arising on the ruins of a premodern slave society. It was going through the process of social change, of modernization that the rest of the nation had gone through a half century or more earlier. But where the rest of the nation had made the change with a social and political structure and an ideology that generally supported such changes, the postwar South was going through the change with the remnants of a social and political structure and an ideology that had been antagonistic to such changes. While slavery, the institution that had been at the core of that nonmodern ideology and social structure, had been forcibly extinguished, its culture and ideology lingered and gave the new society that emerged a peculiar, southern form.

Racism and Southern Backwardness

ROGER L. RANSOM AND RICHARD SUTCH

The South of 1900 was underdeveloped. It remained an agrarian society with a backward technology that still employed hand labor and mule power virtually unassisted by mechanical implements. The rural South of 1900 was stagnant. Crop outputs, yields per acre, and agricultural technology remained virtually the same year after year. Progress was nowhere in evidence. . . .

. . . The impediments to capital formation, the South's subservience to cotton, and the barriers to interregional labor mobility were three of the roots of southern poverty. Each of these explanations can be considered as economic interpretations; these roots were buried deep in the South's economic institutions. There existed another dynamic factor impeding economic growth—one not normally considered as economic in nature—that also appeared during our examination of the South's economic structure. That factor was the pervasive influence of race relations. We believe that the animosity and mutual fear that existed between the races, and in particular the whites' antagonism toward the blacks' economic advancement, were at least as powerful as were economic incentives in motivating individual economic behavior. The effect of racism was felt throughout the entire system; it left no economic institution undistorted.

As a cause of southern poverty, racism may well have been preeminent. One way in which racial animosities restricted southern development is

Roger L. Ransom and Richard Sutch, *One Kind of Freedom*. Cambridge University Press, 1977, excerpts from pp. 174–186. Reprinted with permission of the publisher.

rather obvious. When whites used threats of violence to keep blacks from gaining an education, practicing a trade, or purchasing land, they systematically prevented blacks from following the three routes most commonly traveled by other Americans in their quest for self-advancement. With over half the population held in ignorance and forced to work as agricultural laborers, it is no wonder that the South was poor, underdeveloped, and without signs of economic progress.

While this point is obvious by itself, it is also misleading. If the direct coercive manifestations of racism were the only obstacles to progress, blacks might well have overcome them by outright defiance or, even more likely, they might have bypassed them by finding new roads for self-advancement. It would be presumptuous to argue that whites, by threat, bluster, and force alone, could have kept blacks from advancing their own cause. Moreover, if the impact of racism were restricted only to these direct influences, racism would not explain why southern whites (with presumably all the opportunities denied blacks) did not advance their own fortunes in the forty years following emancipation.

The racism that permeated the southern economy had a more subtle, yet more powerful, impact—more subtle and more insidious because it removed the incentive to self-advancement, not only for the blacks, but for the whites as well. Racism distorted the economic institutions of the South, reshaping them so that the market signals—which normally direct resources toward their most productive employment and provide the incentive to the investments and the innovations that propel economic growth—were either not generated or were greatly weakened. As an example of this mechanism, we shall consider first the case of education.

The Economic Impact of Racism: Education

Slavery . . . produced a largely illiterate black population and left it an easy victim of racial oppression. Perhaps the vulnerability of an illiterate population was recognized, for black education became a primary target of white oppression. The costs of education and skill acquisition were increased by acts of violence and discrimination. A further obstacle to black education was that fewer schools were provided for black children, and these were of inferior quality compared with those provided for whites. Undoubtedly many blacks were discouraged from seeking an education. But what of the black man or woman who persevered, who educated himself, or who braved the whites' hostility and went to school? What did the education mean once it was acquired?

Most blacks who sought an education hoped that literacy and elementary education would make them better farmers or farm managers or open the possibility of becoming independent landowners or artisans. But such individuals were frequently disappointed, not because education was worthless for these pursuits, but rather because blacks were never allowed to pursue those occupations. A literate farmer may well be a better farm manager, but in a rural society where few blacks were educated and where landowners were invariably white, it was not easy for a black man to find employment as an overseer or farm manager. Nor was it easy to lease a farm on better terms than were standard. If a superior job could not be secured, the advantages of the education could not be fully utilized by the laborer. And if it was common knowledge that educated blacks were unable to find employment in occupations that made full use of their acquired skills, then the incentive for others to pursue education would be dampened considerably. With the apparent returns to education kept low by the agricultural system, the net investment in education remained low, the black population remained largely illiterate and the problem perpetuated itself.

The same phenomenon kept many blacks from seeking to acquire artisan or mercantile skills. If racist pressure kept blacks from practicing these skills or prevented them from earning the same incomes from their skills as similarly trained whites, then the incentive to apprentice themselves would be greatly diminished. . . .

Those whites who competed in the same labor markets with unskilled blacks were similarly disadvantaged. The economic system that limited black education required an agricultural economy structured to utilize uneducated labor. Agriculture in the South generated no demand for skilled or literate workers of any color. Once established, such an agricultural system also left little room for educated whites. As a result, the poor white's incentive to educate himself was suppressed nearly as effectively as the black's.

The Economic Impact of Racism: Credit

The capital market was also adversely influenced by white appraisals of Negro ability. Lenders required information on a prospective borrower's assets, on his education, and on his ability as a farmer. Race, in each of these instances, seemed to be viewed as pertinent information by white leaders. Without further investigation, the lender might conclude that a black applicant was less creditworthy than a white. The costs of obtaining more accurate information would be high relative to the possible gains to the moneylender. As a result, the loan application of the black would be denied, limited to a lower amount, or offered at a higher interest rate than to whites. . . .

The racial prejudice of the merchant may also have worked to the detriment of the black when he sought financing to purchase fertilizer. In the Cotton South 33.5 percent of the white-operated family farms purchased fertilizer; only 21.9 percent of the black-operated family farms did so. This is particularly surprising, since the black-operated farms should have had a greater need for commercial fertilizer. They had a relative shortage of untilled land, and they reported fewer animals that could provide manure. We estimate that on small family farms operated by whites there was an average of 1.9 work animals and 9.9 swine compared with only 1.3 work animals and 5.2 swine on black-operated farms. Black-run farms that did purchase fertilizer reported a higher expenditure per acre than their white counterparts, confirming their greater need for this input. Moreover, we suspect that this is also an indication that the black farmer whose need for commercial fertilizer was moderate or low was in many cases unable to obtain financing for this input.

Discrimination in land tenure and labor arrangements and in the market for capital meant that black families had to support themselves with fewer acres of land than did white families. . . .

Racism in the capital markets meant that black farmers had less capital, smaller farms, and fewer acres of untilled land than whites. This meant that the typical black farmer was more dependent upon purchased supplies than his white counterpart and was thereby more susceptible to exploitation by the merchant's credit monopoly. If this was the case, we would expect black farmers to have been locked into cotton overproduction more frequently than whites and to be less self-sufficient. . . . [And, in fact,] black operators of one-family farms devoted a higher percentage of their acreage to cotton, a lower percentage to crops other than cotton and corn, and reported fewer crops grown.

Emancipation removed the legal distinction between the South's two races, but it left them in grossly unequal economic positions. The blacks lacked assets; they lacked education; they lacked skills. From the outset there were whites who sought to preserve the social and political inequalities between the races, and these white supremacists perceived that to do so they would have to maintain the economic inequalities as well. When necessary, a campaign of violence was launched to prevent blacks from acquiring assets, education, or skills. But the violence was only the most visible way in which racial suppression worked. The most powerful and most damaging way was indirect. Southerners erected an economic system that failed to reward individual initiative on the part of blacks and was therefore ill-suited to their economic advancement. As a result, the inequalities originally inherited from slavery persisted. But there was a by-product of this effort at racial repression: the system tended to cripple all economic growth. It caught up whites in its trap, stifled their initiative, and curtailed their economic progress. Lewis H. Blair, a southerner from a prominent Virginia family, perceived this phenomenon and viewed it as the principal cause of the South's lack of prosperity in 1889: "Like a malignant cancer which poisons the whole system, this degradation [of the Negro] seems to intensify all the other drawbacks under which we labor."

✢ *F U R T H E R   R E A D I N G*

Pete Daniel, *The Shadow of the Plantation* (1972)
Ronald F. Davis, *Good and Faithful Labor* (1982)
Stephen J. DeCanio, *Agriculture in the Postbellum South* (1975)
Charles L. Flynn, Jr., *White Land, Black Labor* (1983)
Thavolia Glymph and John J. Kushma, eds., *Essays on the Postbellum Southern Economy* (1985)
Robert Higgs, *Competition and Coercion* (1977)

Gerald D. Jaynes, *Branches Without Roots* (1986)
Jacqueline Jones, *Labor of Love, Labor of Sorrow* (1985)
Jay Mandle, *The Roots of Black Poverty* (1978)
Daniel A. Novack, *The Wheel of Servitude* (1978)
William Alexander Percy, *Lanterns on the Levee* (1941)
Peter J. Rachleff, *Black Labor in the South* (1984)
Roger L. Ransom and Richard Sutch, *One Kind of Freedom* (1977)
Lawrence D. Rice, *The Negro in Texas* (1971)
Theodore Rosengarten, *All God's Dangers* (1975)
Harold Woodman, *King Cotton and His Retainers* (1968)
Gavin Wright, *Old South, New South* (1986) —
———, *The Political Economy of the Cotton South* (1978)

CHAPTER
5

Populism

The dissatisfactions of southern farmers grew in force until a massive political upheaval occurred: the populist revolt. The People's party also flourished in the Midwest and West, but it was strongest in the South, where it posed a major threat to the Democratic party. In its programs and its tactics, Populism represented a serious challenge to the status quo.

The Populists demanded far-reaching changes in the nation's monetary system and thereby frightened both bankers and the leaders of the New South's budding industry. Finding the Democratic party unsupportive, the Populists demanded greater democracy in the political system and began courting the votes of black southerners. This step brought racial issues to center stage, and as a result the battles over Populism involved not only fundamental economic questions but also an alleged threat to white supremacy and the danger of a return to the "evils" of Reconstruction.

The Populist period is stimulating and complex, and historians continue to debate its issues. Were the Populists radicals, or were they would-be capitalists seeking needed economic reforms? Why did their movement create such deep divisions in southern society? How important were racial as opposed to economic issues in the Populists' agenda? And did Populism fail because of its opponents' measures or because of deficiencies inherent in the movement?

✢ DOCUMENTS

One wellspring of Populist strength was the suffering and frustration of thousands of southern farmers, many of whom were in debt and had lost or feared losing their land. Their pent-up anger is conveyed in the first document, containing selections from letters of North Carolina farmers to a state agency inquiring about conditions in agriculture. The political demands and program of the Populist party are summarized in the Ocala platform, the second document. Note its proposals for a subtreasury system and changes in the nation's money supply. Georgia's Tom Watson, the most prominent Populist leader in the South, described the problems of southern farmers in an article in the *Arena*, a national magazine. He also outlined a strategy of political cooperation across racial lines, which became highly controversial. The selections from his article, reprinted as the third document, provide clues on the extent and limits of racial tolerance among Populists. The Populist economic doctrines came under attack, but Democrats often focused on white supremacy as their central issue, as the excerpts from the *Raleigh News and Observer*, the fourth selection, indicate. Populists needed black votes but often shared Democrats' racial sentiments. The last document reveals a Populist speaker's manuevering around the racial issue in 1898 when the Democrats' white supremacy campaign in North Carolina was gaining power.

Farmers Describe the Crisis, 1890s

Remarks.—The average farmer in our county, under existing circumstances, cannot make much money over his living. Wages are low, but on account of the scarcity of money the farmer can't afford to give better wages. I think that we need—that the times imperatively demand—a greater volume of circulating currency. I am nearly eighty-four years old and have seen such a great scarcity of money but twice; when Andrew Jackson vetoed the National Bank bill and during the great negro speculation; but those depressions did not last so long.

Remarks.—Owing to the low price of products the farmers are behindhand. We think the trouble lies in our financial system. With a better system of finance than we have, and with the push and energy that our farmers have, they would certainly overcome all their troubles in a few years. But there will have to be changes in the policy of our National Government before we get much relief. The Farmers' Alliance is doing a grand work on this line.

Remarks.—The farmers in my vicinity are much rejoiced at the result of their labor for 1890. Cotton crops are especially good, but, as the results of bad legislation, the cotton, in many instances, will have to be sold for less than the cost of production, caused principally by an insufficient circulation of money to purchase the agricultural products. I trust that in the near future there will be some means of relief, and think there will be by proper legislation, for such are the demands of our agricultural classes in this and other sections of our country.

Remarks.—The greatest evil we have to contend with is the mortgage system and high time prices.

Remarks.—The cotton crop is above an average; it is the best that has been made in this township since I have been farming (or in ten years). I think the greatest evil that exists in this county is the high rate of interest. It is that that makes the poor poorer and the rich richer. We have to pay eight per cent. per annum and a premium of ten per cent. in advance, making eighteen per cent. per annum. The average farmer is poorer than he was ten years ago, and getting poorer every year. I think the next Legislature ought to fix the rate of interest at about five or six per cent., and make it a misdemeanor to charge any more.

Remarks.—The present debts heavily oppress the people. In fact many are forced to give a mortgage or crop lien at the beginning of the year. We have reached a crisis when many cannot run a farm without first pledging it as security for supplies. Do away with the National Banks and abolish all trusts and combines with the abolition of the tariff, and give us the Sub-Treasury Bill; it would afford much relief.

Remarks.—I will name a few evils the farmer has to contend with, to-wit: The price of everything is fixed by speculators; on all the necessaries of life trusts and combines have been allowed to practice wholesale robbery. Dealing in futures should forever be prohibited. We believe the McKinley tariff bill is a curse to the farmer; it takes from the many to enrich the favored few; it makes exactions, small in amount, from millions of people, which go into the pockets of the few. We have heretofore used too much fertilizers, and allowed our manure to waste in the barn-lot, but I am glad to say there is quite an improvement along this line; more clover was sown last year than in the past ten years. The Farmers' Alliance is a great benefit to the country; we are profited by each others experience, and by co-operation we have saved something financially. Elect men who cannot be bribed by money lords and we will prosper.

Remarks.— . . . Our people are not only not prosperous, but are growing poorer as the years go by. Not a man in all my knowledge is making a dollar to lay up for the future or to enlarge his operations. With farmer and mechanic it is a *pull for life*. Farm laborers get poor wages, because the farmer owning the land and hiring labor is not in condition to pay good wages, and laborers are, for the same reason, not regularly employed, but are strolling over the country a large part of the time looking for work. Scarcely any progress is made on farms, and for these reasons the negroes, who constitute the bulk of our farm laborers, are being driven, from necessity, to leave the State in large numbers. This is to our hurt. If hands could be employed regularly the year round it would be to the great advantage of farmers and laborers. With all this, I think there are not so many mortgages given now as for the past few years.

What is to become of the country under these conditions I cannot imagine. Farming is the great "king-wheel" which moves every other branch of business when it moves easily and prosperously. Without success and prosperity in farming, no prosperity can come to other business in our section of this country.

In my judgment the high tariff, with its offsprings, trusts, combines and monopolies of every sort, is ruining us, and making prosperity and contentment among farmers and farm laborers impossible. It seems to me that we cannot survive this state of things brought about largely by these evils, which are made possible only by the unwise laws of our government. We are working only for a very scanty supply of victuals and clothes. Until this state of things is changed there can be no prosperity for us.

Remarks.—Farming pays in this country; but, on account of high interest and scarcity of money, it pays the wrong man. We are oppressed with debt, time prices and high interest. These hinder business of every kind. Manufactured articles are kept up to usual prices, while the products of farm labor drop lower every year. The need of more money in circulation is felt by the farmers all over the country.

Remarks.— . . . The mortgage system, I believe, has more to do with making hard times than any other one thing. When a man mortgages his property he can't help thinking about it, consequently he can't work like a free man.

Remarks.—Times here are very close in money matters. Sometimes they are higher, at others lower. I could not sell anything for cash at present. The money men have closed in on us farmers again. I believe in money being worth its value, but I do not believe in it being shut off entirely. What is this done for? Only to make slaves of the farmers. How is this to be remedied—free silver? I think so. Is it to reduce the homestead exemption? I think so. Has it been any benefit to the farmer? I think not. Do our leaders legislate more for the sake of party than for the good of the country? I think the majority do. Is the farmer as honorable as anybody else? I think he is. God made all men equal.

Remarks.—Times are very hard here, and money very scarce. There are, in my opinion, two great causes for it. One is we have had bad seasons for the last few years. The wet drowned our lowlands, and we have not had much to sell. Labor is very scarce. It has gone to town, to public works, and some to loafing. A great deal of the farming is done by tenants, and they are not of much force, as they will work only a few months in the year—just enough to *stay* here, not to *live*. The greatest cause is one class is arraigned against another. The farmer has arraigned himself against the capitalist, and the capitalist against the farmer. They will crush the farmer, and bring lots of them to be *tenants*. I would be glad if some plan could be devised to send some immigrants in here who have money to buy some of our lands, and cut our farms down smaller, so we could do our own work.

Remarks.—High interest on money is one of our drawbacks. It oppresses the person who borrows it. Great bodies of land owned by one man or company of men is a drawback to our county. Manufacturing ought to be the moneyed men's object, and not the oppression of agriculture. It is demoralizing to the people to take what belongs to man as a gift from God and force men to be tenants or slaves on the soil of a free country. High taxes, big salaries to our county, State and national officers are also demoralizing. Low wages, low prices for produce, and high prices for manufactured goods, handled by many speculators before they reach the consumers, are demoralizing. We want direct trade from the manufacturer to the consumer at the present prices of our produce. More money is needful to make our produce high. Plant peas for manure, sown one to two bushels per acre, and mow down for hay for stock.

Remarks.—. . . Tobacco is our money crop, and since our products are priced before we plant, the future is quite gloomy. Before the American Tobacco Trust was organized we got much better prices, as we raise bright tobacco in this section; but now the price is just half. Farmers are gloomy, and making no money. We hope to see the time when trusts and futures are to be no more. Money is scarce at this time in this section. I have answered the question as near right as I can, trusting you may be successful in helping us.

Remarks.—Farming in our county, owing to the low price of cotton, has not paid the last year. If people would diversify their crops it would be better for them. We hope the Alliance will do something to relieve the laboring class.

DEAR SIR:—These are extra hard times. I have been an employer of labor for many years, and never before saw such hard times. I am still giving full time, full employment, and full pay, but the Lord only knows how long it can last. As to what would be best for our working people, I hardly know what to say. If all could have constant work, that would be a splendid help. Thousands are idle, not of their own choice, but they just can't help themselves. I had rather belong to a country where everybody had work, and everybody *had to* work, than have it as it is. Call it socialism or what you please. Damn a country where there is nobody prosperous but the bond-holder and the money-lender. I want all prosperous—*give all work,* and money enough in circulation to pay for it.

Respectfully,

J. S. RAGSDALE.

DEAR SIR:—Owing to legislation in favor of monopolies our lands are gradually slipping from the hands of the wealth-producing classes and going into the hands of the few. I do not believe God ever intended that a few should own the earth, but that each should have a home. But we cannot take the lands from the rich and give to the poor; no, but let us have legislation to limit a man's freehold, and all that he may own over and above that the law limits him to levy a special tax, something of the nature of an income tax, on it. By this means we could have a revenue for our State that would enable us to educate the children of the State. Three-fourths of our population are tenants, and are not able to buy land at present prices; they are the men who create the wealth and pay the taxes. Let us have legislation that will do justice to all, protect all, and that will bless us as a nation.

Respectfully,

J. A. WILSON.

The Ocala Platform, 1890

Proceedings of the Supreme Council of the National Farmers' Alliance and Industrial Union

1. a. We demand the abolition of national banks.

b. We demand that the government shall establish sub-treasuries or depositories in the several states, which shall loan money direct to the people at a low rate of interest, not to exceed two per cent per annum, on nonperishable farm products, and also upon real estate, with proper limitations upon the quantity of land and amount of money.

    c. We demand that the amount of the circulating medium be speedily increased to not less than $50 per capita.

    2. We demand that Congress shall pass such laws as will effectually prevent the dealing in futures of all agricultural and mechanical productions; providing a stringent system of procedure in trials that will secure the prompt conviction, and imposing such penalties as shall secure the most perfect compliance with the law.

    3. We condemn the silver bill recently passed by Congress, and demand in lieu thereof the free and unlimited coinage of silver.

    4. We demand the passage of laws prohibiting alien ownership of land, and that Congress take prompt action to devise some plan to obtain all lands now owned by aliens and foreign syndicates; and that all lands now held by railroads and other corporations in excess of such as is actually used and needed by them be reclaimed by the government and held for actual settlers only.

    5. Believing in the doctrine of equal rights to all and special privileges to none, we demand—

    a. That our national legislation shall be so framed in the future as not to build up one industry at the expense of another.

    b. We further demand a removal of the existing heavy tariff tax from the necessities of life, that the poor of our land must have.

    c. We further demand a just and equitable system of graduated tax on incomes.

    d. We believe that the money of the country should be kept as much as possible in the hands of the people, and hence we demand that all national and state revenues shall be limited to the necessary expenses of the government economically and honestly administered.

    6. We demand the most rigid, honest, and just state and national government control and supervision of the means of public communication and transportation, and if this control and supervision does not remove the abuse now existing, we demand the government ownership of such means of communication and transportation.

    7. We demand that the Congress of the United States submit an amendment to the Constitution providing for the election of United States Senators by direct vote of the people of each state.

Tom Watson's Strategy, 1892

Having given this subject much anxious thought, my opinion is that the future happiness of the two races will never be assured until the political motives which drive them asunder, into two distinct and hostile factions, can be removed. There must be a new policy inaugurated, whose purpose is to allay the passions and prejudices of race conflict, and which makes its appeal to the sober sense and honest judgment of the citizen regardless of his color.

To the success of this policy two things are indispensable—a common necessity acting upon both races, and a common benefit assured to both—without injury or humiliation to either.

Then, again, outsiders must let us alone. We must work out our own salvation. In no other way can it be done. Suggestions of Federal interference with our elections postpone the settlement and render our task the more difficult. Like all free people, we love home rule, and resent foreign compulsion of any sort. The Northern leader who really desires to see a better state of things in the South, puts his finger on the hands of the clock and forces them backward every time he intermeddles with the question. This is the literal truth; and the sooner it is well understood, the sooner we can accomplish our purpose.

What is that purpose? To outline a policy which compels the support of a great body of both races, from those motives which imperiously control human action, and which will thus obliterate forever the sharp and unreasoning political divisions of to-day.

The white people of the South will never support the Republican Party. This much is certain. The black people of the South will never support the Democratic Party. This is equally certain.

Hence, at the very beginning, we are met by the necessity of new political alliances. As long as the whites remain solidly Democratic, the blacks will remain solidly Republican.

As long as there was no choice, except as between the Democrats and the Republicans, the situation of the two races was bound to be one of antagonism. The Republican Party represented everything which was hateful to the whites; the Democratic Party, everything which was hateful to the blacks.

Therefore a new party was absolutely necessary. It has come, and it is doing its work with marvellous rapidity.

Why does a Southern Democrat leave his party and come to ours?

Because his industrial condition is pitiably bad; because he struggles against a system of laws which have almost filled him with despair; because he is told that he is without clothing because he produces too much cotton, and without food because corn is too plentiful; because he sees everybody growing rich off the products of labor except the laborer; because the millionnaires who manage the Democratic Party have contemptuously ignored his plea for a redress of grievances and have nothing to say to him beyond the cheerful advice to "work harder and live closer."

Why has this man joined the PEOPLE'S PARTY? Because the same grievances have been presented to the Republicans by the farmer of the West, and the millionnaires who control that party have replied to the petition with the soothing counsel that the Republican farmer of the West should "work more and talk less."

Therefore, if he were confined to a choice between the two old parties, the question would merely be (on these issues) whether the pot were larger than the kettle—the color of both being precisely the same.

The key to the new political movement called the People's Party has been that the Democratic farmer was as ready to leave the Democratic ranks as the Republican farmer was to leave the Republican ranks. In exact proportion as the West received the assurance that the South was ready for a new party, it has moved. In exact proportion to the proof we could bring that the West had broken Republican ties, the South has moved. *Without* a decided break in both sections, neither would move. *With* that decided break, both moved.

The very same principle governs the race question in the South. The two races can never act together permanently, harmoniously, beneficially, till each race demonstrates to the other a readiness to leave old party affiliations and to form new ones, based upon the profound conviction that, in acting together, both races are seeking new laws which will benefit both. On no other basis under heaven can the "Negro Question" be solved.

Now, suppose that the colored man were educated upon these questions just as the whites have been; suppose he were shown that his poverty and distress came from the same sources as ours; suppose we should convince him that our platform principles assure him an escape from the ills he now suffers, and guarantee him the fair measure of prosperity his labor entitles him to receive,—would he not act just as the white Democrat who joined us did? Would he not abandon a party which ignores him as a farmer and laborer; which offers him no benefits of an equal and just financial system; which promises him no relief from oppressive taxation; which assures him of no legislation which will enable him to obtain a fair price for his produce?

Granting to him the same selfishness common to us all; granting him the intelligence to know what is best for him and the desire to attain it, why would he not act from that motive just as the white farmer has done?

That he would do so, is as certain as any future event can be made. Gratitude may fail; so may sympathy and friendship and generosity and patriotism; but in the long run, self-interest *always* controls. Let it once appear plainly that it is to the interest of a colored man to vote with the white man, and he will do it. Let it plainly appear that it is to the interest of the white man that the vote of the Negro should supplement his own, and the question of having that ballot freely cast and fairly counted, becomes vital to the *white man*. He will see that it is done.

Now let us illustrate: Suppose two tenants on my farm; one of them white, the other black. They cultivate their crops under precisely the same conditions. Their labors, discouragements, burdens, grievances, are the same.

The white tenant is driven by cruel necessity to examine into the causes of his continued destitution. He reaches certain conclusions which are not complimentary to either of the old parties. He leaves the Democracy in angry disgust. He joins the People's Party. Why? Simply because its platform recognizes that he is badly treated and proposes to fight his battle. Necessity drives him from the old party, and hope leads him into the new. In plain English, he joins the organization whose declaration of principles is in accord with his conception of what he needs and justly deserves.

Now go back to the colored tenant. His surroundings being the same and his interests the same, why is it impossible for him to reach the same conclusions? Why is it unnatural for him to go into the new party at the same time and with the same motives?

Cannot these two men act together in peace when the ballot of the one is a vital benefit to the other? Will not political friendship be born of the necessity and the hope which is common to both? Will not race bitterness disappear before this common suffering and this mutual desire to escape it? Will not each of these citizens feel more kindly for the other when the vote of each defends the home of both? If the white man becomes convinced that the Democratic Party has played upon his prejudices, and has used his quiescence to the benefit of interests adverse to his own, will he not despise the leaders who seek to perpetuate the system?

The People's Party will settle the race question. First, by enacting the Australian ballot system. Second, by offering to white and black a rallying point which is free from the odium of former discords and strifes. Third, by presenting a platform immensely beneficial to both races and injurious to neither. Fourth, by making it to the *interest* of both races to act together for the success of the platform. Fifth, by making it to the *interest* of the colored man to have the same patriotic zeal for the welfare of the South that the whites possess.

Now to illustrate. Take two planks of the People's Party platform: that pledging a free ballot under the Australian system and that which demands a distribution of currency to the people upon pledges of land, cotton, etc.

The guaranty as to the vote will suit the black man better than the Republican platform, because the latter contemplates Federal interference, which will lead to collisions and bloodshed. The Democratic platform contains no comfort to the Negro, because, while it denounces the Republican programme, as usual, it promises nothing which can be specified. It is a generality which does not even possess the virtue of being "glittering."

The People's Party, however, not only condemns Federal interference with elections, but also distinctly commits itself to the method by which every citizen shall have his constitutional right to the free exercise of his electoral choice. We pledge ourselves to isolate the voter from all coercive influences and give him the free and fair exercise of his franchise under state laws.

Now couple this with the financial plank which promises equality in the distribution of the national currency, at low rates of interest.

The white tenant lives adjoining the colored tenant. Their houses are almost equally destitute of comforts. Their living is confined to bare necessities. They are equally burdened with heavy taxes. They pay the same high rent for gullied and impoverished land.

They pay the same enormous prices for farm supplies. Christmas finds them both without any satisfactory return for a year's toil. Dull and heavy and unhappy, they both start the plows again when "New Year's" passes.

Now the People's Party says to these two men, "You are kept apart that you may be separately fleeced of your earnings. You are made to hate each other because upon that hatred is rested the keystone of the arch of financial despotism which enslaves you both. You are deceived and blinded that you may not see how this race antagonism perpetuates a monetary system which beggars both."

This is so obviously true it is no wonder both these unhappy laborers stop to listen. No wonder they begin to realize that no change of law can benefit the white tenant which does not benefit the black one likewise; that no system which now does injustice to one of them can fail to injure both. Their every material interest is identical. The moment this becomes a conviction, mere selfishness, the mere desire to better their conditions, escape onerous taxes, avoid usurious charges, lighten their rents, or change their precarious tenements into smiling, happy homes, will drive these two men together, just as their mutually inflamed prejudices now drive them apart.

Suppose these two men now to have become fully imbued with the idea that their material welfare depends upon the reforms we demand. Then they act together to secure them. Every white reformer finds it to the vital interest of his home, his family, his fortune, to see to it that the vote of the colored reformer is freely cast and fairly counted.

Then what? Every colored voter will be thereafter a subject of industrial education and political teaching.

Concede that in the final event, a colored man will vote where his material interests dictate that he should vote; concede that in the South the accident of color can make no possible difference in the interests of farmers, croppers, and laborers; concede that under full and fair discussion the people can be depended upon to ascertain where their interests lie— and we reach the conclusion that the Southern race question can be solved by the People's Party on the simple proposition that each race will be led by self-interest to support that which benefits it, when so presented that neither is hindered by the bitter party antagonisms of the past.

Let the colored laborer realize that our platform gives him a better guaranty for political independence; for a fair return for his work; a better chance to buy a home and keep it; a better chance to educate his children and see them profitably employed; a better chance to have public life freed from race collisions; a better chance for every citizen to be considered as a *citizen* regardless of color in the making and enforcing of laws,—let all this be fully realized, and the race question at the South will have settled itself through the evolution of a political movement in which both whites and blacks recognize their surest way out of wretchedness into comfort and independence.

The illustration could be made quite as clearly from other planks in the People's Party platform. On questions of land, transportation and finance, especially, the welfare of the two races so clearly depends upon that which benefits either, that intelligent discussion would necessarily lead to just conclusions.

Why should the colored man always be taught that the white man of his neighborhood hates him, while a Northern man, who taxes every rag on his back, loves him? Why should not my tenant come to regard me as his friend rather than the manufacturer who plunders us both? Why should we perpetuate a policy which drives the black man into the arms of the

Northern politician?

Why should we always allow Northern and Eastern Democrats to en-slave us forever by threats of the Force Bill?

Let us draw the supposed teeth of this fabled dragon by founding our new policy upon justice—upon the simple but profound truth that, if the voice of passion can be hushed, the self-interest of both races will drive them to act in concert. There never was a day during the last twenty years when the South could not have flung the money power into the dust by patiently teaching the Negro that we could not be wretched under any system which would not afflict him likewise; that we could not prosper under any law which would not also bring its blessings to him.

To the emasculated individual who cries "Negro supremacy!" there is little to be said. His cowardice shows him to be a degeneration from the race which has never yet feared any other race. Existing under such con-ditions as they now do in this country, there is no earthly chance for Negro domination, unless we are ready to admit that the colored man is our superior in will power, courage, and intellect.

Not being prepared to make any such admission in favor of any race the sun ever shone on, I have no words which can portray my contempt for the white men, Anglo-Saxons, who can knock their knees together, and through their chattering teeth and pale lips admit that they are afraid the Negroes will "dominate us."

The question of social equality does not enter into the calculation at all. That is a thing each citizen decides for himself. No statute ever yet drew the latch of the humblest home—or ever will. Each citizen regulates his own visiting list—and always will.

The conclusion, then, seems to me to be this: the crushing burdens which now oppress both races in the South will cause each to make an effort to cast them off. They will see a similarity of cause and a similarity of remedy. They will recognize that each should help the other in the work of repealing bad laws and enacting good ones. They will become political allies, and neither can injure the other without weakening both. It will be to the interest of both that each should have justice. And on these broad lines of mutual interest, mutual forbearance, and mutual support the present will be made the stepping-stone to future peace and prosperity.

Democrats Fight Back: The White-Supremacy Campaign, 1898

The Duty of White Men Today.

No man who loves his State can read the daily occurrences of crime in North Carolina where the negro is the aggressor without trembling for the future of the State. There have been more assaults upon white women by negro brutes in one year and a half of Republican rule than in twenty years of Democratic rule. There have been more insults to white girls, more wrongs to white men, more lawlessness and more crime committed by negroes in North Carolina during the last twenty months than during the previous twenty years.

More than this: In all those communities where the negro is the controlling political factor the influence of the old-time religious negro, who loved peace and concord has been supplanted by the influence of the A. L. Manlys, the Lee Persons, the Jim Youngs, and the like, who control the votes of the negroes for their personal ends by appeals to their prejudice.

The difference between Eastern North Carolina of six years ago and today is marked. Then the white men had control of public affairs, and the government was administered with justice to both races, and peace and concord prevailed. Wherever the negro and his allies have obtained power, the politicians have become offensive and the brutal have become law breakers.

There is a cause for the change. The time was when a public officer was a public servant. The fact that public office pays better than private service has converted public officers into public leaders, and, in the Republican party, into public masters. It is the public officers who are responsible for the change in the negro. Senator [Jeter] Pritchard has given them big Federal offices, Governor [Daniel] Russell has foisted them upon the State government, the eastern counties are honeycombed with them, and so powerful have they become that they dictate nominations in nearly half the counties in the State.

The Fusion Candidate for the Senate in Edge-combe County.

MORE NEGRO SCOUNDRELISM

Black Beasts Attempt to Outrage the Young Daughter of a Respectable Farmer.

HER FATHER SWEARS TO IT

Attacked on the Public Highway in Brunswick County While Returning From Sunday-School—Her Screams Saved Her From a Fate Worse Than Death.

(Wilmington Star.)

JOSEPH GORE IS AN HONEST AND RESPECTABLE FARMER OF THE COUNTY OF BRUNSWICK—POOR IN THIS WORLD'S GOODS, BUT ESTEEMED BY HIS NEIGHBORS. HE HAS A WIFE AND CHILDREN, AND THERE IS A CHURCH AND SUNDAY SCHOOL NEAR HIS HOME WHICH ARE ATTENDED BY HIS FAMILY. BUT HE LIVES IN A TOWNSHIP WHERE THE NEGROES OUTNUMBER THE WHITES MORE THAN THREE TO ONE. THIS, COUPLED WITH THE FACT, NO DOUBT, THAT BRUNSWICK COUNTY IS UNDER REPUBLICAN-FUSION RULE, EMBOLDENED TWO BEASTLY NEGROES TO MAKE AN ATTEMPT TO OUTRAGE A YOUNG GIRL ON THE PUBLIC ROAD, AS NARRATED IN THE FOLLOWING AFFIDAVIT:

STATE OF NORTH CAROLINA,
COUNTY OF BRUNSWICK.
PERSONALLY APPEARED BEFORE ME, GEO. H. BELLAMY, A JUSTICE OF THE PEACE FOR TOWN CREEK TOWNSHIP, BRUNS-WICK COUNTY, JOSEPH GORE, WHO BEING DULY SWORN, STATES: "SOME DAYS AGO MY DAUGHTER, AGED 15 YEARS, WAS RETURNING FROM SUNDAY SCHOOL, ACCOMPANIED BY HER LITTLE BROTHER, AGED 12 YEARS, ABOUT 3 O'CLOCK IN THE AFTERNOON. WHEN ABOUT A QUARTER OF A MILE FROM HOME, TWO NEGRO BOYS, AGED ABOUT 16 TO 18 YEARS, RAN AFTER MY DAUGHTER, WITH THEIR COATS TURNED OVER THEIR HEADS TO CONCEAL THEIR IDENTITY, AND ATTEMPTED TO TAKE HOLD OF HER, AND DOUBTLESS WOULD HAVE PLACED THEIR UNHOLY HANDS ON HER PERSON; AND HAD IT NOT BEEN FOR HER SCREAMS, WOULD HAVE DOUBTLESS AC-

COMPLISHED THEIR PURPOSE. THIS WAS DONE IN TOWN CREEK TOWNSHIP, IN BROAD DAYLIGHT. THE VILLAINS HAVE NOT YET BEEN DETECTED.

(SIGNED.)   "JOSEPH GORE."

SIGNED AND SWORN TO BEFORE ME, THIS 19TH DAY OF SEPTEMBER, A. D., 1898.   GEO. H. BELLAMY, J. P.

WHITE MEN OF BRUNSWICK COUNTY, CAN YOU STAND THAT? IS THERE ONE LEFT IN THE BORDERS OF YOUR COUNTY WHO WILL NOT NOW VOTE AGAINST EVERY CANDIDATE WHO CONSORTS WITH NEGROES, AND WHO IS DEPENDENT ON THEM FOR ELECTION? HAS IT COME TO THIS, THAT YOUR DAUGH-TERS CANNOT ATTEND CHURCH OR SUNDAY SCHOOL WITH-OUT HAVING A BODY-GUARD TO PROTECT THEM FROM THE LUSTFUL BLACK BRUTES WHO ROAM THROUGH YOUR COUNTY?

RISE IN YOUR MIGHT, WHITE MEN OF BRUNSWICK. ASSERT YOUR MANHOOD. GO TO THE POLLS AND HELP STAMP OUT THE LAST VESTIGE OF REPUBLICAN-POPULIST-NEGRO FUSION.

The Vampire That Hovers Over North Carolina.

A Populist Speaker Responds, 1898

[In 1896 the Democrats] said "silver! silver! silver!" and on every breeze and every lip it was silver from every Democratic tongue. They ran that campaign on National issues. Why don't they do it again? Silver is just as urgent an issue now as it was then, certainly so far as Congressmen are concerned. No, they go back to their old cry and say "the white metal and the white man," but they don't say much about the white metal. You can pick up Democratic papers and there is nothing about silver or William J. Bryan in them. They have left it off, and it is just "nigger! nigger! nigger!" forevermore. That is all the politics the Democratic party has in the State now; it is all they had prior to 1896, and they took silver up then because they saw the rank and file of their party would leave them and come to the Peoples Party if they did otherwise. Is there a prominent Democrat here who does not believe that? Why, he knows I am telling the living truth; they all know I am telling the truth. . . .

I saw yesterday morning the Raleigh News and Observer. It had a cartoon in it—a picture you know, of Jim young "a negro politician in Raleigh bossing things at the Blind Asylum" in the city of Raleigh. The Democratic party dares not go before the people of North Carolina on any issue of politics and state its belief upon these issues. It therefore howls "nigger." What has Jim Young got to do with the blind institution in the city of Raleigh? Is he on the board? Not at all. There is not a negro on any institutional board in North Carolina except [institutions] for neg[r]oes, and has not been for a matter of some months, with the single exception of a colored man by the name of Peace on the board of penitentiary directors. In the name of common sense and human suffering, is there no question in North Carolina but the question of "negro?" Is that all; and will the Democratic party persist in it and insult the intelligence of men and make light of the poverty of the people by injecting this as the one issue in their campaign? . . .

And that is not all. Let's look a little further. You have heard Democrats talk about the town of Greenville having a negro policeman. Well, let's see. There is one there. How did he get there? The town has four colored and two white councilmen. Two of the colored councilmen proposed to elect Mr. Cherry, a white Republican policeman, if Mr. Blow, the Democratic County Chairman, Mr. Jarvis' law partner, and Mr. Brown, the other white concilman would vote with them. Blow and Brown refused to do it, so the four negroes voted together and elected a negro. Who is responsible for the negro's election? Blow could have prevented it. They could have prevented it if they had wanted to, but they did not want to prevent it. They wanted it for campaign thunder. Well, was that anything

---

"Dr. Thompson's Great Speech" taken from the Torrance-Banks Family Papers, Special Collections, Atkins Library, The University of North Carolina at Charlotte.

out of the way for them to have a negro policeman in the town of Greenville? As far back as 1878, when the town was Democratic, they always elected William Hamahan a negro, for one policeman, and a white man for the other, and in the case of big crowds, when they had to appoint special policemen, they always appointed as many negroes as whites. . . .

You remember the campaign of 1876 was largely upon the issue of "nigger." It was then the cry of negro equality. Now it is the cry of "negro domination." I state here that the Democratic party does not desire to rid itself of the negro in politics. When the Democratic party in North Carolina removes the negro from politics in North Carolina, the Democratic party goes out of existance in North Carolina. If they had desired to get rid of the negro as a disturbing factor in North Carolina, they acquired the power in 1876, when, contrary to all of their professions upon the stump, and their denunciations of the Republican party for putting negroes in office in North Carolina, they proceeded to elect negro magistrates in New Hanover, in Craven and in other counties in the State. They had it in their power to remove the negro from politics from that day until 1895, and yet they left him for the purpose of future campaigns. When they fail of the negro issue in North Carolina, what issue will the Democratic party have?

Why, when Peg-leg Williams in the days of negro exodus was carrying thousands of negroes out of the State of North Carolina, it was a Democratic legislature that rose up and passed a law stopping the business under a penalty of a thousand dollars. I have heard it said that our friend Captain Kitchen felt so outraged at the lessening of the negro population in the county of Halifax that he assaulted poor old Peg-leg Williams who was carrying his thousands further South.

I continue this charge against the Democratic party. It has always howled the nigger, and yet it has given the negro office when it could, notwithstanding its howl. . . .

[Democrats] are the men in North Carolina who have their quiet conferences with negroes, and openly in their public prints say to the negroes, "you do a majority of the voting; therefore you are entitled to a majority of the offices of your party; demand them!" I read this advice in a paper published over here in Dunn, in the same issue of which I found also an appeal for the formation of white supremacy clubs to beat back the waves of negro domination.

What hypocrits these Democrats be. It is astonishing to me that God Himself lets them live. It is a wonder he does not start out and blast them for their hypocrisy.

✠ E S S A Y S

C. Vann Woodward, professor of history emeritus from Yale University, wrote the classic biography of the Populist leader Tom Watson of Georgia. In the first essay, Woodward describes Populism's supporters and examines the racial cooperation in politics that made Populism so controversial in the South. Historian

Lawrence Goodwyn of Duke University, author of a more recent account of the Populist movement, studied closely the programs of the Farmers Alliance, from which Populism grew. He emphasized the importance of cooperative stores and cooperative marketing efforts among members of the Alliance. In the second selection, Goodwyn gives graphic examples of the economic suffering of southern farmers and discusses the cultural significance of their cooperative efforts. Finally, historian Steven Hahn of the University of California, San Diego, analyzes the ideology of the Populist movement, based on his study of Georgia, and asks to what extent limitations in their ideology handicapped the Populists.

The Populists, Race, and Tom Watson

C. VANN WOODWARD

Who were the Populists?

Aside from the new factory proletariat of a few cities (themselves of recent rural origin), the Populists were agricultural and rural. But so were the great mass of people of the state and of the South; and that mass was divided by class and race lines. Were they exploiters or the exploited?

In answering such questions the Populists themselves were confusing. In resolving themselves into the People's party, the Oglethorpe County Alliance referred to its members as "the peasantry of America." On the other hand, a Populist of Douglas County said, "Some of our people were once rich, and most all were well to do . . . and it is no fault of theirs that they are reduced to such straights [*sic*]." Tom Watson struck nearer the truth when he said, "You stand for the yearning, upward tendency of the middle and lower classes." Therefore, they were "the sworn foes of monopoly—not monopoly in the narrow sense of the word—but monopoly of power, of place, of privilege, of wealth, of progress." Individualist and middle-class in tradition and aspiration, they accepted the basic capitalistic system. Watson summed up their objectives: "Keep the avenues of honor free. Close no entrance to the poorest, the weakest, the humblest. Say to ambition everywhere, 'the field is clear, the contest fair; come, and win your share if you can!'"

In general, the Southern Populists were mainly the agrarian masses, including tenant, small landowner, and a surprising member of large landowners, together with the industrial proletariat. They were united by their resentment of the crushing oppression of capitalist finance and industrialism. Watson himself recognized the complexity of his ranks. "There is a gradation in servitude," he said. The laborer was the first to feel the lash, the cropper next, the tenant next, and the landlord next—in Watson's hierarchy of serfdom. "But," he added, "the livery of the serf is there all the same." This livery, he believed, would become the uniform of the army that he led against its oppressors.

Tom Watson was himself one of the largest landowners in the state, with more tenants on his land than his grandfather had slaves. There were other large landowners high in the party ranks, who fought side by side with small farmers and tenants. In this regard a remark of Charles A. Beard upon the battles of Jefferson's day might be recalled: "It is a curious freak of fortune that gives to the slave owning aristocracy the leadership in a democracy of small farmers, but the cause is not far to seek. In a conflict with capitalism, the agrarians rallied around that agrarian class which had the cultural equipment for dominant direction." There is room for doubt whether there was an "aristocracy" of the tidewater sort in Georgia. At any rate, the former slave-owners were divided in the 'nineties. While some became Populists, many of the larger owners became merchants, bankers, and small capitalists, and fought the Populists as bitterly as did the business men of the towns.

It is undoubtedly true that the Populist ideology was dominantly that of the landowning farmer, who was, in many cases, the exploiter of landless tenant labor. But about half of the farms in the state at that time were operated by owners, dirt farmers, and the rank and file of the Populists were of this poverty-ridden small farmer class. They were surely more exploited than exploiting, and the Populist contention that the tenant was in the same boat as the owner had much truth in it. The southern urban proletariat was yet an embryonic class, largely of immediate agrarian background. They were not yet class-conscious, and thought more as farmers than as industrial workers. Obviously the Populist attack did not strike at the whole system of capitalist exploitation, as did socialism, but in its time and section the Populist party formed the vanguard against the advancing capitalist plutocracy, and its fate was of vital consequence to the future.

That class contradiction was not magically resolved in the Populist-agrarian potpourri is indicated by various signs. Once the Colored Farmers' Alliance proposed to call a general strike of Negro cotton pickers. The *Progressive Farmer*, paper of Colonel L. L. Polk, president of the National Alliance (white), did "not hesitate to advise our farmers to leave their cotton in the field rather than pay more than 50 cents per hundred to have it picked." The Negro brethren were attempting "to better their condition at the expense of their white brethren. Reforms should not be in the interest of one portion of our farmers at the expense of another."

The Populist struggle in the South, moreover, was fought under such peculiar circumstances as to set it apart from the history of the national movement, and to call for special treatment. "Political campaigns in the North," wrote a veteran of Alabama Populism, "even at their highest pitch of contention and strife, were as placid as pink teas in comparison with those years of political combat in the South." Taking into comparative account the violence of the passions unloosed by the conflict, the actual bloodshed and physical strife, one is prepared to give assent to that judgment.

What explained the bitterness and violence that characterized the Populist struggle in the South? To answer in a word—"race." And that is much too simple an answer. But if to race be added the complexities of the class economy growing out of race, the heritage of manumitted slave psychology, and the demagogic uses to which the politician was able to put race prejudice—then "race" may be said to be the core of the explanation.

In later life Watson once wrote a retrospective (and quite candid) comparison of his own career with that of William Jennings Bryan. In it he said: "Consider the advantage of position that Bryan had over me. His field of work was the plastic, restless, and growing West: mine was the hide-bound, rock-ribbed Bourbon South. Besides, Bryan had *no everlasting and overshadowing Negro Question to hamper and handicap his progress:* I HAD." There is no doubt that Watson thought of the Negro problem as the Nemesis of his career. He fled it all his days, and in flight sought every refuge—in attitudes as completely contradictory and extreme as possible. At this stage, however, he faced his problem courageously, honestly, and intelligently. As the official leader of the new party in the House, and its only Southern member in Congress, Watson was the logical man to formulate the Populist policy toward the Negro. This he did in a number of speeches and articles.

The Populist program called for a united front between Negro and white farmers. Watson framed his appeal this way:

> Now the People's Party says to these two men, "You are kept apart that you may be separately fleeced of your earnings. You are made to hate each other because upon that hatred is rested the keystone of the arch of financial despotism which enslaves you both. You are deceived and blinded that you may not see how this race antagonism perpetuates a monetary system which beggars both."

This bold program called for a reversal of deeply rooted racial prejudices and firmly fixed traditions as old as Southern history. In place of race hatred, political proscription, lynch law, and terrorism it was necessary to foster tolerance, friendly cooperation, justice and political rights for the Negro. This was no small task; yet Watson met each issue squarely.

It should be the object of the Populist party, he said, to "make lynch law odious to the people." Georgia at that time led the world in lynchings. Watson nominated a Negro to a place on the state executive committee of his party, "as a man worthy to be on the executive committee of this or any other party." "Tell me the use of educating these people as citizens if they are never to exercise the rights of citizens." He spoke repeatedly from the same platform with Negro speakers to mixed audiences of Negro and white farmers. He did not advocate "social equality" and said so emphatically, since that was "a thing each citizen decides for himself." But he insisted upon "political equality," holding that "the accident of color can make no difference in the interests of farmers, croppers, and laborers." In the same spirit of racial tolerance he was continually finding accomplishments of the Negro race at home and abroad to praise in articles and speeches.

Tom Watson was perhaps the first native white Southern leader of importance to treat the Negro's aspirations with the seriousness that human strivings deserve. For the first time in his political history the Negro was regarded neither as the incompetent ward of White Supremacy, nor as the ward of military intervention, but as an integral part of Southern society with a place in its economy. The Negro was in the South to stay, insisted Watson, just as much so as the white man. "Why is not the colored tenant open to the conviction that he is in the same boat as the white tenant; the colored laborer with the white laborer?" he asked. With a third party it was now possible for the Negro to escape the dilemma of selling his vote to the Democrats or pledging it blindly to the Republican bosses. Under Watson's tutelage the Southern white masses were beginning to learn to regard the Negro as a political ally bound to them by economic ties and a common destiny, rather than as a slender prop to injured self-esteem in the shape of "White Supremacy." Here was a foundation of political realism upon which some more enduring structure of economic democracy might be constructed. Never before or since have the two races in the South come so close together as they did during the Populist struggles.

No one was more keenly aware of the overwhelming odds against his social program than Tom Watson. In an article in the *Arena* he wrote:

> You might beseech a Southern white tenant to listen to you upon questions of finance, taxation, and transportation; you might demonstrate with mathematical precision that herein lay his way out of poverty into comfort; you might have him "almost persuaded" to the truth, but if the merchant who furnished his farm supplies (at tremendous usury) or the town politician (who never spoke to him excepting at election times) came along and cried "Negro rule!" the entire fabric of reason and common sense which you had patiently constructed would fall, and the poor tenant would joyously hug the chains of an actual wretchedness rather than do any experimenting on a question of mere sentiment. . . . The Negro has been as valuable a portion of the stock in trade of a Democrat as he was of a Republican.

Henry Grady's statement in 1889 that "The Negro as a political force had dropped out of serious consideration" sounded strange indeed in 1892. The Negro as a political force was the concern of everybody. The Democrats sought industriously to resurrect the scare of the Republican "Force Bill," introduced in the House and defeated in the Senate in 1890. "All agree," said the Augusta *Chronicle*, "that this is the overshadowing issue," and it was obvious that the Populists were "aiding the Republicans in their nefarious schemes." "The old issue of sectionalism is confronting the South," asserted the *Constitution*, and White Supremacy is more important than "all the financial reform in the world."

A Westerner, the most eminent student of Populism, has remarked, "Perhaps only a Southerner can realize how keenly these converts to Populism [in the South] must have felt their grievances." A Southerner might add, "only a Southerner of that period"—which followed close upon Reconstruction. The motives of the most sincere Populists were not above the basest construction by Democrats, many of whom were perfectly honest in their suspicions. It was widely believed that they were in secret alliance with the Republicans, and therefore not only traitors to their section, but to their race as well—enemies of white civilization. The worst slander, however, was the product of editors and politicians who believed that any means was justified by the end they had in view. When a responsible editor wrote that "The South and especially the tenth district is threatened with anarchy and communism" because of "the direful teachings of Thomas E. Watson," there were thousands who believed him literally. Populists were subjected to every type of epithet, scurrility, and insult Democrats could devise. There is record of Populists' being turned out of church, driven from their homes, and refused credit because of their beliefs. Families were split and venomous feuds started. . . . One of Tom Watson's brothers was secretary of the mass meeting that pronounced him a traitor; a second brother, a merchant, remained a Democrat, and a third became a Populist. A Southern Populist leader told a Western writer, "The feeling of the Democracy against us is one of murderous hate. I have been shot at many times. Grand juries will not indict our assailants. Courts give us no protection."

To overcome the harsh penalties attached to revolt—the compulsions of tradition as well as economic pressure making for conformity—there must have been tremendous forces at work upon the Southern masses. It is furthest from the intention of this work to suggest that adequate cause can be discovered in the eloquence of Thomas E. Watson, or the eloquence of anybody else. More eloquent than any orator in the cause of revolt were the hard times of 1891–1892 that opened the "heart-breaking 'nineties."

After a two weeks' tour of observation in the cotton belt of Georgia in December, 1891, the editor of the *Southern Alliance Farmer* wrote that "the farmer has about reached the end of his row." The crop was selling at "the lowest price that cotton has reached in a third of a century," and "hundreds of men will be turned out of house and home, or forced to become hirelings and tenants in fields that they once owned. . . . The doors of every courthouse in Georgia are placarded with the announcements of such [sheriffs'] sales. Hundreds of farmers will be turned adrift, and thousands of acres of our best land allowed to grow up in weeds through lack of necessary capital to work them. . . . The roads are full of negroes begging homes." There was a veritable "epidemic of distress and foreclosures of mortgages now sweeping over our state." The president of the Burke County Alliance wrote Watson: "Our county is in a terrible, terrible condition. Out of fifteen hundred customers at one store only fourteen paid out; five hundred paid less than 50 cents on the dollar." Mrs. W. H. Felton wrote, "We sold our cotton crop in 1892 for a little over four cents the pound, and it did not pay taxes, guano, and farm supplies."

In the factory slums of the New South, where tenement houses had hardly weathered gray yet, hunger and destitution prevailed. The Atlanta *Journal* reported that just outside Atlanta in the workers' district of the Exposition Mills—the mills that occupied the same buildings in which Henry Grady hailed the birth of the New South just ten years before—

"famine and pestilence are to-day making worse ravages than among the serfs of Russia." The mill workers are paid "the magnificent sum of 36 cents a day for their labor, and . . . the average wage fund in the factory district is 9 cents a head divided among the members of the family." The bodies of their dead remain unburied. One may see "rooms wherein eight and ten members of one family are stricken down, where pneumonia and fever and measles are attacking their emaciated bodies; where there is no sanitation, no help or protection from the city, no medicine, no food, no fire, no nurses—nothing but torturing hunger and death."

"There is a song in the fields where the plowshare gleams," wrote the heir to Grady's editorial chair, "a song of hope for the harvest ahead, and the man at the plow-handles seems happier than he has been, as the furrows are formed at his feet." "Yes," answered Tom Watson, " 'there is a song in the field'—and it begins, 'Good-by, old party, Good-by,' and ends with a cheer for the St. Louis platform."

The Cooperative Movement

LAWRENCE GOODWYN

Both the literal meaning and the ultimate dimension of the crop lien were visible in simple scenes occurring daily, year after year, decade after decade, in every village of every Southern state. Acted out at a thousand merchant counters in the South after the Civil War, these scenes were so ubiquitous that to describe one is to convey a sense of them all. The farmer, his eyes downcast, and his hat sometimes literally in his hand, approached the merchant with a list of his needs. The man behind the counter consulted a ledger, and after a mumbled exchange, moved to his shelves to select the goods that would satisfy at least a part of his customer's wants. Rarely did the farmer receive the range of items or even the quantity of one item he had requested. No money changed hands; the merchant merely made brief notations in his ledger. Two weeks or a month later, the farmer would return, the consultation would recur, the mumbled exchange and the careful selection of goods would ensue, and new additions would be noted in the ledger. From early spring to late fall the ritual would be enacted until, at "settlin'-up" time, the farmer and the merchant would meet at the local cotton gin, where the fruits of a year's toil would be ginned, bagged, tied, weighed, and sold. At that moment, the farmer would learn what his cotton had brought. The merchant, who had possessed title to the crop even before the farmer had planted it, then consulted his ledger for a final time. The accumulated debt for the year, he informed the farmer, exceeded the income received from the cotton crop. The farmer had failed in his effort to "pay out"—he still owed the merchant a remaining balance for the supplies

From *The Populist Moment: A Short History of the Agrarian Revolt in America* by Lawrence Goodwyn. Copyright © 1978 by Lawrence Goodwyn. Reprinted by permission of Oxford University Press, Inc.

"furnished" on credit during the year. The "furnishing merchant" would then announce his intention to carry the farmer through the winter on a new account, the latter merely having to sign a note mortgaging to the merchant the next year's crop. The lien signed, the farmer, empty-handed, climbed in his wagon and drove home, knowing that for the second or fifth or fifteenth year he had not paid out.

Such was the crop lien system. It constituted a new and debasing method of economic organization that took its specific form from the devastation of the Civil War and from the collapse of the economic structure of Southern society which had resulted from the war. In the aftermath of Appomattox, the people of the South had very little capital or the institutions dealing in it—banks. Emancipation had erased the slave system's massive investment in human capital, and surrender had not only invalidated all Confederacy currency, it had also engendered a wave of Southern bank failures. Massachusetts alone had five times as much national bank circulation as the entire South, while Bridgeport, Connecticut, had more than the states of Texas, Alabama, and North and South Carolina combined. The per capita figure for Rhode Island was $77.16; it was 13 cents for Arkansas. One hundred and twenty-three counties in the state of Georgia had no banking facilities of any kind. The South had become, in the words of one historian, a "giant pawn shop."

The furnishing merchants, able to get most of their goods on consignment from competing Northern mercantile houses, bought supplies and "furnished" them on credit to farmers, taking a lien on the farmer's crop for security. Farmers learned that the interest they were paying on everything they consumed limited their lives in a new and terrible way; the rates imposed were frequently well in excess of 100 per cent annually, sometimes over 200 per cent. The system had subtle ramifications which made this mountain of interest possible. At the heart of the process was a simple two-price system for all items—one price for cash customers and a second and higher price for credit customers. Interest of 25 to 50 per cent would then be charged on this inflated base. An item carrying a "cash price" of 10 cents would be sold on credit for 14 cents and at the end of the year would bring the merchant, after the addition of, say, 33 per cent interest, a total of 19 cents—almost double the standard purchasing price. Once a farmer had signed his first crop lien he was in bondage to his merchant as long as he failed to pay out, because "no competitor would sell the farmer so much as a side of fat back, except for cash, since the only acceptable security, his crop, had been forfeited." The farmer rarely was even aware of the disparity between cash and credit prices, for he usually had no basis for comparison; "many of the merchants did a credit business so exclusively they set no cash prices." The farmer soon learned that the prudent judgment—or whim—of his furnishing merchant was the towering reality of his life. Did his wife want some calico for her single "Sunday dress," or did his family need a slab of bacon? Whether he got them or not depended on the invisible scales on which the merchant across the counter weighed the central question—would the farmer's crop yield enough money to pay off the accumulating furnishing debt?

In ways people outside the South had difficulty perceiving, the crop lien system became for millions of Southerners, white and black, little more than slavery. "When one of these mortgages has been recorded against the Southern farmer," wrote a contemporary, "he had usually passed into a state of helpless peonage. . . . From this time until he has paid the last dollar of his indebtedness, he is subject to the constant oversight and direction of the merchant." The man with the ledger became the farmer's sole significant contact with the outside world. Across the South he was known as "the furnishing man" or "the advancing man." To black farmers he became "the Man."

The account books of Southern furnishing merchants present grim evidence not only of the gradations of privation between blacks and whites, but the near universality of privation. In South Carolina low farm prices forced a middle-class white farmer, S. R. Simonton, to open a credit account with the furnishing house of T. G. Patrick. While Simonton's first year's expenditures were $916.63, declining prices helped reduce his after-sale "credits" to only $307.31, leaving an unpaid balance of over $600, which he settled by note. The subsequent annual credit extended to him by the furnishing merchant did not exceed $400 per year, showing that he had suffered a drop of well over 100 per cent in his standard of living. Still, he was never able to "pay out." After seven years the debt was settled by a transfer of land to the furnishing merchant. Simonton had become a landless tenant.

Detailed records of the account of a Mississippi Negro farmer over seventeen years reveal an even grimmer degradation. Matt Brown purchased his supplies from the Jones Store at Black Hawk, Mississippi, from 1884 to 1901. Brown was not free of debt at any time in those years. He began the year 1892 with an indebtedness of $226.84 held over from previous years. At final settlement on January 3, 1893, his obligation had increased to $452.41. Though his credits during the year from selling cotton, cutting wood, clearing land, and hauling for the store amounted to $171, his expenditures for the year were $353 for household and farm supplies. By 1895 his credit standing had diminished to the point that his twelve-month expenditure for food totaled $8.42. In that year he spent $27.25 on clothing, $38.30 on farm and household supplies, 95 cents on drugs, $2.35 for a cash advance, and $12.08 on miscellaneous supplies. Matt Brown's account, it appears, was ultimately settled by a mortgage. A 1905 entry is for a coffin and burial supplies. The record was permanently closed by "marking it off."

For millions of farmers of both races throughout the South, those were the realities of life in the last half of the nineteenth century. Southern metropolitan newspapers told farmers they "bought too much and sold too little," but farmers who spent $10.00 to $50.00 a year for food knew better. They could have cited another statistic: the Southern cotton crop of 8.6 million bales in 1890 brought $429.7 million to the farmers; the next year's crop, 9.0 million bales, brought only $391.5 million—a decrease of $38.2 million despite an increase in production.

New South editorialists said that the Southern farmer should diversify and grow perishable food supplies as well as cotton, but both the farmer and the furnishing merchant knew better. The compelling fact was that an acre of corn produced even less financial return than an acre of cotton did. Conservatives who advised the farmer assumed he possessed a degree of autonomy that he simply did not have. Furnishing merchants demanded that their debtors plant the one certain cash crop, cotton. One phrase defined the options: "No cotton, no credit." Moreover, goldbug newspaper editors rarely focused on the reality that the government's reliance on the gold standard meant deflation, which translated into the long postwar fall of farm prices. Farmers, caught between high interest rates and low commodity prices, lost almost all hope of ever being able to pay out. Every year more and more of them lost their land to their furnishing merchant and became his tenants. Merchants began to consider a "run" of fifty to one hundred tenants on their lands as normal. They gradually acquired title to steadily increasing portions of the lands of the country. As thousands, then millions descended into the world of landless tenantry, the annual output expanded, but both the soil and those who worked it gradually became exhausted as a result of the desperate cycle of crop lien, furnish, cotton harvest, failure to pay out, and new crop lien. . . .

. . . Tactically, the rise of the Alliance was a result of its determination to go beyond the cash stores of the Grange and make pioneering efforts in cooperative marketing as well as purchasing. The cooperative effort was helpful because it recruited farmers by the thousands. But in a deeper political sense the Alliance organization was experimenting in a new kind of mass autonomy. As such, it was engaged in a cultural struggle to redefine the form and meaning of life and politics in America. Out of the individual sense of self of leaders like S. O. Daws and William Lamb the Alliance had begun to develop a collective sense of purpose symbolized by the ambitious strivings of scores of groups who were anxious to show the world why they intended to "stand united." Inexorably, the mutually supportive dynamics inherent in these individual and collective modes of behavior began to produce something new among the huge mass that Alliancemen called "the plain people." This consisted of a new way of looking at society, a way of thinking that represented a shaking off of inherited forms of deference. The achievement was not an easy one. The farmers of the Alliance had spent much of their lives in humiliating circumstances; repeated dealings with Southern merchants had inculcated insecurity in generations of farming people. They were ridiculed for their poverty, and they knew it. They were called "hayseeds" and they knew that, too. But they had also known for decades that they could do nothing about their plight because they were locked into the fabric of the lien system and crushed by the mountain of interest they had been forced to pay. But now, in their Alliance, they had found something new. That something may be described as individual self-respect and collective self-confidence, or what some would call "class-consciousness." All are useful if imprecise terms to describe a growing political sensibility, one free of deference and ridicule. Such an intuition shared by enough people is, of course, a potentially powerful force. In whatever terminology this intuition is described, it clearly represents a seminal kind of democratic instinct; and it was this instinct that emerged in the Alliance in 1884–85.

In the succeeding eighteen months their new way of looking at things flowered into a mass expression of a new political vision. We may call it (for that is what it was) the movement culture of Populism. This culture involved more than just the bulking of cotton. It extended to frequent Alliance meetings to plan the mass sales—meetings where the whole family came, where the twilight suppers were, in the early days, laid out for ten or twenty members of the suballiance, or for hundreds at a county Alliance meeting, but which soon grew into vast spectacles; long trains of wagons, emblazoned with suballiance banners, stretching literally for miles, trekking to enormous encampments where five, ten, and twenty thousand men and women listened intently to the plans of their Alliance and talked among themselves about those plans. At those encampments speakers, with growing confidence, pioneered a new political language to describe the "money trust," the gold standard, and the private national banking system that underlay all of their troubles in the lien system.

How is a democratic culture created? Apparently in such prosaic, powerful ways. When a farm family's wagon crested a hill en route to a Fourth of July "Alliance Day" encampment and the occupants looked back to see thousands of other families trailed out behind them in wagon trains, the thought that "the Alliance is the people and the people are together" took on transforming possibilities. Such a moment—and the Alliance experience was to yield hundreds of them—instilled hope in hundreds of thousands of people who had been without it. The successes of the cooperative effort gave substance to the hope, but it was the hope itself, the sense of autonomy it encouraged and the sense of possibility it stimulated, that lay at the heart of Populism. If "the Alliance was the people and the people were together," who could not see that the people had created the means to change the circumstances of their lives? This was the soul of the Populist faith. The cooperative movement of the Alliance was its source.

In 1884–85, the Alliance began developing its own rhythm of internal "education" and its own broadening political consciousness among leaders and followers. The movement culture would develop its own mechanism of recruitment (the large-scale credit cooperative), its own theoretical analysis (the greenback interpretation of the American version of finance capitalism), its own solution (the sub-treasury land and loan system), its own symbols of politics (the Alliance "Demands" and the Omaha Platform), and its own political institution (the People's Party). Grounded in a common experience, nurtured by years of experimentation and self-education, it produced a party, a platform, a specific new democratic ideology, and a pathbreaking political agenda for the American nation. But none of these things were the essence of Populism. At bottom, Populism was, quite simply, an expression of self-respect. It was not an individual trait, but a collective one, surfacing as the shared hope of millions organized by the Alliance into its cooperative crusade. This individual and collective striving generated the movement culture that was Populism.

The Limitations of Populist Ideology

STEVEN HAHN

The defense of private property and common rights illuminates the elements of a nineteenth-century producer ideology embodied in the appeal and program of both the Southern Alliance's radical wing and the People's party. Thus, when Populists assailed the "money kings," the "speculative parasites," the "capitalists" who "grow richer and richer . . . at the expense of those who produce," and associated the third-party cause with "liberty and independence, which can only be realized by giving equal rights to all and special privileges to none," they did not advance a version of political pluralism. They lent wider expression to republican sensibilities founded on social relations quite at odds with the dominant trends of industrializing America—sensibilities at odds with the tenets of bourgeois individualism and the free market. Blaming the concentration of wealth and power on the corruption of the political process, Populists did not wish to unfetter the "invisible hand" of the marketplace; they wished to protect a "liberty tree" rooted in petty ownership of productive resources. The People's party, they proclaimed, "is composed of the yeomanry of the country. The small landed proprietors, the working farmers, the intelligent artisans, the wageworkers[,] men who own homes and want a stable government."

To the hegemony of the marketplace, Populism counterposed the vision of a producers' commonwealth achieved through cooperative enterprise and public regulation of exchange. Included among the party's most far-reaching planks were demands for the Alliance-inspired subtreasury system, for democratization of the money supply through the abolition of national banks and the "free and unlimited coinage of silver" so as to increase the "circulating medium . . . to not less than $50 per capita," and for government ownership of the means of transportation and communication. It was a vision informed by historical experience—by the structure and dynamic of the family farm, the shop, and the local market; by notions of government as the repository of the public will and the defender of the public good—and tailored to the exigencies of an expansive society. As one Carroll County yeoman could write, "Competition may be the life of trade, but it is death to the farmer." Not a proletarian movement, Populism spoke for men and women of "small means" who faced and sought to resist the specter of proletarianization, of "be[ing] forced to work at the pleasure of the money lords," of "becom[ing] a nation of shylocks and serfs."

The republican producer ideology embraced by Upcountry supporters of common rights and, later, of Populism at once facilitated and limited the development of a biracial political coalition of poor Southerners. It was, of course, the prominent Georgia Populist Tom Watson who forcefully argued that the economic woes shared by white and black farmers alike demanded cooperative political endeavor. "[T]he crushing burdens which now oppress both races in the South will cause each to . . . see a similarity of cause and a similarity of remedy," Watson contended. "They will recognize that each should help the other in the work of repealing bad laws and enacting good ones." Such "broad lines of mutual interest" did become increasingly apparent to many Upcountry whites in the years after Reconstruction, as the rise of staple agriculture transformed social relations and jeopardized the independence of small landowners. Tentatively during the Independent campaigns of the 1870s and more dramatically during the stock-law conflict of the 1880s, a new political alignment began taking shape. In large part, overtures to the black community reflected its impressive political mobilization; though relatively few in number, the freedmen stood as a force to be grappled with. But, as the arguments of stock-law opponents suggested, a sense of commonly suffered economic exploitation and political misrule gradually emerged as well. While the Farmers' Alliance excluded blacks, relegating them to a separate organization, more than a few Upcountry Populists looked to narrowing the racial divide. Thus, in an effort to recruit local blacks, the People's party in Jackson County opened meetings to both races, welcomed black delegates at their county conventions, and invited a black speaker from Atlanta.

Blacks contributed significant electoral support to Populist candidates, who were uniformly white. The sympathetic Dallas *Herald* of Paulding County found that the "People's party colored men did splendid work at the polls" in 1894 and 1895 and praised their courage in the face of "protests, persuasions, and the employment of all manner of means by the democrats." The hostile Carroll *Free Press* could blame a local third-party victory in 1894 on a poor Democratic turnout and on blacks who "voted almost solidly for the populists [having been made to] believe that the low price of cotton was attributable to democratic rule." Yet, black political leaders in the Upcountry, and doubtless many of their followers, approached the People's party with some caution and skepticism. For one thing, abandoning the Republican party and its potential network of patronage in favor of a new party whose prospects were uncertain carried risks. Furthermore, numerous blacks justifiably charged that the Populists paid minimal, if any, attention to the special needs of the black community. One announced that he voted for the Democrats in state elections because "Weaver, Watson, and Peek" ignored the issue of public schools, "which is the only hope the colored people can have."

Perhaps more important in steering a considerable number of blacks away from the Populists was the reputation for bitter racism that the party's white constituency had earned. The reign of terror brought upon the freedmen by vigilante bands during Reconstruction left a painful legacy, while

Independent efforts to reform the Democratic party led to the establishment of white primaries in the 1880s. And as P. W. Carter, a black Jackson County Republican, roared in 1892, "many who are now Populists were the strongest kind for the primaries because it shut the 'nigger' out." The less-than-courageous response of third-party faithfuls to Democratic accusations that they encouraged racial mingling and opened the way for "negro domination" did little to allay the suspicions of men like Carter. Indeed, white Populists could hoist the banner of white supremacy even as they assailed its partisan manifestation. Most state Republican leaders, white and black, along with the head of Georgia's Colored Alliance, endorsed the Populists with good effect; but more than a handful of black voters in the Upcountry and elsewhere chose to abstain or to side with the Democrats, who attempted to lure black support with halfhearted denunciations of lynching.

However much it had a life of its own, the enduring racism of Populism's rank and file was rooted in deeper class relations and attitudes. Though often confronting expropriation, though able to style themselves the "laboring poor" and to feel solidarity with the "toiling masses" throughout the nation, these Southern whites had strong cultural ties, if not direct personal experience, with a community of petty proprietors. They adhered to a popular radicalism—widespread in nineteenth-century America—that linked freedom and independence with ownership of productive resources and looked with fear and contempt upon the permanently dispossessed who fell subject to the wills of other men—precisely the image associated with blacks. Some small landowners in the Upcountry had previously owned, or were members of families that had previously owned, slaves; some had a black cropper or two on their farms; others, including white tenants, occasionally hired black hands for day labor. And when, in 1891, the Colored Farmers' Alliance launched a strike of black cotton pickers across the South, it met with a hostile response from, and often brutal repression at the hands of, the white Farmers' Alliance itself—an episode leaving scars of racial anger. Rather than resolving these tensions and contradictions, the republican producer ideology captured and advanced by Populism served to re-emphasize them. "We have in this country two dangerous classes," a Southern Populist could declare. "One a band of capitalist conspirators who enjoy special advantages which they are determined to maintain and increase even at the cost of involving the nation to ruin. The other, homeless and friendless, goaded to desperation by the teaching of designing men, clamoring for something they do not understand themselves, filled with a desire by a reign of riot and confusion, to establish a new order of things based on chimerical values."

The failure of Populism to address the specific plight of blacks and landless farmers generally reflected not only the persisting culture of independent proprietorship but also the particular social relations of the new cotton economy. For if white farmers were increasingly drawn into commercial agriculture and the attendant grip of merchant capital, the household remained the dominant productive unit. Although the raising of staple crops and the acquisition of basic necessities led to spiraling indebtedness and encumbrance and to a growing perception that they "worked for the other fellow" instead of for themselves, heads of farm households continued to rely on family labor. Consequently, they located exploitation in the sphere of exchange rather than at the point of production and looked directly to the credit and money, not the land, question as a solution to their predicament and as a means for rallying political insurgency.

The historical experiences of Southern yeomen that underwrote and gave force to Populism's republican producer ideology created even further obstacles for a movement intent upon reshaping the regional and national landscape in the name of the "laboring classes." A legacy of exclusion from the immediate processes of political decision making, a highly personalized view of economic relations, and a decidedly moral interpretation of political conflict—widely shared by rural folk—made it difficult for the third party to confront the issue of power in an increasingly centralized and bureaucratized society. Nationally, these problems led to dissension, if not confusion, in the ranks when the question of translating the party platform into political reality was faced; and they contributed to the ascendancy of a "shadow movement" committed only to free silver and engineered by political leaders far more interested in electoral success than in radical reform. Locally, these problems hampered the effectiveness of Populist officeholders, who tended to win on symbolic issues such as abolishing the county courthouse—an action which promised, at best, to reduce taxes and ease the burdens of litigation. And the mixed records that third-party officials compiled hardly offered encouragement to debt-ridden constituents already harassed for their political leanings. Drawing upon the elements of rural disaffection, Populism articulated a bitter critique of capitalist relations and values, but it was no accident that much of its specific program came by way of the Greenbackers and other labor radicals.

What appear to be missed opportunities, of course, can partly be attributed to a rather brief presence. Quite simply, the Populists had precious little time or room in which to move. Although the third party lived on into the early twentieth century, it dissolved as a mass movement after 1896—victimized by the superior resources and intense pressure brought to bear by its opponents. But here, too, internal weakness and contradiction contributed to collapse. Robert Preston Brooks, the economic historian, noted after a research trip through the Georgia Upcountry in 1911 that while black tenants and laborers organized, their white counterparts did not. His caveat could have included yeoman farmers, for this form of self-activity seemed virtually absent among white rural common folk. An explanation may be found, not so much in a legacy of sturdy individualism, as in a complex of social relations that continued to link many of the landed and landless by kinship and that promoted cooperative exchanges between neighboring families. These very networks and norms of the household economy partially disguised class distinctions and probably discouraged reliance on supralocal, unfamiliar, and more formalized organizational structures. In this way, white farmers and tenants could rise to protect customary use rights, could sense and express shared grievances, yet make no attempt to mobilize their forces. If the Farmers' Alliance and the People's party provided an institutional focus for such discontent, they had a tenuous foundation to build upon, leaving the emergent rank and file with few means of defense against the fierce, and frequently violent, counterattack of elites who saw in Populism the forebodings of "communism" and "anarchism."

The materials of social unrest, therefore, often flowed into prepolitical forms of administering popular justice. As early as the fall of 1893, amid an unfolding nationwide depression, "white-cappers" of distinctly lower-class origin formulated their own remedy for economic distress: they sent anonymous notes to Upcountry merchants and landlords warning of the torch if cotton were ginned or marketed before the price "reaches 10¢" a pound or if debts were collected before "the monetary stringency is past." The flames that soon engulfed several barns, dwellings, and gins may have evened some personal scores; they signaled the failings of the agrarian movement as well. Only in Texas, where Populism culminated more than a decade of organized activity and benefited from labor support, did the third party show considerable resiliency and unflagging adherence to the full spectrum of Populist demands.

Yet, however beset with contradictions, Populism's commitment to political democracy and cooperative enterprise represented a radical alternative in the Gilded Age and a watershed in the history of industrializing America. On the heels of its demise came formal disfranchisement in the South and a long-range narrowing of political discussion and participation that was national in scope. If later federal farm legislation drew upon Populist programs, it was possible only after the movement's downfall and, not incidentally, served the interests of large landowners. As a further measure of Populism's import and character, defeat gave way to an accelerated process of rural dispossession, which left growing numbers of white Southern farmers in a condition of permanent landlessness and turned political protest in new directions. The scattered popular movements of the early twentieth century, especially the Socialist party which spread through the Southwest, set their sights on organizing tenants and laborers and evinced an increasingly proletarian sensibility. But theirs was a sensibility owing much to the experiences and struggles of Populist predecessors.

✢ *F U R T H E R   R E A D I N G*

A. M. Arnett, *The Populist Movement in Georgia* (1922) ➛
Donna A. Barnes, *Farmers in Rebellion* (1984)
Jeffrey J. Crow and Robert F. Durden, *Maverick Republican in the Old North State* (1977)
Charles Crowe, "Tom Watson, Populists, and Blacks Reconsidered," *Journal of Negro History* 55 (April 1970), 99–116.
Robert F. Durden, *The Climax of Populism* (1966) ➛
Gerald Gaither, *Blacks and the Populist Revolt* (1977)
Lawrence Goodwyn, *Democratic Promise* (1976)

————, *The Populist Moment* (1978)

Sheldon Hackney, *Populism to Progressivism in Alabama* (1969)

Steven Hahn, *The Roots of Southern Populism* (1983)

William Ivy Hair, *Bourbonism and Agrarian Protest* (1969)

Roger L. Hart, *Redeemers, Bourbons, and Populists* (1975)

John D. Hicks, *The Populist Revolt* (1931)

Richard Hofstadter, *The Age of Reform* (1955)

J. Morgan Kousser, *The Shaping of Southern Politics* (1974)

Robert McMath, *Populist Vanguard* (1975)

Stuart Noblin, *Leonidas Lafayette Polk* (1949)

Walter T. K. Nugent, *The Tolerant Populists* (1963)

Bruce Palmer, *"Men Over Money"* (1980)

Norman Pollack, *The Populist Response to Industrial America* (1962)

William Warren Rogers, *One-Gallused Rebellion* (1970)

Theodore Saloutos, *Farmer Movements in the South* (1960)

Michael Schwartz, *Radical Protest and Social Structure* (1976)

Barton Shaw, *The Wool Hat Boys* (1984)

James Turner, "Understanding the Populists," *Journal of American History* 67 (September 1980), 354–73.

C. Vann Woodward, *Origins of the New South* (1951)

————, *Tom Watson* (1938)

CHAPTER
6

Segregation and Disfranchisement

At approximately the same time as the defeat of Populism, there occurred an-
other major development in southern history: the imposition of segregation and
disfranchisement. Black southerners (along with some poorer whites) lost the po-
litical rights they had gained during Reconstruction. In addition, a legally man-
dated system of cradle-to-grave segregation fastened upon southern blacks the
stigma of inferiority. They were ostracized by southern white society as objects of
contempt and discrimination.

Clearly, this institutionalization of white supremacy was in some ways a
culmination of racist trends that had been developing since emancipation or even
before. But it also marked a drastic change in the legal, political, and social
status of black southerners, who had been voting and had not been legally
barred from many areas of southern life. The causes of disfranchisement and
Jim Crow segregation are complex and important and therefore have generated
considerable historical debate. The connection between Populism and segregation,
in particular, is an area of significant disagreement among historians today.

What were the roots of segregation, and how far had it advanced before the
1890s? How did black southerners respond to the rising tide of racism and to
attempts to disfranchise them and impose segregation? How did the new system
affect blacks who lived under it? What was the influence of urban areas, of
racist psychology, and of political exigencies on these developments? Did white
racism compel legal, political, and social changes, or were racist forces manipu-
lated and fostered for their political effects?

⚓ D O C U M E N T S

Legally imposed segregation and disfranchisement were new in the 1890s, but
discrimination against blacks was not new, of course. The testimony of Henry
Adams before Congress, reprinted in the first document, illustrates the disappointment blacks felt when Reconstruction was overthrown and describes one attempt to deal with the changed situation. The second document was written by a
white southerner, George Washington Cable, who assessed the nature of racial
sentiments in the South and spoke out in the 1880s for fairer treatment of black
citizens. Cable was condemned for his stand, but his speeches and writings show

161

that segregation had not yet become the reigning orthodoxy. In 1895, when white-supremacy movements were clearly gaining momentum, Booker T. Washington accepted an invitation to speak at the Atlanta Exposition. The text of his speech in the third document sheds light on black attitudes and reveals one black leader's strategy to preserve some advantageous positions for his race. The North in general, and the United States Supreme Court in particular, abetted the South's move toward segregation. Excerpts from the text of *Plessy* v. *Ferguson*, reprinted as the fourth selection, show the Court's acceptance of the "separate-but-equal" fiction. The legal formulas of disfranchisement—the literacy test, poll tax, and grandfather clause (used to benefit otherwise unqualified whites)—are illustrated by excerpts from a North Carolina statute in the fifth document. Although institutional and political power had swung against them, black leaders protested vigorously, as shown by the remarks of W. J. Whipper and Robert Smalls, black delegates to South Carolina's 1895 Constitutional Convention, in the sixth document. The painful impact of racial segregation is described in the final selection by Pauli Murray, who grew up in the newly segregated society and saw how it worked against the hopes of all black people.

Black Southerners React to the End of Reconstruction, 1879

From Testimony of Henry Adams to the United States Senate, Senate Report No. 693

Q. What is your business, Mr. Adams?—*A.* I am a laborer. I was raised on a farm and have been at hard work all my life.

Q. Now tell us, Mr. Adams, what, if anything you know about the exodus of the colored people from the Southern to the Northern and Western States; and be good enough to tell us in the first place what you know about the organization of any committeee or society among the colored people themselves for the purpose of bettering their condition, and why it was organized. Just give us a history of that as you understand it.—*A.* Well, in 1870, I believe it was, or about that year, after I had left the Army—I went into the Army in 1866 and came out the last of 1869—and went right back home again where I went from, Shreveport; I enlisted there, and went back there. I enlisted in the Regular Army, and then I went back after I came out of the Army. After we had come out a parcel of we men that was in the Army and other men thought that the way our people had been treated during the time we was in service—we heard so much talk of how they had been treated and opposed so much and there was no help for it—that caused me to go into the Army at first, the way our people was opposed. There was so much going on that I went off and left it; when I came back it was still going on, part of it, not quite so bad as at first. So a parcel of us got together and said that we would organize ourselves into a committeee and look into affairs and see the true condition of our race, to see whether it was possible we could stay under a people who had held us under bondage or not. Then we did so and organized a committee.

Q. What did you call your committee?—*A.* We just called it a committee, that is all we called it, and it remained so; it increased to a large extent, and remained so. Some of the members of the committee was ordered by the committee to go into every State in the South where we had been slaves there, and post one another from time to time about the true condition of our race, and nothing but the truth.

Q. You mean some members of your committee?—*A.* That committee; yes, sir.

Q. They traveled over the other States?—*A.* Yes, sir; and we worked some of us, worked our way from place to place and went from State to State and worked—some of them did—amongst our people in the fields, everywhere, to see what sort of living our people lived; whether we could remain in the South amongst the people who had held us as slaves or not. We continued that on till 1874. . . .

Q. Was the object of that committee at that time to remove your people from the South, or what was it?—*A.* O, no, sir; not then; we just wanted to see whether there was any State in the South where we could get a living and enjoy our rights.

Q. The object, then, was to find out the best places in the South where you could live?—*A.* Yes, sir; where we could live and get along well there and to investigate our affairs—not to go nowhere till we saw whether we could stand it.

Q. How were the expenses of these men paid?—*A.* Every one paid his own expenses, except the one we sent to Louisiana and Mississippi. We took money out of our pockets and sent him, and said to him you must now go to work. You can't find out anything till you get amongst them. You can talk as much as you please, but you have got to go right into the field and work with them and sleep with them to know all about them.

Q. Have you any idea how many of your people went out in that way?— *A.* At one time there was five hundred of us.

Q. Do you mean five hundred belonging to your committee?—*A.* Yes, sir.

Q. I want to know how many traveled in that way to get at the condition of your people in the Southern States?—*A.* I think about one hundred or one hundred and fifty went from one place to another.

Q. And they went from one place to another, working their way and paying their expenses and reporting to the common center at Shreveport, do you mean?—*A.* Yes, sir.

Q. What was the character of the information that they gave you?— *A.* Well, the character of the information they brought to us was very bad, sir.

Q. In what respect?—*A.* They said that in other parts of the country where they traveled through, and what they saw they were comparing with what we saw and what we had seen in the part where we lived; we knowed what that was; and they cited several things that they saw in their travels; it was very bad.

Q. Do you remember any of these reports that you got from members of your committee?—*A*. Yes, sir; they said in several parts where they was that the land rent was still higher there in that part of the country than it was where we first organized it, and the people was still being whipped, some of them, by the old owners, the men that had owned them as slaves, and some of them was being cheated out of their crops just the same as they was there.

Q. Was anything said about their personal and political rights in these reports, as to how they were treated about these?—*A*. Yes; some of them stated that in some parts of the country where they voted they would be shot. Some of them stated that if they voted the Democratic ticket they would not be injured. . . .

Q. The result of this investigation during these four years by your committee was the organization of this colonization council. Is that the way you wish me to understand it?—*A*. It caused it to be organized.

Q. It caused it to be organized. Now, what was the purpose of this colonization council?—*A*. Well, it was to better our condition.

Q. In what way did you propose to do it?—*A*. We first organized and adopted a plan to appeal to the President of the United States and to Congress to help us out of our distress, or protect us in our rights and privileges.

Q. Your council appealed first to the President and to Congress for protection and relief from this distressed condition in which you found yourselves, and to protect you in the enjoyment of your rights and privileges?—*A*. Yes, sir.

Q. Well, what other plan had you?—*A*. And if that failed our idea was then to ask them to set apart a territory in the United States for us, somewhere where we could go and live with our families.

Q. You preferred to go off somewhere by yourselves?—*A*. Yes.

Q. Well, what then?—*A*. If that failed, our other object was to ask for an appropriation of money to ship us all to Liberia, in Africa; somewhere where we could live in peace and quiet.

Q. Well, and what after that?—*A*. When that failed then our idea was to appeal to other governments outside of the United States to help us to get away from the United States and go there and live under their flag.

Q. Have you given us all the objects of this colonization council?—*A*. That is just what we was organized for, to better our condition one way or another. . . .

Q. Now, let us understand more distinctly, before we go any further, the kind of people who composed that association. The committee, as I understand you, was composed entirely of laboring people?—*A*. Yes, sir.

Q. Did it include any politicians of either color, white or black?—*A*. No politicianers didn't belong to it, because we didn't allow them to know nothing about it, because we was afraid that if we allowed the colored politicianer to belong to it he would tell it to the Republican politicianers, and from that the men that was doing all this to us would get hold of it, too, and then get after us.

Q. So you did not trust any politicians, white or black?—*A.* No; we didn't trust any of them.

Q. That was the condition of things during the time the committee were at work in 1870 to 1874?—*A.* Yes, that was the condition.

Q. Now, when you organized the council what kind of people were taken into it?—*A.* Nobody but laboring men. . . .

Q. At the time you were doing that, was there anything political in your organization?—*A.* Nothing in the world.

Q. You were simply looking out for a better place in which you could get work and enjoy your freedom?—*A.* Yes, sir; that was all.

Q. When did the idea first enter your council to emigrate to the northern and northwestern States; if you remember, what were the first movements in that direction?—*A.* Well, in that petition we appealed there, if nothing could be done to stop the turmoil and strife, and give us our rights in the South, we appealed then, at that time, for a territory to be set apart for us to which we could go and take our families and live in peace and quiet.

Q. The design of your organization, then, as you understood it, was not so much to go north to live among the white people in the Northern and Western States as it was to have a territory somewhere that you could occupy in peace and quiet for yourselves?—*A.* That is what we wanted, provided we could not get our rights in the South, where we was. We had much rather staid there if we could have had our rights.

Q. You would have preferred to remain in the South?—*A.* Yes, sir.

Q. And your organization was not in favor of your moving, providing you could get your rights and be protected in the enjoyment of them as any other men?—*A.* No, sir; we had rather staid there than go anywhere else, though the organization was very careful about that, and we said so from the first; and then, if that could not be done under any circumstances, then we wanted to go to a territory by ourselves.

Q. Well, about what time did this idea of a territory first occur to you; did it occur at all during the organization of your committee, or after the council was organized?—*A.* After the committee had made their investigations.

Q. Well, what did you do after that?—*A.* We organized the council after that.

Q. About what time did you lose all hope and confidence that your condition could be tolerated in the Southern States?—*A.* Well, we never lost all hopes in the world till 1877.

Q. Not until 1877?—*A.* No, sir. In 1877 we lost all hopes.

Q. Why did you lose all hope in that year?—*A.* Well, we found ourselves in such condition that we looked around and we seed that there was no way on earth, it seemed, that we could better our condition there, and we discussed that thoroughly in our organization along in May. We said that the whole South—every State in the South—had got into the hands of the very men that held us slaves—from one thing to another—and we thought that the men that held us slaves was holding the reins of government over our heads in every respect almost, even the constable up to the governor. We felt we had almost as well be slaves under these men. In regard to the whole matter that was discussed, it came up in every council. Then we said there was no hope for us and we had better go.

Q. You say, then, that in 1877 you lost all hope of being able to remain in the South, and you began to think of moving somewhere else?—*A.* Yes; we said we was going if we had to run away and go into the woods.

Q. Well, what was the complaint after you failed to get the territory?—*A.* Then, in 1877 we appealed to President Hayes and to Congress, to both Houses. I am certain we sent papers there; if they didn't get them that is not our fault; we sent them.

Q. What did that petition ask for?—*A.* We asked for protection, to have our rights guaranteed to us, and at least if that could not be done, we asked that money should be provided to send us to Liberia.

Q. That was 1877, was it?—*A.* Yes, sir; that was in 1877.

Q. Still, up to that time you did not think at all of going into the Northern States; at least you had taken no steps toward going into those States, had you?—*A.* No, sir.

Q. When did that idea first occur to your people?—*A.* In 1877, too, we declared that if we could not get a territory we would go anywhere on God's earth; we didn't care where.

Q. Even to the Northern States?—*A.* Yes; anywhere to leave them Southern States. We declared that in our council in 1877. We said we would go anywhere to get away.

Q. Well, when did the exodus to the Northern States from your locality, or from your country you are acquainted with best, begin?—*A.* Well, it didn't begin to any extent until just about a year ago.

Q. It didn't begin to any extent until 1879, you mean?—*A.* No, sir; not till the spring of 1879.

Q. But you had prior to that time been organized and ready to go somewhere, as I understand you?—*A.* Yes, sir; we had several organizations; there were many organizations; I can't tell you how many immigration associations, and so forth, all springing out of our colonization council. We had a large meeting, some five thousand people present, and made public speeches in 1877 on immigration.

Q. What was the character of those speeches as to what you intended to do?—*A.* We intended to go away, to leave the South, if Congress would not give us any relief; we were going away, for we knowed we could not get our rights.

Q. Where were these meetings held?—*A.* Some were held at Shreveport, in Caddo Parish, some were held in Madison, and some were held in Bossier Parish.

Q. Was there any opposition to these meetings in which you talked about going away?—*A.* No, sir. There didn't nobody say anything to us against our having our meetings, but I will tell you we had a terrible struggle with our own selves, our own people there; these ministers of these churches would not allow us to have any meeting of that kind, no way.

Q. They didn't want you to go?—*A.* No; they didn't want us to go.

Q. Why?—*A.* They wanted us to stay there to support them; I don't know what else. Mighty few ministers would allow us to have their churches; some few would in some of the parishes. There was one church, Zion, in Shreveport, that allowed us to talk there.

Q. Were the ministers opposed to it?—*A.* Yes, sir; they was opposed to it. . . .

Q. Your meetings were composed, then, of men in favor of going away?—*A.* Yes, and of the laboring class.

Q. Others didn't participate with you?—*A.* No, sir.

Q. Why didn't the politicians want you to go?—*A.* They were against it from the beginning.

Q. Why?—*A.* They thought if we went somewhere else they would not get our votes. That is what we thought.

Q. Why were the ministers opposed to it?—*A.* Well, because they would not get our support; that is what we thought of them.

Q. They thought it might break up their churches?—*A.* Yes; that is what they thought; at least we supposed the ministers thought that.

Q. About how many did this committee consist of before you organized your council? Give us the number as near as you can tell.—*A.* As many as five hundred in all.

Q. The committee, do you mean?—*A.* Yes; the committee has been that large.

Q. What was the largest number reached by your colonization council, in your best judgment?—*A.* Well, it is not exactly five hundred men belonging to the council, that we have in our council, but they all agreed to go with us and enroll their names with us from time to time, so that they have now got at this time 98,000 names enrolled

Q. Women and men?—*A.* Yes, sir; women and men, and none under twelve years old. . . .

Q. How many of your people have gone from that part of the country to the North, if you know?—*A.* I don't know exactly how many have gone.

Q. Of course you cannot tell us exactly, but as near as you know; give some idea of the number, if you can.—*A.* My reports from several members of the committee, in parts I have not been in and seen for myself—I take their words and put their words down as mine, because they are not allowed to lie on the subject. And so from what I have learned from them from time to time I think it is about five thousand and something.

Q. Do you mean from that section of country down there?—*A.* Yes, sir.

Q. From Louisiana?—*A.* Yes, sir. . . .

Q. Now, Mr. Adams, you know, probably, more about the causes of the exodus from that country than any other man, from your connection with it; tell us in a few words what you believe to be the causes of these people going away.—*A.* Well, the cause is, in my judgment, and from what information I have received, and what I have seen with my own eyes—it is because the largest majority of the people, of the white people, that held us as slaves treats our people so bad in many respects that it is impossible for them to stand it. Now, in a great many parts of that country there our people most as well be slaves as to be free; because, in the first place, I will state this: that in some times, in times of politics, if they have any idea that the Republicans will carry a parish or ward, or something of that kind, why, they would do anything on God's earth. There ain't nothing too mean for them to do to prevent it; nothing I can make mention of is too mean for them to do. If I am working on his place, and he has been laughing and talking with me, and I do everything he tells me to, yet in times of election he will crush me down, and even kill me, or do anything to me to carry his point. If he can't carry his point without killing me, he will kill me; but if he can carry his point without killing me, he will do that. . . .

George Washington Cable Criticizes Racial Attitudes, 1884

First, then, what are these sentiments? Foremost among them stands the idea that [the black man] is of necessity an alien. He was brought to our shores a naked, brutish, unclean, captive, pagan savage, to be and remain a kind of connecting link between man and the beasts of burden. The great changes to result from his contact with a superb race of masters were not taken into account. As a social factor he was intended to be as purely zero as the brute at the other end of his plowline. The occasional mingling of his blood with that of the white man worked no change in the sentiment; one, two, four, eight multiplied upon or divided into zero still gave zero for the result. Generations of American nativity made no difference; his children and children's children were born in sight of our door, yet the old notion held fast. He increased to vast numbers, but it never wavered. He accepted our dress, language, religion, all the fundamentals of our civilization, and became forever expatriated from his own land; still he remained, to us, an alien. Our sentiment went blind. It did not see that gradually, here by force and there by choice, he was fulfilling a host of conditions that earned at least a solemn moral right to that naturalization which no one at first had dreamed of giving him. Frequently he even bought back the freedom of which he had been robbed, became a taxpayer, and at times an educator of his children at his own expense; but the old idea of alienism passed laws to banish him, his wife, and children by thousands from the state, and threw him into loathsome jails as a common felon for returning to his native land.

It will be wise to remember that these were the acts of an enlightened, God-fearing people, the great mass of whom have passed beyond all earthly accountability. They were our fathers. I am the son and grandson of slave-

George Washington Cable's essay "The Freedman's Case in Equity" from Arlin Turner, ed., *The Negro Question: A Selection of Writings on Civil Rights in the South* by George W. Cable, Doubleday, 1958.

holders. These were their faults; posterity will discover ours; but these things must be frankly, fearlessly taken into account if we are ever to understand the true interests of our peculiar state of society.

Why, then, did this notion, that the man of color must always remain an alien, stand so unshaken? We may readily recall how, under ancient systems, he rose, not only to high privileges, but often to public station and power. Singularly, with us the trouble lay in a modern principle of liberty. The whole idea of American government rested on all men's equal, inalienable right to secure their life, liberty, and the pursuit of happiness by governments founded in their own consent. Hence, our Southern fore-fathers, shedding their blood, or ready to shed it, for this principle, yet proposing in equal good conscience to continue holding the American black man and mulatto and quadroon in slavery, had to anchor that conscience, their conduct, and their laws in the conviction that the man of African tincture was, not by his master's arbitrary assertion merely, but by nature and unalterably, an alien. If that hold should break, one single wave of irresistible inference would lift our whole Southern social fabric and dash it upon the rocks of Negro emancipation and enfranchisement. How was it made secure? Not by books, though they were written among us from every possible point of view, but, with the mass of our slaveowners, by the calm hypothesis of a positive, intuitive knowledge. To them the state-ment was an axiom. They abandoned the methods of moral and intellectual reasoning and fell back upon this assumption of a God-given instinct, nobler than reason, and which it was an insult to a free man to ask him to prove on logical grounds. . . .

. . . For more than a hundred years we had made these sentiments the absolute essentials to our self-respect. And yet if we clung to them, how could we meet the Freedman on equal terms in the political field? Even to lead would not compensate us; for the fundamental profession of American politics is that the leader is servant to his followers. It was too much. The ex-master and ex-slave—the quarterdeck and the forecastle, as it were—could not come together. But neither could the American mind tolerate a continuance of martial law. The agonies of Reconstruction followed.

The vote, after all, was a secondary point, and the robbery and bribery on one side, and whipping and killing on the other were but huge accidents of the situation. The two main questions were really these: on the Freed-man's side, how to establish republican state government under the same recognition of his rights that the rest of Christendom accorded him; and on the former master's side, how to get back to the old semblance of republican state government, and—allowing that the Freedman was *de facto* a voter—still to maintain a purely arbitrary superiority of all whites over all blacks, and a purely arbitrary equality of all blacks among them-selves as an alien, menial, and dangerous class. . . .

To be a free man is [the black man's] still distant goal. Twice he has been a Freedman. In the days of compulsory Reconstruction he was freed in the presence of his master by that master's victorious foe. In these days of voluntary Reconstruction he is virtually freed by the consent of his master, but the master retaining the exclusive right to define the bounds of his freedom. Many everywhere have taken up the idea that this state of affairs is the end to be desired and the end actually sought in Reconstruction as handed over to the states. I do not charge such folly to the best intelligence of any American community; but I cannot ignore my own knowledge that the average thought of some regions rises to no better idea of the issue. The belief is all too common that the nation, having aimed at a wrong result and missed, has left us of the Southern states to get now such other result as we think best. I say this belief is not universal. There are those among us who see that America has no room for a state of society which makes its lower classes harmless by abridging their liberties, or, as one of the favored class lately said to me, has "got 'em so they don't give no trouble." There is a growing number who see that the one thing we cannot afford to tolerate at large is a class of people less than citizens; and that every interest in the land demands that the Freedman be free to become in all things, as far as his own personal gifts will lift and sustain him, the same sort of American citizen he would be if, with the same intellectual and moral caliber, he were white.

Thus we reach the ultimate question of fact. Are the Freedman's liberties suffering any real abridgment? The answer is easy. The letter of the laws, with a few exceptions, recognizes him as entitled to every right of an American citizen; and to some it may seem unimportant that there is scarcely one public relation of life in the South where he is not arbitrarily and unlawfully compelled to hold toward the white man the attitude of an alien, a menial, and a probable reprobate, by reason of his race and color. One of the marvels of future history will be that it was counted a small matter, by a majority of our nation, for six millions of people within it, made by its own decree a component part of it, to be subjected to a system of oppression so rank that nothing could make it seem small except the fact that they had already been ground under it for a century and a half. . . .

. . . Nothing is easier to show than that these distinctions on the line of color are really made not from any necessity, but simply for their own sake—to preserve the old arbitrary supremacy of the master class over the menial without regard to the decency or indecency of appearance or manners in either the white individual or the colored.

See its everyday working. Any colored man gains unquestioned admission into innumerable places the moment he appears as the menial attendant of some white person, where he could not cross the threshold in his own right as well-dressed and well-behaved master of himself. The contrast is even greater in the case of colored women. There could not be a system which when put into practice would more offensively condemn itself. It does more: it actually creates the confusion it pretends to prevent. It blunts the sensibilities of the ruling class themselves. It waives all strict demand for painstaking in either manners or dress of either master or menial, and, for one result, makes the average Southern railway coach more uncomfortable than the average of railway coaches elsewhere. It prompts the average Southern white passenger to find less offense in the presence of a profane, boisterous, or unclean white person than in that of a quiet, well-behaved colored man or woman attempting to travel on an equal footing with him without a white master or mistress. The holders of the old sentiments hold the opposite choice in scorn. It is only when we go on to say that there are regions where the riotous expulsion of a decent and peaceable colored person is preferred to his inoffensive company that it may seem necessary to bring in evidence. And yet here again it is prima-facie evidence; for the following extract was printed in the Selma (Alabama) *Times* not six months ago, and not as a complaint, but as a boast:

"A few days since, a Negro minister, of this city, boarded the eastbound passenger train on the E. T., V. & G. Railway and took a seat in the coach occupied by white passengers. Some of the passengers complained to the conductor and brakemen, and expressed considerable dissatisfaction that they were forced to ride alongside of a Negro. The railroad officials informed the complainants that they were not authorized to force the colored passenger into the coach set apart for the Negroes, and they would lay themselves liable should they do so. The white passengers then took the matter in their own hands and ordered the ebony-hued minister to take a seat in the next coach. He positively refused to obey orders, whereupon the white men gave him a sound flogging and forced him to a seat among his own color and equals. We learned yesterday that the vanquished preacher was unable to fill his pulpit on account of the severe chastisement inflicted upon him. Now [says the delighted editor] the query that puzzles is, 'Who did the flogging?' "

And as good an answer as we can give is that likely enough they were some of the men for whom the whole South has come to a halt to let them get over the "feelings engendered by the war." Must such men, such acts, such sentiments stand alone to represent us of the South before an enlightened world? No. I say, as a citizen of an extreme Southern state, a native of Louisiana, an ex-Confederate soldier, and a lover of my home, my city, and my state, as well as of my country, that this is not the best sentiment in the South, nor the sentiment of her best intelligence; and that it would not ride up and down that beautiful land dominating and domineering were it not for its tremendous power as the *traditional* sentiment of a conservative people. But is not silent endurance criminal? I cannot but repeat my own words, spoken near the scene and about the time of this event. Speech may be silvern and silence golden; but if a lump of gold is only big enough, it can drag us to the bottom of the sea and hold us there while all the world sails over us.

The laws passed in the days of compulsory Reconstruction requiring "equal accommodations," etc., for colored and white persons were Freedmen's follies. On their face they defeated their ends; for even in theory they at once reduced to half all opportunity for those more reasonable and mutually agreeable self-assortments which public assemblages and groups of passengers find it best to make in all other enlightened countries, making them on the score of conduct, dress, and price. They also led the whites to overlook what they would have seen instantly had these invidious distinctions been made against themselves: that their offense does not vanish at the guarantee against the loss of physical comforts. But we made, and are still making, a mistake beyond even this. For years many of us have carelessly taken for granted that these laws were being carried out in some shape that removed all just ground of complaint. It is common to say, "We allow the man of color to go and come at will, only let him sit apart in a place marked off for him." But marked off how? So as to mark him instantly as a menial. Not by railings and partitions merely, which, raised against any other class in the United States with the same invidious intent, would be kicked down as fast as put up, but by giving him besides, in every instance and without recourse, the most uncomfortable, uncleanest, and unsafest place; and the unsafety, uncleanness, and discomfort of most of these places are a shame to any community pretending to practice public justice. If any one can think the Freedman does not feel the indignities thus heaped upon him, let him take up any paper printed for colored men's patronage, or ask any colored man of known courageous utterance. Hear them:

"We ask not Congress, nor the Legislature, nor any other power, to remedy these evils, but we ask the people among whom we live. Those who *can* remedy them if they *will*. Those who have a high sense of honor and a deep moral feeling. Those who have one vestige of human sympathy left. . . . Those are the ones we ask to protect us in our weakness and ill-treatments. . . . As soon as the colored man is treated by the white man as a *man*, that harmony and pleasant feeling which should characterize all races which dwell together shall be the bond of peace between them."

Surely their evidence is good enough to prove their own feelings. We need not lean upon it here for anything else. I shall not bring forward a single statement of fact from them or any of their white friends who, as teachers and missionaries, share many of their humiliations, though my desk is covered with them. But I beg to make the same citation from my own experience that I made last June [1884] in the far South. It was this: One hot night in September of last year [1883] I was traveling by rail in the state of Alabama. At rather late bedtime there came aboard the train a young mother and her little daughter of three or four years. They were neatly and tastefully dressed in cool, fresh muslins, and as the train went on its way they sat together very still and quiet. At the next station there came aboard a most melancholy and revolting company. In filthy rags, with vile odors and the clanking of shackles and chains, nine penitentiary convicts chained to one chain, and ten more chained to another, dragged laboriously into the compartment of the car where in one corner sat this mother and child, and packed it full, and the train moved on. The keeper of the convicts told me he should take them in that car two hundred miles that night. They were going to the mines. My seat was not in that car, and I staid in it but a moment. It stank insufferably. I returned to my own place in the coach behind, where there was, and had all the time been, plenty of room. But the mother and child sat on in silence in that foul hole, the conductor having distinctly refused them admission elsewhere because they were of African blood, and not because the mother was, but because she was *not,* engaged at the moment in menial service. Had the child been white, and the mother not its natural but its hired guardian, she could have sat anywhere in the train, and no one would have ventured to object, even had she been as black as the mouth of the coalpit to which her loathsome fellow passengers were being carried in chains. . . .

. . . I must repeat my conviction that if the unconscious habit of oppression were not already there, a scheme so gross, irrational, unjust, and inefficient as our present caste distinctions could not find place among a people so generally intelligent and high-minded.

Booker T. Washington's Atlanta Exposition Address, 1895

Mr. President and Gentlemen of the Board of Directors and Citizens: One-third of the population of the South is of the Negro race. No enterprise seeking the material, civil, or moral welfare of this section can disregard this element of our population and reach the highest success. I but convey to you, Mr. President and Directors, the sentiment of the masses of my race when I say that in no way have the value and manhood of the American Negro been more fittingly and generously recognized than by the managers of this magnificent Exposition at every stage of its progress. It is a recognition that will do more to cement the friendship of the two races than any occurrence since the dawn of our freedom.

Not only this, but the opportunity here afforded will awaken among us a new era of industrial progress. Ignorant and inexperienced, it is not strange that in the first years of our new life we began at the top instead of at the bottom; that a seat in Congress or the state legislature was more sought than real estate or industrial skill; that the political convention or stump speaking had more attractions than starting a dairy farm or truck garden.

A ship lost at sea for many days suddenly sighted a friendly vessel. From the mast of the unfortunate vessel was seen a signal, "Water, water; we die of thirst!" The answer from the friendly vessel at once came back, "Cast down your bucket where you are." A second time the signal, "Water, water; send us water!" ran up from the distressed vessel, and was answered, "Cast down your bucket where you are." And a third and fourth signal for water was answered, "Cast down your bucket where you are." The Captain of the distressed vessel, at last heeding the injunction, cast down his bucket, and it came up full of fresh, sparkling water from the mouth of the Amazon River. To those of my race who depend on bettering their condition in a foreign land or who underestimate the importance of cultivating friendly relations with the Southern white man, who is their nextdoor neighbor, I would say: "Cast down your bucket where you are"—cast it down in making friends in every manly way of the people of all races by whom we are surrounded.

Cast it down in agriculture, mechanics, in commerce, in domestic service, and in the professions. And in this connection it is well to bear in mind that whatever other sins the South may be called to bear, when it comes to business, pure and simple, it is in the South that the Negro is given a man's chance in the commercial world, and in nothing is this exposition more eloquent than in emphasizing this chance. Our greatest danger is that in the great leap from slavery to freedom we may overlook the fact that the masses of us are to live by the productions of our hands, and fail to keep in mind that we shall prosper in proportion as we learn to dignify and glorify comman labor and put brains and skill into the common occupations of life; shall prosper in proportion as we learn to draw the line between the superficial and the substantial, the ornamental gewgaws of life and the useful. No race can prosper till it learns that there is as much dignity in tilling a field as in writing a poem. It is at the bottom of life we must begin, and not at the top. Nor should we permit our grievances to overshadow our opportunities.

To those of the white race who look to the incoming of those of foreign birth and strange tongue and habits for the prosperity of the South, were I permitted I would repeat what I say to my own race, "Cast down your bucket where you are." Cast it down among the 8 millions of Negroes whose habits you know, whose fidelity and love you have tested in days when to have proved treacherous meant the ruin of your firesides. Cast down your bucket among these people who have, without strikes and labor wars, tilled your fields, cleared your forests, builded your railroads and cities, and brought forth treasures from the bowels of the earth, and helped make possible this magnificent representation of the progress of the South. Casting down your bucket among my people, helping and encouraging them as you are doing on these grounds, and to education of head, hand, and heart, you will find that they will buy your surplus land, make blossom the waste places in your fields, and run your factories. While doing this, you can be sure in the future, as in the past, that you and your families will be surrounded by the most patient, faithful, law-abiding, and unresentful people that the world has seen. As we have proved our loyalty to you in the past, in nursing your children, watching by the sickbed of your mothers and fathers, and often following them with tear-dimmed eyes to their graves, so in the future, in our humble way, we shall stand by you with a devotion that no foreigner can approach, ready to lay down our lives, if need be, in defense of yours, interlacing our industrial, commercial, civil, and re-ligious life with yours in a way that shall make the interests of both races one. In all things that are purely social we can be as separate as the fingers, yet one as the hand in all things essential to mutual progress.

There is no defense or security for any of us except in the highest intelligence and development of all. If anywhere there are efforts tending to curtail the fullest growth of the Negro, let these efforts be turned into stimulating, encouraging, and making him the most useful and intelligent citizen. Effort or means so invested will pay a thousand percent interest. These efforts will be twice blessed—"blessing him that gives and him that takes."

There is no escape through law of man or God from the inevitable:

> The laws of changeless justice bind
> Oppressor with oppressed;
> And close as sin and suffering joined
> We march to fate abreast.

Nearly 16 millions of hands will aid you in pulling the load upward, or they will pull against you the load downward. We shall constitute one-third and more of the ignorance and crime of the South, or one-third its intelligence and progress; we shall contribute one-third to the business and industrial prosperity of the South, or we shall prove a veritable body of death, stagnating, depressing, retarding every effort to advance the body politic.

Gentlemen of the Exposition, as we present to you our humble effort at an exhibition of our progress, you must not expect overmuch. Starting thirty years ago with ownership here and there in a few quilts and pumpkins and chickens (gathered from miscellaneous sources), remember the path that has led from these to the inventions and production of agricultural implements, buggies, steam engines, newspapers, books, statuary, carving, paintings, the management of drugstores and banks, has not been trodden without contact with thorns and thistles. While we take pride in what we exhibit as a result of our independent efforts, we do not for a moment forget that our part in this exhibition would fall far short of your expectations but for the constant help that has come to our educational life, not only from the Southern states, but especially from Northern philanthropists, who have made their gifts a constant stream of blessing and encouragement.

The wisest among my race understand that the agitation of questions of social equality is the extremest folly, and that progress in the enjoyment of all the privileges that will come to us must be the result of severe and constant struggle rather than of artificial forcing. No race that has anything to contribute to the markets of the world is long in any degree ostracized. It is important and right that all privileges of the law be ours, but it is vastly more important that we be prepared for the exercises of these privileges. The opportunity to earn a dollar in a factory just now is worth infinitely more than the opportunity to spend a dollar in an opera house.

In conclusion, may I repeat that nothing in thirty years has given us more hope and encouragement, and drawn us so near to you of the white race, as this opportunity offered by the exposition; and here bending, as it were, over the altar that represents the results of the struggles of your race and mine, both starting practically empty-handed three decades ago, I pledge that in your effort to work out the great and intricate problem which God has laid at the doors of the South, you shall have at all times the patient, sympathetic help of my race; only let this be constantly in mind, that, while from representations in these buildings of the product of field, of forest, of mine, of factory, letters, and art, much good will come, yet far above and beyond material benefits will be that higher good, that, let us pray God, will come, in a blotting out of sectional differences and racial animosities and suspicions, in a determination to administer absolute justice, in a willing obedience among all classes to the mandates of law. This, this, coupled with our material prosperity, will bring into our beloved South a new heaven and a new earth.

Plessy v. *Ferguson,* 1896

BROWN, J[ustice]   This case turns upon the constitutionality of an act of the general assembly of the state of Louisiana, passed in 1890, providing for separate railway carriages for the white and colored races. . . .

The constitutionality of this act is attacked upon the ground that it conflicts both with the 13th Amendment of the Constitution, abolishing slavery, and the 14th Amendment, which prohibits certain restrictive legislation on the part of the states.

1. That it does not conflict with the 13th Amendment, which abolished slavery and involuntary servitude, except as a punishment for crime, is too clear for argument. . . .

A statute which implies merely a legal distinction between the white and colored races—a distinction which is founded in the color of the two races, and which must always exist so long as white men are distinguished from the other race by color—has no tendency to destroy the legal equality of the two races, or re-establish a state of involuntary servitude. Indeed, we do not understand that the 13th Amendment is strenuously relied upon by the plaintiff in error in this connection. . . .

The object of the amendment was undoubtedly to enforce the absolute equality of the two races before the law, but in the nature of things it could not have been intended to abolish distinctions based upon color, or to enforce social, as distinguished from political, equality, or a commingling of the two races upon terms unsatisfactory to either. Laws permitting, and even requiring their separation in places where they are liable to be brought into contact do not necessarily imply the inferiority of either race to the other, and have been generally, if not universally, recognized as within the competency of the state legislatures in the exercise of their police power. The most common instance of this is connected with the establishment of separate schools for white and colored children, which have been held to be a valid exercise of the legislative power even by courts of states where the political rights of the colored race have been longest and most earnestly enforced. . . .

It is claimed by the plaintiff in error that, in any mixed community, the reputation of belonging to the dominant race, in this instance the white race is *property,* in the same sense that a right of action, or of inheritance, is property. Conceding this to be so, for the purposes of this case, we are unable to see how this statute deprives him of, or in any way affects his right to, such property. If he be a white man and assigned to a colored coach, he may have his action for damages against the company for being deprived of his so-called property. Upon the other hand, if he be a colored man and be so assigned, he has been deprived of no property, since he is not lawfully entitled to the reputation of being a white man. . . .

So far, then, as a conflict with the 14th Amendment is concerned, the case reduces itself to the question whether the statute of Louisiana is a reasonable regulation, and with respect to this there must necessarily be a large discretion on the part of the legislature. In determining the question of reasonableness it is at liberty to act with reference to the established usages, customs, and traditions of the people, and with a view to the promotion of their comfort, and the preservation of the public peace and good order. Gauged by this standard, we cannot say that a law which authorizes or even requires the separation of the two races in public conveyances is unreasonable or more obnoxious to the 14th Amendment than the acts of Congress requiring separate schools for colored children in the District of Columbia, the constitutionality of which does not seem to have been questioned, or the corresponding acts of state legislatures.

We consider the underlying fallacy of the plaintiff's argument to consist in the assumption that the enforced separation of the two races stamps the colored race with a badge of inferiority. If this be so, it is not by reason of anything found in the act, but solely because the colored race chooses to put that construction upon it. The argument necessarily assumes that if, as has been more than once the case, and is not unlikely to be so again, the colored race should become the dominant power in the state legislature, and should enact a law in precisely similar terms, it would thereby relegate the white race to an inferior position. We imagine that the white race, at least, would not acquiesce in this assumption. The argument also assumes that social prejudice may be overcome by legislation, and that equal rights cannot be secured to the Negro except by an enforced commingling of the two races. We cannot accept this proposition. If the two races are to meet on terms of social equality, it must be the result of natural affinities, a mutual appreciation of each other's merits and a voluntary consent of individuals. . . . Legislation is powerless to eradicate racial instincts or to abolish distinctions based upon physical differences, and the attempt to do so can only result in accentuating the difficulties of the present situation. If the civil and political right of both races be equal, one cannot be inferior to the other civilly or politically. If one race be inferior to the other socially, the Constitution of the United States cannot put them upon the same plane.

Justice HARLAN, dissenting. . . . In respect of civil rights, common to all citizens, the Constitution of the United States does not, I think, permit any public authority to know the race of those entitled to be protected in the enjoyment of such rights. Every true man has pride of race, and under appropriate circumstances, when the rights of others, his equals before the law, are not to be affected, it is his privilege to express such pride and to take such action based upon it as to him seems proper. But I deny that any legislative body or judicial tribunal may have regard to the race of citizens when the civil rights of those citizens are involved. Indeed such legislation as that here in question is inconsistent, not only with that equality of rights which pertains to citizenship, national and state, but with the personal liberty enjoyed by every one within the United States. . . .

In my opinion, the judgment this day rendered will, in time, prove to be quite as pernicious as the decision made by this tribunal in the Dred Scott Case. It was adjudged in that case that the descendants of Africans who were imported into this country and sold as slaves were not included nor intended to be included under the word "citizens" in the Constitution, and could not claim any of the rights and privileges which that instrument provided for and secured to citizens of the United States; that at the time of the adoption of the Constitution they were "considered as a subordinate and inferior class of beings, who had been subjugated by the dominant race, and, whether emancipated or not, yet remained subject to their authority, and had no rights or privileges but such as those who held the power and the government might choose to grant them." The recent amendments of the Constitution, it was supposed, had eradicated these principles from our institutions. But it seems that we have yet, in some of the states, a dominant race, a superior class of citizens, which assumes to regulate the enjoyment of civil rights, common to all citizens, upon the basis of race. The present decision, it may well be apprehended, will not only stimulate aggressions, more or less brutal and irritating, upon the admitted rights of colored citizens, but will encourage the belief that it is possible, by means of state enactments, to defeat the beneficent purposes which the people of the United States had in view when they adopted the recent amendments of the Constitution, by one of which the blacks of this country were made citizens of the United States and of the states in which they respectively reside and whose privileges and immunities, as citizens, the states are forbidden to abridge. Sixty millions of whites are in no danger from the presence here of eight millions of blacks. The destinies of the two races in this country are indissolubly linked together, and the interests of both require that the common government of all shall not permit the seeds of race hate to be planted under the sanction of law. What can more certainly arouse race hate, what more certainly create and perpetuate a feeling of distrust between these races, than state enactments which in fact proceed on the ground that colored citizens are so inferior and degraded that they cannot be allowed to sit in public coaches occupied by white citizens? That, as all will admit, is the real meaning of such legislation as was enacted in Louisiana. . . .

If evils will result from the commingling of the two races upon public highways established for the benefit of all, they will be infinitely less than those that will surely come from state legislation regulating the enjoyment of civil rights upon the basis of race. We boast of the freedom enjoyed by our people above all other peoples. But it is difficult to reconcile that boast with a state of the law which, practically, puts the brand of servitude and degradation upon a large class of our fellow citizens, our equals before the law. The thin disguise of "equal" accommodations for passengers in railroad coaches will not mislead anyone, or atone for the wrong this day done. . . .

I am of opinion that the statute of Louisiana is inconsistent with the personal liberty of citizens, white and black, in that state, and hostile to both the spirit and letter of the Constitution of the United States. If laws of like character should be enacted in the several states of the Union, the effect would be in the highest degree mischievous. Slavery as an institution tolerated by law would, it is true, have disappeared from our country, but there would remain a power in the states, by sinister legislation, to interfere with the full enjoyment of the blessings of freedom; to regulate civil rights, common to all citizens, upon the basis of race; and to place in a condition of legal inferiority a large body of American citizens, now constituting a part of the political community, called the people of the United States, for whom and by whom, through representatives, our government is administered. Such a system is inconsistent with the guarantee given by the Constitution to each state of a republican form of government, and may be stricken down by Congressional action, or by the courts in the discharge of their solemn duty to maintain the supreme law of the land, anything in the Constitution or laws of any state to the contrary notwithstanding.

For the reasons stated, I am constrained to withhold my assent from the opinion and judgment of the majority.

Literacy Test and Poll Tax, 1899

(Sec. 4.) Every person presenting himself for registration shall be able to read and write any section of the constitution in the English language and before he shall be entitled to vote he shall have paid on or before the first day of March of the year in which he proposes to vote his poll tax as prescribed by law for the previous year. Poll taxes shall be a lien only on assessed property and no process shall issue to enforce the collection of the same except against assessed property.

(Sec. 5.) No male person who was on January one, eighteen hundred and sixty-seven, or at any time prior thereto entitled to vote under the laws of any state in the United States wherein he then resided, and no lineal descendant of any such person, shall be denied the right to register and vote at any election in this state by reason of his failure to possess the educational qualification prescribed in section four of this article: *Provided,* he shall have registered in accordance with the terms of this section prior to December one, nineteen hundred and eight. The general assembly shall provide for a permanent record of all persons who register under this section on or before November first, nineteen hundred and eight: and all such persons shall be entitled to register and vote in all elections by the people in this state unless disqualified under section two of this article: *Provided,* such persons shall have paid their poll tax as requ[i]red by law.

Public Laws of North Carolina, 1899, *chapter 218.*

Black Leaders Fight Disfranchisement, 1895

[*W. J. Whipper:*] I am not here as a suppliant, nor do I put myself and my race in the attitude of a begger. I am here as a man and a representative, not representing simply the negro, but representing the people. The fact that I am a negro has nothing to do with my status here. And just here I will digress to speak of the flippant way the term "nigger" has been used in this convention. I am a negro. There are five others here that are negroes. We are proud of it, and we hope to be able to do something in and out of this convention that the negroes will be proud of and white men compelled to recognize. . . .

Is the negro such a bad citizen that you should violate all law, human and divine, and chain him down? You have the wealth and intelligence. Now you say you musn't let the negro vote because he will vote against you. The negro is an imitative being. This has made him valuable and a necessity. What the negro asks now is that they be treated as men. You say that you must rule this country; that it's white man's country. We are here to ask you to stay your hand and do justice.

When the gentleman from Barnwell [County] comes here and labors long to show that under the 15th amendment that the negroes were not entitled to hold office, I say, wasn't that a small effort. If the negro was not fit, how could he hold office?

Another gentleman—even here in the evening of the nineteenth century—comes and says the Bible justified slavery. He says he would like to have 100 slaves now. If he had them he would be worse off than any one of you. He would be taught that this business was unprofitable and troublesome.

We have only six of us here of the inferior race, and you have 154. Men upon this floor are clamoring for white supremacy, come here and assume dignity and call us niggers with the flippancy of barroom attendants. The trouble is "negro rule" and "white supremacy." Was there ever any such thing as negro rule in South Carolina? It was the rule of white men, supported by the negroes. Ain't there more negroes than white men on your farms? Yet, don't your wife rule? In the convention of 1868 there were less than a dozen negroes and less than a dozen white men engaged in the work done there. I am proud of the work done in that convention. The way it has stood the test has shown that there was nothing dangerous in it. They had simply taken the best parts of other Constitutions. Most of the men were there to vote as they were told.

This convention, 'tis said, is to prevent negro rule and establish white supremacy. Again, as a matter of fact, there never was any negro rule in South Carolina. When was there ever a time when we had a negro governor? We never had a majority of negro officers at any time in this State. Indeed, there were only four colored men who ever held any of the State offices, and that only for a single term each. There never was a county in this State controlled by colored officers. In fact all of the important officers, clerk of the court, sheriff, treasurer, auditors throughout the whole State, with less than half a dozen exceptions, have been filled by white men. Does this look like negro rule? Even in the darkest hours of reconstruction, when the bad legislation led to the fall of the Republican party, white men held the offices; white men did the robberies; many of them Democrats of the deepest die, who reaped the rewards for their purchase of negroes. There never was a negro lobbyist parading the corridors of this house. They were white men. Call them carpetbaggers, scalawags, renegades, what you will, they were white men, and are responsible for the bad legislation. Charge not this up to the account of the negro. There was never a time in even old Beaufort county, where there were not more white officers than negroes. Is that negro rule? Beaufort never had a colored sheriff during the reconstruction period. Talk about negro rule. The negro could have ruled, but he has shown discretion. There was never negro rule in a single county or a single town in this State. He challenged the body to say if there was a town with a negro intendant and a majority of the town council. If I am wrong correct me. We could have elected such in my town of Beaufort. We are 20 to 1 there. Does this look like negro rule? Does that look like we want to trample on the rights of the white man?

Do away with this negro rule howl. When the negroes had a majority in the lower house, the only place where they ever had a majority, white men governed them. Things were done there that were against his protest— white men ruled. Bonds were flooded all over the State. Corruption was rife. I proclaimed it on the floor. The leading Democratic newspaper in Charleston was even subsidized. He thought a negro brought the fact out in full. That is a matter of record. I warned them to stop. But who were the lobbyists that carried it all through? They were all white men. Some of them South Carolinians, some Democrats from New York. They must take the consequences. . . .

. . . We are going to make this fight all along the line. I know that nothing I can say will change a single vote. I do say that sooner or later, God being always right, right will eventually prevail. We want you to understand that we have rights and they must sooner or later be recognized. We are testing the very ground work of this whole matter in the United States supreme court, and we will push it to the bitter end. We may go on to congress. We want this thing to pass in the very worst form it can pass.

Where township governments exist we then know every ra[s]cal in the community. We are now going on with our fight and try to sap the very foundation of this convention. It is a duty I owe to myself and this convention that I tell you this—not in a threatening spirit, however. We go to you now and ask for justice. God is just and justice cannot sleep forever. I have spoken to you in the kindest of spirit. Whatever concerns mankind, this convention, South Carolina, all these concerns me. Your people to-day—the negroes are yours—are deeply concerned.

If you vote down my amendment, then fix the matter in justice to the negro and to yourselves. Remember ever that the oppressor meets a just fate. Remember, too, that

> "The laws of changeless justice bind
> Oppressor with oppressed
> And close as sin and suffering joined
> We march to fate abreast."

General Smalls' Speech

Gen. Robert Smalls' who is known everywhere as South Carolina's "gullah statesman," then took the floor. He said: . . .

I was born and raised in South Carolina, and today I live on the very spot on which I was born, and I expect to remain here as long as the great God allows me to live, and I will ask no one else to let me remain. I love the State as much as any member of this convention, because it is the garden spot of the south.

Mr. President, this convention has been called for no other purpose than the disfranchisement of the negro. Be careful, and bear in mind that the elections which are to take place early next month in very many of the States are watching the action of this convention, especially on the suffrage question. Remember that the negro was not brought here of his own accord. I found my reference to a history in the congressional library in Washington . . . that he says that in 1619, in the month of June, a Dutch man-of-war landed at Jamestown, Va., with 15 sons of Africa aboard, at the time Miles Kendall was deputy governor of Virginia. He refused to allow the vessel to be anchored in any of her harbors. But he found out after his order had been sent out that the vessel was without provisions, and the crew was in a starving condition. He countermanded his order, and supplied the vessel with the needed provisions in exchange for 14 negroes. It was then that the seed of slavery was planted in the land. So you see we did not come here of our own accord; we were brought here in a Dutch vessel, and we have been here ever since. The Dutch are here, and are now paying a very large tax, and are controlling the business of Charleston today. They are not to blame, and are not being blamed.

We served our masters faithfully, and willingly, and as we were made to do for 244 years. In the last war you left them home. You went to the war, fought, and come back home, shattered to pieces, worn out, one-legged, and found your wife and family being properly cared for by the negroes you left behind. Why should you now seek to disfranchise a race that has been so true to you? . . .

Since reconstruction times 53,000 negroes have been killed in the south, and not more than three white men have been convicted and hung for these crimes. I want you to be mindful of the fact that the good people of the north are watching this convention upon this subject. I hope you will make a Constitution that will stand the test. I hope that we may be able to say when our work is done that we have made as good a Constitution as the one we are doing away with.

The negroes are paying taxes in the south on $263,000,000 worth of property. In South Carolina, according to the census, the negroes pay tax on $12,500,000 worth of property. That was in 1890. You voted down without discussion, merely by a vote to lay on the table, a proposition for a simple property and educational qualification. What do you want? You tried the infamous eight-box [required poorly educated voters to place ballots correctly in eight separate ballot boxes, one for each office] and registration laws until they were worn to such a thinness that they could stand neither the test of the law nor of public opinion. In behalf of the 600,000 negroes in the State and the 132,000 negro voters all that I demand is that a fair and honest election law be passed. We care not what the qualifications imposed are, all that we ask is that they be fair and honest, and honorable, and with these provisos we will stand or fall by it. You have 102,000 white men over 21 years of age, 13,000 of these cannot read nor write. You dare not disfranchise them, and you know that the man who proposes it will never be elected to another office in the State of South Carolina. But whatever Mr. Tillman can do, he can make nothing worse than the infamous eight-box law, and I have no praise for the Conservatives, for they gave the people that law. Fifty-eight thousand negroes cannot read nor write. This leaves a majority of 14,000 white men who can read and write over the same class of negroes in this State. We are willing to accept a scheme that provides that no man who cannot read nor write can vote, if you dare pass it. How can you expect an ordinary man to "understand and explain" any section of the Constitution, to correspond to the interpretation put upon it by the manager of election, when by a very recent decision of the supreme court, composed of the most learned men in the State, two of them put one construction upon a section, and the other justice put an entirely different construction upon it. To embody such a provision in the election law would be to mean that every white man would interpret it aright and every negro would interpret it wrong. I appeal to the gentleman from Edgefield to realize that he is not making a law for one set of men. Some morning you may wake up to find that the bone and sinew of your country is gone. The negro is needed in the cotton fields and in the low country rice fields, and if you impose too hard conditions upon the negro in this State there will be nothing else for him to do but to leave. What then will you do about your phosphate works? No one but a negro can work them; the mines that pay the interest on your State debt. I tell you the negro is the bone and sinew of your country and you cannot do without him. I do not believe you want to get rid of the negro, else why did you impose a high tax on immigration agents who might come here to get him to leave?

Now, Mr. President we should not talk one thing and mean another. We should not deceive ourselves. Let us make a Constitution that is fair, honest and just. Let us make a Constitution for all the people, one we will be proud of and our children will receive with delight.

Pauli Murray Recalls Segregation, 1956

Each morning I passed white children as poor as I going in the opposite direction on their way to school. We never had fights; I don't recall their ever having called me a single insulting name. It was worse than that. They passed me as if I weren't there! They looked through me and beyond me with unseeing eyes. Their school was a beautiful red-and-white brick building on a wide paved street. Its lawn was large and green and watered every day and flower beds were everywhere. Their playground, a wonderland of iron swings, sand slides, seesaws, crossbars and a basketball court, was barred from us by a strong eight-foot-high fence topped by barbed wire. We could only press our noses against the wire and watch them playing on the other side.

I went to West End where Aunt Pauline taught, on Ferrell Street, a dirt road which began at a lumberyard and ended in a dump. On one side of this road were long low warehouses where huge barrels of tobacco shavings and tobacco dust were stored. All day long our nostrils sucked in the brown silt like fine snuff in the air. West End looked more like a warehouse than a school. It was a dilapidated, rickety, two-story wooden building which creaked and swayed in the wind as if it might collapse. Outside it was scarred with peeling paint from many winters of rain and snow. Inside the floors were bare and splintery, the plumbing was leaky, the drinking fountains broken and the toilets in the basement smelly and constantly out of order. We'd have to wade through pools of foul water to get to them. At recess we herded into a yard of cracked clay, barren of tree or bush, and played what games we could improvise like hopscotch or springboard, which we contrived by pulling rotted palings off the wooden fence and placing them on brickbats.

It was never the hardship which hurt so much as the *contrast* between what we had and what the white children had. We got the greasy, torn, dog-eared books; they got the new ones. They had field day in the city park; we had it on a furrowed stubbly hillside. They got wide mention in the newspaper; we got a paragraph at the bottom. The entire city officialdom from the mayor down turned out to review their pageantry; we got a solitary official.

Our seedy run-down school told us that if we had any place at all in the scheme of things it was a separate place, marked off, proscribed and unwanted by the white people. We were bottled up and labeled and set aside—sent to the Jim Crow car, the back of the bus, the side door of the theater, the side window of a restaurant. We came to know that whatever we had was always inferior. We came to understand that no matter how neat and clean, how law abiding, submissive and polite, how studious in school, how churchgoing and moral, how scrupulous in paying our bills and taxes we were, it made no essential difference in our place.

It seemed as if there were only two kinds of people in the world—

Excerpts from *Proud Shoes* by Pauli Murray. Copyright © 1956, 1978 by Pauli Murray. Reprinted by permission of Harper & Row Publishers, Inc.

They and *We—White* and *Colored*. The world revolved on color and variations in color. It pervaded the air I breathed. I learned it in hundreds of ways. I picked it up from grown folks around me. I heard it in the house, on the playground, in the streets, everywhere. The tide of color beat upon me ceaselessly, relentlessly.

Always the same tune, played like a broken record, robbing one of personal identity. Always the shifting sands of color so that there was no solid ground under one's feet. It was color, color, color all the time, color, features and hair. Folks were never just folks. They were white folks! Black folks! Poor white crackers! No-count niggers! Red necks! Darkies! Peckerwoods! Coons!

Two shades lighter! Two shades darker! Dead white! Coal black! High yaller! Mariny! Good hair! Bad hair! Stringy hair! Nappy hair! Thin lips! Thick lips! Red lips! Liver lips! Blue veined! Blue gummed! Straight nosed! Flat nosed!

Brush your hair, child, don't let it get kinky! Cold-cream your face, child, don't let it get sunburned! Don't suck your lips, child, you'll make them too niggerish! Black is evil, don't mix with mean niggers! Black is honest, you half-white bastard. I always said a little black and a little white sure do make a pretty sight! He's black as sin and evil in the bargain. The blacker the berry, the sweeter the juice!

To hear people talk, color, features and hair were the most important things to know about a person, a yardstick by which everyone measured everybody else. From the looks of my family I could never tell where white folks left off and colored folks began, but it made little difference as far as I was concerned. In a world of black-white opposites, I had no place. Being neither very dark nor very fair, I was a nobody without identity. I was too dark at home and too light at school. The pride I learned at home was almost canceled out by the cloak of shame I wore at school, especially when my schoolmates got angry and yelled at me, "You half-white bastard! You dirty-faced Jew baby! Black is honest! Yaller is dishonest!"

I was a minority within a minority, shoved down by inexorable pressures from without, thrust up by intolerable frustrations from within. Black ancestry brought the shame of slavery; white ancestry was condemned as bastardy and brought another kind of shame. Since there was no middle ground between these two extremes, I sought neutral territory in my American Indian ancestry, a group nonexistent in my community and which could not challenge my asserted kinship. I fell back on Great-Grandmother Harriet and her Cherokee blood. That she too had been a slave subject to all the evils of slavery was submerged in the more significant fact that the American Indians at least had preferred annihilation to enslavement. This seemed to me a worthier trait than acceptance of bondage as the price of survival.

It is little wonder, then, perhaps, that I was strongly anti-American at six, that I hated George Washington, mumbled the oath of allegiance to the American flag which we children were taught in the second grade and was reluctant to stand up when we sang "The Star-Spangled Banner." I was unmoved by the story of Washington's crossing the Delaware, nor was

I inspired by his truthfulness and valor. My thin knowledge of history told me that the George Washingtons and their kind had stolen the country from the American Indians, and I could lodge all my protests against this unforgivable piece of thievery.

Every February the lower grades buzzed with activities commemorating the birthdays of George Washington and Abraham Lincoln. I dutifully cut out log cabins to symbolize Lincoln's birth but I invariably messed up the hatchets and bunches of cherries. My folks would have been horrified at my private seditious thoughts if they had known of them. Grandfather and my aunts considered themselves part of the noblest of professions—schoolteaching—a profession allied with feelings of deepest patriotism. Aunt Pauline's classroom walls were full of American flags, pictures of American Presidents, and a print of the famous Spirit of '76. I regularly attended church every Sunday where prayers were offered for the "President of the United States and all others in civil authority." Yet, for all their patriotism, the somber fact remained that until the three Negro schools of Durham in my childhood—West End, East End and Whitted—all burned to the ground mysteriously one after the other, the colored children got no new buildings.

⚓ *E S S A Y S*

C. Vann Woodward, professor of history emeritus from Yale University, wrote the best-known study of segregation. The excerpts below from *The Strange Career of Jim Crow* describe "cross currents and contradictions" that prevailed in race relations before the 1890s and argue that a marked change occurred in that decade. In the second essay Howard Rabinowitz, professor of history at the University of New Mexico, who has carefully studied the urban South, deepens Woodward's description of the rise of segregation in housing, public accommodations, welfare services, and education. Rabinowitz notes two ironies: that in governmentally provided services, segregated facilities could represent a gain rather than a loss for black southerners and that black attitudes helped bring about the shift to segregation.

Historian J. Morgan Kousser of the California Institute of Technology presents in the final essay a different assessment of the motives of those who legislated segregation and disfranchisement. Kousser argues that disfranchisement not only was a marvelously effective tool for Democrats to defeat the Populist-Republican coalition coming to power but also proved a highly effective means of ensuring power in the future.

Forgotten Alternatives in Race Relations

C. VANN WOODWARD

Regardless of the law, the discriminatory practice of denying Negroes the use of first-class accommodations nevertheless continued on many railroads throughout Reconstruction and beyond. Not until the arrival of the full Jim

Crow system much later, however, was the separation of the races required in second-class coaches or universal in first-class cars.

Other aspects of segregation appeared early and widely and were sanctioned by Reconstruction authorities. The most conspicuous of these was the segregation of the public schools. While the law might not provide for it and individuals might deplore it, segregation of the schools nevertheless took place promptly and prevailed continuously. There were very few exceptions. The only notable one was the public schools of New Orleans, which were thoroughly and successfully integrated until 1877. Attempts elsewhere were probably restrained by the knowledge that the whites would withdraw if integration were attempted. This in fact did occur at times when desegregation of colleges and other institutions was attempted. This situation prevailed generally throughout major government-supported services and facilities. The law sometimes provided for separate facilities for the races during Reconstruction. But even when this was not the case, and when both races were housed in the same jails, hospitals, or asylums, they were usually quartered in separate cells, floors, or wings. All these practices, legal or extra-legal, had the consent or at least the acquiescence of the Reconstruction governments.

In view of the degree of racial separation developed during Reconstruction, some historians have concluded that the full-blown Jim Crow system sprang up immediately after the end of slavery to take the place of the Peculiar Institution [slavery]. In a full and interesting study of the Negro in South Carolina entitled *After Slavery*, Joel Williamson finds that while "slavery necessitated a constant, physical intimacy," emancipation precipitated an immediate and revolutionary separation of races. "Well before the end of Reconstruction," he writes, "separation had crystalized into a comprehensive pattern which, in its essence, remained unaltered until the middle of the twentieth century."

The experience of South Carolina may have been exceptional in some respects. But in most parts of the South, including South Carolina, race relations during Reconstruction could not be said to have crystalized or stabilized nor to have become what they later became. There were too many cross currents and contradictions, revolutionary innovations and violent reactions. Racial relations of the old-regime pattern often persisted stubbornly into the new order and met head-on with interracial encounters of an entirely new and sometimes equalitarian type. Freedman and white man might turn from a back-door encounter of the traditional sort to a strained man-to-man contact of the awkward new type within the same day. Black faces continued to appear at the back door, but they also began to appear in wholly unprecedented and unexpected places—in the jury box and on the judge's bench, in council chamber and legislative hall, at the polls and the market place. Neither of these contrasting types of contact, the old or the new, was stable or destined to endure for very long, but for a time old and new rubbed shoulders—and so did black and white—in a manner that differed significantly from Jim Crow of the future or slavery of the past.

What happened in North Carolina was a revelation to conservative whites. "It is amazing," wrote Kemp Battle of Raleigh, "how quietly our people take negro juries, or rather negroes on juries." Randolph Shotwell of Rutherfordton was dismayed on seeing "long processions of countrymen entering the village by the various roads mounted and afoot, whites and blacks marching together, and in frequent instances arm-in-arm, a sight to disgust even a decent negro." It was disturbing even to native white radicals, as one of them admitted in the Raleigh *Standard*, to find at times "the two races now eat together at the same table, sit together in the same room, work together, visit and hold debating societies together." It is not that such occurrences were typical or very common, but that they could happen at all that was important.

Southern Negroes responded to news of the Reconstruction Act of March 1867 with numerous demonstrations against incipient Jim Crowism. In New Orleans they demonstrated so vigorously and persistently against the Jim Crow "Star Cars" established in 1864 that General Phil Sheridan ordered an end to racial discrimination on street cars in May 1867. Similar demonstrations and what would now be called "sit-ins" brought an end about the same time to segregated street cars in Richmond, Charleston, and other cities. One of the strongest demands of the freedmen upon the new radical state legislatures of 1868 in South Carolina and Mississippi was for civil rights laws that would protect their rights on common carriers and public accommodations. The law makers of those states and others responded with comprehensive anti-discrimination statutes. Their impact was noted in South Carolina in 1868 by Elizabeth H. Botume, a Northern teacher, on a previously segregated river steamer from Charleston to Beaufort. She witnessed "a decided change" among Negro passengers, previously excluded from the upper deck. "They were everywhere," she wrote, "choosing the best staterooms and best seats at the table. Two prominent colored members of the State Legislature were on board with their families. There were also several well-known Southerners, still uncompromising rebels. It was a curious scene and full of significance." In North Carolina shortly after the adoption of the Federal Civil Rights Act of 1875 Negroes in various parts of the state successfully tested their rights in railroads, steamboats, hotels, theaters, and other public accommodations. One Negro took the railroad from Raleigh to Savannah and reported no difficulty riding and dining unsegregated. Future Congressman James E. O'Hara, a Negro, successfully integrated a steamer from Greenville to Tarboro.

As a rule, however, Negroes were not aggressive in pressing their rights, even after they were assured them by law and protected in exercising them by the federal presence. It was easier to avoid painful rebuff or insult by refraining from the test of rights. Negroes rarely intruded upon hotels or restaurants where they were unwelcome. Whites often withdrew from desegregated facilities or cut down their patronage. Negro spokesmen constantly reiterated their disavowal of aspirations for what they called "social equality," and insisted that they were concerned only for "public equality," by which they apparently meant civil and political rights. Actually there is little evidence of racial mixing on social occasions during Reconstruction, though there was much mixing on public occasions, particularly of a political character. Native white Republicans were conscious of their minority status and their desperate need for black support. As one of them wrote the Governor of Alabama, "we must have men who will mix with the negroes & tell them of their rights. If we don't have such men, we will be defeated." Such men, native white Alabamians, were found, and they worked with a will across the color line.

It would be wrong to exaggerate the amount of interracial association and intimacy produced during Reconstruction or to misconstrue its character and meaning. If the intimacy of the old regime had its unhappy and painful aspects, so did that of the new order. Unlike the quality of mercy, it was strained. It was also temporary, and it was usually self-conscious. It was a product of contrived circumstances, and neither race had time to become fully accustomed to the change or feel natural in the relationship. Nevertheless, it would be a mistaken effort to equate this period in racial relations with either the old regime of slavery or with the future rule of Jim Crow. It was too exceptional. It is impossible to conceive of innumerable events and interracial experiments and contacts of the 1860's taking place in the 1900's. To attempt that would be to do violence to the nuances of history. . . .

More than a decade was to pass after Redemption before the first Jim Crow law was to appear upon the law books of a Southern state, and more than two decades before the older states of the seaboard were to adopt such laws. There was much segregation and discrimination of an extra-legal sort before the laws were adopted in all the states, but the amount of it differed from one place to another and one time to another, just as it did in Virginia.

The individual experiences and the testimony regarding them presented below are not offered as conclusive evidence or as proof of a prevailing pattern. They are the observations of intelligent men with contrasting backgrounds and origins about a fluid, continually changing, and controversial situation. . . .

Southern white testimony on the subject has naturally been discounted as propaganda. If only by way of contrast with later views, however, the following editorial from the Richmond *Dispatch*, 13 October 1886, is worth quoting: "Our State Constitution requires all State officers in their oath of office to declare that they 'recognize and accept the civil and political equality of all men.' We repeat that nobody here objects to sitting in political conventions with negroes. Nobody here objects to serving on juries with negroes. No lawyer objects to practicing law in court where negro lawyers practice . . . Colored men are allowed to introduce bills into the Virginia Legislature, and in both branches of this body negroes are allowed to sit, as they have a right to sit." George Washington Cable, the aggressive agitator for the rights of Negroes, protested strongly against discrimination elsewhere, but is authority for the statement made in 1885, that "In Virginia they may ride exactly as white people do and in the same cars."

More pertinent, whether typical or not, is the experience of a Negro.

In April 1885, T. McCants Stewart set forth from Boston to visit his native state of South Carolina after an absence of ten years. A Negro newspaperman, corresponding editor of the New York *Freeman*, Stewart was conscious of his role as a spokesman and radical champion of his race. "On leaving Washington, D.C.," he reported to his paper, "I put a chip on my shoulder, and inwardly dared any man to knock it off." He found a seat in a car which became so crowded that several white passengers had to sit on their baggage. "I fairly foamed at the mouth," he wrote, "imagining that the conductor would order me into a seat occupied by a colored lady so as to make room for a white passenger." Nothing of the sort happened, however, nor was there any unpleasantness when Stewart complained of a request from a white Virginian that he shift his baggage so that the white man could sit beside him. At a stop twenty-one miles below Petersburg he entered a station dining room, "bold as a lion," he wrote, took a seat at a table with white people, and was courteously served. "The whites at the table appeared not to note my presence," he reported. "Thus far I had found travelling more pleasant . . . than in some parts of New England." Aboard a steamboat in North Carolina he complained of a colored waiter who seated him at a separate table, though in the same dining room with whites. At Wilmington, however, he suffered from no discrimination in dining arrangements. His treatment in Virginia and North Carolina, he declared, "contrasted strongly with much that I have experienced in dining rooms in the North." Another contrast that impressed him was the ease and frequency with which white people entered into conversation with him for no other purpose than to pass the time of day. "I think the whites of the South," he observed, "are really less afraid to [have] contact with colored people than the whites of the North."

Stewart continued his journey southward, rejoicing that "Along the Atlantic seaboard from Canada to the Gulf of Mexico—through Delaware, Maryland, Virginia, the Carolinas, Georgia and into Florida, all the old slave States with enormous Negro populations . . . a first-class ticket is good in a first-class coach; and Mr. [Henry W.] Grady would be compelled to ride with a Negro, or, walk." From Columbia, South Carolina, he wrote: "I feel about as safe here as in Providence, R.I. I can ride in first-class cars on the railroads and in the streets. I can go into saloons and get refreshments even as in New York. I can stop in and drink a glass of soda and be more politely waited upon than in some parts of New England." He also found that "Negroes dine with whites in a railroad saloon" in his native state. He watched a Negro policeman arrest a white man "under circumstances requiring coolness, prompt decision, and courage"; and in Charleston he witnessed the review of hundreds of Negro troops. "Indeed," wrote Stewart, "the Palmetto State leads the South in some things. May she go on advancing in liberal practices and prospering throughout her borders, and may she be like leaven to the South; like a star unto 'The Land of Flowers,' leading our blessed section on and on into the way of liberty, justice, equality, truth, and righteousness." . . .

It would certainly be preposterous to leave the impression that any evidence I have submitted indicates a golden age of race relations in the period between Redemption and complete segregation. On the contrary, the evidence of race conflict and violence, brutality and exploitation in this very period is overwhelming. It was, after all, in the 'eighties and early 'nineties that lynching attained the most staggering proportions ever reached in the history of that crime. Moreover, the fanatical advocates of racism, whose doctrines of total segregation, disfranchisement, and ostracism eventually triumphed over all opposition and became universal practice in the South, were already at work and already beginning to establish dominance over some phases of Southern life. Before their triumph was complete, however, there transpired a period of history whose significance has been neglected. Exploitation there was in that period, as in other periods and in other regions, but it did not follow then that the exploited had to be ostracized. Subordination there was also, unmistakable subordination; but it was not yet an accepted corollary that the subordinates had to be totally segregated and needlessly humiliated by a thousand daily reminders of their subordination. Conflict there was, too, violent conflict in which the advantage lay with the strong and the dominant, as always; but conflict of some kind was unavoidable so long as there remained any contact between the races whatever.

The era of stiff conformity and fanatical rigidity that was to come had not yet closed in and shut off all contact between the races, driven the Negroes from all public forums, silenced all white dissenters, put a stop to all rational discussion and exchange of views, and precluded all variety and experiment in types of interracial association. There were still real choices to be made, and alternatives to the course eventually pursued with such single-minded unanimity and unquestioning conformity were still available.

Emerging Patterns of Segregation

HOWARD N. RABINOWITZ

In the antebellum years the majority of urban blacks, as slaves, lived with their masters in enclosed compounds. Subjected to close supervision, they were nevertheless provided with adequate food and shelter. At the same time many fugitive and hired-out slaves joined free Negroes in colonies located on the periphery of the cities. The emerging pattern of segregation was strengthened at the end of the war as numerous blacks vacated the old slave quarters. By 1890 separate black and white neighborhoods dominated the urban landscape.

As in other areas of Negro urban life, the existence of segregation paradoxically marked both the success of social control and a further threat

---

to it. For if keeping Negroes out of white neighborhoods prevented racial mixture and the lowering of property values, it also brought together large numbers of Negroes in areas that whites could not easily control. As whites discovered, if one part of the city was unhealthy, the rest of the city might suffer. If crime flourished in one neighborhood, it might easily spread to others; fires begun in one locality might inflame the rest of the city. Throughout the period this dilemma baffled whites. How could blacks be kept out of the white neighborhoods without causing even more serious repercussions by compressing blacks into a united mass?

Even by the end of the period whites and blacks could still be found living next to one another in certain sections of the city. The extent of such intermingling is distorted if judged solely by ward population figures, but even house-by-house examination reveals a certain amount of racial intermixture within city blocks. Nevertheless, such occurrences were limited to special circumstances. Negroes either worked for their white neighbors or lived among whites unable to move elsewhere. In the latter case, the pattern was clearly temporary, to be ended either by the death of the whites or their financial improvement.

There were usually one or more main concentrations of Negroes and numerous other smaller clusters. Some of the housing segregation was voluntary: Negroes sought proximity to their jobs, welcomed the freedom from white surveillance, and enjoyed the company of other blacks. Much of it, however, was due to black poverty, which limited housing options, and to white pressures to keep blacks out of their neighborhoods. Some Negro neighborhoods had begun in antebellum times as a result of the concentration of free Negroes and fugitive and hired-out slaves. Others evolved after the occupation by federal forces. Whatever the origin, these areas were in the worst sections of the city: in unkempt alleyways, on low-lying ground near contaminated streams, or near slaughterhouses, flour mills, or other industrial sites. In short, the Negroes occupied land considered unfit for white habitation. . . .

. . . Segregated job opportunities and housing generally constituted setbacks for blacks. Nevertheless, segregation in other areas of Southern life ironically often signified an improvement, for what it replaced was not integration but exclusion. The pattern was clearest in welfare services, education, and militia service, but also was present in a variety of public accommodations and institutions of the black community.

Segregation was neither a tactic invented by the Redeemers to punish blacks nor the result of a bargain between Democrats and Populists in the 1890s to forestall Negroes from becoming a pivotal force in Southern politics. It was the Northerners in the form of the U.S. Army, the Freedmen's Bureau, and Republican politicians who together with their Southern allies inaugurated much of the segregation. White Republicans, elected largely by Negro votes, wanted to improve the lives of their chief supporters; but, as was true of their Northern predecessors, the major concern was an end to exclusion. Integration was rarely considered, although blacks were promised facilities equal to those of whites.

Many Republicans were Southerners who still believed in Negro inferiority; most Northerners had never been free from such prejudice either. Nor were the realities of power lost on these men. Strongly anti-Negro mountain whites in North Carolina, Tennessee, and Alabama formed a major part of the Republican coalition and integration would have constituted an obvious affront, costing many votes. Similarly, if the Republicans elsewhere were to stay in power, allies needed to be attracted from among independents, former Whigs, and even Democrats. The professed policy of separate but equal had the benefit of minimizing white hostility while still presenting the blacks with a significant improvement over their treatment at the hands of earlier administrations.

Negroes themselves favored this policy over exclusion. Along with their white allies, they believed, or at least hoped, that separate treatment could be truly equal. Protests against segregation were primarily confined to the area of public accommodations where from 1875 to 1883 blacks had the law on their side. Equal access rather than integration was their chief aim. As a result, they convinced any doubting whites that they too wanted segregation. Their decision to form separate churches immediately after the war further strengthened this impression. . . .

The Republicans did make an important break with past practice. Even though segregated, some public institutions were opened to blacks for the first time. In other instances such as the Richmond and Nashville almshouses or the Virginia insane asylum, the Radicals administered segregated institutions that the military had forced upon the postwar Conservative governments. The justification, it must be remembered, was equal access. But the Republicans were in power for such a short period that they had time to institute merely a small portion of the welfare apparatus freedmen needed. When the Republicans surrendered office, only Richmond and Montgomery had public hospitals; only Richmond provided for its Negro orphans. Certain state institutions continued to exclude Negroes, and relief and medical aid were still less available for blacks than for whites. Therefore, it was the Redeemers, many of them former slave owners and veterans of the Confederate Army, who determined the quality and quantity of welfare facilities for blacks during the largest segment of the period.

Many of the Redeemers had taken part in the first postwar white governments that had excluded Negroes from health and welfare services. Since 1867 the quality of life for most urban blacks had improved little. Despite pleas that they return to the countryside, the number of urban blacks increased each year. Democratic officials frequently called attention to the miserable living conditions of the Negroes in seeking to account for their high death rates. Sometimes they hedged and blamed the "inherent weaknesses" of the race, a subtle way of extolling the virtues of slavery. But the head of the Richmond Board of Health put the blame for the high mortality rate squarely where it belonged. It was not due to "race constitutional defects," he said. The main causes were poverty and overcrowding.

The search for a solution to this problem of needy blacks divided the Redeemers. Some felt that to provide services would encourage the influx

of more Negroes to the cities, whereas by providing fewer ones, many of
the blacks already there would return to the land. Few expressed such
views openly, preferring instead to oppose new facilities because of alleged
lack of funds. Much of the opposition only can be inferred from the defeats
suffered by proponents of greater aid to Negroes. . . .

Nonetheless, despite an occasional reversion to the policy of exclusion
or its continuation where the Radicals had left it undisturbed, the Redeemers' most frequent response to the legacy of Radical rule was to endorse
the shift from exclusion to segregation. It must be remembered, however,
that the Redeemers were not a monolithic group, even within a given city
or city council. Whether due to fear of Northern intervention if Negroes
did not receive adequate attention or because of paternalistic or political
impulses, some Democrats supported aid to blacks and publicly reaffirmed
the Radical principle that separate treatment was to be equal treatment.
When plans were made in 1876 for the opening of a Jim Crow institution
for Georgia's Negro deaf and dumb, the legislature ordered that "the present
Board of Trustees [of the white institution] will act for this colored institution and conduct it, in all respects as the present one of the whites is
conducted." The annex of Atlanta Hospital to be completed in 1880 was
for Negro patients, "who will receive every attention bestowed on the
whites." And the final justice: "Every grave which the keeper has dug,"
read a Richmond ordinance, "whether for the body of a white or colored
person, shall be at least six feet deep."

But the implementation of plans for Negro accommodations frequently
met with delays, and, in cases such as the Atlanta Hospital, never came
to fruition. In explaining why Negroes were still barred from the Georgia
Institution for the Deaf and Dumb in 1873, the Board of Commissioners
stated that "it was incompatible with the general school law that blacks
and whites should be educated together." They felt that it was now time
to spend $6,000 for the separate accommodation of blacks. Money was
finally appropriated in 1876 for a Negro department to be opened when
there were ten or more applicants. The bill provided that the Negro division

> shall, in all respects, be conducted separate from the other institution; . . .
> the funds appropriated for its use to be a separate fund; the teachers and
> all other employees to be as distinctly separate as though the two insti-
> tutions were in different towns. . . .

Race relations in public accommodations were relatively fluid. Unlike
welfare and education, *de jure* segregation was not widespread until after
1890. As a result, there was a degree of integration throughout the period
not matched in other aspects of Southern life. Nevertheless, *de facto* segregation generally prevailed. And, again, what it ordinarily replaced was
not integration, but exclusion, although the roots of this shift often lay in
the antebellum period.

Before the war blacks, except for servants, had been excluded from
restaurants, hotels, and parks. They were also barred from many theaters
and shows, though managers sometimes provided segregated sections.

Steamboats and railroads segregated those few blacks who traveled as paying passengers, while in New Orleans the use of separate streetcars for blacks superseded earlier exclusion.

Southern whites continued these policies during the years 1865 to 1867. Some places of amusement continued to exclude blacks; others retained their earlier pattern of segregated seating, as did those in New Orleans; and still others—for example, those in Nashville, Montgomery, and Richmond—opened their doors to freedmen for the first time, although also on a segregated basis. Traveling circuses, which were especially popular with blacks, went so far in Montgomery as to establish separate entrances for the races. The states of Texas, Mississippi, and Florida passed laws to strengthen existing segregation on public conveyances. Savannah officials closed their city parks from fear that blacks would have to be admitted. Meanwhile, the leading white restaurants and hotels continued exclusion. But the postwar shift was already evident in the decision of Nashville streetcar owners to provide segregated cars for the previously excluded blacks.

As in education and welfare, Republicans were either unwilling or unable to end segregation in most forms of public accommodation. The Republican-controlled legislature in North Carolina was so averse to the idea of forced integration that, in 1870, it defeated a proposal to assure Negroes the same facilities as whites on steamboats and railroads. Even the spate of antidiscrimination laws passed elsewhere, often over the objections of white Republicans, seem to have had little effect on the pattern of segregation in public conveyances. If they accomplished anything, it was to encourage the railroads and steamboat companies to provide supposedly equal—though separate—accommodations for blacks. Despite the passage of the 1866 Civil Rights Act, a British traveler who extensively toured the South during 1867–1868 concluded that "there are 'nigger cars' open, of course, to white people and often used as smoking cars, but to which all coloured passengers have to confine themselves." Vernon Lane Wharton concluded about Mississippi's antidiscrimination railroad act passed in 1870 that "In spite of its stringent provisions, the law had almost no effect." As demonstrated by the numerous suits by blacks against Southern railroad companies, with few exceptions the best that blacks could hope for were segregated accommodations the equal of the whites. Blacks, for example, were forced to ride on the platforms of cars between Montgomery and Union Springs, Alabama. . . .

Both white Republicans and Redeemers came to embrace the shift from exclusion to segregation in public accommodations. But what helped to assure this shift was the attitude of the blacks themselves.

Blacks on occasion did criticize segregation. During Richmond's celebration of the passage of the Fifteenth Amendment, a Negro minister, the Reverend J. Sella Martin, was accused by the *Richmond Dispatch* of saying that "the negroes must claim the right to sit with the whites in theatres, churches, and other public buildings, to ride with them on the cars, and to stay at the same hotels with them." Similarly, after Tennessee passed its Jim Crow law in 1881, the Reverend W. A. Sinclair of Nashville argued that "no man of color [should] ride in a car simply because it is set apart and *labeled* 'exclusively for negroes,' but rather let every individual choose of the regular coaches the one in which to ride." Six years later when Charles Dudley Warner asked a group of leading Nashville black businessmen, "what do you want here in the way of civil rights that you have not?" the answer was, "we want to be treated like men, like anybody else regardless of color. . . . We want public conveyances open to us according to the fare we pay; we want the privilege to go to hotels and to theatres, operas and places of amusement . . . we cannot go to the places assigned us in concerts and theatres without loss of self respect."

Negroes sometimes opposed segregation by deeds as well as by words. As noted earlier, by 1870 Charleston, New Orleans, Richmond, Mobile, and Nashville were among several cities to experience challenges to the policies of exclusion or segregation on their streetcars. Suits also were brought against offending railroad companies. Challenges to segregation, however, were most pronounced after passage of the 1875 Civil Rights Act. But for the most part blacks failed in their attempts to break down the racial barriers in theaters, hotels, restaurants, public conveyances, and bars. More isolated and equally unsuccessful attempts occurred with decreasing frequency in subsequent years. The few successes were due to special circumstances. During his visit to Atlanta in 1877, for example, Lieutenant Henry O. Flipper, a native of the city and the first Negro graduate of West Point, was invited by a white officer into Schumann's Drugstore for a glass of soda water. Flipper later told a large crowd of blacks that "I know it is not a usual thing to sell to colored people, but we got it." When he added that before coming to the meeting he and J. O. Wimbish, a Negro politician, had joined another white officer for a drink of soda at Schumann's, the crowd, appreciative of the difficulties, loudly applauded.

Despite this opposition to segregation, the majority of blacks, including their leaders, focused their attention elsewhere. The failure of a sustained attack on segregation perhaps resulted from the lack of support from their white allies and the courts. There were other reasons as well. Five prominent Nashville blacks, for example, argued that Negroes would not use passage of the Civil Rights Bill "to make themselves obnoxious" since they had too much self-respect to go where they were not wanted. Besides, they added, such actions would lead only to disturbances and they wanted as little agitation as possible. Bishop Henry M. Turner echoed this view in 1889, telling a reporter that "I don't find much trouble in traveling at [*sic*] the south on account of my color, for the simple reason that I am not in the habit of pushing myself where I am not wanted." A similar attitude might have governed the response of "several really respectable colored persons" in Charleston to the attempt of a Negro to buy a ticket for the orchestra or dress circle of the Academy of Music in 1870. Calling the move a cheap political trick, they "avowed their willingness to sit in the places provided for their own race when they visited the Academy."

Economic pressures also led blacks to accept segregation. Negroes who relied on a white clientele were especially reluctant to serve members of both races. Shortly after the passage of the Civil Rights Act two Negro barbers in Edgefield, across the river from Nashville, refused to serve black customers. The previous year a Negro delegation had been ejected when it demanded shaves at the shop of a black barber in Chattanooga. Asked if their money was not as good as a white man's, the barber, fearful of the loss of his white customers, answered, "Yes just as good, but there is not enough of it." Both whites and blacks understood the focus of economic power. In 1875 the *Nashville Union and American* listed twelve blacks who had been testing compliance to the Civil Rights Act. The fact that "most of them got their reward by losing their situations" helps explain why there were not more protesters.

Other blacks sought to work out an equitable arrangement within the confines of a segregated order. They accepted segregation per se because it was seen as an improvement over the policy of exclusion and because they believed, or at least hoped, that separate facilities could be equal. A rider on the Nashville streetcar set apart for blacks in 1866 did not complain about the segregation, but threatened a boycott unless the company protected black passengers from abusive whites who forced their way into the car and used obscene language in front of black women. A Norfolk, Virginia, Negro observing that the city was building a new opera house suggested that "colored theatre-goers . . . petition the managers to give them a respectable place to sit, apart from those of a lewd character." To Atlanta's C. H. J. Taylor writing during a period of racial tension in his city, it seemed that whites and blacks should "travel each in their own distinct path, steering clear of debatable ground, never forgetting to render one to the other that which equity and good conscience demands [*sic*]." And when William H. Councill, Negro principal of the Alabama State Normal School, brought suit against the Western and Atlantic Railroad on the ground that despite his possession of a first-class ticket, he was ejected from the first-class car and removed to the Negro car, he admitted the right of the company to classify passengers by race, but maintained it was the duty of the railroad to furnish equal facilities and conveniences for both races.

In other ways as well blacks seemed to provide support for white claims that they really preferred segregation. When blacks ran their own railroad excursions or benefit concerts, they provided segregated facilities for their white friends. And when the white community persisted in its policy of exclusion, blacks responded as they had in the areas of education and welfare, by opening their own hotels, ice cream parlors, and skating rinks. Part of this response was an accommodation to white prejudice; but it was also related to the development of a group identity among blacks. Though it cannot be equated with the racism of whites, by moving in this direction, blacks themselves contributed to the emergence of the separate black and white worlds which characterized Southern urban life by 1890.

The separation of the races was accomplished largely without the aid of statutes as long as both races accepted its existence. As early as 1866, an English traveler, William Dixon, noted that the Negro in Richmond, regardless of his legal rights, knew "how far he may go, and where he must stop." He also knew that "habits are not changed by paper law." In 1880 two of the Negro witnesses testifying before a Congressional committee pointed to this difference between the power of law and the power of custom. When asked if there were any laws in Alabama applied solely to one race, James T. Rapier answered: "Custom is law in our country now, and was before the war." Asked again if there were any discriminatory provisions in the constitution or state statutes, he replied, "None that I know of; but what we complain of is the administration of the law—the custom of the country." James O'Hara of North Carolina agreed: "These are matters [segregation in public accommodations] that are and must be regulated purely by prejudice and feeling, and the law cannot regulate."

When integration did occur, it was only at the initiation of whites and was confined as a rule to the least desirable facilities—cheap, inferior restaurants, second-class and smoking cars on trains. Whites were there because they chose to be; blacks were there because they had no choice.

Disfranchisement and Democratic Supremacy

J. MORGAN KOUSSER

Democrats countered Populist economic appeals with the old litany perfected during the Independent campaigns: if whites split, they warned, the Negroes would hold the balance of power. Blacks would then demand offices, favorable laws, appropriations, and ultimately social equality. The South would undergo another Reconstruction. Like the Independents before them, the Populists derided such propositions as bogies conjured up to mislead and frighten white voters. Both sides were partly correct. Certainly the Democrats played on the racism inbred in virtually every white Southerner to cloud over other issues and thereby maintain their control. On the other hand, in localities where Negro political strength was important, blacks did demand and obtain patronage, protection of their political and civil rights, larger funds for governmental programs servicing Negroes, and finally the right to representation by men of their own race—a right that implied a broad, though not necessarily social, equality.

The Democrats' employment of white supremacy rhetoric may have been cynical. While chiding opponents for endangering the racial hierarchy, they often secretly courted black voters. Nonetheless, they undoubtedly internalized their campaign cries, so intertwining the Democratic party with the idea of white domination in their own minds that partisanship and racism became indistinguishable. For example, the official Democratic organ in Louisiana, the *Baton Rouge Daily Advocate*, referred to the Populists as "the most dangerous and insidious foe of white supremacy" and said of the Republican party that "the Africanization of the state was its cardinal

From *The Shaping of Southern Politics* by J. Morgan Kousser, pp. 36–44, 244. Copyright © 1974 Yale University Press. Reprinted by permission of the publisher.

doctrine." Constantly referring to the Democrats as "the party of the white man," it considered the fusion between Populists, Republicans, and sugar planters "a grave menace to our civilization." Conversely, the *Pine Bluff* (Arkansas) *Commercial* appealed to white Democrats to pass the poll tax in order to disfranchise blacks because "the most dangerous foe to democracy [the party] is the Negro. . . . The Negro is an uncontrollable objector to our ticket." A threat to the political establishment was a threat to the racial establishment, and vice versa. Only such rationalizations could have saved thousands of politicians from consciousness of their own self-serving hypocrisy. Few men could live with such an image of themselves.

This equation of the Democratic party with white paramountcy carried with it the implication that Negro domination threatened until all partisan opposition was eliminated. Not only black, but potential white dissent had to be eradicated. From such thinking arose violence, intimidation, gerrymandering, fraud, and curtailment of the suffrage. Even after almost every Negro ceased voting, Democrats instantly charged any partisan adversary with racial treason. The expression "white man's party" became popular dogma.

Not satisfied that the cry of white supremacy would save them, the Democrats also co-opted Populist issues and rhetoric. By the mid-nineties, no stump speech in the South was complete without blasts at the railroads, the trusts, Wall Street, the gold bugs, the saloonkeepers, or some similarly evil "Interest." Political machines likewise became objects of universal denunciation, even by organization stalwarts. Conservatives appropriated the Populists' call for fair elections under the Australian ballot system and employed that system to disfranchise many potential converts to the People's Party. The "horny-handed sons of toil" began to receive rhetorical attention once reserved for Confederate soldiers and Southern industrial magnates. The state Democratic party which could not boast of a leading farmer-turned-politician (or vice versa) during the nineties was poor indeed. The fusion behind Bryan in 1896 was only the last and most effective device to pull agrarians into the Democratic party.

If fraud, racism, and co-optation failed to quash the opposition, there was always disfranchisement. In the eighties and early nineties, Democrats developed a panoply of restrictive measures—registration and multiple-box laws, the poll tax, the Australian ballot, and the educational qualification. Each state became in effect a laboratory for testing one device or another. Indeed, the cross-fertilization and coordination between the movements to restrict the suffrage in the Southern states amounted to a public conspiracy. Since newspapers reprinted comments from their counterparts throughout the South, since politicians could often get firsthand information about the effect of laws through personal friends or through associates in Congress, and since state libraries traded lawbooks, any successful law could easily be copied. Thus, Florida copied South Carolina's eight-box scheme, and Alabama and Florida borrowed from Tennessee's secret ballot law; Tennessee, Arkansas, Florida, and Mississippi followed Georgia's example in enacting a poll tax. There was a slight pause after the first enactment of any particular mechanism, perhaps to test the reaction of Northerners and the state's own electors. When Congress did not intervene, and when voters did not rise up against the disfranchisers, legislators in other states felt free to write similar laws.

Though Mississippi's constitutional disfranchisement certainly impressed contemporaries as the most permanent and effective solution, politicians in the early nineties hesitated to follow Mississippi's lead. One reason was that calling conventions or passing amendments usually required two-thirds majorities in the legislatures, as well as majorities in referenda and in constitutional conventions. Moreover, in a time of political upheaval, few groups with strong interests in any aspect of the status quo dared to invite constitutional change. Many Democrats feared Populists might poll sufficient strength in such conventions to alter other sections of the constitutions; conservatives in South Carolina feared the Tillmanites would permanently enshrine the Dispensary system in the fundamental law; reformers feared that the railroads would destroy utility commissions; where no commission yet existed, railroad men feared reformers might create one. Only after the Democrats had gained secure majorities did they call disfranchisement conventions, and then only in five states.

Tables 1 and 2 demonstrate the efficacy of even simple disfranchising devices in cutting the strength of opposition to the Democrats. At the height of Populist or Republican strength in gubernatorial elections in each Southern state, the opposing parties were unable to garner a majority of the recorded votes. (The Populists were, however, undoubtedly counted out in the Louisiana and Alabama elections shown in the tables.) The opposition

Table 1   The Opposition at Its Crest in the 1890s: Populist or Republican Percentage and Turnout in Key Gubernatorial Races

STATE	YEAR	PARTY	% POPULIST OR REPUBLICAN OF THOSE VOTING	% TURNOUT
Group 1ᵃ				
Arkansas	1896	Republican	25.3	48.7
Florida	1892	Populist	21.3	38.9
Georgia	1894	Populist	44.0	49.6
Mississippi	1895	Populist	27.2	20.8
South Carolina	1894	Independent	30.4	22.3
Tennessee	1896	Republican	46.8	70.5
Group 2ᵇ				
Alabama	1892	Populist	47.6	70.5
Louisiana	1896	Fusion	43.7	69.9
North Carolina	1896	Republican	46.5	85.4
Texas	1896	Fusion	44.4	85.6
Virginia	1893	Populist	40.8	54.3

ᵃ Group 1 is composed of states which adopted effective disfranchising statutes before 1894.
ᵇ Group 2 is composed of states which did not adopt effective disfranchising laws before 1894.

Table 2   Estimated Voting Patterns, by Race, in Key Gubernatorial Contests During the 1890s

			WHITE				BLACK			
STATE	YEAR	CHIEF OPPOSITION PARTY	DEMOCRAT	REPUBLICAN	POPULIST	NO VOTE	DEMOCRAT	REPUBLICAN	POPULIST	NO VOTE
Group 1[a]										
Arkansas	1896	Republican	37	15	12	40	21	5	0	75
Florida	1892	Populist	43	0	17	41	11	0	0	89
Georgia	1894	Populist	35	0	34	31	23	0	15	62
Mississippi	1895	Populist	35	0	19	45	0	0	0	100
South Carolina	1894	Independent	22	0	11	67	12	0	5	84
Tennessee[b]	1896	Republican	42	45	3	10	24	−4[c]	5	74
Group 2[d]										
Alabama	1892	Populist	27	0	53	20	49	0	14	36
Louisiana	1896	Fusion	22	58	0	21	62	7	0	31
North Carolina	1896	Republican	45	31	9	15	20	59	8	13
Texas	1896	Fusion	48	34	0	18	47	50	0	3
Virginia	1893	Populist	40	0	11	47	19	0	46	35

[a] States which restricted suffrage before first Populist Party election.
[b] Tennessee estimates computed by sections, North Carolina and Virginia by splitting the state into counties above and below 30 percent Negro. Estimates in table are weighted sums of the separate estimates.
[c] For an explanation of estimates outside the 0–100% limits, see my "Ecological Regression" article.
[d] States which restricted suffrage after first Populist Party election.

was virtually crushed in four of the six states that adopted restrictive statutes before 1894; in none of the four did the chief opposition party poll one-third of the votes. Less than a majority of the potential electors went to the polls in five of these six states. Low turnout appears to have correlated with Populist defeat.

In states which had restricted the vote, the opposition party survived suffrage restriction only where it had exceptionally strong white support. In Georgia, where the poll tax had long discouraged Negroes from voting, where the Republicans had been so weak since 1872 that whites had almost ceased to fear a return to Reconstruction, and where the Populists produced their most astute leader, Tom Watson, the People's Party did relatively well. The Peach State was the one polity where the Populists prospered despite a minority voter turnout. The mountaineer Republicans of Tennessee also continued to vote despite that state's adoption of a poll tax in 1890. In these two and other states, it is evident that the poll tax requirement was quietly relaxed or that parties raised money to pay the taxes of large numbers of their followers during fervent campaigns.

Table 2 shows that the most accurate estimate is that at least 60 percent of the adult male Negroes in each of the states in Group 1 failed to vote in the decade's hottest elections. The five states that did not restrict the franchise prior to the mid-1890s present quite a different picture. In none of these states did the chief opposition party fail to gather 40 percent of the voters. A majority of the adult males of each state voted in the elections cited. In two of the five states turnout reached astronomical proportions, by twentieth-century standards, as 85 percent of those eligible voted. Estimated Negro turnout and party preferences in the states in group 1 provide a striking contrast with those in group 2. In the former, less than 40 percent of the blacks voted; in the latter, at least 64 percent. In the first group, the Democrats carried the recorded black vote by at least two to one except in Georgia, where the old party won by a five to three margin. In the second group, the majority of blacks supported the dissenters, except in Louisiana and Alabama, where black belt ballot fraud had become a vocation.

The degree to which disfranchising laws adversely affected dissenting parties becomes even clearer when we compare the nineties with the preceding decade in Southern politics. Whereas the Democrats lost governors' races in two states during the eighties, they lost only one in the next decade. In the 1880s, Independents or Republicans had polled at least 40 percent of the votes in seven states; in the 1890s, in six states. Independents scored at least 30 percent of the vote in ten states, Populists or Republicans in only eight. In the 1880s at least 49 percent of the voters participated in the key gubernatorial elections in each ex-Confederate state; in the 1890s, four states fell below that mark. Despite increased economic grievances, a better organization, and a more coherent ideology, the Populists were, on the whole, somewhat less successful politically than the Independents.

The fact that franchise limitation was one of the chief reasons for Populist failure becomes unmistakable when we focus on three states. In Florida, Arkansas, and Mississippi the Independents had gained over 40 percent of the votes; the Populists won less than 30 percent in each state. In the key contests in the 1880s, overall turnout rates varied from 50.8 percent in Mississippi to 79.4 percent in Florida; the range in the nineties was from 20.9 percent to 48.7 percent. From 39 percent to 87 percent of the Negroes are estimated to have voted in these three states in the Independent campaigns; from 0 percent to 25 percent in the Populist elections. Thus, the strong opposition movements in these three states in the eighties faded after the Democrats restricted the suffrage. The lesson must have been clear to politicians elsewhere. . . .

By 1910 the Southern political system which was to last through mid-century had been formed. The new system posed a striking contrast to that of the eighties and nineties. . . . During the 1880s, 64 percent of the Southern adult males, on the average, turned out to vote in the elections selected. This figure increased to 73 percent in the 1890s in those states which passed no major piece of restrictive legislation before 1894, but dropped to 42 percent in those states which did enact such legislation. In the next decade Southern turnout fell to an average of 30 percent. The political system had changed from a democracy to what Dean Burnham has termed a "broadly-based oligarchy."

Likewise, one of every four adult males voted for Republican or Independent candidates during the 1880s; whereas, by the first decade of the twentieth century, the percentage had dropped to one in ten. Post-Reconstruction Southern politics had a moderately active electorate and fairly vigorous, if somewhat sporadic, competition between parties. In the early twentieth century the electorate was tiny and party competition almost nonexistent.

⚓ *F U R T H E R   R E A D I N G*

Eric Anderson, *Race and Politics in North Carolina, 1872–1901* (1981)
Elizabeth Bethel, *Promiseland* (1981)
John W. Blassingame, *Black New Orleans, 1860–1880* (1973)
John W. Cell, *The Highest Stage of White Supremacy* (1982)
Helen G. Edmonds, *The Negro and Fusion Politics in North Carolina, 1894–1901* (1951)
George Fredrickson, *The Black Image in the White Mind* (1971)
Louis R. Harlan, *Booker T. Washington: The Making of a Black Leader, 1856–1901* (1972)
J. Morgan Kousser, *The Shaping of Southern Politics* (1974)
Frenise A. Logan, *The Negro in North Carolina, 1876–1894* (1964)
Gordon B. McKinney, *Southern Mountain Republicans, 1865–1900* (1978)
August Meier, *Negro Thought in America, 1880–1915* (1963)
Pauli Murray, *Proud Shoes* (1956, 1978)
Sydney Nathans, *The Quest for Progress* (1983)
Nell Irvin Painter, *Exodusters* (1977)
Howard N. Rabinowitz, *Race Relations in the Urban South, 1865–1890* (1978)
Donald Spivey, *Schooling for the New Slavery* (1978)
George Brown Tindall, *South Carolina Negroes, 1877–1900* (1952)
Vernon Lane Wharton, *The Negro in Mississippi, 1865–1890* (1947)
Joel Williamson, *The Crucible of Race* (1984)
———, *The Origins of Segregation* (1968)
C. Vann Woodward, *Origins of the New South* (1951)
———, *The Strange Career of Jim Crow*, 3d rev. ed. (1974)
Charles E. Wynes, *Race Relations in Virginia, 1870–1902* (1961)

CHAPTER
7

Progressivism

In the midst of black disfranchisement, escalating racial violence, a flourishing cult of the Lost Cause, the rise of a one-party South, and steadily declining cotton prices, it is strange to talk about reform in the South, let alone a northern-style reform movement. It seems especially strange given that southern society increasingly perceived itself as immutable. If reform implies change, how then could a southern reform movement have developed?

Yet historians have demonstrated that for at least two decades after 1900, a vigorous spirit of reform took root in the South. The region's reforms included child-labor legislation, improved education, railroad regulation, and prohibition. Their champions came primarily from a new middle class emerging in cities and towns. But progressivism also had a rural dimension, designed to improve the quality of life on the farm and break the isolation of the countryside through better schools, scientific agriculture, and good roads.

The reforms represented a desire to direct the changes occurring in southern society in an orderly, efficient, and moral manner. Progressives' success owed in part to their effective use of the new political system in the South and also to their ability to frame their proposals in traditional language. Most believed that the elimination of blacks from southern political life would further the cause of both reform and black progress. Unlike the Populists, the progressives did not offer any radical economic programs; rather, they actively pursued economic development as another method of improving southern society.

In consideration of the cautious nature of the progressives' reforms, what impact did they have on southern society? Did the attempt to reconcile progress and tradition merely result in an improved version of the status quo? Or were the changes more fundamental, and did they establish a foundation for future advances in race relations, labor, and education?

⚓ D O C U M E N T S

The documents reflect both the diversity of southern progressivism and its relationship to regional culture, explicit and implied. Charles W. Dabney was a leading southern educator of the period and president of the University of Tennessee at the time he wrote "The Public School Problem in the South" (1901), reproduced here as the first document. The essay candidly discusses the "disgrace" of public education in the South and its impact on politics and the regional economy. Edgar Gardner Murphy, a Montgomery, Alabama Episcopal priest, typified many of his colleagues in the movement by his participation in a wide variety of reform efforts. These included race relations, education, and, as can be seen from the second document, child labor. The third document presents two excerpts from the North Carolina publication *The Progressive Farmer* that illustrate progressivism's rural dimension. Prohibition advocate John E. White grounds the movement in "southern conditions" and reveals its underlying racial and class biases in the fourth document. The Southern Sociological Congress was a major organizational response to the progressive movement in the South. It was founded in Nashville in 1912 and dedicated to coordinating social reform efforts. The 1914 meeting in Memphis took as its theme "The Solid South for a Better Nation," and the excerpts from the conference proceedings, presented here as the fifth selection, reveal the strong clerical influence in progressive reform, as well as progressives' interest in improving race relations. Georgia's progressive governor Hoke Smith discussed an array of progressive measures in his 1907 inaugural address. His speech, the final documentary selection, makes clear how black disfranchisement, ironically, fit well within the progressive movement.

Charles W. Dabney on the Public-School Problem in the South, 1901

The South waiting for education.—Everything in the South waits upon the general education of the people. Industrial development waits for more captains of industry, superintendents of factories, and skilled workmen. The natural resources of the Southern States are great and varied; capital in abundance is ready for investment in them; only men are wanted who can plan, organize, and direct. This is true of all our industries, even of our agriculture. A director of an Agricultural Experiment Station says: "We can do little more to improve the agricultural methods of the farmers until a new generation is educated, who can read our bulletins, apply scientific methods, and keep simple farm accounts."

The colleges for liberal, and institutions for scientific and technical education as well, wait for preparatory schools and high schools. With the same population there were during 1899 in all collegiate and graduate courses in liberal arts only 16,351 students in the Southern States against 30,741 in the North Central States, where they have public high schools. A system of public education is a pyramid; the primary schools are the foundation; the secondary schools and high schools, the normal schools, the technical schools, and the colleges carry up the structure step by step, and the university is the capstone. Our old system of education in the South, so far as we had any, was a Greek column; the university was a beautiful carved capitol of classic design, supported by a slender column of literary colleges and academies, which stood upon a narrow and unsubstantial base of private schools.

The effects of war and reconstruction.—Good government in town and State and intelligent action in national affairs are impossible without educated voters. Pettifogging politicians, selfish demagogues, and corrupt lobbyists will continue to control our legislative and county governments until a majority of the voters can read and think for themselves. The Republic must have an educated citizenship or go down. The question of educating all the people is more critically important to the South than it is to the remainder of the nation. We must educate all our people, blacks as well as whites, or the South will become a dependent province instead of a coordinate portion of the nation. What, for example, is the cause of the present complete isolation, of the almost entire exclusion from the councils of the nation, of a dozen States which for a long time supplied a majority of the statesmen who directed the affairs of this country, unless it is the political ignorance of their successors, illustrated persistently by the pursuit of absurd financial theories and antiquated political hobbies? The only remedy for the political situation in the South is to be found in public education.

Even religion waits upon general education. How else can we interpret the action of our enlightened and progressive churches, many of which are now actively at work raising their twentieth century educational funds? Evidently they think that the further extension, purification, and strengthening of religion in the South depends also on general education.

This study was undertaken out of a desire to get a true conception of the condition of the public schools in the South, which might be the starting point for efforts at improving them. The writer sincerely hopes that no one will think, because he has tried to tell the truth as he sees it, that he takes a pessimistic or despairing view of the situation. In most aspects the situation of the public schools in the South is indeed a sad one. It is not proposed to discuss at length here the origin or the causes of this state of things, for everyone who knows our history understands them already. The South emerged from the civil war thirty-six years ago, having lost one-tenth of all her white males and three billions of property, which was nearly all her accumulated capital. Reconstruction was even more desolating than war. The spoiler not only stole everything that war had left, but, as Judge Jeremiah S. Black has said, "by their devilish ingenuity they succeeded in running their felonious fingers into the pockets of posterity." They not only looted the treasuries, squandered the school funds, and raised the taxes so high that a general system of confiscation ensued, but in their insatiable lust placed bonded debts upon the Southern States aggregating over $300,000,000. A debt was piled upon the State of North Carolina, for example, of about $38,000,000, which was nearly one-third as much as the total valuation of all its property; upon Alabama they put a debt amounting to over $18,000,000; upon Tennessee one of over $14,000,000. They squandered $140,000,000 for Louisiana and increased her debt $40,000,000! . . .

But the Southern people are too brave and energetic a race to live forever in the shadow of a great sorrow and under the burden of a great wrong. The restoration and recuperation have been rapid; there never was anything like it. The census of 1880 showed that the South had gained nearly $5,000,000,000 in the assessment of property; in the next ten years she gained 50 per cent more, against 22 per cent in New England and in the Middle States. Since 1880 the production of cotton has doubled and the manufactures of all kinds have been more than quadrupled. The capital invested in cotton manufacturing has increased twelvefold in ten years. Thirty thousand miles of railroads have been built in fifteen years and over $1,000,000,000 expended upon them. The coal products have increased fivefold and the production of pig iron in this section has increased from 400,000 tons to over 2,000,000 tons. These figures are only pointers; the progress has been equally great along all other lines. The people of the entire South are now able to have better schools.

Believing that the Southern people have at last overcome most of the financial and political results of war and reconstruction, I hold that the time has come when we must begin seriously upon the work of reconstructing Southern society in all its departments, and that the first thing to do is to establish schools for all the people. God knows we remember the past, even those of us who were nothing but children remember it, and we would not forget or have our children forget any of the lessons of those days, and least of all the inspiring examples of their heroic grandfathers; but our faces are toward the future, and in preparation for the work of rebuilding our institutions it is our duty to study the facts as they are, blinking nothing of the truth, however unpleasant. Some politicians find it desirable to flatter the people and try to make them feel as comfortable as possible in their present position, but all thinking Southerners know that our public schools are a disgrace and such persons demand the truth, and will be glad to learn how to make them better. . . .

. . . In North Carolina only 30 per cent of the children are in daily attendance upon the schools; less than 60 per cent are enrolled in them, and the annual school term is less than seventy-one days. There are in North Carolina on the average 65 enrolled pupils to each school and 54 to each teacher. The schoolhouse which is supposed to shelter the children is valued at $179.60, and the teacher who has charge of them receives $23.36 a month for seventy and eight-tenths days, or about $77 for the term. The amount expended per year per pupil in attendance is but $1.34, which is only 51 cents per capita. In Tennessee less than half of the children between 5 and 18 years of age are in daily attendance; only 70 per cent are enrolled in the schools; the school term is only ninety-six days, and the enrolled pupils attend an average of only sixty-three days in the year. In Tennessee they are taught in a schoolhouse which cost $426, by teachers who receive an annual salary of $134. The total expense per pupil is $5.17 a year, which is only 87 cents per capita. . . .

The laws designed to disfranchise illiterate whites and blacks are likely to have a beneficent influence upon the educational situation in the South. Such laws, if impartially drawn and fairly carried out, will do almost as much good in promoting the elementary education, of males at least, as compulsory laws. The uneducated people of the Southern States, both whites and blacks, esteem their ballot to a degree that is almost ridiculous. In States like North Carolina, where the educational qualification has been applied, the colored people are already showing an earnest desire to get the little education required to qualify as voters. But these laws, even at best, touch only one-half the population. The only perfect solution of the problem is a compulsory attendance law carefully designed to reach every healthy child. We must put all the children in school, but before we do this we must have the schools and the teachers. . . .

One hears a great deal in the South about its natural resources and their development. Shall we not realize that our great resources—our soils, minerals, and timbers—are useless in the hands of an untrained people? We should recognize that our children are our greatest resource and that the first thing to do is to train them in natural science and the industrial arts, so that they may utilize these resources. . . . Moreover, if we do not educate our own people to use these resources intelligently, the skilled men of other States will come in and do so, and make our native population the "hewers of wood and drawers of water" in their industries. We shall then be reduced to an industrial dependency even worse than our present political and commercial dependency.

The improvement of the public schools of the South will come through industrial development. Of all peoples in the world, therefore, we need industrial education; but before we can have it there must be a complete revolution in methods. Book teaching must be replaced in large part by nature study, and simple industrial arts must be introduced in all public schools. It will be exceedingly difficult, however, to do this. The people are by nature very conservative. The normal schools, colleges, and universities are still devoted chiefly to literary work, and turn out few teachers of science and none of manual training. The revolution must begin, therefore, in the higher institutions—in the normal schools and colleges. They must be largely remodeled before we can even begin to educate the kind of public-school teachers we need to make the new schools. . . .

The curse of politics.—The great curse of our public educational system, as of most things in our States, is politics. From the school directors up to the State superintendent politics is the blight of our school administration. Listen to these words from a former superintendent of public instruction of North Carolina. Speaking of the county superintendents, he says: "Why have not the men best qualified to fill these positions been elected in every county in North Carolina? I am sorry to tell you why, should you not already know, but I will do it. Politics was the cause and is the cause to-day." He continues: "The public schools have been in the galling grasp of the court-house politicians for twenty years. The county supervisor owes his election both directly and indirectly to the county officers. They are the men he is supposed to serve; they are the men to whom he must render an account of his stewardship. Away with such! Let us break away from this court-house ring business." Brave man! Would there were more like him.

At the bottom of it all is the want of serious interest in the public schools among the body of the voters. When the people realize their value they will be ready to give money to support them and to see to it that they are administered by competent and faithful men. . . .

The way to improvement.—Our system of school legislation and management and our methods of school taxation must be completely turned round before we can have anything like a system of efficient public schools. The school money must be raised to a larger extent from the State as a whole and be distributed more in accordance with the needs of the people. School management and supervision must be centralized to a considerable degree in the hands of representative and skilled experts. There should be a State board of education composed of the ablest educational authorities to be found, who should be responsible for all the public schools and should elect a State superintendent who should in turn have the fullest authority with regard to the organization of schools, examination of teachers, courses of study, and the distribution of funds, and have the general direction of county and city superintendents. The schools of the counties and the towns should be in the hands of boards of like powers working under the general direction of the State board and its superintendent. Who would think of carrying on any great business reaching every part of the State by the worthless methods, or no methods, which prevail in the South in regard to our schools? We must have a thoroughgoing reform in these things before we can even begin to build good schools. . . .

. . . We should consider the negro as a man to be educated for work, independence, and citizenship like other men. Everything I have said applies to him, therefore, just as it does to the white man. The negro is in the South to stay—he is a necessity for Southern industries—and the Southern people must educate and so elevate him or he will drag them down. The human race is an organism, all its members being bound together by natural affinities and ministering to each other by natural law. If history, philosophy, and revelation teach us anything it is the solidarity of all mankind, that "no man liveth to himself" and "no man dieth to himself," but that we are each "his brother's keeper."

I plead for justice and common sense in the education of the negro. The most encouraging thing about public education in the South is the noble, self-sacrificing way in which the Southern people have given of their limited resources for the education of their recent slaves. That they will continue to do for the black man all that their means will permit, I firmly believe. These attacks upon the negro school fund, these proposals to give him for his schools only what he pays in himself, come from short-sighted people who fail to recognize the basal principle underlying all public education, namely, the duty of all the people to educate all the people. They do not represent the opinion of the best people of the South and their proposals will not prevail. The people of the South realize already that this proposal is not primarily an assault upon the black man, but a movement to undermine the foundation of the country's prosperity, progress, and peace. . . .

But we must use common sense in the education of the negro. We must recognize in all its relations that momentous fact that the negro is a child race, at least two thousand years behind the Anglo-Saxon in its development, and that like all other races it must work out its own salvation by practicing the industrial arts, and becoming independent and self-supporting. Nothing is more ridiculous than the programme of the good religious people from the North who insist upon teaching Latin, Greek, and philosophy to the negro boys who come to their schools. Many of our Southern States make a similar mistake in trying to enforce in the schools of the black districts courses of study laid down for whites.

Edgar Gardner Murphy on Child Labor in Alabama, 1901

*A Reply to the Committee**

On Wednesday, October 30, the following communication appeared in the *Evening Transcript* of Boston, Massachusetts.

To the Editor of the *Transcript*:

My attention has been called to an article in your paper of the 23d inst., signed by gentlemen from Alabama, in reference to child labor.

As treasurer of a mill in that State, erected by Northern capital, I am interested in the subject. From the starting of our mill, I have never been South without protesting to the agent, and overseer of spinning (the only department in which small help can be employed), against allowing children under twelve years of age to come into the mill, as I did not consider them intelligent enough to do good work. On a visit last June, annoyed that my instructions were not more carefully observed, before leaving I wrote the agent a letter of which the following is a copy:—

"Every time I visit this mill, I am impressed with the fact that it is a great mistake to employ small help in the spinning room. Not only is it wrong from a humanitarian standpoint but it entails an absolute loss to the mill. We prepare the stock and make it into roving, and, because of the small spinners, send back to the pickers an excessive amount of roving waste, and meantime lose the work of the spindles. I again express the wish that you prevent the overseer, as far as possible, from employing children under twelve years of age. I know it is sometimes difficult to get at the real age—and in some cases the parents may threaten to leave our employ unless we give work to their small children, but we must take this stand—and I trust an honest effort will be made to carry out my wishes."

In defence of our officials, it is doubtless true that the trouble comes largely from the parents, who make every effort to get their children into the mill, and often because of refusal, take their families containing needed workers, to other mills, where no objection is made to the employment of

---

* Murphy was chairman of the Executive Committee on Child Labor in Alabama.

children. The statement that twice as many children under twelve years of age are employed in mills under Northern control as in Southern mills, if it means, as it should, in proportion to spindles on same number of yarns, is absolutely false so far as relates to our company, and I have reason to believe the same can be said of other mills under Northern ownership.

Now in regard to the attempted legislation of last winter: The labor organizations at the North imported from England a very bright and skilful female labor agitator and sent her to Alabama. She held meetings at central points, and when the Legislature convened appeared at Montgomery with her following, and a bill against employing children was promptly introduced. The manufacturers and other business men of Alabama resented this outside interference, well knowing the source from which it came, and they were also aware that manufacturers at the North were being solicited for funds with which to incite labor troubles in the South.

As they recognized that this bill was only the entering wedge, they determined that action must come from within the State, and not outside. They also felt that the adjoining State of Georgia, having double the number of spindles, should act first. With these considerations in mind, the manufacturers selected among others our agent, a native Alabamian, to appear before the legislative committee, with the result that the bill was defeated. I think it may be said with truth, that the interference of Northern labor agitators is retarding much needed legislation in all the manufacturing States of the South.

As to our mill and the little town of 2300 people which has grown up around it, there is nothing within the mill or without, of which any citizen of Massachusetts need be ashamed. On the contrary, I challenge either of the gentlemen from Alabama whose names are attached to the letter referred to, to mention among the forty mills in the State, of which only four are directly operated from the North, any one which will compare with ours, in the expenditure which has been made for the comfortable housing of the operatives, and the appliances introduced for their comfort and uplift. From the inception of this enterprise, the purpose has been to build up a model town that should be an object lesson to the South, and we are assured that its influences have been helpful. In addition to a school supported by public tax, the company has always carried on a school of its own, with an experienced and devoted teacher, who has been instructed to make special effort to get in the young children, and thus allure them from the mill. We have built and have in operation a beautiful library— the first erected for this special purpose in the State of Alabama, and we have a church building which would be an ornament in any village of New England, and is in itself an education to our people. We are now building a modern schoolhouse from plans by Boston architects which will accommodate all the children of our community. These are a few of the things we have done and are doing, in our effort to meet the responsibility we have assumed, in dealing with a class of people who have some most excellent traits, and who appeal to us strongly, because many of them have hitherto been deprived of needed comforts and largely of elementary advantages.

What we are attempting to do for our operatives may seem to the gentlemen who signed the appeal in your columns as "spectacular philanthropy" and a "heartless policy"; but this is not the opinion of our employees, nor of visitors who have acquainted themselves with the facts, nor of the communities adjacent to us.

J. Howard Nichols,
Treasurer Alabama City Mill, Alabama

A Rejoinder from Alabama

On the afternoon of November 2d, Mr. Edgar Gardner Murphy, of Montgomery, Alabama, the chairman of the Alabama Child-labor Committee, received a copy of the above letter. Mr. Murphy at once wrote and forwarded the following rejoinder:—

To the Editor of the *Transcript*:

I note in your issue of October 30th a reply to a statement to the press and the people of New England, on the subject of child labor in Alabama. Our statement bore the signatures of six representative citizens of Alabama, among them the Superintendent of Public Schools of Birmingham and ex-Governor Thomas G. Jones, of Montgomery. The reply to the address of the committee is signed, not by a disinterested citizen of the State, but by Mr. J. Howard Nichols, Treasurer of the Alabama City Mill, at Alabama City.

I thank you for publishing Mr. Nichols's letter. The well-known citizens of Alabama with whom I have the honor to be associated, have welcomed the discussion of this subject, and they desire the frankest and fullest showing of the facts.

I note, however, with some amazement, that the Treasurer of the Alabama City Mill begins his argument by conceding the two fundamental principles for which we are contending—the social wrong and the economic error of child labor under twelve. He declares that from the starting of that mill he has repeatedly protested against the use of children under this age and that last June he wrote to his local agent that the employment of such help "is not only wrong from a humanitarian standpoint, but it entails an absolute loss to the mill." Now this is substantially, and in admirable form, the whole case of our committee.

Yet what must be our added amazement when, in the next paragraph but one, we read the further admission that, in order to continue this economic and social wrong and in order to defeat a simple and effective remedy for this wrong, the salaried representative of his own mill, during the preceding February, had appeared in this city before our Legislature, in aggressive and persistent antagonism to the protection of little children under twelve! This, in the teeth of protests which Mr. Nichols declares he has made since "the starting" of his mill. Who, then, is the responsible representative of the actual policy of the Alabama City Mill—its Treasurer or its representative before the Legislature? Or is the policy of the mill a policy which concedes the principle, only to deny the principle its fruit? If this be the true interpretation of the conditions, what are we to say to the explanations which are suggested; explanations offered "in defence of our [Mr. Nichols's] officials."

Mr. Nichols assures us that the officials have been put under grave pressure from the parents. Let us concede that this is true. Yet Mr. Nichols himself is not satisfied with this "defence," and he declares wisely and bravely that his officials must take their stand against the pressure of unscrupulous and idle parents. His agents must resist the threat of such parents to leave the Alabama City Mill for mills having a lower standard of employment. Does not Mr. Nichols see that our legislation was precisely directed toward ending this pressure, toward breaking up this ignoble competition, and toward the preservation of the standard of employment which he professes? There could be no pressure to withdraw the children and to enter them in other mills, if such labor were everywhere prohibited by statute. But we are grateful to Mr. Nichols for his declaration. And yet, is he ignorant of the need of legislation in the State at large? His very argument is a confession of knowledge. If the Alabama City Mill is fairly represented by the profession of Mr. Nichols, why should the paid and delegated agent of that mill labor here for weeks to thwart a simple legislative remedy for the abuses he deplores?

Is it sufficient for your correspondent to declare that this legislation met with local opposition simply because such reforms should come "from within the State and not from outside"? This is a strange objection upon the part of one who represents investments from outside. The evils may be supported from the East, but the remedies (sic) must be indigenous! Nor is there the slightest ground for the suggestion that the initiative for our movement of reform came from "a skilful female labor agitator imported from England." We yield sincere gratitude to the American Federation of Labor for their earnest, creditable, and effective coöperation. Their interest in the situation is entirely intelligible. When the younger children are thrust into the labor market in competition with the adult, they contend that the adult wage is everywhere affected. But the agent of the Federation of Labor—earnest and devoted woman that she is—did her work, not in the spirit of interference, but in the spirit of helpfulness. She was not responsible for the beginning of the agitation. The demand for this legislative protection of our children was made by the Minister's Union of Montgomery and by the Woman's Christian Temperance Union of Alabama, before she was ever heard of in the South.

Nothing could be more baseless than the assumption that our local effort for reforms is due to outside forces. But if it were—what of it? There is at stake here to-day the welfare of our little children, the happiness and efficiency of our future operatives; the moral standard of our economic life; and this committee frankly proposes, in every honorable way, to secure all the aid, from every quarter of our common country, which we can possibly command. The criticism of such a policy is a little out of place from the representative of a mill here operated upon investments from Massachusetts.

Mr. Nichols then informs us that the reform legislation was defeated because "the adjoining State of Georgia, having double the number of spindles, should act first." This, we have contended, is to miss the very essence of the statesmanship of the situation. The very fact that Georgia has twice as many spindles as Alabama, makes it twice as hard for Georgia to precede us. The cost of such an economic readjustment must be obviously twice as great in Georgia as in Alabama. That Alabama is not so deeply involved in the system of child labor as some other Southern States is clearly the reason why Alabama should take the lead.

It has been conservatively estimated that in some of the Southern States more than twenty per cent of the mill operatives are under fourteen years of age. Does Mr. Nichols wish Alabama to delay until that becomes the condition of the industry in this State? According to the logical demand of his argument, the State having the most spindles, the State most deeply and inextricably involved, must be the first to face the delicate and difficult problem of readjustment!

Mr. Nichols also declares that our reform measure was defeated because it was believed to be "the entering wedge" of other troublesome labor legislation. We must not protect our little children under twelve, we must not do a compassionate and reasonable thing, because, forsooth, somebody might then demand an inconsiderate and unreasonable thing! Do the corporate interests in Alabama wish to predicate their liberties upon such an argument?

Yet, says Mr. Nichols, "with these considerations in mind, the manufacturers selected, among others, our agent, a native Alabamian, to appear before the Legislative Committee, with the result that the bill was defeated." Mr. Nichols neglects to state that on the second hearing of the bill, his agent appeared alone as the chosen spokesman of all the opponents of reform. He, too, made much of this hoary scare about "the entering wedge."

What iniquities of reaction, what bitter stultification of human progress has that argument not supported! In such a case as this, it is not an argument, it is a provocation. It is a challenge to the common sense and the common humanity of our people. If the corporate interests of this State, whether operated by Northerners or Southerners, are to rest the great cause of their unrestricted development upon the cruel refusal of protection to our younger children, then let them beware lest, having rejected "the entering wedge," they invite the cyclone. What greater folly, viewed from the strictly selfish standpoint of certain corporate interests, than to involve their fate in the issues of so odious an argument?

Such a course must gradually invite the hatred of the people, must inevitably goad the great masses of our population into the fixed belief that the corporation desires to live, not by production, but through destruction; that it is a force to be feared and bound rather than a force to be trusted and liberated. The course of humanity is always the course of wisdom. If the corporate interests of this State desire a long and prosperous career, untrammelled by restrictive legislation, let them disabuse the people of the impression that their liberties represent the refusal of compassion to our children; let them persuade the people of Alabama that they wish to grow, not out of the soil of ignorance and wretchedness, but out of the rich and human fertilities of social justice and the social welfare. Let them go to the popular heart, and base themselves there, not upon the negation, but upon the extension of privilege.

I concur in the claim that the Alabama City Mill is in some respects wholly exceptional. Says Mr. Nichols: "I challenge either of the gentlemen from Alabama to mention among the mills of the State . . . any one which compares with ours in the expenditure which has been made for the comfortable housing of the operatives and the appliances introduced for their comfort and uplift." In one breath the friends of this mill ask us to believe it exceptional, and yet in the next breath they ask that the need for reform legislation in relation to all the mills of the State, shall be determined from the conditions it presents! If the Alabama City Mill is so unique, then it is not representative or typical. If it is not representative of the average conditions of child labor in Alabama, it has nothing to do with this argument.

As to the proportionate number of little children in our Southern and Northern mills, the facts have been accurately stated by the committee. The statement of Mr. Nichols that there are only four mills in the State "directly operated from the North" is unintelligible to me. Upon my desk, as I write, there are the figures from eleven Alabama mills which, upon the word of their own managers, are controlled by Northern capital.

It seems to have grieved Mr. Nichols that we should have characterized certain unique philanthropies in connection with one or two of our Eastern mills as "spectacular." The gentlemen of this committee have no desire to express themselves in the language of impulsive epithet. We are sincerely grateful for every motive and for every work which touches and blesses the lot of the unprivileged. But when large photographs of the exceptional philanthropies of a single mill are seriously brought before the committee of our Legislature as an argument for the perpetuation of the general conditions of child labor in this State, when the advertisements of a unique establishment are used to cloak the wretched lot of the average factory; when, upon the basis of the representations of Alabama City, men are taught to ignore the essential cruelty of the whole miserable system, and are made blind to the misery of hundreds whom that factory can never touch, then I frankly declare that such philanthropies are indeed "spectacular," for they have actually cursed more than they have ever blessed. They have become a mockery of love. They may have benefited the employees of one mill; but they have served to rivet the chains of a heartbreaking and wretched slavery upon hundreds of our little children in the State at large. And no philanthropy, however exceptional, and no institutional compassion, however effective, can ever justify the refusal, at the door of the factory, of legislative protection to the little child under twelve years of age. That is the sole contention of this committee.

Is that asking too much? If Massachusetts protects at fourteen years, may not Alabama protect at twelve? Is this too drastic a demand upon the exceptional philanthropy of the mill at Alabama City? I hope not. I do not mean to write with the slightest personal unkindness, but I do write with an intense earnestness of concern in behalf of the sad and unnatural fate of the little people of our factories. We, for their sakes, do not want enemies anywhere. We want friends everywhere. It is with pleasure therefore that I recur to the instructions forwarded by Mr. Nichols to his agent. Speaking of the employment of little children, he said, "Not only is it wrong from a humanitarian standpoint, but it entails an absolute loss to the mill." There speaks the man of wisdom and the man of heart. Does Mr. Nichols mean it? Does the mill at Alabama City mean it? Will Massachusetts join hands with Alabama?

That mill, with its great influences, has led the fight in this State against the protection of our factory children. Will it continue to represent a policy of opposition and reaction? Or, will it represent a policy of coöperation and of progress? Will it send its representative, with this committee, before our next Legislature and there declare that the cotton industry of the South, as here undertaken by Massachusetts, is too important in its dignity and its value to be longer involved in the odium and the horror of an industrial system which all the world has cast off? If so, that representative may indeed find himself in the company of some of the nobler forces from "outside." The whole world has a way of taking the little child to its heart. But he will also find himself in the company—the increasingly resolute company—of thousands of the people of Alabama.

Edgar Gardner Murphy.

Montgomery, Ala., November 2, 1901.

The Progressive Farmer on Public Schools and Good Roads, 1904

Three Generous Offers to the Public Schools.

The State Superintendent of Public Instruction has received the following encouraging letter from Mr. A. C. Shuford, the President and Treasurer of Startown Nursery Company, at Newton, N.C.:

"Dear Sir:—We have watched closely the work you are doing to better the public schools and advance the cause of education in North Carolina. We feel a deep interest in this matter, and believing, as we do, that local taxation is the one thing needful to supplement the public schools, we desire to make the following proposition, with the hope that it will not only encourage communities where a tax is voted for, but aid in cultivating a love of the beautiful.

"Beginning with the year 1904, we offer $5 worth of ornamental trees, shrubbery, etc., or any class of nursery stock desired, to every community or school where the people vote a tax upon themselves to supplement the public fund. We offer also $10 worth as above stated to every graded school established in the country."

The Poor Farmer.—"I had to lighten this load, though it was only 2,000 pounds, and I am afraid I must get another team to help pull out of this mud hole. Next spring I will have to borrow the money to buy a new team; these skates won't last another season. I am so sorry I did not favor the Brownlow Bill."

His Horses.—"We would rather die in our tracks than to try to get this load to market. No matter how much we eat, we are thin."

The Go-ahead Farmer.—"Since this new road was built I can haul a load of 5,000 pounds to market and make two trips in the time it took me to make one on the old mud road; then, too, I can haul in wet weather when I can't plow. I am so glad I was in favor of the Brownlow Bill."

His Horses.—"It is just play to haul this load on the new road. See how fat we are!"

John E. White on Prohibition, 1908

The people of the South are the historical partisans of personal liberty. They are naturally opposed to sumptuary laws of any kind. Thousands of men are with the Prohibition movement who have always had whiskey in their homes for personal and domestic use. They have not been aroused and are not aroused against whiskey *per se*. And it has gone contrary to the grain to contemplate as they do the limitation which Prohibition will place upon their personal liberty in that matter. But there they are, and it is the hopefulest sign of Southern civilization . . . for it reveals the dawning of a sense of social obligation than which Christianity holds nothing finer for the future of society. They are opposed to the Liquor Traffic, opposed to its investment of millions of dollars in a demoralizing social agency, opposed to its cold blooded attitude toward humanity, its essential lack of patriotism, its interference with industrial efficiency, its consistent alliance with crime and every evil, its necessary antagonism to all the agencies of character building, and to its particular peril to the peace and happiness of the South, which has the great problem of the races on its hands. In short, the intelligent people of the South are looking upon Prohibition, not as a temperance reform, but as statesmanship—a public policy, favorable to religion, favorable to education, favorable to industry, favorable to the coming generation, and as a necessity of Southern conditions in particular and as an ideal of social obligation to a broad general good.

Where these considerations have never been so formulated, and with men who could not formulate such an explanation of their attitude toward the Prohibition movement, they are the real considerations felt with varying degrees of earnestness throughout the rank of Southern society.

In addition to the steady development of the anti-saloon conviction in the South, upon which Prohibition depends, there are conditions not found elsewhere which have contributed to its popular appeal and stand stoutly in support of its permanency. One of these conditions, in the judgment of some, is the probable explanation of the general attitude of the Southern people. I refer to the race question—the presence of eight million negroes.

The feeling of insecurity in the rural sections of the South on account of vagrant and drunken negroes had become a contagion among the country women. A little of this sort of thing goes a long way in the South. Public sentiment has become intensely stimulated by it. Probably no demonstration under Prohibition will be calculated to make a more influential impression on the country people than to show them an end to drunken negro parties, the return from the nearby towns, and the courts uncongested by negro cases.

But more than this in real importance, for several years two ideas have been growing strong in the intelligence of the South, both of which have force in bringing on and fixing Prohibition as a settled policy.

The fact that the negro constitutes a child-people element in our population, that the great mass of the negroes are ignorant and weak and therefore are to be thought for in government and protected from the perils of liberty, is an ascending idea in the legislative scheme of the South. The moral basis of the disfranchisement movement was this: thousands of the best men—the justest men—went with this movement in consideration of the true welfare of the negro race, their thought being that through such limitation only could the discipline of citizenship become possible. This idea of the negro is more pronounced in the Prohibition movement. It stands out more nobly. The saloon was the ravager of the negro people. It plundered them at all points, robbed them of their wages, fed their animalism, and was, as every one knows, a debauching agent let loose by law upon them.

Another fact made constantly more prominent in the South's study of herself is a condition among a considerable mass of the white population not entirely unlike the condition among the negroes—ignorance, poverty and irresponsibility. This constitutes the other half of the race peril. The new movement in public education has made clear this fact as one to be seriously reckoned with. There are these thousands—should we say millions?—of our own Anglo-Saxon stock, not yet raised to a safe level of civilization, not yet, by education and opportunity, strong enough to reckon their social responsibility and to resist the elemental impulse of lawlessness, when racial antipathies are aroused. The obligation of a democracy to make law minister to their development is being felt more and more in the South and has a place in the interpretation of the Prohibition policy.

These are the two elements of Southern society that define the acute dangers of the race problem. It is realized that in any Southern community with a bar-room a race war is a perilously possible occurrence. The danger is not in the upper but in the lower levels of both races. There the inflammable fringes hang loose. Following the racial lines from top to bottom, it became evident to everybody that the lines of both races converged at the saloon, which stood at the acute angle of the inverted social pyramid. It was the attractive social center for the dangerous elements of our population.

At their hearts the intelligent white people of the South are sick of the race issue as a menace to social peace. They are tired of the depraved and criminal negro. They are tired of the irresponsible white man. The Liquor Traffic fostered and encouraged both. I say, therefore, that the negro is not the only nor the chief reason for Prohibition in the South, and yet its permanency as a policy will find always a ready and powerful justification in the fact that there are eight million negroes in the South, constituting the most difficult sociological problem any people ever had, which the Liquor Traffic only tended to complicate.

The Southern Sociological Congress's Agenda for Reforming the South, 1914

The Social Program of the Congress

The Southern Sociological Congress stands:

For the abolition of convict lease and contract systems, and for the adoption of modern principles of prison reform.

For the extension and improvement of juvenile courts and juvenile reformatories.

For the proper care and treatment of defectives, the blind, the deaf, the insane, the epileptic, and the feeble-minded.

For the recognition of the relation of alcoholism to disease, to crime, to pauperism, and to vice, and for the adoption of appropriate preventive measures.

For the adoption of uniform laws of the highest standards concerning marriage and divorce.

For the adoption of the uniform law on vital statistics.

For the abolition of child labor by the enactment of the uniform child labor law.

For the enactment of school attendance laws, that the reproach of the greatest degree of illiteracy may be removed from our section.

For the suppression of prostitution.

For the solving of the race question in a spirit of helpfulness to the negro and of equal justice to both races.

For the closest co-operation between the Church and all social agencies for the securing of these results.

The Challenge of the Congress

The Southern Sociological Congress is a challenge to the men and women of the whole South:

1. It is a challenge to the Southern fathers and mothers and all social workers to lift the burdens of labor from childhood and to make education universal.

2. It is a challenge to the men who make and administer laws to organize society as a school for the development of all her citizens rather than simply to be a master to dispose of the dependent, defective, and delinquent population with the least expense to the State.

3. It is a challenge to all citizens to rally to the leaders of all social reforms, so as to secure for the South civic righteousness, temperance, and health.

4. It is a challenge to Southern chivalry to see that justice is guaranteed to all citizens regardless of race, color, or religion, and especially to befriend and defend the friendless and helpless.

5. It is a challenge to the Church to prove her right to social mastery by a universal and unselfish social ministry.

6. It is a challenge to the present generation to show its gratitude for the heritage bequeathed to it through the toil and blood of centuries by devoting itself more earnestly to the task of making the nation a universal brotherhood.

7. It is a challenge to strong young men and women to volunteer for a crusade of social service, and to be enlisted for heroic warfare against all destroyers of public health and purity, and to champion all that makes for an ideal national life.

The Social Mission of the Church to City Life

RABBI EMANUEL STERNHEIM, GREENVILLE, MISS.

True religion insists on human service, and this is the end toward which the real development of religion should be in the present suborned. One of the signs of the times is a new consciousness of others' needs. All men agree that there are rights which have not been recognized and duties which have not been performed. The desire to serve is forcing men to new and sometimes to strange activities, but nevertheless the desire to determine the relation of the individual to the community is a universal one.

Busy with our trade, and surrounded with the signs of wealth, we, like Jacob, have been met by the angel of our forgotten brother. It is of the struggle of this angel, in the concerted effort to find what we must do for other's needs, that shall make of us princes of God, and enable us to remember that "the rich and poor meet together; the Lord is the maker of them all."

I cannot touch the manifold efforts of modern care for others' needs— the passionate stroke of the reformer, the gentle touch of the comforter— and show the unity of their variety.

I fear I cannot catch the voice of the twentieth century and repeat it as the latest word of God. But I do believe in his presence guiding us all unto truth, and I bow in reverence before the spirit of the age, which is, I believe, socialized religion.

The social worker is everywhere at this time being congratulated upon the increasing interest taken in social questions. I am glad, because the interest reveals the existence of a love which is stronger than mere class. The spirit of the age reveals the fact that love is not dead, even in breasts hardened by success and luxury and fashion. . . .

I propose to devote myself to two or three specific duties of the Church about which there is usually some dispute.

The first claim I make is, that it is the duty of the Church to enter into the work of municipal government. There are arguments pro and con about this, but it seems to me to be axiomatic that the minister is a citizen and a man before he is a parson and he cannot be refused the rights of a citizen; but I am not keen on pressing the point, for my argument is to be that it is a comparatively unimportant thing whether the minister sits on the municipal board or not, but it is an essential to righteous city government that the united voices of the churches of the city shall speak through its personnel the demand for a godly and God-fearing administration. . . .

When one pauses to think of the tremendous influence of municipal government upon the morality and character of the citizens of a city, one can readily foresee the inestimable value of the coöperation of these men trained in the highest ideals of the social application of their religious convictions. A superficial objection will undoubtedly be the fear of infusion of sectarian differences. I am utterly unable to sympathize with the objection, for the very basis of socialized religion is the subordination of dogma before the ideal of universal human service.

Anticipating much the same objection and giving to it much the same reply, I am going to be sufficiently controversial to advocate the extension of the duty of the church to the domain of education. With a very complete and long experience of the evils of the infusion of religious differences into education, I am nevertheless anxious about the growth of a paramount utilitarian and materialistic education system. . . .

. . . I am pleading now for an aesthetic outlook, for an intellectual renaissance, and not for any dogmatic religious expression. It may well be that the Church cannot as an organization wisely attempt to interfere in school management, but it may be sympathetic and may voice that broad and enlightened conception of education that sees in it great possibilities for redemption and achievement.

By virtue of the position of the Church in regard to guidance, it should so coöperate with every educational effort in the city that every teacher in the city may thank God and take courage.

The last point with which I shall deal is the duty of the Church with regard to recreation. . . .

What I am advocating here, however, is not so much the erection of the institutional church to which, of course, there can be no objection in the light of the principles enunciated in this address, but rather a conception of the duty of the Church in the fostering and the encouragement of every possible form of clean and wholesome amusement within the city limits. Perhaps there is no greater authority on this aspect of socialized religion than the late Canon S. A. Barnett, of London, England, for many years the presiding genius of the prototype of the social settlement, the concrete expression of the zeitgeist. He says: "Somehow Sunday must be rescued from its present degradation, saved from being a day of sleep and of eating and drinking, to become a day of learning, enjoyment, and rest. Somehow the people must be brought within a refining influence, such as that which comes from knowledge of the best things within men's reach." Hear him again on the art exhibition: "The admiration of beautiful things will not, we know, keep men from being selfish and sensual; neither is there any other nostrum which, by itself, will cure evil. The sight of pictures and works of art makes them conscious both of power and capacity, and does something to bring them nearer eternal life." Finally, relative to the point that I am endeavoring to emphasize: "Service by doing rather than service by giving is the true ideal, but service by giving has also its place so long as it is properly subordinated."

Poverty, it must be recognized, cannot afford the pleasures which human nature demands. A poor neighborhood cannot support high-class amusements. The best has always to be given away, and if poverty is to enjoy pleasure, then means for giving it must be discovered. Here pre-eminently is the duty of the Church to the city clearly distinguishable. The advocates of pleasure for the people cannot find in the modern church, even yet, the material generosity of those who advocate the gospel. It will not be until the gift of pleasure is seen to be required by God that rich men will set with earnest purpose to the work of making gladder the lives of the very poor.

Finally, it must be the conception of the Church that it is its function to stand for every effort to beautify the city. In the simple yet majestic words of Browning,

> If you get simple beauty and naught else,
> You get about the best thing God invents.

In an ideal city all these things will be. The mission of the Church to the city is to make it ideal, and therefore all these things must be. In an ideal city none will be very rich and none will be very poor; knowledge and good will will join together to give to every child the best education; to render every house and street as healthy as the healthiest hillside in the world; to provide the most comfortable hospital for every one who is sick and to have at hand a friend for every one in trouble.

In our ideal city art will grow out of common life, undisturbed by contrasts of wealth and poverty. The people will have pleasure in their work and leisure to admire what is beautiful.

The Southern Sociological Congress as a Factor for Social Welfare

BOOKER T. WASHINGTON, LL.D., TUSKEGEE, ALA.

In the brief space that has been allotted to me on this program, I want to speak of some special ways in which it seems to me this Congress can promote the welfare of the people of the South.

First of all, it can serve as a medium for direct and candid expression of opinion on the part of the members of both races in regard to matters of common interest. No one living in the South, or out of the South, should expect everything to be done in a day. When we consider all that the South has been called upon to do and to bear in connection with the readjustment of its economic and social program, the wonder is that so much has been accomplished within so brief a space of time. What we want to be sure of is that progress in the right direction is constant and steady. One direction in which meetings of this kind can help is in bringing about a better understanding between the races. In spite of difficulties that grow out of the situation in the South, the races have many fundamental interests in common and there is much that should be done for the welfare of each race which can only be done with the hearty coöperation of both.

How can the negro in the South do his part, through this organization, to bring about better conditions? The leaders of our people, for example, can do much to spread the influence of this meeting to all parts of the South. They can let the masses of the people know that there is an organization made up of Southern white people who are interested in their welfare, to whom they can speak frankly about their desires and their needs. The influence of this meeting spread abroad among the masses of the colored people will lead them to feel that the South is their home, and that they have a share, no matter how humble, in all its weal and woe, in everything that concerns its welfare.

We should learn from this meeting, all of us, to manifest as much pride in whatever concerns our own community, our own city, or our own State as the white people do. We should feel as much humiliation on account of anything that hurts the reputation of the community in which we live as is true of the white race.

In the past, I fear that the white people and the black people have talked too much about each other and not enough to each other. We can use this Congress as a means of appealing directly to the white people. There are certain things we want them to do. The simplest and most practical way is to go frankly to the white people of the South and ask for what we want.

In every county of the South the colored people should get hold of the city, county, and State officials and make it possible for them to see the better life of our race. It is most important that we get hold of the Governor, sheriffs, judges, and other officials and bring them into direct contact with the needs and conditions of our people. Our leaders can use this organization for making it easier for the liberal-minded white people who are desirous of helping us to come into contact with us in a manner that will not embarrass them.

We have friends among the Southern white people. You will hardly find a colored man in the South, no matter how humble, and no matter, I was going to say, how worthless, who has not some white friend to whom he is accustomed to go when he is in trouble. It is these friendships between individual white people and individual black people which form the basis for coöperation between the races.

We can use this organization to create a sentiment among our people throughout the South which will serve to stop so much crime. In spite of all that may be said in palliation, there is too much crime committed by our people in all parts of the country. We should let the world understand that we are not going to hide crime simply because it is committed by black people.

We can use this Congress, too, in a way to impress upon the white people throughout the South that education does not unfit us for the common labors and duties of life; but in proportion as we get education we will be more useful in field and shop, in kitchen and laundry, as teachers, and in every walk of life.

We can use this Congress to let the world understand that in proportion as the negro is educated he does not wish to intermingle with the white people in a purely social way; but in proportion as the negro gets intelligence he finds happiness and satisfaction in social intercourse with members of his own race.

We can use this Congress to impress the world with the idea that we are proud of being negroes, and this pride should increase in proportion as the negro goes forward in all the useful lines of our civilization.

How can the white man use this Congress in promoting better conditions between the races in the South?

First, it can be used, as I have suggested, as a medium through which white people may get acquainted with the most useful and best type of black people in every community. The average white man, I sometimes fear, knows more about the criminal negro than he does about the law-abiding, self-respecting, and successful negro.

The white people can use this Congress to help advertise the better side rather than the worse side of negro life throughout the South. Too much space, I often fear, is given in newspapers to reports covering negro crime and not enough to reports covering the useful living and strivings of our race.

This Congress can be used to put in motion a public sentiment throughout the South that will insist that in the courts the negro may be sure of equal justice. The average black man has a notion that the court is a place of punishment rather than a place of protection. The total amount of time the best white people of the South lose every year in dealing with petty negro crime through the courts, if it were reckoned up, would represent a sum so large as to be startling. This Congress, directly and indirectly, can do much to stop the practice of arresting so many of our people for petty and trivial offenses, all of which impose a tremendous burden upon black people and white people in every community throughout the South.

This Congress can be used as a means of letting the people throughout the country know that the educated negro seldom commits crime, and in proportion as we get more education and better education the cost of punishing criminals will disappear.

This Congress can be used in creating a sentiment in every county in favor of better schools for negro children. It is often said that education for the negro has been a failure. We cannot say that a policy has failed until it has been actually tried. Education for the negro, especially in the rural districts, has not been tried in any effective way or upon a comprehensive scale. I say this although I am fully aware that in many counties it is poverty which retards white education as well as negro education.

The negro is going to get some kind of education at the hands of somebody, somewhere and at some time; and I believe the time has come when the white officials in every county should become the leaders and guides in the matter of giving to every negro child an opportunity to get a common school education. The Sociological Congress can do much to encourage the colored people in what they are doing to educate themselves, and to guide and foster every effort that is being made, from whatever direction, to improve the colored people and make them valuable and useful citizens of the communities in which they live.

As no color line is drawn in the courts in the matter of punishing crime, neither should any color line be drawn in the opportunity to get education in the public schools. The schools can always be supported out of the return that they bring to the State in the form of more efficient labor and better social order. The more money spent in educating the negro child, the less the State will have to pay for punishing crime. It should be the aim of this organization, in connection with those who are directing the schools, to prove to the South that education is one of the best investments that any country can make.

The white leaders in attendance on this Congress can use their influence in seeing to it that the negro gets fairer and more just treatment on the railroads throughout the South. In this connection I cannot forbear to commend to other portions of the South what has been done in the city of Memphis at the Union Station in providing adequate, comfortable, and even attractive accommodations for colored passengers. The time has come, too, when the strong white leaders of the South should no longer permit the negro to be used as a political "scarecrow." Too many selfish politicians have used the negro as a political "bogey man" in a way to deceive white people, and even to discourage some of the best black people in their communities. The negro is not seeking either social equality or political domination over the white man in any section of the South.

I want to see both races advance in the South. I have no racial prejudice. I want to see the negro lifted up for his own sake, but just as emphatically do I want to see the negro lifted up for the sake of the white man. I was born a slave here in the South. I love the South, and no white man can excel me in my devotion to the South. But I am aware of the fact that so long as the white man is surrounded by a race that is in a large measure ignorant, weak, and in poverty, so long will the white man be tempted to injure himself by unjust treatment of the weaker race by which he is surrounded. So long as there are hordes of ignorant colored women in any community, so long will they prove a temptation for some of the best white men of the South to degrade themselves.

There are millions of black people throughout the world. Everywhere, especially in Europe, people are looking to us here in the South, black and white, to show to the world how it is possible for two races, different in color, to live together on the same soil, under the same laws, and each race work out its salvation in justice to the other.

I do not wish to be misunderstood. Tremendous progress in all these directions has been made within the last fifty years. I speak as I do with frankness, and yet with love, because I want to see still greater progress brought about.

The negro here in the South, supported and encouraged as he is by the best element of the white people, has made progress in getting property, education, and a high Christian character that is not approached by any similar group of black people in Christendom. We must go on, patiently but courageously, year by year, devoting our best energies to the great big things, the fundamental things that underlie the progress and civilization of white people and black people throughout the South.

And this Southern Sociological Congress, in my opinion, as one of the great mediums in God's providence, has been brought into existence for this purpose.

Hoke Smith's Gubernatorial Inaugural Address, 1907

A government fails to reach its highest sphere if it does not protect the right of property, and at the same time constantly broaden opportunities for mental, moral and financial growth to the less fortunate.

A government by the people furnishes the only hope for such a result. To make it sure, ballot boxes must be pure, and legislative halls must be free from the influences of predatory wealth.

Every frank man admits more power has been exercised by the great corporations than has been consistent with the full protection of popular rights.

The time has come when it is necessary to determine whether certain favored interests or the state shall rule.

Suppress Lobbyists

What has been told of hired political agents infesting legislative halls is no idle story. They have been the curse of national legislation; their influences for evil has been felt in nearly every state, and Georgia has been no exception to the rule.

The great body of the people interested in legislative matters are busy at home with their daily labors.

The hired political agent has been permitted to press his master's interest, not only by using his own personal influence, but by bringing from different parts of the state his little strikers to sit around hotels, and present in the presence of members of the legislature, with professed impartiality, what he terms the wishes of the people, while at the same time, secretly, he is hired to defeat their interests.

I believe that you will pass legislation to make it a crime for any attorney or agent, hired to support or oppose legislation, to discuss his client's interest in the presence of those who are to vote upon it, except where that discussion is at a public hearing, or with members of the legislature officially named for conference.

The proposed legislation also requires that any one employed to support or oppose a legislative measure must promptly enter an appearance with the secretary of state in a book to be kept open to the public, describing the nature of his employment. . . .

Stop Free Passes

I also urge the passage of a bill which will put an end to the free pass system between local points in Georgia.

This practice began, and was followed for a long time, with but few harmful results. It has grown to be a crying evil. It has become a means of petty political bribery.

Our common carriers have no right to charge for transportation more than a sum reasonably sufficient to pay them for their services. If some ride free, those who pay must be charged sufficient rates to cover the legitimate cost of their transportation and the passage of the free pass holders. . . .

Money in Politics and Clean Elections

The best results from popular government can only be had where the individual voter approaches the ballot box influenced alone by a patriotic purpose to serve his country, his state and his nation.

One of the evils which has polluted elections and debauched voters has been political contributions by the great corporations and special interests. Their money has been given not to advance principles, but to debauch character and defeat popular rights. . . .

Make it a crime for a corporation or special interest to contribute money to politics. Make it a crime to buy a voter or hire a striker at the polls. Place upon every candidate the duty of showing, under oath, a detailed statement of what he spent, how he spent it, and where the money came from.

With these three provisions enacted into law, a great step forward will be made. Then let us make elections so clean in Georgia that other states, seeing our good works, may follow our example.

Constitutional Amendment Fixing Franchise Standard

I realize how difficult it will be to reach the standard for which I plead when a great number of qualified voters are hopelessly ignorant and purchasable. The difficulty is greatly increased when a class of voters has for generations inherited incapacity, and must transmit the same incapacity for generations to come.

I favor an amendment to the constitution of the state which will fix a new standard for the elective franchise. . . .

Six Classes of Voters

The proposed constitutional amendment is along the line of the Alabama law. It provides that a person to register and vote must have all the qualifications now required for that purpose, and also belong to some one of the six classes following:

First—All persons who served in any war of the United States, the confederate states or the state of Georgia; or

Second—All persons lawfully descended from any of such soldiers; or

Third—All persons of good character who understand the duties and obligations of citizenship; or

Fourth—All persons who can read correctly and who can write correctly when read to them in the English language any paragraph of the constitution of the United States or the state of Georgia; or

Fifth—Any person who is the owner of forty acres of land on which he lives; or

Sixth—Any person who owns five hundred (500) dollars worth of property in the state of Georgia as shown by the tax digest. . . .

Control Over Rates

The great problem of local freight and passenger rates is one for regulation by the state. . . .

Railroad Employees

The state owes a duty to the faithful men who discharge the labor for railroad and public service companies. . . . Especially is it unjust to free the corporation from liability in those cases defended upon the ground that the employee knew of the negligence of the company and assumed the risk of such negligence. An employee may know of the existence of a defect, known also to his superior officer. He cannot afford to quit work nor can the public afford to have him quit. To deprive him in case of injury of the right to recover is a rule so harsh that it is only defended upon the theory of precedent. . . .

Liquor Legislation

While my sympathies in a local election are with those who oppose the sale of liquor, for the present, local option may furnish the best plan for controlling the liquor traffic.

But after the people of a county vote liquor out, it is not fair to permit the daily inpouring of liquors by jug trains.

Our platform demands that the dry counties of Georgia be kept dry. . . .

Education

The chief object of government should be to prevent special privileges and to give to all equal rights and opportunities. To this the men and women of Georgia are entitled, and you are preparing legislation which insures it to them.

The relation of the state to the children goes much further. It is the duty of the state to see that the children are given an opportunity for all preparation which their probable life work requires.

Education from books alone is not always of much value. It should be accompanied with practical training, having in view the future of the child.

Negro Children

Let me refer to the negro children in this connection. Any plan for the negroes which fails to recognize the difference between the white and black races will fail. The honest student of history knows that the negro had full opportunity for generations to develop before the days of slavery; that the negro race was improved by slavery, and that the majority of the negroes in this state have ceased to improve since slavery. Few have been helped by learning from books. All have been helped who have been taught or made to work.

It is not the difference of environment; it is the difference of race, deep seated, inherited for generations and generations through hundreds of years.

The large majority of negroes are incapable of anything but manual labor and many taught from books spurn labor and live in idleness. Few negroes are willing to work beyond the procurement of the hardest necessities of life.

The negro child should be taught manual labor and how to live. The negro teacher should be selected less by book than by character examinations. The negro school to be useful needs less books and more work. I favor a complete change in the examination of teachers for the negro schools, and for them a different plan of management; I would have the schools help the negro, not injure him. . . .

White Children

The white children of Georgia are prepared for the highest development: but I do not mean by this that they will necessarily obtain it through literary and classical studies.

For them it is at this time most important to improve the manual training and agricultural schools, and the rural schools. With a view to progress, I ask you to consider the unorganized condition of the educational work of Georgia.

University and Branches

. . . We must require the corporations in Georgia to pay their just taxes. We must equalize taxation among all the people of Georgia. Who will object to paying taxes when he realizes that the money is to be intelligently spent for the children of the state? Instead of a burden, it should be a great privilege to help in so noble a cause.

⚓ *E S S A Y S*

Dewey W. Grantham, professor of history at Vanderbilt University, summarizes a generation of scholarship on southern progressivism in the first essay, focusing on the origins, background, and programs of progressives. While acknowledging the cultural boundaries of the progressive movement in the South, Grantham notes that the reform activities—not only by middle-class white men but also by blacks and women—helped to establish a liberal tradition in the region. C. Vann Woodward's chapter on southern progressivism from his seminal book *Origins of the New South, 1877–1913* reflected the standard view until the early 1970s. Reprinted here as the second selection, the essay argues that the movement was strictly urban and middle class and that it generally failed to alter the life of the average southerner, black or white. Woodward's emphasis on state administrations reflects the prominence of politics as both means and end to the progressive agenda. The final selection—by historian James L. Leloudis II of the University of North Carolina, Chapel Hill—provides an example of the direction of recent scholarship on southern progressivism. Leloudis demonstrates the active role of women in educational reform in North Carolina, but as with earlier writers, he questions whether the involvement meant a significant departure from the traditionally subordinate status of women in the South.

The Promise of Southern Progressivism

DEWEY W. GRANTHAM

The April 1946 issue of the *North Carolina Historical Review* contained a pioneering article by Arthur S. Link on "The Progressive Movement in the South, 1870–1914." While noting that most writers "ignore the pro-

Dewey W. Grantham, "The Contours of Southern Progressivism," *American Historical Review* 86 (December 1981), pp. 1035–1056. Reprinted by permission of the author and the American Historical Association.

gressive movement in the South altogether," Link contended that the Southern states were the scene of "a far-reaching progressive movement." At
the time the young Princeton historian wrote these words, he had virtually
no scholarly literature on which to rely, particularly for developments of
the early twentieth century. This was still largely true five years later when
C. Vann Woodward's interpretation, "Progressivism—For Whites Only,"
appeared as chapter 14 of his *Origins of the New South, 1877–1913* (1951).
Except for a few scholarly articles and a handful of monographs on such
topics as child labor reform and prohibition, Woodward was forced to
quarry his building materials from primary sources. But the situation was
already beginning to change.

During the 1950s the Progressive era in the South became a new historical frontier. The field attracted a growing number of historians, especially young scholars stimulated by Woodward's seminal volume, and their
research merged into the larger historiographical assault on the Age of
Reform in the United States. Some of the products of this research are
apparent in George B. Tindall's *The Emergence of the New South, 1913–
1945* (1967) and in other general studies published by Hugh C. Bailey in
1969 and Jack Temple Kirby in 1972. In the preface to an edition of *Origins
of the New South* that appeared in 1971, Woodward spoke of "the outpouring of historical scholarship" during the past twenty years, a statement
amply substantiated in the 112-page bibliographical essay prepared for the
new edition by Charles B. Dew. The number of books, articles, and essays
on the Progressive era in the South continued to mount during the 1970s.
Evidence of this historiographical vitality can be found in the selected
bibliography published annually in the *Journal of Southern History* and in
almost any recent volume of a Southern state's historical journal.

The scholarly writings on the Progressive era in the South are so extensive that it is now possible to think in terms of a comprehensive historical
synthesis. This essay attempts to outline the dimensions of such a synthesis.
In sketching the contours of Southern progressivism, the essay addresses
several questions. First, what were the origins of the progressive impulse
in the South? Second, who were the Southern progressives and what were
their social values? Third, what were the most important progressive campaigns in the Southern states and what pattern did they assume? Fourth,
to what extent did these regional movements eventually become national
in orientation? And what effect did Woodrow Wilson's first administration
and World War I have on Southern progressivism? Fifth, what of the
aftermath of progressivism in the South? Did it have an enduring impact
on Southern politics and social attitudes? . . .

Perhaps the most fundamental of the dynamics that contributed to Southern
progressivism were changes that had occurred by the end of the nineteenth
century in the social landscape of the region, particularly the coming of
industry, increasing urbanization, and the growing importance of a new
middle class made up of business and professional groups. The increasing
economic diversification of the South brought with it what one observer
described as "radical changes in the social tendencies" of the section's

inhabitants. A spirit of commercialism had become pervasive, and "business" was exalted as never before. Distinct "capitalist" and "laboring" classes were emerging. Social differentiation based on wealth and business success was becoming more pronounced, especially in the cities, and institutions like the church were less "democratic" than in earlier years. The varied forces of economic and social change disrupted many established patterns of life in the South, threatened the stability of the countryside and small town, and precipitated a new awareness of human problems and needs. According to a Vanderbilt professor, writing in 1909, "The most capable business men, lawyers, doctors and preachers are practically all leaving the country for the town and city." This meant that "the great centers of life and influence and authority" were shifting from the country to the city, and "as a result the city is more and more setting the pace of and dominating Southern life and Southern thought."

The expanding role of cities in Southern life brought notable social changes. The growth of this urban South mirrored the industrialization of the region, but its implications went far beyond the organizing and servicing of the economy. The city sorted out people along economic and social lines, facilitated the formation of functional organizations, and fostered a heightened concern for social order, stability, and efficiency. New social types were especially prominent in the South's developing cities, which provided the setting for what Rupert B. Vance later referred to as "a hustling, urban type—the rising merchants, lawyers, and doctors." A new and growing class of supply merchants and bankers provided credit for farmers. In the larger cities and favorably located rural communities a group of industrial entrepreneurs came into existence, mainly in lumber, food, and textile industries. Many small merchants, salesmen, technicians, and clerical workers entered the South's amorphous but expanding middle class.

The emerging urban-industrial system, in the South as elsewhere, demanded a host of services and skills. These were provided by traditional professions such as law, medicine, engineering, education, and journalism and by a wide range of newer professions and specialities in industry, the service trades, public administration, public health, social work, and so on. The vocational and professional concerns of these increasingly differentiated and specialized groups tended both to isolate them from their local communities and to encourage their organization on the basis of function and skill. Industrialists and businessmen came together in trade associations, merchant organizations, bankers' groups, and chambers of commerce. The various professions either reorganized older associations or created new ones for the purpose of elevating professional standards and restricting admission. Other interest groups reflected common social characteristics such as race or ethnicity or common attitudes on particular social issues such as the regulation of community morals. These proliferating organizations, representing the developing middle segment of Southern society, provided an indispensable matrix for the growth of progressivism in the South. They turned to collective action, not only to obtain entrepreneurial and professional advantages but also to help control the social environment in which they operated.

Social reform in the early twentieth-century South was also rooted in the idea of Southern progress. The idea was inherent in the longing for economic development and regional rehabilitation. It found expression in many ways, most notably in the creed of the New South. The forward-looking ideas of the New South advocates embodied a compelling vision of regional progress. The benefits to be derived from industrialization seemed boundless. The spokesmen for industrialism in Tennessee, for example, "equated prosperity, progress, and civilization with smoking factory chimneys, booming cities, and rising indices of industrial production." An early student of Southern industrialization in this period concluded,

> All of our social gains in the South have been associated with the advance of industry—employment for the poor whites, urban growth with all the activity this implies, sound banking, establishment of a wage system, greater productivity of wealth and its more even distribution, larger tax yields, better schools and roads, improvement of farming methods, and the growth of many governmental services.

Economic advances promised to bring the South "a larger point of view," help diminish "prejudice and emotionalism in southern life," and further national integration.

The idea of Southern progress was promoted not only by the concept of economic development but also by a group of critics who wanted to improve life in the region by reforming various institutions and practices. The new social criticism, more restrained and more hopeful than the searing agrarian indictment of the 1890s, began to have an effect early in the twentieth century. Suddenly, it seemed, ministers, women, professors, writers, and publicists were singling out an assortment of evils in Southern life: in farm conditions, factory work, corporate practices, political life, and so forth. The critics included a liberal sprinkling of crusading journalists, a group of educators and scholars who had recently come out of the new graduate schools, a handful of socially conscious ministers, Southern expatriates like Walter Hines Page and William Garrott Brown, and an occasional politician, usually a state legislator. Some of the critics began to complain about the intolerance—even the tyranny—of public opinion in a section where, as one writer observed, everything must conform to "the Democratic platform, the Daughters of the Confederacy, old General So-and-So, and the Presbyterian creed."

Nevertheless, there was an optimistic note in most of this social commentary. "Here," wrote a contributor to the *South Atlantic Quarterly* in 1905, "is the supreme opportunity of the Southern newspaper, the Southern college, and Southern criticism of today, to learn from the records of the past the essentials of human progress and to bring these lessons of life to bear on the solution of our own particular problems." A few years later a Southern progressive declared, with considerable satisfaction, that the South had become "a laboratory for the study of sociological forces." The region was "a-making," he wrote, citing its rapid material development, the way its educational system was "democratizing society," the retreat of Southern sectionalism and the "revival of loyalty to the Nation," the "statesman-like way" religious agencies were adjusting to the demands of social change, the "rare insight and initiative" Southern women were demonstrating in furthering social changes, the breaking up of "political crystallization," and the emergence of industrial leaders as "a new power in public affairs." Withal, the instincts of the masses remained "sound and conservative," thus preserving "the ideals of personal honor," and "the traditions of loyalty to home and state" continued "to enrich present forces in Southern life."

Another reform dynamic was incorporated in the growth of a more vigorous humanitarian spirit in the South. The church was the major source of this social compassion. Although Southern Protestantism did far more to conserve than to undermine the dominant culture in the region, Southern churches were agents of change—and reform—as well as of continuity. An impressive number of ministers stood in the vanguard of social reform in the South. The clergy spoke out with greater frequency against social evils, religious bodies showed a deepening interest in the improvement of social conditions, and all of the major Protestant denominations established social action agencies of one kind or another. As Kenneth K. Bailey has written of the three leading white Protestant churches in the South, "Absorbed at the turn of the century in evangelism and little mindful of social needs beyond blue laws and prohibition, they emerged during the next fifteen years as advocates of social justice, proclaiming the Christian obligation to fashion Christ's kingdom on earth." Christian faith continued to center in the gospel of personal redemption, but the churches succeeded in giving a moral-religious tone to much of the region's reformism. The social justice activities of women in the South took shape, appropriately enough, in "church work," particularly in the women's missionary societies and the Woman's Christian Temperance Union. Religion remained "a central aspect" in the lives of many Southern women at the turn of the century, and, as Anne Firor Scott has pointed out, its form gradually changed from "intense personal piety to a concern for the salvation of the heathen and for social problems."

The origins of Southern progressivism can also be traced to the changing political scene and the transformation of Southern politics in the late nineteenth century. The most distinctive attribute of political affairs in the South at the turn of the century was the overwhelming dominance of the Democratic party. Despite the fissures in the section's political solidarity caused by the Populist revolt of the 1890s, Democratic supremacy in the states from Virginia to Texas was more secure than ever before. This meant that the competition for political leadership and public office, the formulation and discussion of political issues, the fate of reform movements, and the outcome of legislative action were all decided within the confines of one-party politics. This simple fact had a profound influence on the nature of Southern progressivism.

Several features of the South's altered political system were especially significant in shaping Southern progressivism. One of these was the drastic shrinkage of the electorate as a result of the restructuring of Southern politics in the 1890s and early 1900s. Disfranchisement and restrictive election laws not only deprived most black Southerners of the ballot but also, in conjunction with the persistence of poverty, illiteracy, and cultural barrenness, sharply limited the political involvement of millions of whites. A second important feature of Southern politics in the Progressive period was the direct primary and other democratic devices, whose adoption introduced new elements into the region's politics and promised changes in the complexion of state government. These innovations contributed to a third notable development in the politics of the South: the vigorous competition in the Democratic party and the prevalence of bifactional cleavages in most Southern states. The implications of these developments for social reform were ambiguous, but such changes facilitated the emergence of interest-group politics and enhanced the political influence of middle-class organizations and professional groups, whether in mobilizing mass support or bringing pressure to bear on legislators and other public officials. Although the remodeled system was restrictive and undemocratic, it nonetheless provided a setting for insurgent political campaigns, for broad appeals to the public, for the open discussion of issues, and for the organization and conduct of reform movements.

The political context in which Southern progressivism developed was also affected by populism. In appealing for solidarity in the white community, Democratic leaders were moved to make some concessions to the agrarian reformers, particularly in their rhetorical obeisance to the ideal of popular government. There was, to be sure, an indigenous reformism in the Democratic party of the various Southern states. Many Southern Democrats were genuine advocates of reform and were not motivated by a desire merely to propitiate Populists. But populism challenged Democratic commitments and served as a catalyst for selective change in Southern politics. Populist proposals for stringent railroad regulation, liberal agricultural credit, abolition of convict leasing, and support of public education became part of the reform agenda of the region's progressives. Southern Democrats increasingly accepted the Populist concept of the positive state—of a more active governmental role in promoting economic growth and protecting society—and this notion found fertile ground in the new climate of interest-group politics. A goodly number of former Populists became leaders in the Democratic party, and agrarian radicals often discovered compatible allies in the Bryanized wing of the party. The persistence of agrarian radicalism also seems to have contributed to the vigorous intraparty factionalism that developed in the one-party South during this period.

Politics, of course, constituted an essential medium for the waging of progressive campaigns. State and local governments were the primary agencies for the resolution of conflicts in the community and for the regulation of business practices and social behavior, as well as the source of public services. The South's economic growth and diversification increased the demands on state and local governments for franchises, services, and regulations. The expanding cities and towns were confronted with especially troublesome problems, which often required action by state legislatures. With the enhanced role of government came a dramatic enlargement in the part played by economic and professional organizations in the formulation and enactment of public policy. Chambers of commerce, freight bureaus, farmers' organizations, labor unions, professional associations, and scores of other groups were soon participating in local and state politics throughout the region.

All of these tendencies—social change, the emergent ideology of Southern progress, a broadening humanitarianism, and the transformation of politics—converged around the turn of the century to provide a favorable setting for Southern progressivism. The divisions and frustrations of the 1890s formed a somber backdrop for the sunnier outlook of the new decade. The ending of the economic depression lifted Southern spirits, and talk of the South's imminent agricultural and industrial expansion assumed a new animation. With the passing of the political turmoil of the 1890s, the public mood became more relaxed. The threat to the integrity of the "Southern" community had faded away. Democratic hegemony having been re-established, politicians paid greater heed to the widespread revulsion against the political corruption and electoral fraud of earlier years. The "race question" was apparently being settled through disfranchisement and segregation laws. The possibility of outside interference in the politics and social arrangements of the South, despite campaign rhetoric, seemed increasingly remote, and "Northern" opinion was, for the most part, agreeably acquiescent. The South's enthusiastic support of the Spanish-American War appeared to symbolize the final achievement of intersectional harmony and national integration.

Identifying the Southern progressives continues to pose a challenge to historians of reform movements in the early twentieth-century South. In his 1946 essay Arthur S. Link suggested that after 1900 the leadership of the Progressive movement passed from "the hands of the farmers to progressive editors, politicians, and other urban groups." As a general rule, Link wrote, the progressives found recruits in "the middle classes of the South among the more prosperous farmers, small businessmen, school teachers, editors, and other professional groups." C. Vann Woodward, in *Origins of the New South*, advanced a similar interpretation. "Southern progressivism," in his view, "was essentially urban and middle class in nature, and the typical leader was a city professional man or businessman, rather than a farmer." In pushing for reform, Woodward added, small businessmen and the urban middle class "joined hands with the discontented farmers." Subsequent interpretations have generally confirmed the Link-Woodward thesis. George B. Tindall, in *The Emergence of the New South* (1967), located the wellsprings of the progressive cause in "the aspirations of the middle-income groups to own and develop productive property"; progressivism in the South drew strength from "merchants, mechanics, farmers, small manufacturers, and the brokers and factors who serviced the farm economy." Writing in 1979, Willard B. Gatewood described the progressive coalitions as including "businessmen, professionals, certain agricultural interests, and a medley of social uplift agents." These judgments, while persuasive, were for the most part based on impressionistic evidence; there are as yet few studies that convincingly identify rank-and-file supporters and opponents of the various progressive campaigns in the South.

Although the composition of the progressive coalitions in the South remains inadequately analyzed, it is clear that many of them involved what Sheldon Hackney has called "the politics of pluralistic interest groups." These groups were primarily concerned with their own survival and competitive position, but their increasing resort to collective action made them a major consideration in reform politics. The commercial-civic elites and other organized elements often opposed social reforms, of course, and their character differed from state to state. Urban influences were obviously stronger in Tennessee than in Mississippi. Cultural traditions were more significant in Virginia than in Oklahoma politics. Farmer and labor groups were better represented in the politics of the Southwestern states than in the states of the Southeast. In general, however, the politics of pluralistic interest groups reflected the strength and vigor of the new commercial and professional classes centered in the region's cities. These groups included lawyers, editors, teachers, ministers, doctors, businessmen, agricultural scientists, demonstration agents, city planners, labor leaders, social workers, YMCA directors, railroad commission experts, and legislative lobbyists. These middle-class men and women were the quintessential Southern progressives.

Nevertheless, rural Southerners played an important part in the South's progressivism, particularly in legislative enactments and support of such causes as disfranchisement, public education, railroad regulation, and prohibition. One aspect of this question, the relationship between populism and progressivism in the South, has evoked differing interpretations. Raymond H. Pulley has found no continuity between the two movements in Virginia, arguing instead that progressivism there developed as "a direct reaction" to populism. In the case of Alabama, Hackney has contended, progressivism was an alternative to populism that represented "a substantially different reaction by a separate set of men to the same enemy Populism faced—the dominant industrial wing of the Democratic Party." Tindall, however, though not directly concerned with the roots of Southern progressivism, has characterized it as "an amalgam of agrarian radicalism, business regulation, good government, and urban social justice reforms." Kirby has depicted progressivism in the South as "dichotomous" and "multidirectional," but he has also suggested that "the most potent force for southern reform lay in the frustrations and yearnings of the rural and small town masses." And he has cited the pervasive antimonopoly spirit among Southerners as "the great connecting link between the rural protests of the nineteenth century and those of the twentieth." More substantial agreement on this important question must await the completion of additional studies like that of Hackney on Alabama. Meanwhile, historians should be wary of exaggerating the discontinuity between the reform movements of the 1890s and those of the early twentieth century. The concept of "a continuing and potent agricultural influence," to borrow the phrase James Tice Moore applied to the Age of the Southern Redeemers, may have considerable validity in the case of the Progressive era in the South.

Southern progressives were no doubt a rather disparate collection of social reformers, but they were unified in some measure by common goals and social values. They shared a yearning for a more orderly and cohesive community. Such a community, they believed, was a prerequisite for economic development and material progress. Its realization depended upon the effective regulation of society in the interest of ethical business practices and good government, and in the elimination of political corruption, machine politics, and the insidious power of large corporations and other special interests. Social controls were also indispensable to the preservation of moral values, to the purification of social institutions, and to the protection of men from their own weaknesses. Optimistic about future prospects but alarmed by the tensions and turmoil that pervaded the South in the late nineteenth century, Southern progressives looked toward the creation of a clearly defined community that would accommodate a society differentiated by race and class but one that also possessed unity, cohesion, and stability. The search for community may explain the reformers' obsession with the virtues of rural life and with means of improving it.

Progressives in the South, like other American reformers in this period, talked about the virtues of "the people," identified morality with majority rule, and urged the desirability of preserving and expanding traditional democratic principles. But, characteristically, their concept of democracy was limited. The ideal they invoked was that of "*Herrenvolk* democracy" — a democratic society for whites only. Racial segregation and black disfranchisement, some white leaders claimed, were the touchstones through which the distinctions separating white men could be softened, white unity maintained, and a broader white democracy achieved. But well-to-do and middle-class Southerners, including many social reformers, often revealed a deep distrust of the masses, whether black or white. While the social critics and reformers in the early twentieth-century South worked for the education and uplift of the common man, they were fully aware of his prejudices and narrow-mindedness, of his extreme sensitivity to criticism, obsession with the race question, and susceptibility to sentimentalism. Thus, Southern progressives demonstrated a proclivity toward paternalistic solutions in dealing with many social problems. It is significant that progressives sometimes coupled education, which they emphasized as an instrument of material progress and social control, with the need to cleanse the political process and limit participation to those who were prepared for responsible citizenship.

For all of their emphasis on social order and their faith in social controls, many Southern progressives revealed a strong commitment to social justice and the amelioration of human suffering in their communities. A growing number of Southerners were genuinely worried about the consequences of industrialization for ordinary people, aware of the increasing need for social services, and sensitive to the social roles and responsibilities opening up to them as part of an emerging class of trades people, professionals, and experts. The creative response of Southern women to the plight of the poor and disadvantaged was especially notable in the South's uplift campaigns. The cause of social justice in the South was also fostered by the monetary and moral support of Northern philanthropists during the Progressive era.

Most Southern progressives were convinced that much of the South's social distress could be relieved or prevented through economic development. They accepted, like so many contemporary Southerners, the basic assumptions of the New South program of regional progress through rapid economic growth, industrialization, and a more diversified economy. These objectives led directly to an emphasis on efficiency and rationality not only in the production of goods but also in such areas as education, the treatment of criminals, race relations, and the prohibition of alcoholic beverages. The theme of social efficiency was prominent, for instance, in the efforts of Southern progressives to improve farm life, in their approach to industrial labor, in their municipal reforms and innovations, and in their advocacy of a larger role for state governments as promoters, regulators, and arbiters. The search for efficiency in these diverse areas of Southern society, while not exclusively or even primarily a manifestation of social reform, was nonetheless a significant aspect of the progressive mentality and program in the South.

These social values—order, morality, benevolence, efficiency, and development—were not separate categories of progressive concern. Rather they were, as Hackney has written of the Alabama progressives, "interrelated facets of a single, economically self-interested, ethically shaped, middle-class attitude toward life." These areas of social concern and commitment, moreover, were mutually reinforcing, and in seeking to give them effect Southern progressives began to develop an expanded concept of governmental responsibilities. They moved beyond the regulatory state to advocate a broadening array of public services. In other words, Southern progressivism became "a movement for positive government."

Identifying the major movements that comprised Southern progressivism and categorizing them on the basis of their fundamental purposes may be helpful at this point. The reform movements were often interrelated, and in many cases the same reformers were prominent in several progressive campaigns. In Virginia and South Carolina, for example, the educator Samuel Chiles Mitchell was an ardent champion of public schools, child labor reform, prohibition, public health, better roads, improved race relations, and public welfare programs. Furthermore, the progressive endeavors were inspired by a variety of motives; thus, the classification suggested in this essay is somewhat arbitrary. One group of reform efforts appears to have been primarily concerned with governmental regulation and the imposition of social controls in troublesome areas such as race relations. The race settlement of the 1890s and early 1900s was one such manifestation of Southern progressivism. The white consensus that developed during this period reflected a widespread conviction that disfranchise-ment, segregation, and black proscription not only made up a workable system of racial control but also promised a greater measure of social stability and public calm. Such a milieu, it was said, would make it possible for progressives to address themselves to other pressing social causes. It might also help establish a new national consensus of "enlightened" and "liberal" opinion on the race question.

Prison reform, centering on efforts to abolish the leasing of convicts, to introduce prison farms, and to develop a new system of road work for prisoners, constituted another example of Southern progressivism largely concerned with the application of more efficient social controls. Antimo-nopolism represented another manifestation of the regulatory impulse among the region's progressives. The movement to control railroads and other large corporations and to destroy their political dominance became a major objective of progressives in many Southern states. Corporate reg-ulation also served as one of the key issues in providing a rallying point for progressive politics in the South. For big business, so often identified with powerful outside interests, entrenched political "machines," unethical business practices, and the destruction of competition, seemed to demand stronger public control no less than did black workers, criminals, and al-coholic beverages. The concentrated attack of Southern governors and legislatures upon railroads and other corporations in 1906 and 1907 soon spent itself, and much of the regulatory force during the next decade found an outlet in the antiliquor crusade, first in the drive for statewide prohibition and subsequently in the campaign for a national law. Prohibition offered a means of moral reaffirmation of traditional values, an assurance of cleaner politics, and a way to employ the power of the state in the pursuit of moral and social progress.

A second significant category of progressive campaigns in the South was dominated by the theme of social justice. One of the principal reform movements in this sphere was devoted to the regulation of child labor. The child-labor campaigns brought the section's social reformers together in a common cause, gave them valuable experience in organizing for reform purposes, and stimulated their interest in the establishment of juvenile courts and programs for the care of dependent children. No aspect of social reform in the South during the Progressive era touched the immediate lives of more of the region's inhabitants than the great educational awakening soon after the turn of the century. Education was the entering wedge and the sustaining focus for unprecedented Northern philanthropy as well as a major element in the rationale of interregional accommodation that flour-ished during these years. It was almost always viewed by reformers as a redemptive force in the development of a better South. A third area of social justice concern was the organized charity movement. By the end of the first decade of the twentieth century, social welfare in the South had begun to move away from the long-dominant emphasis on relief of the destitute and to put greater stress on casework, surveys, and organization. The cause of social justice also included an embryonic movement to ameliorate the conditions of black people in the South. During the Progressive period, the primary concerns of white Southerners, including most social reformers, in their approach to the "race problem" were social efficiency and the means of social control. Yet some whites sought to ease the terrible burden of racial injustice borne by the Negro. Their program, as one scholar has recently observed, was based on "an updated version of paternalism in which whites would offer blacks help, guidance, and protection in exchange for a commitment to the New South values of thrift and hard work, as well as a continued subservience."

There was also a black approach to racial progress and better social conditions. Given sustenance by an emerging Negro middle class, it envisioned "an expanded concept of social justice, a more efficient pattern of living, and a greater emphasis upon local organizations." Blacks, as John Dittmer has written, "built their own institutions behind the walls of segregation, preaching race pride and practicing self-help." Negro civic organizations, boards of trade, public welfare leagues, and community betterment groups, particularly in the larger cities, labored to extract worthwhile concessions in education and other public services from the white system, to secure more adequate correctional facilities for black juveniles, to improve housing and sanitation in Negro areas, and to promote moral conduct, social order, and efficiency in the black community. The community work of Negro club women was a prominent feature of this black progressivism. The glimpses that recent studies provide into the world of social reform among blacks, like those into the world of inarticulate Southern whites, suggest that much research remains to be done on the intricacies of progressivism in the South.

Social efficiency, especially as it related to economic development, was a motif in several of the reform movements. A multifaceted attack on the ills of Southern agriculture made up one such movement. Despite the frequent invocation of rural values, the effort to rehabilitate the Southern farmer basically entailed programs to improve agricultural techniques, increase production, and raise farm income. Municipal reform was also an important part of Southern progressivism. It embodied all of the major themes of Southern reformism in the early twentieth century—regulation and social control, humanitarian efforts to relieve social distress, and the drive for efficiency. Protective labor measures and other reforms affecting industrial workers provide still another example of the emphasis on social efficiency in Southern progressivism. As a rule, the legislative concerns and social policy preferences of the state labor federations, railroad brotherhoods, and labor councils were compatible with the program and rationale of Southern progressivism.

The progressive campaigns for efficiency in agriculture, municipal government, and industrial labor led to greater emphasis on scientific knowledge, expertise, and effective administration in the public arena. Similar pressures emanated from other reform campaigns, such as the movements for public education, public health, and good roads. The state was increasingly viewed not only as the source of regulatory action but also as the provider of vital new services. This expanded role of government was in harmony with the widespread commitment in the South to economic development and with the entrepreneurial aspirations of diverse groups and specialized organizations representing farmers, industrial workers, and business and professional men and women. The steadily mounting demand for public services formed an important dimension of Southern progressivism.

Perhaps this sketch of reform movements will suggest the varied and overlapping incentives that underlay Southern progressivism. The campaign for public education, for example, was inspired by the reformers' interest in social order, efficiency, and development as well as in social justice. A similar mixture of motives is apparent in most other progressive endeavors in the South. The reform movements unfolded more or less simultaneously during the first decade of the twentieth century, except for disfranchisement and the race settlement, which were well under way by 1900. Beginning as scattered and loosely organized efforts in the late 1890s and early 1900s, the more significant reform movements soon moved to the creation of state organizations and campaigns. The pace of these campaigns varied from state to state, but in many cases they led to coordinated or parallel activities throughout the South, although the process was occasionally reversed, as in the launching of the Southern education movement. The campaign against child labor, the education crusade, and several other reform movements were set in motion during the first two or three years of the new century. The railroad regulatory campaigns, led by several reform governors, reached their height in 1907, and during the next year or two the prohibition movement enjoyed spectacular success, before losing momentum during the years 1910–13.

Virtually all of the progressive campaigns had assumed a regionwide character by 1910, and they were promoted as "Southern" reforms. A kind of progressive balance had emerged: the claims of numerous social groups were given a hearing and tensions were modulated between classes, races, rural and city dwellers, South and North, tradition and innovation. In other words, progressives were able to create a strong sense of community as a setting for their pursuit of social reform.

By the time Woodrow Wilson assumed the presidency in March 1913, a new stage had arrived in the evolution of Southern progressivism. Reform movements in the Southern states, as in other sections, were increasingly influenced by national organizations, standards, and solutions. This tendency was evident in the formation of the Southern Sociological Congress, a regional civic organization established in Nashville in the spring of 1912. Characterized by a zeal for uplift and an evangelical spirit, the congress was intended to serve as a medium for organizing and coordinating various social reform groups. Its creation reflected the growth of social services in the South during the previous decade, the organization of several state conferences on charities and correction, and a heightened awareness among Southern progressives of social reforms in other parts of the country. The congress stimulated interest in attacking social problems, including racial injustice, encouraged the establishment of other social welfare groups, and exerted some influence in the enactment of social reform legislation in the individual states.

The nationalization of reform after 1912 was apparent in two of the Southern progressives' most vigorous regulatory movements: the campaign to control railroads and the prohibition crusade. The barriers to effective regulation of railroads by state legislatures and commissions, including the inherent problem of dealing with interstate companies and the restraints imposed by federal court decisions and Interstate Commerce Commission rulings, brought a shift from reliance on state regulation to national control. Meanwhile, the vexatious task of enforcing state and local prohibition in dry areas, not to mention the defeat of the antiliquor cause in Florida, Texas, and Alabama, led many Southern reformers to fall in line with the American Anti-Saloon League's call for national prohibition. The tendency to look for national remedies was also evident in numerous other progressive campaigns: in the child labor reform movement; in the demand by the Farmers' Union and other agricultural pressure groups for federal regulations, credit facilities, and farm demonstration programs; and in the willingness of organizations such as the Southern Commercial Congress to turn to Washington for assistance in dealing with problems like flood control. This transition from state to federal action was hastened by the activities of such organizations as the National Child Labor Committee, the American Anti-Saloon League, the Commission on Country Life, and the National Association of Charities and Correction.

The South was slower in lending support to the National American Woman Suffrage Association's efforts to secure the enfranchisement of women through congressional action and a constitutional amendment. Although tiny woman suffrage groups were formed in most Southern states in the 1880s and 1890s, they were feeble and many of them soon disappeared. There was little concerted activity in behalf of the votes-for-women cause before 1910. Nevertheless, the intensity of "the woman's movement" in the region had increased, and feminine involvement in the campaign to regulate child labor, the educational crusade, and the prohibition movement, not to mention numerous community projects, indicates the distance the reformers had come since joining the missionary societies and the women's clubs. As time passed this feminist reformism tended to find greater focus in the drive for the suffrage. During the five or six years before the United States entered World War I, Southern suffragists developed statewide associations, organized hundreds of local societies, and launched campaigns to influence legislators and the public. Their objective was to win the vote with favorable decisions in the statehouses, but they encountered formidable resistance. As their strength grew and their frustrations mounted in the wake of setbacks at the state level, Southern suffragists began to work more actively for a federal amendment.

Meanwhile, Southern politics showed signs of increasing involvement in the debate over national issues and elections. In 1910 the Democrats won control of the House of Representatives, and, when the House organized for business in 1911, the seniority rule brought a group of Southerners to prominence as chairmen of important committees. Southern interest in national politics rose to new heights with the nomination and election of Woodrow Wilson as the nation's twenty-eighth president. Southerners such as Walter Hines Page and William G. McAdoo were prominent in promoting Wilson's candidacy. The movement for his nomination was closely identified with progressive politics in the South, and in a broader sense its impact upon the diffused currents of social reform in the region was profound. In short, the Wilson movement marked an important stage in the course of Southern progressivism. Furthermore, during the Wilson years the region took a long step in the direction of a more positive role in national politics.

Southern congressmen, who dominated the standing committees in both houses of Congress, strongly supported the principal legislation of Wilson's New Freedom. Nevertheless, there was strong Southern opposition to many of the more advanced progressive measures considered during Wilson's first term. For example, Southerners were in the vanguard of the successful opposition in 1914 and 1915 to a constitutional amendment to enfranchise women. The Southern lawmakers were much more inclined to support certain measures of social control, such as national prohibition, immigration restriction, and especially Negro proscription in Washington and the federal service. In general, however, public opinion in the South and the section's congressmen found much to applaud in Wilson's New Freedom. Meanwhile, the progressive spirit, stimulated by the Wilsonian example, became manifest in new reform campaigns and in new advances in state services and administration in the South.

In some respects the First World War weakened and redirected the currents of social reform in the United States, particularly after the nation entered the conflict in April 1917. Yet the war also created new opportunities for social planning and even nourished the progressive belief that "by altering the environment it was possible to reconstruct society." The war had a momentous effect on Southern society. It contributed to the region's prosperity, brought an expansion in the functions of government, encouraged civic cooperation, enhanced the role of voluntary groups, and opened new avenues of social control, efficiency, and social justice. Preoccupation with the war effort was evident in virtually every aspect of Southern life. The region's congressmen, entrenched in powerful committee positions, provided indispensable legislative assistance in the enactment of the administration's wartime program. The mobilization of community resources for military purposes had important consequences for the development of new social services in the Southern states. As Hastings H. Hart of the Russell Sage Foundation wrote during the war, in reporting on the social agencies and institutions of South Carolina, that state had an opportunity "so to direct its war work in production and food conservation, in guarding the health and morals of the soldier, in the care of invalid, crippled, and insane soldiers, and in the training of youth for patriotic service as greatly to improve the quality and efficiency of the social work of the State for all future time.''

Some Southern states took advantage of the wartime atmosphere to adopt new social welfare legislation. North Carolina, for example, reorganized its public welfare program during the years 1917–19. The war also brought to fruition three reforms for which Southern progressives had long struggled. One of these was national prohibition, an achievement that owed much to Southern congressmen, state legislators, and public opinion. Another was the adoption of the Nineteenth Amendment enfranchising women. During the war the woman suffrage movement had emerged as a serious reform cause in the South. Although a majority of the Southern congressmen voted against the amendment and it encountered powerful opposition in the section's state legislatures, it was supported by an increasing number of Southerners. The third reform occurred in the search for progress in race relations. The attention given this perennial question by the Southern Sociological Congress and the efforts of people like Willis D. Weatherford, James H. Dillard, and Will W. Alexander helped pave the way for tangible action. Even so, the exigencies and opportunities of the war and its aftermath provided the immediate impetus for the establishment of the Commission on Interracial Cooperation in 1919.

The end of the war and the collapse of the Wilson administration in 1919 and 1920 coincided with and contributed to the disintegration of Southern progressivism. By that time the regional focus of the reformers had been disrupted, and they were no longer united by a common program of social reforms and values. They had also lost much of their élan and optimism as progressives. Social change, accelerated by the war, created new tensions, and the postwar years were exacerbated by sharp conflicts among Southerners and between the South and other sections. The intersectional struggle for control of the Democratic party eroded the progressive balance in the South and added to the saliency of cultural issues like prohibition. In other words, the harmony that had held the major components of Southern progressivism in balance no longer existed. The earlier successes of Southern progressivism may also have contributed to its loss of vitality in the 1920s. There were signs that the progessives had about reached the limits of their concept of reform. A new generation of leaders was coming to the fore. Furthermore, many professional groups were making the transition from ''the missionary era to one of institutionalization and professionalism.'' Caught up in the struggle to develop effective agencies and services in their particular fields and in their professional growth and recognition, they found the old kinds of social reform increasingly irrelevant and unsatisfying. Southern social workers, for example, like their counterparts in the rest of the country, now seemed more concerned with ''procedure and the adjustment of the individual to his environment'' than in transforming the social environment in which the individual lived.

Nevertheless, progressivism in the South did not disappear in the 1920s.

Instead, as George B. Tindall has shown, it was "transformed through greater emphasis upon certain of its tendencies and the distortion of others." One of the surviving strains of Southern progressivism expressed itself in the zealous campaign to enforce prohibition, in the fundamentalist movement, and in other efforts to protect moral standards and traditional cultural values. Another was what Tindall has termed "business progressivism"— the intensified emphasis on "good government," administrative efficiency, and more adequate public services. Racial attitudes and practices provide a third example. Southern reformers, building upon their modest efforts of earlier years to soften the harsh rigidities of race relations and to continue the limited interracial cooperation of the war period, undertook a major reform initiative in this period. The creation of the Commission on Interracial Cooperation represented an organized endeavor for harmonious race relations and, unlike earlier white reformism in this area, pointed to a concrete and realistic mode of action. But at the same time the commission was carefully restricted by the bounds of white orthodoxy. . . .

Progressivism in the South had a marked effect on the region's politics, social action, and social thought during the early twentieth century. This was true in large part because Southern progressives brought together in tolerable equipoise a number of assumptions and ideas about the nature and development of the South and elicited support from diverse social elements, including the section's civic-commercial elites and upwardly mobile urban groups. The progressives, as Tindall has argued, effected a synthesis of the antithetical approaches of the Bourbons and Populists. There was room in this complex of ideas for material progress, efficiency, ethical standards, social order, a more vigorous regulatory state, social justice, public services, and especially the vision of a revitalized regional community. In the early twentieth-century setting the progressives were able to function both as agents of modernization and as guardians of Southern tradition.

The legacy of Southern progressivism was also important. The social values, approach, and style of the progressives created an enduring design in the modern South. Thus tradition and modernization, both encompassed in Southern progressivism, strongly influenced the section's political culture during the 1920s. One aspect of Southern progressivism looked toward intersectional accommodation, national involvement, and national solutions to regional problems, and those Southerners who represented this approach welcomed the New Deal and later liberal administrations in Washington. Other Southerners were upset and increasingly alienated by this brand of national social action. Keenly aware of the South's pressing social problems and the many regional barriers to progress as well as the fragility of their own strength and resources, Southern liberals were, in Gunnar Myrdal's words, "inclined to stress the need for patience and to exalt the cautious approach, the slow change, the organic nature of social growth." While the early twentieth-century progressives were cautious reformers, they were the first Southerners to make a concerted effort to cope with social problems growing out of the new industrial and urbanized system. The liberal tradition they did so much to establish survived in the antitrust and consumer protection politics of men like Hugo L. Black, Claude Pepper, and Estes Kefauver. But, in general, the South's recent political leaders, including most liberals, continued to emphasize the essential role of economic development in the rehabilitation of the region. Like the progressives, moreover, they also continued to emphasize the need to broaden and unite the middle class in order to deal with contemporary social problems.

The Limits of Southern Progressivism

C. VANN WOODWARD

The Southern counterpart of a Northern progressivism developed nearly all traits familiar to the genus, but it was in no sense derivative. It was a pretty strictly indigenous growth, touched lightly here and there by cross-fertilization from the West. It sprouted in the soil that had nourished Populism, but it lacked the agrarian cast and the radical edge that had frightened the middle class away from the earlier movement. Southern progressivism was essentially urban and middle class in nature, and the typical leader was a city professional man or businessman, rather than a farmer. Under the growing pressure of monopoly, the small businessmen and urban middle class overcame their fear of reform and joined hands with the discontented farmers. They envisaged as a common enemy the plutocracy of the Northeast, together with its agents, banks, insurance companies, public utilities, oil companies, pipelines, and railroads. Southern progressivism often took a sectional character, identifying the popular enemy with "foreign" interests. These interests were defended by Southern apologists who were strongly entrenched within the old party and frequently controlled it through bosses and state machines. William E. Dodd, then a college professor in Virginia, described the situation in his state to Walter Clark, a critic of machine rule in North Carolina. "This state," wrote Dodd, "is no more self-governing to-day than the Catholic Church. Thomas F. Ryan is our master and he lives in New York. Thomas S. Martin is his henchman and we have powerful newspapers to defend both with none to oppose either." The struggle for progressive democracy was directed against such bosses as Martin and was carried on within the old party between conservative and reform factions.

Several circumstances favored the reform factions in the first decade of the new century. The Populist party, bearing the odium attached to any threat to white solidarity, had in large measure constituted an obstruction to the spread of reform ideas in the South. The collapse of the third party not only removed a stigma from reformism, but it brought back into the old party its disaffected left wing. Returning, the Populists brought along with them their ideological baggage, for which room had to be found.

Reprinted by permission of Louisiana State University Press from *Origins of the New South, 1877–1913* by C. Vann Woodward, pp. 371–388. Copyright © 1971 by Louisiana State University Press and The Littlefield Fund for Southern History, University of Texas.

Whether as a cause or a result, the direct-primary system of nominating party candidates appeared with progressive movements all over the South. The direct primary was not invented in Wisconsin in 1903, as is sometimes said, for by that time a majority of the Southern states were already practicing the system, and by 1913 all the remaining ones had adopted it except North Carolina, which fell into line in 1915. A part of the paraphernalia of progressivism in all sections, the primary was one of the first demands of the reformers. "In the South this demand was even stronger than at the North," because in the one-party system nomination meant election. The adoption of the primary was in part the fulfillment of the implied pledge of the disfranchisers that once the Negro was removed from political life the white men would be given more voice in the selection of their rulers. In part also it was a gesture of welcome to the returning Populist prodigals. The great hope of the progressives was that since the old convention system of nomination had facilitated boss and machine control, the substitution of the primary would restore popular control. In at least five states, Alabama, Arkansas, Florida, Mississippi, and Texas, the change to the primary was an immediate, or nearly immediate, antecedent of the victory of a reform administration. It is probable that in those cases the primary paved the way for reform.

The joker in the Southern primaries was the fact that they were *white* primaries. Southern progressivism generally was progressivism for white men only, and after the poll tax took its toll not all the white men were included. The paradoxical combination of white supremacy and progressivism was not new to the region, but it never ceased to be a cause of puzzlement and confusion above the Potomac—and not a little, below. The paradox nevertheless had its counterpart in the North, where it was not uncommon for one man to champion both progressivism and imperialism. In such instances it was a matter of white supremacy over browns instead of blacks. Hiram Johnson was apparently no more troubled by his advocacy of proscription of Japanese in California than Hoke Smith by his treatment of Negroes in Georgia. The Southern leader who professed reactionary racial views and advanced political and economic reforms in the same breath was known as a "demagogue," unless he happened to be a political ally, in which case he was a "progressive."

Had La Follette and White undertaken the most casual survey of legislation and platforms in the South they would have discovered there all the progressive doctrines and experiments familiar to Wisconsin and Kansas and their latitudes. Southern reformers sought to "bust the trusts" and regulate them at the same time. They strengthened their railroad and public-utility commissions, hauled railroads and other malefactors into court, reduced rates, fought discrimination, and passed unfair-practice laws, safety and inspection laws for mines and factories, pure-food and drug bills, penitentiary reforms, and much humanitarian legislation. Progressives here and there experimented with all the political inventions associated with the movement. Besides the direct primary, these included the initiative, referendum, and recall; preferential primaries; and corrupt-practices and antilobby acts.

In command of the movement was a group of "reform governors" who were almost as picturesque a lot of leaders as those who arose in the nineties. Like their contemporaries and counterparts, the Western reform governors La Follette of Wisconsin and Albert B. Cummins of Iowa, the Southern governors had no co-ordinated, interstate organization, although their programs were similar. The men themselves ranged in type from a spellbinder to a dignified factory owner.

Napoleon Bonaparte Broward came of a line of planters, soldiers, and theologians impoverished by the war. He was left an orphan at the age of twelve in the palmetto scrub of eastern Florida. The boy worked through the hard-bitten, hungry years of Reconstruction on the St. Johns River as raftsman, cook, deck hand, and fireman. In his teens he shipped north to Boston on a freighter. For two years he followed the sea as a fisherman off the Newfoundland Banks or aboard oyster boats and lumber vessels. Returning to the Florida river life, he became a bar pilot and later the skipper of a steamboat. Broward entered politics in 1888 at the age of thirty-three as sheriff of Duval County, in which Jacksonville lies. In 1896 he returned to the sea and became an evader instead of an enforcer of the law. As designer, part-owner, and sometimes captain of the steamer *Three Friends*, the erstwhile sheriff turned filibusterer [military adventurer] and ran the blockade with arms and ammunition for the Cuban revolutionists. His adventures brought him fame and popularity. But it was Broward's championship of the "crackers" against the predatory railroads, his efforts to save the remaining public lands from the "land pirates," and his Paul Bunyan–like ambition to drain the Everglades which made him a folk hero, elected the former deck hand governor in 1904, and founded Broward progressivism in Florida.

Born in 1856, William Goebel of Kentucky was the son of a German immigrant cabinetmaker and his German wife who moved to Covington from Carbondale, Pennsylvania, in 1863. Goebel escaped a jeweler's apprenticeship, studied law, and rose rapidly and brilliantly in the profession. His political career opened in the state senate, where he served twelve years and rose to leadership of the reform faction of the Democratic party. Outwardly a cold and taciturn man with no oratorical gifts and few intimates, Goebel succeeded by his consummate political ability and the popular appeal of his struggle to tax and regulate the corporations and railroads.

Charles B. Aycock and James K. Vardaman, though men of very different types, both rose to power on the white-supremacy issue and waves of racial bitterness. The youngest of ten children of a small farmer and local politician, Aycock was born in Wayne County, North Carolina, in 1859. His mother was unable to write her own name. Aycock managed to attend the state university and qualify for the bar. In 1893 he became United States attorney for the eastern district of his state. His great political passion, aside from white supremacy, was education, and apparently he meant education for both races. Beyond that he rarely ventured. The party boss and Aycock's campaign manager, Furnifold M. Simmons, frankly admitted that Aycock had reached an understanding with "the large corporations." In comparison with the simple, unassuming figure of Aycock, Vardaman presented a spectacular contrast, with his long, flowing hair and long, flowing coattails. The Mississippian campaigned for the hillbilly vote mounted upon a lumber wagon drawn by oxen and won the devotion of this element both by his reactionary race doctrine and his progressive program of economic and social reform. Even his opponents found it "impossible to determine where his idealism ended and his demagoguery began." He was defeated twice in his attempts to secure the Democratic nomination for governor but was successful in 1903 after the adoption of the direct primary.

In August, 1906, within the same week, Braxton Bragg Comer of Alabama and Hoke Smith of Georgia were elected governors in those states by strong reform movements. Smith, the Atlanta editor and publisher, and Comer, the Birmingham manufacturer, were both prosperous members of the urban middle class. Like the earlier reform governor Altgeld and the Cleveland mayor Tom Johnson, Comer was a man of considerable wealth, reported to have been worth a half million or more at the time of his election. Yet under Comer's leadership the Democratic party of Alabama for the first time since Reconstruction dropped the word "Conservative" from its official title. Comer was jolted out of the complacency of his class by the impact of freight rates and railroad discriminations upon his interests as a planter, banker, and cotton manufacturer. Hoke Smith was probably carried farther along the road to reform than was his natural inclination by his coalition with Tom Watson, who swung the old Populists to his support. These oddly matched teammates—a former member of Grover Cleveland's cabinet and the leader of the Populist party—pulled together awkwardly until Watson kicked over the traces, but while they pulled they carried Georgia farther toward progressivism than Watson and all the hosts of Populism had in the nineties.

Southern progressivism had a fringe that was less lunatic than comic, less radical than burlesque. It is best typified by Jeff Davis of Arkansas. In the dialectics of this "Karl Marx for Hill Billies," the class struggle was waged between the "red necks" and their mortal enemies, the "high-collared roosters" of the city. In that struggle, so he assured the dispossessed, the "one-gallus" [having only 1 suspender to hold up pants] proletariat had nothing to lose but their plowlines—whereas the trusts had plenty. Jeff Davis tilted with the corporation monster at every crossroad in Arkansas and made trustbusting the favorite sport of the rustic barbecue. If his battles were largely bloodless and the results intangible, the same was often true of more celebrated combats in far-off Washington, and Jeff's were more exciting. There was a compensatory satisfaction in watching the enemy being bullied and slain in pantomime, especially when one had fought in vain for years without so much as coming to grips with the foe.

Jeff Davis loved his trade and practiced it with gusto and without shame.

He abjured all elegancies save his habitual Prince Albert suit of Confederate gray, and he could demolish an opponent by calling him a gentleman. "If you red-necks or hillbillies ever come to Little Rock," he would say, "be sure and come to see me. . . . If I am not there tell my wife who you are, that you are my friend and belong to the sunburned sons of toil. Tell her to give you some hog jowl and turnip greens. She may be busy making soap, but that will be all right." And they loved him with a devotion unshaken by his defiance of both Baptists and prohibitionists and elected him governor and then to the Senate, where he died unbeaten and unbeatable.

The first Southern reform movement to make a determined fight for power ended in an assassination and came near plunging a state into civil war. This was the fight led by William Goebel of Kentucky in 1899–1900. A man of remorseless determination, Goebel fought ruthlessly against equally ruthless foes and inspired hatred as well as devotion. In the Democratic convention of 1899, he outmaneuvered the L and N machine, which led the fight against him, and won the nomination for governor in a struggle that split the party. Goebel then faced the opposition not only of a strong Republican party, which nominated William S. Taylor, but also of the bolting Democrats who nominated former Governor John Young Brown, a friend of the railroads.

Goebel campaigned on his reform record in the state senate, where he had labored to tax hidden capital, to increase the taxation of railroads and public utilities, and to secure labor and franchise laws. He also demanded a new state antitrust law and increased power for the state railroad commission. Above all, however, he carried home his fight against the Louisville and Nashville Railroad, its president Milton H. Smith, its lobbyist Basil W. Duke, and the chairman of its board of directors, August Belmont. In scarcely a speech did Goebel fail to mention the railroad or one of its officials. It was time, he declared, that "the Louisville and Nashville became the servant instead of the master of Kentucky." He charged that Brown had entered the race only "after Basil Duke had called at the office of August Belmont in New York City, and found out what the attitude of the L & N Railroad would be in this fight."

There is no question that the railroad was deeply interested in the election. Belmont published correspondence revealing that Goebel's campaign had been the subject of resolutions by the board of directors. The fight centered in Louisville, where the power of the Louisville and Nashville was concentrated and where tension was so great that the Republican governor called out the militia to police the polls. William Jennings Bryan toured the state speaking in Goebel's behalf. In spite of Bryan's aid the Republican candidate Taylor won by a plurality of 2,383 votes and was inaugurated on December 12.

Goebel was not to be stopped by the inauguration of an opponent. Contending that the election had been corrupted by the railroads, he organized his forces in the legislature to contest the election. When it became apparent that the Democratic majority in that body intended to unseat the

Republican administration, tension in the capital became dangerous. Threats and insults had been loosely exchanged during the campaign. In answer to Goebel's charge that he was a "corruptionist" for the Louisville and Nashville, Basil Duke replied that he would "not submit to an attack from a liar, slanderer and an assassin because he happens to be a self-selected candidate for governor." This was the customary challenge to a duel. It was a day of hair-trigger politics. Goebel himself had killed a political opponent three years before in an exchange of shots. Toward the middle of January a train loaded with more than a thousand armed men from the mountains pulled into the capital, transported by the Louisville and Nashville. On the thirtieth, as Goebel was approaching the state capitol, several shots rang out from one of the offices occupied by a Republican official and Goebel dropped in his tracks, fatally wounded. His assassin was never identified.

Ignoring the Governor's order, the Goebelite members of the legislature met and proclaimed the wounded man governor. Goebel died four days after taking the oath and was succeeded by his lieutenant governor, J. C. W. Beckham. Kentucky now had two governments, one of which proclaimed a state of insurrection. The deadlock was eventually broken by the courts, which decided in favor of the Democrats. Governor Taylor became an exile from the state. The reformers pushed through their bill extending the powers of the railroad commission, but the death of their leader and the very violence of their struggle for power seemed to leave them enervated. They failed to rally to the support of the commission during its prolonged litigation with the Louisville and Nashville, which virtually tied its hands for nearly fifteen years.

While no other reform movement encountered resistance that went to the extreme of assassination, they all met stiff opposition. This was always supported and often led by the railroads. It was natural that railroad regulation should have headed the list of reforms. The lobbyists and lawyers of the large systems were in many cases closely allied with the political machines which the reformers were seeking to overthrow. Moreover, the farmers and the urban middle class nursed long-accumulated grievances against the railroads. In the lexicon of the reformers, the locomotive came to replace the steam roller as a symbol of oppression.

The development of railroad regulation in the various states was closely parallel. In the seventies and eighties the nine Southern states east of the Mississippi River created railroad commissions. They ranged in type from the weak Virginia commission of 1877, which had only advisory capacity and narrowly restricted jurisdiction, to the powerful Georgia commission of 1879, which had authority to fix and enforce uniform rates, prevent discrimination, and establish freight classifications. These early commissions, although they performed useful functions in their day, came under attack toward the end of the century. The reformers were dissatisfied, not only with the law, but with the performance of the commissions. From Georgia came the cry that the comparatively strong commission of that state was "nothing more than a pretense, a sham, an imposition on the tax payers and an insidious prop to the present system of corporative robbery."

Within the decade beginning in 1897 nearly all the Southern states revised their commissions, increased the authority they exercised, and usually made the members elective instead of appointive. Florida and Tennessee, both of which had repealed their earlier commissions, revived them in 1897 in a strengthened form and made membership elective. Louisiana in 1898 and Arkansas in 1899 created their first commissions, and Kentucky revised her old one in the following year. North Carolina pioneered with "the first corporation commission created in the United States" in 1899, extending jurisdiction not only to all carriers of freight and passengers but to other public utilities, private and public banks, and loan and trust companies. Virginia followed her example in 1901, Georgia and Alabama in part in 1907, and Oklahoma in her new constitution of the same year. A comparison of state commissions in 1902 revealed that those with strongest authority were in the South and Middle West.

The fierce antimonopoly and antirailroad spirit probably reached its climax in the South, as it did in other parts of the country, in 1906 and 1907. In the latter year, wrote a North Carolina college professor, the various state legislatures of the South were furiously at work "reducing freight and passenger rates, prohibiting discriminations and rebates, establishing penalties for delay in the transportation of goods, enforcing liability for damages to passengers, prohibiting free passes, reducing the hours of labor of railroad employees, requiring the introduction of safety appliances, prohibiting combinations and traffic agreements." The commissions or legislatures of Alabama, Arkansas, Georgia, Mississippi, North Carolina, South Carolina, Tennessee, Texas, and Virginia were considering drastic reductions in passenger fares, while before the Texas legislature alone were pending eighty-three antirailroad measures.

In considerable degree the railroads had themselves to blame for the bitterness of the crusades against them in the South. Practices of discrimination, rebates, stockjobbing and stock watering, favoritism, and overcharging continued in spite of regulations against them. Certain of the larger roads, in particular, evaded or ignored the orders of the state commissions, or tied them up in litigation. Scarcely an order of importance made by the Louisiana commission was left uncontested. Resentment was aroused by the way in which railroads punished certain states—for example, Georgia and Texas—by retaliating against their commissions through control over interstate rates. The fighting blood of the reformers was especially stirred by the ease with which the railroads, after they had lost a long struggle over some piece of legislation, would secure an injunction from a Federal judge. This happened repeatedly.

North Carolina reformers in the legislative session of 1907 had as their *cause célèbre* a uniform reduction of passenger rates to two and one-fourth cents a mile. Josephus Daniels, who had recently adopted red-ink headlines, led a sensational campaign in the press. In spite of a multitude of lobbyists, a subsidized opposition press, and the threats and promises of the railroads, the reformers won their new law by a narrow margin. Daniels proclaimed it "the most brilliant victory in the history of legislation in North Carolina." Some of the carriers complied promptly with the law, but a group headed by the Southern Railway quickly obtained an injunction. The reformers were outraged. Daniels called on state officials to indict the railroads and ignore the Federal judge, and the speaker of the house of the state legislature declared that state officials would have to "choose between obeying Federal decisions and their oaths to enforce the state laws." Governor Robert B. Glenn, though a former employee of the Southern Railway, was prepared to enforce the law if it took "every dollar in the treasury and put arms in the hands of every available man in the state." Shades of Calhoun and nullification were invoked when a North Carolina superior-court judge then defied the Federal-court injunction, indicted and imprisoned a railroad agent for violating the state law, and fined the Southern Railway $30,000. The president of the Southern and other railroad officials were also arrested. According to a contemporary review of the proceedings, "never before has so sharp a conflict between the State and the United States Courts been presented." Fortunately, [President Theodore] Roosevelt was denied the opportunity of playing Jackson to Daniels' Calhoun, for the Southern capitulated to state authority, and differences were adjusted by compromise.

The Southern, the Seaboard, and the Atlantic Coast Line came to adopt a more conciliatory policy toward state commissions and legislatures—an example that came to be generally followed by railroads. But not by the Louisville and Nashville, not while President Milton Hannibal Smith had breath in his body and "legislative agents" on his payroll. A stocky figure with a pointed beard and an unconcealed contempt for "demagogues" and "blatherskites," Smith charged head on through the age of reform bearing the banner of *laissez faire*. At one and the same time his railroad was defying regulations and orders of the four sovereign states of Kentucky, Florida, Tennessee, and Alabama. In Governor Comer of Alabama, a man of his own class who had gone over to the reformers, Smith met something like his match, and in that state the battle was fought to a finish.

Comer's position was that high freight rates were thwarting the development of manufactures in cotton, lumber, iron, and steel, and keeping the state on a raw-material economy. The new reform legislature of 1907, elected on Comer's platform, rapidly enacted his program, greatly expanding the authority of the railroad commission, reducing rates, and prohibiting passes to public officials, lobbying, and various unfair practices. Passenger rates were reduced and maximum freight rates were fixed on 110 commodities.

Milton Smith descended upon Montgomery with an army of retainers and lobbyists and took the field in person, touring the state denouncing the Governor as a "highwayman" and his legislation as "populistic." He later admitted that he directed the expenditure of $34,800 in one campaign against Comer, that he subsidized a newspaper to the extent of $15,000, and that these were not his only political expenditures in Alabama. The very thought of Comer enraged the railroad president: "An impossible man," he declared. "A disordered mind. He will not be placated." The Governor replied in an address to the legislature that Smith "admitted that his road has dominated the policies and politics of Alabama for years," and charged that his corporation had "done more to debauch the State of Alabama than any other interest in the State."

The railroads applied to the Federal district court in Montgomery for an injunction against enforcement of certain of the new acts. This court was presided over by Judge Thomas G. Jones, inveterate foe of the Populists in the nineties, moderate champion of the Negro in the convention of 1901, and now Federal judge by grace of the support of Booker Washington. The reformers had not forgotten Jones's long service as attorney for the Louisville and Nashville, and perhaps with that in mind enacted their "Outlaw Bill," a measure revoking the license of any foreign corporation that instituted in the Federal court a suit that had started in a state court. Jones not only declared this act unconstitutional but on the same ground enjoined the enforcement of all but one of the acts complained of, and for good measure declared the rate-making power of the railroad commission unconstitutional. Off the bench, he said that Comer was inciting the people to riot and sedition and that in all probability he was slightly mad.

After a conference with Governor Smith of Georgia and Governor Glenn of North Carolina, both of whom had succeeded in bringing the railroads to terms, Comer appeared before a special session of the legislature with what he believed a means of evading Judge Jones. The assembly enacted an "injunction-proof" bill, so called because in order to be effective against it an injunction would have to extend to every citizen of the state—a manifest absurdity, so it was thought. But that was precisely the kind of injunction Judge Jones granted, upon the application of the Louisville and Nashville, thereby nullifying the work of the special session completely. The battle continued, and after governor and judge were both retired from office, Milton Smith was still defying the law of Alabama. He did not give up the struggle until 1913. The capitulation of this fortress of *laissez faire* might almost mark the end of an era.

The railroads were only one of several strongholds of economic privilege attacked by the Southern reformers. . . .

If the antitrust laws on the statute books of the states were any indication, the monster of monopoly would have been slain forever in the South. The statutes of North Carolina, for example, forbade virtually all of the practices by which the tobacco trust built up and maintained its monopoly. Yet the American Tobacco Company continued to thrive without embarrassment in that state. It remained for Jeff Davis of Arkansas to press the antitrust crusade to its logical and preposterous conclusion. As attorney general he filed 126 suits against fire-insurance companies, and while he was in the mood he brought action against express companies, tobacco companies, oil companies, and cotton-oil companies. The metropolitan press of the East was indignant. Representatives of the leading insurance companies of the United States and Great Britain resolved to boycott

Arkansas and immediately began canceling policies and withdrawing from the state. Representatives of the budding business community of the state met in convention and desperately implored relief. But Jeff was adamant. When the courts ruled against his construction of the law, he took the issue to the people and was elected governor. He made the trust "the paramount issue" in three campaigns, but nothing very practical came of his efforts.

The only effective fight made on the trust was extralegal, not to say illegal, and it was inspired by zeal for no theory but by desperate economic pressure. It started in the Kentucky and Tennessee "Black Patch" among the dark-leaf tobacco farmers as a protest against the market monopoly of the American Tobacco Company, which had driven the price of tobacco down below the cost of production and threatened the farmers with ruin. Organized at Guthrie, Kentucky, in September, 1904, the Planters' Protective Association took in all classes of farmers from planters to share-croppers. At its peak it was estimated to have 30,000 members in western Kentucky and Tennessee and 8,000 in Virginia. A similar association was organized in Henderson, Owensboro, and Bowling Green, Kentucky, which reached a total of about 20,000 members, and another of Burley-tobacco growers in Central Kentucky attained a membership of approximately 35,000. Finding no satisfactory relief in the peaceful methods originally adopted, and obtaining no help from the heirs to Goebel's reform movement, the farmers in 1906–1908 took the law in their own hands. Masked bands of night riders dynamited factories, burned down scores of warehouses, and destroyed hundreds of thousands of dollars worth of property belonging to the tobacco trust and its friends. In order to compel co-operation, the night riders scraped plant beds, laid waste to crops and farms, brutally whipped, beat, and sometimes murdered men and women, intimidated courts, and terrorized whole towns and counties. Frankly revolutionary in method, the night riders justified their lawlessness by invoking the spirit of the Boston Tea Party. Before violence was curbed by military force in 1908, the movement spilled over into the cotton states of Arkansas, Mississippi, Alabama, and Louisiana and threatened to awaken such a spirit of lawlessness as had not existed since the time of the Ku Klux. The farmers secured higher prices, but their victory was bought at an appalling cost in property, suffering, life, and moral deterioration. . . .

In municipal reform progressives held up two innovations as the cures for the "shame of the cities." These were the commission plan and the city-manager plan of municipal government. Both of them originated in the South. The first city in the country to adopt the commission plan was Galveston, Texas. The devastating hurricane and tidal wave of September, 1900, not only swept away a large part of the city but the antiquated city-council form of government as well. In the crisis of reconstruction and relief that followed, the city commission proved its efficiency by rebuilding the city, restoring its credit, and constructing a mighty sea wall. Houston followed the example of her neighbor in 1903, and by 1907 Dallas, Denison, Fort Worth, El Paso, Greenville, and Sherman had adopted the commission plan. The movement spread eastward and was taken up by Memphis, New

Orleans, Jackson, Birmingham, and Charlotte. By 1913 most of the larger cities in the South and many of the smaller ones were using the new type of government. Des Moines, Iowa, adopted it in 1907 and from there it spread over the North and West under the name of the "Des Moines Idea." Likewise, the city-manager plan was first tried by Staunton, Virginia, in 1908, then by Sumter, South Carolina, in 1911, but it spread over the rest of the country under the name of the "Dayton Idea" after that city adopted it in 1914.

Partly by chance the prohibition crusade made juncture with the progressive movement in the South, and the two forces marched together for a time. Occasionally they quarreled, but common enemies more often drew them together, and they fought many of their battles in close alliance.

Until 1907 no state-wide prohibition law existed in the South; only three survived in the country, and none had been passed since 1889. Then in August, 1907, Georgia passed a drastic statewide law that touched off the third national prohibition wave, the first since the eighties. In rapid succession within the next nine months Oklahoma, Alabama, Mississippi, and North Carolina followed Georgia's example, and Tennessee joined them in January, 1909. Four of the six states acted through their legislatures, two by popular vote. Florida and Texas came within a handful of popular votes of adopting prohibition, and the remaining states crowded the saloons into the cities and diminishing pockets of territory. The suddenness with which the prohibitionists appeared to seize whole states was deceptive. For years they besieged the demon rum in county campaigns by the local-option method. In Georgia 125 of the 145 counties were already dry before state-wide prohibition was adopted, and in Alabama, 90 per cent of the state. In Mississippi 69 of the 76 counties, and in North Carolina 62 of the 97 counties had banished the saloon before the states took action.

Even in Kentucky the cause of good bourbon whisky had been lost in 94 of the 119 counties by 1908. One computation at the beginning of 1907, before the prohibition "wave" was heard of, found 825 of the 994 counties in the ex-Confederate states under prohibition laws.

The remarkable success of the movement in the South was often attributed to the presence of the Negro, but a close study of the region concludes that "the negro has been an inconsiderable factor" and that "the saloon has been abolished and retained in the communities of the South without apparent reference to the presence of the negro." There was, however, a pronounced correlation between the success of prohibition and a high percentage of native-born, rural, Protestant elements in the population. In Georgia, Alabama, Mississippi, North Carolina, and Tennessee, which were among the strongest and earliest prohibition states, the native-born constituted 99 per cent or more of the population, the rural element ranged from 88 to 79 per cent, and Protestants comprised from 99 to 92 per cent of the church population. More specifically, it was the nine tenths of the Protestants included in the Baptist and Methodist folds who filled the dry ranks, for their ministers carried the crusade into their pulpits and preached not temperance but teetotalism. Hand in hand with the Anti-

Saloon League and the temperance organizations, the parsons gradually perfected their methods in local campaigns. They tapped the sources of reformism that sustained the contemporary education and child-labor crusades, but they also used revival tactics and stormed polls with mobs of singing and praying women and children. Their success earned for the South the name of being "the mainspring" and "the propagandic base of the national agitation." The region was "well-nigh puritanized" by the White Ribboners.

Even though prohibition was primarily a countryman's cause, it won converts among the urban progressive leaders. Reform governors Glenn of North Carolina, Comer of Alabama, and Smith of Georgia took up the cause, and their reform legislatures enacted state prohibition. . . .

. . . [T]here were other Southerners, many of them, who were relatively unmoved by these triumphs of the righteous and whose political urges were not fulfilled by progressivism. They had nothing to ship by classified freight rates, no oil wells to protect against pipelines, and no insurance policies to bother about. Perhaps they were also deficient in righteousness, for come Saturday night they wouldn't mind if they had a drink. But they did harbor deep and abiding grievances and powerful, if inarticulate, political urges. Those of them who had sought satisfaction in the independent rebellions and the Populist revolt came away frustrated and cheated. It is doubtful that many of them were later able to identify themselves completely with citified reformers like Comer the manufacturer, and Smith the publisher, nor with Glenn, Campbell, Goebel, and Broward. Jeff Davis they could claim as their very own, and Vardaman and Tillman could speak their idiom. But Tillman, harsh and ascetic as ever, drew away from them, and both he and Vardaman ascended unto Washington and left their flocks untended. In their absence, a new type of shepherd took charge of the fold.

By some obscure rule of succession, Bleases tended to follow Tillmans and Bilbos to succeed Vardamans. The new type of leader could hardly be said to have had a program or a party. Instead, he had prejudices and a following. Abuse by the city press was grist to his mill, and the more he was badgered and set upon by respectable politicians, reforming parsons, and Northern liberals, the more readily and joyfully did a slandered, misunderstood, and frustrated following uphold his cause and identify themselves with the persecuted leader. The leader often flouted sober conventions, sometimes consorted with lewd company, and in numerous ways proclaimed himself one of the boys. Cole Blease, Jeff Davis, and Tom Watson were periodically embroiled with parsons, missionaries, and prohibitionists. But they oftener tilted with foes more vulnerable and farther afield.

In one instance the transition from the old to the new type of leadership was accomplished by a single individual, though at tragic cost to his integrity and mental health. Tom Watson, who in his Populist days had stepped forth alone like a young David to battle the Goliath of his people's foe, spent his latter days rallying villainous mobs to bait and hound minorities. Turning against the progressive Hoke Smith, whom he had helped to elect, he defeated him in 1908 by combining with the reactionary Joseph M. Brown. Meanwhile, he diverted his following with a seven-year crusade against the Pope, forays upon the Socialists, and tirades against his onetime allies of the Negro race that were matchless in their malevolence. For two years he poured forth a flood of obscene and incendiary slander against the Jewish defenders of Leo Frank, who was eventually lynched and brutally mutilated by a mob that drove the Governor from the state. By such devices he recouped his lost political power and for sixteen years virtually bossed the Democratic party of Georgia while acknowledging no loyalty to it.

As an understudy of Tillman, Cole L. Blease imitated the master but improved his technique and expanded his appeal. For Blease embraced within his fold the people the master had described as "the damned factory class," and with them the large depressed rural element that had been entranced by the violence of Tillman's language but disappointed by the mildness of his performance. Agricultural colleges were very nice, but these people, when they were so much as literate, rarely aspired to more than grade school. Not that Blease gave them anything more tangible than Tillman, but he was more lavish with the intangibles—which were better than nothing. In vain his opponents pointed out that Blease had knifed labor bills, opposed child-labor laws, and repeatedly betrayed the classes he professed to love. Those classes cherished him for voicing their bitter hatreds and frustrations and for his unabashed defiance of the self-righteous and respectable. They loved him when he humiliated the old state by praising lynchers before the Governors' Conference of 1912 and threatening to "wipe the inferior race from the face of the earth." After two Blease administrations, Tillman had more than he could stand. "It makes me sad and angry," he said in a premature "farewell address" in 1914, "to be told that Tillmanism is the direct cause of Bleaseism," though he admitted that "there is just enough likeness to deceive the ignorant." To defeat Blease and save his own failing political fortunes, Tillman joined hands with his old conservative enemies, the very people he had taught the Bleaseites (and onetime Tillmanites) to hate. Blease's rise was temporarily scotched, but the future of Calhoun's onetime Greek Democracy lay in Cole Blease's hand as surely as it had once lain in Tillman's.

The relationship between Vardaman and his heir apparent Theodore G. Bilbo was much the same as that between Tillman and Blease. Perhaps the difference between master and understudy was not so great, and Vardaman could never be persuaded to renounce his successor. But even Vardaman's enemies, whom Bilbo inherited along with his following, admitted that the Great White Chief had mixed a modicum of idealism with his demaguery. On the other hand, the majority of them would never admit that his heir ever rose above the level of an obscene clown. An extensive reading in the literature of billingsgate by which such offenders have been characterized leads to the conclusion that the invective employed to describe Bilbo set a new mark. In 1910 the Mississippi senate resolved by a vote of twenty-five to one that he was "unfit to sit with honest upright men in a respectable legislative body" and called upon him to resign. But he thrived on abuse and was even then on the threshold of a long career.

Progressivism had its day in the South as elsewhere, but it no more fulfilled the political aspirations and deeper needs of the mass of people than did the first New Deal administration. Otherwise, there is no explaining the rise of the Bleases in the earlier instance—nor of Huey Long in the latter.

Women and School Reform in North Carolina

JAMES L. LELOUDIS II

"Revolutionize the state!" With that injunction, Charles D. McIver opened his address before a gathering of young women on the evening of March 20, 1902. His audience was receptive, but it was hardly a revolutionary cadre. McIver, president of the North Carolina Normal and Industrial College for Women at Greensboro, was speaking to two hundred juniors and seniors whom he had called together to discuss means of upgrading the state's white public schools. The revolution he envisioned was the industrial transformation of North Carolina. He implored his listeners to pursue that goal by improving the physical condition of schools with the same energy they devoted to keeping their homes and churches "neat and attractive." If such "housekeeping" seems tame as a revolutionary act, it nonetheless inspired the students. After President McIver's speech, they founded the Woman's Association for the Betterment of Public School Houses (WABPS) and urged the press to spread word of their organization across the state. The association flourished in subsequent years as a major voice in the crusade for New South industrialism and as a primary channel for white women's participation in public affairs.

The WABPS won wide acclaim and support from the outset. The *Raleigh News and Observer* greeted its creation as "an event of deep satisfaction," while editors of the *Biblical Recorder* and the *Progressive Farmer* offered to promote the group's work. With that assistance the association quickly enlisted thousands of women in programs designed to make schools more attractive, sanitary, and comfortable. By 1905 those programs had proved so successful that teachers attending the Summer School of the South at Knoxville, Tennessee, decided to implement them on a regional basis. The educators formed the Interstate Association for the Betterment of Public School Houses and elected delegates to establish state chapters modeled on the North Carolina association. Within two years the delegates had organized women in Alabama, Arkansas, Georgia, Kentucky, South Carolina, Tennessee, Texas, and Virginia. North Carolina's WABPS maintained a position of regional leadership in school-improvement

James L. Leloudis II, "School Reform in the New South: The Woman's Association for the Betterment of Public School Houses in North Carolina, 1902–1919," *Journal of American History* 59 (March 1983), pp. 886–909.

work until 1919, when many of its local chapters began to merge with the newly founded North Carolina Congress of Parents and Teachers. A subsequent decline in membership forced the association to close its state headquarters during the same year, although several local chapters continued to operate independently through the mid-1920s.

The North Carolina WABPS was one of many reform organizations that emerged during the Progressive Era offering women new public roles as agents of social change. By joining those groups, women moved from the home into public life and wielded new forms of power. Their activities raise a host of questions concerning female reform and the emergence of the New South: How did women activists organize their campaigns? What motivated their efforts? How did sex role prescriptions and class identity affect their strategies? What was the place of male authority in female voluntary societies? How did women influence the course of regional and national development? These queries remain largely unanswered by a historical literature that is centered upon more prominent male reformers and national organizations. Nevertheless, they are of vital importance to students of southern education and of progressivism in general. The southern movement for improved schools drew its strength from local groups comprised mostly of women; therefore, any attempt to explain the content and legacy of educational progressivism in the region must begin by placing women's studies in the mainstream of historical inquiry.

A focus on women is helpful in two ways. First, it sheds new light on the debate over the ideological foundations of progressive schools. Educational reform in the New South cannot be understood in the simple terms of either altruism or self-interest. Association women and their supporters among state school officials exhibited genuine concern for poor whites and struggled to improve standards of health and material comfort among school children and their families. The women, especially, viewed their work as "a labor of love" that would relieve "present hard conditions of ignorance and illiteracy, weakness and poverty." Yet these humanitarian concerns ultimately supported a program of social control. The association was intent upon training children "to fill the positions defined by circumstances" without going "so far as to make [them] discontented with their lot or [to] fill their minds with vain ambition." It sought to aid students by molding them into a manageable labor force rather than by preparing them to be critical participants in the reshaping of southern society. This paradox was not the product of hypocrisy but resulted instead from a unified vision of uplift and development that both informed and constrained school-improvement programs. Although sympathetic toward the poor, that vision could not satisfy their needs. It faltered in both its boosterism and philanthropy by refusing to address the issues of racial, class, and regional inequality that underlay the southern condition.

The study of women reformers also reveals the mixture of personal need and public enterprise that guided educational work during the early twentieth century. Women joined the association not only out of commitment to a New South but also in response to anxiety over their womanhood generated by the effects of economic development. As the twin forces of urban and industrial growth began to transform the South in the late nineteenth century, many women found their mothers' lives inappropriate models for feminine behavior and turned to reform activities as a means of adapting old values to a new society. Thus the WABPS was related to the New South on two levels: it would help modernize the region and would aid white, middle-class women in coping with the personal consequences of that process. Association women used the organization to restructure both their lives and the southern economy. Their actions, in turn, established a pattern of reform that has persisted as a central factor in regional development policy.

The connection between the association and women's private lives became apparent when its founders held their first public meeting in Greensboro on April 3, 1902. President McIver's students adopted a constitution that contained strict gender-specific requirements for membership. Female members of the WABPS paid no dues but were expected to participate regularly in the association's work and to vote in the annual election of officers. Men, on the other hand, were required to pay one dollar a year to join as "associate members" with no voting privileges. The association requested that its male patrons limit their services to the provision of money, labor, and advice. As a female officer explained on a later date, the organization was "purely feminine." "We allow the men to pay the money to carry on this work," she boasted. "We do not pay one cent, but every man that becomes an associate member gives one dollar and then he does the work we ask him to do. When we come to our election of . . . officers . . . we never let him vote. The women do all the voting in this Association and the men pay all the money—taxation without representation, if you please." The officer's assertive tone, however, belied the association's compliance with ordinary forms of male-female relations. Women modeled the organization after their own households, assuming responsibility for its affairs yet relying upon male support and approval to conduct their work. The association represented a translation of the white, middle-class home— itself a female institution sustained by male labor and money—into public life.

This adherence to domestic forms enabled the association to enter the traditionally male domain of public affairs without fear of condemnation. Indeed, men generally applauded women's involvement in school-improvement work. When a chapter of the association was organized in Wake County in 1902, the mayor of Raleigh and the superintendent of the Wake County Board of Education joined to wish the ladies immediate success. Similarly, in 1908, the superintendent of the Vance County Board of Education informed Lula M. McIver, Charles's wife and colleague, that he was "very anxious" for her to visit his county and begin the improvement work there. Women in the WABPS enjoyed such enthusiastic approval because they accepted the primacy of male authority. The association looked for guidance to what its members considered superior "man's judgment" and pursued aims that had been proposed originally by Charles D. McIver and other men in positions of public leadership.

Male endorsements helped the WABPS to grow rapidly. With permission of the state Board of Education, the North Carolina Teachers' Assembly sponsored the association's first annual conference in June 1902 for the purpose of proselytizing teachers and inaugurating a membership drive. Ten of President McIver's students volunteered during the conference to stump the state and to organize local auxiliaries. They spent the summer lecturing to church meetings, county teachers' institutes, community picnics, and intimate gatherings in private homes. The students' tireless labor met with remarkable success, especially in urbanized counties. They recruited more than two thousand members by September 1902 and over the next four years established branch associations in seventy of the state's ninety-six counties. Never before, except through the church, had so many North Carolina women been brought together in a single organization.

The popularity of the WABPS among women was due in large measure to the changing status of white, middle-class housewives. These women had grown up in rural homes in which their mothers had held responsibility for rearing large numbers of children and had played important roles as producers by growing food and making clothes. The industrial transformation of the southern economy in the late nineteenth century brought with it a move to town, a decline in family size, and greater access to commercial goods such as canned food and ready-made clothing. These changes combined to undercut women's traditional domestic duties and to reduce housewives to a position of lesser importance as consumers and symbols of their husbands' economic success. This loss of responsibility robbed many women of their sense of purpose in life. One lady noted that "women who had been fully occupied with the requirements of society . . . were now tossed to and fro amidst the exigencies and bewilderments of strange and for the most part painful circumstances, and were eager that new adjustments should relieve the strained situation, and that they might find out what to do." She and other middle-class women found the cure for their malaise in a strategy of role perfection. Rather than taking up feminist demands for the reorganization of social authority, WABPS members created new public activities that affirmed their identity as wives and mothers. Participation in school reform enabled them to regain a sense of personal dignity by expanding and elaborating upon traditional notions of femininity.

The reformers employed prevailing conceptions of women as housekeepers, guardians of virtue, and counselors of youth to legitimate their work. As Elvira Evelyna Moffitt, leader of the association in Wake County, observed, the women in the WABPS meant, not to "invade the kingdom of men," but only to assist local school committees. She explained that men were unfamiliar with the basic elements of child rearing because they worked away from home and left their wives to take "charge of the children." The men on school committees therefore often became so involved in "larger undertakings," such as hiring teachers and managing school funds, that they lost sight of the " 'little things' that in reality make the sum and substance of educational success." The women desired to remedy that neglect by using their domestic skills to make schoolhouses into "school homes" where children could learn virtues that were both the benchmarks of middle-class propriety and the behavioral ideals of industrial society. In performing that work, the women regained their lost self-esteem and perfected their traditional role in a public as well as private capacity. As one recruiter explained, women who had felt worthless as housewives flocked to her meetings and left with assurance that through the association they could once again attain the noble standards of motherhood.

The WABPS mobilized women in its school-improvement programs through a tripartite hierarchy of state, county, and district associations, which ensured that the psychic benefits of betterment work were distributed according to individual need. Groups at each level of the hierarchy held specific responsibilities. The state association included members of the county and district branches and was in fact synonymous with the WABPS. Delegates from the branch organizations met in annual conventions and elected five executive officers and five field agents, all of whom worked out of a central office in Greensboro. The executive officers dealt primarily with matters of planning. They consulted with the state Departments of Public Instruction, Agriculture, and Public Health on the development of improvement programs; issued regular advisory bulletins; and sent the field agents on lecture tours intended to create a sense of urgency and opportunity among local women. Officers of the county associations, in turn, used information from the state headquarters to establish improvement priorities in their communities and to direct the work of subordinate district associations. Together, these management activities shaped the efforts of individual members into a coherent campaign.

District associations were the workhorses of the WABPS. Local women organized themselves around individual schools and assumed responsibility for actually conducting improvement programs. Their chances of success depended upon support from lower-class parents who viewed the school as an avenue to economic security and social mobility for their children. District associations generally financed their projects with money solicited from students and parents at school picnics and plays. A teacher in Edgecombe County, for instance, raised more than thirty dollars by having her students bring lunch baskets for a class auction. On occasion, the district organizations also sponsored larger events. In 1906 the women in Raleigh directed a performance of "Cinderella in Flowerland" with a cast and crew of children from all of the city's schools. The operetta drew a large crowd and raised more than enough money to support the Raleigh Township association during the following year.

The neat division of labor within the association provided rewarding positions for a variety of members. Some women, such as Moffitt and Lucy Bramlette Patterson of Winston-Salem, felt compelled to assume leadership and win recognition as figures of importance. Both ladies spent their later adult lives as executive officers of the WABPS and satisfied their ambitions by managing the association's programs. They also found opportunities for personal growth and development in the traveling and speaking engagements connected with executive work. Patterson, for example, was a shy woman who succumbed to "stage-fright" whenever she spoke to more than a small group of friends. Several months of work as a state organizer, however, helped her to cultivate new self-confidence. With exuberant pride, she reported to Charles D. McIver in August 1903 that she had addressed "a big crowd for fifteen minutes and didn't get frightened!" Her short involvement in the association's campaign had taught her that despite her inhibitions she was capable of expressing herself in public with poise and persuasive force.

Such self-discovery often had a profound impact upon women's perceptions of themselves. Patterson and her colleagues adhered to the comfortable and familiar precepts that had defined their mothers' lives but in practice established a new standard of feminine conduct. Organizers who felt "unwomanly" when they began their work quickly came to accept public agitation as a respectable female activity. After addressing several audiences, Leah D. Jones no longer found herself "embarrassed and frightened" by seeing her name "posted quite publicly on trees and houses as a lecturer." "I felt that I was certainly doing nothing unwomanly," she wrote, "when I sat in some school house, with women and children close around me . . . or . . . stood in front under the trees and discussed with fathers as well as mothers the need to have the school attractive." Association work taught Jones and other women that they could succeed in what had previously been considered strictly male undertakings.

The women's view of themselves as competent and resourceful individuals, however, did not constitute a feminist consciousness. This fact became clear in 1912 and 1913 when the association joined the North Carolina Teachers' Assembly and Federation of Women's Clubs in a campaign to have women appointed to local school boards. Edith Royster, president of the Wake County association and of the Teachers' Assembly, argued that board membership was appropriate for women because it was a position of "trust and honor" rather than a political office. That distinction was crucial, for it avoided the issue of social authority and implied acceptance of sexual inequality. Royster considered board membership a privilege that men should bestow upon women in recognition of their special interest in education rather than a right to which women held legitimate claim. Her attitude reflected the peculiar blend of old and new values that pervaded the work of state and county leaders. These women wished to move out of the home and involve themselves in public affairs, yet they remained unprepared to question their subordinate status. They sought to expand the feminine sphere within the established structure of social relations without altering the sexual division of power.

The issue of feminism remained even more remote for the association's rank and file, most of whom acted out of motherly concern for children in their communities. Young teachers without children and middle-aged women whose children were grown comprised 87 percent of the female membership. Unable to fulfill their maternal role within the home, these women became "school-mothers" by participating in district associations. They adopted neighborhood children as their own and labored to nurture their new charges by carefully monitoring the details of school life. This work resolved the women's longings for the emotional warmth of a family and confirmed their feminine identity. As Hortense Turlington of Smithfield explained, "I miss my own children less because of the love I give the school children and the love they give me in return. It is a better solace than fancy work, bridge whist, or transcendentalism."

The district associations' focus on individual schools made these psychic rewards both personal and immediate. Local WABPS women acquired certain knowledge that they were "doing some real sure enough good" by observing directly the results of their handiwork, an experience that would have been impossible in more diffuse campaigns to enhance entire school systems. This high rate of return on investments of time, energy, and self-esteem was crucial to the association's survival, for it sustained women through terms of membership that commonly ranged between five and ten years. Such devotion marked the association's success in fitting the benefits of betterment work to the needs and uncertainties of individual lives.

Association women maintained their loyalty and enthusiasm in the face of what must have seemed insurmountable odds. North Carolina's white public schools were in utter disrepair when the WABPS began its work in 1902. The state had at that time 8,094 school districts, 840 of which had no school facilities of any kind. Another 829 had only log huts. Children in the remaining districts attended school in what Charles Lee Coon, City Superintendent of Public Instruction in Salisbury, described as "shabbily built board structures." He noted that the typical building of this type consisted of a single room with six windows, none of which had curtains or blinds. The children sat on uncomfortable homemade benches facing a teacher who had a chair but no desk. A "dilapidated wood stove . . . red with rust and dirt," stood in the center of the room. In winter, it barely warmed the cold wind that blew through cracks in the walls. The schoolhouse had no steps, but instead an inclined plane of dirt leading to its door. The yard was always muddy, and the general appearance of the surroundings was "anything but attractive." Coon concluded from these observations that North Carolina's schools provided a totally inadequate environment in which to prepare children for adult life.

The association's goal was to transform these "unattractive, cheerless schools" into "places of beauty and refinement." Its members pursued that objective through improvement projects which they divided into two categories: health and beautification. The health programs addressed matters of sanitation and comfort in the classroom. They included such tasks as removing rubbish from around school buildings, cleaning out wells, replacing water buckets with coolers, installing ceiling vents, and constructing sanitary privies. The association also encouraged its members to provide their schools with efficient heating systems and comfortable desks and chairs. The beautification projects complemented these health measures by creating a pleasant environment in and around the school. Inside the building, WABPS members hung maps and pictures of famous men, installed window shades, constructed display cases and bookshelves, painted walls, and polished stoves. Outside, they removed underbrush and stumps from the yard, set out saplings, planted vegetable and flower gardens, built paved walkways, and laid out large grassy plots for students to use as playgrounds. Once completed, these improvements were to provide children with a haven in which to develop fully their moral and physical capacities.

The association hoped that it could eventually remodel North Carolina's educational facilities to conform with the ideal schoolhouse depicted in photographs that adorned its annual reports. That school was a one- or two-room structure nestled in a grove of trees and surrounded by flowers. A small steeple or cupola sat atop its roof and housed the school bell. The building possessed all the idyllic charm of a modest Victorian cottage and represented the transfer of woman's aesthetic talents and motherly skills from the domestic sphere into the public realm. Through the model school, association women attempted to give substance to their conception of the surroundings required in rearing children to responsible adulthood. That conception emerged from a combination of their personal experiences as mothers and the cultural conventions of middle-class life.

The association's efforts to provide young white southerners with a healthy and beautiful environment were part of a larger educational crusade devised to breathe new life into the faltering industrial campaigns of the New South movement. That movement had begun during the last quarter of the nineteenth century as northern and southern businessmen, financiers, and publicists joined to rebuild the region. These men chose, not to revitalize the Old South's cash-crop economy, but rather to build a new economic order based upon factory production and diversified agriculture. They dreamed of developing a prosperous South that would "out-Yankee the Yankee" as a national center of commerce. That vision inspired bold new ventures in manufacturing and agricultural experimentation, yet its fulfillment constantly eluded its proponents' grasp. The South remained so firmly bound to cash crops in the 1890s that it had to import grain to feed its population. The region also failed to keep pace with the North and West in industrial growth. In 1900 it held a smaller percentage of the nation's factories and investment capital than it had claimed before the Civil War. Furthermore, its inhabitants continued to live in relative poverty. The estimated per capita wealth of the United States in 1900 was $1,165 as compared to $509 for the South. Despite the efforts of New South advocates, the region remained at the turn of the century the poorest and most underdeveloped section of the nation.

Southern boosters blamed their homeland's persistent problems on the shiftlessness of lower-class whites. Walter Hines Page, editor of the *Raleigh State Chronicle* and a member of the prominent group of middle-class reformers known as the Watauga Club, characterized the common white as "the real curse of the land. He is the fellow for whom Southern civilization sacrifices itself. . . . Better white men cannot rise for . . . the sorry Southern white man. His like exists in other parts of the country, but he does not set the pace elsewhere." In Page's view, southern laborers, whether farmers or factory operatives, had "become not only a dead weight but a definite opponent of social *progress*."

Page and his associates traced the inertia of southern labor to a combination of poor public health conditions and the "narcotic influences" of the Old South's aristocracy. They charged that the old elite preserved on their plantations and in their lifestyle both the South's love affair with cotton and the antebellum ideal of leisure. Because aristocrats occupied positions of political and economic power, common men and women respected and imitated their behavior. Thus a "smothering atmosphere" of "old thoughts" stifled efficiency, thrift, and innovation among southern workers and farmers. The white laboring classes remained "listless . . . and backward-looking" and denied the South the benefits of modernity.

Directors of public health agencies added that the effects of disease compounded those of cultural stagnation. In 1902, for example, Charles W. Stiles identified the hookworm as "the cause of the proverbial laziness of the 'cracker.' " He and others attributed the chronic ill health of poor whites to their "filthy" habits of personal hygiene. Perhaps most disturbing was the widespread failure to build and use sanitary privies:

> Although the privy was in old times called a "necessary," it is startling to find how many persons do not consider such a structure to be a necessary adjunct to the human dwelling. The absence of a privy can fairly be called uncivilized. . . . It ought to go without saying that every person should have the opportunity to use a properly constructed privy at all times, and should also be compelled to use it, and never under any circumstances be allowed to deposit his discharges in any other place.

The health officials' concern in reporting and attempting to police such intimate aspects of personal life was both to relieve human suffering and to increase worker productivity. Malaria, hookworm, and the wide variety of gastrointestinal ailments common among southern laborers seldom proved fatal. They instead produced days of debilitating fever and nausea, which made their victims lethargic and nearly unable to work. According to the International Health Board, a Rockefeller Foundation agency concerned primarily with health problems in the South, the "loss of efficiency" from such diseases was "probably the most serious obstacle to the development of civilization in the region."

Leaders of the New South movement turned to school reform as a primary means of reshaping "habits of life" and improving living conditions among southern working people. They formulated their strategy in the annual sessions of the Conference for Education in the South. The conference began in 1898 at Capon Springs, West Virginia, as an informal gathering of ministers, businessmen, and educators who were interested in southern economic and social development. Its meetings attracted little attention until the fourth session convened in Winston-Salem in April 1901. Delegates attended from each of the southern states, and Robert Curtis Ogden, a clothing manufacturer from New York and president of the conference, brought along a number of prominent northerners, including John D. Rockefeller, Jr. After several days of deliberation, the conferees decided to undertake a campaign to improve public education in the South. Ogden appointed the Southern Education Board (SEB) to supervise the project. Over the next eight years, Rockefeller donated more than $53 million to support the board's work and that of its affiliated agencies.

The SEB chose to begin its campaign in North Carolina because of the state's reputation for regional leadership in public education. Ogden placed the program under the direction of Charles D. McIver, the board's secretary, and Governor Charles Brantley Aycock. On February 13, 1902, these men organized the state's educational leaders into the Central Campaign Committee for the Promotion of Public Education and charged them with persuading individual counties to consolidate small school districts, adopt local school taxes, and repair or replace deteriorating schoolhouses. Five weeks later, Charles D. McIver established the WABPS as a woman's auxiliary to the all-male committee. Like its parent organization, the association received substantial funding and direction from the SEB. The board provided five hundred dollars a year to cover the expenses of the state field agents and helped finance most of the association's organizational and public relations activities. Through Charles D. McIver and the committee's careful supervision, the SEB also shaped the women's projects in accordance with its own program for reform.

McIver organized the WABPS as a middle-class association devoted to the rehabilitation of the laboring poor. Membership lists for the Raleigh Township and Wake County chapters demonstrate the class dimensions of the association's work. These local groups had 108 members in 1904, 44 of whom were women teachers and principals. The remaining associate members and the husbands of the regular female members were all merchants, bankers, professional men, and prosperous farmers. These men and women viewed themselves as the vanguard of a New South and considered it their duty to train the children of less-fortunate whites in the ways of progress. Moffitt likened herself to a diver probing "the depths of darkness to bring to light the pearls that need but to be polished." Sue V. Hollowell, president of the association in 1903, expressed a similar sense of mission. She explained that WABPS women assumed the responsibility of "those who are more fortunate . . . to make bright, beautiful spots in the lives of those who know not what sunshine and brightness is." Through their school-improvement work, the women strove to "raise the masses to a higher plane of life."

The WABPS based its mission of uplift upon the belief that a child's environment was the major factor shaping its character. "As a child's surroundings are," exclaimed Mary Taylor Moore, "so is he liable to be." Like progressive reformers elsewhere, the association women had come to view the perceived moral defects of the laboring classes as products of their "social environment" rather than inherent personal evil, and they were moving to replace traditional attempts at individual uplift with broader programs of environmental management. Moffitt explained the assumptions underlying this new outlook in a speech before the Raleigh Township association. She noted that "there is an embryo" of a productive citizen "in every human being that grows to good or evil, governed by circumstances and ambition." That embryo often withered and died in laboring-class children simply "for the want of direction" and a suitable environment. The association's duty was to correct this situation by creating schools that would motivate children "to aspire to higher ideals and perfect them to the highest place." It sought to meet that responsibility by addressing its reforms specifically to the deficiencies of laboring-class life identified by New South spokesmen.

The association designed its beautification programs to free children from their antebellum legacies of laziness and cash-crop farming. The beautiful schoolhouse and yard were to break the bonds of idleness by altering children's outlook on life and imbuing them with new values. "A child seeing the pleasant school house and its attractive surroundings gets a new impulse," Moffitt declared, and "new hope springs up in his breast and a new life opens to his view." Each aspect of the school contributed to that awakening. The pictures of famous men provided students with role models, fostering in them "a spirit of self-reliance and individuality." "A single picture" of Sir Galahad or of a minuteman might, "by its silent influence," call "youth to high and noble endeavor." The pleasing atmosphere created by freshly painted walls, clean window shades, and landscaped lawns added a contempt among pupils for their "low, groveling, canine conditions of life." When these effects combined, they imparted to schoolchildren both the desire and self-confidence to strive for a better life. In pursuit of that desire, Moffitt observed, a child was "driven to labor."

School gardens presumably operated in a similar manner to liberate southern children from the region's ancient commitment to cash crops. The association advised teachers that most children grew up on small cotton or tobacco farms where they had little or no exposure to diversified planting and learned the "practical part of tilling the soil, but not the science of it." The agricultural practices of their ancestors therefore became habitual with them before they reached adulthood. WABPS field agents claimed that school gardens could circumvent that cycle of ignorance by demonstrating the benefits of crop rotation and diversification to children while they were still at an impressionable age. Children witnessed "the fundamental principles of farming" in the gardens just as they learned the "fundamental truths of arithmetic, geography, or grammar" in the classroom. That experience then sparked an enthusiasm among rural students for adopting "new discoveries in farming" and "bringing up their farms by the well-tried experiments made at the A[gricultural] and M[echanical] College." The agents predicted that such enlightened pupils could reverse the direction of southern agriculture within a single generation if every school had its own garden.

The WABPS maintained, however, that beautification would be ineffectual unless accompanied by improvements in public health. Association members shared with health officials a belief that intellectual and physical development were inseparable and that the school's duty was to educate the "whole child." . . .

. . . Having mastered the inner reaches of children's minds, it now remained for the WABPS to apply the principles of management and control to their bodies. Association women undertook that task through health programs designed to transform sick and feeble children into a productive citizenry.

These programs were to work in three ways to invigorate students' minds and bodies. First, the comfort-oriented improvements would help students gain proficiency in basic intellectual skills by providing a correctly designed school environment. Ceiling vents removed from classrooms the "vitiated" air that produced headaches, while the installation of contoured desks and chairs cured the back pains caused by sitting on uncomfortable homemade benches. Once liberated from these distracting ailments, students could focus their full attention on learning to read, write, and cipher. The WABPS considered this concentration of effort a vital component of proper schooling because training in the three R's constituted an education for "progress and efficiency." Literacy and numeracy made working-class children accessible to the New South elite who relied upon the written word and the statistical rhetoric of the social sciences to promote and validate their social vision. Unless children were prepared to accept that vision, Moffitt warned, they would become unruly citizens incapable of comprehending or attacking "the difficult problems of life" in the factory and on the farm. Laborers who could not read or perform simple arithmetic also could not be governed.

The sanitation projects were meant to make the work force dependable as well as tractable by guarding children's physical strength against the effects of disease. Moffitt took special interest in these projects and regularly invited physicians to attend meetings of the Raleigh Township association. The doctors lectured on the need to drain school yards and to construct sanitary privies, advising the women that such efforts would help reduce the incidence of yellow fever, malaria, typhoid, and cholera. Moffitt also led a campaign to replace water buckets with pressurized coolers. "Children," she observed, "are often careless to put the dipper back into the bucket with water in it." As a result, the entire water supply became contaminated with the "germs of disease." Coolers remedied the problem by providing children with "unpolluted water" and flushing waste water down a drain. Moffitt and state health officials believed that these simple techniques of sanitary engineering would begin to bring the human body and its maladies under control, thereby diminishing the South's health-related problems of labor inefficiency.

Finally, the sanitation and comfort projects would work together to secure the South's industrial transformation within the routines of domestic life. Moffitt explained that the projects made schools into "models of cleanliness'' where students learned to ''hate ugliness in the home and in the street.'' As children became disgusted with the conditions in which they lived, they would encourage their parents to adopt the principles of ''sanitation, ventilation, and neatness'' they were taught in the classroom. Moffitt believed that the parents, embarrassed by their children's low opinion of them, would consent readily and begin to reinforce rather than undermine the redeeming influence of the school. In this way, the school would ultimately become a ''community center'' through which the values and habits of an entire population could be transformed, managed, and controlled.

Association members trusted that this broad package of reform activities would bring the New South dream to fruition by enabling educators to produce the ''abundant supply'' of farmers and laborers, ''properly trained and disciplined,'' that the region's economy seemed to require. Improved schools would change lethargic southerners into a ''happy and progressive'' people no longer content to lounge on their porches and in the doorways of factories. They would instead employ the principles of scientific agriculture in their fields and work diligently at their machines to produce the ''industrial progress'' and ''material prosperity'' the ''Great Southland'' needed to rise above and dominate the North. In the minds of its members, the WABPS appeared to hold the key to the South's future. With the association's assistance, North Carolina and her neighbors could at last take their rightful place as jewels in the ''diadem of the nation's crown.''

These expectations became a source of both satisfaction and disappointment for association members. In the area of school improvement, the women experienced astounding success. Their public relations activities helped raise the tax revenues necessary to build on the average more than one new schoolhouse a day during the years 1902–1910. This construction program, when combined with the association's renovation projects, increased the value of North Carolina's public school property from $1,466,770 to $5,862,969. These accomplishments, however, proved inadequate either to alter the state's economy or to alleviate poverty. The land devoted to cotton and tobacco rose from 21 percent to 31 percent of the state's total cultivated acreage between 1900 and 1920. As a result, farm tenancy increased by 26 percent and per capita farm income fell to a level less than half the average for nonsouthern states. Although North Carolina's industries more than doubled the value of their products during the same decades, they too posted a discouraging record. Manufacturers remained locked into a system of primary production that severely depressed industrial wages. In 1919 factory workers earned an average of $757 a year— the forty-fifth lowest industrial wage in the nation. Programs of moral and physical uplift could not cure these ills, for they mistook poverty's symptoms for its causes. North Carolina's plight was rooted far more deeply in the structure of its economy than in the health and character of its poor white population. . . .

The failure of association women to recognize the basic structural problems of the southern economy originated in their class background and role expectations. As members of the white middle class, they envisioned a

New South developed and governed by managers of capital such as their husbands. The women had little reason to question the institutional arrangement of southern society or to seek a fundamental redistribution of power and authority. From their perspective, the nascent industrial order seemed just, progressive, and replete with opportunities for self-improvement and social mobility. This view rendered the association incapable of explaining the misery of poor whites in terms other than the inadequacies of lower-class life. The WABPS argued that common whites suffered penury and disease because they mismanaged their land, lived in squalid homes, and lacked ambition. It sought to remedy that situation by engineering a new environment that would imbue workers' children with middle-class values and thereby lead them to prosperity. This tactic placed the burden of change on the victims of social inequality by focusing on perceived defects in white working-class culture and ignoring the structural roots of poverty, illness, and despair. It also revealed the dilemma of reformers caught unwittingly between humanitarian impulses and the limitations of their own world view. Association women voiced genuine concern for white laborers but were unprepared to provide the working class with the political and economic resources necessary to improve its condition.

The strictures of class also made the association unresponsive to the plight and special needs of southern blacks. The racial ideology of the New South dictated that blacks receive only that education necessary to prepare them for their "place" in the segregated social and economic order. White school officials therefore sought to limit black schooling to instruction in proper forms of racial deference and the technical skills of agricultural and manual labor. The WABPS generally had no cause to challenge these measures, since they were grounded in social arrangements that made possible the achievements of the white middle class. On occasion, however, its members found their class identity overcome by a sense of feminine duty toward the welfare of children. In 1905, for instance, Hollowell violated the association's constitution by attempting to organize an integrated chapter in Granville County. Charles D. McIver and the state superintendent of public instruction, James Yadkin Joyner, quickly censured her, proclaiming that WABPS members might aid blacks in forming independent betterment associations but never were to become directly involved in black school improvement. That reprimand stood as clear warning that the participation of white women in public school reform was contingent upon their willingness to subordinate humanitarian concerns to prior racial and class loyalties.

The reformers' conception of womanhood left them little choice but to abide such restrictions. Within traditional roles as wives and mothers, they had limited access to the channels of power controlled by men and were confined to the practices of housekeeping as means of ordering their society. Their position enabled them to pursue social reform only in accordance with priorities established by their husbands, priorities that had the effect of tidying up the world rather than making it anew. The women therefore ignored black education altogether and sought to rehabilitate lower-class whites by translating the concerns of the home for beauty and cleanliness into public life. This strategy misdirected the association into an obsession with aesthetics and environmental purity and an interest in the outward appearances of poverty rather than the inequities from which it grew. The irony of civic domesticity, however, was that it contributed to a growing self-awareness among white women even as it restricted the scope of reform. Social action organized around traditional conceptions of womanhood pushed against the boundaries of feminine propriety and awakened women to their capacity for public expression. Progressive school reform ultimately proved more liberating for its practitioners than for its subjects. The WABPS failed to bring prosperity to North Carolina, yet it offered white, middle-class women a new measure of dignity and self-respect.

This blend of success and failure shaped the decision of local chapters to merge with the Congress of Parents and Teachers in 1919. Having achieved their short-term goal of school improvement, the women in the WABPS lacked a strategy capable of directing further efforts to build a New South. Their emotional involvement in the association and the psychological rewards of their work, however, were too great for them to allow their local associations to become inactive or to disband. This situation generated intense frustration and anxiety for the women, which they in turn projected onto parents. Patterson voiced the sentiments of association members in 1918, explaining that the subversive influence of "ignorant parents" had prevented the WABPS from realizing any permanent benefits from its work. This diagnosis of the association's failure placed the onus of guilt outside the organization and mandated a fresh approach to the task of school reform. It transformed abandonment of the WABPS from an act of betrayal into one of devotion and prepared the women to join the Congress of Parents and Teachers with a clear conscience. Association women transferred their loyalty to the new organization in an attempt to revitalize their betterment work and their pursuit of psychic gratification.

Membership in the congress required little change in local WABPS chapters. The women who established the congress adopted both the association's organizational structure and its desire to modernize the South. They altered only its methods. The congress worked to bring parents and teachers into a close relationship. Its leaders believed that through such contact teachers could educate parents "so that [they] might better be able to cope with existing conditions and meet more intelligently the problem of rearing a child in a changing civilization." In embracing this plan of action, members of the WABPS appropriated a new means of attaining their original objectives. They moved to perpetuate their local organizations and their quest for a New South by joining the congress and carrying the school's lessons on ambition, cleanliness, and economic progress directly into children's homes. The women proposed to make their state both modern and affluent by raising "the standards of home life" and developing "wiser, better trained parenthood." They would no longer seek to create a New South by simply molding children within the school but would now reach directly into the home to gain more complete control over the process of child rearing.

The association's merger with the Congress of Parents and Teachers ended a reform enterprise that illustrated both the limitations and the complexities of southern educational progressivism. School reform in the New South was concerned only marginally with matters of curriculum and children's cognitive development. It focused instead upon promoting social change and adjusting southerners to industrial life. Women used school reform to restructure their lives in a manner that satisfied their need to feel useful and respected without violating established notions of womanhood. Their efforts, like those of progressive reformers elsewhere, marked a pervasive feminization of American politics and culture. As never before, the domestic realm of women had become a model for social policy.

While they worked to resolve personal crises, the women also labored to develop a healthy and tractable population capable of sustaining a conservative modernization of southern society. The association's work derived from a truly benevolent attitude. Conditions among poor whites were indeed deplorable and demanded attention. Members of the WABPS, however, grounded their projects in a sense of moral superiority that generated inappropriate tactics and robbed their humanitarianism of meaning. The women sought to save white, working-class children from the world of their parents by remaking them in a middle-class image rather than freeing them to shape their own lives. This approach to reform perpetuated social inequality by denying poor whites a voice in the restructuring of the southern economy. It also helped lay the foundation for a school system that historically has claimed the noble purpose of social amelioration, while failing to recognize the structural roots of poverty in the New South. Since 1920, southern educators have instituted new programs such as vocational high schools and community colleges, each of which has fallen short in its promise of uplifting the poor. Like members of the WABPS, these policy makers accepted industrialism and public education as cures for the South's ills without considering the roles of class and race in distributing the rewards of economic development. The disappointment of the WABPS and its successors in their search for regional prosperity and social betterment has not grown from a lack of concern or sincerity. It has instead been the natural product of a reform ethos both unable and unwilling to confront fundamental questions of power, authority, and social justice.

✢ *F U R T H E R   R E A D I N G*

Raymond Arsenault, *The Wild Ass of the Ozarks: Jeff Davis and the Social Bases of Southern Politics* (1984)

Hugh C. Bailey, *Edgar Gardner Murphy: Gentle Progressive* (1968)

———, *Liberalism in the New South: Southern Social Reformers and the Progressive Movement* (1969)

Paul D. Casdorph, *Republicans, Negroes, and Progressives in the South* (1981)

Bruce Clayton, *The Savage Ideal: Intolerance and Intellectual Leadership in the South, 1890–1914* (1972)

John Dittmer, *Black Georgia in the Progressive Era, 1900–1920* (1977)

Elizabeth E. Etheridge, *The Butterfly Caste: A Social History of Pellagra in the South* (1972)

J. Wayne Flynt, *Cracker Messiah: Governor Sidney J. Catts of Florida* (1977)

Dewey W. Grantham, *Hoke Smith and the Politics of the New South* (1958)

———, *Southern Progressivism: The Reconciliation of Progress and Tradition* (1983)

Sheldon Hackney, *Populism to Progressivism in Alabama* (1969)

Louis R. Harlan, *Separate and Unequal: Public School Campaigns and Racism in the Southern Seaboard States, 1901–1915* (1958)

———, *Booker T. Washington: The Wizard of Tuskegee, 1901–1915* (1983)

Carl V. Harris, *Political Power in Birmingham, 1871–1921* (1977)

William F. Holmes, *The White Chief: James Kimble Vardaman* (1970)

Jack Temple Kirby, *Darkness at the Dawning: Race and Reform in the Progressive South* (1972)

J. Morgan Kousser, *The Shaping of Southern Politics: Suffrage Restriction and the Establishment of the One-Party South, 1880–1910* (1974)

———, "Progressivism—For Middle-Class Whites Only: North Carolina Education, 1880–1910," *Journal of Southern History* 46 (1980), 169–194

Lester C. Lamon, *Black Tennesseans, 1900–1930* (1977)

William E. Larsen, *Montague of Virginia: The Making of a Southern Progressive* (1965)

Arthur S. Link, "The Progressive Movement in the South, 1870–1914," *North Carolina Historical Review* 23 (1946), 172–195

William A. Link, *A Hard Country and a Lonely Place: Schooling, Society, and Reform in Rural Virginia, 1870–1920* (1986)

John Patrick McDowell, *The Social Gospel in the South: The Woman's Home Mission Movement in the Methodist Episcopal Church, South, 1886–1939* (1982)

William D. Miller, *Memphis during the Progressive Era, 1900–1917* (1957)

Raymond O. Pulley, *Old Virginia Restored: An Interpretation of the Progressive Impulse, 1870–1930* (1968)

Linda D. Vance, *May Mann Jennings: Florida's Genteel Activist* (1985)

LeeAnn Whites, "The De Graffenried Controversy: Class, Race, and Gender in the New South," *Journal of Southern History* 54 (1988), 449–478

George C. Wright, *Life behind a Veil: Blacks in Louisville, Kentucky, 1865–1930* (1985)

CHAPTER
8

The Religious South

Religion is one of the major defining characteristics of southern identity. Yet prior to the 1970s, historians had not studied religion as systematically as they had other cultural elements such as race relations and political culture. Since then, scholars have discovered that evangelical Protestantism took hold during the nineteenth century and became central to the perspectives of black and white southerners, though they responded to its theology in different ways. After the Civil War, the black church provided social services, recreational facilities, education, and leadership training for black communities, especially in towns and cities. The black minister emerged as a powerful leader, a role prefigured in the antebellum era. Whereas some ministers deflected racial tensions to otherworldly concerns, others were active in social ministries and urged their congregations to persevere—and even to protest.

For whites after the Civil War, the institutional church was less important than the evolving evangelical theology that helped to explain their defeat and to provide hope for eventual redemption, personally and regionally. The key focus remained the individual's relationship with God; collective objectives and social concerns were secondary. Religion justified and became inseparable from southern culture, what theologian Samuel S. Hill called Culture-Protestantism.

Yet at the same time, especially after the 1890s, southern religion promoted reform. Churchmen and churchwomen were prominent in the progressive movement, for example. Is southern religion a force for inspiring change—or for sanctifying the status quo?

✢ D O C U M E N T S

The strict separation of church and state is a standard evangelical tenet. However, as the first document, a sermon by Baptist minister C. C. Lloyd, reveals, the tenet is easier preached than practiced. The Reverend Lloyd's sermon supported Alabama's embattled Democratic Party against the Populists. Evangelical theology, however, is not of one piece; there are disparate black and white interpretations and numerous differences among the denominations. In black and white sacred music, the past figured significantly but in contrasting ways. Negro spirituals from the slavery era often had double meanings, as indicated in "Steal

Away to Jesus" in the second selection. Hymns in white churches after the Civil War sanctified the Lost Cause, as this 1901 variation on "When the Roll Is Called Up Yonder," also in the second selection, reveals. Black leader W. E. B. Du Bois reflects on the pervasiveness of religion in the life of southern blacks in the third document. The fourth document presents a mainstream perspective on the role of the white church in the South. Victor I. Masters, a Baptist minister and an official with the Home Mission Board of the Southern Baptist Convention, was concerned about the growing gap between rural and urban Baptist churches during the early twentieth century, which he attributes to the country churches. The excerpt shows the growing urban and middle-class leadership of the major evangelical denominations. Few causes stirred evangelical zeal in the 1920s more than the attempt to outlaw the teaching of evolution. In the fifth document, a sermon delivered in Raleigh, North Carolina, the Reverend Amazi Clarence Dixon attributes an array of global evils, including World War I and divorce, to Darwin's theory. The final document is from the Pentecostal Holiness church. The provincialism that Victor I. Masters sought to exorcise is evident, and he would probably disapprove of some of the rituals as well.

Reverend C. C. Lloyd on the Separation of Church and State, c. 1892

The State of Alabama is just now shaken from centre to circumference by a question which has been agitating the minds of its people for several years. What power is to settle it? The church has no power to legislate either civilly or ecclesiastically. It can only execute the laws given it by its Head. Then it must be the work of the State and if so we ask in all candor, how can preachers, godly men, leaders set for the defense of christ's church dare to take such an active part with the State without jeopardizing this tenet of the church for which we have ever contended? Are we not blending the two powers that are and should ever be kept separate and distinct in one common effort to do the work the State alone should do? Is the Church a coercive power? And to take my brother by the throat and in the language of a tyrant or law-giver say: "In the name of my Master Jesus of Nazareth" I command and will force you to obedience? Or like "Peter the hermit" shall we in this day of gospel liberty and gospel light engage to conquer the world for Christ by force of arms or civil authority? "The Kingdom of God cometh not with observation": that is, it was not established with carnal weapons amidst the confusion of battles and victories over conquered armies. Are Ministers of the gospel set apart to be Messengers of "peace on earth and good will to men" to abandon the sacred desk and entering the Political arena transform themselves into messengers of confusion, strife and discord to advance a cause that bids fair to forever sunder the life-long ties of christian love and christian fellowship? Is this the character of the church established by the Savior of men?

Nay—His Kingdom is not to be defended and perpetuated by carnal weapons. The weapons of our warfare are not carnal but spiritual and mighty through God to the pulling down of strong-holds and every vain thing. Again knowing the terror of the Lord we persuade men. We love men and by love we would persuade men.

Further are we not or rather have we not already drifted into political strife? How true the prediction of a prominent Senator some two years ago, "the tendency is to the disruption of the Democratic Party." Today we find that faithful custodian of our liberties disrupted, divided, torn with dissensions, the freedom of our citizens both civil and ecclesiastical threatened with destruction and a reign of civil and religious intolerance set up in the Commonwealth of Alabama. And this too accomplished largely by leaders in the Churches whose duty it is to exalt Christ. . . .

Let preachers return to thier [*sic*] pulpits long prostituted to political ends hold up the Banner of Christ now trailing in the mire and filth of political shame and disgrace and never never forget that this same unholy alliance of Church and State by Catholic Rome in the dark ages of the world was fraught with perils and persecutions of Christs Church. . . .

Back to your holy calling, leave this many cornered fight to Catholics, Protestants, Fanatics, False teachers, Political aspirants, Statesmen and all whose creeds exercise no restraining influence to keep them out of this unholy Crusade.

Have we forgotten that civil and religious intolerance drove our forefathers to the wilds of America to escape the hand of tyrany [*sic*] and oppression?

Two Hymns

"Steal Away to Jesus," a Negro Spiritual, N.D.

Chorus

> Steal away, steal away, steal away to Jesus!
> Steal away, steal away home,
> I ain't got long to stay here.
> Steal away, steal away, steal away to Jesus!
> Steal away, steal away home,
> I ain't got long to stay here.

> My Lord, He calls me,
> He calls me by the thunder,
> The trumpet sounds within-a my soul,
> I ain't got long to stay here.

Chorus

> Green trees a bending, po' sinner stand a-trembling,
> The trumpet sounds within-a my soul,
> I ain't got long to stay here,
> Oh, Lord I ain't got long to stay here.

"When the Roll Is Called Up Yonder," 1901

When this time with us shall be no more and final taps shall sound,
And the Death's last cruel battle shall be fought;
When the good of all the armies shall tent on yonder camping ground,
When the roll is called up yonder, let's be there.

On that mistless, lonely morning when the saved of Christ shall rise,
In the Father's many-mansioned home to share;
Where our Lee and Jackson call us to their homes beyond the skies,
When the roll is called up yonder, let's be there.

If all's not well with thee, my comrades, for thy entrance at the gate,
Haste thy calling and election to prepare;
You will find that precious peace, sweet peace,
When the roll is called up yonder, let's be there.

W. E. B. Du Bois on the Faith of the Fathers, 1903

It was out in the country, far from home, far from my foster home, on a dark Sunday night. The road wandered from our rambling log-house up the stony bed of a creek, past wheat and corn, until we could hear dimly across the fields a rhythmic cadence of song,—soft, thrilling, powerful, that swelled and died sorrowfully in our ears. I was a country school-teacher then, fresh from the East, and had never seen a Southern Negro revival. To be sure, we in Berkshire were not perhaps as stiff and formal as they in Suffolk of olden time; yet we were very quiet and subdued, and I know not what would have happened those clear Sabbath mornings had some one punctuated the sermon with a wild scream, or interrupted the long prayer with a loud Amen! And so most striking to me, as I approached the village and the little plain church perched aloft, was the air of intense excitement that possessed that mass of black folk. A sort of suppressed terror hung in the air and seemed to seize us,—a pythian madness, a demoniac possession, that lent terrible reality to song and word. The black and massive form of the preacher swayed and quivered as the words crowded to his lips and flew at us in singular eloquence. The people moaned and fluttered, and then the gaunt-cheeked brown woman beside me suddenly leaped straight into the air and shrieked like a lost soul, while round about came wail and groan and outcry, and a scene of human passion such as I had never conceived before.

Those who have not thus witnessed the frenzy of a Negro revival in the untouched backwoods of the South can but dimly realize the religious feeling of the slave; as described, such scenes appear grotesque and funny, but as seen they are awful. Three things characterized this religion of the slave,—the Preacher, the Music, and the Frenzy. The Preacher is the most unique personality developed by the Negro on American soil. A leader, a politician, an orator, a "boss," an intriguer, an idealist,—all these he is, and ever, too, the centre of a group of men, now twenty, now a thousand in number. The combination of a certain adroitness with deep-seated earnestness, of tact with consummate ability, gave him his preëminence, and helps him maintain it. The type, of course, varies according to time and place, from the West Indies in the sixteenth century to New England in the nineteenth, and from the Mississippi bottoms to cities like New Orleans or New York.

The Music of Negro religion is that plaintive rhythmic melody, with its touching minor cadences, which, despite caricature and defilement, still remains the most original and beautiful expression of human life and longing yet born on American soil. Sprung from the African forests, where its counterpart can still be heard, it was adapted, changed, and intensified by the tragic soul-life of the slave, until, under the stress of law and whip, it became the one true expression of a people's sorrow, despair, and hope.

Finally the Frenzy or "Shouting," when the Spirit of the Lord passed by, and, seizing the devotee, made him mad with supernatural joy, was the last essential of Negro religion and the one more devoutly believed in than all the rest. It varied in expression from the silent rapt countenance or the low murmur and moan to the mad abandon of physical fervor,—the stamping, shrieking, and shouting, the rushing to and fro and wild waving of arms, the weeping and laughing, the vision and the trance. All this is nothing new in the world, but old as religion, as Delphi and Endor. And so firm a hold did it have on the Negro, that many generations firmly believed that without this visible manifestation of the God there could be no true communion with the Invisible. . . .

The Negro church of to-day is the social centre of Negro life in the United States, and the most characteristic expression of African character. Take a typical church in a small Virginian town: it is the "First Baptist"—a roomy brick edifice seating five hundred or more persons, tastefully finished in Georgia pine, with a carpet, a small organ, and stained-glass windows. Underneath is a large assembly room with benches. This building is the central club-house of a community of a thousand or more Negroes. Various organizations meet here,—the church proper, the Sunday-school, two or three insurance societies, women's societies, secret societies, and mass meetings of various kinds. Entertainments, suppers, and lectures are held beside the five or six regular weekly religious services. Considerable sums of money are collected and expended here, employment is found for the idle, strangers are introduced, news is disseminated and charity distributed. At the same time this social, intellectual, and economic centre is a religious centre of great power. Depravity, Sin, Redemption, Heaven, Hell, and Damnation are preached twice a Sunday with much fervor, and revivals take place every year after the crops are laid by; and few indeed of the community have the hardihood to withstand conversion. Back of this more formal religion, the Church often stands as a real conserver of morals, a strengthener of family life, and the final authority on what is Good and Right.

Thus one can see in the Negro church to-day, reproduced in microcosm, all that great world from which the Negro is cut off by color-prejudice and social condition. . . .

Such churches are really governments of men, and consequently a little investigation reveals the curious fact that, in the South, at least, practically every American Negro is a church member. Some, to be sure, are not regularly enrolled, and a few do not habitually attend services; but, practically, a proscribed people must have a social centre, and that centre for this people is the Negro church. The census of 1890 showed nearly twenty-four thousand Negro churches in the country, with a total enrolled membership of over two and a half millions, or ten actual church members to every twenty-eight persons, and in some Southern States one in every two persons. Besides these there is the large number who, while not enrolled as members, attend and take part in many of the activities of the church. There is an organized Negro church for every sixty black families in the nation, and in some States for every forty families, owning, on an average, a thousand dollars' worth of property each, or nearly twenty-six million dollars in all.

Victor I. Masters on the Crisis in the Country Church, 1916

Outstripped by material progress. Material progress in the country has gone a hundred miles while the country church has not yet decided whether it would take a leisurely stroll down to the spring. The church has marked time, while population has doubled and farm practice has gone forward tenfold. And in this implicitly are all the problems of the country church. It has dealt in eternal verities, and the material forces have dealt in the things which serve this present life, but while it has whispered in the far-away accents of last month's sermon, they have shouted into the farmer's ear every hour of every day, and their cry is so loud and insistent that they not seldom make him forget there was a sermon over at the church last month. When our mothers and grandmothers used the hand-loom and spinning wheel, they accompanied the hum of the wheel by the quaint and soul-stirring melodies which they had heard at the church. Exit now the spinning wheel; enter the automobile, whose nervous hum at the gate speaks of friends to be visited, of city shops, of sylvan beauties afar by the roadside. No longer does the countryman fill in the vacant hours of a month digesting the one sermon he heard during the month in the single assembly of men which has met within his reach. But the pioneer church, with its practice little changed, goes on its traditional way, wondering what it all means. It means that modern life goes forward on springs and cushions over good roads by gasoline, while pioneer life went forward by ox-cart over cobble-stones and gullies. Can the church live in the dead past?

Slow to understand. The country church has been slow to grasp the meaning of these changes. With admirable tenacity it has clung to its faith that only the gospel of Christ can save men in any day. In this our churches have done better than some at the North, which, in their confusion, have seemed ready to substitute a social service program, of which experts told them, for a religion which never forgets to go back to the task of bringing men into right relations with God. Our churches begin to realize that something is wrong, but few of them have come to definite diagnosis, and far fewer to adequate treatment. The religious needs of humanity are fundamental and undying, and the souls of country people who drive automobiles and raise 200 bushels of corn to the acre will respond to the challenge of the spiritual to-day as surely as they did when they rode in ox-carts and raised fifteen bushels to the acre. But the challenge will have to be so strong and sustained that so intensely occupied a man will come to know what the preacher and church are driving at. "The old time religion" song was not written by the pioneers we picture when we sing it, but by a later dreamer, whose vision was of a languid past, in which with hands folded in untroubled contemplation those red-blooded forerunners were supposed to comfort themselves by such inert sentimentalities. But the pioneer was another kind of person. Of all things, anaemic sentimentality found in him the least chance of an abiding place. For his life was given to the business of wilderness-conquering, and he was much of a man. His descendants have no wilderness to conquer. Among some of his more unfit descendants, we must look for the anaemic poets who confirm our later day in a fatal static indolence, seeking to glorify this laziness by crowning it with a halo from the past. The country church of to-day is in need of a red-blooded moral equivalent for the rugged manliness and efficiency of those wilderness-conquerors. Either let us go back to chopping down forests, fighting Indians, and plowing an ox across new-ground roots, or else, in very shame, forsake our indolent assumption of the sacredness of the once-a-month preaching in a log house. It was the best the pioneer could do. Would not such a man be ashamed of descendants who made his limitations an excuse for their confirmed indolence! . . .

The interest of the church. The country church should be a positive force in seeking to turn the tide against increasing farm tenancy, and the country preacher should do his best to go to the bottom of the subject, in order that he may instruct the people and help to stay the perverse tide. It would be helpful if our country preachers could take a course in rural sociology and economics at an agricultural college which is awake to its business, or else in an aroused theological seminary. The country preachers are the leading force which drove out the whiskey traffic from the South. Equally informed and stirred, they could in another channel do a work in its own way equally vital to the South's welfare, by helping to save it from an era of farm tenancy and the consequent profound depression of all social, religious, and political life. The tenant system depresses the standard of the home, for families which "move on" at the end of one or a few years, do not develop strong local attachments. The land exploitation of owners who buy to sell at a bargain, is also ruthlessly violating the sacred associations of the old Southern country home. A generation ago, a typical rural Southern home was rich in the traditions of generations, a place where common joys and sorrows were shared by a little group, who looked into the flickering flame of the fire on the domestic hearth and learned the love of home, and then into the changing face of nature out-of-doors and sought not in vain to learn something there of the goodness and mercy of nature's God. Now farmers sell out and move and buy elsewhere as a speculation, or buy and hold the land for a rise in price and then sell. The country church and its friends have every reason to seek to understand and remedy this exploitation of the land.

Better homes. Improved farm practice is making more headway in the South than improved home-making. One of the things that leads country youth from the farm home to the town or city is the belief that they will by the change have about them more attractions and conveniences, and this same thing influences the rural housewife. Farmers often spend hundreds and even thousands on machinery and land improvements, but do nothing to make the farm home a more comfortable and attractive place. With acres to build on, the farm houses are often narrow at the base, poorly proportioned, and two stories high, and placed near the roadside, instead of back from it. Before the Civil War the South had a stately, simple, and well proportioned architecture of its own, adapted to the climate. Once it recovered from the distressing poverty which followed the conflict, the towns imported an unadapted architecture from the North and the country was so busy trying to get ahead in the economic game by devotion to all-cotton that it took no time to study architecture. It would hold more of its splendid boys and girls, if it did.

Domestic conveniences. The most comfortably arranged room in the farm home should be the kitchen. The farm woman's scheme of life calls for the preparation of three meals a day in all seasons endlessly till death. Yet the husband often buys improved machines to make some particular farm operation easier for perhaps a month in the year, while he leaves his wife to potter with pans and stoves and pots and dishes in the same way through all the years. There is a tradition that farm women furnish an exceptionally large number of the inmates of insane asylums. If it is true, there is a reason in the endless monotony and routine which they too often endure. Dr. C. C. Brown, of South Carolina, on reading this chapter in manuscript, said: "I saw a woman, in a country home in Darlington County, drop into a seat, holding a little black pot in her hand, and exclaim: 'I have half a mind to break it with a hatchet. I've cooked rice in this one pot every day for twenty-eight years. It makes me tired and sick to look at it.' " In midwinter, years ago, in a remote corner of Horry County, South Carolina, Dr. Brown, Dr. Harvey Hatcher, and this writer hunted the deer. We were most hospitably entertained in the humble homes of the people. One night we were sitting with a family circle before the open fire. Dr. Hatcher, with that matchless charm and understanding which made him so universally beloved, discoursed for the family group about things out in the big world. The worn housewife, in a plain dress and with her hair pulled back and knotted behind her head, sat quietly in a chair and listened, her eyes glued on the venerable speaker. At last she sighed deeply and said:

"It is mighty good to hear you-all tell about all them things out yonder. I ain't never gone nowhere much. Once I did go with John [her husband] down to Conway, but it's been a mighty long time ago." Southern farm housewives complain that the Negro women are less and less to be depended on as cooks. Instead of allowing this to drive the family from the farm, the most approved labor-saving appliances should be installed in the kitchen. By such measures the slavery of the cook stove can be lightened into a much less grievous and soul-consuming burden. A builder informs me that running water can be put in a house for a minimum cost of $200. Other labor-saving and sanitary provisions would not be expensive. . . .

A comparison in wages. There is an influential though relatively small group of country churches which do not treat the pastor's salary with neglect, but cheerfully provide for his support. There are some such churches or groups of churches in most of the States in the South. They pay the pastor $1,000 or more and possibly furnish him with a parsonage. But, glad as the author is to note these exceptions and to look upon them as harbingers of a better day, he must yet seek faithfully to portray with something of its real force the chronic inertia which through generations the great mass of our rural churches have manifested toward the duty of honestly seeking to support the men who give their lives to preaching to them. Averages do not tell the whole story, but they may yet be profoundly significant. The average country Baptist preacher's salary in the South to-day is not so much as $500. Street car conductors and motormen in Atlanta get $700 to $900. Railway conductors and engineers are paid from $1600 to $2100; railway mail clerks get from $900 to $1500; brick masons and carpenters from $2.50 to $5.00 per day; many cotton mill operatives make $400 to $500 a year; responsible clerks in stores are paid from $500 to $3000; stenographers from $500 to $1200. None of these workers gets more than he earns. But a country church in a prosperous community usually feels that it is doing pretty well if it pays $150 for a minister to serve the spiritual interests of the people, and it is well above the average if it pays $200 for a once-a-month preaching service. Much may be said to explain why these churches are doing so poorly in the support of the gospel, but nothing can disguise the fact that it is a discreditable and even shameful situation.

The Reverend Amazi Clarence Dixon on the Evils of Evolution, 1922

Evolution with its "struggle for existence" and "survival of the fittest," which gives the strong and fit the scientific right to destroy the weak and unfit is responsible for the oppression and destruction of the weak and unfit by the strong and fit. It has fostered autocratic class distinctions and is no friend to those who stand for the protection of the weak against the oppression of the strong. The greatest war in history, which has drenched the world with blood and covered it with human bones, can be traced to this source. If the strong and fit have the scientific right to destroy the weak and unfit, that human progress may be promoted, then might is right, and Germany should not be criticized for acting upon this principle.

The "Superman"

Nietzsche, the neurotic German philosopher, hypnotized the German mind with his Pagan brute philosophy. "The weak and botched," said he, "shall perish; first principle of humanity. And they ought to be helped to perish. What is more harmful than any vice? Practical sympathy with the botched and weak Christianity." "If what I publish be true," he wrote to an invalid woman, "a feeble woman like you would have no right to exist."

"Christianity," he said, "is the greatest of all conceivable corruptions, the one immortal blemish of mankind." And he hated it because of its sympathy with the botched and weak. He glorified his ideal "blond beast" and gave to the world a "superman," one-third brute, one-third philosopher. Under the spell of his daring brutality, Germany adopted the motto, "Corsica has conquered Galilee." Nietzsche's philosophy of beastliness has its roots in the evolutionary assumption that the strong and fit, in the struggle for existence, have the scientific right to destroy the weak and unfit.

The Super-Nation

Under the spell of Nietzsche's "superman" there came into the heads of the German politicians and militarists the vision of a super nation, with the scientific right to destroy weaker nations and build its throne upon their ruins. . . .

I tremble for the future of the world if the millions of China are to be moulded and dominated by a philosophy which gives to the strong and fit the scientific right to destroy the unfit. It is easy for the patriotism of any nation to make its people believe that they are the fittest nation in the world; only, if China with the conviction should become conscious of her strength, she could become, under masterful military leadership, the menace of the future. Any nation that teaches this pernicious delusion to its youth is now a menace to the peace of the world; and if all nations teach it, war will be the normal method of settling all disputes. Universal peace can never come until nations turn from this voice of the jungle to the song of the angels floating from the skies above the plain of Bethlehem: "Peace on earth among men of good will."

If the home is to be preserved as a sacred institution, the Bible which teaches that marriage came down from God and not up from the beast must be believed. The jungle theory as to the origin of marriage is today keeping busy the divorce courts of the civilized world. If government came down from God, so that "the powers that be are ordained of God," law will rule in righteousness and courts will mete out justice, but if the basis of government came from the jungle where brute force prevails, the Bolshevist rule by bullet and bayonet is scientific and the scientific mind ought to accept it. This jungle origin of government is today a world-wide peril. If the Bible is a revelation from God through inspired men, its teaching is authoritative and its truths have in them an irresistible dynamic, but if the Bible is a mere record of human experience as men have struggled upward from their jungle origin, its teaching has no authority and its sayings are to be accepted or rejected by the inner consciousness of men, which is itself a product of the jungle.

If man came down from God, created in His image and has been wrecked by sin, then sin is an intrusion, an enemy that ought to be expelled; but, if man came up from the beast through the jungle, sin is "embryonic goodness," "righteousness in process of formation," even a search after good; of course such sin has no guilt and may be condoned, if not coddled. Such a delusion makes it easy to believe that sin has no existence and all things, even theft, falsehood and murder are good, because there is no evil in the world.

If the church came down from God in the sense that its members are "born from above," we have on this world a unique spiritual organism, of which Jesus Christ is the head, endued with an irresistible dynamic, "power from on high." But if the church came up from the beast through the jungle and is the expression of man's struggle out of beastliness into spirituality, we have simply one earth-born institution among many and cannot be optimistic regarding its destiny.

If Christ came down from heaven, as He says He did, "the only begotten Son of God" in the sense that He is the only one in the universe begotten of God in a virgin's womb, "God manifest in the flesh," "the Word made flesh and dwelling among men," we have in Him a unique personality; God, who is a Spirit, made concrete, thinkable, approachable and lovable; God, lowering Himself to our level, that He may lift us to His level. But if Christ is the expression of humanity's struggle up from the beast through the jungle, we have in Him simply a combination and culmination of jungle life in body, soul and spirit, detached from heaven, on the same plane with others, with little power to lift or transfigure.

The Beast-Jungle theory of evolution robs a man of his dignity, marriage of its sanctity, government of its authority, the church of her power and Christ of His glory.

Discipline of the Pentecostal Holiness Church, 1937

Basis of Union

1. We believe that Jesus Christ shed His blood for the remission of sins that are past; and for the regeneration of penitent sinners, and for salvation from sin and from sinning (Rom. 3:25; 1 Jno. 3:5–10; Eph. 2:1–10).

From *Discipline of the Pentecostal Holiness Church* (Franklin Springs, GA, 1937), pp. 11–14, 41–43, 73–74. Used with permission of the Pentecostal Holiness Church of Franklin Springs, GA.

2. We believe, teach and firmly maintain the Scriptural doctrine of justification by faith alone. (Rom. 5:1).

3. We believe also that Jesus Christ shed His blood for the complete cleansing of the justified believer from all indwelling sin and from its pollution, subsequent to regeneration. (1 John 1:7–9.)

4. We believe also that entire sanctification is an instantaneous, definite, second work of grace, obtainable by faith on the part of the fully justified believer. (John 15:2; Acts 26:18).

5. We believe also that the Pentecostal Baptism of the Holy Ghost and fire is obtainable by a definite act of appropriating faith on the part of the fully cleansed believer, and that the initial evidence of the reception of this experience is speaking with other tongues as the Spirit gives utterance. (Luke 11:13; Acts 1:5; 2:1–4; 8:17; 10:44–46; 19:6).

6. We believe also in divine healing as in the atonement. (Isa. 53:4, 5; Matt. 8:16, 17; Mark 16:14–18; Jas. 5:14–16: Ex. 15:26).

7. We believe in the imminent, personal, premillennial second coming of our Lord Jesus Christ, (1 Thess. 4:15–18; Titus 2:13; 2 Peter 3:1–4; Matt. 24:29–44), and we love and wait for His appearing. (2 Tim. 4:8).

8. The Pentecostal Holiness Church is utterly opposed to the teaching of the so-called Christian Scientists, Spiritualists, Unitarians, Universalists and Mormons. We deny as false and unscriptural, Seventh-day Adventism, annihilation of the wicked, conditional immortality, antinomianism, absolute perfection, so-called come-outism, the so-called resurrection life, the so-called redemption or glorification of the body in this life, the doctrine of the restitution of all things, as set forth in millennial-dawnism, and the teaching that we are not born of God until we are sanctified wholly.

9. The Lord says, "Marriage is honorable in all, and the bed undefiled," and the Pentecostal Holiness Church firmly holds that there are certain relations between husband and wife which are strictly private according to the Word of God, and into this sacred privacy no one has any right to inquire. (Heb. 13:4; 1 Cor. 7:1–5).

General Rules

1. All members of The Pentecostal Holiness Church shall take as their rule of conduct the Bible, known as the Old and New Testaments, including sixty-six books, and shall conform to its simple teachings inwardly as well as outwardly in their daily walk and conversation. (Gal. 6:16.)

2. All our members are forbidden to hold membership in or have fellowship with oath-bound secret societies, social clubs, and corrupt partisan politics; to attend places of worldly amusement, such as moving picture shows, baseball games, picnics, circuses, dancing halls, county and state fairs; and to follow after anything that is calculated to destroy their spirituality. (2 Cor. 6:14–17; Eph. 5:11; Rom. 12:2; 2 Tim. 3:5.)

3. The preceding paragraph is not intended to prohibit consistent association with a legal effort on the part of labor, to prevent oppression and injustice from capitalism. (Jas. 5:1–5.) Furthermore, picnics shall not apply

to any Sunday school or church outing for recreation, and to promote fellowship among the members.

4. The use of tobacco in any form is forbidden, also its growth; its· sale as a merchant, and its manufacture as a proprietor.

5. The Pentecostal Holiness Church is utterly opposed to the manufacture, sale, and use of all intoxicants, and any other drink or drug detrimental in its effects. (II Cor. 7:1.)

6. Filthiness of speech, foolish talking, jesting, and speaking evil of others are also forbidden. (Eph. 4:29–31; Col. 3:8, 17; 1 Thess. 5:22.)

7. All of our members are forbidden to follow immodest and extravagant styles in dressing, or to wear needless ornamentation. (I Tim. 2:9; I Pet. 3:3.)

8. All our members are required to observe the first day of the week as the holy Sabbath, according to the teachings of the Old and New Testaments, and to abstain from doing their own pleasure thereon. (Ex. 20:8–11; Isa. 58:13; Mark 2:27, 28.)

9. Also, to abstain from mentioning the faults of an absent person, and refuse to listen to those who do, except it be absolutely necessary for the glory of God, and the good of the cause and the person concerned. (Lev. 19:16; Ps. 15:3.)

10. All our members are required to be patterns of frugality, diligence, faith and charity, taking up the cross daily, and true to the abiding baptism of the Holy Ghost. . . .

Appendix

The absolute separation of church and state is a fundamental principle in the constitutional law and polity of the American nation, and unqualified loyalty to this principle is essential to its preservation and welfare in all departments of government, both state and national, and The Pentecostal Holiness Church affirms its adherence to said principle and polity without reservation.

In view of this all-important fact, we can but place upon any deviation therefrom our unqualified condemnation. This declaration leads us to note with pain the subtle encroachment into every branch of our government, municipal, state and national, of the Roman Catholic Church, seeking to fill and control the same for the purpose of placing its authority above other ecclesiastical bodies, restricting their liberties, restraining their privileges, in harmony with the false claim of the Roman pontiff to dictate all the affairs of all nations and governments of the whole world.

We deny such a claim, and pledge ourselves to wage unflinching warfare against the encroachment of the Roman Catholic Church ("For the weapons of our warfare are not carnal, but mighty through God to the pulling down of strongholds," 2 Cor. 10:4), or any other ecclesiastical body, seeking to control any or all branches of government in its own interest, which we deem contrary to the fundamental law of our national and state constitutions.

⚓ E S S A Y S

Samuel S. Hill, professor of religious studies at the University of Florida, has been a pioneer in southern religious historiography for the past two decades. He has been especially outspoken about the historical missed opportunities of southern religion to advance the cause of social justice in the South. In the first essay, he discusses how a religious faith that "accentuates love of God and neighbor" nevertheless supported an oppressive racial system. In the second selection, Charles Reagan Wilson of the Center for the Study of Southern Culture at the University of Mississippi accounts for one of the major sources of "Culture-Protestantism"—the Lost Cause. In the final selection, J. Wayne Flynt, professor of history at Auburn University, offers a more optimistic assessment of the southern church's reform tendencies, though he acknowledges that such efforts diminished after 1920.

The Southern Church as Conservator

SAMUEL S. HILL

How are race and religion correlated in southern experience? Two facts concerning the religion of Southerners stand out. In the first place, they take their religion seriously. They entertain scant doubt of the ultimate truthfulness of the Christian claim, a trait reflected in the high proportion of the population having formal affiliation with a church and by the absence of ideological alternatives. . . . Few societies in modern Christendom can compare with the American South for proportion of religious affiliation or intensity of religious conviction. The second unavoidable fact is the rootage of Christianity, the religion the people embrace so zealously, in the claim that love is the ultimate power and purpose of reality, and the norm for human behavior. No serious reading of Christian teaching can challenge the conclusion that in its preachments concerning both the divine government of the world and man's call to responsible living, the central, all-dominating motif is love defined as creative good will.

If then the people of the American South can be said to owe supreme loyalty to a religious faith which accentuates love of God and neighbor, how does it happen that racial discrimination can have been practiced for so long by so many? Putting the question more fruitfully, what brought about the peculiar relations which prevail between the *two* cultures, Southernness and religion, in which the love ethic of the latter is modified by the values of the former and largely accommodated to them? It is important, if also difficult, to describe this strange interrelation—this paradox—and to offer some explanation for it. But we must begin by disregarding any argument which maintains that white Southerners have been typically insensitive to the needs and feelings of people. Nor does it advance our understanding of the paradox to impugn them as egregiously immoral people, either inherently or by comparison with other societies. On the contrary, their reputation for hospitality and friendliness is often supported by the quality of life they embody. They do prize helpfulness, courtesy, and amicable relations. Of course the temptation to romanticize southern society must be resisted, inasmuch as mores of this kind are common to simple societies. Even so, one is impressed by the lengths to which sons of Dixie are frequently willing to go for the sake of cultivating warm personal relations, in the process manifesting admirable grace and charm.

Morally, they have often acted with courage and resolution in expressing concern for public problems, for example, the adverse effects of alcoholic beverage consumption, gambling, crime, encroachment on Sunday rest, and so on. . . . They are a people whose hearts can be touched, who can be appealed to for the alleviation of human distress, whether they perceive this rightly to take the form of Christianizing the heathen in foreign lands or relieving misery at home.

Yet these same God-fearing Christians have subscribed to white supremacy. It is true that many of the most conspicuous advocates of racism are classifiable as "red necks," people who are not governed by good will and a noble sense of responsibility for others. But this is by no means the whole picture. Without flamboyance, the educated, the magnanimous, the religious also practice white supremacy. . . . Whence and why the shocking contradiction that generous, benevolent, and amiable Christians are racists? . . .

. . . The region's religious leaders, according to their own convictions and in their own ways, have frequently involved themselves in issues which have been directly related to the internal life of the churches. That is, the creed of many has transcended the common notion of the "spirituality of the church"—that the church should confine itself to preaching and teaching the Gospel and cultivating religious growth in its members, steering clear of secular involvements and objectives. The most prominent investment of church crusading has been toward the control of liquor sales and use. Look upon this issue as one may, it is partially social in character, a component in public morality, and southern churches have endeavored to render a social service by directing its supervision. For readers familiar with the history of Christianity, it is instructive to draw a contrast with the classical Anabaptist communions which have kept their absolute convictions on various moral matters within their own ranks, abstaining from efforts to legislate morality by imposing their views on the wider society. The churches of the American South have not been asocial or apolitical, rather, selective in the public causes to which they have devoted their passions.

The importance—and subtlety—of the prevalence of a sense of social responsibility within the churches of the South is well illustrated in a collision which took place in Lubbock, Texas, in 1932, pitting the conservative Protestant clergy against the issue of academic freedom on the campus of Texas Technological College. What generated the clash was the activity of a few faculty members and YMCA staff, several having been trained in the tradition of theological liberalism at the University of Chicago, who were acquainting students with the ways of heterodoxy, socialist economic and political views, and modern academic skepticism. When two consecutive

ministers of the huge First Baptist Church, the fundamentalist superintendent of city schools, and other religious leaders learned of the religious
and social heresies being promoted under their noses, they mounted an
assault upon the Tech staff members, eventually securing their dismissal.
(They were able to do this in spite of the tenured status of one of them,
who happened also to be a departmental chairman.)

These events of the early years of the national depression on their face
do not suggest that the ministers in question were assuming any social
obligation. In fact we might initially conclude the opposite. But, on a closer
look, it appears that they, perhaps especially the two ministers of a two
thousand member congregation numbering many of the community's most
influential citizens, endeavored to act in what they judged the highest interests of their society. For these and many other religious conservatives,
the essence of social responsibility is the preservation of orthodoxy, primarily religious, but with social orthodoxy in a supporting role, as we see
in their own words: "All our troubles, hard times on the farm, our present
drought, all—are caused by sin"; "Christian people of this nation are going
to have to take a definite stand (against evolution) some of these days and
the sooner it comes the better"; the liberals at the college are seeking to
"subvert the moral code."

Without being able to rationalize their instincts, in all probability such
leaders saw clearly the need for a culture-ethic, that is, a framework of
meaning and order for fruitful life in the society. They looked with disfavor
upon pluralism. Moreover they were convinced that a people's greatness
stems from purity in private morality among individuals and from God's
systematic blessing of those who adhere to doctrinal orthodoxy. Rightly
then they crusaded to eradicate "poisonous propaganda" and loose morality, *for the good of the civilization,* not alone of the churches. Southern
religious leadership in Lubbock, Texas, in 1932, and generally throughout
the South during this century especially, has perceived more than it knew
in working to establish orthodox religion as the basis for a culture-ethic.
An item in the bulletin of a Lubbock church on November 8, 1929, speaks
volumes: "Evidently God has a special mission for the First Baptist Church.
She stands in a strategic place in a strategic section of the nation. This
section is being filled by emigration from the great Anglo-Saxon centers of
the South. . . . We have a pure-blooded, homogeneous population that can
be directed into a remarkable social order."

This Lubbock scenario provides us with a set of conditions exceptionally transparent to the intimate correlation between the South's two cultures, regionality as (simple) culture and religiosity as cultural system. What
the Lubbock fundamentalists set out to do, in the terms of this analysis,
was to legitimate, consolidate, and perpetuate the secular culture through
the instrumentality of conservative Protestant Christianity. Intoxicated by
the growth of west Texas, yearning for stability and approval, needing a
feeling of cosmic significance, and in quest of both comfort and scapegoat
during a stressful economic period, religious spokesmen ballyhooed the
status quo—practices of speech, dress, eating, organizing, doing business,

racial relations, ideological preference, education, and the like. All threats to conformity and to recognition of their mores' superiority were to be resisted. The most effective device for sealing and confirming, one eminently accessible and universally approved, was orthodox Christianity—of the fundamentalist sort. It was the cultural system needed to tighten and sanctify the culture. That is, religion provided a formulated, coherent framework of meaning for ordering the west Texas culture which, like all cultures, was largely an accident of historical circumstances, migration patterns, geography, climate, politics, social conditions, and so on. Fundamentalist Protestantism when imposed upon the culture thus had much to recommend it functionally. It performed two complementary roles by providing a culture-ethic for ordering life in the society, and casting legitimation in the mold of ultimate truth. Mentalities and sensibilities in Lubbock, and elsewhere analogously, have been locked in by the powerful double grip of secular effectuality and metaphysical confirmation.

In the context of southern society, often it has been especially difficult to discover viable arrangements for the maintenance of constructive social patterns. Life has had to go on, of course, but sometimes under taxing conditions, produced variously by racial strains, the challenge of developing stability in a frontier setting, and severe economic hardship. Historian Avery Craven marshals considerable evidence pointing to the "frontier" nature of antebellum southern society, from the Atlantic to the Mississippi. Thus Lubbock's case may not be so exceptional, despite its rather late date and its situation on the territorial "edge." We may then take rather seriously Merton Dillon's interpretation of the churches' functionality in that burgeoning frontier city.

> . . . the church served from the beginning as a means of social control. As one of the few institutions which impinged upon a large portion of the community, it lent itself well to such use. Life in a new country has always given some men an opportunity to shed conventions and restrictions; as they step from the threshold of ordered society, they are tempted to leave its trammels behind. . . .
>
> There is ample evidence to suggest that the leaders of Lubbock from the beginning looked upon churches not alone as a means for assisting souls otherwise lost to enter the kingdom of God or as a means for gathering together the saved remnant of humanity, but also for the secular purpose of molding the social order. The churches were not to be set apart from the world; they were to be placed directly in the midst of it. Ranchers and a few merchants, most of whom were also church leaders, dominated the town. They and the preachers joined in the enterprise of creating an orderly community safe for churches and secure for business enterprise.

Having seen something of the churches' involvement in responsibility for the culture's well-being, we return directly to the paradox, the practice of racial discrimination by a people who affirm love as the norm for human behavior. It is incumbent to recall that a variety of factors in southern life have helped stifle the influence of Christian teaching with respect to the immorality of slavery and segregation. First, the aftermath of the Civil War was a critical period in that the perceptions and aspirations of white people obligated them to defend their accustomed ways by hardening the lines of separation between the two races. The formation of Jim Crow laws was necessary for white southern society to achieve self-respect, a major point demanding fuller elaboration presently. A related though somewhat different matter is the observation of most whites, according to their own criteria, that the Negro is inferior. In empirical terms, especially by white standards, it is simply the case that the achievements of black people are sparse. To this day there are multitudes of whites who have never seen an accomplished member of the Negro race—except by means of television, a fact which itself is beginning to make a difference. In the southern social context, to see is to believe; perhaps examination of the causes of the black man's empirical inferiority would be far too painful to engage in, so that avoidance of subtleties has been a means of self-defense. Also, living as he has in a relatively homogeneous culture, the white Southerner has had little incentive to acknowledge the inherent strengths of a culture (the southern black) different from his own. It has been typical of folk-cultures to build figurative walls around their own, and to be uncomfortable over awareness of alternatives. Finally, the economic and political emergence of the blacks has produced negative responses among white Southerners. The new prominence and upward mobility of black people threatens the social status of numerous whites, particularly among the working classes. "Forget, hell" on the front license plates of revved-up older model cars expresses the genuine sentiments of many who suffer from status anxiety. Of very recent origin is a companion response to black emergence, namely taking offense at what is judged to be arrogance on the part of a people heady with the wine of new pride and self-consciousness.

The moral sense of white people, not surprisingly, is dimmed somewhat by this welter of circumstances. When cultural memory draws to mind, first, the slave status of Negroes, followed by Jim Crow arrangements for interracial living, this image being bloated by the convincing evidence of Negro inferiority, and these factors are joined with the unsettling facts of black competition and black arrogance, the white man's intended good will is easily made ambivalent or diverted. In other words, practical circumstances have militated against any transformation of racial attitudes. Since practical experience is regularly more determinative of one's behavior than his formal ideological (theological) commitments, we need not wonder that the southern value system, with its traditional convictions about the appropriate coexistence of the black and white races, has stifled much of the aspiration to holiness which rightly translates as love of God and neighbor.

Despite the powerful presence of these social forces, however, we might have expected church teaching to be sufficiently effectual to create tension between the Christian mandate and the accepted racial attitudes of the white South. For the most part, such has not been the case. Instead, the parallel secular and religious currents actually have issued in a reversal of what is from the Christian standpoint the ideal situation. That is, religion has further tightened the hold of racially discriminating convictions, at least that has been the net effect of the churches' influence. What seems to have happened is that religious assumptions deflected moral earnestness. This is ironic and poignant, the more so since few Christians ever have longed with greater passion to build the kingdom of God on earth or been as confident that they were engaged in that enterprise. Perhaps we may account for the disjuncture between intention and accomplishment, in terms common to this analysis, as the churches' failure to see that "Christian teaching" does not exist in a cultural vacuum, that it is always apprehended through the vehicles by which people perceive and communicate.

Theologically speaking, religious assumptions deflect moral earnestness because southern churchmen have been taught that the high God of heaven, who is life's ineluctable reference point, issues a single directive to each person: find forgiveness for your personal sins. This being the divinely imposed, overriding obligation of mankind, consideration of the unloving character of relations between persons, and especially between persons of distinct races, is bound to be depreciated—though not intentionally abrogated. In other words, when religion is defined as status, that is, how one stands before a morally requiring God, it follows that racial concerns will not have more than proximate significance. In recent years, an expanding company of southern ministers and lay leaders have been affirming the unity of black and white under God in church and society—sometimes at their personal peril. Despite their courageous proclamation and example, when the evangelical concern shapes perceptions, this message is viewed as "tacked on," perhaps very important, but neither the central concern nor an organic by-product of the religious life. This is to say, the main practical impact of the churches' message does not penetrate the racial situation of the South. Indeed, in recent years, no doubt as reaction to rapid social change, many ministers have declared that the primacy of evangelism is being eroded by undue attention to economic and racial matters. A number have asserted that what occurs in the marketplace or the county courthouse is only indirectly the business of the church, which is rightly understood as a "spiritual" organization.

This rather curious role of the church, as contributor to the preservation of unloving racial patterns, becomes stranger still when we recall that southern evangelicalism is presented in distinctly moral categories. The Christian life is depicted as a *doing* existence. Note the familiar verbs: one *makes* decision, *remembers* his identity, *practices* what he *preaches, bears* witness, *lets* his light *shine, wins* the world, *grows* in grace, *gets right* with God. These are hardly metaphors of passivity or complacency. The faithful are continually reminded that it is not enough to "call me Lord, Lord"; such vocation must issue in doing what the Lord says. They believe that the gift of salvation from sin is accompanied by the gift of moral empowerment. Moreover, the basic characterization of God is moral: He has standards, is altogether holy, cannot countenance evil, sends his son to pay the sin-debt, and requires total loyalty. Accordingly, man is defined as moral: one who by (Adam's) choice is alienated, can decide, must decide, and is capable of considerable spiritual attainment. Perhaps this breadth of moral awareness, dominating theology, man's nature, and man's calling, has played into the prevalence of Southerners' sense of moral ambiguity on the racial question. They have handled this awareness, partly by being kind to Negroes as individuals (often in a paternalistic framework), partly by expressing interest in the salvation of the Negro's soul, and also by the conviction that the reign of justice can be deferred until the divine day of judgment in the world to come.

To summarize this interpretation of the churches' complicity in the hierarchical pattern of racial relations: ultimate confidence of personal re-demption deflects the painful ethical question of white supremacy, thus relegating it to secondary importance. In order to do so, an unconventional conception of morality has had to guide the ethical understanding of south-ern religion. That is, morality is construed in ahistorical categories, for it is associated with *being,* rather than with doing. The rhetoric of doing, so common to southern church life, is actually self-contradictory, since doing, according to this view, consists of *interior* states, resolutions, and convic-tions. Rhetoric notwithstanding, the principal mode of southern religious sensibilities is not operationally the moral—and no one supposes that it is the aesthetic. In the classical philosophical division, it must then be the ontological. In other words, this form of religious knowledge is delineated by a vivid sense of inferiority: one *is* a forgiven sinner; one *hears* God's call; one *knows* he is going to heaven; one *talks* with God in prayer; one *deepens* his devotional life; one *reads* his Bible; one *becomes* the vehicle for the recurrence of all this in the interior lives of others. These are the distinguishing events in the Christian life, as the southern (evangelical) church teaching has it. In standard fashion, it is said that these events, having been drunk to the dregs, *will* bear fruit; we have here a "stages model"—first do this, then that follows. It may be questioned whether human behavior can be so ordered, in the first place. But even assuming that it can be, the habit of mind which generates this form of religious consciousness emanates from a fundamental conviction that the locus of religious reality is "heaven" or "between heaven and earth" or "the in-terior self." Because history must be defined as "outer" as well as "inner," having to do with public events and relationships, the interpretation is seen to be ahistorical. For, in the final analysis, it views the primal *modus operandi* as being, one *is* a forgiven sinner—and not as doing one *should love* his neighbor as God loves him. . . .

. . . Tersely stated, religion is dominantly a conservative or reinforcing agent for the traditional values held by white southern society. Pattern-maintenance has been the primary result, if not the declared intention. Granted, some prophetic activity has taken place. Nevertheless, the overall impact of the church leadership has been priestly in that secular traditions and values have been "baptized" and accorded legitimacy. Usually this happens in line with natural law interpretations. For, articulately or not, white culture has decreed such beliefs as that the Negro's inferior status is in the nature of things, that agrarian or quasi-agrarian society is the most moral type of arrangement for human living, and that the southern churches are the purest in Christendom. In a word, many southern whites have regarded their society as God's most favored. To a greater degree than any other, theirs approximates the ideals the Almighty has in mind for mankind everywhere. Clearly, an attitude of this kind contains few incentives for self-criticism or efforts to redirect southern ways.

In exploring the history of the churches' role as reinforcer of secular traditions, one is struck by the increase in religious expressiveness, of both personal and institutional sorts, which occurred during the period following the Civil War. . . .

Historian C. Vann Woodward describes this phenomenon for the New South era: "Instead of withering away before the advance of industry, science, and urbanization, the Southern legions of Christian soldiers multiplied in numbers and, to judge from appearances, waxed in zeal." In 1890, white church membership figures stood at 6,130,023 while sixteen years later the total was 9,260,899. This amounts to a growth rate of fifty-one percent during a span when population increased by thirty-nine percent. Causation is hard to assess, of course, and any attempt must consider a variety of factors, such as greater population concentration in towns and cities and heightened institutional awareness which accompanied the new complexification of life, as the agrarian mind-set yielded to the urban. Even so, the burgeoning religious statistics are impressive, and call for inquiry into social determinants.

In the nineteenth-century South, there was plenty of "socio-psychological strain." During the period before the Civil War the dominant white society was caught in an intricate web of ambiguity. After all, slavery was a profound moral contradiction to a people who (like all Americans) had participated in the spirit of liberal democracy. During the last quarter of the eighteenth century, their own kinsmen had been nearly peerless as the architects of national documents which spiritually forbade regarding human beings as property. Moreover, the moral teachings of their Christianity stirred restiveness on the matter of slavery, as did personal friendship with Negroes whom they could relate to appropriately only as beings in their own species.

The role of the clergy in southern society between the Revolution and Reconstruction illuminates the tension existing between the political-religious traditions on the one hand, and the fundamental processes of life in the society on the other. Within the early postrevolutionary generation, the Protestant clergy endeavored to build social cohesion by transforming a scattered, isolated people into community-conscious citizens. With respect to black citizens, they hoped to avoid effective differentiation by including both races in a single social arrangement. For complicated reasons they failed in this ambition, and compromised by working to save the souls of individual Negroes.

For the clergy who flourished in the 1830s and 1840s the primary accomplishment was the formation of denominational solidarity, even regional separateness, by the three largest groups. In helping construct southern Methodist, southern Baptist, and southern Presbyterian organizations, they

were leading the masses toward a sense of identification with an intermediate collectivity, a group larger in size than the local congregation or
community, but smaller than the total society. The effect of this was the
development of a social image by which white Southerners saw themselves
in corporate terms; here we witness a major, if unwitting, contribution of
religion to secular society, specifically, to the crystallization of the Solid
South image and the powerful self-consciousness of the Southern Baptist
Convention. Of great significance is the fact that during these two decades
clergymen moved into a central role in the society, as educators, guardians
of the collective life, and models of the good life for the privileged. Perhaps
more than any other vocational group they were effective in promoting
social integration.

Over the last fifteen years before the Civil War, southern ministers
developed a proslavery argument. As the one strategic elite for the entire
society, they attempted to integrate it on the basis of a moral philosophy
of public responsibility. This is not to suggest that they were "clean" in
their support of slavery, however. Rather, it had now fallen their lot to
hold the (white) society together, to sanctify its ways, and to generate *elan*
for its causes, so that approval of slavery would be automatic and casual.
They perceived that its demise would spell the doom of southern ways.

There was continuity between the place of the church before the war
and its role after 1865. Yet because conditions had been altered so dramatically, the exact function was different. Following Reconstruction, the
institutional life of the churches really flowered in that, as we have noted,
they grew in numbers, size, and fervor. The new factor appears to have
been the sense that one had a societal obligation to belong to the church.
Whereas in antebellum days, the clergy were the foundation of social coherence, now the whole population must perform that function. Mass solidarity was required for the legitimation of an entire society. Accordingly
in the postwar era, the elite was broadened to include every (white) person.

Religion's coming to the fore as a conspicuous and indispensable quality
in southern life served a number of social and psychological functions for
a defeated, disorganized, and poverty-stricken people. In terms of "strain
theory," it helped them cope with the anguish of social-psychological dis-
equilibrium and afforded them a measure of conquest over anxiety. And
we must highlight the salient fact that it was a particular form of Christianity,
Evangelical Protestantism, which flourished. The denominations embodying
this outlook had become parochially southern owing to schism from their
respective national bodies before the war, as we have seen. Following
Reconstruction these communions, especially the Methodist and Baptist,
presented themselves attractively to the populace. This was due in part to
their being organizations whose leaders and membership were confined to
the southern region. But more than this, their approaches to theology,
ethics, and churchmanship struck a responsive chord within southern
sensibilities.

Southern whites had lived with feelings of guilt for a long time. Many
slaveholders viewed their economic-social system with ambivalence. In this

context, Evangelical preachments struck home by virtue of the emphasis on man's propensity for breaking the law of God. But once his deep moral disquietude (with some traces of masochism) had been sated by vivid re-iteration, the churchgoer experienced relief. He was told that forgiveness is a *state* which one enters upon conversion. This recognition enabled him to ignore his society's complicity in discriminating between races because he could relegate moral questions to the periphery. According to the message he heard, the Christian is merely a sojourner in this world; evils have to be endured, and the evangelical gospel makes them endurable. Ironically, many southern whites got relief from the guilt of perpetuating an immoral social-economic system by subscribing to the tenets of a guilt-oriented theology. Such hymns as "The Old Rugged Cross," "Nothing but the Blood," and "Blessed Assurance" possessed deeper meaning than most perceived.

In connection with "interest theory," evangelical Christianity communicated to southern whites some sense of power. Since the end of Reconstruction, acquisition of power has been a particular temptation to a people beset by inferiority feelings and stung by criticisms from outside—a factor which may partially explain the southern infatuation with championship football teams and beauty contests, and Southerners' brashness in making claims for the superiority of regional social amenities. In tapping this aspect of southern consciousness we are probing the powerful appeal of a religious interpretation which exalts eternal spiritual victory. Whether or not this comes through a memorable single experience, it carries un-assailable interior knowledge. Existential conquest, indeed even the capacity for controlling the circumstances of one's life, has escaped many citizens because of the region's poverty and isolation. But religious victory, in this simplistic form, has been within reach and becomes for many a *fait accompli*. Only Evangelical Protestantism from among all the families of Christianity provides so grandiose a promise of assurance.

In addition, religion has delivered the consolation of *ultimate* advantage, at both personal and denominational levels. Many a sermon has magnified texts like, "If God be for us who can be against us?" the sentiment being that though worldly conditions may be oppressive, the heavenly home awaits. Small wonder that much popular hymnology has pointed to dependent trust, faithful waiting, and the promise of sweetness in the by-and-by. One is inclined to associate the popular Baptist stress on the "eternal security of the believer" with this psycho-social need, and similarly the Methodist confidence, reached by a different means but achieving the same goal, that reclamation by grace may occur repeatedly. As far as denominational issues are concerned, we can only be impressed by the self-consciousness and immodesty of the southern bodies. From Reconstruction forward, ecclesiastics compared the religious situation of the South with that prevailing elsewhere—itself a revealing disposition and always to the South's advantage. From many quarters came assessments of the superior purity of regional Methodism, Presbyterianism, or Baptist life, with the implication or even the assertion that their brand was the hope of the world.

Important as these factors are in pointing to the solid appeal of Evangelical Protestantism to southern whites, in my judgment they stop short of the most telling component in the linkage between church and culture. For, beyond enabling them to cope with strain, stake out their superiority, and assuage their guilt, both as souls before God and as crisis-ridden society, religion legitimated the (white) Southern Way of Life. What was most fundamental to the experience of the people was Southernness, not religious faith, truth, or integrity as such. Everything, the unfinished business of the society, the primary issue in their shared memory, the matters of most vital concern, focused upon the legitimation of a way of life. Public and private health were dependent upon absolution from guilt over the most serious departure in history from the nation's moral tradition, and the restoration of its sense of self-esteem. This deep-going need was met in numerous ways, including the ebulliency of "New South" plans for turning the region's God-given superiority into a magnificent civilizational accomplishment. But given the South's history and actual resources, the route *par excellence* was bound to be spiritual, combining moral, affective, and metaphysical aspects. The popular version of Christianity supplied the palliative. . . .

Tying this in with a previous discussion, we are now ready to assert that the South, or Southernness, because of the intensity with which people practice it owing to defensiveness, guilt, defeat, and isolation, is itself a kind of cultural system. To say this is to go beyond describing it as merely a culture. The concept of system adds the qualities of rationality, coherence, consciousness, and order to culture which is relatively accidental and one-dimensional. . . . Stated simply, southern mores are accorded a certain divine quality. They are not only the way things are, they are the way things should be. Perhaps only by this exponential activity could white Southerners have tolerated themselves in the midst of a time-space which valued, in addition, democratic ideals and industrial progress.

Consider some of the elements comprising the (white) Southern Way of Life: the Confederate flag; "Dixie"; distinctive speech accents; regional foods and culinary styles; the sense of regional apartness and superiority; specifiable convictions about the appropriate relations between the races; the same about the role of women; the notion that trade unions are both unnecessary and conspiratorial; belief that all social disputes can be resolved through personal diplomacy; *Gemeinschaft* assumptions about human collectivities, including cities; a preference for personality extroversion; the tendency to identify "American" as Anglo-Saxon; pride in agrarian or small-town manners; etc.

I am suggesting that to a peculiarly intense degree Southernness as a cultural system provides the framework for living, complete with metaphysical claims (unformulated) and moral constraints. Whereas the resident of Kansas or Wisconsin, for example, also lives in a culture with eminently visible patterns, typically he has not felt the need to construct a defense of it and invest it with some kind of ultimate sanction—to create a Midwest mythology. The relatively greater ease with which one moves from Midwest to another culture than has been true of the mobile Southerner is some indication of the point being made. At least until recently it was no more possible to forget that one is a Southerner than for the Jew to have a comparable lapse of memory. It is this regional-historical cultural system by which southern people have identified themselves, which they have defended, which they have carried as baggage wherever they go, which many have sought to spread as an evangel. For millions, most having few opportunities to compare or proselytize, Southernness has been the ultimate social good news. In a descriptive sense, society is God.

What is at issue here is another form of the paradox which wends its way through this entire essay. Here the form is not, how can Christian identity and racism coexist, but rather its cultic projection, how can one belong to two moral communities, church and South? Potential conflict is aroused by the fact that the Christian Church demands a total loyalty, while the South as a cultural system presents itself as a nurturing and teaching agency lacking in self-critical powers. In very different ways both Christianity and Southernness lay exclusive claim upon the white people of the region.

Does it follow that southern men and women practice duplicity or betrayal? What of the millions of them who intend to profess faith in religion's deity, the God of Abraham, Isaac, and Jacob, and of Jesus Christ, in the setting of Christian theism? To the query, are they merely deceiving themselves, I think we must reply "no," in a great many cases. Rather, they are participants in *two* primary frameworks of meaning, two cultural systems. Their lives are governed by two culture-ethics, God who is society and God who is the subject of existential experience within the Christian community. *Both* provide context, identity, community, and moral constraint. . . .

. . . Down South, there has been a *societal obligation* to belong. That is, pursuing the logic of this essay's central contention, regional citizens who abstain from lining themselves up with the church fail to ratify the churches' ultimate legitimation of the southern heritage and culture system, leaving room for the judgment that the South may in fact bear massive corporate guilt or to be inferior in its attainments. The pressure upon every last citizen to affiliate is heavy, often compulsive, so much so that there would appear to be other incentives than the evangelical. Cultural forces give the unchurched person the impression that he is somehow a threat to the entire society, a traitor to the cause, an inauthentic member of the regional community. Accordingly, the white Southerner must belong to the church for the sake of establishing the solidarity and legitimacy of his culture. It follows that the churches are shielded from being prophetic, for any affirmation or testimony which serves to impede or make difficult the act of affiliating would amount to a disruption of the Southern Way of Life.

Bringing these observations about the South's two cultures, regionality and religiosity, into the present, we may observe what effect the decline in regional self-consciousness, particularly among the young and more cosmopolitan, is likely to have upon the place of the church in southern society.

As Southernness becomes less important, uncritical subscription and loyalty to church religion is apt to follow a parallel course. This constitutes the crisis of the southern churches in the early 1970s. What is not clear at this juncture is whether the churches can tie their attractiveness to other features of life than the reinforcement and legitimation of the traditional (white) Southern Way of Life, and thereby preserve for their ministry a constructive role in the society.

Theology of the Lost Cause

CHARLES REAGAN WILSON

In times of adversity Christians frequently stress that suffering is a means to greater faith, and the postbellum era was no exception. Some preachers called for Southerners to draw closer together in adversity. In a typical sermon near the war's end, H. C. Hornady, a Baptist pastor, exhorted that the common suffering of Southerners should bind them together in "that best solace of the afflicted—true and steady friendship." Southern clerics told their congregations that they had experienced the great problems of existence, not in philosophy, poetry, or history, but in life itself, and that their common experiences should unite them. Stephen Elliott noted in the 1866 survey of his Georgia diocese that his people were "suffering and depressed, but united in spirit." He claimed that most Georgians believed their suffering to be "unnecessary and cruel," but in his opinion it was a condition "very favorable for religious impression of a deep nature." Suffering could lead to "unbelief and indifference"; in contrast, the clergy should use the situation to lead their followers "to the foot of the Cross, that emblem of humiliation and suffering." Elliott's eventual successor as bishop of Georgia, John Beckwith, preached a series of sermons in the immediate postwar years which attempted to explore the role of suffering as a catalyst for faith. In his view, one virtue of suffering was that it led to patience: "Without suffering there would be no room for patience, and without patience man would lose possession of his soul." Moreover, periods of prosperity and happiness were historically times of "spiritual lukewarmness and indifference," while eras of "affliction, suffering, trial and humiliation have always exhibited the church in her greatest purity, and earnestness and activity." Making yet another Southern analogy to Christ, he remarked that before Jesus "wore His crown of glory, He was pierced with one of thorns." If God wanted to ensure "our eternal ruin," Beckwith said, He would crown man's efforts "with perpetual prosperity, giving us unmarred health and insuring us against suffering: Nothing more effectively causes us to forget God than prosperity." He concluded that "it is part of our destiny to suffer," but that from suffering would emerge a stronger Christian.

Reprinted from *Baptized in Blood: The Religion of the Lost Cause, 1865–1920* by Charles Reagan Wilson. Copyright 1980 by the University of Georgia Press.

The war's results prompted sermons and periodical articles on the book of Job, urging Southerners to accept their burdens without murmurings. While the Baptist minister Henry C. Renfro of Texas allowed that Southerners had endured "havoc and desolation," he castigated them for their failure "to meet their calamities in the spirit and language of Job." The most popular quote from Job was "Though He slay me, yet will I trust him." Baptist minister S. G. Hillyer of Georgia decided that, in addition to Job, other biblical stories provided models for the development of Southern piety in the face of adversity. "It was," he stated, "when Isaac lay upon the altar of sacrifice that Abraham's faith was made perfect by works; it was when the Hebrew children walked in the midst of the fiery furnace that the glory of the Lord was revealed before the eyes of His enemies." Hillyer concluded that under similar circumstances "our Southern churches may make all men know that our religion is to us a sublime reality." Adversity, then, should provide an opportunity for Southern Christians to testify to their religion's truth.

These reactions to defeat rested ultimately on the belief in God's omnipotence and control of history. In this Southern context the clergymen elaborated on the traditional Christian interpretation of history—that God was working from a plan, a design, which man was unable to understand. "God is working out larger ends than those which concern us as a people," said Stephen Elliott. "His ends embrace the universe: His purposes are co-extensive with Time." Elliott advised his parishioners that the foundation of the Christian faith was "a scheme, which, beginning in the cradle of the world, is to go on, until the kingdoms of this world shall become the kingdoms of Christ." Each event in the history of a nation was a link in the chain of events that would eventually bring the Christian's hopes to fulfillment. Given this scheme of things, the duty of the Southern Christian was to be patient and submissive in the postwar world and to take care, in Elliott's words, "that we do not perish in the wilderness." In an 1866 sermon Elliott's successor, John Beckwith, agreed, stating that "the evidence of a *plan* is stamped upon the history of the world: a plan of mercy in wh.[ich] God works for our good and turns even the *wrath* of man to His own glory and the salvation of souls." The meaning of God's plan was beyond human comprehension; furthermore, it was not important that man know that meaning. This, of course, was a traditional Calvinist explanation, a call for faith in the benevolence of Providence. To expect God to be accountable to man would be to deny His omnipotence. "As the ruler of the universe, and the supreme arbiter of events, He disposes of all things in accordance with His own secret purposes," said John L. Girardeau. "For wise purposes," He sometimes allowed his saints, including His Southern ones, to undergo "apparent defeat" and to experience "a tempest of opprobrium, oppression and scorn."

Girardeau's use of the phrase "apparent defeat" suggested that Southerners clung to the hope of future vindication. Though they accepted the Confederacy's defeat as final, they repeatedly speculated that God might allow Confederate principles to succeed in another guise, in another time.

In June, 1865, William Nelson Pendleton surmised that God had sent defeat because Southerners had become idolatrous of their region; now they had to be a people without a country for a while. Yet he anticipated that God's order in the future would "enable us to achieve the independence which is our birthrite and of which we have now been despoiled by a mighty combination. . . ." Girardeau predicted the same future in 1866, that Confederate ideals would "in another day, in some golden age, sung by poets, sages and prophets, come forth in the resurrection of buried principles and live to bless mankind, when the bones of its confessors and martyrs shall have mouldered into dust." In short, as good Christians, they left their case with God. As a poet put it in 1871:

> From each lost cause of earth
> Something precious springs to birth,
> Tho' lost it be to men,
> It lives with God again.

The Methodist minister J. L. Gilbert, writing in 1869, believed that he knew the specific form this future success would take. He concluded that Confederate defeat was not an "unmitigated calamity," but "a necessary disciplinary ordeal, chosen by God, in his wisdom, by which he designed to prepare the Christian Churches of these States for their high and holy mission, as the custodians of an unadulterated evangelism, and as his honored instruments for the development of a pure Christian civilization throughout this continent and throughout Christendom." He confidently assumed that the evangelism of the Southern churches would eventually vanquish the menace of the politically oriented religion in the Northern churches. Soon all Americans would seek "a pure and unadulterated gospel from the lips of the ministry of the Churches of our Southern States."

However specifically envisioned, the general idea of future vindication became even more ingrained as time passed, so that Southerners remained unwilling to call it a lost cause. "Can a cause be lost which has passed through such a baptism as ours?" asked Benjamin Morgan Palmer. "Principles never die, and if they seem to perish it is only to experience a resurrection in the future." In 1889 Moses Drury Hoge told Southerners not to worry about the Confederate cause, because other Southerners would eventually put on the knightly armor "and in God's good time vindicate the principles which must ultimately triumph." In a 1901 oration Methodist Bishop Warren A. Candler even suggested that the goals of the Confederates had been achieved, although he (like others who made this argument) saw the achievement as one of political goals, making the tenuous claim that local self-government was more respected in 1901 than before the Civil War.

Speaking in 1897 before a church service preceding the yearly Confederate Veterans' reunion, James I. Vance, the pastor of Nashville's First Presbyterian Church, told the audience that ideals can survive defeat in war. A democratic majority could alter the externals of life, but "truth is truth, whether it have a conquering army at its back or wear the chains of imprisonment, like Paul in his cell at Rome." Vance explicitly made the connection between the Southern Lost Cause and Christianity: "His enemies could nail Christ to the cross, but they could not quench the ideals he embodied. His seemed to be a lost cause as the darkness fell on the great tragedy at Calvary, but out of what seemed Golgotha's irretrievable defeat has come the cause whose mission it is to save that which is lost." The implication was that Confederate principles might yet be the basis for a similar magnificent destiny. Vance stated that life itself is a lost cause, in a sense, because it is only preparation for certain death. As a result, human affairs had to be placed in a long perspective. "The incidents of life have more about them than the present," he said. "All the ages gather around them. Destiny is to speak a word over the lost causes of earth. Then it will appear that what we retain is not what we have acquired, but what we have become." The Confederate devotion to principle was a legacy that could inspire generations of Southerners to nobility. His analysis of how Confederate values could be vindicated in the character of Southerners was more subtle than Candler's political view. Vance's philosophical treatment of the Lost Cause was based on a more perceptive understanding of the nature of its impact.

The idea that Confederate defeat was a form of discipline from God, preparing Southerners for the future, was fundamental to the belief in ultimate vindication. The report of an 1865 Southern Presbyterian church committee said as much, proposing that God had sent disasters to the South in order to develop "that spirit of liberality which distinguished the primitive churches, in like poverty, and which may be the means of uniting us as one common brotherhood for any trials or triumphs He may have in reserve for us." The same committee a year later went so far as to conclude that God's chastisement, if it yielded the desired "fruits of humility, submission, love, and forbearance," would do more than any amount of money "to promote the interests of his kingdom among men." Similarly, John Girardeau denied that all afflictions were penal, since some "constitute a salutary discipline which is intended to benefit and not to destroy." They were not so much harsh retributions from a judge as loving corrections from a father. Suffering was a crucial element of "the moral economy of the world," said William Nelson Pendleton, because without it "virtue could not be what it is." He was sure that "virtue the most approved" might be sorely tried, but that ultimately it would triumph.

The metaphor used most frequently in this connection was that of the purification of metals. In March, 1866, W. B. W. Howe told his church members that their postwar sorrows should "purge us as gold and silver, that we may offer unto the Lord an offering in righteousness." James I. Vance predicted that "the period of struggle was the period of discipline. It was providence placing the idle ore in flame and forge." As a result, the South in his generation was "awakening to an inheritance that eclipses all her past." Southerners were now of great worth, as precious metals are when purified.

After the turn of the twentieth century, the writings of Southern clergymen expressed faith that God's plan included an important role for the South. Randolph McKim, for example, while granting that "It was not the will of God that we should succeed," nevertheless insisted that "the Southern people were necessary then, they are necessary now, for the accomplishment of the designs of Providence." McKim guessed that "the Lord could not trust the North to fulfill His great purposes on this continent without the aid of the Southern people." According to the pastor, the common sense, conservatism, and Anglo-Saxon tradition of the South were the traits that God wanted the South to preserve in the American nation. R. A. Goodwin, in a 1909 memorial sermon, outlined an almost identical manifest destiny for the South. "God is in our history as truly as He was in the history of Israel," he commented, later adding that the defeat of the Confederacy "was a part of the wilderness through which we were led" by God. Refusing to admit that Confederate defeat was anything but evil, he reminded his audience of biblical examples of God bringing good out of evil. The good was apparent to Goodwin in 1909: the Southern destiny was to be a necessary part of the American nation. He continued:

> Without the welding together of our people by the fiery trials of war, of reconstruction, of threatened servile domination, we could not have been the conserving power we have been. If this government is still to stand for liberty and freedom, it will be the South which will preserve it, and in the good providence of our God, bringing good out of evil, our sufferings will help to bring a blessing to all people.

The South's real cause was not lost, since a fight for "right and truth and honor" is never lost. "The spirit of the men of '61 goes marching on!" he said. And His truth goes marching on.

Confederate defeat ultimately brought a renewal of faith for Southern Christians. The harsh lesson of evil triumphing—by God's command—strengthened an already present strain of fatalism. But Southerners learned a more important religious lesson from their defeat in a holy war: God's chosen people did not give up that chosen status when defeated. Like the Reverend George B. Eager, they eventually decided that "behind a frowning providence Thou did'st hide a smiling face." Southerners thus retained their pride. They believed that God would bring good out of triumphant evil: the new good would be a purer, more holy chosen people prepared to face a special destiny. The stress was on the future, the need for communal solidarity, and the conviction that God would demand great achievements from Southerners, especially Southern Christians. The relation between Southern defeat and the development of a Southern religious mind prepared to combat evil could be seen in the words of Bishop Stephen Elliott in 1866: "Arouse yourselves, children of God; and while you humble yourselves under the mighty hand of God, forget not that you are Christ's servants, bound to do His work in the church militant upon earth, and to advance His kingdom wherever He may spread the banner of the Cross. Instead of permitting suffering to overcome your faith, let it rather lead you on to perfection." In the postbellum years Southern religious leaders believed that the South was almost Zion; nevertheless, they also understood that if they risked being "at ease in Zion," the punishment would be another divine chastisement, such as had occurred when their Confederate crusade against evil failed. They would have to demand even higher standards of themselves and their society. As a result of facing defeat in a holy war, therefore, Southerners emerged with a paradoxical blend of fatalism and a heightened sensitivity to the need to combat evil.

The Southern Church as Reformer

J. WAYNE FLYNT

W. R. Meroney spent 1919 writing his doctoral dissertation at Southern Baptist Theological Seminary in Louisville, Kentucky. Facts gathered, analysis complete, he took up his pen and began to write. His work was entitled "The Old Church in the New Era," and as he warmed to his subject, the paragraphs flowed. The church that he loved must come to terms with the new age: She "must wage common war with socialism against the festering evils of human society. She must preach the gospel to the poor in a far richer way than she has ever yet done. She must proclaim liberty to those who are bound and make as her supreme social task the elevation of human society."

Of course, every religious group produces its nonconformists, and the Reverend Dr. Meroney was by no means typical of Southern Baptist ministers. But those who judge the character of the past by the conservative uniformity of the present ignore the many W. R. Meroneys who flourished in the South between 1890 and 1920. Although they were atypical, they challenged southern Christianity at numerous points, sometimes with frenzied prophecies like those of Jeremiah, sometimes with quiet reasonableness like that of Luke.

To look at the South without discussing religion is like examining modern American culture without reference to sex: it is possible, but one certainly misses the drift of things. All scholars of the South interested in the dynamic interaction of religion and society owe a debt to Samuel S. Hill, Jr. Although others had made the point earlier, no other work so changed the direction of scholarship on southern religion as did his *Southern Churches in Crisis*. Hill insisted that historians, in their efforts to understand the shaping of the South, had taken religion too lightly. Along with white supremacy, the biblical heritage was central to southern continuity. Hill postulated that the frontier, a rural mode of life, and cultural insulation have been as influential on southern religion as the Puritan covenant, immigrant subcultures, and other factors have been on religion elsewhere in the nation.

Reprinted by permission of Louisiana State University Press from *Varieties of Southern Religious Experience*, edited by Samuel S. Hill, pp. 135–154. Copyright © 1988 by Louisiana State University Press.

Hill's chief premise—that there has been a symbiotic relationship between biblical Christianity and secular southern culture—is now conventional wisdom. When George Tindall described the reformist Southern Sociological Congress, he noted, "One finds in the annals of this and later social reform movements a fundamental conditioning influence of the churches which gave to middle-class liberalism in the South a unique moral-religious tone." Charles R. Wilson has examined the rise of a civil religion in the South between 1865 and 1920 that developed quite separately from the mainstream American version. The variety based in Dixie was less optimistic, less liberal, less democratic, less tolerant, and more homogeneously Protestant. Applying southern liberalism exclusively to the complex question of race, Morton Sosna observed that most twentieth-century southern racial reformers were either newspaper editors, academics, "or people with a religious motivation who took ideas about Christian brotherhood seriously." Furthermore, as race increasingly became the quintessential issue of southern liberalism, those who viewed it in terms of the ethics of Christian brotherhood were more likely than journalists or academics to transcend the old separate-but-equal stance to embrace one of true racial brotherhood. Finally, the late John Lee Eighmy insisted that southern campaigns for social justice in the first decades of this century, though conducted generally under the "secular banner of Progressivism," sprang from the "South's religious resources."

In years past, when historians generally agreed on the nature of progressivism, the task of relating religion to southern progressivism would have been simple enough. I could construct my syllogism as follows: the Progressive Era was a period of political, economic, and social reform; southern Protestants endorsed and even pioneered some of these reforms; therefore, many southern Protestants were social reformers. But there is wide disagreement among historians today over the nature of progressivism. The most widely accepted recent interpretation has it that the Progressive Era, which lasted from approximately 1900 to about 1916, was essentially conservative, concerned with preserving traditional values, restoring status to middle-class professionals and business groups, and asserting social control. By applying expertise, scientific data, and professional skills, middle-class reformers hoped to create a rational new social order out of a chaotic urban, industrial, immigrant society. Yet, such a view displays an enormous amount of presentism. Progressivism may now appear to have been bland and conservative and bureaucratic, but in its day it challenged many established ideas and institutions. Nowhere is this more evident than in what happened within the southern churches.

For my purposes, progressivism needs to be defined in more specific, regional ways. Southern progressivism, like all things southern, is a bird of a different feather, no matter how much it may resemble the rest of the flock. . . .

The people's visions were not entirely of burgeoning cities and a new industrial order. Down endless dirt roads, among countless sharecroppers, on small farms where depressed agricultural prices and rural blight threatened to drive children to cities and parents to tenancy, alienated Baptists, Methodists, and Pentecostals were angry.

Because the evangelical gamut stretched from sharecroppers to millionaires, rural religion was not homogeneous. Among better-educated ministers who were pastors of affluent "First Churches," edited denominational newspapers, or held state convention posts, one was more likely to find traces of liberal theology mixed with conservative economic and social ideas. But at the forks of the creeks, where the poorly educated jackleg preachers held forth, other views were common.

One reason historians ignored this story so long is that though they assumed that religion is heavily conditioned by culture, they did not follow the assumption to its logical conclusion, which is that different subcultures produce different religious expressions. Beyond the prevalent conservatism of the Redeemer South were different views, in coal-mining camps, in textile mills, and on tenant farms. These environments spawned labor unionism, Populism, socialism, racial demagoguery, and other nontraditional by-products that sometimes also provoked new tasks for the church.

In Bibb County, Alabama, Baptist pastor Samuel M. Adams served as president of the state Farmers' Alliance, as head of the Populist party in the 1890s, and as a state legislator. A reporter for a conservative Democratic newspaper listened to Adams address a farmers' institute in 1891 and wrote: "Mr. Adams is an easy and fluent speaker, but if he had stuck to his text we think it would have been more in accord of our idea of a Farmer's Institute. He is so full of politics that it was a hard matter for him to keep in the road."

Adams was not an isolated case. Robert H. Jackson, a Baptist minister from Heard County, was elected to head the Georgia Farmers' Alliance in 1887. He also was elected county judge and a member of both houses of the state legislature. Another Baptist preacher, Richard Manning Humphrey, was chosen general superintendent of the Texas Alliance. Mrs. Bettie Gay, of Columbus, Texas, managed a large farm after her husband's death, represented her church at the state Baptist convention in 1886, and became a champion of woman suffrage, prohibition, the Farmers' Alliance, and the Populist party. One enthusiastic southern churchwoman spoke for many Baptists when she announced, "I am going to work for prohibition, the Alliance, and for Jesus as long as I live."

Baptists and Methodists whose interests lay with more conservative causes chastised their reformist brothers and sisters. The editor of the *Alabama Baptist* worried about reports of unrest in the rural churches. He warned that many Baptist pastors had "gone wild over politics." Laymen were so engrossed with secular affairs that "they talked politics during Sunday School and outside church, not coming into worship until after the prayer and Scripture reading." A county preacher wrote that his members had become so divided over politics that bad feelings and a general coldness prevailed. In 1893 the pastor of Shiloh Church in Pike County wrote, "The dreadful political excitement of last year had almost torn the church to pieces." A state denominational leader returned from a mission tour and summarized conditions in almost exactly the same words: "Many of our churches are torn to pieces on account of last year's politics."

Conservative Protestant leaders branded Populism a radical heritage and insisted that pastors had no business forsaking hallowed sanctuaries for tarnished legislative chambers. State denominational papers were full of such admonitions, and "First Churches" rang with denunciations of political parsons. . . .

Obviously, evangelicals were not of one mind in the 1890s; nor did they reach a consensus with their urban brethren in the years to come. The crisis in rural America attracted attention on two levels between 1900 and the 1920s. The initial response came from religious leaders who perceived the complex crisis threatening southern rural life and believed that the churches must adopt new strategies to cope with this danger.

Although agricultural conditions improved after the 1890s, they remained bad. Rural people, especially the young, left farms for alluring cities; many of those who remained behind believed cities to be centers of crime and vice, where people were depersonalized, couples were divorced, and families were broken. One religious leader, J. C. Hiden, expressed the opinion of many Baptist rural folk when he proclaimed, "Men, like hogs, are bred in the country to be consumed in the towns."

The malaise in rural America caused general concern about all areas of country life. In 1908 President Theodore Roosevelt appointed a Country Life Commission to study rural America, diagnose its problems, and propose solutions. One of the commission's recommendations was that the institutionalized church should exert social as well as spiritual influence on rural life.

Rural-life reformers, most of whom were urban, educated, middle-class Protestants with roots in rural America, blamed country churches for much of the crisis. Country churches clung to a narrow doctrinal emphasis and outworn orthodoxy, which admitted no link between religious and social problems. Poorly paid ministers presided over declining congregations worshiping in dilapidated buildings. Their vision was no broader than criticism of Saturday-night dancing or Sunday-afternoon baseball. Such attitudes among rural clergymen were understandable; seminaries offered no courses in rural sociology or the rural church.

Religious leaders documented the problems of the rural church with statistical surveys. They condemned farm tenancy, which was robbing the church of thousands of members, and urged churches to consolidate and become concerned for the welfare of their communities.

The earliest Southern Baptist treatment of the crisis of the rural church was Victor I. Masters' insightful book *Country Church in the South*. Masters was superintendent of publicity for the Home Mission Board, and his book, published in 1916, belonged to the literature of the national country life movement. He compiled statistics to document the decline of rural Baptist churches, stressing their inadequate programs, absentee pastors, and dilapidated buildings. He traced many of the problems to the Baptist pioneer legacy of excessive individualism, exclusive concern for personal salvation, and the notion that ministers should not be paid.

Masters illustrated the troubles resulting from this legacy with poignant case studies. One untrained, dedicated pastor in the mountains of southwest Virginia preached at two churches for a year, conducted three weeks of revival annually, and received a total salary of $13.20. He lived with his family in a two-room cabin on thirty acres of rented land. He worked for a neighbor part-time in exchange for a horse to plow his cornfield. On Sundays he walked to his churches, one of which was six miles away, the other five. Another pastor in the same region worked at a gristmill during the week and earned a salary from his part-time churches that totaled less than $30. A 1913 survey of 5,400 Southern Baptist churches with quarter-time pastors indicated that the average pastor's salary was $378, but that some made less than $30 a year.

Even when rural pastors were promised an adequate salary, they did not always receive it. Baptist farmers were subject to capricious weather and fluctuating agricultural prices. Pledges made in the winter were contingent upon good crops and high prices the following fall. Even in good times pledges were not paid until harvest, and in bad times they were not paid at all. Masters recalled a case where a rural pastor with seven children and a salary of $700 received only $555 because of poor crops. He preached three times each Sunday at different part-time churches, a feat he accomplished by walking thirty miles each Lord's day. Another rural pastor with two children was promised $600 but received only $340. He raised $500 to buy lumber to repair the church, and the deacons offered to pay him $2.50 per day as carpenter. Ironically, the church agreed to pay him more per day as a carpenter than he earned as a pastor. But the irony was only theoretical: after he worked eighty-three days as a carpenter and was due $207, the deacons paid him only $5.

Masters acknowledged that part of the problem could be traced to rural poverty. He called the growth of farm tenancy the most alarming fact in southern rural life. Tenancy meant "the serious crippling, or the actual destruction of the treasured social, religious, and personal resources of the country." Tenancy was developing a class of white peasants that would in time destroy southern civilization. The country church must find ways to halt the growth of tenancy if rural religious life was to be stabilized, Masters believed.

Besides cataloging problems, he also advanced a number of proposals to rescue the country church. Rural churches should discuss frankly the "fictitious and harmful" elements of city life, he said. They should enlarge their social ministry to include women's societies and activities for the young. They should encourage organizations of farm people, which would improve community morale and reduce isolation. They should encourage better schoolhouses and salaries for teachers, give moral sanction to efforts to improve farming practices, use lay preachers on Sundays when pastors were unavailable, create circulating libraries to educate members, and

standardize hymnbooks. Country pastors should take courses in rural sociology and economics at agricultural colleges and should have "an intelligent comprehension of . . . the problems of soil fertility, animal husbandry,
and the growth of crops." Although the social function of the church must
be recognized, Masters maintained, he cautioned against a social gospel
that promised "a millennium without the cross of Christ."

Masters used his own position with the Home Mission Board to
strengthen rural church work. Begun through his efforts in 1913, the board's
Enlistment Department (actually a country church department) immediately
began to spend $20,000 annually to aid rural churches. The department also
inaugurated annual financial canvasses of all members of rural churches.
The board employed twelve enlistment workers, who were paid jointly by
the board and the state conventions. One each served in North Carolina,
Georgia, and Kentucky, two each were employed in South Carolina, Mississippi and Louisiana, and three served in Alabama. Masters recommended
that state boards refuse to provide aid to missionary pastors unless the
local churches were willing to pay an amount that would provide a salary
of at least $900 annually when combined with state funds. For years he
used the monthly magazine of the Home Mission Board to emphasize
country church problems and propose solutions.

Not everyone was so interested in country life. Masters criticized the
Southern Baptist Convention for devoting little time to rural church problems. Denominational colleges and seminaries drew from the country but
turned little back to it. They tended to produce graduates who were ashamed
of their rural heritage and sought urban pastorates.

Masters was responsible for another step forward in July, 1922. At a
joint meeting of the Home Mission and Sunday School boards in Atlanta,
members agreed to sponsor a survey of rural church life to be undertaken
by the Sunday School Board's Department of Survey, Statistics, and Information. This massive statistical survey of 2,043 white Southern Baptist
rural churches was published in the *Southern Baptist Handbook* for 1923.
The publication provided graphic, incontrovertible proof of the problems
facing the rural church.

John W. Jent was the first person to mine the new information. Born
on a farm in southern Kentucky and reared in rural southwest Missouri,
Jent was a third-generation rural Baptist preacher. Although his father and
grandfather had little education, Jent obtained degrees from Baylor University and Southwestern Baptist Theological Seminary. He continued his
training in rural sociology at Columbia University and then joined the faculty
of Oklahoma Baptist University, where he taught applied Christianity and
conducted church conferences.

In 1924 Jent was invited to deliver the Holland Lectures at Southwestern
Seminary. The lectures were published as *The Challenge of the Country
Church*. Although he spent more time on the theological rationale of his
proposals and elaborated them in more detail, his analysis of the crisis in
the rural church and his recommendations closely paralleled Masters' earlier
work.

Using statistics from the 1922 survey, Jent developed a point system for evaluating a "standard" rural Baptist church. The church received points for having a full-time, resident, college- and seminary-trained pastor; an adequate church building with kitchen, sanitary water, toilets, and a parsonage; a complete organizational structure and a regular program of community service; organized activities for young people to help keep them in the country; a regular budget system; and a minimum pastor's salary of $1,200 a year. A score of less than fifty points indicated that the rural church was "inefficient." As a result of his role at conferences on the country church and his call for more attention to rural sociology, Jent became a major authority on the subject within the Southern Baptist Convention. Unfortunately, the proposals of Masters and Jent came as the South was entering a prolonged agricultural depression that drove millions of rural white southerners off the land and left the rest too impoverished to upgrade churches.

Doubtless many Protestant leaders were surprised and disappointed by the reaction of rural people to their attempts to save farm life. Reformers did not convince the rural churches that they should consolidate or become more socially conscious. Traditional evangelical religion, with its appeal for salvation of the soul, still dominated the rural churches' vision.

This fact did not mean that the rural church of the Progressive Era was of one mind any more than it had been in the 1890s. The same social and economic cleavage remained, as was demonstrated in a bitter political conflict brewing in the Southwest.

Too often the Fundamentalist mind has been depicted as theologically warped, and little attempt has been made to comprehend its mainsprings or its complexity. The life of one of Fundamentalism's greatest champions, J. Frank Norris of Fort Worth, Texas, suggests how rural poverty affects religious perceptions. Norris was born in 1877 at Dadeville in east-central Alabama. Eleven years later his family moved to Hubbard, Texas, where his father drowned the sorrows of sharecropping, not in the balm of Gilead but in the tonic of John Barleycorn. He lived with his wife and children in a dilapidated, unpainted shack. The boy grew up in a setting of deep family tension. On one occasion his father beat young Norris so severely that he broke the boy's nose and lacerated his body. Yet, when horse thieves threatened his father's life, the boy went to his aid, receiving three bullet wounds in the process. Gangrene set in, followed by inflammatory rheumatism that left Norris speechless and paralyzed. He spent two years in a wheelchair and a third year completing his recovery. In his thirteenth year he had been converted in a brush-arbor revival, and his mother sustained his faith by assuring him that someday he was destined to be a leader of men. The J. Frank Norris of the Fundamentalist 1920s is well known, but the tortured young boy, growing up in the grinding poverty, demented violence, and wracking pain of the southern tenancy system is barely remembered. Norris' response to rural poverty—flamboyant Fundamentalism and repudiation of social reform—is familiar; in fact, it has become a stereotype. Other responses are less well known.

In the latter years of the Progressive Era agrarian socialism swept across the parched prairies and rolling hills of Oklahoma and Texas, blossoming like young cotton in the first warmth of summer. From 1912 to 1916 the Socialist party captured nearly 20 percent of statewide votes in Oklahoma. The party's primary strength was in rural counties with high rates of tenancy. Although fiercely partisan, socialism in the Southwest differed in many ways from the predominantly urban, eastern variety, which was often oriented toward immigrants. For one thing, Socialist ministers in the Southwest used camp-meeting fervor and a Fundamentalist idiom to create a "Socialist Gospel" that transformed secular socialism into a millenarian and transcendent faith in the possibility of reform. They generally ignored the genteel and intellectual brand of communitarianism advocated by men like George D. Herron. While clinging tenaciously to their individualistic cultural traditions, they also resisted the encroachments of capitalistic commercial agriculture and mainstream urban values on the rural community.

Baptists, Methodists, and the Churches of Christ produced more than their fair share of Socialists from rural congregations, despite the conservatism of most of their leaders. But the Holiness wing of revivalism produced the most converts to socialism. "The radical asceticism and hopeful postmillennialism" of the Pentecostals provided fertile ground for the radical Red seed. Eugene V. Debs held one of his 1905 rallies in southern Oklahoma in a Holiness tabernacle. A few years later a Socialist organizer reported that he had founded a local among tenants near Romney, Texas, and had left "a holiness preacher in charge to keep them right." He added that "holiness people make good Socialists." One Oklahoma newspaper concluded that Socialists were like simple-minded children who "took up one enthusiasm after another." After leaving the Socialist party, they would probably "join up with Holy Rollers," the writer speculated. He was probably right about the close association of these two enthusiasms, though he almost certainly had their chronology reversed.

When historians speak of progressivism, they usually do not mean the radical agrarianism spreading across the South's impoverished farm belt. They usually mean the political and bureaucratic reforms sponsored by urban businessmen and professionals. But even the urban South, home of the more traditional progressive reforms, did not escape the attention of concerned clerics.

Across the entire nation the social gospel emphasized the achievement of the Kingdom of God in this world, the relevance of Christian ethics to everyday life, and the power of Christianity to reconcile classes at war. It sought to replace the stress on church membership with the idea that all citizens could be part of the Kingdom of God, which would establish justice and love as the basis of all of American society. It arose primarily in response to the plight of industrial labor in cities and largely ignored the question of race. Most blacks still lived on farms, and the social gospel, even in the South, was tilted toward the emerging crises of the cities.

If Samuel Hill is right—if the South's frontier, its rural life-style, and its cultural insulation produced a unique southern religion—it follows logically (albeit incorrectly) that there was "virtually no recognition of any responsibility to redeem the secular dimensions of community and national life, inasmuch as life and the Christian life are construed to be essentially individualistic." Such a conclusion assumes a static quality in southern religious thought; yet, during the intellectual ferment of the early twentieth century, southern religious thought was not static. Even southern ministers were attending the University of Chicago, studying rural sociology, attending conferences on social reform, and reading books.

The Reverend G. C. Hamilton, a Methodist minister from Crowell, Texas, conducted several heated debates with a Socialist lawyer in 1911. After one particularly spirited exchange, Hamilton accepted his antagonist's challenge to read Walter Rauschenbusch's *Christianity and the Social Crisis*. Shortly after finishing the book, Hamilton announced his conversion to socialism. The parson's new conversion experience did not sit well with the stewards of his Crowell church, who expelled him; afterward, he was welcomed as a lecturer by the local Church of Christ. Such conversions occurred with increasing frequency between 1900 and 1920.

The fact that the social gospel did indeed flourish in the urban South (though with some opposition from rural people) demonstrates that southern religion was far more resilient and flexible than its confined roots in the rural frontier might suggest. Although they seldom accepted liberal theology—with its "higher criticism" of scripture, its attempt to rationalize science with religion, and its humanism—well-educated Protestant divines were receptive to the new and more relevant gospel message.

The issues that most often attracted the attention of reformist ministers were the obvious ones: prostitution, alcohol abuse, child labor, and the convict lease system. Campaigns against prostitution and Demon Rum often have been dismissed as pietist attempts to enforce private moral standards in the entire community. But it was precisely these movements, requiring political involvement and shrewd use of ecclesiastical power, that first caused many ministers and lay people to apply Christian ethics to social problems. Having entered the fray, they found it difficult to disengage.

During the two decades in which Frank W. Barnett served as editor of the *Alabama Baptist*, he conducted a successful campaign to restrict child labor in Alabama. Barnett was an early ally of Montgomery's Episcopal priest Edgar Gardner Murphy, who launched the national campaign to end child labor. In 1907 Barnett waxed eloquent during a debate in the Alabama legislature on a bill to control such work: "The South is harboring a system of slavery more horrible than that which existed before the civil war, or which now exists in the Siberian mines—the slavery of child labor. Children from five to twelve years of age, working twelve and fourteen hours a day; babies . . . tramping wearily all day, before flying and buzzing machinery, pitiful little wrecks of humanity that wring the hearts of all who behold their thraldom, save their brutish masters, the mill owners."

As in the 1890s, conservative ministers and laymen chided pastors like Barnett for moving beyond the proper ministerial sphere, the salvation of souls. But the times had changed, and Barnett responded that any sincere minister must sometimes enter aggressively into the struggle over grave social issues. He had no use for "ultra-conservative and timid church members who elevate their eyebrows and rub their pious hands in deprecation" every time their pastor entered politics to improve the moral quality of life. Nor did he accept a definition of Christianity that assumed that religion had nothing to do with business and politics, "as if it were simply a question of private life, with no social obligations."

Barnett was not exceptional. In 1882 Baptists from North and South had organized the Baptist Congress. By 1893 the congress had attracted enough southern delegates to move the meeting south, gathering at the First Baptist Church of Augusta, Georgia. Walter Rauschenbusch opened the session with an address entitled "The Church and the Money Power," which included a scathing attack on the church's acquiescence to wealth. Dr. James B. Gambrell, president of Baptist affiliate Mercer University in Macon, Georgia, praised the speech in his response.

Over the years the social activism and intellectual ferment of the congress influenced a new generation of Southern Baptist leaders, including Edgar Y. Mullins, William O. Carver, William J. McGlothin, John R. Sampey, all of Southern Baptist Theological Seminary, and Dr. William L. Poteat, who was later to head Wake Forest College. Professors and ministers from throughout the Southern Baptist Convention imbibed an activist theology that contributed directly to the creation of the church's Social Service Commission in 1908.

Although the Social Service Commission focused more narrowly on temperance in later years, it did include a broader social agenda in the teens. In 1913 Poteat became chairman of the commission and attempted to address the South's social distress, but he met increasing resistance from fellow Baptists.

In search of a more daring organization, many ministers, including Poteat, joined the Southern Sociological Congress, whose motivation was religious. Poteat addressed the congress in 1913, maintaining that "in the thought of Jesus, the Kingdom of God is not formal or institutional. . . . It is rather a social spirit which will transfigure" all institutions, he said. Furthermore, the local church was responsible for making its community "a little province of the Kingdom of God." Dr. Arthur J. Barton, at that time superintendent of Southern Baptist educational work in Texas, helped write a report that called attention to the need for health services, equitable justice, an end to lynching, and welfare and economic reforms.

Charles S. Gardner, professor of sociology at Southern Baptist Seminary, also attended the Southern Sociological Congress. He praised the social gospel as "the insistent Christian ideal . . . not only for the individual, but for the social life." Gardner's *The Ethics of Jesus and Social Progress*, published in 1914, argued the primacy of the Kingdom of God. The Kingdom, as he defined it, was a "social order, a system of human relations, progressively realized, in which the will of God is the formative principle and all the functions of which are organized and operated for the purpose of helping all men to realize the spiritual possibilities of humanity."

John N. Prestridge, editor of Kentucky's *Baptist World*, served with Poteat on the Social Services Commission. At the 1908 Southern Baptist Convention, Prestridge agreed with Gardner's definition of the Kingdom. As the chairman of the Committee on Civic Righteousness, he reported to the convention that "Civic righteousness and the Kingdom of God are bound up in each other. We are learning anew that Christ's commission to his followers is not primarily to increase the census of heaven, but to make down here a righteous society in which Christ's will shall be done, his kingdom come."

Southern Baptist Theological Seminary's biblical scholar, Archibald T. Robertson, was not renowned for his liberalism. Yet, even he caught a new vision of the Kingdom. In his book *The New Citizenship*, published in 1919, Robertson argued that Christians need not wait for the millennium to achieve social justice. They should go to work immediately to deal with "the white-slave traffic, the bondage of childhood in the factory, the oppression of labour by capital," he said. "The rights of labour are unquestioned and the labouring man must have the opportunity of educating his children," he added. Robertson advocated woman suffrage and praised Woodrow Wilson's New Freedom: "At least we can all do our part as citizens of the colony of heaven to make our commonwealth and our world as nearly like heaven as possible. This [the New Freedom] is the new crusade of the new citizenship and it is worth the best that is in the statesman and social reformer. And more, it has the promise of the blessing of the King of the Kingdom of God."

Since they were under the tutelage of professors with such views, it is no wonder that a new generation of Baptist ministers arose with a social definition of the Kingdom of God. Doctoral dissertations written at Southern Seminary during these years confirmed the new influences. In 1919, along with Meroney's essay advocating a Christian-Socialist alliance, there was a dissertation by James C. Stivender titled "The New Interpretation of Democracy." It called for applying the Christian perception of the brotherhood of man to the complex social problems of the day. "The Christian religion is working for the realization of the brotherhood of men which will take form in an ideal social order—the Kingdom of God." Also in 1919, James E. Welsh's dissertation, "Our Future Toward the Criminal," applied Christian ethics to another arena. The problem of criminality, he reasoned, "is a social one, and must be solved, to no small degree, by principles social."

In 1916 James R. Quisenberry submitted a dissertation grounded in the sociology of religion. In "The Primitive Church Congregation as a Social Organism," he probed the relation of the New Testament church to society and social conditions. He concluded that the task of Jesus had been "to establish the reign of heaven on earth; he taught his followers that loyalty to *him* was that alone which constituted them citizens of the Kingdom of God, and he taught them that the purpose of their lives was to be the promotion and reign of God."

The same winds of change that stirred Southern Baptist life swept with greater velocity through the Methodist denomination. Kirby noted in his study of southern progressivism that women professionals played a key role in reform. Specifically, Methodist laywomen launched a widely based social-settlement ministry in the South.

The earliest concrete effort by Methodist women to initiate a ministry to the South's cities occurred in 1893. Meeting in Saint Louis, the women entrusted the new urban evangelical emphasis to the Woman's Parsonage and Home Mission Society. Economic depression delayed the work until 1900, when three pioneer settlements were begun in Nashville, Dallas, and Atlanta. Four others were opened in 1904. Predicated on the notion that ministers must live near settlement houses, Methodist social workers tackled the problems of the inner city.

One of their first controversies concerned the term *settlement house,* which had a nonevangelical and even secular connotation to Methodists, and as a result many pastors criticized the work. The women employed a shrewd stratagem in 1906; noting that Presbyterians did their downtown settlement house work in what was called Church House and Episcopalians in the Parish House, they changed the name of their facilities to Wesley House. In later years they distinguished mission efforts in black communities by the name Bethlehem House.

The New South industrial city of Birmingham was a perfect setting for expanded social ministries. As early as 1877, women of the Home Mission Society of First Methodist Church had begun an industrial school for deprived children. The women gradually broadened their work to include home visitation and poor relief. They organized the Board of City Missions in 1903 and rented a cottage in a working-class neighborhood. This cottage became the city's first settlement house. A deaconess and a city missionary were employed as residents. They operated a day school for children whose parents worked, a night literacy school for working boys, and a free kindergarten. By 1905 three thousand children from lower-class families had attended the church-sponsored kindergartens. Funding proved a major problem, and the work was closed from 1905 to 1908, when the Board of City Missions opened a Wesley House in a different neighborhood. The ministry grew rapidly, requiring a larger house, which was purchased in 1909. A deaconess and assistant were employed, and Wesley House broadened its scope to include the textile operatives at Avondale Mills.

In 1912 the Board of City Missions established a Wesley House to minister to five thousand Italian immigrants employed at the Ensley mills of the Tennessee Coal and Iron Company. The company donated a house, a playground, heat, lights, and two thousand dollars. The Board of City Missions employed a trained social worker—Dorothy Crim—and two assistants. The house staff conducted a night school three evenings a week, formed a community band, sponsored games, and set up two free medical clinics, the first in the Birmingham district. Behind the house, a 50-by-150-foot block of land was divided into plots so the children could learn gardening. Classes in cooking, sewing, first aid, and home nursing were conducted for women. In 1916 Wesley House established a housekeeping center consisting of a bedroom, kitchen, and dining room. There young women learned housekeeping skills, which were important in their social and cultural assimilation. On Sunday afternoons, Bible stories and songs attracted the children of Ensley for more traditional religious services.

Such ministries quickly spread throughout the urban South. By 1920 there were at least twenty-six Methodist settlement houses for whites and blacks in southern cities. Methodists also constructed other types of facilities, all essentially rescue missions, during these years.

Training workers for ripe urban mission fields was a major task. Scarritt Bible and Training School, which opened in Kansas City in the fall of 1892, provided a steady supply of Methodist social workers for inner-city work. In 1902 Belle H. Bennett, who headed the Woman's Board of Home Missions, petitioned the general conference for creation of the office of deaconess. The conference granted the request and consecrated the first five young women in 1903. The deaconesses provided the staff for most urban social work. They received no salary at first, only room and board and ten dollars a month. Belle Bennett could not understand how the church could insist on adequate compensation for laborers while refusing deaconesses a living wage, and in time the monthly stipend became a regular salary.

By no means were these pioneer ventures of Southern Baptists and Methodists the only regional expressions of the social gospel. Many Episcopal and Presbyterian congregations sponsored "institutional churches," which were open each day of the week to provide social services. In fact the growth of these institutional churches is one of the notable achievements of the Progressive Era in the South.

As with the rural church, this urban progressivism can be viewed as a genteel movement of social uplift growing from middle-class paternalism. But as with agrarian Socialist church folk, the urban social gospel produced its radical underside.

The Reverend S. R. Emerson, Alabama's state chaplain to prisoners, penned an essay in 1910 on the state's twenty thousand miners. Few of them attended church, he maintained, because they had no respect for pastors. If Methodism wanted to reach the miners, he wrote, pastors of churches in mining camps should each purchase a miner's lamp, suit, and cap, and enter the mines where their people worked. The denomination should build its own churches and reject offers to use buildings owned by the company. Such arrangements had caused miners to view ministers as company men, "and it is a known fact that in many places there is not the best of feeling between the men and the company." Furthermore, the pastor should be an advisory member of the United Mine Workers. Emerson believed that "the pastor makes a great mistake to oppose" the union.

In 1907 another Methodist minister, the Reverend W. P. Blevins, addressed a district conference of his church meeting in the mining center of Dora, Alabama. There were fewer converts in mining camps than in foreign mission fields, he said. Even the membership figures for mining-camp churches were misleading, because Methodists in such churches were mostly farmers from adjacent areas or company officials. Miners preferred not to worship in the same congregation with company men. Mining communities needed institutional churches devoted exclusively to miners, with reading rooms, games and tables, a small gynmasium and baths, a night literacy school, a glee club, and religious services two evenings a week conducted "as often as possible by a miner in the interest of miners."

Such sophisticated institutional churches usually developed in urban textile mill communities rather than mining towns. But in both types of communities bivocational ministers did supply a pastorate more sympathetic to workers. Because Baptists maintained a strong anti-intellectual tradition, one commonly found pastors in the denomination who made their living the same way as their parishioners: as tenant farmers, cotton mill operatives, or coal miners. Because depression, injustice, low wages, poor housing, and company oppression affected their lives the same way it did their members, they often expressed their anger in identical fashion. When Florida phosphate miners struck for higher salaries in 1919, the pastor of the church attended by most of the strikers offered his building in case of rain. He attended their rallies and led them in prayer. . . .

. . . During the Progressive Era, new thoughts were circulating among the evangelical denominations of the South, which had been spawned by the great revivals of 1801 and nurtured by frontier individualism and isolation. Although these groups were more conservative, more emotional, and more oriented toward salvation than their counterparts in other regions, important new ideas charged the atmosphere. Many of the better-educated ministers who had been exposed to European and northern thought came to believe that the concept of the Kingdom of God applied to the social conditions of this world. And among uneducated rural church people—who were staunchly Fundamentalist and barely literate—millennialistic and Pentecostal religion fueled a raging fire of Populist and Socialist radicalism.

In later decades prohibition would become a central focus for religious reformers rather than only one element of a broad reform movement. Baptists and Methodists would move into the middle class, leaving the voice of social prophecy, as well as religious ecstasy, to the Pentecostals. But for a brief historical moment between 1890 and 1920, many southern evangelicals sounded more like Jeremiah than Jerry Falwell.

✢ *F U R T H E R   R E A D I N G*

Kenneth K. Bailey, *Southern White Protestantism in the Twentieth Century* (1964)
John B. Boles, *The Great Revival, 1787–1805: The Origins of the Southern Evangelical Mind* (1972)
———— et al., eds. *Religion in the South* (1985)
Dickson D. Bruce, Jr., *And They All Sang Hallelujah: Plain-Folk Camp-Meeting Religion, 1800–1845* (1974)
Mark Cowett, *Birmingham's Rabbi: Morris Newfield and Alabama, 1895–1940* (1986)
Leonard Dinnerstein and Mary Dale Palsson, eds., *Jews in the South* (1973)
John Lee Eighmy, *Churches in Cultural Captivity: A History of the Social Attitudes of Southern Baptists* (1972)

Eli N. Evans, *The Provincials: A Personal History of Jews in the South* (1973)

J. Wayne Flynt, "Baptists and Reform," *Baptist History and Heritage* 7 (1972), 211–222

Jean E. Friedman, *The Enclosed Garden: Women and Community in the Evangelical South, 1830–1900* (1985)

Willard B. Gatewood, Jr., *Preachers, Pedagogues and Politicians: The Evolution Controversy in North Carolina, 1920–1927* (1966)

David Edwin Harrell, Jr., *White Sects and Black Men in the Recent South* (1971)

———, *All Things Are Possible: The Healing and Charismatic Revivals in Modern America* (1975)

———, ed. *Varieties of Southern Evangelicalism* (1981)

Samuel S. Hill, Jr., *Southern Churches in Crisis* (1966)

———, *The South and the North in American Religion* (1980)

E. Brooks Holifield, *The Gentlemen Theologians: American Theology in Southern Culture, 1795–1860* (1978)

Anne C. Loveland, *Southern Evangelicals and the Social Order, 1800–1860* (1980)

Robert F. Martin, "A Prophet's Pilgrimage: The Religious Radicalism of Howard Anderson Kester, 1921–1941," *Journal of Southern History* 48 (1982), 511–530

Donald G. Mathews, *Religion in the Old South* (1977)

James Sellers, *The South and Christian Ethics* (1962)

Shelton Smith, *In His Image, But . . . : Racism in Southern Religion, 1780–1910* (1972)

Noreen Dunn Tatum, *A Crown of Service: A Story of Woman's Work in the Methodist Episcopal Church South, from 1878 to 1940* (1960)

James J. Thompson, Jr., *Tried as by Fire: Southern Baptists and the Religious Controversies of the 1920s* (1982)

Edward L. Wheeler, *Uplifting the Race: The Black Minister in the New South, 1865–1902* (1986)

New Realism in Southern Culture

⚓

In 1917, journalist H. L. Mencken referred to the South as ''the Sahara of the Bozart.'' By the 1930s, millions of Americans were reading the novels of Thomas Wolfe and William Faulkner; sociologist Howard W. Odum and his colleagues at the University of North Carolina had established national reputations for their social-scientific explorations of southern problems; and a creative group at Vanderbilt University, the Nashville Agrarians, had offered a stunning critique of urban-industrial society.

The literary renaissance and accompanying developments in critical thought and the social sciences were in some ways continuations of the self-analysis and self-criticism initiated during the progressive era. More open challenges to prevailing racial, class, and political orthodoxies characterized the cultural revival, though few suggested such radical changes as racial integration or trade unionism. Southerners developed firmer intellectual connections with other parts of the nation. Financial support from northern foundations, for example, promoted social-science research in the South. The South's image underwent a positive change, and this metamorphosis accounted to some degree for the receptivity of regional literature and research in the rest of the nation. To Americans at large, the South was still exotic, leisurely, and romantic in an era of the corporate man, dense cities, and troubling racial and ethnic problems. As the rest of the nation reached south to remember what it was losing, the South merely tried to remember. Perhaps this was the significance of the renaissance era—to introduce the regional memory to reality in small doses.

Why did the cultural renaissance occur at this particular time? What factors motivated the literary and academic writers, and what were their objectives? Finally, were they chroniclers of, or contributors to, the tensions in southern society between the world wars?

✠ D O C U M E N T S

Journalist H. L. Mencken was a persistent gadfly to the South during the 1920s. Perhaps his most notorious dissection of the region may be observed in the first document, which demonstrates Mencken's sharp wit, exaggerated rhetoric, and some truth about the South's cultural condition in 1917. The *Journal of Social Forces* began publishing at Chapel Hill, North Carolina, in the early 1920s and quickly established a reputation for tackling sensitive issues relating to religion, race, and politics. In the second excerpt, journalist Gerald Johnson challenges southerners, in the name of patriotism, to adopt a critical attitude toward regional conditions. Nell Battle Lewis took up Johnson's challenge, as the third document attests. A rare female columnist for the *Raleigh News & Observer* in the 1920s, she became an outspoken critic of numerous southern conventions. The pressure of criticism led to Lewis's suffering a nervous breakdown in the early 1930s. Thomas Wolfe so chafed against these conventions that he eventually went into exile in New York, a favorite venue for displaced southerners. In the fourth excerpt, taken from his great novel *Look Homeward, Angel*, Wolfe attacks the stifling conformity of the South through the thoughts of Eugene Gant. The Nashville Agrarians were rebels of a different sort. In their manifesto, entitled *I'll Take My Stand*, they warned that modernization of the South would destroy some important regional values. Vanderbilt English Professor John Crowe Ransom's introduction to the volume is excerpted here as the fifth document. The sixth document typifies the detailed, quantitative assessment of regional problems (in this case, agriculture) that Howard W. Odum and his colleagues undertook from the early 1920s to World War II. Regional values, or at least certain of them, drove black novelist Richard Wright of Mississippi away from the South. In the final document, an excerpt from his autobiographical novel *Black Boy*, he demonstrates how the rigid place of blacks in southern society distorted the perceptions of both races toward blacks.

H. L. Mencken, "The Sahara of the Bozart," 1917

Alas, for the South! Her books have grown fewer—
She never was much given to literature.

In the lamented J. Gordon Coogler, author of these elegaic lines, there was the insight of a true poet. He was the last bard of Dixie, at least in the legitimate line. Down there a poet is now almost as rare as an oboe-player, a dry-point etcher or a metaphysician. It is, indeed, amazing to contemplate so vast a vacuity. One thinks of the interstellar spaces, of the colossal reaches of the now mythical ether. Nearly the whole of Europe could be lost in that stupendous region of fat farms, shoddy cities and paralyzed cerebrums: one could throw in France, Germany and Italy, and still have room for the British Isles. And yet, for all its size and all its wealth and all the "progress" it babbles of, it is almost as sterile, artistically, intellectually, culturally, as the Sahara Desert. There are single acres in Europe that house more first-rate men than all the states south of the Potomac; there are probably single square miles in America. If the whole of the late Confederacy were to be engulfed by a tidal wave tomorrow, the effect upon the civilized minority of men in the world would be but little greater than that of a flood on the Yang-tse-kiang. It would be impossible in all history to match so complete a drying-up of a civilization.

I say a civilization because that is what, in the old days, the South had, despite the Baptist and Methodist barbarism that reigns down there now. More, it was a civilization of manifold excellences—perhaps the best that the Western Hemisphere has ever seen—undoubtedly the best that These States have ever seen. Down to the middle of the last century, and even beyond, the main hatchery of ideas on this side of the water was across the Potomac bridges. The New England shopkeepers and theologians never really developed a civilization; all they ever developed was a government. They were, at their best, tawdry and tacky fellows, oafish in manner and devoid of imagination; one searches the books in vain for mention of a salient Yankee gentleman; as well look for a Welsh gentleman. But in the south there were men of delicate fancy, urbane instinct and aristocratic manner—in brief, superior men—in brief, gentry. To politics, their chief diversion, they brought active and original minds. It was there that nearly all the political theories we still cherish and suffer under came to birth. It was there that the crude dogmatism of New England was refined and humanized. It was there, above all, that some attention was given to the art of living—that life got beyond and above the state of a mere infliction and became an exhilarating experience. A certain noble spaciousness was in the ancient southern scheme of things. The *Ur*-Confederate had leisure. He liked to toy with ideas. He was hospitable and tolerant. He had the vague thing that we call culture.

But consider the condition of his late empire today. The picture gives one the creeps. It is as if the Civil War stamped out every last bearer of the torch, and left only a mob of peasants on the field. One thinks of Asia Minor, resigned to Armenians, Greeks and wild swine, of Poland abandoned to the Poles. In all that gargantuan paradise of the fourth-rate there is not a single picture gallery worth going into, or a single orchestra capable of playing the nine symphonies of Beethoven, or a single opera-house, or a single theater devoted to decent plays, or a single public monument (built since the war) that is worth looking at, or a single workshop devoted to the making of beautiful things. Once you have counted Robert Loveman (an Ohioan by birth) and John McClure (an Oklahoman) you will not find a single southern poet above the rank of a neighborhood rhymester. Once you have counted James Branch Cabell (a lingering survivor of the *ancien régime:* a scarlet dragonfly imbedded in opaque amber) you will not find a single southern prose writer who can actually write. And once you have— but when you come to critics, musical composers, painters, sculptors, architects and the like, you will have to give it up, for there is not even a bad one between the Potomac mud-flats and the Gulf. Nor an historian.

Nor a sociologist. Nor a philosopher. Nor a theologian. Nor a scientist. In all these fields the south is an awe-inspiring blank—a brother to Portugal, Serbia and Esthonia.

Consider, for example, the present estate and dignity of Virginia—in the great days indubitably the premier American state, the mother of Presidents and statesmen, the home of the first American university worthy of the name, the *arbiter elegantiarum* of the western world. Well, observe Virginia to-day. It is years since a first-rate man, save only Cabell, has come out of it; it is years since an idea has come out of it. The old aristocracy went down the red gullet of war; the poor white trash are now in the saddle. Politics in Virginia are cheap, ignorant, parochial, idiotic; there is scarcely a man in office above the rank of a professional job-seeker; the political doctrine that prevails is made up of hand-me-downs from the bumpkinry of the Middle West—Bryanism, Prohibition, vice crusading, all that sort of filthy claptrap; the administration of the law is turned over to professors of Puritanism and espionage; a Washington or a Jefferson, dumped there by some act of God, would be denounced as a scoundrel and jailed overnight. Elegance, *esprit,* culture? Virginia has no art, no literature, no philosophy, no mind or aspiration of her own. Her education has sunk to the Baptist seminary level; not a single contribution to human knowledge has come out of her colleges in twenty-five years; she spends less than half upon her common schools, *per capita,* than any northern state spends. In brief, an intellectual Gobi or Lapland. Urbanity, *politesse,* chivalry? Go to! It was in Virginia that they invented the device of searching for contraband whisky in women's underwear. . . . There remains, at the top, a ghost of the old aristocracy, a bit wistful and infinitely charming. But it has lost all its old leadership to fabulous monsters from the lower depths; it is submerged in an industrial plutocracy that is ignorant and ignominious. The mind of the state, as it is revealed to the nation, is pathetically naïve and inconsequential. It no longer reacts with energy and elasticity to great problems. It has fallen to the bombastic trivialities of the camp-meeting and the chautauqua. Its foremost exponent—if so flabby a thing may be said to have an exponent—is a statesman whose name is synonymous with empty words, broken pledges and false pretenses. One could no more imagine a Lee or a Washington in the Virginia of to-day than one could imagine a Huxley in Nicaragua.

I choose the Old Dominion, not because I disdain it, but precisely because I esteem it. It is, by long odds, the most civilized of the southern states, now as always. It has sent a host of creditable sons northward; the stream kept running into our own time. Virginians, even the worst of them, show the effects of a great tradition. They hold themselves above other southerners, and with sound pretension. If one turns to such a commonwealth as Georgia the picture becomes far darker. There the liberated lower orders of whites have borrowed the worst commercial bounderism of the Yankee and superimposed it upon a culture that, at bottom, is but little removed from savagery. Georgia is at once the home of the cottonmill sweater and of the most noisy and vapid sort of chamber of commerce, of the Methodist parson turned Savonarola and of the lynching bee. A self-respecting European, going there to live, would not only find intellectual stimulation utterly lacking; he would actually feel a certain insecurity, as if the scene were the Balkans or the China Coast. The Leo Frank affair was no isolated phenomenon. It fitted into its frame very snugly. It was a natural expression of Georgian notions of truth and justice. There is a state with more than half the area of Italy and more population than either Denmark or Norway, and yet in thirty years it has not produced a single idea. Once upon a time a Georgian printed a couple of books that attracted notice, but immediately it turned out that he was little more than an amanuensis for the local blacks—that his works were really the products, not of white Georgia, but of black Georgia. Writing afterward *as* a white man, he swiftly subsided into the fifth rank. And he is not only the glory of the literature of Georgia; he is, almost literally, the whole of the literature of Georgia—nay, of the entire art of Georgia.

Virginia is the best of the south to-day, and Georgia is perhaps the worst. The one is simply senile; the other is crass, gross, vulgar and obnoxious. Between lies a vast plain of mediocrity, stupidity, lethargy, almost of dead silence. In the north, of course, there is also grossness, crassness, vulgarity. The north, in its way, is also stupid and obnoxious. But nowhere in the north is there such complete sterility, so depressing a lack of all civilized gesture and aspiration. One would find it difficult to unearth a second-rate city between the Ohio and the Pacific that isn't struggling to establish an orchestra, or setting up a little theater, or going in for an art gallery, or making some other effort to get into touch with civilization. These efforts often fail, and sometimes they succeed rather absurdly, but under them there is at least an impulse that deserves respect, and that is the impulse to seek beauty and to experiment with ideas, and so to give the life of every day a certain dignity and purpose. You will find no such impulse in the south. There are no committees down there cadging subscriptions for orchestras; if a string quartet is ever heard there, the news of it has never come out; an opera troupe, when it roves the land, is a nine days' wonder. The little theater movement has swept the whole country, enormously augmenting the public interest in sound plays, giving new dramatists their chance, forcing reforms upon the commercial theater. Everywhere else the wave rolls high—but along the line of the Potomac it breaks upon a rock-bound shore. There is no little theater beyond. There is no gallery of pictures. No artist ever gives exhibitions. No one talks of such things. No one seems to be interested in such things.

As for the cause of this unanimous torpor and doltishness, this curious and almost pathological estrangement from everything that makes for a civilized culture, I have hinted at it already, and now state it again. The south has simply been drained of all its best blood. The vast blood-letting of the Civil War half exterminated and wholly paralyzed the old aristocracy, and so left the land to the harsh mercies of the poor white trash, now its masters. The war, of course, was not a complete massacre. It spared a decent number of first-rate southerners—perhaps even some of the very best. Moreover, other countries, notably France and Germany, have survived far more staggering butcheries, and even showed marked progress thereafter. But the war not only cost a great many valuable lives; it also brought bankruptcy, demoralization and despair in its train—and so the majority of the first-rate southerners that were left, broken in spirit and unable to live under the new dispensation, cleared out. A few went to South America, to Egypt, to the Far East. Most came north. They were fecund; their progeny is widely dispersed, to the great benefit of the north. A southerner of good blood almost always does well in the north. He finds, even in the big cities, surroundings fit for a man of condition. His peculiar qualities have a high social value, and are esteemed. He is welcomed by the codfish aristocracy as one palpably superior. But in the south he throws up his hands. It is impossible for him to stoop to the common level. He cannot brawl in politics with the grandsons of his grandfather's tenants. He is unable to share their fierce jealousy of the emerging black—the cornerstone of all their public thinking. He is anaesthetic to their theological and political enthusiasms. He finds himself an alien at their feasts of soul. And so he withdraws into his tower, and is heard of no more. . . .

What is needed down there, before the vexatious public problems of the region may be intelligently approached, is a survey of the population by competent ethnologists and anthropologists. The immigrants of the north have been studied at great length, and any one who is interested may now apply to the Bureau of Ethnology for elaborate data as to their racial strains, their stature and cranial indices, their relative capacity for education, and the changes that they undergo under American *Kultur*. But the older stocks of the south, and particularly the emancipated and dominant poor white trash, have never been investigated scientifically, and most of the current generalizations about them are probably wrong. For example, the generalization that they are purely Anglo-Saxon in blood. This I doubt very seriously. The chief strain down there, I believe, is Celtic rather than Saxon, particularly in the hill country. French blood, too, shows itself here and there, and so does Spanish, and so does German. . . . It is very likely that in some parts of the south a good many of the plebeian whites have more than a trace of negro blood. . . . But the Celtic strain is far more obvious than any of these others. It not only makes itself visible in physical stigmata—*e.g.*, leanness and dark coloring—but also in mental traits. For example, the religious thought of the south is almost precisely identical with the religious thought of Wales. There is the same naïve belief in an anthropomorphic Creator but little removed, in manner and desire, from an evangelical bishop; there is the same submission to an ignorant and impudent sacerdotal tyranny, and there is the same sharp contrast between doctrinal orthodoxy and private ethics. . . . The most booming sort of piety, in the south, is not incompatible with the theory that lynching is a benign institution. Two generations ago it was not incompatible with an ardent belief in slavery.

It is highly probable that some of the worst blood of western Europe flows in the veins of the southern poor whites, now poor no longer. . . .

Obviously, it is impossible for intelligence to flourish in such an atmosphere. Free inquiry is blocked by the idiotic certainties of ignorant men.

The arts, save in the lower reaches of the gospel hymn, the phonograph and the chautauqua harangue, are all held in suspicion. The tone of public opinion is set by an upstart class but lately emerged from industrial slavery into commercial enterprise—the class of "hustling" business men, of "live wires," of commercial club luminaries, of "drive" managers, of forward-lookers and right-thinkers—in brief, of third-rate southerners inoculated with all the worst traits of the Yankee sharper. One observes the curious effects of an old tradition of truculence upon a population now merely pushful and impudent, of an old tradition of chivalry upon a population now quite without imagination. The old repose is gone. The old romanticism is gone. The philistinism of the new type of town-boomer southerner is not only indifferent to the ideals of the old south; it is positively antagonistic to them. That philistinism regards human life, not as an agreeable adventure, but as a mere trial of rectitude and efficiency. It is overwhelmingly utilitarian and moral. It is inconceivably hollow and obnoxious. What remains of the ancient tradition is simply a certain charming civility in private inter-course—often broken down, alas, by the hot rages of Puritanism, but still generally visible. The southerner, at his worst, is never quite the surly cad that the Yankee is. His sensitiveness may betray him into occasional bad manners, but in the main he is a pleasant fellow—hospitable, polite, good-humored, even jovial. . . . But a bit absurd. . . . A bit pathetic.

Gerald Johnson on Critical Attitudes North and South, 1924

The fact of prime importance . . . is the existence in the South of a thought-ful minority capable of making the necessary allowance for human fallibility, and in the North and elsewhere of publicists interested in finding out and publishing the exact truth about the South. There is at this hour more willingness on the part of the rest of the country to give the South a fair hearing than has been manifest for three quarters of a century. There is a new realization that Southern problems are necessarily American problems, that Southern progress is American progress, and that complete under-standing of the South is essential to complete understanding of America. It is conceded that the South has a contribution to make to the spiritual and intellectual progress of the nation, and that the nation cannot hope to achieve its highest destiny without that contribution. America, at last, is ready to lend us her ears.

But shall she be required to lend us her tongue, also? It is nothing to wonder at that the South has hitherto been silent. In addition to her moral exile, she has been engaged for two generations in the task of reconstructing a shattered civilization. Although the oldest section of the country, she was thrown back, by the cataclysm of seventy years ago, to something ap-proximating frontier conditions, and the atmosphere of the frontier is no-

Gerald W. Johnson, "Critical Attitudes North and South," *Journal of Social Forces* 2 (May 1924), pp. 578–579.

toriously inclement to the arts, especially to the highly sophisticated art of criticism. When the house has been knocked down, and it is imperatively necessary to construct some sort of shelter for the family, one able-bodied hod-carrier is worth a platoon of interior decorators. Up to the beginning of the century the South literally was unable to spare from the more immediately necessary work of reconstruction a single man of sufficient mental calibre to make an effective critic.

Those desperate and laborious days are over now. The civilization of the South has been rebuilt, and stands stronger and firmer than ever before. At last we can afford to take time off to answer questions, and to question ourselves as to what we intend to do and how we propose to go about it. At last we can afford to listen to what the neighbors think of our work, to obtain suggestions from them as to its improvement, and to explain to them its good points.

But who is to speak for us? Heretofore we have depended upon bringing in an outsider, showing him over the place, and leaving it to him to explain it to the rest of the world. That method has proved unsatisfactory. The man may do his best, but it is out of the question for him to know as much about it as those who have watched it all their lives.

If the work of building the new South is to go forward to best advantage, the South must develop its own critics. They can criticise most effectively, in the first place because they have the Southern viewpoint, and can therefore be understood, and in the second place because they have the most reliable information, and therefore can most frequently spot the joints in Southern armor. For the same reasons they can best interpret the South to the rest of the nation.

But if they are to affect either the South or the outside world, they must be critics, not press-agents. Too much has been said of the South's need for "sympathetic" criticism. This demand has resulted in some so-called criticism that is sympathetic, not with the South, but with the South's least admirable traits, with bigotry, intolerance, superstition and prejudice. What the South needs is criticism that is ruthless toward those things— bitter towards them, furiously against them—and sympathetic only with its idealism, with its loyalty, with its courage and its inflexible determination. Such criticism will not be popular, for it is not in human nature to hold in warm affection the stern idealist who relentlessly exposes one's follies and frailties and continually appeals to one's better nature. But it will be respected and in the end admired. And above all, it will be effective.

The *Journal of Social Forces* has faith to believe that there are in the South men and women who are capable of producing such criticism, and it is the wish of the magazine to afford them a mouthpiece. This endeavor has been misinterpreted, of course, and doubtless will continue to be misinterpreted; but that is of small importance if the magazine can continue to find contributors who are able and willing to present the facts as they exist, and to interpret them in the light of Southern conditions, Southern history, and—if there is such a thing—of Southern psychology. It is too much to claim that the South has nothing of which it should be ashamed; if that were true it would be a terrestrial paradise. But the worst that can be said truthfully of the South is by no means so bad as to justify a conspiracy of silence concerning it, for if we deny our faults no one will believe us when we admit our virtues.

Nell Battle Lewis on Southern Customs and Dissent, 1926

To the Tainted Tar Heels

I thank the Lord that you were never able
To swallow down the patriotic pap,
But for the current local blah and fable
Cared something less, to toto, than a lap.
It is a comfort to me, recollection
That ballyhoo quite patently absurd
About the glories of your native section
Moved you to thumb your noses at the herd;
I'm proud you wouldn't let them do your thinking,
The noisy boys who set the styles in thought,
That, faced by facts which all the rest were blinking
You held opinions which you hadn't ought.
I sing the small, perverse minority
That died unsung, unpopular,—and free.

The Four Inch Shelf

The conventional Southern idea of the Negro is that of a shiftless, good-humored inferior still pretty close to the brutes. Good humor and light-heartedness are emphasized by most Southern whites as the Negro's outstanding characteristics. One of the most familiar figures in the plantation tradition,—still so influential in Southern thinking,—is that of the Negro as a funny-man. People who still hold this conventional view will not understand nor approve Paul Green's "Lonesome Road," a collection of six one-act plays for the Negro theatre published by McBride. Mr. Green presents the Negro not as a comic but a tragic figure, which, of course, essentially he is. Southerners like to think the Negro comic because it is much more comfortable to contemplate a comic semi-savage than a tragic human being, especially when your own race has contributed to the tragedy. That, I believe, is the basic psychology of the Southern white's conventional idea of the Negro.

Thomas Wolfe on Conformity, 1929

His feeling for the South was not so much historic as it was of the core and desire of dark romanticism—that unlimited and inexplicable drunkenness, the magnetism of some men's blood that takes them into the heart

Reprinted with permission of Charles Scribner's Sons, an imprint of Macmillan Publishing Company, from *Look Homeward, Angel* by Thomas Wolfe. Copyright 1929 by Charles Scribner's Sons; renewed © 1957 by Edward C. Ashwell, Administrator, C.T.A. and/or Fred W. Wolfe.

of the heat, and beyond that, into the polar and emerald cold of the South as swiftly as it took the heart of that incomparable romanticist who wrote *The Rime of the Ancient Mariner*, beyond which there is nothing. And this desire of his was unquestionably enhanced by all he had read and visioned, by the romantic halo that his school history cast over the section, by the whole fantastic distortion of that period where people were said to live in "mansions," and slavery was a benevolent institution, conducted to a constant banjo-strumming, the strewn largesses of the colonel and the shuffle-dance of his happy dependents, where all women were pure, gentle, and beautiful, all men chivalrous and brave, and the Rebel horde a company of swagger, death-mocking cavaliers. Years later, when he could no longer think of the barren spiritual wilderness, the hostile and murderous intrenchment against all new life—when their cheap mythology, their legend of the charm of their manner, the aristocratic culture of their lives, the quaint sweetness of their drawl, made him writhe—when he could think of no return to their life and its swarming superstition without weariness and horror, so great was his fear of the legend, his fear of their antagonism, that he still pretended the most fanatic devotion to them, excusing his Northern residence on grounds of necessity rather than desire.

Finally, it occurred to him that these people had given him nothing, that neither their love nor their hatred could injure him, that he owed them nothing, and he determined that he would say so, and repay their insolence with a curse. And he did. . . .

Leonard [Eugene Gant's neighbor] himself was not a bad man—he was a man of considerable character, kindliness, and honest determination. He loved his family, he stood up with some courage against the bigotry in the Methodist church, where he was a deacon, and at length had to withdraw because of his remarks on Darwin's theory. He was, thus, an example of that sad liberalism of the village—an advanced thinker among the Methodists, a bearer of the torch at noon, an apologist for the toleration of ideas that have been established for fifty years.

John Crowe Ransom Takes a Stand for the Agrarian Way of Life, 1930

Nobody now proposes for the South, or for any other community in this country, an independent political destiny. That idea is thought to have been finished in 1865. But how far shall the South surrender its moral, social, and economic autonomy to the victorious principle of Union? That question remains open. The South is a minority section that has hitherto been jealous of its minority right to live its own kind of life. The South scarcely hopes to determine the other sections, but it does propose to determine itself, within the utmost limits of legal action. Of late, however, there is the

From "Introduction" by John Crowe Ransom, from *I'll Take My Stand* by Twelve Southerners. Copyright 1930, © 1962 by Harper & Row Publishers, Inc. Reprinted by permission of Harper & Row Publishers, Inc.

melancholy fact that the South itself has wavered a little and shown signs of wanting to join up behind the common or American industrial ideal. . . . The younger Southerners, who are being converted frequently to the industrial gospel, must come back to the support of the Southern tradition. They must be persuaded to look very critically at the advantages of becoming a "new South" which will be only an undistinguished replica of the usual industrial community.

But there are many other minority communities opposed to industrialism, and wanting a much simpler economy to live by. The communities and private persons sharing the agrarian tastes are to be found widely within the Union. Proper living is a matter of the intelligence and the will, does not depend on the local climate or geography, and is capable of a definition which is general and not Southern at all. Southerners have a filial duty to discharge to their own section. But their cause is precarious and they must seek alliances with sympathetic communities everywhere. The members of the present group would be happy to be counted as members of a national agrarian movement.

Industrialism is the economic organization of the collective American society. It means the decision of society to invest its economic resources in the applied sciences. But the word science has acquired a certain sanctitude. It is out of order to quarrel with science in the abstract, or even with the applied sciences when their applications are made subject to criticism and intelligence. The capitalization of the applied sciences has now become extravagant and uncritical; it has enslaved our human energies to a degree now clearly felt to be burdensome. The apologists of industrialism do not like to meet this charge directly; so they often take refuge in saying that they are devoted simply to science! They are really devoted to the applied sciences and to practical production. Therefore it is necessary to employ a certain skepticism even at the expense of the Cult of Science, and to say, It is an Americanism, which looks innocent and disinterested, but really is not either.

The contribution that science can make to a labor is to render it easier by the help of a tool or a process, and to assure the laborer of his perfect economic security while he is engaged upon it. Then it can be performed with leisure and enjoyment. But the modern laborer has not exactly received this benefit under the industrial regime. His labor is hard, its tempo is fierce, and his employment is insecure. The first principle of a good labor is that it must be effective, but the second principle is that it must be enjoyed. Labor is one of the largest items in the human career; it is a modest demand to ask that it may partake of happiness.

The regular act of applied science is to introduce into labor a labor-saving device or a machine. Whether this is a benefit depends on how far it is advisable to save the labor. The philosophy of applied science is generally quite sure that the saving of labor is a pure gain, and that the more of it the better. This is to assume that labor is an evil, that only the end of labor or the material product is good. On this assumption labor becomes mercenary and servile, and it is no wonder if many forms of modern labor are accepted without resentment though they are evidently brutalizing. The act of labor as one of the happy functions of human life has been in effect abandoned, and is practiced solely for its rewards.

Even the apologists of industrialism have been obliged to admit that some economic evils follow in the wake of the machines. These are such as overproduction, unemployment, and a growing inequality in the distribution of wealth. But the remedies proposed by the apologists are always homeopathic. They expect the evils to disappear when we have bigger and better machines, and more of them. Their remedial programs, therefore, look forward to more industrialism. . . .

Religion can hardly expect to flourish in an industrial society. Religion is our submission to the general intention of a nature that is fairly inscrutable; it is the sense of our rôle as creatures within it. But nature industrialized, transformed into cities and artificial habitations, manufactured into commodities, is no longer nature but a highly simplified picture of nature. We receive the illusion of having power over nature, and lose the sense of nature as something mysterious and contingent. The God of nature under these conditions is merely an amiable expression, a superfluity, and the philosophical understanding ordinarily carried in the religious experience is not there for us to have.

Nor do the arts have a proper life under industrialism, with the general decay of sensibility which attends it. Art depends, in general, like religion, on a right attitude to nature; and in particular on a free and disinterested observation of nature that occurs only in leisure. Neither the creation nor the understanding of works of art is possible in an industrial age except by some local and unlikely suspension of the industrial drive.

The amenities of life also suffer under the curse of a strictly-business or industrial civilization. They consist in such practices as manners, conversation, hospitality, sympathy, family life, romantic love—in the social exchanges which reveal and develop sensibility in human affairs. If religion and the arts are founded on right relations of man-to-nature, these are founded on right relations of man-to-man.

Apologists of industrialism are even inclined to admit that its actual processes may have upon its victims the spiritual effects just described. But they think that all can be made right by extraordinary educational efforts, by all sorts of cultural institutions and endowments. They would cure the poverty of the contemporary spirit by hiring experts to instruct it in spite of itself in the historic culture. But salvation is hardly to be encountered on that road. The trouble with the life-pattern is to be located at its economic base, and we cannot rebuild it by pouring in soft materials from the top. The young men and women in colleges, for example, if they are already placed in a false way of life, cannot make more than an inconsequential acquaintance with the arts and humanities transmitted to them. Or else the understanding of these arts and humanities will but make them the more wretched in their own destitution. . . .

The tempo of the industrial life is fast, but that is not the worst of it; it is accelerating. The ideal is not merely some set form of industrialism, with so many stable industries, but industrial progress, or an incessant extension of industrialization. It never proposes a specific goal; it initiates the infinite series. We have not merely capitalized certain industries; we have capitalized the laboratories and inventors, and undertaken to employ all the labor-saving devices that come out of them. But a fresh labor-saving device introduced into an industry does not emancipate the laborers in that industry so much as it evicts them. Applied at the expense of agriculture, for example, the new processes have reduced the part of the population supporting itself upon the soil to a smaller and smaller fraction. Of course no single labor-saving process is fatal; it brings on a period of unemployed labor and unemployed capital, but soon a new industry is devised which will put them both to work again, and a new commodity is thrown upon the market. The laborers were sufficiently embarrassed in the meantime, but, according to the theory, they will eventually be taken care of. It is now the public which is embarrassed; it feels obligated to purchase a commodity for which it had expressed no desire, but it is invited to make its budget equal to the strain. All might yet be well, and stability and comfort might again obtain, but for this: partly because of industrial ambitions and partly because the repressed creative impulse must break out somewhere, there will be a stream of further labor-saving devices in all industries, and the cycle will have to be repeated over and over. The result is an increasing disadjustment and instability.

It is an inevitable consequence of industrial progress that production greatly outruns the rate of natural consumption. To overcome the disparity, the producers, disguised as the pure idealists of progress, must coerce and wheedle the public into being loyal and steady consumers, in order to keep the machines running. So the rise of modern advertising—along with its twin, personal salesmanship—is the most significant development of our industrialism. Advertising means to persuade the consumers to want exactly what the applied sciences are able to furnish them. It consults the happiness of the consumer no more than it consulted the happiness of the laborer. It is the great effort of a false economy of life to approve itself. But its task grows more difficult every day.

It is strange, of course, that a majority of men anywhere could ever as with one mind become enamored of industrialism: a system that has so little regard for individual wants. There is evidently a kind of thinking that rejoices in setting up a social objective which has no relation to the individual. Men are prepared to sacrifice their private dignity and happiness to an abstract social ideal, and without asking whether the social ideal produces the welfare of any individual man whatsoever. But this is absurd. The responsibility of men is for their own welfare and that of their neighbors; not for the hypothetical welfare of some fabulous creature called society.

Opposed to the industrial society is the agrarian, which does not stand in particular need of definition. An agrarian society is hardly one that has no use at all for industries, for professional vocations, for scholars and artists, and for the life of cities. Technically, perhaps, an agrarian society is one in which agriculture is the leading vocation, whether for wealth, for pleasure, or for prestige—a form of labor that is pursued with intelligence and leisure, and that becomes the model to which the other forms approach as well as they may. But an agrarian regime will be secured readily enough where the superfluous industries are not allowed to rise against it. The theory of agrarianism is that the culture of the soil is the best and most sensitive of vocations, and that therefore it should have the economic preference and enlist the maximum number of workers.

These principles do not intend to be very specific in proposing any practical measures. How may the little agrarian community resist the Chamber of Commerce of its county seat, which is always trying to import some foreign industry that cannot be assimilated to the life-pattern of the community? Just what must the Southern leaders do to defend the traditional Southern life? How may the Southern and the Western agrarians unite for effective action? Should the agrarian forces try to capture the Democratic party, which historically is so closely affiliated with the defense of individualism, the small community, the state, the South? Or must the agrarians—even the Southern ones—abandon the Democratic party to its fate and try a new one? What legislation could most profitably be championed by the powerful agrarians in the Senate of the United States? What anti-industrial measures might promise to stop the advances of industrialism, or even undo some of them, with the least harm to those concerned? What policy should be pursued by the educators who have a tradition at heart? These and many other questions are of the greatest importance, but they cannot be answered here.

For, in conclusion, this much is clear: If a community, or a section, or a race, or an age, is groaning under industrialism, and well aware that it is an evil dispensation, it must find the way to throw it off. To think that this cannot be done is pusillanimous. And if the whole community, section, race, or age thinks it cannot be done, then it has simply lost its political genius and doomed itself to impotence.

Howard W. Odum Analyzes the Agrarian Way of Life, 1936

Key to the Southeast is the agrarian South, old and new. This is true not only because of the economic and romantic aspects of the Old South, but because of more recent developments and the prospects for regional agricultural reconstruction. On the one hand, it is often assumed that the South is the most fertile field in the Union for agrarian recovery; and, on the other, it is known that internal agricultural readjustment is an irreducible minimum for survival on any adequate cultural basis. In addition to deficiency units in agricultural production and farm and home standards . . . there are certain other aspects of the agrarian heritage and promise which give definitive character to the region.

Inherent in its dynamic part in the region's past and future are the meanings and implications of agrarian culture. There was, of course, the

From *Southern Regions of the United States* by Howard W. Odum. © 1936 the University of North Carolina Press, pp. 55–67. Reprinted by permission.

spell of the old plantation economy, significant not only for its way of life but for its subsequent influence upon the tenant system and other aspects of cotton economy. To many, agrarianism means a trend back toward the glory that was the Old South. Yet the substance of the nostalgic yearnings of this particular group of agrarians is little more than this: the culture of the Old South, if it had been what it was purported to be, which it was not, would have constituted a magnificent contribution to a richer civilization; therefore, go to, let us turn back to that agrarian ideal as relief from the maladjusted industrialism of the new era. Manifestly, there is little realism here.

There remain, however, some aspects of this agrarian ideal which yet retain the motivation of agriculture as a way of life, to be adapted to a new equilibrium between rural and urban, between agricultural and industrial life. Here are included the ideals of those who, as Julia Peterkin points out, yearn for the peace and quiet of country places with leisure to possess their own souls and with abundance of things for the comfort of minds and bodies. "To realize the earth's generosity to those who have joy in sowing and reaping," so runs the theme, "gives a deep sense of security and a faith in the rightness of things." For such an ideal the Southeast is peculiarly well equipped by nature and awaits that new planning which will transvaluate the poverty-breeding system of tenant and landlord into that abundant life so pictured.

Another meaning is that which sets the agricultural economy simply but clearly over against industrialism. This envisages the imbalance between country life and urban trends and their contrasting character of life and labor. Such an ideal, however, allows liberally for suitable industrial development, decentralized and featuring the coördination of small industries and village industrial centers with small-scale farming. It allows for new developments in subsistence farming and in the great natural increase of basic consumption of farm commodities. The new agrarian culture, furthermore, is fabricated upon the assumption of reasonable advances in rural electrification, good roads, and ample tools and facilities for richer living. Here again the Southeast excels in its natural equipment and awaits only the technics of a new day.

The most realistic implication of the agrarian South, however, is found in the actual picture of the present Southeast. After all, the region is primarily rural, constituting in area almost the whole landscape; in people, three-fourths and more of the population, either in actuality or in experience and interest. The region ranks second only to the great agricultural Middle States in composite measure of its commodity production. Moreover, the Southeast receives more than 25 per cent of its income from agriculture as opposed to about 12.5 per cent for the nation. Its percentage of gainfully employed in extractive work, 45.7, is the highest of any region, as is its ratio of farm population to the total. The burden and implications of agrarianism include further the processes of change and conflict reflected in a heavy migration cityward and the whole recent decade of country life bankruptcy. Likewise, part of the agrarian problem is that of attaining an

enduring balance between rural and urban civilization. A part is the reconstruction of cotton economy. A part is the problem of securing the
southeastern farmer in a normal procedure whereby he adapts his crops to
climate, soil, transportation, human-use requirements, rather than primarily
to a colonial, commercial agriculture. A part is the marginal standard of
living and housing of five millions of the region's rural folk; a part is the
prospect of a new sort of American peasantry. In fine and in sum, the
agrarian problem is *the region,* for better or for worse, and the agrarian
statecraft which is involved. . . .

This preëminently rural Southeast enumerates a larger number of farm
families than any other region of the nation. Of the 6,266,000 odd farms in
the United States, the Southeast has 2,380,000 compared with the other
regions: in round numbers the Far West, 265,000; the Northwest, 648,000;
the Northeast, 618,000; the Southwest, 744,000; and the Middle States,
1,622,000. Mississippi alone has a larger number of farms than all of the
great agricultural Far West. The Southeast is different, among other respects, in having the lowest average acreage per farm; namely, 71 acres.
Mississippi averages only 53 acres per farm. A similar small farm division
is found in the other "plantation states"; in Louisiana where the average
size is scarcely 58 acres; in Arkansas, only 66; and in Alabama, only 68.
For the whole Southeast nearly 80 per cent of the total farms are under
100 acres and less than one per cent over 500 acres. Moreover, the size
of these farms has been steadily decreasing since 1900. And before that
time the break-up of the plantation system into small farms constituted an
unprecedented revolution in the economic and cultural ways of the region.

The visible ends of this revolution have been manifest primarily in
cotton economy, which is the most dominant and definitive factor of all
the region's agrarian culture. Basic to any adequate regional analysis and
reconstruction are the understanding and mastery of this situation. First of
all, there is the dominance over all other crops of cotton culture in eight
cotton states, including Oklahoma and Texas of the Southwest, with conflicting patterns of production, harvesting, marketing. The Southeast produces nearly 60 per cent and the Southwest nearly 40 per cent of the nation's
annual cotton crop, which ranges from 12,500,000 to 17,000,000 bales, with
the Southwest's meteor-like rise within the last few decades. Of this crop
in 1932–33, 66.2 per cent was exported. And of the 24,800,000 bales world
consumption of the same year, 58.2 per cent was American grown. Furthermore, this raw cotton constitutes about a fifth of the total exports of
the United States.

In the production of this gigantic cash-crop commodity more than half
of all the crop land of the region involved is utilized at one time or another.
There are, moreover, in these states more than 2,000,000 cotton farm families or nearly a third of all the farm families in the nation. Furthermore,
half of the people and more depend for their cash income upon cotton and
its related economy, which in turn is a hard master over the whole human
culture of the region. For one thing, over half of these farmer families are
tenants and their number and ratio are increasing, white tenancy increasing

faster than Negro. In some of the subregions of the Southeast the proportion of tenants is much larger. Thus, in the Delta it is 90 per cent; in the Red River Bottoms it is 80 per cent; in the Bluffs it is 75 per cent; in the Black Belt, 73; in the Cotton Piedmont, 64; in the Interior Plain, 61; in Southern Cotton and Tobacco, 60. In at least ten of the subregions white tenancy averages more than 50 per cent.

The Negro tenant constitutes a special aspect of this agrarian situation, although in many ways he may play a quite different rôle from that commonly assumed. The Negro tenant numbers at least a quarter million fewer than the whites, and during the last decade his number actually decreased, while white tenants increased nearly a quarter million. In certain subregions of the Southeast, however, the concentration of Negro tenancy still constitutes a more acute problem than in others. Thus, the Delta shows 95 per cent Negro tenancy; the Red River Bottoms, 89; the Black Belt, 88; the Bluffs, 86; the Cotton Piedmont, 85; the Interior Plain, 79; and the semitropical, Interior Ridge, both the southern and northern Cotton and Tobacco, more than 70 per cent. The increase of tobacco growing has accentuated the trends toward tenancy, giving the region two major money crops especially suited to tenant cropping instead of one. The size of this factor is indicated by the fact that of the 1,600,000,000 pounds of the American weed grown annually the Southeastern States account for 85 per cent.

The picture of the cotton-tobacco agrarian South may almost be described as a landscape of dilemmas. The tenant type bordering on poverty and hopelessness is only one. . . . The instability that comes from great mobility and lack of purpose on the part of millions of citizens is another problem. Disgracefully low standards of housing follow a logical shiftlessness and irresponsibility. Instability of prices and income, speculation and tragedy of lost fortunes, lack of capital for efficient farm management and machinery, the low standard of wages due partly to the Negro, the debtor character of the southern economy—these and others cry out for a more adequate analysis and long-time planning.

The region's dilemmas are increased by the falling off of exports and the trend toward economic nationalism. Sixty per cent of the cotton and perhaps a fourth of the tobacco grown are normally exported. This falling off of exports itself offers multiple dilemmas. It may deprive the South of its place in the world markets. It will certainly throw the South back into intolerable deficiency of income, throwing a million and a half farm families tragically out of gear and forfeiting millions of dollars in equipment and good will. On the other hand, if there should be maximization of exports and domestic demand, the South will resort to new highs in production and consequent drain of land and people, slaves to the one-crop system. There is, moreover, the dilemma of ineffective competition with southwestern cotton culture, or inventions which may make cotton less exclusively necessary for world markets. Still other dilemmas envisage a better machine cultivation and harvesting which will throw millions out of employment and the spectacle of an already over-populated rural cotton South unable to absorb any of the stranded folk set free from city and industry. To these are added the great agrarian discontent, partly due to the cumulative plight of the depression years with the cotton farmer's few dollars worth about 42 cents each, and none left to pay taxes, debts, and interest, or to recoup his depreciated tools and buildings.

What then is the picture and the promise of the agricultural South in the production of other commodities? First of all, the inventory of its natural resources presented justifies the conclusion that the region now featuring commercial farming in a sort of continuing colonial policy is peculiarly well adapted to a more balanced agriculture in subsistence and self-sufficing economy. In the meantime, here is the Southeast's quota of the nation's major farm commodities: wheat, less than 2 per cent; corn, about 15 per cent; beef cattle, nearly 12 per cent; milk, about 12 per cent; butter, about 13 per cent; eggs, about 15 per cent; hay, not quite 8 per cent. The Southeast's ratio of vegetables, exclusive of potatoes, nearly 20 per cent; cabbage, cantaloupes, and onions, nearly 10 per cent; white and sweet potatoes, nearly 23 per cent. The ratio of fruits: apples, peaches, and pears, about 18 per cent; grapes and strawberries, about 5 per cent; oranges and grape fruit, about 43 per cent. The corresponding ratio of farm animals: sheep and lambs, about 4 per cent; horses and colts, nearly 9 per cent; mules and mule colts, 52 per cent; milk cows and heifers, nearly 16 per cent; all cattle and calves, 13 per cent; hogs and pigs, 15 per cent.

Set over against these is the Southeast's 85 per cent of all tobacco production; 60 per cent of cotton, yielding recently to the great Southwest's nearly 38 per cent. In contrast to this abundance of cotton and tobacco are the scarcity of special commodities necessary for health and vitality and for balancing the agricultural program of seasonal work, land conservation and enrichment, and seasonal stability. Thus, the production requirement deficit in eggs for the Southeastern States shows an increase of from 90 per cent in Virginia to 374 per cent in South Carolina needed to meet reasonable standards. The other greatest deficits are found in the states listed below as requiring the following percentage of increase necessary for meeting the minimum dietary standards: Florida, 341; Georgia, 313; Louisiana, 302; North Carolina, 250.

The situation with reference to dairy products merits special treatment in view of not only the production-requirement deficits but also because of the relation to the whole program of balanced agriculture. Some of the deficiencies and problems have already been noted. The production requirement is met in only the state of Kentucky with the other states requiring percentages of increase from 30 per cent for Tennessee to 403 for Florida. The other four low states are Louisiana, 224; South Carolina, 198; North Carolina, 139; Georgia, 130. The minimum dietary requirements for the whole Southeast may be set at 2,450,000,000 gallons, of which there is a production deficit of no less than 1,161,455,000, which is more than a tenth of the nation's total milk production. Thus the deficit must be made up at home.

Some of the explanations of this deficit will indicate also the practicability of reconstructing the whole dairy industry such that within so short a time as ten years the whole region can be remade. Thus, only 62 per cent of all farms in the Southeast reported cows milked and the average number of gallons per animal was only 394 as compared with 618 for the Northeast, 638 for the Far West, and 530 for the Middle States. So, too, the number of purebred cattle per farm is less than one per cent as compared with 28 per cent for the nation. Furthermore, the low ratio of pasture land, the excellent conditions for dairying and other factors make it clear that the problem presents no insurmountable obstacles, but requires special emphasis upon initiating, financing, and management. Yet the fact that one answer to the question often asked as to why millions of southern folk working on the richest land in the world are living on standards close to the margin of slow starvation and deterioration may be found in this deficit of dairy products, eggs, and vegetables, indicates the critical nature of this phase of southern agrarian life.

The place of commercial fertilizer as a leading factor in human culture also deserves a special twofold appraisal. One is the quantitative problem and the other is its relation to the whole farm economy of the region. Both are fundamental. First, as to the size of the fertilizer bill, the Southeast, cultivating barely a sixth of all crop lands harvested in the United States, uses two-thirds of the total national tonnage of commercial fertilizer. The Southeast, accounting for a fifth of the agricultural income, expends three-fifths of the fertilizer bill. Further comparison with other regions shows that although the Far West, the Northwest, and the Southwest account for nearly 50 per cent of all crop land and nearly 40 per cent of all agricultural income, they account for only five per cent of the total fertilizer tonnage. Furthermore, the Southeast spends more than seven per cent of its gross income for fertilizer as compared with less than one per cent for the Northwest and Southwest and only one per cent for the Middle States. In costs for farm operation, the Southeast shows a still greater preponderance with 41 per cent for fertilizer, 27 per cent for feed, and 32 per cent for labor as contrasted with the great Middle States farming areas of 6 per cent for fertilizer, 51 per cent for feed, and 42 per cent for labor; or contrasted with the Southwest with less than 4 per cent for fertilizer, 36 per cent for feed, and 60 per cent for labor. Thus, exclusive of debt service and taxes, the fertilizer bill amounts to nearly a half of the base cost of operation for southeastern agriculture, and has nearly four times the importance as for the Northeast, seven times as for the Middle States, and about 150 times that of the Northwest.

The significance of this to the cultural region is manifold. In the first place, this tremendous expenditure is not reflected in crop yields except in relation to commercial crops of cotton and tobacco, and, even with these, they have a very special significance in comparison with southwestern culture of cotton, where, with little fertilizer, yields are far greater than on millions of acres of run-down land in the Southeast. The southeastern yield for corn is only 15 bushels per acre compared to 43 for the Northeast, 36 for the Middle States, and 28 for the nation. Similar comparison for other crops and for fruits and vegetables mark striking contrasts to other regions and indicate the relation of fertilizer, not only to the past development of the Southeast, but to any adequate reconstruction which departs from the present commercial-colonial policy supported by the tenancy system.

Richard Wright on the Place of Blacks, 1937

"What grade are you in school?"

"Seventh, ma'am."

"Then why are you going to school?" she asked in surprise.

"Well, I want to be a writer," I mumbled, unsure of myself; I had not planned to tell her that, but she had made me feel so utterly wrong and of no account that I needed to bolster myself.

"A what?" she demanded.

"A writer," I mumbled.

"For what?"

"To write stories," I mumbled defensively.

"You'll never be a writer," she said. "Who on earth put such ideas into your nigger head?"

"Nobody," I said.

"I didn't think anybody ever would," she declared indignantly. . . .

A few days later my classmates came to me with baffled eyes, holding copies of the *Southern Register* in their hands.

"Did you really write that story?" they asked me.

"Yes."

"Why?"

"Because I wanted to."

"Where did you get it from?"

"I made it up."

"You didn't. You copied it out of a book."

"If I had, no one would publish it."

"But what are they publishing it for?"

"So people can read it."

"Who told you to do that?"

"Nobody."

"Then why did you do it?"

"Because I wanted to," I said again.

They were convinced that I had not told them the truth. We had never had any instruction in literary matters at school; the literature of the nation or the Negro had never been mentioned. My schoolmates could not understand why anyone would want to write a story; and, above all, they could not understand why I had called it *The Voodoo of Hell's Half-Acre*. The mood out of which a story was written was the most alien thing conceivable to them. They looked at me with new eyes, and a distance, a

---

From *Black Boy* by Richard Wright. Used by permission of Madame Ellen Wright.

suspiciousness came between us. If I had thought anything in writing the story, I had thought that perhaps it would make me more acceptable to them, and now it was cutting me off from them more completely than ever.

At home the effects were no less disturbing. Granny came into my room early one morning and sat on the edge of my bed.

"Richard, what is this you're putting in the papers?" she asked.

"A story," I said.

"About what?"

"It's just a story, granny."

"But they tell me it's been in three times."

"It's the same story. It's in three parts."

"But what is it about?" she insisted.

I hedged, fearful of getting into a religious argument.

"It's just a story I made up," I said.

"Then it's a lie," she said.

"Oh, Christ," I said.

"You must get out of this house if you take the name of the Lord in vain," she said.

"Granny, please . . . I'm sorry," I pleaded. "But it's hard to tell you about the story. You see, granny, everybody knows that the story isn't true, but . . ."

"Then why write it?" she asked.

"Because people might want to read it."

"That's the Devil's work," she said and left.

My mother also was worried.

"Son, you ought to be more serious," she said. "You're growing up now and you won't be able to get jobs if you let people think that you're weak-minded. Suppose the superintendent of schools would ask you to teach here in Jackson, and he found out that you had been writing stories?"

I could not answer her.

"I'll be all right, mama," I said.

Uncle Tom, though surprised, was highly critical and contemptuous. The story had no point, he said. And whoever heard of a story by the title of *The Voodoo of Hell's Half-Acre*? Aunt Addie said that it was a sin for anyone to use the word "hell" and that what was wrong with me was that I had nobody to guide me. She blamed the whole thing upon my upbringing.

In the end I was so angry that I refused to talk about the story. From no quarter, with the exception of the Negro newspaper editor, had there come a single encouraging word. It was rumored that the principal wanted to know why I had used the word "hell." I felt that I had committed a crime. Had I been conscious of the full extent to which I was pushing against the current of my environment, I would have been frightened altogether out of my attempts at writing. But my reactions were limited to the attitude of the people about me, and I did not speculate or generalize. . . .

I was building up in me a dream which the entire educational system of the South had been rigged to stifle. I was feeling the very thing that the state of Mississippi had spent millions of dollars to make sure that I would never feel; I was becoming aware of the thing that the Jim Crow laws had been drafted and passed to keep out of my consciousness; I was acting on impulses that southern senators in the nation's capital had striven to keep out of Negro life; I was beginning to dream the dreams that the state had said were wrong, that the schools had said were taboo.

Had I been articulate about my ultimate aspirations, no doubt someone would have told me what I was bargaining for; but nobody seemed to know, and least of all did I. My classmates felt that I was doing something that was vaguely wrong, but they did not know how to express it. As the outside world grew more meaningful, I became more concerned, tense; and my classmates and my teachers would say: "Why do you ask so many questions?" Or: "Keep quiet."

I was in my fifteenth year; in terms of schooling I was far behind the average youth of the nation, but I did not know that. In me was shaping a yearning for a kind of consciousness, a mode of being that the way of life about me had said could not be, must not be, and upon which the penalty of death had been placed. Somewhere in the dead of the southern night my life had switched onto the wrong track and, without my knowing it, the locomotive of my heart was rushing down a dangerously steep slope, heading for a collision, heedless of the warning red lights that blinked all about me, the sirens and the bells and the screams that filled the air. . . .

The white South said that it knew "niggers," and I was what the white South called a "nigger." Well, the white South had never known me— never known what I thought, what I felt. The white South said that I had a "place" in life. Well, I had never felt my "place"; or, rather, my deepest instincts had always made me reject the "place" to which the white South had assigned me. It had never occurred to me that I was in any way an inferior being. And no word that I had ever heard fall from the lips of southern white men had ever made. me really doubt the worth of my own humanity. True, I had lied. I had stolen. I had struggled to contain my seething anger. I had fought. And it was perhaps a mere accident that I had never killed . . . But in what other ways had the South allowed me to be natural, to be real, to be myself, except in rejection, rebellion, and aggression?

Not only had the southern whites not known me, but, more important still, as I had lived in the South I had not had the chance to learn who I was. The pressure of southern living kept me from being the kind of person that I might have been. I had been what my surroundings had demanded, what my family—conforming to the dictates of the whites above them— had exacted of me, and what the whites had said that I must be. Never being fully able to be myself, I had slowly learned that the South could recognize but a part of a man, could accept but a fragment of his personality, and all the rest—the best and deepest things of heart and mind—were tossed away in blind ignorance and hate.

I was leaving the South to fling myself into the unknown, to meet other situations that would perhaps elicit from me other responses. And if I could meet enough of a different life, then, perhaps, gradually and slowly I might learn who I was, what I might be. I was not leaving the South to forget the South, but so that some day I might understand it, might come to know what its rigors had done to me, to its children. I fled so that the numbness of my defensive living might thaw out and let me feel the pain—years later and far away—of what living in the South had meant.

Yet, deep down, I knew that I could never really leave the South, for my feelings had already been formed by the South, for there had been slowly instilled into my personality and consciousness, black though I was, the culture of the South. So, in leaving, I was taking a part of the South to transplant in alien soil, to see if it could grow differently, if it could drink of new and cool rains, bend in strange winds, respond to the warmth of other suns, and, perhaps, to bloom . . . And if that miracle ever happened, then I would know that there was yet hope in that southern swamp of despair and violence, that light could emerge even out of the blackest of the southern night. I would know that the South too could overcome its fear, its hate, its cowardice, its heritage of guilt and blood, its burden of anxiety and compulsive cruelty.

✠ E S S A Y S

In the opening essay, C. Vann Woodward of Yale University explores the various theories accounting for the southern literary renaissance and finds problems with each. Richard H. King, a professor of history at the University of Nottingham, England, takes Woodward's essay as his base and expands the definition of the renaissance to include social science and journalistic efforts. King asserts that the key to understanding the cultural awakening and its participants lies in examining how the writers perceived and dealt with the past. The final essay, by historian George B. Tindall of the University of North Carolina, Chapel Hill, summarizes the early cultural contributions of the era, especially in the context of Mencken's remarks to the contrary.

The Difficulty of Explaining the Southern Renaissance

C. VANN WOODWARD

Why the Southern Renaissance ever occurred is still something of a mystery. All that is attempted here is an analysis of some explanations that have been offered by others and a few additional speculations. Before turning to the critical *why,* however, it is necessary to determine just what it is we are talking about. In the first place, we are stuck with a misnomer in the very word "renaissance." For neither in its literal sense nor in its classic historical usage is this French word really applicable to what happened in the South. As for the literal meaning when applied to that phe-

C. Vann Woodward, "Why the Southern Renaissance?", *Virginia Quarterly Review* 51 (Spring 1975), pp. 222–239. Used with permission of the publisher.

nomenon, Allen Tate has observed that "it was more precisely a birth, not a rebirth." Certainly nothing comparable had happened before in the South that could conceivably be said to have been reborn in the twentieth century. The second and more common historical usage of "renaissance" is the one to describe the evocation of the ghost of a dead civilization, as the ghost of Hellenic culture was evoked in thirteenth to fifteenth-century Italy. And surely nothing of that sort took place in the South. Nevertheless, we are stuck with this misnomer and will continue to use it. It has been applied with comparable looseness to New England in the early nineteenth century and by F. O. Matthiessen to Northern letters in the 1850's.

In continuing to apply the word "renaissance" to the twentieth-century Southern phenomenon it is well to remember that the movement was pretty strictly limited to the literary arts—poetry, fiction, and drama. It did not spill over to any significant degree to the visual or performing arts. There was no Southern Renaissance in music, painting, sculpture, or architecture, so far as I am aware. To turn H. L. Mencken's famous quip in "The Sahara of the Bozart" upside down, one could say that an oboe player or a drypoint etcher was much rarer than a poet down there at a time when poets—to use another Menckenism—had become as common as evangelists or snake-oil salesmen.

Assuming agreement, therefore, that our subject is confined to an explosion of literary productivity, the next question is *what* literary products we are talking about. There is no doubt whatever that Southern writers were remarkably active in this period, that the presses roared with their products, and that hucksters sold some of them by the millions. With their special regard for numbers, the sociologists have come forward with a sort of quantification of the Renaissance. Howard Odum estimated that in the first half of the twentieth century Southern writers turned out no fewer than five thousand titles of what he described as "full-sized-book literature." Classifying half of these as "literature in the traditional sense," he broke these down into 1,000 volumes of fiction, 500 of biography, 400 of poetry, 125 of drama, and threw in 800 volumes on history and 800 on Negro life for good measure. Not content with purely quantitative standards, he ventured into what he called "the qualitative measure" by pointing out that "Pulitzer awards have been made to Southern authors in more than half of the years since the first awards in 1917" and that "of the eleven best sellers that have exceeded or approximated a million copies, ten were by Southern authors."

We immediately run into difficulties with the quantitative standard, however, when we discover that "the most widely read American writer of the twentieth century" was Erskine Caldwell, that one of his works sold more than 6,500,000 copies and six others more than 2,000,000 copies each. And this at a time when all of William Faulkner's novels save "Sanctuary" had gone out of print. Clearly there is something misleading about market figures in this field. The case for them is not very much improved by a literary critic who has compiled a list of some 700 so-called "Renaissance authors" of "book-length volumes which have been issued by reputable publishers of more than local prestige.'' He even apologizes for inadvertent omissions. One trouble is that in scanning the columns of this list state by state compiled ten years ago one so rarely runs across a recognizable name. If we are not talking in terms of millions of books or hundreds of authors, then in just what terms are we talking? Briefly, the answer is, in much smaller terms.

When Allen Tate was pressed to ''invoke certain names'' a decade ago he said that ''if the Elizabethan Age would still be the glory of English literature without Shakespeare, the new literature of the Southern states would still be formidable without Faulkner.'' He then suggested in support of that view the names of twenty additional writers. How that list will stand up after another fifty or a hundred or three hundred and fifty years one cannot know. About some of the names there is already dispute among critics. But if as many as ten remained undisputed by the end of the century and as many as three after another century, that would still constitute a formidable record indeed—a phenomenon worthy of comparison with distinguished periods in Western literary history.

If this suggests the scope of the phenomenon, it remains to agree roughly on the time of its appearance and its duration. It is sometimes said to have taken place between the two world wars. There would probably be less difficulty agreeing about its beginnings than its endings. Some of the major figures are still alive and still productive, while some of the younger writers may not yet have reached their full stature. It is generally agreed that the Renaissance began in the 1920's, though there is some dispute about just how early in that decade.

I like to think of the year 1929 and those immediately following as specially significant. In 1929 appeared Faulkner's ''Sartoris'' and ''The Sound and the Fury'' and within three years ''As I Lay Dying,'' ''Sanctuary,'' and ''Light in August''—all with blinding suddenness and little comprehension from critics or public. In 1929 came Thomas Wolfe's first novel, ''Look Homeward, Angel'' and first books by Robert Penn Warren and Merrill Moore. Katherine Anne Porter's first book ''Flowering Judas'' came in 1930 and on its heels followed the first books of Caroline Gordon, Andrew Nelson Lytle, and Lillian Hellman. Tate, Ransom, and Davidson had already published. A second generation of authors was already in the wings and a third one was to come. Together they dominated the literary scene in America for three, perhaps four, decades. Their influence fluctuated over that period, as did individual productivity, and full recognition of the stature of some was slow in coming. But the dramatic suddenness of the coming was unmatched by any previous burst of creative literature in American history. . . .

Turning to the question of *why* one should remember first how crude and inappropriate for the task at hand are the instruments of the historian. Typically history deals with groups rather than individuals—with nations, classes, political parties, governments, industries, interests. True, writers may be described as a group, but their significant acts, motives, purposes, values, habits, and achievements at the level we are talking about are highly individual. I have rarely met one who could give me a coherent account of what made him tick—much less a convincing account of his peers. His is a lonely trade. The only important thing he does in his whole life, so far as we are concerned, he does alone in a room by himself, quite unobserved. The task of explaining and understanding him is better suited to the skills of the biographer or the psychologist than to those of a historian.

Those historical forces the historian deals with in writing of wars, revolution, religious and ideological conflicts, and movements like industrialization and urbanization are ill adapted to fathoming the mysteries of human mind in its rare moments of high creativity. It is important to remember that we are dealing here not with thousands of people or hundreds, but with a mere handful—fewer than one in a million. And remember too that they are scattered over a vast area, in villages, towns, cities, or remote country places. Their formative years are behind them before they meet each other. They may congregate briefly in Nashville, Charleston, Richmond, or New Orleans in small numbers, but what they do in common is of less significance than what they do alone. And the important shaping influence on the writer's art may not be his daily drinking companion in Nashville or New Orleans but a man he has never met in Dublin or Rome or for that matter in sixteenth-century London or thirteenth-century Florence.

Some skepticism is advisable toward historians who are willing to tell you just why it was that Sophocles, Aeschylus, and Euripides appeared in fifth-century Athens, or a handful of poets suddenly got active in second-century Rome, or a Dante and a Petrarch turned up in Italy when they did. . . .

First, to dispose of a few explanatory hypotheses that will not take much time. They are predominantly sociological in character and seek to correlate the Renaissance with various social changes in the South. Among the social variables that have been suggested are increasing prosperity, the industrial revolution, the rise of cities, the "leaven of liberalism," changing attitudes toward the Negro, and a transfusion of "new blood" from the North. Were I an impatient man—and such hypotheses certainly provoke impatience—I would simply say "nonsense" and pass on. But I am an academician indoctrinated with the creed that sociologists (and historians who imbibe their theories) like other disciplines must be treated with due respect and their arguments patiently answered.

In the first place the Renaissance was a depression phenomenon and if correlated with any social condition it was certainly not prosperity. Secondly, both industries and cities had been growing at a desultory rate for several decades without producing any literary phenomenon of this sort, and when cities and industries really did start booming in the forties and fifties they produced no discernible effect on literary output. Thirdly, if the major literary figures can be tagged with any ideological identification (and I am reluctant to do so), it was not liberalism. If there were any appreciable change in attitudes toward the Negro in the twenties and thirties, the two major Negro figures in the Southern Renaissance, Richard Wright and Ralph

Ellison, failed to note such change. And, incidentally, in the period since such changes in racial attitudes *have* occurred, no black author in the South has attained the stature of Wright or Ellison. And finally, whatever "new blood" came South, it is distinctly old blood that we are dealing with here.

Donald Davidson, among others, has taken particular delight in making paradoxes out of the sociological determinants. Pointing out that "By every cultural standard that the sociologist knows how to devise, Mississippi rates low in the national scale during William Faulkner's formative period," Davidson challenges the sociologists to explain why Faulkner "or some novelist of comparable stature, did not appear, during this period, somewhere north of the Ohio—say in Massachusetts or Wisconsin." He goes on to say that in view of the "extremely forbidding" and backward condition of Mississippi in that period he "can hardly see how Mr. Faulkner survived, much less wrote novels," and that in view of reliable sociological evidence "a William Faulkner in Mississippi would be a theoretical impossibility" and "would have to originate in, say, Massachusetts, where the cultural factors were favorable to literary interests." Allen Tate has taken the argument a step further by expressing his "paradoxical conviction . . . that the very backwardness of Mississippi, and of the South as a whole, might partially explain the rise of the new literature. . . ."

It is now time to turn to theories of more substance. One of these is the theory that the basic impulse behind the sudden release of Southern literary creativity, the "cause" if you prefer that tricky word, was profoundly defensive—an urge to defend the native region from unjust attack and repel the invasion of alien values. This theory had perhaps its most explicit formulation from W. J. Cash, who called it "the decisive factor." As he put it, "the outburst proceeded fundamentally from, and represented basically the patriotic response of men of talent to, the absorbing need of the South to defend itself, to shore up its pride at home, and to justify itself before the world." Since this theory, or some variation on it, has also received support from some of the major Southern men of letters, it cannot be dismissed out of hand and must be weighed with care. . . .

Two things about this assault of South-baiters complicate the problem. One is simply the substantial amount of truth in it. That is precisely what constitutes the main mystery of the sudden flowering of literature in such a desert. In the second place, one difficulty about explaining that phenomenon as a defensive reaction to the assult is the initial response of many of the alleged defenders. The fact is that many of them joined the assault. As Cash himself remarks, "baiting the South in [the American Mercury's] pages was one of the favorite sports of young Southerners of literary and intellectual pretensions." It was the surest way of establishing one's credentials, of shaking off the abhorred stigma of provincialism. Sufficient stridency about the boobs and yokels below the Potomac might even overcome the handicap of a young Southerner's tell-tale accent during visits to New York.

The most curious manifestation of this foible was its outcropping among those who later became the most militant defenders of the South. In fact, Mencken is said to have "long been an ideal of the literary young men at

Vanderbilt" and that "even Tate went around with Mencken under his arm." In 1925 young Tate, a temporary exile in New York, published in the Nation an essay he called "Last Days of the Charming Lady," in which he declared that the Southerner "does not inherit . . . a native culture compounded of the strength and subtlety of his New England contemporary" and that an "essential" Southern literature was made impossible by the inability of Southerners to repudiate "outmoded general notions which have lost their roots in an existing reality" and consequently had "no tradition of ideas, no consciousness of moral and spiritual values." About the same time his friend Donald Davidson despaired of finding "a single Southern writer of merit who in his thinking and manner of expression is as clearly of the South as Robert Frost is of New England." Southerners felt that "the gallantries of the Lost Cause, the legends of a gracious aristocracy, the stalwart traditions of Southern history" had been "mouthed over and cheapened." They felt homeless between the abhorred slogans of "New South" and "the treacly lamentation of the old school." John Crowe Ransom declared that "If there is a significance in the title of the magazine [The Fugitive], it lies perhaps in the sentiment of the editors (on this point I am sure we all agree) to flee from the extremes of conventionalism, whether old or new." And in the preface to the first number of that journal he wrote, "The Fugitive flees from nothing faster than the high-caste Brahmins of the Old South."

The turning point for these three and for others of the Nashville group came in 1925 with the trial of Scopes at Dayton, Tennessee, for the violation of the state law against teaching evolution. This brought the whole tribe of South-baiters, boob-jeerers, and yokel-tormentors led by Mencken himself to Nashville's doorstep. From there they broadcast their mockery of the moronic idiocy of the Southern boobs. It was too much for the Nash-villians and then and there they "took their stand." Tate declared, "I've attacked the South for the last time" except in so far as it has produced the "New South." Davidson replied that he was "delighted at your own annunciation of the True Southern Spirit," and Ransom rallied to the colors. Dayton "broke in upon our literary concerns like a midnight alarm," wrote Davidson. To him it seemed that a " 'cold Civil War' began from about that moment . . . a long sustained bombardment. . . . We were religious bigots. We were Ku Kluxers. We were lynchers. We had hookworm, we had pellagra, we had sharecroppers, we had poll taxes, we had poor whites, we had fundamentalists. We did not have enough schools . . . paved roads . . . skyscrapers . . . modern plumbing. . . . Our women were too hoity-toity about ancestors. Our men all chawed tobacco or drank mint juleps and sometimes did both." It seemed to him incredible "that nobody in the South knew how to reply to a vulgar rhetorician like H. L. Mencken," and that "no real defense was being made," that "a kind of wholesale surrender was in progress," and that "the Trojan Horse of liberalism had disgorged a horde of social scientists" within the walls.

Avoiding the discredited strategy of the late Confederates, the Nash-villians decided promptly that the best defensive was an offensive and assumed the aggressive posture from the start. Taking their native South as "the best available existing model of the traditional society," they professed to set it in contrast "with the giant industrialism, anti-traditional in all its features, that had possessed the North" and was making inroads into their own region. "In championing this South," wrote Davidson, "we were abandoning the defensive attitude of the nineteenth-century South" of Henry Grady "and the servile collaborationism of the modern Southern liberals. For the first time since Lee's invasion of Pennsylvania in 1863 we were taking the South into an offensive movement. We were attacking not retreating. But this time it was an intellectual offensive, executed at the highest level and in the broadest terms we could command." . . .

There were really very few active participants, and of the Twelve Southerners who took part in their major manifesto, "I'll Take My Stand," in 1930, only five, Ransom, Tate, Davidson, Warren, and Andrew Nelson Lytle could be said to have figured in an important way in the literary Renaissance. Other prominent Southern writers of no connection with the Nashville group were no doubt influenced and excited by some of their ideas. The very posture of cultural defiance and independence, coming as it did on the heels of the Panic of 1929 and accompanying the deflation of industrial pretensions, suffused among many Southerners a new mood of release and autonomy from dominant national values. As Davidson wrote Tate in late October, 1929, "The terrific industrial 'crises' now occurring almost daily . . . give present point to all the line of thinking and argument we propose to do. . . . It all means more ammunition to us." There is some truth in the observation of Edward Weeks in the Atlantic that "it is the Depression which really marks the fountainhead of Southern genius. . . . No area of North or West could match that quality of competition."

I personally recall a visit to Vanderbilt in the early 1930's in the company of a small delegation of Chapel Hillians who had the temerity to accept a challenge to debate the Agrarians on their own turf. The visitors were clearly suspected of having emerged from the Trojan Horse. The verve, confidence, and spirited conviction of the Agrarians gave them an enormous advantage and an overpowering sense of purpose. It is quite probable that the values they invoked often found their way into work of serious literary character.

It is one thing to grant the excitement of a defensive movement voiced by a few eloquent and passionate men, some of whom were then or later became distinguished writers. It is quite another thing to say, as W. J. Cash did, that the defensive purpose was "the decisive factor" behind the Southern Renaissance, or that its literary treasures "represented basically the patriotic response . . . of the South to defend itself." What sort of Southern defense is "The Sound and the Fury" or "The Violent Bear It Away" or "Flowering Judas" or "Brother to Dragons?" What mad propagandist would perpetrate such works to defend any cause, just or unjust? For the language of defense or attack is the language of propaganda, however high a cause it serves. It finds no place in literature of the level that commands worldwide acclaim. . . .

Here I quote from an essay I first published in 1956. "The best of the Southern novelists have never set out to defend the values or the prejudices or the errors of any particular age or section. It is true that their books are often filled with tales of horror and lust and betrayal and degradation. But they have not paused to reckon their popularity in attacking the values of their own age or any other. They have not set up as defenders of a cause, either one lost or one still sought. They have proved themselves able to confront the chaos and irony of history with the admission that they can fit them into no neat pattern and explain them by no pat theory." I have found no reason to change these views after nineteen years. None of these writers was a purveyor of what Warren once labeled "The Great Alibi"—and incidentally Warren never implied that they were.

Abandoning the defense thesis as hopeless, I turn next to one of wider currency and more acclaim. This is Allen Tate's "backward-glance" theory. "With the war of 1914–1918," he writes, "the South re-entered the world— but gave a backward glance as it stepped over the border: that backward glance gave us the Southern renaissance, a literature conscious of the past in the present." In an earlier essay he had said: "The Southern novelist has left his mark upon the age; but it is of the age. From the peculiar historical consciousness of the Southern writer has come good work of a special order; but the force of this consciousness is quite temporary. It has made possible the curious burst of intelligence that we get at a crossing of the ways, not unlike, on an infinitesimal scale, the outburst of poetic genius at the end of the sixteenth century when commercial England had already begun to crush feudal England. The Histories and Tragedies of Shakespeare record the death of the old régime, and Doctor Faustus gives up feudal order for world power."

Robert Penn Warren offers a similar theory by suggesting "a parallel between New England before the Civil War and the South after World War I to the present. The old notion of shock, a cultural shock, to a more or less closed and static society—you know, what happened on a bigger scale in the Italian Renaissance or Elizabethan England. After 1918 the modern industrial world, with its good and bad, hit the South; all sorts of ferments began. . . . There isn't much vital imagination, it seems to me, that doesn't come from this sort of shock, imbalance, need to 'relive,' redefine life."

There is a generous amplitude and an imaginative insight about these theories that inspires credibility. Of "the peculiar historical consciousness of the Southern writer" there can be no question. It is the hallmark of the regional genre. And scores of instances spring to mind that substantiate the characterization of "the Southern renaissance [as] a literature conscious of the past in the present." It is in the present or the recent past rather than in the Old Régime that the major Southern fiction writers have most often sought their subject matter. No matter how contemporary or recent the period they treat, however, the past is always a part of the present, shaping, haunting, duplicating, or reflecting it. The past is indeed an essential dimension of the present. As one of Faulkner's characters says, "The past is never dead. It's not even past." Examples from the work of Robert Penn Warren, Katherine Anne Porter, Eudora Welty, Andrew Lytle, Allen Tate, Thomas Wolfe, and Tennessee Williams provide ample illustration.

It is, indeed, difficult to imagine this body of literature without resort in some measure to the "backward-glance" or "crossroads" hypothesis. It was almost a necessary condition of the phenomenon. Without it there is no satisfactory accounting for powerful inner conflicts of these writers, the unrelenting tensions between what Warren once called "the Southerner's loyalties and pieties—real values, mind you" and "his religious and moral sense, equally real values." The "pieties"—blood kin, regional pride, manners, history—clashed with moral values of the present. It was the conflict between a traditional society and a modern one. The conflict necessitated a coming to terms with the past. The "crossroads" and the "backward-glance" are necessary conditions to what happened.

But "necessary conditions" are not historical explanations. The logicians properly insist on a distinction here. The conditions can exist without the historical event to which they are necessary occurring. After all, feudalism was overwhelmed by commercialism in many other countries without producing the Elizabethan literary phenomenon. And when we rely on the "crossroads" theory to explain the Southern Renaissance we have to admit that our "crossroads" are not as fixed in time or place as firmly as would be convenient to accounting for the suddenness and apparent co-ordination of this cultural happening. Or for that matter its continuation. Southerners had been encountering historic crossroads for quite a while before the 1920's. It is true that the major figures of the first generation of Renaissance writers were all born within a few years around the turn of the century. But that leaves a second and perhaps a third generation of writers missing the crossroads or facing different ones. Yet they manifested many of the characteristics and inner conflicts of the first generation. I am thinking here particularly of the generation of Flannery O'Connor and William Styron.

Perhaps the historian had best concentrate on "necessary conditions" and leave causation and explanation to nonhistorians, who are less hobbled by logic. Cleanth Brooks presents a promising list of what he calls "the elements in the life of the South which have an important bearing on its literature." Without his permission, I shall call them "necessary conditions." They are as follows: "(1) the concreteness of human relationships, including the concreteness of moral problems; (2) the conflict and tension which everywhere confront one in the Southern scene and which, because they are conflict and tension, make for drama; (3) the pervading sense of community; (4) the sense of religious wholeness—I dare say that the South is the last part of the country which still believes instinctively in the supernatural; (5) the belief that human nature is mysterious and relatively intractable, and that it is not a kind of social putty which can be shaped as the politician or the social scientist may be tempted to shape it; and (6) a sense of the tragic dimension of life." He adds that "If the South still believes in the 'American dream,' it is at least chastened in its belief, not naïve and uncritical." In his opinion these "elements" brought the South "closer to the older European tradition" than were any other parts of America.

Brooks admits that his six "elements" are only a few of many that might have been named, only a few of what I choose to call "necessary conditions." He would be the first to concede that his elements had been there a long time—waiting for a Renaissance to happen. They can, therefore, hardly qualify as "causes"—only conditions. It is one of the most important contributions the critic and literary historian can make to define, explore, and understand such necessary conditions. The task is endless, for there is no end to the conceivable number of them. But assuming the impossible and imagining that we did succeed in putting together a complete and accurate compilation of them, what then? I am afraid our task of finding the cause of it all would still be a failure, and like some modern Sisyphus we would be condemned to start all over again.

I suppose I am forced in the end to agree with Donald Davidson when, in seeking the explanation for just one aspect of the Renaissance, he wrote: "I do not think the literary historian can ever explain, by piecing together bits of fact and theorizing from cause to effect, just how this particular group of young men happened to become a group of poets in Nashville, Tennessee." He then promptly and rashly and inconsistently proceeds to "venture an hypothesis"—another hypothesis, which takes the form of a question: "Suppose that Ransom had been a Californian, Tate a native of Iowa, Warren of Kansas, Davidson of Maine," etcetera, etcetera. Of course, the obvious answer to Davidson's question is that thousands of young men of equally authentic Southern heritage gathered in those same years at scores of other Southern colleges—and nothing much happened.

Besides, we are left with an endless number of other questions, many of them yet unasked, which might be equally important. For example, why was it that of the major writers all over the South, as Warren has observed, "almost all of them of that period had some important experience outside the South, then returned there—some strange mixture of continuity and discontinuity in their experience—a jagged quality." And if we venture beyond the South, as we most certainly should in any thorough search for the causes of things, the mysteries thicken and multiply. What about that strange young man of Dublin, Paris, and Trieste and how his influence happened to penetrate to Oxford, Mississippi, at a particular moment? And there are similar questions about the influence of an American exile from St. Louis who settled in London and of another American exile from Idaho who wound up in Rapallo.

Explaining the Southern Renaissance

RICHARD H. KING

In 1975 the leading historian of the South in the post–World War II era, C. Vann Woodward, sought to define the Southern Renaissance and to specify the conditions of its emergence. "Why the Southern Renaissance?" was characteristically Woodwardian in its lack of dogmatism, its lucid summations and deft criticisms, and its tendency toward equivocation. Locating the origins of the Renaissance in 1929, the year that saw the publication of Thomas Wolfe's *Look Homeward, Angel* and William Faulkner's *The Sound and the Fury*, Woodward characterized it as a flowering of the "literary arts—poetry, fiction and drama." Although Woodward suggested no point at which the literary well ran dry, one might conveniently locate the end of the main phase of the Renaissance somewhere around 1955. After that year the South was preoccupied with "other voices, other rooms." . . .

Woodward was properly skeptical that any determinate relationship between historical causes and cultural results could be drawn; but he was also perhaps overly defensive. Indeed it is difficult to imagine what a scientific (in the sense of "natural" scientific) explanation of the Southern Renaissance would look like. Besides this knotty theoretical issue, however, Woodward's essay suggested other matters that called for further analysis.

First, the Southern Renaissance was more than "just" a literary movement. It was certainly that; but it also represented an outpouring of history, sociology, political analysis, autobiography, and innovative forms of journalism. W. J. Cash, James Agee, Lillian Smith, Howard Odum, and William Alexander Percy were as central to the Southern Renaissance as William Faulkner, Robert Penn Warren, Allen Tate, and John Crowe Ransom. To be specific, Woodward's biography of the Georgia Populist leader Tom Watson, which appeared in 1938, deserved the kind of attention which Warren's novel about a Huey Long–like figure, *All the King's Men* (1946) attracted. This is not to say that *Tom Watson* and *All the King's Men* are the same kind of book. They are, however, embedded in the same historical context and informed by a "structure of feeling and experience" (to use Raymond Williams's phrase) common to the writers and intellectuals of the Renaissance. In that sense they can and should be considered together.

Woodward's essay presents other problems. He never identifies the source of the sociological explanation of the Renaissance, and it seems to me a straw man. Though he attributes the "defensive" thesis to W. J. Cash, nowhere in *The Mind of the South* does Cash claim that the Southern Renaissance was the product of Southerners under siege, except in the case of the Agrarians, where there is a lot to be said for Cash's claim. Cash paid high tribute to the realistic romanticism of Thomas Wolfe, Faulkner, and Erskine Caldwell. They were examples of the newly emerging critical spirit at work in the "mind" of the South after World War I. But though he mentions Faulkner and Caldwell together, Cash never equates them, as Woodward claims he does.

Finally, though there is no gainsaying some of the regional characteristics that Woodward draws from Brooks, it should be noted that they are generally conservative traits or tend to be most eagerly embraced by the party of the past. But the Renaissance was by no means the exclusive property of the conservative spirit and those who protested the appearance of the modern world. Second, some of these alleged characteristics of the Southern experience are questionable. It is difficult to see, for instance, how one can speak of the Southern fear of abstraction when the section

has been addled over the years by all sorts of chimerical causes and collective delusions. Nor does the Southern claim on the tragic sense appear
very strong if one assumes that the tragic sense requires insight into the
circumstances which have led to grief. The South has rarely shown much
of that insight. More generally, Woodward might have placed greater emphasis upon what is implied in the Tate thesis: the *dissolution* of the social
and cultural context that nurtured these characteristics made way for the
literary and intellectual resurgence in the South circa 1930. . . .

What then was the Southern Renaissance? Put briefly: the writers and
intellectuals of the South after the late 1920s were engaged in an attempt
to come to terms not only with the inherited values of the Southern tradition
but also with a certain way of perceiving and dealing with the past, what
Nietzsche called "monumental" historical consciousness. It was vitally
important for them to decide whether the past was of any use at all in the
present; and, if so, in what ways? Put another way, the relationship between
present and past which the Renaissance writers explored was fraught with
ambivalence and ambiguity. . . .

Ante-bellum Southern intellectuals provided one of the few sources of
dissent from the prevailing American cultural ethos and historical consciousness. More generally, if American intellectuals have traditionally been
marginal to actual political and economic power, post–Civil War Southern
intellectuals were even more so. As provincials they suffered under the
suspicion (from others and from themselves) that they were "rustic and
boorish," out of touch with the main action in the centers of cultural
ferment. Though this subjective burden, mixed with envy and resentment,
was shared with other American intellectuals, it was accentuated by the
South's trauma of defeat and occupation during Reconstruction and the
South's historical association with racial bigotry, religious primitivism, and
lack of cultural achievement. If this were not bad enough, the Southern
intellectual has measured his status in the South and the nation against the
dominant intellectual role played by the Virginians in the founding and
formation of the nation. As Allen Tate wrote in "Aeneas at Washington":
"The city my blood had built I knew no more." Thus not only has the
South been a cultural province, it has had to live with a decline from prior
cultural and political pre-eminence.

Historically, the choices open to the white Southern writer or intellectual have been limited, though not as restricted as those imposed on black
Southerners, or, say, upon the intelligentsia in Czarist Russia. He could
leave the South, perhaps under pressure, assimilate to the national culture,
and "forget" his origins. Or he could leave, but remain a "Southerner"
in manner and sympathies, serving as an explainer of the region to the rest
of the nation. As recently as the 1960s, under the editorship of Willie Morris,
many émigré white Southerners found in *Harper's* an outlet for their writings, which offered a mixture of criticism and nostalgic good feelings toward
the land they had left. There are several ironies in the title of Morris's
autobiography *North Toward Home*.

Those intellectuals who remained in the South could either become spokesmen, however sophisticated, for the Southern tradition, or speak out for change. To take the latter position was to run the obvious risk of being accused of "fouling one's nest," of being a fifth column for alien, that is, "Yankee," notions. For spokesmen of the tradition, the problem was that as intellectuals they were alienated from those to whom and for whom they spoke. To be an intellectual in the South was to talk to oneself or at best a close group of sympathizers—or to be set upon as an arrant traitor for daring to suggest that intellect might be used for something other than the exigencies of regional self-defense. For instance, in the 1920s, sociologist Howard Odum came under heavy fire from ministerial and business groups in the Piedmont for allowing essays on modern science and religion and industrial working conditions to appear in the newly founded journal *Social Forces*. Either no one listened—or the wrong sort listened.

One of the chief problems was that the South had neither a strong "enlightenment" tradition nor mass tradition of intellectual or educational concern. The Jeffersonian ideal of intellectual curiosity about whatever bore on man's fate had long since faded. By the 1930s the Jeffersonian legacy was a rather tame affair, something honored more in the breach than observance. Virginius Dabney's attempt to show the pervasive influence of Jeffersonian liberalism served mainly to show how weak and amorphous it had been. And of course no better example exists than the Scopes "Monkey" trial in Dayton, Tennessee, in 1925, about the teaching in public schools of Darwin's theory of evolution, and the controversy surrounding it to show that it was not simply a matter of hostile and fundamentalist masses against a beleaguered intelligentsia. Humanism and a defense of the Christian tradition in the South were considered compatible with religious fundamentalism. Nor did the Populist movement in the 1890s provide any lasting education of the masses, whatever its immediate political successes.

On the institutional level, the university tradition in the South was notably weak, though by the 1920s several departments of history and sociology (along with Vanderbilt's English department) were beginning to make their mark. As Howard Odum would note in *Southern Regions* (1936), no Southern university belonged in the top rank of American universities. There was but a small and rather precarious space of freedom within which to consider, much less advocate, new ideas. There was certainly no tradition of academic radicalism in Southern institutions of higher education. Nor, needless to say, was there a vital and intellectually astute clergy in the largely Protestant and fundamentalist South. In general, the steadiest voices of moderate enlightenment came from newspapermen. Dabney, George Fort Milton, John Temple Graves, and—a bit later—Ralph McGill, Hodding Carter, and Mark Ethridge would stand for a certain civil dissent, but they were either unable or unwilling to break any lances against mass opposition.

In addition, Southern cities such as Atlanta or Birmingham, New Orleans or Charleston, lacked strong, dissident artistic communities or influential universities. While black scholars such as W. E. B. Du Bois, earlier at Atlanta, and Charles Johnson at Fisk did important sociological work, the black minority lacked the power or opportunity to be a major factor in Southern intellectual ferment.

All this is to say that, prior to the 1930s, there was little contact between the political and cultural elites, a point made in W. J. Cash's gloomy conclusion to *The Mind of the South*. Agrarian conservatives ruled as they always had—according to tradition and self-interest, which were often synonymous. Neo-populist leaders depended more upon the life of the mouth than of the mind, more on rhetoric than applied intelligence. Business progressives went to school at the Chamber of Commerce and business-men's clubs. Put simply, by around 1930, Southern intellectuals inhabited another country.

And yet, as Cash might have said, something began happening in the 1920s. The "introspective revolution" of the 1930s and 1940s was prepared by a series of historical events which had profound symbolic reverberations among Southern writers and intellectuals. These events served as historical precipitates, crystallizing cultural themes and solidifying individuals into groups, thus setting the stage for much of the *Kulturkampf* in the 1930s.

The first of these events was World War I itself, which marked the end of a century of European peace and the stable bourgeois order which marked that period. Though less so than among the intellectuals of the European nations, the war profoundly affected American writers. The center did not hold. For sensitive Southerners, World War I represented the occasion for the South, as Allen Tate put it, to "rejoin the world."

Nor was the effect of that war lost on young Southern writers such as William Faulkner, who wrote of the disillusionment of the returning veteran in *Soldier's Pay* and *Sartoris*. William Alexander Percy, then a young poet, was later to write in *Lanterns on the Levee* of the exhilaration of combat—and then the sense of being adrift after his return from the trenches. Many young Southerners must have seen World War I not only as a great adventure but also as a sort of historical second chance. Having grown up in a Southern tradition powerfully shaped by the Civil War and Reconstruction, young Southerners saw World War I as a chance to demonstrate the heroism which had been drummed into them as one of the transcendent virtues of the Southern tradition. In the long run the war's cultural reverberations gave a final blow to the genteel tradition in literature. In this sense the Southern Renaissance, at least in its literary manifestations, drew less from the Depression experience than from the cultural impact of the war.

In these years the most frontal (and notorious) assault on Southern cultural esteem came from H. L. Mencken. His "Sahara of the Bozart" (1917) was read by many devoted Southerners, including liberals, as an unfair attack by an outsider. It is less well known that Mencken did not attack only to withdraw and gloat at the havoc he had wreaked. Rather, he helped keep alive fledgling literary magazines such as *The Double Dealer* in New Orleans and *The Reviewer* in Richmond, and later opened the pages of *The American Mercury* to young Southerners, such as W. J. Cash and Gerald Johnson, who were critical of the region's cultural aridity. For him, as for the poets associated with *The Fugitive* in Nashville, the enemy was the genteel tradition, New South boosterism, and the cultural wasteland of rural society. Indeed, when it suited his purposes, the sage of Baltimore fancied himself a Southerner of sorts. His reading of the region's history told him that a golden age had existed in the South sometime prior to 1800; and he even bemoaned the decline of aristocratic influence in the post-Civil War South. Thus, Mencken's attack on the contemporary South was grounded in a certain nostalgic fondness for the Virginia dynasty, and his later championing of Howard Odum and Cash was a strange one. Mencken was no modern liberal, and his affection for the aristocratic ethos should logically have placed him nearer the Agrarians. But Mencken, unlike most American conservatives, had even less use for the clergy and the spirit of religious fundamentalism than he had for social reform. What led to the enmity between Mencken and the Vanderbilt group was the publicist's savage dissection of the fundamentalist mentality at work in the Scopes trial. It was in response to Mencken's attack on the South in Dayton that poets and intellectuals in Nashville readied the counterattack which was to appear in 1930 as *I'll Take My Stand*.

By then even for defenders of the Southern tradition, not to mention its critics, the tradition had become an "entity" which could not be simply assumed; it had to be reappropriated. Accompanying this reification of the tradition was an upsurge in historical self-consciousness, a sign itself of the distance between self and tradition. As Allen Tate was to write in 1930, "[T]radition must, in other words, be automatically operative before it can be called tradition." The very act of trying to re-present the tradition pointed to its absence. In fiction and poetry the tradition was often symbolized in the portraits of the heroic generation, the presiding presences of the tradition, who had wrested the land from the Indians and defended it against the Yankees and the aggressions of Reconstruction. The portraits of these men—stern, untroubled, and resolute—hung in the entrance halls or the parlors of the homes; and from there they judged the actions of their successors. Their example was a standing rebuke to a decline in energy and will. The next generation was of necessity less heroic; charismatic origins were institutionalized, perpetuated by hard work, and marked by less glamor, for the generation between the heroic one and the one that experienced the tradition as absent had to live in the world rather than die heroically. They were too near their sons to be quite heroic. The meaning of the Civil War was, in Donald Davidson's words:

> Something for grandfathers to tell
> Boys who clamor and climb.
> And were you there, and did you ride
> With the men of that old time?

> ("Sequel of Appomattox")

And yet, a crucial segment of the third (and in some cases fourth) generation, which was born around the turn of the century and lived through the cultural crisis of World War I, came to feel increasingly estranged from the tradition. That tradition loomed distressingly distant and overpoweringly strong, insupportable yet inescapable.

This in turn raises the question which has haunted the modern world and has remained central to the culture of modernism: what does it mean to live without a tradition? Insofar as Southern writers and intellectuals were concerned with this question, they expressed a central concern of the modernist movement. The answers to the question are various, some of which this century has seen embodied in ghastly forms. Here Hannah Arendt's work sheds light, for the loss of "the thread which safely guided us through the vast realms of the past" renders memory helpless. In the face of these difficulties "old verities which have lost all concrete relevance" may be "rehashed." Also in the absence of its traditional authorizations, present authority may degenerate into the application of violence which in turn provokes counterviolence. Or finally the world may grow "fantastic."

Certainly of the rehashing of old verities there was no end in the 1930s. One thinks here of the Agrarians or of William Alexander Percy. Calling upon the past to aid the present, they attempted to revitalize the tradition by turning it into a conservative, even reactionary ideology. Some, like Percy, realized that the tradition could not be revitalized in any binding, collective way and that it had become "merely" a personal code by which they could at least live.

Nor was violence far from the surface of much of the writings in the 1930s. One thinks here of Tate's call for violence to reclaim the lost Southern tradition or his evocation of the lost possibility of an expansionist slave empire in his biography of Jefferson Davis. And no matter how far removed they were from the ideological violence of contemporary European fascism, the fictional fantasies of Faulkner's Gail Hightower in *Light in August* or the lacerating self-destructiveness of Bayard Sartoris in *Flags in the Dust* and the sophisticated poetry of Tate or Donald Davidson in his "Lee in the Mountains," all testified to the barely submerged violence that threatened to surface in the Southern tradition at its time of dissolution.

Certainly Arendt's description of reality become "fantastic" could stand as a general characteristic for much of the literature of Renaissance, a sort of modernist gothic style. What else is Faulkner wrestling with in his work up through, say, *Absalom, Absalom!*? And surely W. J. Cash and Lillian Smith were preoccupied with the fantastic aspects of Southern culture, the ways in which historically shaped desires and their inverse, self-destructiveness, had woven a texture which stifled rather than gave comfort. Though the question of when a culture becomes fantastic is terribly complicated, not least because all cultures are based upon certain fantasies, a provisional answer might apply the pragmatic criterion: when it no longer "works." Themes and motifs split off and become isolated from the whole;

they are spun out into whole visions. One might also say, following Freud, that in fantasy there is a refusal to acknowledge that we must die, that we have a body which imposes certain limits on us, and that we must live in a world with other people. In cultures grown fantastic, the regressive or reactionary form of memory is dominant. Time is denied. . . .

But in the Southern Renaissance a second movement of memory despaired of the repetition which marked the culture of melancholy and set about scrutinizing the tradition of the family romance itself. As seen in Faulkner's Quentin Compson of *Absalom, Absalom!* and in Tate's work, beginning with "Ode to the Confederate Dead" and culminating in *The Fathers*, this form of historical consciousness ends in a tragic confusion between past and present, fantasy and reality. Neither repetition nor recollection can triumph. What recollection reveals is the violence and horror at the heart of the tradition itself, or its weakness and contradictions. Time becomes an obsession, and the founding of the tradition and the costs thereby incurred are emphasized.

The third mode of historical consciousness moved toward a reconstitution of "reality" after having carried through on a demystification of the family romance. Building upon the agonized analysis of the second stage, it incorporated and transcended the Southern tradition as previously conceived. As seen in Faulkner's "The Bear" and the writings of W. J. Cash and Lillian Smith, memory emerges from the trap of fantasy which is organized around the judgments of the founding fathers. Recollection triumphs over repetition; not only the impossibility but the undesirability of resurrecting the tradition become clear.

These three stages of historical consciousness present analogies to the unfolding and transformation of memory in psychoanalysis. In both instances, the past is problematic: now overpowering, now completely absent from memory, it is debilitating. What had been assumed as "mine" now appears as "other" and strange. In the final stage this "otherness" is demystified and reassimilated after having been worked through. It is incorporated into a new synthesis. The movement is from incapacitating repetition to recollection and then to self-consciousness, from identity to estrangement and back to incorporation at a higher level. Beyond Nietzsche's monumental and critical forms of historical consciousness, a new form—the analytic or the ironic—emerges. One awakens from the nightmare of history.

Thus the modes of historical consciousness which emerged in the 1930s and 1940s were manifestations of the ambivalent spirit of cultural modernism. The prototypical historical consciousness of the modern period is obsessed with the past and the precarious possibilities of its survival. In addition, the preoccupation with the past among Southern writers and intellectuals in this period was typically Southern. Still, they were by no means united in their attitudes toward the past in general or toward the family romance in particular. The decades after 1930 were to see a reassessment of the Southern tradition.

The Flowering of the Sahara

GEORGE B. TINDALL

When the stream of Southern history broke upon the social and economic rapids of the 1920's, no gifted critic found reason to prophesy that it would nourish a flowering of Southern literature. Professional Southerners claimed to cherish the sixteen-volume *Library of Southern Literature* which had been collected to "make clear that the literary barrenness of the South has been overstated." But few professional critics cherished any Southern writers except the Virginians Ellen Glasgow and James Branch Cabell, and Miss Glasgow still worked in relative obscurity. Several monuments from an earlier day, like Grace King and Mary Johnston, stood until the 1930's, but their era ended when Thomas Nelson Page, Mary Noailles Murfree, George Washington Cable, and James Lane Allen all died between 1922 and 1925.

In 1917, when H. L. Mencken set about constructing his image of the benighted South in his essay, "The Sahara of the Bozart," it was with the sterility of Southern literature that he began. . . .

But Mencken's metaphor had missed the mark, Gerald Johnson suggested. The South was "not the Sahara, but the Congo of the Bozart. Its pulses beat to the rhythm of the tom-tom, and it likes any color if it's red." If Mencken presumed to doubt, he should explore "the trackless waste of the Library of Southern Literature, where a man might wander for years" through the literary equivalent of Sir Harry Johnson's Sierra Leone: "the mammalian fauna of chimpanzis, monkeys, bats, cats . . . large eared earth-pigs, little known duiker bush-buck, hartebeeste, and elephant." By way of prophecy Johnson quoted one Mattie J. Peterson, the Tar Heel counterpart of Coogler and author of the classic lines:

> I seen Pa coming, stepping high,
> Which was of his walk the way.

"He who has the vision to see Southern literature coming at all . . ." Johnson said, "needs must see it stepping high, for that is of its walk the way. . . . It may be outlandish. . . . It may be gorgeously barbaric, but it will not be monotonous. For all I know, it may be in some manifestations tremendously evil—it may wallow in filth, but it will not dabble in dirt."

Johnson anticipated a stereotype that long hampered critical understanding of the new literature, but he identified one of the major forces that motivated it, emancipation from the genteel tradition. Another factor, which became clear only with greater perspective, was that the South had reached a historical watershed, that it stood between two worlds, one dying and the other struggling to be born. The resultant conflict of values, which

Reprinted by permission of Louisiana State University Press from *Emergence of the New South, 1913–1945* by George B. Tindall, pp. 285–299, 306–317. Copyright © 1967 by Louisiana State University Press and the Littlefield Fund for Southern History, University of Texas.

aroused the Ku Klux and fundamentalist furies, had quite another effect on the South's young writers. "After the war," wrote one of them (Allen Tate), "the South again knew the world, but it had a memory of another war; with us, entering the world once more meant not the obliteration of the past but a heightened consciousness of it; so that we had . . . a double focus, a looking two ways, which gave a special dimension to the writings of our school." The peculiar historical perspective of that generation, Tate said on another occasion, made possible the "curious burst of intelligence that we get at a crossing of the ways, not unlike, on an infinitesimal scale, the outburst of poetic genius at the end of the sixteenth century when commercial England began to crush feudal England."

Increasingly adrift in a sea of rooming houses and filling stations, the old gray stone house of Ellen Glasgow at One West Main in Richmond aptly symbolized Southern literature, poised between two eras. There, in the Victorian twilight at the turn of the century she had commenced a lonely revolt against the "twin conventions of prudery and platitude." In the years since, she had patiently composed her "Novels of the Commonwealth," which comprised a realistic social history of Virginia from the Civil War. The series was completed with *Life and Gabriella* (1916), which made the best-seller list, but Miss Glasgow still enjoyed the critics' "benevolent neglect." She was, her neighbor Cabell said, "that other Virginian woman who wrote books," lost "in the obscuring shadow of the famousness and the large sales of Mary Johnston," author of cape-and-sword romances— in third place after still another Virginian, Henry Sydnor Harrison.

She had broken with tradition but, she later confessed, still felt "the backward pull of inherited tendencies." With *Barren Ground* (1925), she wrote, however, "I knew I had found myself." That book was the response to a fresh creative impulse. "All that came after . . . was the result of this heightened consciousness and altered perspective." *Barren Ground* brought the critical recognition so long withheld. In the story the central figure, Dorinda Oakley, daughter of an impoverished dirt-farmer, returned from an unhappy love affair to convert the barren farm into a prosperous dairy and to marry a prosaic storekeeper who later died a hero in a train wreck. In the end Dorinda herself became a heroic figure of endurance, one of those who existed "wherever a human being has learned to live without joy, wherever the spirit of fortitude has triumphed over the sense of futility."

For many a reader the novel represented almost a tract for diversified farming, a timely fact that perhaps had something to do with its reception. Vanderbilt's Donald Davidson felt impelled to object that it was almost a piece of fictionalized advice to young Southern women: "Go, become scientific dairymaids, study agricultural manuals and join the uplift." Davidson's colleague, Edwin Mims, regarded it with more favor: "There is not a single progressive movement in the South to-day that may not find enlightenment and inspiration in some one of her novels." But Ellen Glasgow had set off on a new tack. Entering now her most fruitful years, she turned to the satirical comedy of manners in Queenborough, a thinly-disguised Richmond, and brought forth amid growing plaudits *The Romantic Comedians* (1926), *They Stooped to Folly* (1929), and *The Sheltered Life* (1932).

The new release of powers came in an act of return from the "long distant view" of Virginia history to the more familiar ground of her class and environs. For all the "blood and irony" of her realism, Ellen Glasgow remained a Virginia gentlewoman, inhabiting a new world she had not made. Now she turned to communities "in which the vital stream was running out into the shallows," to social orders that had outlived their functions, a declining aristocracy whose "spirit of adventure had disintegrated into an evasive idealism, a philosophy of heroic defeat" and the thinning stock of rural pioneers whose "fortitude had degenerated into a condition of moral inertia." Like the younger writers of the day she looked backward and forward, and turned her irony both ways. "I do not like the twin curses of modern standardization and mass production," she said in 1931. "I do not like filling stations and smoke stacks in place of hedges. Yet I like even less the hookworm and pellagra and lynching of the agrarian scene, the embattled forces of religious prejudice and the snarling feature of our rural dry-nurse prohibition."

After *Vein of Iron* (1935), which featured a stoical heroine like Dorinda Oakley, the long-delayed award of a Pulitzer Prize came with her last novel, *In This Our Life* (1941), written in the shadow of a lingering illness. Before she died in 1945, Ellen Glasgow found herself again, as she had begun, a rebel against the prevailing fashion. Looking over "the multitude of half-wits, the whole idiots, and nymphomaniacs, and rakehells in general, who populate the modern literary South," she began to suspect that one "was as little likely to encounter truth in the exposed features of the new barbarism as under the mask of civilized conduct." Readers hardened to a new generation of writers would find her earlier work sentimental and strongly tinged with old-fashioned romance. They would find little evidence of the experimental techniques essayed by younger writers. But she had introduced a multitude of new types, new classes, new characters, new themes to Southern literature; and there was still good reason to endorse a judgment passed in 1930: "The novelist who gives the most nearly complete picture of the South is undoubtedly Ellen Glasgow."

The novels of Ellen Glasgow's neighbor, James Branch Cabell, offer a puzzle for chroniclers of regional literature. In 1920 he shared with two obscure poets the distinction of being the only Southern writers worth mentioning in Mencken's "Sahara of the Bozart." An abortive attempt to suppress *Jurgen* (1919) in New York suddenly thrust Cabell into notoriety, and after 1920 he enjoyed a subterranean reputation as the writer of "sexy" books together with critical acclaim and a following that grew almost into a cult of "exquisites." Probably the best-known Southern writer of the period, he was little concerned with the movements and themes that animated his contemporaries: "Ellen Glasgow and I are the contemporaneous products of as nearly the same environment as was ever accorded to any two writers," he said. "From out of our impressions as to exactly the same Richmond-in-Virginia, she has built her Queenborough, and I my Lichfield; yet no towns have civic regulations more widely various."

After an early career of light romances for *Harper's* and other magazines, several Virginia genealogies, and two novels that gently mocked Virginia conventions—*The Cords of Vanity* (1909) and *The Rivet in Grandfather's Neck* (1915)—he retreated more and more into the dream world of Poictesme, a medieval province of his own invention. There began the lengthy "Biography of the Life of Manuel," of which *Jurgen* comprised one installment. If Ellen Glasgow's novels might be entitled, as he suggested, "The Tragedy of Everywoman, As It Was Lately Enacted in the Commonwealth of Virginia," his own might be called "The Fantasy of Everyman, As It Was Once Enacted in the Province of Poictesme." Everyman—were he Manuel the Redeemer whose own history and legend developed in *Figures of Earth* (1921) and *The Silver Stallion* (1926) or one of his descendants, some of them in Lichfield—was moved to feats of chivalry, gallantry, and poetry, traversed the realms of time and space, entered heaven and hell, pursued and possessed the seductive females of history and myth. Finding only disillusionment, he returned at last to a prosy and matronly wife, to middle-aged comfort and routine, much as Cabell himself descended from his study to dinner with his Priscilla. "Art," he once wrote, "is in its last terms an evasion of the distasteful." Only in the deliberate cultivation of myth and dream did man transcend mortality. Yet these, too, ultimately failed to satisfy his appetite for certainty and purpose.

Remote as Poictesme seemed, its genesis was in the Virginia of Cabell's youth. The growth of the myth of Manuel bore a striking resemblance to the rise of the myth of the Confederacy, which Cabell experienced as a youth and described years later in *Let Me Lie* (1947). Each myth, though false to its origins, had its uses, as Cabell saw it, in bolstering the morale and virtue of its adherents, and finally merged indistinguishably with reality.

No other Southern writer during the 1920's equaled the achievement of Richmond's patricians, but all across the barrens of Mencken's "Sahara" new shoots began to stir in the soil; by mid-decade they had flowered into a literary revival. It may be too much to claim, as Oscar Cargill did, that Mencken anticipated the development and in his backhanded way sought to cultivate it. But there can be little question that within a few years, "Like Aaron's rod Mencken's goad had proved itself a symbol of fertility." That Mencken pricked Southern awareness in more than one nerve was apparent from the frequency of references to him among the literary groups that were springing to life. Of late years, the Poetry Society of South Carolina noted in its first *Year Book* (1921), "it has not been *comme il faut* to wave the ensanguined chemise. . . . 'South-Baiting' from now on is going to be more of a dangerous sport than formerly, and will have to be carried on by matadors who wield a brand that does not too closely resemble the animal which they desire to slay." The Sahara had cases where the fig tree was not entirely barren, the *Year Book* asserted, and missiles from the editor of the *Smart Set* had "the irony of the boomerang."

The Poetry Society of South Carolina (mainly Charleston) stood in the vanguard of the Southern Renaissance. It grew out of weekly meetings at which two aspiring poets, DuBose Heyward, an insurance agent, and Hervey Allen, a high school teacher, submitted their verses to a "fanging" by their mentor, John Bennett, an established writer known chiefly for the children's classic, *Master Skylark* (1896). Formal organization came in the fall of 1920, and the first *Year Book* in the spring of 1921 revealed no small element of chauvinism in its effort to prove that "culture in the South is not merely an *ante bellum* tradition." Convinced that they represented "a force that needs only to be directed and coordinated in order to stimulate a genuine *south-wide* poetic renaissance," the Charlestonians set afoot a feverish campaign to awaken the literary South. "Their humorless intensity," said their historian, "would be almost laughable were it not for the fact that they succeeded."

The group drew a miscellany of local poetasters, including some who achieved a degree of success: Josephine Pinckney, Beatrice Ravenel, Katherine Drayton Mayrant Simons, and from upstate, Henry Bellaman and Julia Peterkin. It brought in for lectures and readings outsiders such as Carl Sandburg, Harriet Monroe, Vachel Lindsay, and Robert Frost. It sponsored prize contests that afforded early recognition to young authors such as Donald Davidson, Robert Penn Warren, Olive Tilford Dargan, and others. Heyward, as secretary, neglected his business to carry afar a missionary campaign of lecturing, reading, and fomenting new poetry societies. Within a decade similar groups had sprung up in Maryland, Virginia, Georgia, Florida, Louisiana, and Texas, and active local groups in Norfolk, Suffolk, Nashville, Birmingham, Winter Park, and elsewhere.

The quality of the Charleston group found expression in a collection of verses by Heyward and Allen, *Carolina Chansons* (1922), a self-conscious effort to capture in lyric form the history and legends of the Low Country. It found more explicit expression the same year in *Poetry*'s "Southern Number," which Heyward and Allen edited. They filled it mostly with Charleston authors and inserted an essay, "Poetry South," which predicted a coming Southern poetry "decidedly regional in spirit . . . strongly local in tone," based largely on local color, tradition, and legend.

The Charlestonians betrayed a fatal addiction to the delicate tints of local color, but some of their contemporaries flaunted more garish hues of detached sophistication. At the beginning of 1921 a little group in New Orleans, intoxicated by the exuberance of revolt against Philistia, brought forth *The Double Dealer*—the title was explained by a cryptic quotation from Congreve's play of the same name: "I can deceive them both by speaking the truth." Julius Weis Friend and Basil Thompson were associate editors; later John McClure, newspaperman and poet, became editor. One "need not expect to find in these pages sympathy for presto change reforms, nor for syndicates for the propagation of brotherly love," the editors warned in the first issue; it would avail nothing to seek "an unground ax, a moral purpose, a political affiliation." Their concern was rather the "dissemination of good readable matter and the telling of the truth regardless of whom it disquiets."

But they, too, felt the inexorable pull of regional loyalty. *The Double Dealer*, they said, wanted "to be known as the rebuilder, the driver of the first pile into the mud of this artistic stagnation which has been our portion since the Civil War . . . a movement, a protest, a rising up against the intellectual tyranny of New York, New England, and the Middle West." In the sixth issue Basil Thompson championed a new Southern literature to replace "the treacly sentimentalities" of "lady fictioneers" and "the storied realm of dreams, lassitude, pleasure, chivalry and the Nigger." Hundreds of towns, he said, fairly bubbled "with the stuff of stories," with something "vital to the soil—the physical, mental and spiritual outlook of an emerging people—the soul-awakening of a hardy, torpid race, just becoming reaware of itself." In the seventh issue the slogan on the masthead changed from "A Magazine for the Discriminating" to "A National Magazine from the South."

During its five years of existence *The Double Dealer* became the focus of a minor writers' colony. Its office in an unused third floor on Baronne Street, just outside the French Quarter, became a center for literary talk and beaux arts balls. In and out of the group moved Roark Bradford, Oliver LaFarge, E. P. O'Donnell, Lyle Saxon, the teen-aged Hamilton Basso and James K. Feibleman. For brief periods the exotic charm of the Vieux Carré drew Sherwood Anderson and William Faulkner into a kind of domestic expatriation in the Quarter. The place had, as Faulkner described it in a parody of Anderson's style, an "atmosphere of richness and soft laughter, you know . . . a kind of ease, a kind of awareness of the unimportance of things that outlanders like myself were taught to believe important." There Faulkner wrote his first novel, *Soldiers' Pay* (1926), a story of postwar *Weltschmerz*, and gathered material for the second, *Mosquitoes* (1927), a caricature of the New Orleans Bohemians. After knocking about Europe and the Gulf Coast, he returned home to pursue Anderson's admonition that "all you know is that little patch up there in Mississippi where you started from," and Anderson after the success of *Dark Laughter* (1925) bought a farm near Marion, Virginia, thereby assuming residence at least on the fringes of the Southern literary pantheon.

In May, 1926, *The Double Dealer* expired with the forty-third issue. Like many another such publication, it never paid for itself, but it performed better than most the little magazine's function of uncovering new talents. It printed some of the earliest work of Faulkner, Basso, Feibleman, Ernest Hemingway, Jean Toomer, Thornton Wilder, Hart Crane, Matthew Josephson, Malcolm Cowley, Edmund Wilson, and Kenneth Fearing, among others—surely achievement enough to justify one short-lived journal. . . .

In April, 1922, the first issue of *The Fugitive*, a little magazine devoted to poetry, issued forth to an unexpectant world from Nashville, Tennessee, and thus announced the existence of the most influential group in American letters since the New England Transcendentalists. In several respects the Fugitive poets differed from the transient groups in Charleston, New Orleans, and Richmond: they had a rigorously intellectual tone and academic connections with Vanderbilt; they sustained an intensive devotion to excellence; they were gestating the "New Criticism" that later worked a revolution in the English classroom; and quite ironically in the light of later developments, they were self-consciously cosmopolitan in attitude and opposed to the promotion of Southern literature as such.

At the time Vanderbilt's English department enjoyed a healthy diversity: Edwin Mims, New South progressive and inspirational champion of nineteenth-century literature; Walter Clyde Curry, author of the erudite *Chaucer and the Mediaeval Sciences* (1926); and John Crowe Ransom, who had just published his *Poems About God* (1919). Ransom, in his thirties, was dean and mentor of the Fugitives, though never in any sense their leader. The beginning was in a group of faculty and student intellectuals that began to gather for discussions in 1915. Scattered by the war, the group reassembled in the fall of 1919 at sessions in the home of James Frank, around the chaise longue of his brother-in-law, Sidney Mttron Hirsch, an esoteric dilettante "whose doctrine skittered elusively among imaginary etymologies." Gradually the discourse turned from philosophy to literature and then to biweekly reading and criticism. At the end of 1921 there were seven members and eventually sixteen in all. Of these, four stood out in their ultimate commitment to literature as a profession: Ransom, Donald Davidson, Allen Tate, and Robert Penn Warren.

Under the stimulus of discussions and critiques they began to create new poetry distinguished by attention to form and language, by complexity of content and allusion that yielded only to the closest study. The chief quality which set apart the poetry of the Fugitive group, their historian wrote, was "its embodiment of the fundamental beliefs of the society out of which it came." But their "Southern quality" came through only later, for they started in revolt against the twin images of the sentimental traditionalist and the New South booster. A literary phase "known rather euphemistically as Southern Literature has expired," Ransom announced in the first issue. "*The Fugitive* flees from nothing faster than from the high-caste Brahmins of the Old South." In 1923, ruffled by *Poetry* editor Harriet Monroe's calls for a "strongly localized indigenous art" in a region "jewel-weighted with a heroic past," Davidson retorted that it was "not the province of any critic to dictate the material [Southern poets] shall choose" and expressed fear of too much stress "on a tradition that may be called a tradition only when looked at through the haze of a generous imagination."

The "Southernness" of the Fugitives was least obtrusive in the poems of John Crowe Ransom, who perfected a personal style before any of the others and who, indeed, published few poems after his *Chills and Fever* (1924) and *Two Gentlemen in Bonds* (1927). "Antique Harvesters" did evoke the Agrarian myth of the Old South, which Ransom later espoused, in the picture of a fox hunt:

> . . . The horn, the hounds, the lank mare coursing by
> Straddled with archetypes of chivalry. . . .

The fieldworkers, who had paused to watch the gentry, he enjoined:

> Resume, harvesters. The treasure is full bronze
> Which you will garner for the Lady. . . .

And in the Lady Ransom evoked a semi-religious image of the South:

> The sons of the fathers shall keep her, worthy of
> What these have done in love.

"Necrological" was one among many examples of Ransom's gift for "the conjunction of a stylized, formal attitude of discourse and some of the most vicious, sanguinary subject matter in all of modern America." In that poem a friar slipped away to view the carnage of a battlefield:

> So still that he likened himself unto those dead
> Whom the kites of Heaven solicited with sweet cries.

But the common qualities in Ransom's poems were those of a lofty yet unpretentious elegance, a blend of archaic and modern language, a "fury against abstractions," a dualism that dwelt upon the gap between human aspiration and achievement, a gentle and civilized irony that underscored the terrors which lie below the surface of life. In "Bells for John Whiteside's Daughter," whose "wars were bruited in our high window," the poet was

> . . . sternly stopped
> To say we are vexed at her brown study,
> Lying so primly propped.

In September, 1925, *The Fugitive* expired, less from want of support than from want of time. Its founders had become busy authors with other outlets; some of them, including Tate and Warren, had left Nashville. They still thought themselves detached from the South, but an event remote from the realm of poetry, the Scopes trial, worked a sharp change in their thought. The Mencken-Darrow image of the benighted South stirred defensive attitudes and brought a dawning realization that they "shared pretty much the same assumptions about society, about man, nature, and God." In 1926 Davidson produced an ambivalent essay in which he scored "civic boosters" and "the treacly lamentations of the old school," but called attention to certain Southern qualities: "Exuberance, sensitiveness, liveliness of imagination, warmth and flexibility of temper," which "properly realized, might display an affirmative zest and abandon now lacking in American art." Fundamentalism, he argued, expressed "a fierce clinging to poetic supernaturalism against the encroachments of cold logic; it stands for moral seriousness." About the same time Ransom began to compose *God Without Thunder: An Unorthodox Defense of Orthodoxy* (1930), which used religious myth to counter the deification of science. Tate, in New York, had begun a search for roots, a search that led to biographies of Stonewall Jackson (1928) and Jefferson Davis (1929). In March, 1926, he wrote to Ransom, "I've attacked the South for the last time." The next year Tate published "Ode to the Confederate Dead" and Davidson "The Tall Men," both poems about the Southerner's relation to—or rather alienation from—his heritage. By then the Agrarian Manifesto, *I'll Take My Stand* (1930), had begun to take shape in their minds; Warren and new allies from outside the Fugitive group were being drawn in. The Fugitives, who had begun in flight from the South, stood finally at the very center of the new historical focus in Southern literature. . . .

"Literature in the South as well as trouble," Shields McIlwaine submitted, "seems to start with the 'darkey.' " As it was with the local-color movement of the 1880's, so it sometimes seemed with the new revival. The difference was that, although stereotypes dogged the Negroes' footsteps, it was less as "darkies" and more as people that they were appearing. To be sure a hard core of lachrymose ladies perpetuated mammy and the pickaninnies; and successful humorists followed the advice of Irvin S. Cobb's Jeff Poindexter, "don't mess wid no race problem": men like Hugh Wiley, Arthur Akers, E. K. Means, and most notably Octavus Roy Cohen, a *Saturday Evening Post* regular, whose Florian Slappey perpetrated "a Negro dialect never heard on land or sea—compounded more of Dogberry and Mrs. Malaprop than of Birmingham Negroes." Not far removed from this was Roark Bradford, whose *Ol' Man Adam and His Chillun* (1928) became a stage success as Marc Connelly's *Green Pastures* (1930), a travesty on Bible stories as they might be seen by unlettered Negroes.

In 1922 three authors broke sharply away from this pattern, with problem novels of the aspiring Negro, novels of sociological realism strongly motivated by the urge to right wrongs. H. A. Shands' *White and Black* presented an ambitious Texas Negro sharecropper who was finally lynched for his pains. Clement Wood's *Nigger* took a strikingly new approach, the history of a Negro family from slavery in the Black Belt to bondage in the Birmingham slums, a story suffused with the futility of the former slave Jake's search for the "emancipation" he had heard of, at least for his grandchildren. T. S. Stribling's *Birthright*, the most successful of the three, announced a major new talent. It was the story of Peter Siner, Negro graduate of Harvard, who returned with missionary zeal to "Niggertown" in Hooker's Bend only to find himself cut off from his own people and swindled out of his school by a white banker who supported African missions. Eventually he fled North with Cissie, a girl who had been violated by a white rapist. A basic quality of the novel, which recurred in Stribling's later writings, was satiric irony directed at the racial double standard and at the white man's complacent assurance that he understood the Negro. Walter White's *The Fire in the Flint* (1924), motivated in part by the feeling that Stribling had not truly comprehended the Negro middle class, carried forward the author's antilynching crusade with the story of a Negro doctor lynched by Georgia crackers who could not understand his entry into a white home to save a girl's life. In *Flight* (1926) White retold the classic story of "passing" by a near-white girl.

Other authors turned away from the older stereotypes to exploit themes from Negro folklore. Close to the Uncle Remus tradition were Ambrose Gonzales' stories from the South Carolina Gullahs: *Black Border: Gullah Stories of the Carolina Coast* (1922), *With Aesop Along the Black Border* (1924), and others. John B. Sales's *The Tree Named John* (1929) presented a collection of Mississippi folklore in dialect. R. Ernest Kennedy in *Black Cameos* (1924), *Gritny People* (1927), and *Red Bean Row* (1929) wove original stories about Louisiana Negroes, "unlettered folk who have not lost the gracious charm of being natural: wonderfully gifted and fairly tingling with poetic tendencies." Howard Odum amused himself with stories about Left Wing Gordon, a roguish character based on a highway worker Odum knew, an extroverted, one-armed roustabout who moved from place to place, from woman to woman in three books: *Rainbow Round My Shoulder* (1928), *Wings on My Feet* (1929), and *Cold Blue Moon* (1931). But the masterpieces of the genre were *Congaree Sketches* (1927) and *Nigger to Nigger* (1928), stories about Negroes in the Congaree swamps told by a Columbia physician, E. C. L. Adams. In tales and poems that ran from high comedy to satire on the white man's justice, Adams succeeded in permitting Negro characters to speak for themselves.

In 1921, not far from Adams' Congaree swamps, Julia Peterkin, mistress of Lang Syne Plantation, was hostess to Carl Sandburg, just up from a visit to the Poetry Society in Charleston. He urged her to write down stories of Negroes she had learned around the plantation. The result was a series of sketches, too strong for Mencken's *Smart Set*, that found outlet in *The Reviewer* and grew eventually into *Green Thursday* (1924). *Black April* (1927) and the Pulitzer-Prize winning *Scarlet Sister Mary* (1928) focused on the violent, amoral lives of Negroes in the quarters, struggling not against the injustice of white men but against an overpowering fate that hedged them in with superstition and helplessness: Black April, a plantation foreman with a gigantic appetite for battle and a fatal attraction for women; Scarlet Sister Mary, the feminine equivalent, a matriarch who, abandoned by a footloose husband, bred an indiscriminate brood and struggled against fate with unbending will. The characters were presented with sympathy and respect but with an uninhibited candor that shocked Julia Peterkin's neighbors who had not discovered what James Branch Cabell called the vicarious enjoyment of sin in literature. "I said things that no nice South Carolina lady ever says," she confessed, "and so I must be disciplined a bit even by my friends."

In Charleston, meanwhile, DuBose Heyward followed the counsel of Sidney Lanier to "kill his Egyptian," fled the insurance business for the profession of letters, and poetry for higher achievement in the novel. *Porgy* (1925), a novel about primitive Negroes brought "from the woods to town," differed from Julia Peterkin's works in its brooding awareness of history, in its suggestion of capturing the life of disappearing types: "Are they an aeon behind, or an aeon ahead of us?" Heyward had pondered in a 1923 article. "Who knows? But one thing is certain: the reformer will have them in the fullness of time." A further contrast to Julia Peterkin was the rich tincture of romantic haze cast over a Golden Age "when men, not yet old, were boys in an ancient, beautiful city that time had forgotten before it destroyed." But his characters, if somewhat romanticized, were believable people, with human hopes and emotions, drawn in such high colors as to constitute a gallery of unforgettable portraits: Porgy of the goat cart, Bess, Crown, and others. Popularized in a successful Broadway play (1927), then in George Gershwin's opera, *Porgy and Bess* (1935), the inhabitants of Catfish Row became more widely known than any other characters from the Southern literature of the decade.

Two other unforgettable characters appeared in *Mamba's Daughters* (1929): Mamba, outwardly a handkerchief-headed mammy, inwardly a sly old woman fanatically obsessed with her granddaughter's chances; and Hagar, the slow-witted giant of a daughter who did a man's work in the phosphate mines and finally submitted to her mother's will. But *Mamba's Daughters* added another dimension—a remarkable depiction of the new currents in Negro life. Lissa, beneficiary of Mamba's and Hagar's sacrifice, moved into the genteel circles of Charleston's Negro élite and finally on to triumph as a singer in New York. And Saint Julien Wentworth, willing instrument of Mamba's purpose, stood as the incarnation of "the dilemma of the liberal but nonrevolutionary Southern aristocrat confronted by a world he never made," unwilling to challenge the Southern racial credo but quietly helping in Lissa's triumph.

Both Julia Peterkin and DuBose Heyward arrived at an opportune moment. For one thing it was what F. Scott Fitzgerald had labeled the Jazz Age, a time when the world was just becoming aware of Negro music. The forms that were then working a revolution in the popular music of the nation were forms that had gestated for years in the Negro subculture of the South. There the sorrows—and joys—of the Negro experience had found one free outlet in the music of the people, and the makers of jazz were able to draw upon a rich heritage of African, European, and American elements; upon work songs, field hollers, blues, ragtime, minstrelsy, spirituals—and above all a fashion of wild improvisation.

New Orleans was not the only incubator of jazz, but already by 1900, in the age of the legendary cornetist Buddy Bolden, something that might later have been recognized as jazz was being played by bands that marched in parades and played the street corners and dance halls. Occasionally one of the "spasm" or "jass" bands would venture forth for engagements elsewhere, or upriver on one of the excursion boats. By the early teens a few of the musicians had begun to drift into the gin mills of Chicago, which was destined to be the next major center of jazz.

But the Jazz Age may be dated from January, 1917, when a group of white musicians from New Orleans via Chicago, Nick LaRocca's "Original Dixieland Jass Band," hit solid at Reisenweber's Restaurant in New York. In March the Victor Talking Machine Company released their "Livery Stable Blues" and "Dixieland Jass Band One-Step" on the first commercial jazz record. The dissemination of jazz was soon under way in earnest; hundreds of Negro jazzmen joined the Great Migration. In 1917 Ferdinand "Jelly Roll" Morton, ex-piano-playing "professor" of the Tenderloin, left New Orleans for California. In 1918 Joseph "King" Oliver left for Chicago, whence in 1922 he summoned Louis Armstrong, his successor as cornetist with Edward "Kid" Ory. Kid Ory, meanwhile, had gone to California in 1919. W. C. Handy, "father of the blues," a native of Florence, Alabama, who had knocked about the Mississippi Valley as a bandleader and had already scored success as the composer of "Memphis Blues" (1912) and "St. Louis Blues" (1914), moved from Memphis' Beale Street to Broadway in 1918 for a new career as music publisher. In 1920 Fletcher Henderson of Georgia finished Atlanta University with a major in chemistry and mathematics and went to New York for postgraduate study, but hired out to Handy as a pianist and launched a career as band-leader and arranger.

Soon the record companies discovered a Negro market for "Race Recordings" of hot jazz and blues singers like "Ma" Rainey and Bessie Smith of the Rabbit Foot Minstrels, often too "mean" and "low-down" for the uninitiated whites. But by 1924, when band-leader Paul Whiteman staged a "symphonic" jazz concert in New York's Aeolian Hall, with George Gershwin playing his own "Rhapsody in Blue," the new music had begun to achieve respectability and had moved along the way to recognition as perhaps the one truly original American contribution to the arts.

And as Southern Negroes poured into New York, they created in Harlem the largest center of Negro population in the world and mingled with others from the North, from Africa, from the West Indies. Harlem became a segregated melting pot out of which there boiled up a renaissance in Negro literature and the arts, a rediscovery of Africa and of the folk culture so often derogated by the black bourgeoisie—for many sensitive Negroes an emancipation not only from the genteel tradition but from the race problem itself. Southern emigrés were at the center of the movement: Charles S. Johnson, editor of *Opportunity*, who opened its pages to much of the new writing; Zora Neale Hurston, folklorist and student of anthropology; Countee Cullen, poet and novelist, who explored the Negro past and present in "Heritage" and other poems; James Weldon Johnson, NAACP secretary and author, who rendered old-fashioned sermons in verse in *God's Trombones* (1927) and pictured the Negro mecca in *Black Manhattan* (1930).

After Carl Van Vechten presented a titillating picture of Negro cabaret life in *Nigger Heaven* (1926), adventurous whites in large numbers ventured into the "black and tan" night clubs of Harlem and other cities to sample forbidden fruits. With the Negro Renaissance, Eugene O'Neill's *Emperor Jones* (1921), Sherwood Anderson's *Dark Laughter* (1925), and the writings of Southern folklorists and novelists, the Negro as exotic primitive was for a few years all the rage—to the dismay of a scandalized Negro middle class. But it was, one critic remarked, "a shallow literary vein soon worked out." Still, it wrought an emancipation from old stereotypes even by creating new; the old molds would never again be quite adequate.

In retrospect the supreme creation of the Negro Renaissance was Jean Toomer's novel *Cane* (1923), which a later critic counted among four "Major" novels by American Negroes. Toomer, a grandson of Louisiana's Reconstruction Lieutenant-Governor P. B. S. Pinchback, was born in Washington, D.C., studied at the University of Wisconsin and the City College of New York, moved in a white literary clique devoted to mysticism, and before he wrote his book, made a pilgrimage to Georgia as a rural schoolteacher to establish contact with his Southern roots. The book, a disjointed collection of stories, vignettes, and poems, pictured with a sensitivity that transcended propaganda, the life of simple Negroes in Georgia's Black Belt and sophisticated Negroes in Washington's brown belt. Toomer's book, Waldo Frank asserted in a preface, was "a harbinger of the South's literary maturity," of its release from the racial obsession. Other writers, he said, escaped through "sentimentalism, exoticism, polemic, 'problem' fiction, and moral melodrama." Toomer wrote "not as a Southerner, not as a rebel against Southerners, not as a Negro, not as apologist or priest or critic," but "as a *poet*." His book unfortunately was so strong in its experimental character that it met a cold reception and the rebuff caused Toomer to retire from further literary effort.

During the 1920's the mountaineer, popular as he was with ballad hunters, had little vogue in literature outside the folk plays; his day had come and gone with writers like Mary Noailles Murfree. DuBose Heyward, like all proper Charlestonians, had a summer home at Flat Rock in the North Carolina mountains and used that background for some of his poems and for one novel, *Angel* (1926). But it was written hastily to capitalize on the reputation established by *Porgy*. Perhaps most successful in exploiting the folk mountaineer were Mary and Stanley Chapman, a Tennessean and her British husband who wrote as Maristan Chapman, in *The Happy Mountain* (1928) and *Weather Tree* (1932), which self-consciously utilized peculiarities in mountain speech and customs, usually to the disparagement of cultivated flatlanders.

T. S. Stribling, on the other hand, inverted the Chapman image and subjected the Tennessee hill people to devastating satire. He wrote, Shields McIlwaine said, "like an old-fashioned scalawag." In *Teeftallow* (1926) and *Bright Metal* (1928) he reacted almost directly to the Scopes trial and flayed with mordant irony the stupid cruelties of religious fanaticism and hypocrisy. Stribling eventually would suffer neglect and obscurity at the hands of critics who derogated liberalism and social satire, but he was a significant innovator who opened up a broad range of the Southern experiences that novelists had never before explored. And his novels published in the 1920's, it turned out, were but preparation for a trilogy of the New South, his *magnum opus*, which appeared in the 1930's.

In contrast to Stribling's scalding satires of village life, the sociological novels of tenancy were sympathetic, and usually pointed the way to progressive reform. The salient example of the type was Dorothy Scarborough's *In the Land of Cotton* (1923), outstanding neither for qualities of artistry nor for its picture of local peculiarities of the Brazos River valley, but for its panoramic view of the cotton culture and of people entangled in an almost deterministic system. "If Job was a character today he'd be a cotton farmer," one rustic opined, "a share-cropper, I reckon." One striking feature of the book was a foreshadowing of the New Deal farm programs in an outline of necessary reforms given by one of the characters: credit, tenant rehabilitation, crop limitation, warehouses, cooperation, diversification. Miss Scarborough's *Can't Get a Red Bird* (1929)—the title reflects her primary concern with folklore—further treated the cotton system and farm problems, while Jack Bethea in *Cotton* (1928) told about an Alabama tenant farmer's son who achieved an education and came back to promote co-operative marketing.

At the same time there developed a different artistic perception of the Southern poor-white, not as an object of satire or reform, but as a prototype of man's universal fate: his tribulations, his endurance, his limitations, his ultimate tragedy—a new treatment "compounded of sensibility and idealism in character and of rather hard realism in situation and background." The new perception focused at first upon women characters, possibly because women authors led the way, possibly because the family was the basic Southern social unit and families become matriarchies—the natural superiority of woman is manifested repeatedly in Southern fiction and drama.

Ellen Glasgow's *Barren Ground*, while it did not deal with tenants, paralleled the development, but two ladies in Kentucky led it with remarkably similar novels: Edith S. Kelley's *Weeds* (1923) and Elizabeth Madox Roberts' *The Time of Man* (1926). *Weeds* traced the story of Judy Pippinger, a bright, tomboyish girl growing up in the Kentucky tobacco fields, a girl who somehow expected to escape the usual fate of tenant wives, old before their years, bowed down by inexorable fate. But it was not so ordained. Married to a tenant farmer, she finally bent under the burden of perennial defeat, the inability to have that good year that would put them ahead. In the end she arrived at quiet resignation: "peace was better than struggle, peace and a decent acquiescence before the things which had to be."

The story of Ellen Chesser in Miss Roberts' *The Time of Man* was much the same, but told by an author of greater sensitivity and talent, largely from Ellen's own viewpoint. Ellen Chesser, more than Judy Pippinger or Dorinda Oakley, possessed a lively sensibility, filled with the wonder of earth and the things she had seen and heard. "Here I am," she cried out at the beginning. "I'm Ellen Chesser! I'm here." More than the others she longed for something better, something vaguely spiritual, but also for a home "fixed up, the shutters mended and the porch. . . . To sit on a Saturday when the work is done. A vine up over the chimney. Once I saw a far piece from here. . . ." But again it was out of reach. The only surviving child of parents who were wagoners, then tenants, Ellen gradually moved from vernal exuberance through adolescent disillusionment to adult resignation as the wife of a tenant farmer unjustly accused of barn burning, forever on the move. The book ended as it began, with Ellen on a wagon, the shoddy accumulation of the years piled about, going she knew not where, listening to the children's talk—so much like her own in the years now dead. And yet the enduring hope of some fair land. "Some better country. Our own place maybe. Our trees in the orchard. Our own land sometime. Our own place to keep."

Publication of *The Time of Man* disclosed the existence of still another major talent nourished apart from the little groups and movements elsewhere in the South. The talent bloomed late; Miss Roberts was forty-five when the novel appeared. In her youth, prevented by ill health and uncertain finances from continuing her studies at the University of Kentucky, she settled down to a career of spinster school marm conducting classes in the family's living room. But in 1917, with the assistance of interested friends and a sympathetic professor at the state university, she entered the University of Chicago at the age of thirty-six. There under new stimuli, her interests in philosophy and literature quickened and she began to write the poems collected in *Under the Tree* (1922). Its success stimulated her to finish *The Time of Man*, begun the same year. Often on the move to New York, Massachusetts, California, and Florida in search of health, she always returned to Springfield, in the center of the state and the "Pigeon River" country of her novels.

Other books followed in the fifteen years that remained to her, but *The Time of Man* remained the best. Set in the Kentucky tobacco country of the early twentieth century, it had about it a quality of universality and timelessness in the central theme of man's eternal seeking. Her sensibility grew from a unique combination: a concrete sense of earth and soil and landscape mixed with a Berkeleian turn of philosophy in which ultimate reality resided in the spiritual, all woven together by a rich imagery "physicalizing the spiritual." The language vibrated with music and poetry, the idiom of her Kentucky tenants colored by the English ballad themes of contemporary folklore scholarship. But with remarkable success Elizabeth Madox Roberts presented also scenes of violence: a scene in which Ellen experienced childbirth alone and unaided, and other scenes of realism that broke sharply with the genteel tradition and again marked the transition of the 1920's toward even starker scenes that would soon appear in Southern writing.

The first novel was followed by *My Heart and My Flesh* (1927), which explored themes of madness, incest, and miscegenation, from which the heroine finally emerged into greener pastures; *Jingling in the Wind* (1928), a piece of fantasy and social satire that ridiculed contemporary absurdities of religious prejudice, politics, and high pressure advertising; *A Buried Treasure* (1931), the lighthearted story of what happened to a farmer who discovered it; *The Great Meadow* (1932), which rivaled her first novel in its reception, a story of Harrodsburg pioneers with a sensitive heroine much like Ellen Chesser; *He Sent Forth a Raven* (1935), an allegory of the spirit triumphant over the evils of modern civilization; and *Black Is My Truelove's Hair* (1938), about the spiritual rebirth of a "ruined" woman in the discovery of true love.

With remarkable suddenness after 1920 Mencken's cultural Sahara had turned into a literary hothouse that germinated an increasingly prolific vegetation. With growing frequency after the South Carolina Poetry Society's first *Year Book* called for "a genuine *south-wide* poetic renaissance," the term renaissance appeared and reappeared in discussions of the Southern literary scene. Within two years the Poetry Society complacently confessed "that further assertion on our part that the South has brought forth a literary revival would be to stress the obvious." By mid-decade the major literary journals were taking cognizance of the development in surveys of Southern writing by DuBose Heyward, Frances Newman, and Donald Davidson. Mencken himself, who followed the scene closely, used the little magazines of the South as bush-league training grounds for *The American Mercury*. And in the *Mercury*'s first two years, he noted not without satisfaction, the South supplied fifty-five contributions from twenty-three authors while New England supplied only forty-one by twenty-four authors.

And as the decade advanced there were signs that the flowering of the 1920's foretokened a harvest of ripened fruits in the future. Ellen Glasgow and Elizabeth Madox Roberts were in the full tide of creativity and books published in 1929 heralded the emergence of still other mature talents: Thomas Wolfe's *Look Homeward, Angel* and William Faulkner's *Sartoris* and *The Sound and the Fury*. "One may reasonably argue," wrote Howard Mumford Jones in 1930, "that the South is the literary land of promise today."

⚓ *F U R T H E R   R E A D I N G*

Joseph Blotner, *Faulkner: A Biography*, 2 vols. (1974)

John M. Bradbury, *Renaissance in the South: A Critical History of the Literature, 1920–1960* (1963)

Wayne D. Brazil, "*Social Forces* and Sectional Self-Scrutiny," in Merle Black and John Shelton Reed, eds., *Perspectives on the American South: An Annual Review of Society, Politics and Culture*, vol. 2 (1984), 73–104

Cleanth Brooks, *William Faulkner: The Yoknapatawpha Country* (1963)

Wilbur J. Cash, *The Mind of the South* (1941)

Louise Cowan, *The Fugitive Group: A Literary History* (1959)

F. Garvin Davenport, Jr., *The Myth of Southern History: Historical Consciousness in Twentieth-Century Southern Literature* (1970)

David Herbert Donald, *Look Homeward: A Life of Thomas Wolfe* (1987)

E. Stanley Godbold, Jr., *Ellen Glasgow and the Woman Within* (1972)

William C. Havard and Walter Sullivan, eds., *A Band of Prophets: The Vanderbilt Agrarians After Fifty Years* (1982)

Fred C. Hobson, Jr., *Serpent in Eden: H. L. Mencken and the South* (1974)

———, *Tell About the South: The Southern Rage to Explain* (1983)

Hugh C. Holman, *Three Modes of Southern Fiction: Ellen Glasgow, William Faulkner, Thomas Wolfe* (1966)

Myra Jehlen, *Class and Character in Faulkner's South* (1976)

Michael O'Brien, *The Idea of the American South, 1920–1941* (1979)

William Alexander Percy, *Lanterns on the Levee: Recollections of a Planter's Son* (1941)

Darden Asbury Pyron, "Nell Battle Lewis (1893–1956) and 'The New Southern Woman,' " in James C. Cobb and Charles R. Wilson, eds., *Perspectives on the American South*, vol. 3 (1985), 63–85

Louis D. Rubin, Jr., *The Wary Fugitives: Four Poets and the South* (1978)

———, *Writers of the Modern South: The Faraway Country* (1963)

———, ed., *The American South: Portrait of a Culture* (1980)

Louis D. Rubin, Jr., and Robert D. Jacobs, eds., *Southern Renascence: The Literature of the Modern South* (1959)

Daniel J. Singal, *The War Within: From Victorian to Modernist Thought in the South, 1919–1945* (1982)

Walter Sullivan, *A Requiem for the Renascence: The State of Fiction in the Modern South* (1976)

George B. Tindall, "The Significance of Howard W. Odum to Southern History: A Preliminary Estimate," *Journal of Southern History* 24 (1958), 285–307

CHAPTER
10

The New Deal

When the Great Depression struck, the South was already reeling from agricultural and industrial miseries. By 1932, the meager financial resources of states and localities had disappeared quickly under the avalanche of unemployment and low crop prices. A few years later, the southern economy was scarcely better, but posters bearing the likeness of President Franklin D. Roosevelt seemed to be tacked to every tobacco barn, county courthouse bulletin board, and filling station in the South. The New Deal gave southerners some work and much hope.

The Roosevelt administration did not intend to change the region's society and traditions. Southern politicians held important committee posts in the U.S. Congress and Senate and were wary of massive federal expenditures and bureaucracies that could short-circuit their economic and political control over some whites and most blacks. Intentions aside, it would have been unusual if the introduction of vast sums of federal money (at least $4 billion in the major programs) and the farm upheaval caused by low staple prices and the Agricultural Adjustment Act had not generated some changes in the region.

Historians are just now sorting out the extent of those changes and, more particularly, their legacy for the modern South. What did it mean, for example, to receive a paycheck from the federal government instead of from the county, the plantation owner, or the local grocer? What did it mean to long-time farming families and to rural traditions to leave the land? How did blacks perceive the policies of the Roosevelt administration? Were the 1930s a continuation of the critical self-assessment initiated earlier in the century, or did the decade represent a genuine watershed, laying the foundation for fundamental change in southern society?

✥ DOCUMENTS

Southern labor responded actively to the economic and policy changes of the 1930s. One of the most famous, and bloody, strikes of the decade occurred in coal-mining Harlan County, Kentucky, in 1931. Florence Reece, a local balladeer whose husband was a member of the striking National Miners Union, wrote "Which Side Are You On?" on the back of a calendar. The song, the first document here, became a classic protest song for the American labor movement. The grim conditions on the farms and in the mines and factories played a role in thrusting the author of the second document, Louisiana governor and senator Huey P. Long, into the national spotlight. The "Kingfish," as he was known, was a dyed-in-the-cotton demagogue in a region already famous for the genre, but his deeds matched his rhetoric more closely than others. The selection demonstrates why he generated such loathing and love in the South and elsewhere. The Great Depression muted the brash boosterism of the 1920s and caused even those parts of the South not given to introspection to broach topics heretofore forbidden. The third document, by the Mississippi Department of Education, is a remarkably candid assessment of black education in that state. Note the great reliance on funds from outside the state. The federal government also joined efforts to portray the South in more realistic terms. The federal Farm Security Administration sent photographers, including such noted artists as Walker Evans and Dorothea Lange, into the South during the late 1930s and 1940s to record the impact of the New Deal and what remained to be accomplished. The photographs in the fourth document reveal that New Deal policies were disruptive in some areas of the South, but traditional agricultural labor patterns prevailed in other parts of the region. Another New Deal program, the Federal Writers' Project, sent interviewers into six southern states and gathered more than four hundred "life histories." W. T. Couch, director of the University of North Carolina Press, headed the project and published some of the accounts in 1939. The fifth document is an excerpt from one of them. The final selection is a candid (and, some said, outrageous) report filed by the President's Emergency Council in 1938 detailing how much the South lagged behind the rest of the country in economic, educational, and social development.

Florence Reece's "Which Side Are You On?", 1931

Come all of you good workers,
Good news to you I'll tell,
Of how the good old union
Has come in here to dwell.

REFRAIN: Which side are you on?
            Which side are you on?

We've started our good battle,
We know we're sure to win,
Because we've got the gun thugs
A-lookin' very thin.

They say they have to guard us
To educate their child;
Their children live in luxury
Our children's almost wild.

With pistols and with rifles
They take away our bread,
And if you miners hinted it
They'd sock you on the head.

They say in Harlan County
There are no neutrals there;
You either are a union man
Or a thug for [Sheriff] J. H. Blair.

Oh workers, can you stand it?
Oh tell me how you can.
Will you be a lousy scab
Or will you be a man?

My daddy was a miner,
He is now in the air and sun [blacklisted
    and without a job]
He'll be with you fellow workers
Until the battle's won.

Huey Long, "Every Man a King," 1933

The increasing fury with which I have been, and am to be, assailed by reason of the fight and growth of support for limiting the size of fortunes can only be explained by the madness which human nature attaches to the holders of accumulated wealth.

What I have proposed is:—

The Long Plan

1. A capital levy tax on the property owned by any one person of 1% of all over $1,000,000; 2% of all over $2,000,000 etc., until, when it reaches fortunes of over $100,000,000, the government takes all above that figure; which means a limit on the size of any one man's fortune to something like $50,000,000—the balance to go to the government to spread out in its work among all the people.
2. An inheritance tax which does not allow any one person to receive more than $5,000,000 in a lifetime without working for it, all over that amount to go to the government to be spread among the people for its work.
3. An income tax which does not allow any one man to make more than $1,000,000 in one year, exclusive of taxes, the balance to go to the United States for general work among the people.

The foregoing program means all taxes paid by the fortune holders at the top and none by the people at the bottom; the spreading of wealth among all the people and the breaking up of a system of Lords and Slaves in our economic life. It allows the millionaires to have, however, more than they can use for any luxury they can enjoy on earth. But, with such limits, all else can survive.

That the public press should regard my plan and effort as a calamity

Huey P. Long, "The Maddened Fortune Holders and Their Infuriated Public Press," in *Every Man a King: The Autobiography of Huey P. Long* (New Orleans: National Book Co., 1933), pp. 338–340.

and me as a menace is no more than should be expected, gauged in the light of past events. According to Ridpath, the eminent historian:

> The ruling classes always possess the means of information and the processes by which it is distributed. The newspaper of modern times belongs to the upper man. The under man has no voice; or if, having a voice, he cries out, his cry is lost like a shout in the desert. Capital, in the places of power, seizes upon the organs of public utterance, and howls the humble down the wind. Lying and misrepresentation are the natural weapons of those who maintain an existing vice and gather the usufruct of crime."
> —Ridpath's History of the World,
> Page 410.

In 1932, the vote for my resolution showed possibly a half dozen other Senators back of it. It grew in the last Congress to nearly twenty Senators. Such growth through one other year will mean the success of a venture, the completion of everything I have undertaken,—the time when I can and will retire from the stress and fury of my public life, maybe as my forties begin,—a contemplation so serene as to appear impossible.

That day will reflect credit on the States whose Senators took the early lead to spread the wealth of the land among all the people.

Then no tear dimmed eyes of a small child will be lifted into the saddened face of a father or mother unable to give it the necessities required by its soul and body for life; then the powerful will be rebuked in the sight of man for holding that which they cannot consume, but which is craved to sustain humanity; the food of the land will feed, the raiment clothe, and the houses shelter all the people; the powerful will be elated by the well being of all, rather than through their greed.

Then, those of us who have pursued that phantom of Jefferson, Jackson, Webster, Theodore Roosevelt and Bryan may hear wafted from their lips in Valhalla:

EVERY MAN A KING

The Mississippi Department of Education on Negro Education in Mississippi, 1935

Mississippi, according to the census of 1930, has a population of 2,009,831 people. Of this number 1,009,718, or 50.2% are Negroes. Mississippi, therefore, has the largest percentage of Negro population of any state in the Union, South Carolina being second with 45.6% of its total population Negro. The latest available figures give Mississippi a total of 463,465 educable Negro school children, while only 299,261 are enrolled in our public schools, thus leaving 164,204 of school age who are not enrolled in school. Of those enrolled in school only 72% or 217,313, are in average daily attendance. Less than half of those who are supposed to be in school are

P. H. Easom, "Negro Education," in Mississippi Department of Education, *Biennial Reports and Recommendations of the State Superintendent of Public Education for the Scholastic Years 1933–1935*, pp. 40–43. Used with permission of the Mississippi Department of Education.

in regular attendance. The teaching force, numbering 5,863 teachers, has an average of 50 enrolled pupils each. This average situation is rarely ever found, for teachers in the lower grades frequently have in their charge from seventy-five to one hundred and fifty pupils. In a great many cases these teachers are forced to teach double sessions each day—one group in the forenoon and a totally different group in the afternoon. Small enrollments are found in the upper grammar grades and in the high school grades. By the time the sixth or seventh grades are reached, pupils begin to leave school in large numbers.

School Buildings

Of the 3,753 Negro schoolhouses in Mississippi, 2,313 are owned by public school authorities. The other 1,440 schools are conducted in churches, lodges, old stores, tenant houses, or whatever building is available. Last winter, with the aid of the CWA [Civil Works Administration], a considerable number of the best buildings were repaired. Up to the present time there has been only one PWA [Public Works Administration] Negro school project. It is a farm shop building at the Hopewell School in Covington County. One of the great difficulties in getting Federal aid for these buildings is the lack of local funds for meeting the requirements of the government. The Negroes themselves, in some cases, are building and repairing their schoolhouses out of their own meager savings and with their own labor.

School buildings need to be erected to displace the many little shanties and churches now being used. The Julius Rosenwald Fund, while it was operating in the South, tried to place in every county a good example of how schoolhouses should be built; but it never intended to help build a house everywhere one was needed. Now that this Fund has discontinued operations, the people are left to their own initiative in meeting this need. In the country, Negro farmers should be encouraged to raise funds for building and improving school plants by planting crop projects. One community in Neshoba County raised twenty bales of cotton in one year by each farmer planting one acre for his school. In Newton, during the past year the sum of $493.00 was raised by means of cotton projects for repairing school buildings and for providing school furniture.

There is also dire need for school furniture and teaching materials— comfortable seating facilities, stoves, blackboards, erasers, crayon, supplementary reading materials, maps, flash cards, and charts.

In many of the 3,763 colored schools of the State there is not a decent specimen of any one of the above mentioned items. In hundreds of rural schools there are just four blank, unpainted walls, a few old rickety benches, an old stove propped up on brickbats, and two or three boards nailed together and painted black for a blackboard. In many cases, this constitutes the sum total of the furniture and teaching equipment.

The only aid received during the past biennium from the Julius Rosenwald Fund was for the purchase of elementary libraries, for Rosenwald School Day Programs, for the School Plant Improvement and Beautification Program, and for a county-wide school Plant Improvement Program in Coahoma county. In the latter instance the Fund is cooperating with the school authorities of Coahoma county in employing a full-time carpenter who works throughout the year on building, repairing and beautifying school plants and school grounds. This experiment has been under way only a year, but is proving very helpful.

The Anna T. Jeanes Fund

During the past biennium a healthy interest has been manifested in the improvement of Negro rural schools through the agency of Jeanes teachers. Such teachers are employed jointly by the County Superintendent and the State Department of Education. These teachers act as assistants to the County Superintendent, and devote their entire time to Negro schools. Their activities include aiding Negro schools in the improvement of instruction, in the improvement of health work, in promoting home industries, in promoting live-at-home programs, in promoting parent-teacher association work, and in raising money from the private sources for books and other needed school equipment.

The table below summarizes part of their activities for the two years:

	NO. TEACHERS EMPLOYED	NO. SCHOOLS SUPERVISED	NO. SUPERVISORY VISITS MADE	AMOUNT JEANES FUND	AMOUNT RAISED FROM PRIVATE SOURCES
1933–34	28	1685	6416	$6,886.00	$48,646.12
1934–35	34	2030	7513	$8,799.75	$31,058.78

John F. Slater Fund

Certain sums of money, given annually by the John F. Slater Fund, are used in assisting some schools of the state known as county training schools. These funds are given for the purpose of developing high schools, and for the training of boys and girls along lines of industrial work, such as agriculture, farm shop work, and home economics.

The following summary shows the amount received for the two years of the past biennium:

1933–34	$6,450.00
1934–35	$5,760.00

General Education Board

No other agency has rendered a greater service to the southern states than the General Education Board of New York. From time to time this board has paid the salaries of different people in state department of education, given fellowships to outstanding teachers and school administrators, and promoted various and sundry other worthwhile phases of education. This Board has been exceedingly helpful to the Department of Education in Mississippi. On many occasions it has come to the rescue in time of great need.

The General Education Board has for a long time given financial assistance to the training of Negro teachers in summer schools. During the current biennium special instructors for the training of teachers in one, two, and three-teacher schools were employed with funds granted by this Board.

Negro High Schools

The development of Negro accredited high schools has been very slow. In 1932 the first attempt at accrediting such schools was made, at which time three schools were accepted by the State Accrediting Commission on the same basis as white schools are accredited. At the present time there are only fifteen fully accredited Negro high schools in this state. There are only eighty high schools for Negroes of any description in Mississippi at the present time. Many of these are private schools. The present program is to develop at least one accredited high school to each county. Fourteen counties of the State do not have a single high school or a high school grade taught within their boundaries. Curriculum offerings in Negro high schools tend strongly toward vocational subjects. There is also a great need for the establishment of a normal school for the training of rural and elementary teachers.

Photographers Record the Rural South, 1937, 1939, 1941

Tractor driver and tractor in front of empty sharecropper cabin, Leland, Mississippi, June 1937

Tenant's shack with cotton and sweet potatoes stacked on porch, Perthshire, Mississippi, October 1939

Picking cotton in Greensboro, Alabama, September 1941

Federal Writers' Project, Tore Up and a-Movin', 1939

"We hain't had no Christmas here, not a apple or a nut or nothin': I told the chil'en not to look for no Santa Claus this year, but to thank their God if they had meat and bread." Gracie Turner folds her arms across her husband's brown shirt which she wears over her worn red dress for a sweater and leaves her wash tub in the back yard to show the way to the cheerless fire-place where green wood smolders.

"Dis here is my father, Sam Horton. He has seen some years. He's ninety-one and in tole'ble good health, except his 'memb'ance ain't strong and he can't eat much grease. I've been takin' care o' him now for seven years, best I could. For the past three months he's been gettin' seven dollars and a half for de old age pension, and dat's been a help here.

"Dat's Ola in de corner." Gracie indicates an attractive mulatto girl who looks almost dainty in spite of her ragged clothes. Her feet are bare. "Ola is twenty-four. Awhile back she married a drinkin' man, but he scrapped so bad she couldn't stay wid him; so she come back home to live. Dis girl is Amy, fourteen years old. She's got bad kidney trouble; her leg swells up big as two sometimes. Dr. Simpson started givin' her treatments in de clinic, but she ain't had none in some weeks now." Amy is also barefooted.

"De littlest boy is Raymond Farmer. Dr. Farmer 'fore he died named him for his brother, Judge Raymond Farmer. Stephen is de oldest boy at home. Sam and Will belongs to my daughters, but I raised 'em. Will, go tote in some wood and stir up dis here fire! Will's mama married de second time, and I didn't know how dat new man would treat de child. Wid my husband, James Turner, and Papa and me, dat makes nine of us to stay in dese two rooms. Come on; I'll show you over de house.

"Most of us sleeps on dese three beds in here where we keeps de fire. In here is de kitchen. Mr. Jake Anderson give me dat range; it's de one Miss Bettie fust cooked on when she was married." The old stove is coated with grease, but the kitchen is orderly and fairly clean. At the table, covered with colorful oilcloth, are two long benches where the Turners sit to dine. The bowl of cold collards gives off a penetrating odor even to the front door.

"Right across de hall is de other bedroom. Come on see dat too. De girls covered dese chairs and dis settee wid de flowered cloth deyselves. Dat victrola ain't no good now. We tries to keep dis room sort o' dressed up for comp'ny, but dey ain't no fire in de heater; so we better set in de fireplace room. Today's a cold day if you ain't about stirrin'.

"Now, 'bout de other chil'en: Hattie May lives on some island down here 'bout Portsmith—Hattie May Williams she is now. Her husband does public work and seems to be a right good man, but I didn't know where he'd be good to Hattie May's Will or not. May married Montgomery, and dey sharecraps for Miss Sallie Simpson over toward Benton. Edward's married and farms for Mr. Peter Ellis at Martinsburg. Lillian Turner—now I can't tell you 'bout her, 'cause I hain't heard from her in three years. Marcy works for rich folks in Philadelphia. She sent us a box o' old clothes 'fore Christmas, and dat's de onliest string we've had this fall. De rich folks is always givin' Marcy wrist watches and necklaces and things for presents. Dey sends her down town any time wid a hund'ed dollars to buy things for 'em, and she takes every cent back to 'em it don't cost. Dey has learnt to trust Marcy. I's tried to raise my chil'en to be trusty and mannerable, to mind dey mama and papa, to be honest. 'Show favor to your mother and father,' I tells 'em, 'dat your days may be lengthened on God's earth.' If dey does wrong it shore ain't 'cause I hain't tried to learn 'em right.

"Dey ain't been much schoolin' for none of 'em. Will's in de fif', and Lillian got to de ninth. None de rest got past de fou'th grade. Turner went to school enough to write his name, but he can't do no figgerin' to 'mount to nothin'. I never went a day in my life, can't write my name or add or keep track of our account on de farm. I want dese youngest chil'en to go long enough to do dat much.

" 'Tain't no while to say dis is de hardest year we's ever had. Every year's been hard, de forty-nine years I been here. Dat's all dey is to expect—work hard and go hongry part time—long as we lives on de other man's land. Dey ain't nothin' in sharecrappin', not de way it's run. My folks has always sharecrapped. Papa farmed round Gum Springs when I was a girl, and all I learnt was to work in de field. When I married Turner, we lived in Hawley, Virginia, 'bout six months. He done public work, railroadin' and sech dere. From Hawley we moved to a farm near Gum Springs, where we worked by de day for a year. From dere we moved to my brother's and sharecrapped for him five years. Den we moved to Mr. Calep Jones', where we stayed three years. Next we moved to Mr. Hughes Whitehead's and farmed wid him two years. Our next move was to No'th Ca'lina on Mr. Jake Anderson's farm at de Woollen place. We stayed wid him thirteen years. Den last year we moved here to de Willis place, dat Mr. Dick Henry rents from Mr. Bob Willis in Gum Springs, and here we is now. But we got to move somewhere dis next year. Another man's a-comin' here. I don't know where we'll go; houses is sca'ce and hard to find. Mr. Makepeace told Turner he'd help him all he could, but he ain't got no house we can live in. Plenty o' land everywhere, but no house! Turner has been huntin' a place for weeks, and every night when he comes home I runs to de door to hear de news. Every day it's de same tale: 'I hain't found no place yet.' I hates to move; nobody knows how I hates to move!

"Yonder's somebody movin' now," Ola exclaims, looking out the window. All eyes turn toward the road. Over the deep ruts in the sand, wagon wheels grind slowly eastward; two wagons loaded with shabby furnishings wind around the curve out of sight.

"Dat's de way we'll be soon—tore up and a-movin'. I wish I could have me one acre o' land dat I could call mine. I'd be willin' to eat dry bread de rest o' my life if I had a place I could settle down on and nobody could tell me I had to move no more. I hates movin'. . . .

"When we started farmin' in March for Mr. Dick Henry, he 'lowed us five dollars a week. On de tenth o' June dey took him to de State Horspital, and Miss Annie got her brother, Mr. Bates, to tend to de farm for her. He owned up he didn't know nothin' 'bout farmin'. Fust, dey started out lettin' us have $3.50 a week; den it dwindled down to two, den to nothin'. Miss Annie said she dreaded for Sad'dys to come 'cause we was lookin' to her for money for rations, and she didn't have it. I couldn't fuss wid her, 'cause I knowed she was tellin' de truth. Mr. Bates brought some hogs here and told us to raise 'em on halves [half for the Turners; half for Mr. Bates]. I toted 'em slops all th'ugh de summer and fed 'em co'n; here dis fall he took 'em away from us, on our debt he claimed. . . .

"Mr. Henry come home 'fore Christmas and 'pears to be all right now. We hain't had no settlement wid him yet, but he told us dey wouldn't be nothin' for us this year, not to look for it. De account on de book 'gainst us is $300. How it got dat much I can't tell you. We raised 224 bags o' peas and 1800 pounds o' seed cotton on twenty acres. I knowed we couldn't make no crap, wid just twenty-four bags o' plaster 'lowed us to fertilize twenty acres. We was just about to get hongry here, with all de money cut off and no crap comin' in. Long as dey was cotton to pick or peas to shake some of us could get a day o' work now and then, enough to buy a sack o' flour and a little strip o' meat. Work has been sca'ce dis fall though. So Turner got him a WP and A [Works Progress Administration] job a-diggin' stumps. He's done had three pay days, $12.80 at de time, though he don't get but $12 'cause eighty cents has to go to Mr. Sickle for haulin' him to work. I makes dat twelve dollars do all it will, but dey's eight of us to live out'n it four weeks to de month.

"Turner ought not to be a-workin' wid de WP and A. De gover'ment's got no business a-payin' out relief money and a-givin' WP and A jobs to farmers. De old age pensions is all right for old folks dat's 'flicted and can't do. Take Papa dere; he can't work in de field now. He knocks up our wood to burn in de fireplace, but he's seen too many years to get out and work by de day. But able-bodied landers has got no business a-havin' to look to de gover'ment for a livin'. Dey ought to live of'n de land. If 'twas fixed right dey'd make all de livin' dey need from de ground. Dey ain't no sense in diggin' stumps for dollars to buy co'n and flour-bread and meat, when here's plenty o' land to raise 'em on. Every lander ought to raise his somethin' t' eat de whole year round and some to sell. Everybody's got to eat; dat's 'bout all wages comes to anyhow, somethin' t' eat. If I had de say half de land would be planted in stuff to eat; nobody would have to furnish me and overcharge me when settlement time come. . . ."

Gracie raises her head, but she remains downcast in spirit. "Dis year has been so hard we've had to drop our burial insurance. We enrolled wid de burial association in Ga'ysburg some years back. All it costs is twenty-five cents when a member dies. But dey don't come many twenty-five centses in dis house.

"Every night I prays to de Lord: 'Please keep death off till I get out'n dis shape.' Dey ain't a decent rag to bury me if I was to die right now, and I hates for de county to have to put me away."

The President's Council Reports on Southern Economic Conditions, 1938

The President's Letter

To the Members of the Conference on Economic Conditions in the South:

My intimate interest in all that concerns the South is, I believe, known to all of you; but this interest is far more than a sentimental attachment born of a considerable residence in your section and of close personal friendship for so many of your people. It proceeds even more from my feeling of responsibility toward the whole Nation. It is my conviction that the South presents right now the Nation's No. 1 economic problem—the Nation's problem, not merely the South's. For we have an economic unbalance in the Nation as a whole, due to this very condition of the South.

It is an unbalance that can and must be righted, for the sake of the South and of the Nation.

Without going into the long history of how this situation came to be—the long and ironic history of the despoiling of this truly American section of the country's population—suffice it for the immediate purpose to get a clear perspective of the task that is presented to us. That task embraces the wasted or neglected resources of land and water, the abuses suffered by the soil, the need for cheap fertilizer and cheap power; the problems presented by the population itself—a population still holding the great heritages of King's Mountain and Shiloh—the problems presented by the South's capital resources, and problems growing out of the new industrial era and, again, of absentee ownership of the new industries. There is the problem of labor and employment in the South and the related problem of protecting women and children in this field. There is the problem of farm ownership, of which farm tenantry is a part, and of farm income. There are questions of taxation, of education, of housing, and of health.

FRANKLIN D. ROOSEVELT.

The White House
Washington, D.C., July 5, 1938.

Report to the President

Population

The population of the South is growing more rapidly by natural increase than that of any other region. Its excess of births over deaths is 10 per thousand, as compared with the national average of 7 per thousand; and already it has the most thickly populated rural area in the United States. Of the 108,600,000 native-born persons in the country in 1930, 28,700,000 were born in the Southeast, all but 4,600,000 in rural districts.

These rural districts have exported one-fourth of their natural increase in sons and daughters. They have supplied their own growth, much of the growth of southern cities, and still have sent great numbers into other sections. Of these southerners born in rural areas, only 17,500,000 live in the locality where they were born, and 3,800,000 have left the South entirely.

This migration has taken from the South many of its ablest people. Nearly half of the eminent scientists born in the South are now living elsewhere. While some of these have been replaced by scientists from other sections of the country, the movement from the South has been much greater than this replacement. The search for wider opportunities than are available in the overcrowded, economically undeveloped southern communities drains away people from every walk of life. About one child of every eight born and educated in Alabama or Mississippi contributes his life's productivity to some other State.

The expanding southern population likewise has a marked effect on the South's economic standards. There are fewer productive adult workers and more dependents per capita than in other sections of the country. The export of population reflects the failure of the South to provide adequate opportunities for its people.

The largely rural States of the South must support nearly one-third of their population in school, while the industrial States support less than one-fourth. Moreover, in their search for jobs the productive middle-age groups leave the South in the greatest numbers, tending to make the South a land of the very old and the very young. A study of one southern community in 1928 showed that about 30 percent of the households were headed by women past middle age. Since 1930 most of these women, formerly able to live by odd jobs and gardening, have gone on relief. Relief studies in the eastern Cotton Belt have shown recently that 15 percent of the relief households were without a male over 16 years of age and 15 percent more, or 31 percent altogether, were without any employable male. Even if the southern workers were able, therefore, to secure wages equal to those of the North on a per capita basis dollar for dollar, a great gap would still remain between the living standards of southern families and those of other regions. . . .

Private and Public Income

Ever since the War between the States the South has been the poorest section of the Nation. The richest State in the South ranks lower in per capita income than the poorest State outside the region. In 1937 the average income in the South was $314; in the rest of the country it was $604, or nearly twice as much.

Even in "prosperous" 1929 southern farm people received an average gross income of only $186 a year as compared with $528 for farmers elsewhere. Out of that $186 southern farmers had to pay all their operating expenses—tools, fertilizer, seed, taxes, and interest on debt—so that only a fraction of that sum was left for the purchase of food, clothes, and the decencies of life. It is hardly surprising, therefore, that such ordinary items as automobiles, radios, and books are relatively rare in many southern country areas.

For more than half of the South's farm families—the 53 percent who are tenants without land of their own—incomes are far lower. Many thousands of them are living in poverty comparable to that of the poorest peasants in Europe. A recent study of southern cotton plantations indicated that the average tenant family received an income of only $73 per person for a year's work. Earnings of share croppers ranged from $38 to $87 per person, and an income of $38 annually means only a little more than 10 cents a day.

The South's industrial wages, like its farm income, are the lowest in the United States. In 1937 common labor in 20 important industries got 16 cents an hour less than laborers in other sections received for the same kind of work. Moreover, less than 10 percent of the textile workers are paid more than 52.5 cents an hour, while in the rest of the Nation 25 percent rise above this level. A recent survey of the South disclosed that the average annual wage in industry was only $865 while in the remaining States it averaged $1,219. . . .

Since the South's people live so close to the poverty line, its many local political subdivisions have had great difficulty in providing the schools and other public services necessary in any civilized community. In 1935 the assessed value of taxable property in the South averaged only $463 per person, while in the nine Northeastern States it amounted to $1,370. In other words, the Northeastern States had three times as much property per person to support their schools and other institutions.

Consequently, the South is not able to bring its schools and many other public services up to national standards, even though it tax the available wealth as heavily as any other section. In 1936 the State and local governments of the South collected only $28.88 per person while the States and local governments of the Nation as a whole collected $51.54 per person.

Although the South has 28 percent of the country's population, its Federal income-tax collections in 1934 were less than 12 percent of the national total. These collections averaged only $1.28 per capita throughout the South, ranging from 24 cents in Mississippi to $3.53 in Florida.

So much of the profit from southern industries goes to outside financiers, in the form of dividends and interest, that State income taxes would produce a meager yield in comparison with similar levies elsewhere. State taxation does not reach dividends which flow to corporation stockholders and management in other States; and, as a result, these people do not pay their share of the cost of southern schools and other institutions.

Under these circumstances the South has piled its tax burden on the backs of those least able to pay, in the form of sales taxes. (The poll tax keeps the poorer citizens from voting in eight southern States; thus they have no effective means of protesting against sales taxes.) In every southern State but one, 59 percent of the revenue is raised by sales taxes. In the northeast, on the other hand, not a single State gets more than 44 percent of its income from this source, and most of them get far less. . . .

Women and Children

Child labor is more common in the South than in any other section of the Nation, and several Southern States are among those which have the largest proportion of their women in gainful work. Moreover, women and children work under fewer legal safeguards than women and children elsewhere in the Nation.

Low industrial wages for men in the South frequently force upon their children as well as their wives a large part of the burden of family support. In agriculture, because of poor land and equipment, entire families must work in order to make their living.

The 1930 census, latest source of comprehensive information on child labor, showed that about three-fourths of all gainfully employed children from 10 to 15 years old worked in the Southern States, although these States contained less than one-third of the country's children between those ages. . . .

In a region where workers generally are exploited, women are subjected to an even more intense form of exploitation. Many women work more than 50 hours a week in cotton and other textile mills, and in the shoe, bag, paper box, drug, and similar factories in certain Southern States.

The South has two of the four states in the entire Nation that have enacted no laws whatever to fix maximum hours for women workers. Only one of the Southern States has established an 8-hour day for women in any industry. Only four of the Southern States have applied a week as short as 48 hours for women in any industry.

Reports for a number of industries, including cotton manufacturing, have shown wage earners receiving wages well below those estimated by the Works Progress Administration as the lowest which would maintain a worker's family.

Women's wages ordinarily amount to less than men's. However, only two of the Southern States have enacted a law providing a minimum wage for women, though several others are attempting to pass such legislation. Recent pay-roll figures show women textile workers in an important southern textile State receiving average wages 10 percent below the average outside the South. Other figures show that a week's wage of less than $10 was received by more than half the women in one State's cotton mills, and by a large part of the women in the seamless hosiery plants of three States and in the men's work-clothes factories of two States.

Many women, even though employed full time, must receive public aid because their wages are insufficient to care for themselves and their children. The community thus carries part of the burden of these low wages and, in effect, subsidizes the employer.

One condition tending to lower women's wages is the system by which factories "farm out" work to be done in homes. Women have been found at extremely low pay doing such work as making artificial flowers, sewing buttons on cards, clocking hosiery, embroidering children's clothing, stuffing and stitching baseballs. Although this is a relatively recent tendency in the South, there are indications that such work is increasing. Usually the pay is far below that paid in the factory. A study of industrial home work on infants' wear disclosed that the women worked much longer hours than in the factory, though half of them received less than $2.73 for their week's work.

A low wage scale means low living standards, insufficient food for many, a great amount of illness, and, in general, unhealthful and undesirable conditions of life.

✣ E S S A Y S

Numan V. Bartley, professor of history at the University of Georgia, argues that the New Deal represented a major turning point in southern history, with the breakdown of the plantation as a major event. Pete Daniel of the Smithsonian Institution analyzes that major event, detailing the dislocation, the consolidation of landholding, and, above all, the missed opportunities of New Deal agricultural policy to provide land for tenants and sharecroppers. Gavin Wright, an economics professor at the University of Michigan, effectively demonstrates how New Deal legislation, in this case an industrial minimum wage, produced change in the region but not at the expense of more fundamental cultural patterns, particularly race relations.

The New Deal as a Turning Point

NUMAN V. BARTLEY

While it would not be entirely appropriate to insist that nothing very important happened in the 1860s and the 1890s, those decades no longer seem, at least to me, to be the great watersheds that they have often been depicted.

From "The Era of the New Deal as a Turning Point in Southern History" by Numan V. Bartley, in James C. Cobb and Michael Namorato, eds., *The New Deal and the South*, pp. 138–143. Copyright © 1984 by University Press of Mississippi. Reprinted with permission.

Instead, contemporary scholarship increasingly suggests that far more fundamental changes occurred during the middle years of the twentieth century, with perhaps 1935 to 1945 best qualifying as the latest crucial decade of New South historiography. Developments set in motion during these years produced massive changes in southern life.

Among the most fundamental was the breakdown of plantation agriculture. Despite Civil War and emancipation, the plantation was the South's basic economic and social institution and essentially remained so until the 1940s. Pete Daniel entitled a recent article not "The End of Slavery" but "The Metamorphosis of Slavery." Gilbert C. Fite concluded: "Farming throughout much of the South in the 1930s was little different than in the 1870s." Jack T. Kirby noted that the planters who "organized and dominated much of the flatland and hill South" transformed their plantations during the 1930s and 1940s into capitalist "neoplantations." . . . New Deal farm programs, mechanization, and other factors precipitated an upheaval in regional life. No longer was a country philosopher apt to observe that "as soon as a farmer begins to keep books, he'll go broke shore as hell." Neoplantations kept books, and machines too, but they did not keep very many people.

The vast migration off the southern land was a fundamental demographic fact of the postdepression era. Between 1935 and 1970 more than thirteen million people left southern farms. During just the period from 1940 to 1945, more than 20 percent of the South's farm population abandoned agriculture. Both Daniel and Kirby have specifically, and in my opinion correctly, alluded to this massive exodus as a southern enclosure movement. In a traumatic kind of way, the process did more or less conform to contemporary theories of modernization. By 1930, the South had developed a dual economy of sorts, with the cities far more affluent and more "modern" than the poverty-stricken, "traditionalist" countryside, and "new ideas" did "spread outward" from the advanced "islands" to the backward areas. The process, however, was hardly benign; it uprooted a rural people from the land and cast them into the nation's cities.

The upheaval disrupted the foundations of the southern social order. Tenancy and the furnishing system, race and sex, clan and class, and related arrangements defined proper social behavior. Labor relations were usually personal and often paternal as well as being exploitive and often coercive. These patterns carried over into other areas of southern enterprise, most notably in the case of the mill villages but also in mining villages, lumber and turpentine camps, and elsewhere. This system of labor relations appeared in such odd areas as shrimp fishing, where shrimpers sometimes lived in company houses, sailed company boats, received company credit, and fished on shares. "Crewmen gets everything furnished and the factory gets a share of the shrimp," a shrimper explained to a WPA [Works Progress Administration] interviewer. "Working on a factory boat is like being a share cropper."

The network of dependency relationships was a basic feature of the southern work place. In the 1890s Edward Atkinson, a Boston textile magnate, observed that southern industrial promoters thought in terms of a large textile factory constructed largely with imported capital and operated in part by skilled workmen enticed from Massachusetts. Actually, Atkinson explained, healthy industrial growth was "a single great factory surrounded by a hundred little work shops." The lack of the "hundred little work shops" was a severe impediment to economic growth, and Atkinson's explanation for this absence was that the "idea of caste and class still prevails" in the region. With regard to capitalist development, Atkinson was precisely accurate. The "single great factory" did not threaten social stability and the patriarchal order; the "hundred little work shops" suggested a free-labor capitalism and a more dynamic social system that might threaten the "idea of caste and class." Although buttressed by a paternalistic ideology that encompassed the cult of the Lost Cause and other mythologies, the system ultimately rested on the bedrock of white supremacy, which helps to explain why virtually all establishment spokesmen placed defense of white supremacy above all other public and political virtues.

The South was by no means static, of course, and by the 1920s the growing cities nurtured an increasingly self-confident "business-oriented middle class" anxious to encourage what Blaine A. Brownell has called "the urban ethos in the South." Numerous other town and city dwellers and yeomen farmers did not live in company houses or shop on credit at company stores. Nevertheless, southerners generally were caught up in the web of marketing and credit arrangements that were a part of the South's colonial dependence on the North and were influenced by the prevailing regional commitment to social stability and a hierarchical order. W. J. Cash had a definite point when he described the southern factory as "a plantation, essentially indistinguishable in organization from the familiar plantation of the cotton fields." At any rate, New Deal wage and hours legislation, World War II economic expansion, and changing social conditions consigned factory communities to approximately the same fate as tenant farmers.

The enclosure movement in agriculture and the passing of the relatively self-contained workers' villages along with the decline of isolation and provincialism generally freed southern labor to flow unhindered in response to market forces. The result was not free labor, at least not as that term has been defined by Eric Foner and others. Instead, the collapse of paternal forms of labor control—and the word collapse is fitting despite the fact that the change extended over several decades—spurred the creation of what might best be termed commodity labor. . . . The southern work place became depersonalized and possibly dehumanized while at the same time it became less coercive and possibly less exploitive. The behavior of southern working people changed, and so too did southern society's attitudes toward work.

The decline of ideological paternalism encouraged an expanding commitment to economic growth. The urban boosterism of the 1920s gained momentum after the depression of the 1930s had exposed the bankruptcy of southern agriculture. The state planning agencies funded by the New

Deal quickly evolved into industrial promotion boards, and in 1936 Mississippi established its Balance Agriculture With Industry program. Thereafter, all of the southern states created industrial development commissions and, as James C. Cobb has demonstrated, competed vigorously with a variety of programs and policies designed to offer favors and services to national and international corporations that chose to expand into the South. Southern assistance to corporate enterprise was sufficiently generous to perhaps justify a wag's remark that the South believed in "socialism for the rich and free enterprise for the poor." By 1964 Leslie W. Dunbar of the Southern Regional Council could appropriately muse: "Southern governors have become the de facto executive directors of the state chambers of commerce, and spend their time competing with each other as supplicants for new plants. We have talked of state socialism and state capitalism, but what do we call governments whose chief affair it is to entice and propitiate business?"

Whatever the answer to Dunbar's question, the economic growth ethos came to dominate the formulation of southern state policy. Changes within southern society and most directly the black civil rights movement made institutionalized white supremacy no longer compatible with social order and led prevailing elites to identify social harmony with more factory payrolls and office parks. As the locus of southern political and economic power shifted from plantation-oriented county seats to corporation-oriented metropolitan areas, economic expansion came to be championed as the panacea for southern public problems.

This outlook, incidentally, coincided with the changing views of northern elites. In 1938 the Roosevelt administration released its *Report on Economic Conditions of the South*, which was a sound summary of the region's economic disasters. The *Report* associated virtually all of these debilities with the South's colonial dependency relationship with the North. President Roosevelt's covering letter declared the region to be "the Nation's No. 1 economic problem—the Nation's problem, not merely the South's." The document symbolized shifts in federal policies that made the national government a significant sponsor of southern economic growth. Northern liberal journals, one study has reported, tended to agree with this assessment and to favor federal aid to the South. Although the *Report* for a time made national liberals suspicious of private economic penetration of a colonized region, the dominant view soon came to be that northern corporate expansion into the region was the best solution to southern "backwardness." Thus, for much of the post–World War II era, southern elites and northern liberals were in essential agreement that northern corporate enterprise would solve southern problems.

The expansion of northern enterprise into the South and the growth of federal programs supporting southern "progress" contributed to the depopulation of rural areas and the growth of cities and factories. Commodity labor replaced the more personal labor relations of an earlier era and a growth-oriented metropolitan elite replaced a county-seat elite committed to traditional social stability. Such upheavals led to profound and as yet ill-understood changes in social structures, ideology, and personal interrelationships.

Federal Farm Policy
and the End of an Agrarian Way of Life

PETE DANIEL

At last there is a New South. Its most obvious manifestations are the gleaming towers of Atlanta, the burgeoning sunbelt culture of neocarpet-baggers, and puffing factories. Yet the rural traveler sees constant reminders of the agricultural system that once characterized the South—vacant and decaying tenant houses, sagging barns, and empty mule lots. These museum pieces stand juxtaposed with brick houses and mobile homes, bulk tobacco curers, irrigation equipment, tractors, and picking machines. The revolution in southern agriculture happened so quickly that artifacts of the old days linger on; indeed, the change has come in little more than a generation. What forces shook the rural South that since the Civil War had wallowed in an almost feudal agricultural system? What caused an evolution from a labor-intensive mode of production to one that was capital-intensive? What drove both mule and man from those primitive communities dominated by a crossroads store and a scattering of churches and schools?

In material measures the South, characterized today by huge farms, small factories, retirement villages, and even some labor unions, is prosperous beyond the dreams of the sharecroppers who used to sit on the galleries of those crossroads stores. A culture of rural poverty disappeared, one that now attracts itinerant antique dealers looking for farm bells or discarded and rusting plowpoints and anthropologists poking for cultural clues in sagging architecture, remnants of folklore, and songs.

The rural transformation has been memorialized more by novelists and autobiographers than by historians. As materially successful as the South is, such writers approach it not with praises of accomplishment but rather with a sense of loss tempered with the realization that the old ways were in themselves enervating. Whether one reads in William Faulkner of the destruction of the big woods and their traditions paralleled by the steady progress of the ruthless Snopeses, in Erskine Caldwell of the destruction of Jeeter Lester, in James Agee's text and Walker Evans's photographs of the courage and simplicity of "famous men," in Nate Shaw of the love for mule and work, in H. L. Mitchell of the failure of agrarian unionism, or in Harry Crews of the profound sense of place and suffering, there is a common element that binds this literature—reverence for the land and the constant struggle of man and often mule against nature. Since the founding of Jamestown, the southerner has been firmly planted in the soil, has strug-

From "The Transformation of the Rural South, 1930 to the Present" by Pete Daniel. *Agricultural History* 55, No. 3 (July 1981), pp. 231–244, 245–248. Copyright © 1981 by Agricultural History Society. Reprinted by permission.

gled to produce from the land the elements of survival. Institutions sprang from the necessities of people struggling with nature, and tensions that fueled that culture have supplied the dynamics that still give the South its distinctiveness.

The rural tradition that evolved over three hundred years was threatened with extinction in a generation. Challenged by depression, war, federal agricultural policy, and technological change, the old structure crumbled. Millions of people were sacrificed to modernization, whether they were the inhabitants of the valleys flooded by the Tennessee Valley Authority or the hapless croppers forfeited to the prosperity of their landlords. That country music in its various manifestations has become a national nostalgia industry only underscores the extent of change.

Literary sources and the letters and documents that make up the agricultural records of the National Archives reveal that rural life in the South, characterized by sharecropping, tenancy, and at times peonage, cannot be measured by the material standards that generally measure prosperity. For example, a sharecropper was legally a wage hand, selling his labor to a landlord, receiving his wage in a share of the crop, and likely as not moving on to another nearby farm at the first of the year to experience the same routine. The legal definition does not explain, as do the human sources that survive, that even sharecropping retained some of the traditional paternalistic protections that evolved from slavery, and a man, a family, not only took the accepted "furnish" but also chopped wood from the forest, cultivated an occasional garden, had hunting rights, and often picked up odd jobs at logging, ginning, or other manual labor. All of this added up to a meager but, for some, a satisfactory existence.

Paternalism and the customs generated by the southern agricultural system did not lead to an idyllic life. Perhaps Harry Crews puts the harsh life of tenants as graphically as anyone. "Whether on shares or on standing rent, they were still tenant farmers and survival was a day-to-day crisis as real as the rickets in the bones of their children or the worms that would sometimes rise out of their children's stomachs and nest in their throats so that they had to be pulled out by hand to keep the children from choking." Yet, farmers continued to till the land through the seasons and the years, and this created a rural population that was both tough and vulnerable. "It was a world in which survival depended on raw courage," Crews observes, "a courage born out of desperation and sustained by a lack of alternatives."

This grim existence was made bearable by church services, family visits, schools, conversations at the crossroads store, and any number of singings, drinkings, marryings, and, if the literature is any guide, fornications and adulteries. At the center of this life was a natural harmony—the seasonal plowing, planting, hoeing, harvesting, and settlement. It was a primitive way of life, a struggle for survival, as Harry Crews observed, but the human race has often found grim satisfaction in living as close to the margin of absolute failure as possible.

The legal definition aside, a sharecropper extracted more from landlords than a yearly settlement. The rules were so dictated by custom that when the Agricultural Adjustment Administration [AAA] tried to reform the system in the late 1930s both the landlords and the tenants refused to adopt the model contracts; they trusted custom more than the law. When the New Deal acreage reduction forced them off the land, sharecroppers did not ask for reform. They wanted to continue sharecropping; they wanted to stay on the land.

This rural southern culture that existed when the Great Depression struck in 1929 evolved from the Civil War labor settlement. During those years, many yeomen lost their land and became first tenants and then sharecroppers. Ever fewer owners controlled the land, and small farms rented or sharecropped typified southern agriculture. For over sixty years sharecroppers held to a status that in their minds was a cut above being a wage hand. Significantly, landlords made most of the business decisions, and the cropper tilled the leached-out soil with another man's mule, implements, and fertilizer. In this mechanically backward region, a man could farm cotton with a mule, a fertilizer distributor, a plow with a few sets of points, a few hoes, a bag to pull among the stalks at picking time, and scales to weigh-up. Tobacco culture added to this sleds, curing barns, a packhouse, and some sticks on which to hang the tobacco in the barns. Rice culture, taking a cue from midwestern wheat growers, mechanized earlier, and by the time of the depression was using binders and tractors to do much of the work and sophisticated canal networks to furnish water.

Yet there were too many people on the land, and the soil was unable to support them, at least in the traditional one-crop manner. In many areas the forest, the big woods, had been cut over, depriving croppers of fuel for their stoves, game for their tables, and winter jobs in the logwoods or at the sawmills. Simultaneously, the depression swept through the South, and odd jobs at the cotton gins or local businesses also disappeared. The old system had been able to withstand an occasional bad year, low prices, and even the boll weevil, but when depression continued and other options disappeared at the same time, poor farmers had nowhere to turn.

There had been relief experiments earlier with short-term disasters. The 1927 Mississippi River flood immersed 16.5 million acres and sent a million people scudding across the water in search of high ground. The Red Cross stepped in to feed them, and landlords feared that their hands were being spoiled. Yet planters learned that it was preferable to have their workers fed by outside agencies, and laborers discovered that being a refugee was in many ways preferable to being a sharecropper. The drought that came three years later reiterated the lesson. The Red Cross fed millions of people throughout the South, and landlords greedily accepted the aid—after the picking season was over.

The question was, of course, what role would the federal government play in relief. Under Herbert Hoover, relief proved to be piecemeal and insufficient. As the New Deal began, propaganda led farmers to believe that a new day was dawning when settlements would be fair, crop prices would soar, and a nice home would be available to all. At this point, the beginning of the New Deal, numerous forces emerged simultaneously to complicate the South's modernization. The collapse of the old plantation system was imminent, but whether the ensuing changes would be gradual or revolutionary hung in the balance.

The millions of letters that poured into Washington outlined the dreams of people faced with extinction. Most humbly asked for aid—for a cow, pigs, chickens, a small home, a loan to get started. They asked for opportunity not alms. The AAA, various alphabetical agencies of rural hope, and the president implied that there would be a new start, a New Deal. Perhaps both Congress and the president believed that the prescribed legislation would lead to such a deal, but in practice and implementation other factors intervened.

Despite the legal protection guaranteed to croppers by the AAA, many were evicted, lost whatever protection sharecropping provided, and became wage hands. In many ways this revolutionary transition paralleled the enclosure movement that centuries earlier had run some of their forebears off the land in England and in Europe. Robbed of their cropper status, they possessed only their labor to sell, and there were few buyers in the depression years. Even as they were driven off the land, the payments that went to the landlords were often used to purchase tractors or other labor-saving machines. The AAA gave protection to the landowners by price supports in the form of rental and parity payments. Using labor only at peak seasons, landlords could save the costly furnish. As mechanization increased, the demand for labor dropped off even more, and instead of landlords supplying their workers, ultimately the federal government took the place of the landlord, disbursing relief as stingily as any Snopes ever dispensed furnish. In some cases the landlords followed their croppers off the land as low prices and hard times conspired to bankrupt them. Land concentrated into yet fewer hands, and machinery allowed farmers to become more specialized. The rural work force dropped drastically, beginning a trend that continues.

New Deal agricultural policy must be measured by its stated goals, which were, primarily, to raise commodity prices and purchasing power by reducing output, to prevent a parallel reduction of tenants and sharecroppers, and to provide a new start for farmers threatened with failure. The most obvious and most researched aspect of the U.S. Department of Agriculture's [USDA] failure was its inability to solve the problems connected with the collapse of cotton tenancy. There were other manifestations of how the USDA failed to aid poor farmers while propping up commercial farmers. The examples below raise the question of whether the USDA and the AAA were attempting to save those most threatened by the forces of change or attempting to revolutionize agriculture by clearing off the old order at any cost and establishing a new structure of agriculture.

More than any other program, the Resettlement Administration and its successors the Farm Security Administration [FSA] and the Farmers' Home Administration [FHA] sought to provide relief for those families disrupted by the reduced acreage formulas of the AAA. Numerous books and articles have evaluated these programs and the political mechanics that existed within them. In a simple evaluation, however, statistics show the failure of these schemes.

In its first decade of operation, from 1937 to 1947, the FSA and its successor the FHA made tenant purchase loans totaling nearly $294 million to over 47,000 families. Since in 1945 there were still 1.9 million tenants, one historian figured that it would take the tenant purchase program "nearly 400 years to make them all owners at the rate that has prevailed so far." The FSA did not cater to those who were displaced, for it gave preference to farmers who could make down payments and had their own stock and equipment. The loan program saved those who could not obtain credit from traditional sources, usually a bank. The FSA thus helped farmers who were a cut below owners, got them started, and then closely supervised them.

Of all the farmers helped, 17.1 percent were sharecroppers and 0.6 percent were wage hands. Share renters, farmers who furnished their own workstock, tools, and fertilizer, got nearly 60 percent of the loans, and cash or standing renters, even higher up the prosperity scale, received almost 22 percent. Those aided were hardly those on the bottom rung. In essence the FSA tenant loan program did not correct the problems created by acreage reduction and eviction. Within the bounds of survival (which meant satisfying Congress that it was a financial success and safe from ideological radicalism), the FSA did stabilize the best risks left on the land.

Landlords manipulated the AAA parity and rental payments, and croppers suffered rather than prospered from this program. In the cotton program, especially, landlords took not only the rental payment, to which they were entitled, but a portion of the parity payment and in some cases all of it. When the AAA began investigations into this, landlords quickly evaded the legal obligations by forcing croppers off the farms or making them wage hands who had no claim to government money. Comparatively little of the money trickled down to the croppers.

Lawrence J. Nelson's recent article on Oscar Johnston suggests where the money went and why it went where it did. Not only did Johnston, finance director of the AAA, establish the payment rules, but also in 1934 the company that he managed received $124,000 in government payments. From 1933 to 1935 the Delta Pine and Land Company, the English corporation that Johnston managed, received $318,000 in government subsidies and a smaller plantation also managed by Johnston received nearly $78,000. Only in 1939 did the government set a cap of $10,000 in soil conservation payments to a single recipient but not until 1970 did it place a ceiling on cotton price adjustment payments—$55,000.

Many individuals and firms had multiple farms under contract, and in 1936 a published Senate Document revealed that insurance companies held large amounts of farmland and reaped significant amounts of federal money. For example, Metropolitan Life Insurance Company of New York held contracts on 1,141 cotton farms and 232 tobacco farms, John Hancock on 1,580 cotton and 7 tobacco farms, Prudential on 999 cotton and 206 tobacco farms, Union Central on 509 cotton and 58 tobacco farms, and Phoenix

Mutual on 517 cotton and 54 tobacco farms. There were 55 multiple land-owners each reporting 150 or more farms under AAA contract. These 55 concerns held almost 11,000 cotton farms and over 1,000 tobacco farms, but unfortunately the report did not reveal landowners who held less than 150 farms or received less than $10,000 in payments.

Although these large landholders received only 2 percent of cotton and 0.75 percent of tobacco payments, when coupled with checks to other sizable landlords it can be seen that the AAA program provided a large subsidy to people and institutions not directly connected to the land. Agricultural wage hands, conversely, did not receive any AAA money, croppers and share tenants received only the percentage of parity payment that was their share of the crop, while managing share tenants and renters received the entire parity payment. No matter how one analyzes the statistics, landowners, in many cases large corporations far removed from the land, received the bulk of the federal money, and they often found ways to ensure that even a greater share would go to them.

Changes in lending patterns also supported large institutions at the expense of the poorer farmers. The redistribution of farm credit between 1929 and 1934 shows a radical shift from the private to the public sector. In 1929 individuals held 44 percent of new mortgages—in 1934, 14 percent; insurance companies held 14 percent in 1929 and 3 percent five years later; banks 23 percent to 8 percent, while federal land banks increased their mortgages from 5 percent in 1929 to 68 percent five years later.

This drastic redistribution of farm credit, however, did not destroy private lending agencies; indeed, the opposite was true. As a study of the Farm Credit Administration showed, land banks moved in to fill the void left by private lending sources. From 1933 to 1939 land banks lent $2.5 billion, and 71 percent went to refinance mortgages originally held by other credit agencies, particularly banks and insurance companies. "In addition to strengthening the assets of banks and insurance companies," the report concluded, "this government lending had the effect of easing the breakdown in the private credit structure and restraining demands for its reconstruction." Thus, federal lending programs saved the private lending agencies and strengthened them through the worst of the depression. Fortunately, many struggling owners held on to their land.

After weathering the worst of the depression, private agencies again asserted themselves and by 1939 new mortgages by federal land banks had fallen to 11 percent while individuals had advanced from the 1934 figure of 14 percent to 31 percent; insurance companies from 3 to 19 and banks from 8 to 30 percent. In effect the federal loan program had financed not the farmers so much as the private lending agencies.

This readjustment was more subtle than the statistics reveal. Insurance companies, for example, had foreclosed on many mortgages and taken control of the land. They often rented land to tenants and, as discussed above, complied with the AAA programs, taking the landlord's share of the payments. By the mid 1930s they began to sell the land, again taking mortgages on it. A study by the Land Tenure Section of the Bureau of

Agricultural Economics (BAE) showed that farmers who bought land found themselves again in debt to the insurance companies, and insurance companies found themselves holding mortgages that in hard times could default to them. The depression, then, destroyed the assets of millions of indebted farmers. In 1932, for example, the twenty-six largest insurance companies acquired almost 15,000 farm properties.

The question follows, then: who owned the land in the South? There were people on the land, but they were in effect only squatting there. "Even more alarming than the high rate of tenancy," a 1935 BAE report notes, "is the small equity that the farmers of the South have in the land they operate. In addition to the tenant class, who have no equity in the farms they operate, owner-operators have no equity in the land which they rent, and due to heavy mortgage indebtedness only partial equity in the land they own." Not only did southern farmers possess little equity in the land they held but most land was held by people who were not directly connected with farming. "In all seven of that block of Cotton Belt States that included South Carolina, Georgia, Alabama, Mississippi, Arkansas, Louisiana, and Texas," the report continues, "between 60 and 70 percent of the value of the farm real-estate belonged to persons or agencies other than the farm operator." One economist calculated that "more than 84 percent of the land in the Old Plantation Piedmont section of Georgia is owned by credit companies, banks, and mortgage corporations." Such concentration also occurred in South Carolina and Alabama and no doubt throughout the South. . . .

During the first seven years of the Agricultural Adjustment Administration's acreage reduction policies, the thirteen cotton states lost over 30 percent of their sharecroppers, 12 percent of other tenants, and 9 percent of the farm owners. Georgia lost 40 percent of its sharecroppers, Alabama and Arkansas both lost 32 percent. Increasingly, tractors replaced those cut from the land.

The war siphoned off unemployed farmers into either the military or into defense industries. The havoc created by New Deal policies had in some respects been ameliorated by the war. During the war, when labor was scarcer and more expensive, farmers bought even more machinery. Those who had the foresight to invest before the war were in a good position to utilize machinery, and others, even in the restricted implements market of the war, bought what they could. Land prices, the price of farm goods, and labor prices increased, and generally farmers prospered, as can be measured by the decreasing debt during those years.

Land became increasingly concentrated into fewer hands. The BAE made numerous studies of this trend and offered suggestions, but the forces of change ground on. "In a competitive system," the BAE concluded, "family-size farms are no match for efficient large-scale operators, and 'the irresistible march of invention and machinery must foretell the doom of the small farmer just as it destroyed the small craftsman.'" Farmers discovered that the pot at the end of the rainbow contained better seeds, more fertilizer, and larger machines. The message was clear: sharecropping, which "carried" a laborer all year and in many ways cared for him, had become outdated.

The trend begun during the New Deal has continued, and price supports give stability to the larger operators while acreage reduction and increasing costs drive small farmers from the land. Whether this came about because of the executive planning of Franklin Roosevelt, the execution of it by the USDA, the successful commercial agricultural lobby, the persistent congressional revisions, or the inevitable working out of the forces of capitalism, the U.S. farm count dropped from 6.8 million in 1935 to 2.3 million in 1979. In the eleven southern states, farms declined from 2.4 million in 1940 to 723,000 in 1974, while the average size grew from 86 to 235 acres. Commercial farms dominate agriculture, for the smallest 50 percent of farms, a recent Government Accounting Office report notes, "have less than 5 percent of the sales, while at the other end of the size spectrum the situation is almost reversed, the largest 5 percent grabbing nearly 50 percent of the market."

The old cotton belt of the Carolinas and the Black Belt purged itself of tenants and the old cotton culture. Arkansas, the Mississippi Delta, and Texas continued to grow cotton, utilizing machinery, heavier fertilizer, and better seeds to increase production on fewer farms of larger acreage. Soybeans moved in to replace cotton in many areas of the South. . . .

The tobacco culture endured, in part because the AAA tobacco section proved less ruthless than the cotton section and also because mechanization came slower to tobacco. The reduction in tobacco farms has come recently, for in 1954 there were 136,000 tobacco farms in North Carolina, more than in 1934, but increasing mechanization cut tobacco farms by 90,000 in two decades. Yet North Carolina grew 300,000 pounds more tobacco in 1974 than it had in 1934.

Mechanization in the tobacco belt continues rapidly. Early tobacco harvesters in the 1950s, resembling spindly-legged birds, were inefficient. With automatic stringers, bulk barns, and finally efficient mechanical harvesters, the old fashioned hand-cropping, stringing, and wood-fired barns have all but disappeared.

Rice fared quite differently from cotton and tobacco. Rice had migrated, like cotton, from the Carolinas to Louisiana, Texas, Arkansas, and then to California. There was a steady demand for rice, and because growers and millers were highly organized, the AAA did not cut into the acreage. Because rice farmers owned a substantial amount of machinery, the AAA gave allotments to producers—not just to landlords. Although rice farms have decreased by 3,500 in Louisiana since 1934, farmers till 287,000 more acres there. In Arkansas, a booming rice area, the number of farms has increased by over 2,100 and the acreage by over 500,000.

Until the mid 1950s, the rice industry had been quite stable and had grown during the war due to a high international demand for rice. More important, rice farmers had used machines much earlier than did cotton or tobacco farmers. By the 1930s, rice farmers used tractors and binders, and during the war combines and dryers became common. Until the 1950s, tenants had protection from the policies of eviction characteristic of tobacco and cotton because of the producer allotments. Tenants in the early years could even take their "hip pocket" allotment and move from farm to farm or state to state, driving the best bargain they could with their allotment. When rice acreage was reduced in the mid 1950s, farmers urged the government to reduce the acreage progressively, like the income tax, but the USDA argued that such a plan would be unworkable. At any rate, the rice culture was less disrupted by government policies, mostly because of a consistent and then increasing demand and in no small part because of the producer allotments and earlier mechanization.

Rice, the most technologically advanced crop, and tobacco, the most retarded, have suffered least from government policies. In the early years, these programs stabilized prices and gave some security to growers. Although the tobacco culture is still characterized by small farms, federal policies since the mid 1950s and increasing mechanization have encouraged large-scale operations and forced consolidation. The depression caught cotton growers at just the wrong point between feudalism and modernization, and the Cotton Section of the AAA did not ease the transition. One disaster after another—boll weevil, flood, drought, the AAA program, tractors, war, and picking machines—swept croppers, wage hands, and small owners from the land.

In the transition from labor-intensive to capital-intensive operations, the USDA did little to protect the victims of displacement. Producer allotments in rice and minimum acreage holdings in tobacco helped some, but overall USDA policy encouraged a change in structure. Whether one looks at the size and management of farm units, the landowners, the manner of production, the ease of entry, the inheritance laws, or the credit structure, nearly all policies favored large versus small farmers. In the face of mechanization and the other dynamics of change, perhaps there was no option. Farming as a culture was superseded by large-scale farming as a commercial enterprise.

Once the forces of commercialization began, no check on them seemed possible. For the southern farmer to survive meant that he had to turn from cotton to soybeans, from mules to tractors, from stoop labor to harvesters, from prayers for rain to irrigation systems, from the almanac to the science of growing, from harmony with nature to a war against it.

In the century since the Reconstruction labor settlement set up the sharecropping system, the South has at last succumbed to the forces of capitalism. A vast enclosure movement swept millions of rural workers from the land. Who can judge or even find the statistics, the facts, to judge whether the erstwhile croppers who now inhabit urban areas North and South are better or worse off than their forebears who walked behind the plow? Does television substitute for the gallery of Will Varner's store at Frenchman's Bend? Is any pavement as solid as the soil?

By material standards the South today is prosperous. While no one would mourn the improvement in race relations or federal programs that combat hunger, the road not taken—stabilizing and upgrading sharecroppers and tenants—was the one that could have both preserved the rural culture and absorbed integration and welfare. The weeds continue to encroach on the old shacks and barns, and the decaying material remains of the plantation South are constant reminders of the death of the old culture. The agrarian values of the South are fading, just as the Vanderbilt Fugitives prophesied, buried beneath federal policy and machines.

How New Deal Wage Policy Influenced Southern Industry

GAVIN WRIGHT

The National Recovery Administration (NRA) raised the wage level for many other southern industries besides textiles. This tumultuous program was so short-lived (less than two years) and so chaotic in its operation, and is so far removed from present-day conceptions of sound economic policy, that historians have assumed it was merely a fiasco with little lasting influence. But this is not so for the South. The idea behind the NIRA (the act that created the NRA) was that recovery would be encouraged by allowing industries to prohibit unsavory forms of "cutthroat competition," thereby stabilizing both company profits and the purchasing power of labor. When the early industry response was slow (after cotton textiles), President Roosevelt announced the President's Re-employment Agreement (PRA), the so-called blanket code, in July 1933. The PRA established a limit of thirty-five hours per week per employee for industrial workers, and a forty-cent per hour minimum wage. Under this sort of pressure, codes were hastily approved in over 450 industries covering 23 million workers, or more than 90 percent of all industrial workers in the country. It was, in effect, a national minimum wage, more drastic and universal in its coverage than any that have since been passed.

The effects of the NRA were far greater on low-wage than on high-wage industries, hence far greater on the South than on the North. . . . The overnight increases in the southern hourly wage ranged from 21.5 percent in paints and varnishes to more than 70 percent in lumber [for example]. . . .

Wages did begin to slip in some industries with the demise of NRA in 1935. Plans to continue the NRA standards voluntarily were announced by some businesses, such as Dan River Mills, the Virginia-Carolina Chemical Corporation, and the American Tobacco Company. By contrast, most firms in lumber and furniture beat a quick retreat. But the retreats were limited for several reasons. Wage increases are often difficult to reverse for firms with experienced employees. In this instance, the federal government supported higher southern wages in another way, through the policies of the work-relief programs, especially the Works Progress Administration (WPA).

Originally mandated to pay local "prevailing wages," the WPA minimum rates in the southern states were only half the levels for the northern states. But between 1935 and 1939, the southern rates steadily increased while the northern rates were unchanged (in some cases they actually fell). By 1939, WPA minimums in the South were up to 80 percent of northern minimums. These rates were often more than double the farm wage, perhaps more cash money than southern workers had seen before. The WPA certainly did not employ all people who might have wanted to work at these wages. Indeed, there were cases in which whole classes of workers were dismissed from WPA jobs to work on the cotton or sugar harvest, even at lower pay. But the work-relief wage set a standard that workers could hope to get if they waited their turn; this must surely have affected wage rates in other jobs.

A second way that the federal government raised southern wages in the 1930s was through the encouragement to unionization and liberal labor legislation. The unionization rate was still far lower than that of the rest of the nation in 1940 (10.7 percent compared to 21.5 percent), but even this figure was a significant increase, and in some industries, the effect was important. Though the textile strike of 1934 was decisively defeated, when the National Labor Relations Act (NLRA) of 1935 put the federal government firmly on the side of organizing, some millowners simply accepted their legal obligation to bargain and desist from "union busting." In other cases, such as where unions would have had no chance given the balance of local power in depressed conditions, unionization was achieved only with the support of federal authorities. National unions like those of the steel and rubber workers were important forces in bringing about the full equalization of industry wages in subsequent decades. For the most part, the South remained nonunion, but the organizational efforts focused national attention on southern conditions, and the state labor departments established under New Deal pressure were a continuing presence.

In the 1930s, however, the most direct federal effect on southern wage levels came through the minimum wage provisions of the Fair Labor Standards Act (FLSA) of 1938. Though southern industries may have been of incidental concern to the drafters of the NIRA and the NLRA, the FLSA was clearly passed by Congress with its eye on the South. The act provided for an initial floor of twenty-five cents an hour, to be increased by steps of five cents a year to a limit of forty cents. Few employers outside the South were affected by these rates. Of the 690,000 workers earning less than thirty cents an hour in the spring of 1939, fully 54 percent were southern. The thirty-two and one-half cent law which went into effect in October 1939 affected 44 percent of textile workers in the South, but only 6 percent in the North. The average percentage wage increase in the southern seamless hosiery industry between 1938 and 1940 was three times as large as that in the North. The hourly wage of black workers for independent leaf-tobacco dealers actually doubled between 1935 and 1940. Certainly most of the opposition was southern and was spearheaded by the Southern Pine Association, which considered the bill "by far the most important question facing our industry.'' Cotton Ed Smith spoke for many employers when he told congress:

> Any man on this floor who has sense enough to read the English language knows that the main objective of this bill is, by human legislation, to overcome the splendid gifts of God to the South.

It is pretty good evidence that a minimum wage is effective, when the wage frequency distribution shows a marked ''heaping'' at or near the legal minimum. Many southern industry distributions came to look just this way. In lumber and timber products, half the workers in 1939–40 earned exactly the national minimum wage of thirty cents per hour. The southern lumbermen had good reason to lead the fight against the FLSA.

Why was the New Deal administration so determined to raise southern wage levels? Certainly ''high-wage'' thinking was in the air in the 1930s; many, and perhaps most, supporters simply felt that industry should be required to pay a decent wage, and that was that. The WPA, for example, was not defensive about paying wages above local levels. Its spokesmen argued that ''if any industry is paying less, somebody should investigate that industry,'' and that raising wage levels was ''good public policy in areas of extremely low living standards.'' For many advocates, the ideas that higher wages might stifle the progress of southern industry or reduce the job opportunities open to unskilled workers by stimulating mechanization were merely remote theoretical possibilities they would rather not confront. At the 1938 session of the Southern Regional Conference on Labor Legislation, a lone economics professor finally protested: ''I have been profoundly impressed with the fact that you people do not answer the arguments that are brought against you.''

But if many people were unconcerned about possible economic repercussions of higher southern wages, it is equally clear that many others were looking closely at these effects, and that slowing the progress of low-wage southern industry was precisely what they wanted to do. The concerns of northern labor and industry groups about cheap labor competition from the South were of course not new, particularly in textiles. Between 1900 and 1903, the American Federation of Labor (AFL) had employed a young Englishwoman named Irene Ashby (later Mrs. Macfadyen) in a campaign for child labor laws in Alabama, Georgia, and South Carolina. At the time of the debate over the Federal Child Labor Act of 1916 (which sought to prohibit the interstate shipment of goods produced by workers under sixteen), southern textile interests were firmly opposed but many northern producers were in support. The widespread depression and suffering in New England textiles in the 1920s led the AFL to give some priority to southern organizing by the end of that decade, and . . . industry groups gave implicit or explicit backing to efforts to raise labor standards in the southern mills. But all of these efforts intensified during the 1930s, precisely because the forces of labor were pushing wages up in the North and feared that southern competition would undermine all of their achievements.

The NRA, for example, did not question the opinion it received from the Department of Labor in 1933 that "there were no economic reasons for wage differences between regions and that these should be eliminated as soon as feasible," despite the fact that wage differences in excess of 50 percent for unskilled labor had lasted for more than a half-century at that point. Once wage rates became direct objects of national decision, the inclination to move toward this conclusion was difficult to resist. . . . Once the higher standards had been accepted as a fait accompli in the North, many northern businessmen did come to see that they too had an interest in the matter. When H. C. Berckes, chief officer of the Southern Pine Association, canvassed business contacts in preparation for the fight against the FLSA in 1937, he found "very little sympathy among a number of those contacted toward our problem in the South." . . .

It is also interesting to ask, however, why southern industrialists did not put up a better fight. In part, they simply lacked unity and regionally based organization. . . . Though southern industrialists later argued that "the NRA was devised, to a very large extent, to reform the South," it was only the following year that a concerted regional interest began to be expressed by the Southern States Industrial Council. By then, many of the changes were hard to reverse. In another dynamic that has frequently played a role in the extension of labor legislation, some *southern* firms found themselves paying high wages for one specific reason or another, and wanted to make sure that they were not undercut by "wage chiselers."

But there was another, deeper, reason why southern industrialists were defeated, namely that the political forces of the New Deal were able to mobilize a *southern* labor and voting constituency in favor of these measures. Though the secretary of the Southern States Industrial Council claimed that "practically every one" of his organization's seventeen thousand southern industrialist members opposed the Black-Connery labor standards bill (forerunner of the FLSA), the Gallup poll reported in the same year that 56 percent of Southerners were in favor. The decisive turning point in the legislative history of the FLSA came after two strong southern supporters were decisive winners in the 1938 primaries: Claude Pepper of Florida, and Lister Hill of Alabama; the latter had run for the seat vacated by the Supreme Court nomination of Hugo Black, himself the coauthor of the original bill.

It must be said, however, that not many blacks were voters in southern Democratic primaries in 1938, and black industrial workers were among the casualties of this line of policy. Just as an economist would predict, when jobs were made scarce by upward pressure on wages, racism became easier to indulge, and blacks were the first to be laid off. This tendency was unquestionably present in the interwar South well before the New Deal arrived, as demonstrated by the 1930 campaign slogan of the Atlanta Black Shirts: "Niggers, back to the cotton fields, city jobs are for white folks." But the severity increased after 1933. Black spokesmen in Washington faced a cruel choice when the proposal for a racial wage differential was advanced in the early debate over the NRA. Recognizing the risks involved, the majority felt they could not support such an "official stamp of inferiority" and worked actively against the differential. As right as they may have been for the long haul, the short-term consequences were severe. The Cowles Commission estimated that "directly or indirectly because of minimum-wage provisions of codes, about 500,000 negro workers were on relief in 1934." Even for those still working, the cuts in hours stipulated or induced by the NRA often resulted in little or no increase in weekly pay. Black newspapers derided the NRA as the "Negro Removal Act," and it is easy to understand the source of this attitude when reading the bitter complaints expressed by black tobacco workers:

> I just haven't been able to see too much good in this NRA business. I don't believe its their [the Government's] fault either. I believe its just that the employers don't do what they ought to do. They say they are under the code and they don't act like it. They try to have you think you got a raise but they cut your hours and days down so much you don't draw what you think you should draw. You don't get any more money.
>
> I was raised twice under the NRA. I worked 10 hours and 5½ days a week before the NRA and I got less money. Then they put in machines to stem since the NRA and they put me on the machines. They laid off a hundred people when that NRA come in, and they put in that machine.
>
> They made us work harder now because they takes one or two hands and tries to make them work for four or five hands. I got raised under the NRA once and then got put off because of the machines they put in.

The trend toward eliminating black jobs through mechanization and replacement by whites continued long after the NRA, under the FLSA and other sources of upward pressure on the unskilled wage. A 1941 survey found that 95 percent of new job openings in Georgia were reserved for whites. In the tobacco industry, where in 1930 two-thirds of the workers were black, the labor force was only one-fourth black by 1960.

The fact that the burdens of displacement could be largely shifted onto blacks has to be counted as an additional reason why the South succumbed to the "Yankee plot" to impose northern wages. At the 1938 Southern Regional Conference on Labor Legislation, speakers objected to the whole idea of a "southern wage differential," saying that the apparent gap was merely due to the "abundance of colored labor." The representative from Mississippi commented:

> There are industries who pick the most unskilled labor and the people that can do the least work and put them on jobs that somebody else should be doing. . . . We should try to get these people to employ more competent workers.

It does not take much reading between the lines to see the implication for black workers. Yet not much more than a decade later, a reputable economist could write that "it is unlikely that minimum wage legislation in the United States has had much effect," and that the North-South differential was largely attributable to the high percentage of nonwhites in the South. What a complete misreading of cause and effect.

⚓ *F U R T H E R   R E A D I N G*

Anthony J. Badger, *Prosperity Road: The New Deal, Tobacco, and North Carolina* (1980)
Roger Biles, *Memphis in the Great Depression* (1986)
George T. Blakey, *Hard Times and New Deal in Kentucky, 1929–1939* (1986)
Dan T. Carter, *Scottsboro: A Tragedy of the American South* (1969)
Pete Daniel, *Breaking the Land: The Transformation of Cotton, Tobacco, and Rice Cultures since 1880* (1985)
Anthony P. Dunbar, *Against the Grain: Southern Radicals and Prophets, 1929–1959* (1981)
Charles W. Eagles, *Jonathan Daniels and Race Relations: The Evolution of a Southern Liberal* (1982)
Gilbert C. Fite, *Cotton Fields No More: Southern Agriculture, 1865–1980* (1984)
Frank Freidel, *FDR and the South* (1965)
Donald H. Grubbs, *Cry from the Cotton: The Southern Tenant Farmers' Union and the New Deal* (1971)
Ronald L. Heinemann, *Depression and New Deal in Virginia: The Enduring Dominion* (1983)
John W. Hevener, *Which Side Are You On? The Harlan County Coal Miners, 1931–1939* (1978)
James A. Hodges, *New Deal Labor Policy and the Southern Cotton Textile Industry, 1933–1941* (1986)
Donald Holley, *Uncle Sam's Farmers: The New Deal Communities in the Lower Mississippi Valley* (1975)
Preston J. Hubbard, *Origins of the TVA: The Muscle Shoals Controversy, 1920–1932* (1961)
Jack Temple Kirby, *Rural Worlds Lost: The American South, 1920–1960* (1987)
A. Cash Koeniger, "The New Deal and the States: Roosevelt Versus the Byrd Organization in Virginia," *Journal of American History* 68 (1982), 876–896
Thomas A. Krueger, *And Promises to Keep: The Southern Conference for Human Welfare, 1938–1948* (1967)
Michael J. McDonald and John Muldowny, *TVA and the Dispossessed: The Resettlement of Population in the Norris Dam Area* (1982)
Paul Mertz, *New Deal Policy and Southern Rural Poverty* (1978)
H. L. Mitchell, *Mean Things Happening in This Land: The Life and Times of H. L. Mitchell, Co-Founder of the Southern Tenant Farmers Union* (1979)
Chester M. Morgan, *Redneck Liberal: Theodore G. Bilbo and the New Deal* (1985)
Lawrence J. Nelson, "Welfare Capitalism on a Mississippi Plantation in the Great Depression," *Journal of Southern History* 50 (1984), 225–250
Theodore Rosengarten, *All God's Dangers: The Life of Nate Shaw* (1974)
John A. Salmond, *A Southern Rebel: The Life and Times of Aubrey Willis Williams, 1890–1965* (1983)
Harvard Sitkoff, *A New Deal for Blacks: The Emergence of Civil Rights as a National Issue*, vol. 1: *The Depression Decade* (1978)
Morton D. Sosna, *In Search of the Silent South: Southern Liberals and the Race Issue* (1977)
Tom Terrill and Jerrold Hirsch, eds., *Such As Us: Southern Voices of the Thirties* (1979)
Nancy J. Weiss, *Farewell to the Party of Lincoln: Black Politics in the Age of FDR* (1983)
T. Harry Williams, *Huey Long* (1969)
Billy H. Wyche, "Southern Industrialists View Organized Labor in the New Deal Years, 1933–1941," *Southern Studies* 19 (1980), 157–171

CHAPTER
11

The South and the Second World War

Historians are beginning to probe the impact of World War II on the South, though contemporary observers sensed and commented on the enormous changes swirling about the region. The migration from the farm accelerated, sparked by increased employment opportunities in cities; the war heightened blacks' hopes for racial progress in the courts, on the battlefields, at polling places, and in their towns; and a flickering of prosperity dampened the chronic poverty and dependence of the South and its people. The South was on the move as millions left their communities—some for the first time in their lives—to work in distant cities or fight in even more remote places. The effect of these movements on family life and southern traditions remains largely unexplored. In addition, millions of young men from all over the country trained for war on military bases in the South. The images they carried and the impressions with which they left are still being sorted out. What impact these encounters had in forming northern opinions during the civil-rights era is another interesting and unanswered question.

There was a darker side to the South during the war years. While blacks hoped for a racial reconciliation, many whites feared it. Further, migration physically and psychologically overwhelmed some southern communities. Prosperity and hope notwithstanding, the war laid bare southerners' fears and shortcomings even more than had the Great Depression.

One historian has asked if this era was ''more important than the Civil War.'' As in the case of the New Deal, it is not yet clear whether the war was a watershed or the continuation of earlier trends in southern society.

⚓ DOCUMENTS

The war meant a rediscovery of the South for the nation. The opening and expansion of defense plants and military training bases attracted soldiers, journalists, and government bureaucrats into the region, many of whom recorded their impressions. The first two documents, one from *Fortune* magazine and the other from *Washington Post* journalist Agnes E. Meyer, not only reveal the impact of war on southern cities and on the attitudes of their people but indicate, especially in the Meyer excerpts, the condescension of the visitor. W. T. Couch, director of the University of North Carolina Press, commissioned a book written by blacks designed to explicate their aspirations during and after the war. The resulting manuscript, edited by Howard University history professor Rayford W. Logan and excerpted in the third selection, was more than he bargained for, as Couch's introduction demonstrates. The excerpts from Logan and veteran black educator Gordon B. Hancock reflect the differences between the younger, less patient generation of blacks that sought national solutions to regional racial problems, and an older generation that favored a gradualist approach to race relations undertaken by an interracial coalition within the South. The fourth document gave southern blacks considerable cause for hope. The decision in *Smith* v. *Allwright*, involving a challenge to the white primary in Texas by a black Houston dentist, held the potential of opening up the most important election in southern states—the Democratic party primary—to black voters. H. Clarence Nixon, a writer from northern Alabama and a member of the Nashville Agrarians briefly in the 1930s, summarizes in the final document the significant changes that needed to occur in the South following the war.

Fortune Magazine on Opportunities for the Deep South, 1943

For the first time since the "War Between the States," almost any native of the Deep South who wants a job can get one. The region may not have a proportionate share of wartime industry, but it has achieved a degree of industrialization unheard of five years ago. From New Orleans to North Carolina, from Memphis to Miami, the change has quickened imagination and ambition as they have not been quickened since 1861. It is a step toward what Southerners wanted for years—a broad economic basis for the solution of apparently insoluble problems like their Tobacco Roads and race question. But now that they have it, they're worried about how they will keep it—and expand it—in the face of what they regard as obstacles imposed from the outside. "We must have more than the crumbs from the North's table," say bankers, editors, merchants, liberals, conservatives, radicals, union leaders, white and Negro. Next to the war itself, no topic is hotter in the Deep South today. . . .

The National Campground

When the southern governors organized in 1941 to demand a greater share of war contracts, they complained that the South had become a campground and not an arsenal. This is still partly true. Chiefly because of the mild

"The Deep South Looks Up," *Fortune* 28 (July 1943), pp. 95–100, 218–225. Reprinted courtesy of *Fortune* Magazine, © 1943 Time, Inc.

climate, nearly a third of the U.S. armed forces in training are encamped in the Deep South. The government has spent about $1,500,000,000 or 13 per cent of all expenditures on supply depots and cantonments in the Deep South. The enormous military concentration in Florida has in a way compensated for loss of tourist trade. Miami Beach hotels have been as much as 90 per cent military. Boosters have drawn graphs to show how Florida, which has boomed after every war because soldiers came back to the sunshine, will boom again. Unlike the rest of the Deep South, the Florida east coast has few postwar worries.

In other states, soldier money has also converted cities into the equivalent of tourist resorts. Towns wisely or unavoidably have made the minimum of addition to their service facilities. Many have added little or nothing. Troops are handled as an increment—but an increment nearly as big as the thing added to. Civilians, while still trying to be extremely hospitable, are beginning to grumble that troops on leave are eating up the food and monopolizing entertainment. Landlords prosper as they never have. In places like Macon, where $40 or $50 used to be high for a six-to-eight-room house, single rooms now bring as much. Storekeepers make hay while they can. Soldiers from northern cities, where prices are ordinarily higher, have a hard time finding anything cheap down south.

One permanent effect of this military occupation may be a more widespread understanding of the Deep South's problems, or at any rate of its poverty. Another will certainly be the education of Southerners in the services. Even a few of the folks at home are becoming international-minded by firsthand contact. They have seen Russian sailors at Tampa, Dutch flyers at Jackson, Mississippi, and French *aspirants* at Columbus, Georgia. Recently a group of British sailors shocked poor whites in a coastal town by talking British Labor party politics. The natives thought they were Communists. Says a sign in a bar at Biloxi, Mississippi (a "dry" state): NO DRINKS SERVED AFTER MIDNIGHT TO MEMBERS OF THE ARMED FORCES OF THE UNITED NATIONS. At Macon, Georgia, even southern speech has been affected. Generally the soft southern accent is dominant; crossed with any other it tends to come out on top. But local girls, who would give almost anything to go out with the British air cadets stationed at nearby Cochran field, began to talk with noticeably English accents.

The biggest benefit resulting from the South's military position is the development of aviation. Florida contains upwards of ninety camps and airfields. Miami has been the chief jumping-off-place for Africa. Pan American's Thirty-sixth Street airport, now being enlarged by the Army, will probably be a main terminal for lines to South America after the war. A plane factory (managed by Vultee) is located next door, and natives see in the juxtaposition an almost infallible indication of Miami's prime importance in the new era of international air transport. Miami abounds in people who will solemnly tell you that Miami someday will be bigger than New York City. Skeptics, far in the minority, point out that merely having a yard and roundhouse never converted a railroad division point into a great metrop-

olis, and that many military fields elsewhere are badly located for commercial use. But even the smallest towns near new airports talk glowingly
of the ability of the plane to overcome what used to be the handicap of
not having railroads and harbors. Provincialism has already suffered mea-
surably. Many Southerners who had been content to let the world slip by,
who sentimentally turned their eyes inward to the imaginary glories of an
overrated past, are becoming men with world vision. . . .

Of Factories and Ships

Southern shipyard cities present some of the most acute population and
social problems in the nation. In 1940 the ship and boat yards of the Deep
South employed about 7,500 workers. Today the approaching figure is
200,000. About a quarter of them are at Mobile. . . . Next is New Orleans,
where 18,000 work for Delta (Liberty ships) and some 9,000 for Higgins.
The two boomingest shipyard towns are Panama City, in northwest Florida,
and Pascagoula, Mississippi. Panama City had a population of 20,000 in
1940, has some 60,000 today. Pascagoula had 4,000 a few years ago, has
some 30,000 today. Chambers of Commerce no longer drag out figures
proudly; they hate to look for fear they have jumped overnight.

Workers have been largely recruited from nearby rural areas. People
are living in government-built houses, in trailers, in tents, in boats. Rustics
who never learned a trade in their lives have now acquired at least part of
a skill. Women who never made more than $5 a week now consider $40
fair. Crackers who counted themselves lucky to take in $500 cash in a year
can do almost that in a month. "Hit's got me right bothered," said one
standing in front of the Hotel Marie in Panama City, "how I'm a-goin' to
spend it all." . . .

. . . Only a few of the large shipyards in the Deep South hope to survive
on any scale. Tampa Shipbuilding, which closed down after the last war,
now has a drydock and repair yard. The company fabricates bridges, makes
hydraulic mixers and pumps. It hopes to keep going after the war on these,
but not the way it is going now. Alabama Drydock & Shipbuilding of Mobile,
with more than 30,000 employees, runs the biggest drydock and ship-repair
plant on the Gulf, plans to survive on its maritime business as it has since
the last war. The city of Mobile, already on the ascendant in 1939 after
generations of tranquillity, is very active in postwar planning. It looks
forward to a big coastal and South American trade for which it is ideally
located. But Alabama Drydock anticipates only part of current volume. . . .

. . . With the possible exception of the aluminum industry, heavily
concentrated in Alabama and Tennessee, the rest of the wartime addition
to the Deep South's industrial plant also has dubious prospects. Much of
it has been in not readily convertible shell-loading plants. Though the South
will have gained a pool of semiskilled labor and machine tools, these may
mean little unless somebody arises with a workable program for making
and distributing industrial products. . . .

Race Against Race

In any other region these problems would be less noticeable even if they were greater. What complicates and intensifies them here is that six million of the Southeast's seventeen million people are Negroes. The fundamental fact to remember is that the white's attitude toward the Negro is not peculiar to the South. Because there are so many Negroes in the South, the attitude there is merely more intense and less conscious. The *average* Southerner just doesn't *think* at all about the Negro, any more than he ponders the rising and setting of the sun. He just naturally regards the Negro as inferior. . . .

Southern politicians, who know the all too human characteristics of their constituents all too well, still run the race issue ragged. "White southern boys . . ." says Governor Sam Jones of Louisiana, "do not improve in morale when they are told that one of the things they are fighting for is social equality of the Negro. They would renounce any such war aim, rightly or wrongly." A prominent southern legislator remarked recently: "If the Republican party would come out on the issue of white supremacy, it would sweep the South." Liberal Mark Ethridge, publisher of the Louisville *Courier Journal*, then Chairman of the President's Committee on Fair Employment Practice (of which more later) had to concede: "He [the Negro] must recognize that there is no power in the world—not even all the mechanized armies of the earth, Allied and Axis—which could now force the southern white people to the abandonment of the principle of social segregation."

Nevertheless, this unity of whites against Negroes is not what it once was. Developed in a feudal agrarian South, it has tended to soften up partly as the result of union activity. Since 1935, it is estimated, nearly one million white Southerners have joined trade unions with 100,000 Negroes. White and Negro members of the U.M.W. [United Mine Workers] in Birmingham are meeting together as industrial equals. Ninety per cent of the members of the Transport Workers Union in New Orleans are Negroes. Both the Farmers' Union and the conservative Farm Bureau have Negro members. Even the A. F. of L. [American Federation of Labor] last year set up an "integrated" Transport Workers Union in Mobile.

In constantly harping on white racial unity, demagogues have probably kept it more lively than it otherwise might be. For probably only a small minority of the white Southerners believe that economic and political equality is bound to end in social equality and "mongrelization." Of course, only a very small percentage of intellectual whites believe in total equality for the Negro. The bulk of the whites have no objection to the Negro's attaining a greater degree of economic opportunity, or the right to hold jobs. Despite the official stand on the poll tax, many favor political equality, or the right to vote. But they are against social equality, or the right to mingle with the other race. Unfortunately they really don't think much about it. Sometimes their demagogues denounce social equality when they are really bucking political and economic equality, and the people don't bother to think through the distinction.

What the articulate southern Negro hopes for and wants first of all is the right to take jobs for which he is qualified and the right to vote—some of the very things for which he and whites alike are fighting. He has neither. So he is either very cynical, very indignant, or very discouraged. "Seems like they're only out to lynch Hitler and Mussolini," as one Negro worker doped it out. "That's why the white folks down here got so het up about it right away." Others express their resentment in requests for a better deal from employers, both industrial and domestic. Even the humblest Negro is aware of the gap between what has been promised and what is being given. "Ask any Negro sharecropper or worker what his neighbor is thinking," says one leader, "and if he has sense enough to come out of the rain he will say that the white man cannot lick Hitler with his right hand and keep the Negro down with his left."

The contradictions of the war, in other words, have naturally made the body of Negroes restless. Their leaders reflect their restlessness in various degrees. Many do what they can within the rigid framework of southern customs. In order to get the other equalities, they tactically avoid discussion of the issue of social equality. This is the tradition of schools like Tuskegee Institute and Atlanta University. As Dr. Rufus Clement, president of the latter, puts it: "I think it is foolish to assume that we can reach our ultimate goals tomorrow."

But more and more Negro leaders and white sympathizers are becoming impatient. There are all shades of viewpoints. Labor leaders and organizations like the Southern Negro Youth Congress are concentrating on specific objectives like war jobs and the right to vote, and do not stress social equality. Most white liberals, many represented in the Southern Conference for Human Welfare, are with them. Northern Negro newspapers like the Pittsburgh *Courier* and Chicago *Defender* plug the issue of segregation. Less patient are militant little papers like *South Today*, published by whites who believe that democracy should and can be enforced now. Not to be confused with any of these are demagogues like Ethelbert Broaster of New Orleans, General Messenger of International Reassemble of the Church of Freedom League, Inc.

"The Time to Act Is Now"

Meantime, Negroes are having a hard enough time getting economic opportunity. A common attitude is exemplified by the remark of a go-getting foreman at a new shipyard: "I wouldn't hire one of the black bastards," he explained, anxious to show his discernment. "They all right on the business end of a rake or shovel, but they no good on this kind of work. Besides, the whites wouldn't stand for it. One nigger told me the law says I *had* to hire him—he was a trained welder, and we need 2,000 welders.

'I have to hire you, eh?' says I. 'Well, you insolent, uppity black so and so, you get the hell out of here before I call the *po*-lice.''

It was this kind of attitude, by no means confined to the South, that the President's Committee on Fair Employment Practice tried to fight. The committee's activities drew letters from Negroes all over. In Jackson, Mississippi, several hundred met in a church and framed a fourteen-page statement on discrimination in a local plant, and sent it to the President and Congress. The committee held enough hearings to establish proof of general racial discrimination in southeastern war industry. One of the worst examples was Gulf Shipbuilding in Mobile. Though Negroes comprise a third of the city's population the Negro percentage of Gulf employees was exactly .0013. The company blamed the A.F. of L. local union; the A.F. of L. blamed the company; training officials blamed everybody else. Today the percentage of Negroes at Gulf Shipbuilding is no more than 8. There have been few Negro training programs anywhere. According to the War Manpower Commission, only 10 per cent of war workers trained in the Southeast since 1941 have been Negroes, and many of them have had to go north for skilled employment.

When the committee started south in 1942 it got a reception from businessmen hardly more cordial than that accorded Sherman's army. Industrial leaders appealed to Governor Dixon, who tried to head it off. There were rumors of impending "race riots." There was talk of Negro "Eleanor" clubs [clubs named after the First Lady and allegedly formed by black domestics to promote civil rights; the clubs were figments of nervous white imaginations], which the FBI later found to be nonexistent. In the course of the hearings at Birmingham, rattled white witnesses found themselves saying "yessuh" to Negro interrogators.

The event not only incensed white leaders but provided some with a chance to play anti-New Deal politics. The pressure grew into one of the tensest the South has known since the Atlanta race riot in 1906. Although Mark Ethridge had made his speech of appeasement . . . in which he said the committee was not interested in promoting social equality, the politicians were not appeased. Governor Dixon refused to sign an Army contract for prison-made textiles because, he said, the contract required equality for Negroes. Judge Horace C. Wilkinson, a powerful political figure in the state, made a much-quoted and reprinted speech before the Bessemer, Alabama, Kiwanis Club. ''. . . There is need of a League to Maintain White Supremacy . . . The time to act is now. An organization should be formed so strong, so powerful, and so efficient, that this menace to our national security and our local way of life will rapidly disappear.''

The race line is still taut. There have been numerous minor clashes on busses. Segregation is being more strictly enforced. Several stores in Birmingham have erected partitions and installed cash registers on each side— one for Negroes and one for whites. Some urbanites are forming "home guard" units, and spend spare time at target practice. Out in the Delta of Mississippi, where 80 per cent or more of some counties are Negro, planters too are arming. . . .

A Better South

Informed southern leaders do not expect greater industrialization to solve automatically the Deep South's problems, economic or social. They see in it a chance to put the good will of the region, the progress made so far, on a sound economic basis. That progress has been considerable. Allowing for its starting point, the South has probably come further in the past twenty-five years than the rest of the nation. While other parts of the world were slipping into an orgy of visceral reactions, the South, at least on certain levels, was developing a remarkable capacity for self-criticism and even some tolerance for ideas alien to its traditions. While totalitarians were perfecting the art of legal lynching, the South was gradually abandoning illegal lynching. Whereas the South used to vent its emotions in bombast, it has been channeling them into some of the most arresting novels and stories in the language.

Southern liberals are speaking up boldly. "We must quit playing Ole Massa and Ole Missus (the South is the greatest stage in the world's history)," says Mark Ethridge. "We got into the trouble we are in because intelligence abdicated in favor of sentiment and immediate economics. There is no way out if we stick to sentiment; if we are not ready to abandon every prejudice, or at least re-examine it. Leadership is crystalizing; intelligent people can help . . . by creating the ferment."

More and more men are talking that way, and more and more people are listening to them. In the summer of 1942 cocky Gene Talmadge, who ousted liberal educators at the University of Georgia and used race prejudice in his campaign, was dumbfounded to find himself beaten. Credit is due in large part to the fact that people listened not to rabble rousers but to liberals. As Edna Cain Daniel, editor of the Quitman, Georgia, *Free Press*, puts it: "There was less rabble to rouse than they thought."

Agnes E. Meyer on Wartime Conditions in the Urban South, 1943

Beaumont and Port Arthur, Texas: Local War Problems

In Beaumont, East Texas, the production of the Pennsylvania Shipyards and the health of the entire East Texas area, a population of a quarter of a million people, are being endangered by a nauseous garbage dump. The shipyards used to be a half mile away from the dump, but they have now taken up this whole space.

When the wind comes one way, it blows a stench so vile over the Pennsylvania yards that the whole shift has to be pulled off the ships, causing the loss of thousands of man-hours of work. If the wind changes, the people of Beaumont are nauseated and nearly choked by the unwholesome fumes. I can testify that the experience is sickening. The city fathers have put hogs on the dump to keep down the amount of green, rotting vegetable matter, but that emergency measure scarcely improves the odor.

M. W. McMaster, director of the Pennsylvania company and its public relations officer, said: "The flies we get from the dump in the executive offices are so thick that it is almost impossible to concentrate on our duties. Twice a day the rooms are sprayed and the dead flies swept out with a broom. As soon as it gets warm we have to send people around the yard to spray the men on the job, or they would be eaten up by mosquitoes and flies. The dump is not only a hindrance to production but a menace to the health of the city of 100,000 inhabitants and the entire area from which the workers are drawn. With doctors and nurses as scarce as they are around here, an epidemic would quickly become a major disaster." . . .

Pascagoula, Mississippi: Community Co-operation on War Problems

Pascagoula is a port on the Gulf of Mexico between New Orleans and Mobile. In spite of its "newness," it has a small shipyard that has been in the same family for a hundred years. Most of the people worked at the sawmills. After the collapse of the lumber business, the small population eked out a meager subsistence by fishing, growing pecans, and gathering oysters, until Governor White started his plan to balance agriculture with industry. Under this act, Hermes Gautier, vice president of the Jackson County Board of Supervisors, managed to get a woolen mill started, which gave 600 farm girls a chance to earn a living; the dilapidated farmhouses got a coat of paint and began to "perk up" all over the county.

Through a real stroke of foresight, the little town in 1938 voted a $100,000 bond issue to improve the harbor and induce the Ingalls Iron Works of Birmingham to open shipbuilding yards for the construction of barges. The next year this concern was asked by the Maritime Commission to build merchant ships and the war orders have now put the shipyards and the town on the map as one of our important shipbuilding centers. . . .

The schools are on a double shift, and the usual trailer and tent colonies are still squatting in their disorderly huddles. The cafeterias are too crowded to be kept clean. When the health authorities placed notices on the dirtiest one that they were "out of bounds," these restaurants welcomed the idea, as it reduced their trade slightly and gave them some rest. . . .

What worries a rather inaccessible spot such as Pascagoula most is the food problem. Rationing has eased the acute shortage somewhat, but not very much. One butcher has had what is called a "display" supply of meat now and then, but anybody getting there an hour after the meat arrived did without. Nobody can spend his meat ration tickets because there is never enough. This part of the South has produced neither market gardeners nor large dairy herds; vegetables and milk are very scarce indeed.

At the high school there has been some milk just 14 times since school began last year, and 10 of these times were the result of shipments that came by carload all the way from Minnesota. At the shipyards they need

10,000 quarts of milk per day. With great effort, they manage to get 3,000. . . .

What makes the chance of panic greater is the fact that a mass of very primitive, ignorant people from the backwoods are now jammed together in the industrial centers. For weeks they have already felt the pinch of a limited food supply. They have been saying to themselves that the food situation would soon be stabilized. If it should now become worse instead of better, their restlessness and general feeling of unhappiness in a strange environment could easily reach the breaking point.

Especially here in the Gulf area there is a type of warworker from the country districts of Mississippi, Tennessee, Louisiana, and Alabama, the like of which I have never seen anywhere else. They are not only illiterate but they have transported to Pascagoula and Mobile their native habits of living; even now that an ample supply of housing units has been completed, many of them are vacant because these people cannot be induced to leave their dirty tents and unsanitary trailer communities and move into clean quarters. When the social workers begged one man with a large family to transfer them from a small tent to the housing unit, he replied, "What's good enough for the boys in Africa is good enough for me."

The unattached men and boys have almost wrecked the new dormitory. The wild specimens of sixteen and seventeen years, recruited by the National Youth Administration training schools from the mountain areas, are the most ferocious and unreliable of the lot. Nobody had a good word to say for the kind of training the NYA gives these boys. They come to the dormitory with two shirts and a pair of pants and disappear with the first check. One of them ran amuck after getting drunk, kicked holes in the walls, broke all the windows, and rammed his knife in the floor so hard that his hand slid down the blade, nearly severing the fingers. He was found sleeping it off the next day in the girls' dormitory.

There are about 2,500 people still living in tents and trailers. I visited a number of these families. Most of them are pitiful. The children are especially pathetic, dirty, ragged, undernourished and neglected from every aspect. The parents are old before they turn forty. One man who looked eighty to me spoke of himself as "an old man of fifty-one." . . .

Some of the little girls are adorned with cheap rayon taffeta dresses, trimmed with lace, that do not wash or wear well, and look pathetic when they get dirty.

In the expensive trailers, the people are of a better grade, but equally unhappy and fearful.

"Those folks in houses think trailer people are vermin," one man said to me resentfully. They feel like outcasts and resent fiercely the cleavage between them and the housed population. A sense of impermanence governs their psychology and behavior.

Many of them were misfits at home and flocked to the war centers because they did not do well among their own people. In the grocery stores they are lost, because they do not know what to buy, cannot make up their minds quickly in the crowd, and get jostled around by the others, who know their own minds and can push for the things they want. A campaign to force these people to leave their trailers and live in houses would only drive them out of Pascagoula to overrun some other industrial center. . . .

Mobile, Alabama: The War's Impact on Children

One of the pathetic aspects of the child situation in Mobile is that the girls and boys who come alone from the country to work live in dormitories with no guidance of any sort. There is not even a suitable place for them to eat. There are dirty little holes in the wall that fix them up some kind of lunch to take along for their midday meal; but when they are through with the day's work, the cheap cafeterias are crowded, and they literally never get a decent, quiet meal.

Even the highest type of children are getting into serious trouble. Middle-class mothers who now have to do all their own cooking and housework frequently neglect their children as much as those who have jobs. In one blue-blooded family of substantial means that used to have two servants, the mother, who now does her own work, has let her two children, eight and ten, get so completely out of control that they divert themselves by pulling firegongs and stealing.

It is conceded that Mobile's worst problem is the sex-delinquency of very young girls. The police chief told me that girls as young as eleven are picked up for this offense. They run away for days and weeks. Two girls, of good background, went off recently to live for a week with some young men who had a trailer. One taxi driver organized a trailer as a rendezvous and persuaded a fourteen-year-old girl who had married a departed sailor to bring in her friends. This place was discovered when the mother of a fifteen-year-old girl who had disappeared asked the police to hunt for her.

Illegitimacy is high. Many of these young mothers do not know more than the first name of the baby's father, which makes his apprehension somewhat difficult. The sex epidemic, I was told, infects the whole community to such an extent that no young girl is safe from its pervading influence. That is one reason why Mobile thinks it must establish a curfew law.

The girls, moreover, are the aggressors, and pursue not only sailors and soldiers but warworkers. They are frequently the ones who buy contraceptives, and when one druggist refused to sell these articles to a group of very young girls, they informed him contemptuously that he was an old fogey. There is a heavy baby traffic. So many people are anxious to have children that these unmarried mothers can get rid of their babies without any difficulty.

It must be said in Mobile's defense that the city has an overwhelming influx of the worst type of warworkers to be found anywhere. . . .

. . . The beautiful old city of Mobile is up to its ears in trouble. The moss-hung trees seem to be mourning its fate.

When the authorities have had time to trace back the reasons for the deplorable condition of their children, they will find that the explanation lies in their unwillingness to pay for good schools, recreational outlets, and welfare work for the youth of the city. . . .

To save its children from further degeneration, this city must have new playgrounds, a city-wide recreation program, and liberal support of the character-building youth organizations, all of which are now lacking.

Mobile needs at least 10 more war nurseries and a real social welfare program, staffed with workers experienced in family welfare and child guidance. Above all things, it needs nine new schools to keep thousands of children off the streets, together with teachers able and willing to take hold of this extremely difficult situation.

These schools should be open from 6 A.M., when the parents leave home for work, until 6 P.M., when they return. The schools will have to reach out into the community and stabilize it if the trend toward juvenile delinquency and parental negligence is to be arrested.

Mobile cannot possibly be expected to meet this great crisis with its own resources. However responsible it may be for its social deficiencies, it is not responsible for the overwhelming influx of warworkers.

What to do? is the question. The Catholic bishop wrote a letter saying that mothers should not work, but stay home and look after the children. This is, of course, contrary to the policy of the Manpower Act; but even if it were not, such admonitions are useless. Many of these workers have been half starved all their lives. The parents are both making big money for the first time, and they will fight like wild animals to keep their jobs. They have the conviction that all their past misery was due to lack of money, and here is their first big chance. Obviously the bishop's solution is not going to be followed. . . .

The parents in Mobile are obviously remiss when you find them calling up the USO to ask whether their daughters of fourteen and fifteen may entertain the soldiers. There is something lax by this time about the whole moral tone of Mobile. In the parade, for example, of the Catholic school children, while I was in Mobile, the pretty little drum majors in white hip-length tights and satin skirts, performed gyrations as they led the various bands which were anything but decorous. These little girls ended their performances by doing the split on the cold and not too clean asphalt of the city streets. I could not but wonder what the hillbillies who looked on open-mouthed were thinking of this exhibition.

Perspectives on "What the Negro Wants," 1944

Publisher's Introduction

I have argued at length elsewhere ("The Negro" in *Culture in the South*) that many of the customs and practices and discriminations of the South are a terrible burden on the region and ought to be removed. But I have also argued, and see no reason to change my view, that "no worse pun-

From W. T. Couch, "Publisher's Introduction;" Rayford W. Logan, "The Negro Wants First-Class Citizenship;" Gordon B. Hancock, "Race Relations in the United States: A Summary;" in *What the Negro Wants*, edited by Rayford W. Logan. © 1944 The University of North Carolina Press. Reprinted by permission.

ishment for Negro children in the South could be imagined than to send them to schools with white children.'' I believe that if complete elimination of segregation would be accomplished overnight—as many of the authors of this volume assume it ought to be—the consequences would be disastrous for everyone and more so for the Negro than the white man. . . .

I believe that regardless of the Negro's abilities the same justice that is good for the white man is good for the Negro. But this justice does not, cannot operate on the basis of a mechanical equality. To be just, distinctions and discriminations have to be made. If the distinctions and discriminations are made in directions that some people say are wrong—who can take such charges seriously in a world that denies the existence of any real right and wrong? I can and do, because I believe standards of right and wrong are necessary to civilization. . . .

Rayford W. Logan on What the Negro Wants

We [black people] do not stand alone. Even the conservative *Washington Post* admonished editorially that Negroes ''can scarcely be expected to give full devotion to the democratic cause unless it affords some recognition of their legitimate aspirations.'' But the more we assert these ''legitimate aspirations,'' which the *Post* did not enumerate, the more the advocates of the *status quo* become determined to deny them. Mr. Duncan Aikman reported almost a year before Pearl Harbor, before these aspirations had become resoundingly vocal, that Southerners of various economic brackets were saying: '' 'We're not going to let the Negro come out of this war on top of the heap as he did in the last one.' [!] That means,'' Mr. Aikman continued, ''and plenty of Southerners stated it specifically, no Negro officers this time; no Negro skilled labor training and, if avoidable, not even any combat regiments.'' Investigations by the National Association for the Advancement of Colored People, the National Urban League, and the Committee for Participation of Negroes in National Defense revealed at the same time a shockingly large number of Northern manufacturers and laborers, both organized and unorganized, just as determined not to use or permit to be used skilled Negro labor or to train it.

Negroes quite naturally became angry. Their anger increased when our entry into the war did not materially alter the situation. Fixed patterns of segregation in the armed forces that carried segregation into sections of the nation where it had not previously existed, limitations upon advancement, insults and violence inflicted upon men and women in uniform added to the resentment. The insistence by the Red Cross that blood from Negroes for the blood bank should be labeled Negro—in spite of the facts that a Negro physician, Dr. Charles Drew, had made significant contributions to the development of the idea of the blood bank and that science denies that blood types are determined by race—provoked extreme bitterness. The failure to give adequate publicity to white America of the feats of Negro heroes also produced much caustic criticism. The conspicuous absence of the Chairman of the Senate Committee on Foreign Relations [Tom Connally, D-Tex.] from official dinners given by the President of the United States to the Presidents of Liberia and of Haiti more than offset the fact that the Speaker of the House [Sam Rayburn] who is also from Texas rose above his racial provincialism sufficiently to perform his official duties. The discrimination imposed upon dark-skinned individuals from some Latin American nations, even when they were guests of our government, was not likely to decrease the resentment. American Negroes have been particularly distressed by the humiliations inflicted upon black French soldiers and sailors in this country. Reports of discrimination by Americans against Negroes in foreign theatres of war have cast an added pall of gloom. The little consideration given to Negroes in all parts of the world by many planners for world peace and the apparent acceptance of Prime Minister Jan Christiaan Smuts of South Africa as the spokesman for all of English Africa— all of these have caused many Negroes to ask bitterly, "What are we fighting for?"

The tension has at times become so great that periodically some "liberals," both North and South, have warned us to keep quiet. At least one rather well-known Southern colored educator publicly preaches the same doctrine. But most Negroes remember public lethargy on the Negro question in time of peace. They ask this question: If they can not assert their rights at the very time that they are risking their lives in the name of the very rights which they are asking, when will they receive consideration? We have no wish to obstruct the war effort. Rather we believe that the recognition and implementation of at least some of our legitimate aspirations will materially aid the winning of victory. Unfortunately, as this book goes to the press, the debates over the soldier vote bill, the publicly declared determination of some Southerners to filibuster the anti-poll tax bill to death reveal that the Old Guard dies but never surrenders. Many Negroes therefore remind themselves of the famous passage that William Lloyd Garrison wrote in the first issue of the *Liberator*: "I am in earnest. I will not equivocate—I will not excuse—I will not retreat a single inch. AND I WILL BE HEARD." . . .

What We Want

Negroes in the United States want first-class citizenship. There is, of course, still a considerable number who are willing to settle for less. This number is, however, growing smaller: a current expression among us asserts that "it is time for the leadership to catch up with the followship." There is also the growing conviction among us that the privileges and opportunities of the "talented tenth" are curtailed by the proscription of those privileges and opportunities to other Negroes, just as many white persons realize the danger for themselves in the proscription of these privileges and opportunities. In the name of democracy for all Americans we ask these irreducible fundamentals of first-class citizenship for all Negroes:

1. Equality of opportunity
2. Equal pay for equal work
3. Equal protection of the laws

4. Equality of suffrage
5. Equal recognition of the dignity of the human being
6. Abolition of public segregation . . .

How to Get What We Want

My own methods for achieving first-class citizenship for the Negro take as their point of departure the fact that the Negro problem in the United States is today a national problem. . . .

What must be avoided, however, is the attempt of a group in any region or locality to solve its problems without the advice, counsel, consultation, or even the "interference" of "furriners." Sectionalism has been the bane of American progress. Any attempt, therefore, to seek a sectional solution by only the inhabitants of that section runs counter to one of the most unmistakable lessons of our nation's history and of its inexorable trend. The world trend, moreover, is toward ever more distant horizons rather than toward provincialism.

The Durham, Atlanta, and Richmond conferences in which Southern Negroes and Southern whites drafted a program for the solution of the problem in the South must, therefore, be deplored so long as the participants come only from the South. So long as trains, automobiles, planes, the telephone, telegraph, printing presses, and nation-wide business, church, educational, labor and other national organizations exist, the South will not be able to make the Negro problem in the South exclusively a Southern problem. So long as we have a national Constitution, a national Congress, a Supreme Court of the nation, and national armed forces, there can be no South apart from the rest of the nation. Northern Negroes and Northern whites have the right and the duty to accept or reject any program for the South just as long as the South is a part of the nation. The only way by which the South can make its problem exclusively a Southern problem is for it to secede from the Union and surround itself with a Chinese land, sea and air wall. Even then the radio and television would penetrate this medievalism.

Gordon B. Hancock on a Southern Solution to Race Relations

The Durham Conference

What is probably the most constructive departure in race relations since the emancipation of the Negro was made in the historic conference held at Durham, North Carolina, October 20, 1942. Sixty of the most influential Negroes of the South representing all shades of thought and occupational affiliation met of their own free will and accord—and at their own expense—and drew up a statement now known as the Durham Manifesto, which has had a far reaching effect on the thought and thinking of this country. Six thousand copies of the printed statement have been sent upon request to every state of the Union where interested persons are seeking more intimate knowledge of a document that has had such dramatic reception throughout the country. The conferees not only brought forth the statement, but assumed the financial responsibility for its publication. This forthright statement by a group of Southern Negroes caught the imagination of the country and the first edition of seven thousand copies is nearing exhaustion. A prominent churchwoman recently requested sufficient copies to supply the missionary circles of her entire state where it is to be used for study groups. In the *Statement of Purpose* we read:

> The inception of this conference hinges about the tragedy that took place at the close of World War I, when returning Negro soldiers were met not with expressions and evidences of the democracy for which they had fought and for which thousands of their fellow race men had died. Instead, there was a sweeping surge of bitterness and rebuff that in retrospect constitutes one of the ugliest scars on the fair face of our nation. Interracial matters were left adrift and tragic was our experience and distressing was our disillusionment. Today the nations are again locked in mortal combat and the situation is desperate and dangerous, with the scales of fortune so delicately poised that we dare not predict what a day may bring forth; but this we know, that the Negro is again taking the field in defense of his country. Quite significant also is the fact that whereas the pronounced anti-Negro movement followed the last war, it is getting under way before the issues of the current war have been decided. In an hour of national peril, efforts are being made to defeat the Negro first and the Axis powers later. Already dire threats to throw again the Negro question into the politics of the South is becoming more and more dangerous. This is a direct challenge to the Negroes of the South who have most to gain if this threat is throttled and most to lose if it is fulfilled.
>
> The purpose then of this conference is to try to do something about this developing situation. We are proposing to set forth in certain "Articles of Cooperation" just what the Negro wants and is expecting of the post-war South and nation. Instead of letting the demagogues guess what we want, we are proposing to make our wants and aspirations a matter of record, so clear that he who runs away may read. We are hoping in this way to challenge the constructive cooperation of that element of the white South who express themselves as desirous of a New Deal for the Negroes of the South.
>
> In our "Articles of Cooperation" we are seeking for a common denominator of constructive action for the Negroes and this element of whites who are doing many of the things that we want done, and cannot do ourselves. In other words, we are proposing to draft a "New Charter of Race Relations" in the South. The old charter is paternalistic and traditional; we want a new charter that is fraternal and scientific, for the old charter is not compatible with the manhood and security of the Negro, neither is it compatible with the dignity and self-respect of the South. It ever leaves the South morally on the defensive! The Negro has paid the full price of citizenship in the South and nation, and the Negro wants to enjoy the full exercise of this citizenship, no more and no less.

The Durham Manifesto broke down the whole area of race relations into seven categories relating to political and civil rights, industry and labor, service occupations, education, agriculture, military service, social welfare and health. The statement was widely and favorably received throughout the nation, with white and Negro press not only lavish in their praise of the document but generous in the space allotted to its publicity. By its very nature it presupposed a like conference of the Southern whites which met in Atlanta, April 8, 1943, attended by over a hundred representatives from all the Southern states. The righteousness of the Negro's cause and contentions were readily conceded and full assurances of cooperation given in any reasonable plan for the achievement of the objectives outlined in the Durham Manifesto. Members of a Collaborating Committee were named to meet with a like committee representing the Durham Conference. The Collaboration Conference was held in Richmond, June 16, 1943, attended by sixty-six committeemen representing the Durham and Atlanta conferences. The Durham statement was heartily indorsed and was accepted as the "blue print" for the improvement of race relations in the South. The profound and sympathetic understanding evinced by the participating conferees can best be appreciated by an excerpt from the final report which reads in part:

> This is the problem of two great peoples caught up in the midst of transition between the powerful heritage of the past and the mighty pull of the future. For here is the white South, a great people often doing little things and good people often doing bad things. And here is the Negro South, caught as always between the upper and nether millstones of conflicting forces and as also paying the price of extraordinary transition from level to level of cultural achievement, and needing plenty of understanding and cooperation. And here is the white South inexorably conditioned by cultural complexes, suffering terribly, too, and needing sympathy and help as few peoples have ever needed in the annals of man. And, even more important, the two, white South and black South, are part and parcel of the nation whose people need, scarcely less than the two regional peoples, the sense of time and wisdom. . . .
>
> This is a rare challenge to the leadership of the South; to the white leadership to find new ways of cooperation and to justify increased confidence of Negro leadership in the white South; to sense the difficulties involved and to meet increasing demands without slowing down their essential efforts.

. . . All things considered, it is safe to say that the ground work for some constructive developments in race relations has been laid by the Durham, Atlanta and Richmond Conferences and that great things are possible if ways and means and moral courage can be found to implement the spirit of these pronouncements. If the South can be organized by states and counties into councils on race relations committed to the implementation of this spirit of the new South, there are evidences that we are heading somewhere in particular in the area of race relations. Somebody has said that the study of philosophy is like unto a blind man, in a dark room, looking for a black cat that is not in there. No such futility surrounds honest efforts at interracial adjustment in the South; for what we are trying to do must be done in defense of the Negro, the South and the nation.

Smith v. Allwright, 1944

Mr. Justice Reed delivered the opinion of the Court: . . .

Primary elections are conducted by the party under state statutory authority. The county executive committee selects precinct election officials and the county, district or state executive committees, respectively, canvass the returns. These party committees or the state convention certify the party's candidates to the appropriate officers for inclusion on the official ballot for the general election. No name which has not been so certified may appear upon the ballot for the general election as a candidate of a political party. No other name may be printed on the ballot which has not been placed in nomination by qualified voters who must take oath that they did not participate in a primary for the selection of a candidate for the office for which the nomination is made.

The state courts are given exclusive original jurisdiction of contested elections and of mandamus proceedings to compel party officers to perform their statutory duties.

We think that this statutory system for the selection of party nominees for inclusion on the general election ballot makes the party which is required to follow these legislative directions an agency of the state in so far as it determines the participants in a primary election. The party takes its character as a state agency from the duties imposed upon it by state statutes; the duties do not become matters of private law because they are performed by a political party. The plan of the Texas primary follows substantially that of Louisiana, with the exception that in Louisiana the state pays the cost of the primary while Texas assesses the cost against candidates. In numerous instances, the Texas statutes fix or limit the fees to be charged. Whether paid directly by the state or through state requirements, it is state action which compels. When primaries become a part of the machinery for choosing officials, state and national, as they have here, the same tests to determine the character of discrimination or abridgment should be applied to the primary as are applied to the general election. If the state requires a certain electoral procedure, prescribes a general election ballot made up of party nominees so chosen and limits the choice of the electorate in general elections for state officials, practically speaking, to those whose names appear on such a ballot, it endorses, adopts and enforces the discrimination against Negroes, practiced by a party entrusted by Texas law with the determination of the qualifications of participants in the primary. This is state action within the meaning of the Fifteenth Amendment. . . .

The United States is a constitutional democracy. Its organic law grants to all citizens a right to participate in the choice of elected officials without restriction by any state because of race. This grant to the people of the opportunity for choice is not to be nullified by a state through casting its electoral process in a form which permits a private organization to practice racial discrimination in the election. Constitutional rights would be of little value if they could be thus indirectly denied. . . .

The privilege of membership in a party may be . . . no concern of a state. But when, as here, that privilege is also the essential qualification for voting in a primary to select nominees for a general election, the state makes the action of the party the action of the state.

H. Clarence Nixon on the South After the War, 1944

The South, by whatever comparative test, will emerge from this war with more social change and more unfinished business than any other section of the country. It will have fewer share-croppers, but more welders and pipefitters. It will have an agriculture with relatively less plowing and hoeing, but more sowing and mowing. It will have more interest in good cattle and green pastures. It will have more industry and industrial capital, with less rural isolation and more urban sophistication. In the language of Donald Nelson, it will have more of the indispensable managerial "know-how." It will have more than a million men and women in the ranks of organized labor. It will have a Negro population with varied new skills and war experience on or beyond the seven seas. It will know a standard of living for the common man that was undreamt of in its prewar philosophy.

This region will have a few headaches along with its hopes. It will not be easy to cushion the business disruption that will accompany the withdrawal or drastic reduction of the personnel in the large military establishments which have spread over the South. This will affect wholesale and retail merchandizing, hotels and restaurants, and a host of service activities. It will take more than wishful thinking or efforts of individual Congressmen to convert expansive ordnance plants, powder factories, and munition depots into peacetime establishments with commensurate employment. It will be impossible to continue the great shipbuilding program which the war brought to the Gulf Coast and to the South's Atlantic ports, with giant payrolls and population gains as illustrated by Mobile County, Alabama, where the increase was 69 per cent from the census of 1940 to February, 1943. The inevitable curtailment of wartime airplane production will drastically affect the operation of this industry's branch plants in the South. . . .

Cotton farming and cotton textiles are important to this region in both war and peace. But the South cannot return to its traditional reliance on cotton economy in the face of national and world competition from other fibers and in the face of competition from non-American cotton. Even under the most favorable conditions, cotton could not meet our modern demands for employment and living standards, not to mention the significant factor

From H. Clarence Nixon, "The South After the War," *Virginia Quarterly Review* 20 (1944). Reprinted by permission of the publisher.

of soil exhaustion. It will require more than cotton, its processing, and its by-products for the South to hold its own in the American economic procession—more than cotton and tobacco, too.

The real postwar hope for Southern economic expansion lies in the diversified development of physical and human resources in the creation of goods and services that will constitute a net addition to the nation's total sum of goods and services, with the South at the same time increasing its own consumption *pari passu* with its increased production.

The South has many products in the earth, including coal, iron, petroleum, and sulphur, which the South and the nation need. Trees grow faster in the South than elsewhere in America, and these trees go into naval stores, lumber, furniture, paper, and other useful products, with new possibilities in the realm of plywood and plastics. Timber is spread widely over the South, and a substantial amount grows on farms. There are new hundreds of millions of sustained income from the combined timber industries through the practice of scientific conservation, cultivation, and selective cutting. With proper safeguarding, there is a regional fortune in this growing timber as well as aids to soil protection and stream control.

In addition to its timber and minerals, the South can bank on "white coal" through the actual and potential development of hydro-electric power. This is made possible by a combination of mountains and rivers, with an adequate rainfall. The Tennessee Valley Authority has demonstrated how cheap electricity can pay its own way through increased consumption by municipalities, rural co-operatives, old and new industries, and defense projects. The TVA program has constituted a solid contribution to the economic life of the Valley. It has been the prime factor in the setting up of high-class industrial plants in the South, significantly during the war. David E. Lilienthal, chairman of the TVA directorate, has a basis of experience and insight for his prophecy of a greater rôle for the TVA and a more abundant life for the South after the war. Adaptations of the TVA multiple-purpose plan might be applied to other Southern river valleys. This has been officially proposed for the Coosa-Alabama river system, which, as a stream, ranks next to the Tennessee in the Southeast.

There is a great future for the South in the utilization of its scenic, climatic, and recreational resources, and these resources do not wear out like the soil. The South's mountain, stream, shore, and sunshine together suggest recreation, vacationing, and the pursuits of leisure in summer or winter. Tourists were bringing hundreds of millions of dollars annually into the Southern states before the soldiers came, the estimate being $104,000,000 for Tennessee alone in 1941. The tourist tribe should increase after the war. The industrialization of society increasingly requires plans and provisions for rest and recreation. The region of military campgrounds in time of war should become a greater region of civilian playgrounds in time of peace. Aside from bringing in tourist dollars, the recreational facilities will enrich the lives of Southerners themselves. The South has always emphasized sports, a sense of leisure, and the art of living. It can lead the nation in providing and sharing all-year play. . . .

`    ` . . . Conservation, river and water power development, and great open spaces for recreation cannot be left to private enterprise or handled within a policy of states' rights. Governor Arnall, of Georgia, has aptly urged a shift of emphasis from states' rights to states' responsibilities. This observation is prophetic for the postwar South, which will have and desire close ties with the national government as great public programs take shape in the Southern region. The South will fare better under a sympathetic national administration with progressive leanings, and more so by meeting such an administration half way and on the level. With extensive absentee ownership and control of its private industry, the South will fare the worst under a reactionary policy of laissez-faire or minimum government.

Along with a reorientation toward governmental relations, the South is also going through a somewhat painful process of reorientation in the sphere of labor relations. In the first place, there is a steady shrinkage in the wage differential between North and South, as in various other interregional differences, whether in freight rates, interest rates, cost of living or productivity. This tendency, which was speeded by the war, will continue after the war, and the whole body of differentials may fittingly have the epitaph of the little dog named Rover, "When he died, he died all over." . . .

Falling within and without the labor picture is the problem of race relations in the South. Informed observers see a postwar crisis. Negroes can point to significant social gains in the last six years, thanks to Negro leadership, the Supreme Court, the New Deal, the CIO [Congress of Industrial Organizations], and the war, with its manpower needs affecting all races and with a United Nations' emphasis on interracial democracy. This development has put much of the white South in a paradoxical dilemma, with forward thinking in international affairs and backward thinking in interracial affairs. One horn of the dilemma will have to go. Science, statistics, and ethics oppose extravagant assumptions of "white supremacy." The Southern cultural pattern will have to change, as has the American constitutional system, to permit more economic, educational, and political opportunity to Southern Negroes, whose Northern brothers have an important strategic voting power. There is no hope for a prewar status quo through either national political party. . . .

Cutting through all economic and social relations in the postwar South, will be the central problem of community life and organization. . . .

The war has brought economic activity to many a rural community in the South without restoring its civic unity or civic spirit. This is true of my native Possum Trot in the hills of a North Alabama industrial district. Members of that neighborhood go out daily in different directions to work at distances ranging from four to fifty miles. Practically every farm family furnishes one or more industrial workers or shares rooms with industrial workers or rents a house to an industrial worker. Agriculture and industry are fused into a human balance, but organized social life is sadly lacking, much more than was the case fifty years ago. When the war is over, there will be serious need for a plan for Possum Trot or for the people of Possum

Trot, for productive employment and for participation in recreational activities and other phases of the good life. . . .

The South's greatest need for leadership and statesmanship after the war will be in education. Only through education and continuous training can the wartime gains in industrial science, technical ability, and vocational skills be maintained and expanded. Only in that way can Southern agriculture hold its own and improve in a complex world. Only in that way can community disintegration be retarded or reversed. Only in that way can demagogy and political spoils or privilege be prevented in favor of government that is efficient and democratic.

Since it is the region of the greatest proportion of children and of unschooled adults, the South needs more education upward, downward, and outward. This is needed, not only for civic and cultural values, but for a sustained capacity to produce and consume. Educated communities or regions produce more and consume more. The South cannot prosper by selling the bare necessities and a few gadgets to unskilled laborers and sharecropper farmers.

✢ E S S A Y S

George B. Tindall's essay on World War II, reprinted as the opening selection, was the first major survey of the period undertaken by a historian. Tindall juxtaposes the South's national leadership in foreign affairs with the persistence of regional customs, despite changes. In the next essay, Morton Sosna, historian, and Associate Director of the Stanford Humanities Center is more impressed by the changes, arguing that the war may well have been a "critical turning point of southern history."

Change and Resistance in the South During World War II

GEORGE B. TINDALL

In the late 1930's when the storm of war swept Asia and Europe, the main focus of American politics moved abruptly from domestic to foreign affairs. Once again, as twenty years before, a Democratic administration built its foreign policy on a foundation of Southern support. "The South's legislative role," one writer has said, "was not only marginally decisive; it furnished the bedrock of support without which United States policy might well have been paralyzed." It furnished also the cement that bound together a divided party; the phenomenon of "internationalism" spanned the entire spectrum of Southern politics from Carter Glass to Claude Pepper.

Reprinted by permission of Louisiana State University Press from *Emergence of the New South, 1913–1945* by George B. Tindall, pp. 687–692, 694–731. Copyright © 1967 by Louisiana State University Press and the Littlefield Fund for Southern History, University of Texas.

The region's devotion to a vigorous foreign policy arose from a number of factors: traditional, ethnic, economic, psychological, and political. Sentimental identification with the British, and to a lesser degree with the Chinese (because of the missionary impulse), merged with economic interests. German conquests menaced the cotton and tobacco trade with Europe and Britain. Japanese textiles, if they used Southern cotton, competed with Southern mills. The region's population included few of the German, Italian, or Irish elements that formed anti-British or isolationist nuclei in other areas. Moreover, Southern history had bred a psychology of danger and defense, and a military-patriotic tradition. The basic explanation of regional attitudes, Carter Glass said, was the Southerner's "superior character and exceptional understanding of the problem." The explanation, Erskine Caldwell said, was the Southerner's ignorance.

For whatever reasons, as the world crisis deepened, Southerners more than other Americans favored measures against Nazi, Fascist, and Japanese expansion. In the years before the Pearl Harbor attack they repeatedly displayed in the opinion polls a greater conviction that the United States would be drawn into war again, that overseas events were vital to American interests, that the nation should help France, Britain, China, and ultimately Russia, that the army and navy should be enlarged, that young men should be drafted, that neutrality legislation should be revised or repealed. In October, 1941, the Gallup poll found 88 per cent of the Southerners convinced that the defeat of Germany was more important than keeping out of war; in other regions from 63 to 70 per cent thought so. The isolationist America First Committee, despite persistent efforts, made little headway in the South.

For many senior Democrats the Wilsonian legacy remained a living force. In 1919–1920 they had gone the last mile with Wilson on the Versailles Treaty. In the end they had been frustrated by the partisan machinations of Henry Cabot Lodge, arch-foe of the South, one-time sponsor of the 1890 "Force Bill." The resultant failure to join the League of Nations led in time to the collapse of collective security and new threats to world peace. . . .

Until the spring of 1940 Southern Congressmen sustained a perfunctory lip service to neutrality and noninvolvement. But when the Nazi *blitzkrieg* overran Western Europe, Florida's Senator Claude Pepper passionately championed aid to the Allies. In May, when Hitler's forces reached the English channel, Pepper demanded the sale of American aircraft to the desperate Allies. "It is not written in the holy writ of Americanism," he asserted, "that America should be a mere spectator at Armageddon." When Paris fell he demanded mobilization. In September he defended Roosevelt's swapping American destroyers for Atlantic and Caribbean bases. A year later, in October, 1941, he declared his readiness to vote for an American expeditionary force. As early as the spring of 1941, Carter Glass, honorary chairman of the Fight For Freedom Committee, favored "doing everything possible to bring about the downfall of Hitler and his gang."

Pepper and Glass were in the vanguard. But Southern Congressmen

successively recorded their abandonment of neutrality in votes for inter-
ventionist measures. In August and September, 1940, only Senator "Cotton
Ed" Smith and three Republican representatives from Kentucky and Tennessee voted against the first peacetime draft. Conscription was necessary,
Alabama's Luther Patrick said, "to keep our Southern boys from filling up
the army." On the Lend-Lease Act of 1941 all the Representatives from
seven Southern states and a majority from the rest recorded favorable votes;
in the Senate only Reynolds of North Carolina registered opposition. Indeed
the aberrant Reynolds was the only Southerner among the twenty-six Senators who voted most consistently as isolationists on Roosevelt's proposals.
In August, 1941, only Smith and W. Lee O'Daniel joined him in voting
against renewal of the draft. In the House Speaker Rayburn barely fore-
stalled reconsideration of a 203–202 vote for extension, and thus preserved
the new army just four months before the attack on Pearl Harbor. . . .

   . . . [I]n the late 1930's and early 1940's Southern Democrats ranked
above all other regional and party groups in their devotion to intervention
and internationalism. V. O. Key, for example, in his classic study of Southern politics, recorded an analysis of thirty-four foreign policy votes in the
Senate, divided into four categories. On reciprocal trade agreements, on
preparedness and neutrality, on the lend-lease program, and later, on the
United Nations and international bank agreement in 1945, Southerners recorded more solid support than other Democrats or Republicans. Without
their overwhelming support the administration would have lost on neutrality
revision in 1939 and 1941, the Lend-Lease Act, draft extension, and authorization for seizing foreign and arming American merchant ships. . . .

   World War II activated another cycle of change in the South. To a
greater degree than the previous war it put people on the move: to shipyards,
war plants, training camps, and far-flung battlefields. It intensified established trends: in economic development, race relations, and politics. The
initial impact of the defense effort was defined by President Roosevelt in
December, 1940, when he received newsmen aboard ship in Charleston
Harbor. Asked what distinctive role the South could play in national defense, he responded: "of these million four hundred thousand people that
are going to be trained, how many are going to be trained in the South?"
Before the war ended Texas alone had accommodated over a million. Once
again the climate and open spaces of the region were the magnet for training
camps and airfields. Altogether more than four billion dollars went into
military facilities in the South, some 36 per cent of the total for the con-
tinental United States. In six states—Florida, Georgia, Mississippi, the
Carolinas, and Virginia—the expenditure exceeded that for war plants.

   Early in 1941 *Time* printed a marveling report on the "Defense Boom
in Dixie": the construction of new training camps, powder mills, shipyards,
activity in such established fields as steel and textiles, payrolls that
"bounced from one merchant's cash register to another." The "whole draft
business is just a Southern trick . . . put over by Southern merchants to
hold the big trade they get from the training camps," an irate New Jersey
trainee blurted to a reporter in Alabama that summer.

The defense effort, however, held a potential for economic development more fundamental than an "ice-cream-and-powder-mill-boom." In September, 1940, the Southern Governors' Conference urged decentralization of defense industry and called on the government to utilize the South's "vast reservoirs of natural resources and available labor." In March, 1941, after hearing Chester C. Davis of the National Defense Advisory Commission, the governors appointed a committee to wait on the President and the Office of Production Management. "Nothing short of the most rigorous and most positive efforts to achieve recognition . . . will suffice," Davis asserted. To March 1, he noted, plans for 302 defense plants included only 24 in the former Confederate states. From June, 1940, through January, 1941, those states had received only 7 per cent of the $7,500,000,000 in defense contracts; "we have followed the same pattern of regional concentration that was followed in 1917 and 1918." Davis' figures, however, omitted shipbuilding and supplies. During the first year of activity after the National Defense Act of June, 1940, the eleven Southeastern states got 11.7 per cent of the $16,824,069,000 in defense contracts, a proportion below their 21.5 per cent of the population but about equal to their proportion of existing industrial capacity.

Throughout the war the South remained more campground than arsenal, but war production increasingly moved southward. In the early period urgent need dictated that defense contracts go to areas that had the established facilities and skills. When those areas became saturated, defense production spread, partly to utilize new resources and labor, partly to decentralize for traffic and security reasons. But no policy was ever established to exploit the war effort for region building.

However, Roosevelt, who had favored shipyards in the South since his World War I experience, backed arguments by the National Resources Planning Board in favor of using the "large numbers of workers . . . available for unskilled work or for training" in "a low-income area" which needed "supplementary employment opportunity." Shipyards mushroomed around the Atlantic and Gulf coasts, even at some inland points. Newport News Shipbuilding and Dry Dock Company, the oldest in the country, experienced at making all kinds of vessels up to battleships and aircraft carriers, became the major Southern producer, chiefly for the navy. But the Norfolk and Charleston navy yards and private yards at Houston and Orange, Texas, added substantial contributions. And the Maritime Commission, a civilian agency, sponsored new or greatly enlarged shipyards in 1940 at Norfolk, Tampa, Mobile, Pascagoula, Beaumont, and Orange; in 1941 at Wilmington, New Orleans, and Houston; in 1942 at Brunswick, Jacksonville, and Panama City.

Unseasoned managers struggled with green workers to produce steel, concrete, and wooden vessels: Liberty ships, tugs, barges, landing craft, and other types. J. A. Jones, a general contractor from Charlotte, operated the Brunswick and Panama City yards with a labor force that included farmers, several prize-fighters, one Ph.D., thirteen clergymen, and in one of the pipe-welding departments an entire colored troupe, "The Original

Silas Green New Orleans Shows.'' At Pascagoula, Mississippi, Robert Ingersoll Ingalls, steel manufacturer of Birmingham, took over a dilapidated World War I shipyard and in 1940 launched the first arc-welded cargo ship, made of steel from the parent company. Pascagoula boasted the champion woman welder of the world. The most celebrated miracle-worker was Andrew Jackson Higgins, a former lumberman who had made motorboats in New Orleans before the war and who specialized in smaller craft for the army and navy. One of his many exploits was to deliver finished lighters at Norfolk in 1941 two weeks after the order, having had them painted on flat cars en route. When the war ended, seventeen Southern yards had accounted for $6,092,000,000 or nearly 23 per cent of the cost of vessels delivered by seventy principal shipyards.

Parallel to the shipyards, a line of aircraft plants sprang up, mostly at inland points from Dallas–Fort Worth, where Consolidated-Vultee began making B-24 Liberators in 1942, to Marietta, Georgia, where Bell Aircraft brought its first B-29 Superfortresses off the line in December, 1943. Important component or assembly plants appeared at Dallas, Tulsa, New Orleans, Nashville, Birmingham, and Miami. The production of ships and planes gave the South its greatest industrial thrust. In value added the census category of "transportation equipment, except automobiles" jumped suddenly from fifteenth place among Southern industries in 1939 to third place in 1945; in the number of wage earners from fourteenth to second, exceeded only by textiles.

In chemicals and related processes, war production catalyzed many new developments. By the opening of 1942 the landscape was sprouting ordnance plants that made smokeless powder and other explosives from cotton linters, wood cellulose, and petroleum products. Every Southern state participated—in six (North Carolina, Alabama, Arkansas, Kentucky, Mississippi, and Tennessee) ordnance plants were the largest item in the war expansion; in four (Louisiana, Oklahoma, Texas, and Virginia) they placed second. The largest plant was the du Pont Alabama Ordnance Works at Childersburg, near Birmingham. Other significant operations were the Holston Works at Kingsport, the Radford Works in Virginia, the Oklahoma Works at Choteau, and the Volunteer Works at Chattanooga. These were supplemented by loading plants and lesser amounts of gun and ammunition manufacture. In a class by itself, and greatest of all, was the Oak Ridge plant of the Manhattan District, twenty miles northwest of Knoxville, which processed uranium for the atomic bombs that ended the war with Japan. Altogether, the project employed some 110,000 construction workers from 1942 to 1945; peak employment in the plant was 82,000 in May, 1945.

Petroleum refineries faced a need to convert from automobile fuel to high-octane aviation gasoline, fuel oils, butadiene and styrene for synthetic rubber, toluene for explosives, and alcohol for explosives and rubber. The need for high-octane gasoline hastened conversion to a new catalytic cracking process. More than half the nation's synthetic rubber capacity centered near the petroleum resources in Louisiana and Texas, with another concentration around Louisville. The co-ordination of refinery and chemical plants suggested further potentialities for the future. Oil requirements in the East, and the operations of submarine "wolf-packs" against tankers offshore, hastened the completion of new pipelines. The Plantation line from Baton Rouge to Greensboro and the Southeastern line from Panama City to Chattanooga began to flow in 1941. In January, 1943, the "Big Inch" (24 inches) was completed from Longview, Texas, to Norris City, Illinois, and by August it extended to Philadelphia. In December, 1943, the "Little Big Inch" (20 inches) was completed from Beaumont to Linden, New Jersey.

An important growth occurred also in nonferrous metals. At Texas City a subsidiary of Jesse Jones's Reconstruction Finance Corporation built the world's largest tin smelter. Magnesium production issued from new plants at Freeport, and Austin, Texas, and Lake Charles, Louisiana. In aluminum war broke the ALCOA monopoly, which dated from 1893. In 1940 Robert S. Reynolds, whose aluminum foil plant at Richmond was an offshoot of the family's tobacco business, secured loans from the RFC [Reconstruction Finance Corporation] for alumina plants at Listerhill, Alabama (named for the Senator, who urged expansion), and Longview, Washington. After the war, Reynolds Metals Company acquired government-owned plants at Louisville and at Hurricane Creek and Jones Mill, Arkansas, as part of a deliberate program to encourage competition in the industry. Kaiser Aluminum Company, a new entry after the war, took over a government plant at Baton Rouge. ALCOA itself greatly expanded production in Tennessee and North Carolina, and established a new plant at Mobile.

The total expenditure for Southern war plants was some $4,442,000,000, or 17.6 per cent of the national total—less than the region's share of the population but more than its portion of prewar industry. Nearly a billion of this was private investment, and one study estimated another $600,000,000 in private investments not reported or not connected with the war effort. The over-all investment in the end exceeded that for military facilities, but much of it occurred later at inflated prices. The geographical balance of new capacity tilted heavily toward the Gulf Southwest. More than half the total investment went into Texas, Louisiana, and Alabama, in that order; more than a fourth into Texas alone, or some $1,435,000,000. Indeed, the South Atlantic states below Virginia ranked behind all those farther west, except Mississippi, which ranked last with $64,000,000. Virginia was fifth, after Tennessee. In 1945 Texas temporarily displaced North Carolina as the leading Southern state in value added by manufacturing.

"A bird's-eye view of large-scale Southern industry makes you feel that the South has rubbed Aladdin's lamp," War Production Board Chairman Donald M. Nelson told an Atlanta audience in 1944. Within the next generation, he suggested, Southern resources, skills, and capital would "bring the South into the vanguard of world industrial progress." The region, he noted, had the country's largest combination powder and explosive plant near Birmingham, the largest repair and supply depot at San Antonio, the largest bomber and modification plant in Marietta, one of the largest airplane factories at Dallas, the largest chemical warfare plant at

Huntsville. But the catalog suggested a serious imbalance, a preponderance of capacity ill-suited to peacetime. The region got about 43 per cent of the war-plant expenditure for chemicals and coal and petroleum products (mainly synthetic rubber and aviation gas), 36 per cent of that for ordnance, 12 for guns and ammunition, 24 for ships and aircraft, and 21 for nonferrous metals, but only about 8 per cent of the investment in iron and steel plants, 3 in machinery and electrical equipment, 1 in vehicles.

Much of the expansion, therefore, proved ephemeral, especially in the shipyards, aircraft plants, and ordnance works. Still, the war boom created permanent assets. If the South later slid back from the wartime peaks, it remained on a plateau higher than ever before. In all, Hoover and Ratchford estimated, the wartime expansion raised the region's effective industrial capacity about 40 per cent. From 1939 to 1947 the number of manufacturing establishments grew from 26,516 to 42,739, the value added from $3,124,000,000 to $10,744,000,000 and from 12.7 to 14.4 per cent of the national total. The number of production workers swelled from 1,349,000 to 2,835,000 in November, 1943, and remained at 2,023,000 in 1947. After reconversion, therefore, the South retained about half the addition to its factory force.

The significance of wartime growth did not lie in expanded capacity alone. The war introduced new dynamics of economic growth. Income payments in the South multiplied about two and a half times during the war—in 1944 governmental payments accounted for a quarter of the total, but the over-all rise continued after they slacked off. The new prosperity drew industries oriented to the market. The newly developed pool of skilled workers and experienced managers drew others. In addition the South had accumulated some amounts of local capital. More important than physical assets, perhaps, were the intangibles: the demonstration of industrial potential, new habits of mind, a recognition that industrialization demanded community services. The South had acquired certain essential ingredients of economic "take-off."

But it acquired them at a heavy cost of wartime tribulation. . . . By the spring of 1943, John Dos Passos reported, Mobile looked "trampled and battered like a city that's been taken by storm. Sidewalks are crowded. Gutters are stacked with litter. . . . Garbage cans are overflowing. Frame houses on treeshaded streets bulge with men in shirtsleeves. . . . Cues wait outside of movies and lunchrooms." Community services collapsed. Housewives kept water taps open to catch the trickle. The police force of nineteen was overwhelmed. Murphy High School, built for 2,200, had 3,650 in double shifts; it reported 1,688 absences the first twelve days of April. Juvenile delinquents ran wild; gangs robbed stores, teen-aged girls pursued sailors and war workers. Discontent wracked the shipyards with absenteeism, strikes, and racial conflict. Not until mid-1944 did federally aided services and housing begin to catch up with the problem. But somehow ships were built. . . .

Other communities seethed with anarchy, in greater or lesser degree. Every war town, Marvin Schlegel noted in his account of Norfolk, had its

uniform-crazy "V-girls" who became "VD-girls" through their contribution
to morale. Norfolk itself, a center of naval and shipbuilding activity,
achieved an unequaled reputation for squalor, perhaps because it was so
easily reached by Eastern muckrakers. Walter Davenport of *Collier's*
started the exposés in 1942 with "Norfolk Nights," which reported, among
lesser sensations, a "girlie" trailer camp with Hollywood titles over the
doors: "It Happened One Night," "All That Money Can Buy." *American
Mercury* tagged Norfolk "Our Worst War Town." *Architectural Record*,
PM, *Business Week*, and *Domestic Commerce* joined the indictment. When
a reporter appeared from Baltimore the local paper announced wearily,
"The *Sun* also rises." In 1943 the notoriety finally brought a Congressional
investigation which sparked belated action on housing, vice, and other
problems. Norfolk, like Mobile, began to overtake its problems before the
war ended.

Estimates based on war ration books showed that from 1940 to 1943
civilian population in the South shrank by 1,422,000. Nevertheless thirty-
nine of forty-eight metropolitan areas gained. Savannah grew 29 per cent,
Charleston 37, Norfolk 57, Mobile 61. Over the decade to 1950 urban
population rose 35.9 per cent. Military service and war plants drew off
people long chained to the farm, broadened their horizons, gave them new
skills. From 1940 to 1945 the South's farm population decreased by
3,347,000, or 20.4 per cent, with the greatest losses in Depression problem
areas: the Ozark-Ouachita region, the Eastern and Western upland cotton
areas, the North-South border region, and to lesser degree, the Appalachians. Meanwhile farm owners increased and the number of tenants
dropped, though less sharply than farm population, from 1,449,293 to
1,165,279. A substantial number flowed into the stream of out-migration.

But those who stayed on the land enjoyed a rare prosperity. Farm
prices rose steadily after a period of sharp uncertainty in the fall of 1939.
Tobacco went from 15.4 cents per pound in 1939 to 42.6 cents in 1945;
cotton from 9.89 to 22.52 cents. Tobacco farmers, after their disastrous
experiment with *laissez-faire* in 1939, stabilized production at a level somewhat below the bumper crop of 1939 until 1944 and 1945, when the crop
reached nearly two billion pounds in each year. In the cotton market domestic needs offset a decline in exports, and production stayed around
eleven to twelve million bales until bad weather brought a drop to nine and
then eight and a half million in 1945 and 1946. However, the stabilization
reflected improved yields, for the acreage dropped from 22,811,000 in 1939
to 17,584,000 in 1945. Army camps and industrial complexes offered outlets
for foodstuffs and spurred expansion in dairying and truck farming. Heightened demand for oilseed products raised the production of peanuts, especially in Georgia, Alabama, and Texas. In the Black Belts of Alabama
and Mississippi the transition to livestock, spurred first by the boll weevil,
got new impetus.

But the failure to diversify further was the story of an opportunity lost.
"The outstanding example of misused . . . resources in agriculture during
the war effort," Walter W. Wilcox wrote afterward, "occurred in the Cotton

Belt." Despite an urgent demand for foods, despite a domestic carry-over that never fell much below 10,500,000 bales, despite labor shortages, cotton still absorbed vast amounts of manpower and fertilizer. The wartime drive for diversification assumed the familiar character of exhortation. "There's no sense in continuing to pile up cotton," Secretary of Agriculture Claude A. Wickard told a Memphis audience in September, 1941. "The country needs milk and eggs and meat a lot worse." "We cannot eat surplus cotton," Georgia Farm Bureau President R. L. Wingate said in 1944. "We cannot eat tobacco. . . . We have got to grow food." The Department of Agriculture publicized a system of "goals" for "essential war crops" and Congress extended price support to such crops, but continued the same support for "basic" crops like cotton. Cotton farmers, therefore, preferred to stay with the familiar rather than risk the unknown. . . .

. . . "A prosperous farmer's the most conservative man on earth," an Alabama farmer told John Dos Passos. "We were plenty sick for a while. Now we feel about ready to throw away our crutches. Just leave us alone. Get us good prices and let us produce." With a preponderance of political power in the South, John Temple Graves observed, "the farmer was apparently swinging it against his New Deal patrons and being encouraged by the industrialists, most of whom were long-standing anti-New Dealers." As late as 1937 Ed O'Neal was calling Virginia's Senators "reactionary"; by the early 1940's he was joining Harry Byrd in attacks on the Farm Security Administration (FSA).

The FSA, as an independent power structure, became a prime target of the agricultural establishment. It came under attack for its co-operative farms, mostly inherited from the Resettlement Administration, for its loans to land-leasing and land-purchasing associations, for its tenant-rehabilitation and tenant-land-purchase programs, for helping Negro farmers. "Now comes the New Deal," a Mississippi Delta planter wrote in 1942, ". . . with a law to acquire our plantation . . . and divide the land up again into family sized farms of 40 acres and a mule—the same promise the other Yankees made to the negroes during the other Civil War."

Will Alexander, FSA's first administrator, was an "off-color politician," Georgia's Representative Eugene Cox said. Calvin B. "Beanie" Baldwin, a small-town businessman from Virginia who succeeded him in 1940, grew into an intransigent liberal, inept at maneuver, unwilling to compromise. Baldwin's FSA became increasingly militant in defense of small farmers, tenants, and laborers, but unequal to the growing attack. In 1942 FSA assumed responsibility for most of the wartime farm labor programs, through which it undertook to move workers from submarginal lands to areas of labor shortage and sought to assure minimum standards for its recruits. Among other things, it found jobs for displaced members of the Southern Tenant Farmers Union. Instead of "devoting your efforts to the development of agriculture in the South," Georgia's Representative Malcolm C. Tarver stormed at Baldwin, "you are going out after this fly-by-night program of trying to move some hundreds of thousands, if not millions, of farmers and their families out of the South."

The attack built slowly to a crescendo during the war. In 1942 Harry Byrd investigated the FSA for extravagance and Kenneth McKellar asserted flatly, "I think Mr. Baldwin is a Communist." An Alabama judge created a momentary sensation with a charge that FSA provided funds for poll-tax payments. Closer scrutiny revealed only that it included poll taxes in its clients' family budgets. In truth, FSA's fatal weakness was the absence of an organized political constituency. Yet it did not altogether lack defenders, including John Bankhead, who quarreled with the Farm Bureau on this point. Clarence Poe's *Progressive Farmer* accused Ed O'Neal of "a tragic mistake in joining hands with those elements that are seeking to destroy the Farm Security Administration" and driving "a wedge of bitterness between land-owning farmers and other farmers all over the South." In a public letter leaders of several farm, labor, and church organizations charged that the attacks came "solely from farm interests committed to the high-price-through-scarcity concept" and defended FSA on the ground that it would contribute to war food production. In 1943 this rather dubious idea became the basis of a desperate effort by Baldwin to save FSA by enmeshing it with the Agriculture Department's credit and war production programs.

Meanwhile a conservative-minded Congress whittled away his powers. In 1942 it slashed the FSA budget by 30 per cent, most heavily in the migratory labor camp and tenant purchase programs; forbade further loans to co-operatives; prohibited direct land purchases, collective farming, and homestead associations; and required reports every six months on liquidation of the resettlement program. Early in 1943 North Carolina's Representative Harold D. Cooley put through a resolution for an investigation. Witnesses paraded their charges before his committee while the Farm Bureau and its allies kept up a drum-fire of opposition. Oscar Johnston's National Cotton Council joined the fray with charges of "mismanagement, waste of funds, decreased production, and Communistic activities," and requested that "general rumors" of this nature be forwarded to the council. "But how can they call a program to build up the family-size farm communistic?" John Dos Passos asked an Alabama dairy farmer. "Well, around here communism's anything we don't like," the man replied. "Isn't it that way everywhere else?"

In 1944 the Cooley Committee published its inventory of FSA sins: farm collectives, stretching executive orders, uprooting families, deception, loans to unqualified persons, backing industry in competition with business, and enlarged and inefficient organization. But the report was anticlimactic. Late in 1943 Baldwin had resigned under pressure to be replaced by a "safe" administration under former Representative Frank Hancock of North Carolina. Liquidation proceeded apace and in 1946 Congress replaced FSA with the Farmers Home Corporation, which administered a reduced tenant purchase program.

Commercial farmers who, like businessmen, had manpower problems of their own, viewed labor in much the same perspective. The price-control and food-subsidy disputes set them against urban workers as rivals for shares of the national income. "Farmers resent the efforts of organized labor leaders to influence agricultural policies that are intended to force farmers to toil and sweat unlimited hours at price levels far below industrial wages and industrial prices," Ed O'Neal said. Labor shortages and rising wages came closer home. From 1940 to 1945 the average rate for picking seed cotton rose 211 per cent, from 62 cents a hundred pounds to $1.93. The American war worker "has so much money he doesn't know what to do with it," O'Neal complained. "How can the farmer compete for labor. . . ?" The protest broadened out into generalized attacks. "We must realize that the present administration is not a Democratic party," Mississippi Farm Bureau President Ransom Aldrich told a Greenville meeting. "It is a New Deal party, a labor government. We are letting creep in with the labor policy of the government a lot of communism and state socialism." President Craig Smith of the Alabama Cotton Manufacturers Association, speaking to the Talladega Kiwanians, denounced efforts by metropolitan papers and "professional labor leaders" to portray farmers as war profiteers.

Organized labor, despite substantial gains during the war, remained too weak to temper the rural orientation of most Southern politicos. Quite the contrary, the antilabor obsession quickened movements for antiunion legislation. In Houston Vance Muse, whose "Christian American Association" had explored thin veins of racial and religious prejudice since 1936, finally struck pay-dirt in the antiunion cause. In 1941, after Governor O'Daniel put through a law forbidding violence or threats on the picket line, they began to promote "Anti-Violence-in-Strikes" laws, "God-Given Right-to-Work" laws, and union registration laws. In 1942 Mississippi adopted an antiviolence law on the Texas model. In 1943 Texas, Alabama, and Florida enacted restrictions that required union financial statements and licenses for union agents; limited union fees; prohibited jurisdictional strikes, secondary boycotts, and mass picketing; regulated union elections and the expulsion of members; and banned union political contributions. In 1944 Arkansas and Florida by constitutional amendment set in motion a wave of right-to-work legislation that would crest in 1947 when Georgia, North Carolina, Tennessee, Texas, and Virginia adopted laws against the closed shop and other union security devices. Once started, the movement developed its own momentum, but Vance Muse admitted collecting $67,873.49 to ballyhoo the Arkansas amendment and confessed to significant influence on labor legislation in Alabama, Florida, Mississippi, and Texas.

But the most inflammable issue ignited by the war was the question of Negro participation in the defense effort. From the beginning Negro leaders kept up an unremitting demand for full recognition. In September, 1940, Walter White, A. Philip Randolph, and T. Arnold Hill presented at the White House a program for full integration of Negroes into the armed forces and defense industries. Soon thereafter White House Press Secretary Stephen Early announced a policy of receiving Negroes into the Army in proportion to population, but in separate units. Walter White indignantly denied the implication that the Negro group had endorsed this. Such units as were authorized, he protested, were mainly service and supply units. And the Navy had openings only for Negro mess attendants, stewards, and cooks.

A few significant appointments did little to quiet the outcry. In October, 1940, shortly before the election, Benjamin O. Davis became the first Negro brigadier general, and Negro assistants were named for the Secretary of War and the Director of Selective Service. But as the armed forces grew, Negroes did find a greater variety of positions than in any previous war. Eventually about a million served, in every major branch and in every theater. But they served under circumstances that mirrored the society from which they came, usually in segregated units. In April, 1942, the Navy began to accept Negroes for general service and because it lacked traditional Negro units developed a variegated pattern that ranged up to fairly thorough integration in places. In 1944 the Navy began to commission Negro officers.

But most Negroes served in the Army, which maintained its tradition of separate units through the war. Every camp had its little Harlem, its separate facilities, its periodic racial "incidents." The most publicized departure from the pattern was a 1944 order that banned segregation in recreational and transportation facilities on Army bases, an order honored chiefly by evasion. More important was a 1940 decision to give up segregation in all officer candidate schools except those for Air Force cadets. A separate flight school at Tuskegee, Alabama, trained about six hundred Negro pilots, many of whom saw action over Europe. The nearest approach to integration in ground combat forces occurred during the Battle of the Bulge early in 1945, when the Army distributed platoons of Negro volunteers from the Service of Supply, about 2,500 in all, among eleven white divisions. They fought through the subsequent drive across Germany.

War industries were even less accessible to Negro influence and pressure than the armed forces, although government policy theoretically opposed discrimination. In July, 1940, the National Defense Advisory Commission appointed Robert C. Weaver to the staff of its Labor Division and in August it urged employers not to discriminate, but buried the recommendation in a long statement on labor policy. In October an appropriation act prohibited discrimination in defense training, but local officials in the South frustrated enforcement with the sophism that Negroes should get training only for jobs already open to them. As the defense programs advanced, Negroes saw little evidence that nondiscriminatory policies were implemented. During the fall of 1940 A. Philip Randolph conceived the idea of a mass march on Washington to dramatize job demands and in February, 1941, a meeting in New York organized the March on Washington Movement, with July 1 as its target date. As the movement grew, its leaders promised to mobilize 100,000 marchers. The Office of Production Management, in a letter signed by Sidney Hillman but not by his colleague William S. Knudsen of General Motors, again called upon defense contractors to hire Negro workers, and Roosevelt demanded "immediate steps to facilitate the full utilization of our manpower." Negro leaders rejected these as empty gestures and the administration, alarmed at the prospect of a mass descent on Washington, maneuvered desperately to forestall the march. Finally, a series of conferences produced a recommendation for a Presidential directive against discrimination and the establishment of a grievance committee. This Randolph's group accepted. On June 25 President Roosevelt issued Executive Order 8802 which forbade discrimination in defense industries and training programs, required a nondiscrimination clause in defense contracts, and established the Committee on Fair Employment Practice (FEPC).

Chaired first by Mark Ethridge, publisher of the Louisville *Courier-Journal*, the FEPC wielded chiefly a moral influence, since it had no power to enforce directives and refused to recommend the ultimate weapon, cancellation of defense contracts. Moreover, it initiated investigations only upon complaint. Its first major action was to seek information and publicize the President's policy through regional hearings: in Los Angeles, Chicago, New York, and Birmingham. At Birmingham in June, 1942, Ethridge undertook to mollify Southern whites with the assurance "that Executive Order 8802 is a war order, and not a social document." It was to the South's interest, he said, "even to our economic salvation, that we give our people skills while we can and while they are needed." But in a widely quoted paragraph he denied any intention to challenge segregation: "there is no power in the world—not even in all the mechanized armies of the earth, Allied and Axis—which could now force the Southern white people to the abandonment of the principle of social segregation."

Birmingham itself accepted the three-day hearings with surprising equanimity, Brooks Atkinson reported to the New York *Times* two weeks later. The Birmingham *News*, after noting statements by FEPC representatives that the community had less discrimination than any other Southern town, commented: "Birmingham and the committee seem well met." Other newspapers in the South, however, called the hearings a "three-day inquisition" and wrote of "Roosevelt racial experts," "halo-wearing missionaries of New Deal socialism," "a group of snoopers," and "dat cummittee fer de purtechshun uv Rastus & Sambo." The committee's most outspoken defenders were CIO and Negro organizations, whose voices were lost in a storm of hostility.

The FEPC assumed a low status among war agencies. It cancelled hearings in El Paso because the State Department feared the revelation of discrimination against Spanish-Americans. After the Birmingham hearings the President transferred the committee from the jurisdiction of the War Production Board to the War Manpower Commission [WMC] and in January, 1943, WMC Chairman Paul V. McNutt "indefinitely postponed" hearings on complaints against Southern railroads and unions. This brought the resignation of three members, including Ethridge, and the organization of a new committee.

In May, 1943, Roosevelt established a second FEPC in the Executive Office of the President under, first, Monsignor Francis J. Haas, then Malcolm Ross, with six other members. It still lacked enforcement powers but enlarged the staff, established twelve regional offices (at Dallas and Atlanta in the South), and worked closely with the WMC Minority Groups Branch under Will Alexander. It immediately faced a crisis over an earlier directive that grew out of the Birmingham hearings. On May 24 the Mobile shipyard promoted twelve Negroes to jobs as welders. The next day white workers rioted and more than twenty people were injured before an army detachment quelled the disturbance. In this case the FEPC managed to negotiate an agreement setting aside four segregated shipways on which Negroes could win promotion. In September the committee held the delayed railroad hearings and in November directed the roads and brotherhoods to cease discrimination. But the Southern roads defied the order, the FEPC certified the cases to President Roosevelt, and he, faced by the exigencies of war and politics, permitted the issue to expire in a special mediation committee.

Still the FEPC persisted, hounded by hostile investigations and impassioned critics—"Oh! This is the beginning of a communistic dictatorship," Mississippi's John Rankin erupted—until it expired for want of funds in June, 1946. One measure of its effectiveness was the fact that the very maintenance of a regional office in downtown Atlanta was a major victory over local efforts to have it removed; another, that the Atlanta and Dallas offices spent much of their time fighting discrimination in other governmental agencies such as the War Manpower Commission and the United States Employment Service. Among 1,108 complaints handled by the Southern offices only 227 were successfully adjusted. Scattered reports attested to significant employment gains by Negroes in shipyards, ordnance, aircraft and other defense plants, but more because of intense demand and willing employers like A. J. Higgins in New Orleans than because of governmental policy—and mostly in the "h jobs": hot, heavy, and hard.

In their drive for wartime participation Negroes broadened the front on which battle had already developed against lynching, discrimination, educational inequalities, and voting restrictions. Before the war ended, the great sectional compromise of 1877, which had left the white South unhampered in developing its institutions of white supremacy, faced challenge. And segregation itself became, at last, an open question. "It was as if some universal message had come through to the great mass of Negroes," Howard Odum wrote in 1943, "urging them to dream new dreams and to protest against the old order."

New attitudes were reflected in reports of young Negroes testing barriers at soda fountains, in railroad dining cars, and elsewhere, in stories of Negro defiance like that of a soldier telling his white tormentors: "If I've got to die for democracy, I might as well die for some of it right here and now." On a Southern trip Sterling A. Brown found among Negroes "a sense of not belonging, and protest, sometimes not loud but always deeply felt. . . . The protest I heard ranged from the quietly spoken aside, through twisted humor and sarcasm, to stridency." If protest was more voluble in the North, J. Saunders Redding warned, it was only because "the Negro North has always been the tongue of the black South."

The rising wind of Negro aspirations soon fanned the flames of racist reaction. On July 22, 1942, one month after the Birmingham hearings, Horace C. Wilkinson, a lawyer-politician and former Klansman, stoked the fires with a speech to the Bessemer Kiwanis Club. He began with the story of a Birmingham bus driver who said, pointing to a group of Negroes, "Right there, mister, is where our next war will break out, and it may start before this one is over." This prophecy introduced a sequence of atrocity stories: Negroes who resisted Jim Crowism on buses and trains, took white men's jobs at Republic Steel, threw kisses at white college girls, "practically took over" a liquor store in Dothan, and brought suit to force Negro posts on the Alabama American Legion. "If there is room for a National Association for the Advancement of Colored People," Wilkinson declaimed, "there is need of a League to Maintain White Supremacy." Soon afterward Governor Frank Dixon, with a flourish of publicity, refused to have Alabama convicts supply cloth for the Defense Supplies Corporation because the contract included a standard clause forbidding discrimination. After that Senator Bankhead found the situation so inflamed that he urged the Army to train Northern Negroes only in Northern camps. By September Martin Dies had smelled out a plot: "throughout the South today," he told the House of Representatives, "subversive elements are attempting to convince the Negro that he should be placed on social equality with the white people; that now is the time for him to assert his rights."

Rumor mills went into overtime production, fabricating tales of insolence in crowded buses, warnings that Negroes planned to "take over" white women, and wild fantasies that they were gathering ice picks for a mass insurrection. The stories followed time-worn patterns, different mainly in their prevalence and the urgent significance assigned them. But there was one ingenious original: the legend of the "Eleanor Clubs," named for Mrs. Roosevelt, groups of domestics organized to put "a white woman in every kitchen." Diligent search never uncovered a single one, but the stories had a foundation in labor shortages created by the war boom. White women might not understand the danger of Hitler, Will Alexander remarked, "but white women in the South certainly recognized what a crisis the loss of a cook is."

For Southern liberals tutored in the interracial school the "rumor crisis" threatened a cataclysm. "Indeed," Jonathan Daniels wrote Eleanor Roosevelt, "I have never known a time when well informed friends of the colored people in the South and elsewhere were so alarmed about the situation." One after another such people counseled caution. Segregation "is not an argument in the South," John Temple Graves admonished. "It is a major premise." "A small group of Negro agitators and another small group of white rabble-rousers are pushing this country closer and closer to an interracial explosion," Virginius Dabney wrote. "Let them beware," warned David L. Cohn. "He who attempts to change [the mores of a people] by law runs risks of incalculable gravity." In 1944 W. T. Couch, director of the University of North Carolina Press, having invited fifteen Negro leaders to explain *What the Negro Wants*, felt impelled to cushion the shock of revelation with a "Publisher's Introduction" in which he argued that a sudden end to segregation "would be disastrous for everyone and more so for the Negro than the white man."

Inevitably the tensions challenged the old Commission on Interracial

Cooperation, which had sprung from the crisis of another war. But the Commission, Will Alexander had decided with uncommon detachment, had outlived its generation. William E. Cole, a University of Tennessee sociologist whom Alexander secured to make an analysis, reinforced the judgment. The staff, Cole said, had grown jaded and inefficient. Negro leaders felt that the Commission was "static, colorless . . . not charged with social action . . . 'Uncle Tomish' in nature." He suggested a revival of Howard Odum's proposed Council on Southern Regional Development.

Meanwhile, Mrs. Jessie Daniel Ames, one of the Commission's stalwarts, had unknowingly provided the way. Fearing the reaction that Northern "radicals" might provoke, she had prodded Gordon B. Hancock, dean of Virginia Union University, to call a conference of Southern Negroes which met at Durham in October, 1942, to challenge the "cooperation of that element of the white South who express themselves as desirous of a New Deal for the Negroes." In December a committee of the Durham Conference published a statement detailing demands for the ballot, civil rights, employment opportunity, and access to public services. In April, 1943, 115 whites meeting in Atlanta issued a response and proposed a joint conference which convened in Richmond on June 16. The Richmond Conference in turn undertook to plan a new interracial organization and on February 16, 1944, the Southern Regional Council (SRC) replaced the Committee on Interracial Cooperation in Atlanta. Howard W. Odum, its first president, and Guy B. Johnson, its executive secretary, laid plans for a broad program of regional development, with commissions on race relations, economic affairs, community life and welfare, cultural development, and public affairs.

But dissenters plunged them unwillingly into segregation controversies. "The habit of thought that would tear the Negro problem out of its national context is a southern habit of thought," J. Saunders Redding asserted in the little magazine, *Common Ground*, "and . . . it is potentially more harmful than beneficial." The only appropriate strategy, he argued, was "to storm and defend advanced positions . . . so that when the forces of the native enemy build themselves up for the counterattack, no retreat will be made beyond the lines now—in the spring of 1944—held." "Do we want the tangled race skein completely unraveled? Or don't we?" Lillian Smith asked. "Are we merely trying to avoid . . . more 'tensions' which embarrass white folks, or are we trying to secure for the Negro his full human rights?" "*Common Ground*," Odum fumed, "like a good many of the others, seems to think that when they set up an argument and get people to split among themselves, they are doing something liberal."

On the other side Birmingham columnist John Temple Graves proposed a conference "of Southerners of just plain decency and enlightenment, *plus power,* to do something big for the Negro this side of the segregation line." Odum demurred. "If we could just stop talking about social equality and segregation and go to work," he wrote Graves, "it would be a day for us, wouldn't it?" Several militant groups, North and South, "insist that we must declare ourselves on what they assume to be the one definitive issue," he told the SRC's first membership meeting in December, 1944. He proposed to work for more equal facilities, full equality before the law, and economic opportunities, but not "to go on record as approving the principles and philosophy, the practice and pattern of legal segregation." Carter H. Wesley, Negro publisher of Houston, introduced a resolution endorsing Odum's position: "We shall center our efforts on gaining equal facilities as provided by law and equal opportunities for all people of the South."

At the same meeting the members endorsed a program for equal employment opportunity, Negro policemen and firemen, equalization in education and public transportation, Negro voting, and increased public financing for medical and dental care. The organizational program, like the resolutions, emphasized racial considerations. As it evolved, the SRC continued on the paths developed by the Interracial Commission. During 1945 it revived interracial groups in ten states, surveyed bus segregation in Atlanta, prompted the use of Negro police, established a Veterans Service project to promote equal treatment for returned servicemen, provided informational services, began the periodical *New South*, and advised an official Kentucky Commission for the Study of Negro Affairs, which recommended the abolition of segregation in higher education.

A Conference on the South's Postwar Economy, which met in Atlanta, April 11–12, 1945, drew little attention because it adjourned on the day President Roosevelt died. This and a survey of reconversion problems constituted the only significant departures from interracial activities. Racial controversy and the failure to secure broad support frustrated the SRC in its larger plans. "It seems foolish," Odum wrote Johnson early in 1945, ". . . to talk about getting the South back of the movement when there is no indication anywhere of leadership or of business and professional people following," not even "that brilliant coterie of liberals we counted on." Many of the liberals still had confidence in the Southern Conference for Human Welfare, which experienced a sudden membership growth in 1945, but it virtually collapsed in 1946 and disbanded in 1948. Nevertheless, the SRC survived, essentially as a reincarnation of the Commission on Interracial Cooperation.

In politics the gathering storm of wartime discontent—with Negro demands, price controls, labor shortages, rationing, and a hundred other petty vexations—reinforced the prevailing winds of conservatism. In 1942 the Congressional elections registered a national swing against the New Deal. Republicans gained forty-six Representatives and nine Senators, chiefly in the Middle States farm areas. In Oklahoma they defeated the arch–New Deal Senator Josh Lee. Democratic losses outside the South strengthened the Southern delegation's position within the party, and the delegation itself reflected a conservative trend in Southern primaries. In 1942 Arkansas and Mississippi added John L. McClellan and James O. Eastland to the rebel forces in the Senate. Conservative incumbents Bailey, Glass, and O'Daniel returned; only O'Daniel faced serious opposition. Many primary campaigns mirrored the growing obsession with race. In the Little Rock Congressional district Brooks Hays had to fend off the charge that he had attended unsegregated meetings of the Southern Conference for Human Welfare. In Louisiana, E. A. Stephens, senatorial candidate against Allen J. Ellender, conjured up eerie visions of "colored organizations . . . sitting around midnight candles." In South Carolina, Eugene S. Blease, Cole's brother, accused the NAACP of backing [Burnet R.] Maybank and promised to reform Washington, where "white ladies are ordered to call Negro officials Mister."

But the cry of white supremacy alone was not enough, as Eugene Talmadge discovered to his dismay. In Georgia Talmadge had set the stage during 1941, when he had purged the state's board of regents in order to dismiss five men from Georgia's institutions on vague and unsupported charges of advocating "racial equality." Instead of political profit he reaped a whirlwind of opposition. The Southern Association of Colleges and Secondary Schools withdrew accreditation from state institutions and in the 1942 gubernatorial race students, parents, and an aroused press rallied to the support of Ellis G. Arnall, the young attorney-general, who defended academic freedom and took care to neutralize Talmadge's racist appeal in the boondocks: "Over in west Georgia, where I live," said Arnall, "we don't need any governor to keep Negroes out of our white schools." During his four-year term Arnall restored the independence of the state university system, increased teacher pay, put through a new state constitution, reformed the state's penal and parole systems, cut the voting age to eighteen, sponsored the first state law for soldier voting, and personally argued before the Supreme Court the suit that precipitated action against regionalized freight rates. The "liberal majority within the Democratic Party," he wrote before leaving office, should "retain control of the party; make it the vehicle for acceptance of new ideas; and utilize it for that experimentalism required to solve our problems."

But Georgia under Arnall moved against the political currents. In January, 1943, the "Victory Congress" convened, with Southern Democrats in revolt. In the House Southerners dominated the party caucus, took four additional seats on the steering committee to secure a majority, and rejected a proposal to give the American Labor party's Vito Marcantonio a committee seat for service to New York Democrats. In the Senate Southerners maneuvered deftly to downgrade Bronx Boss Edward J. Flynn by demanding that he quit both the national chairmanship and the national committee before being considered as Ambassador to Australia and then blocking confirmation.

These steps were but the prelude to more substantive assaults on New Deal policies and agencies. "Government by bureaucrats," said Eugene Cox, "must be broken, and broken now." While Bankhead led the farm bloc against food subsidies and price controls, Harold Cooley investigated the FSA, Virginia's Howard W. Smith chaired a "Special Committee to Investigate Acts of Executive Agencies Beyond the Scope of their Authority," and Harry F. Byrd led a drive by the Joint Committee on Non-Essential Expenditures (established in 1941) to eviscerate "non-essential" New Deal agencies. During 1943 Congress abolished the WPA, the NYA,

and the CCC, brought the FSA to heel, and liquidated the National Resources Planning Board by refusing it funds. Tom Connally and Howard
Smith sponsored antistrike legislation which authorized the government to
seize struck plants, required pre-strike plebiscites, and outlawed union
political contributions. Martin Dies produced a list of forty "irresponsible,
unrepresentative, crackpot, radical bureaucrats," and won passage of an
appropriation amendment against paying the salaries of three alleged radicals. Mississippi's John Rankin, previously known as a friend of inflation,
public power, and veterans, now emerged as the foe of bureaucrats, labor
unions, and the "Communist-Jewish world plot" while his senatorial colleague, Theodore G. Bilbo, on most things a New Dealer, warred against
the FEPC and proposed to resettle American Negroes in Africa.

After the 1942 elections two Deep-South governors, Dixon of Alabama
and Jones of Louisiana, tentatively lofted trial balloons of insurgency. The
position of Southern Democrats was "anomalous in the extreme," Dixon
told the Southern Society of New York in December. "It is their own party
that is dynamiting their social structure. . . . Ways and means are being
discussed daily to break our chains": a Southern party, unpledged electors.
The South had gotten better treatment from the Republican party, Sam
Jones declared in New Orleans. "The fact is," he said in a *Saturday Evening
Post* article, "that political booby trap known as the 'Solid South' . . . is
about to fall apart of its own absurdity." New Deal "worthies, perhaps
with the best intentions in the world, are doing the Negro race a grave
long-term disservice." War industries went mostly to the North, New Dealers were "blind and deaf" to freight-rate differentials, the South carried a
disproportionate burden of education, Federal grants went mostly to "the
pampered and protected industrial North and East," public housing was
for Northern slums, and the New Deal had tried to wipe out rice and sugar
production. Both Jones and Dixon raised the banner of insurgency again
at the Southern Governors Conference in Tallahassee in the spring of 1943.

What was happening, Thomas Sancton wrote in the *New Republic*,
was a duplication of the strategy that beat the Populists. Negroes could
not vote. The whites had been poisoned against Negroes. Farmers and
laborers were set at odds. "At all events, the New Deal in the South is
dead," he concluded. "And this is where the New Deal helped the most."
Other observers agreed. Columnist Paul Mallon found "all of the Southern
and border states, with the possible exception of Florida . . . in an extreme
condition of psychological political revolution." But reports of the New
Deal's demise were premature. Reporter Seldon Menefee decided during
wartime travels that the great majority of the people, unlike the "nostalgic
upper-class Southerners," supported the administration wholeheartedly,
"with far less 'beefing' over minor restrictions than I had grown used to
hearing in Washington." A Gallup poll in mid-summer, 1943, showed 80
per cent of the Southern voters in favor of Roosevelt's renomination.

Events early in 1944 charged the political atmosphere with additional
tensions. In February came a rebellion against an administration request
for a tax increase to combat inflation and finance the war. Instead of the

$10,500,000,000 the Treasury demanded, the finance committees headed by Robert Doughton and Walter George put through a measure that yielded an additional $2,300,000,000. The President responded with a biting veto; it was, he said, "a tax relief bill . . . not for the needy, but for the greedy." Alben Barkley angrily resigned as Majority Leader, only to be re-elected unanimously. Both houses promptly overrode the veto by large votes despite Claude Pepper's plea that such a vote would "alter the understanding of the Nation concerning the fundamental spirit . . . of the Democratic Party" and persuade the public "that we are no longer the crusading party."

The reverberations from this incident still echoed when, in March, the question of soldier voting came to a decision. Proposals for a simplified Federal soldier ballot raised the prospect of increased voting by Negroes and by young people likely to support New Dealers. In 1942 a limited law provided for distribution of postal cards with which servicemen could request state absentee ballots. It even abrogated state registration and poll-tax requirements, but came so late that only 28,000 voted under it. The President appealed for a simple and uniform servicemen's ballot in 1944, but a states' rights bloc led by Mississippians in each house, Eastland and Rankin, sidetracked the proposal for a truncated version that required the consent of the state. The President let the bill become law without his signature. That fall twenty states accepted some 111,773 Federal ballots, and probably more than four million servicemen cast state absentee ballots.

With spring the focus centered more sharply on Negro voting. On April 3, in the case of *Smith* v. *Allwright*, the Supreme Court reversed *Grovey* v. *Townsend* (1935) and struck down the Texas white primary on grounds that it was part of the election procedure and subject to the Fifteenth Amendment. Texas Democrats, who had fought the issue for two decades, yielded. But the Allwright opinion seemed to offer a loophole by suggesting that the party acted as an agency of the state because the state regulated primary procedures. South Carolina's Governor Olin D. Johnston, therefore, summoned a special session of the legislature to repeal all laws pertaining to the primary and turn the Democratic party into a "private club." Should this prove inadequate, he warned, "we South Carolinians will use the necessary methods to retain white supremacy in our primaries and to safeguard the homes and happiness of our people."

The South, Senator Maybank said the day before Johnston's message, would handle the problem as it saw fit "regardless of what decisions the Supreme Court may make and regardless of what laws Congress may pass." In May the Senate faced an anti-poll tax bill, a wartime perennial. Again, as in 1942, the Senators buried it, this time after a subdued debate and a prearranged cloture vote that was foredoomed to failure. Allen Drury, a young Texan covering the Senate for the United Press, recorded his impressions in his diary: "We seem to be perched on a cliff, in Washington, above a vast and tumbled plain that stretches far away below us: the South, unhappy, restless, confused, embittered, torn by pressures steadily mounting. As far as the eye can see there is discontent and bitterness, faint intimations of a coming storm like a rising wind moving through tall grass."

Spring primary victories by Lister Hill in Alabama and Claude Pepper in Florida, however, suggested that the New Deal retained some vitality in the South. In South Carolina, where Roosevelt did not intervene again, Olin D. Johnston finally toppled the aging Cotton Ed Smith. But in each case the New Deal candidate deemed it prudent to reaffirm his allegiance to white supremacy. Pepper assured the voters that Florida primaries would be "kept white," and Johnston came to the campaign fresh from his effort to circumvent the Supreme Court.

As the spring advanced, anti-Roosevelt conservatives attempted to mobilize a rebellion in the national convention. In May a movement that came to be known as the "Texas Regulars" captured that state's Democratic convention and named anti-Roosevelt delegates and an anti-Roosevelt electoral slate. Aroused conservatives greeted Lyndon Johnson with cries of "Throw Roosevelt's pin-up boy out of there." Mississippi's convention took similar action. But it was abundantly clear, more so after the Normandy invasion began in June, that Roosevelt the war leader was impregnable. The anti-New Deal campaign then focused on the more vulnerable Henry Wallace, who as vice president had swung increasingly toward the liberal-labor wing of the party but had antagonized the harassed President in 1943 by a bitter embroglio with Secretary of Commerce Jesse Jones over rubber and quinine stockpiling. Wallace, however, carried the battle to the enemy with a bold proclamation in the convention: "The future belongs to those who go down the line unswervingly for the liberal principles of both political democracy and economic democracy regardless of race, color or religion. . . . The poll tax must go. Equal educational opportunities must come. The future must bring equal wages for equal work regardless of sex or race."

Wallace earned the enmity of both Southern conservatives and Northern city bosses who feared the rising CIO Political Action Committee. Yet he retained a substantial degree of Southern support, 43 per cent of the voters, the Gallup poll reported as late as June 6. But in the convention he commanded only the vote of Ellis Arnall's Georgia delegation, about half the Florida votes, and scattered support in Alabama, which voted as a unit for favorite-son John Bankhead. Roosevelt, who won easily over scattered votes for Harry Byrd, apparently considered and rejected James F. Byrnes, since 1943 head of the Office of Economic Stabilization which supervised civilian war agencies, because Byrnes had the fatal opposition of organized labor, Negroes, and city bosses who feared the effect of his early departure from the Catholic church. The outcome, amid complicated maneuvers for the Presidential nod, was a convergence upon Missouri's Harry S Truman, who had established a solid reputation as chairman of the Senate War Investigating Committee, and was acceptable to Southern conservatives because of his Confederate antecedents and his Border-State background. Even so the Republicans under Thomas E. Dewey gained an increased percentage of the vote in every Southern state except Texas, where the unpledged Texas Regulars drew a substantial portion of the anti-Roosevelt vote.

Roosevelt had hardly begun his brief fourth term in January, 1945, before he provoked one of the sharpest major political battles of his era— and the last—by proposing to replace Jesse Jones with Henry A. Wallace as Secretary of Commerce. This, Roosevelt said, was the former vice president's expressed preference as a reward for services rendered in the 1944 campaign. The controversy that followed, said the London *Times*, might come to rank "with the Hayne-Webster debate as pregnant with significance in the future," for it involved "all those mighty issues which agitate men's minds when they look forward to the world after the war . . . the true function of Government in a democratic state; the yearning to be rid of the scourge of unemployment; the conflict between the social conscience and the nostalgia for the old days." Senators Bailey and George led the fight against Wallace, and only Pepper among the Southerners rallied to his defense. The argument raged on through February while Roosevelt flew off to the Yalta Conference with Churchill and Stalin, and reached its end in March when the Senate approved Wallace only after the post was separated from control of the Federal Loan Agency and the Reconstruction Finance Corporation. In a similar battle during March a conservative co-alition blocked confirmation of Aubrey Williams as head of the Rural Electrification Administration.

But unity on foreign affairs persisted through the war. Several Southerners in Congress stood forth as champions of internationalism: Claude Pepper, Lister Hill, William Fulbright, and Tom Connally. In 1943 Hill joined with Senators Hatch, Ball, and Burton to sponsor the "B_2H_2 Resolution" that called for a strong international organization with a military force of its own. In the House, Fulbright, "the Rhodes scholar from the Ozarks," pushed a resolution for "appropriate international machinery with power adequate to establish and maintain a just and lasting peace." The House passed the Fulbright Resolution, 360 to 69. Then Tom Connally, chairman of the Senate Foreign Relations Committee, worked out a compromise, the Connally Resolution, which reaffirmed the principles of national sovereignty, a proviso designed to fend off isolationist attacks. Roosevelt worked closely with Connally in cultivating Senate Republicans in order to avoid partisan divisions like those which had undermined Wilson's postwar program, and Connally himself ultimately participated in the San Francisco Conference that formulated the Charter of the United Nations.

But on April 12, 1945, two weeks before the charter conference convened, Franklin D. Roosevelt quietly and unexpectedly passed away in his cottage at Warm Springs, Georgia. In Knoxville the next day a TVA driver who took David E. Lilienthal to his plane for a sad mission to Washington ventured a few words about the dead President. "I won't forget what he done for us, beginning with the NRA," said the man, who had been a textile worker at sixteen cents an hour. But, he asked, "Who are the little people like me going to have to take their part?" Roosevelt's death indeed "cast the southern liberals adrift," and the accession of Truman heartened the conservatives who had helped to engineer his nomination. "President Truman," the Speaker of Mississippi's House of Representatives wrote in

May, "has begun well and is making rapid progress towards returning this country to Fundamental Americanism." . . .

In 1945 the South emerged from the war . . . more an integral part of the Union and of the world than ever before. But its political leaders, internationalist and parochial at the same time, embodied a curious paradox. In foreign affairs they had advanced boldly toward new horizons in their support of plans for "winning the peace." But in domestic affairs they had retreated back within the parapets of the embattled South, where they stood fast against the incursions of social change. The inconsistency could not long endure, and a critical question for the postwar South, facing eventful issues of economic and racial adjustment, was which would prevail, the broader vision or the defensive reaction.

World War II as a Watershed in Southern History

MORTON SOSNA

Anyone about to suggest that World War II rather than the Civil War is the crucial event of southern history should begin with an explanation. The very proposition seems ludicrous. At least I thought it was ludicrous when I first tendered it before the dozen or so souls who had the fortune (or misfortune) to be taking a recent southern history course I happened to be teaching. We were in that spongy middle of the course; Reconstruction was over and the civil rights movement had not yet begun. It was, moreover, a time when the students' initial enthusiasm had yielded to two well-known dampeners of youthful scholarship: the onset of spring weather and the realization that, while mid-terms were over, finals were still weeks away. Under the circumstances, it was not without trepidation that I found myself having to lecture on "The South and World War II." What could I possibly say on this subject that would be of remotest interest to these students? Given my predicament, I resolved to say anything provided that it be the least bit provocative. Thus I uttered the fateful words that "all in all, World War II probably had a greater impact on the South than the Civil War."

The statement had the desired effect. Looks ranging from bemusement to outrage emanated from the students. Although my own argument of the case was far from compelling, the discussion that followed was stimulating and exciting, speaking directly to the nature of historical experiences and our constant need to interpret them.

The problem was that the notion of World War II being a critical turning point of southern history, which obviously had intrigued the students, soon began to intrigue me. Without a doubt, since 1940 changes of the profoundest sort have affected the South and its regional identity. In speaking of his kinsman, William Alexander Percy, whose 1941 *Lanterns on the Levee* captured much of the flavor of the South as loser and scapegoat, Walker Percy has written: "If anyone had told him in 1940 that in thirty years the 'North' (i.e., New York, Detroit, California) would be in the deepest kind of trouble with race, violence, and social decay, while the South had become, by contrast, relatively hopeful and even prosperous, he would not have believed it." And well he might not. Although it would be simplistic to look upon the entire period from the end of Reconstruction (or, perhaps more accurately, the end of the Populist struggles) as an unbroken continuum, these are years when the idea of a "Benighted South" based on racial segregation, misguided politics, violence, and poverty seemed meaningful both to southerners and outsiders. Like contemporaries, historians have debated just how benighted this South actually was, but however harsh or mild their judgment, it was one totally at odds with the current idea of the South as part of the "Sunbelt."

Yet the South's linkage to the Sunbelt is something that the historian of its recent past must confront. Imprecise as that term may be, it suggests a region of economic growth and social vitality rather than one of stagnation and decline. In the language of presidential commissions, the South has gone from being "the Nation's No. 1 Economic Problem" to a region finally realizing the benefits of "deep-rooted and inexorable historical transformation." To the extent that the concept of the Sunbelt has validity and that the South is part of it—my own opinion is that it does and it is— historians have a duty to explain how such a profound historical change has occurred. Since the one point on which all who speak of a Sunbelt can agree is the crucial importance of World War II to the diffusion of economic and political power within the United States, there would seem to be on this ground alone compelling reasons for looking more closely at the war's impact on the South.

In addition to the idea of the Sunbelt, two other developments suggest that the impact of World War II on the South is a subject worth pursuing. One of these relates directly to major issues in southern historiography. The other suggests some interesting new directions for regional history.

As Carl Degler has noted, "another foray into Southern history is gathering momentum and beginning to change our conception of the South's past." Degler was referring to the work of economic and social historians who have begun to look more intensely at the South's transition from slavery to sharecropping, its experience with industrialization, and the political and economic significance of the region's traditional elites. The works of Robert Ransom and Richard Sutch, Robert Higgs, Stephen De Canio, Gavin Wright, Jonathan Wiener, Jay Mandle, Dwight Billings, William Cooper, and Roger Hart, while they disagree with one another over a number of particulars (e.g., the extent to which racism adversely affected the output of the freed slaves, or whether planters fostered or retarded industrial development) agree on three critical points: (1) the institutional transition from slave labor to free labor did not fundamentally alter the

South's continuation as a plantation society; (2) the region's economic problems were not the result of and indeed went far beyond the war's destructiveness and the economic consequences of emancipation; (3) the same groups that dominated southern society and politics before the Civil War continued to dominate it afterwards. Taken together, this new work strongly suggests that, despite the wrenching political and institutional changes attributable to the Civil War and Reconstruction, life for most southerners, whites as well as blacks, went on much as it did before the conflict. To say this is not to question the value of works by historians who have argued otherwise. But in their understandable eagerness to give large events equally large consequences, they have tended to exaggerate the social and economic results of what undoubtedly is the most dramatic episode in southern and perhaps even our national history.

The other relevant historiographical trend is the growing literature on war and society. In pathbreaking works, Richard Polenberg and John Morton Blum have claimed that, for the United States, the social, economic, and cultural world of today had its roots during World War II. The implications of this for the South would seem to be obvious, but despite the suggestive concept of a "Bulldozer Revolution," which C. Vann Woodward offered in 1958, and George Tindall's perceptive chapter on the South and World War II in *The Emergence of the New South* (1967), southern historians have steered away from applying a "war and society" approach to a regional context. Indeed, the void has been so glaring that in his southern history text published in 1978, I. A. Newby noted that the "history of the South during World War II is still largely unwritten."

Scholars, though, continue to demonstrate the value of studying the domestic results that modern wars have upon the societies engaged in them. Limited neither to the United States nor to World War II alone, studies such as those by Alan Milward and David Kennedy have shown that the social and economic context of wars exist almost independently from their military one. Inasmuch as a main focus of this literature is upon "change versus continuity"—a long and much debated subject within southern history—its relevance for regional history would seem to be self-evident. Yet the only sustained effort to bring a war and society focus to regional history has been applied, with significant success in my opinion, to the Midwest by Alan Clive through a vehicle that has long been the bread and butter of southern history: the state study. In *State of War: Michigan in World War II*, Clive perceptively analyzed how the wartime experiences of prosperity, the growth of the federal government, heightened race consciousness, consolidations within both business and labor, rural industrialization, the suburbanization of cities, and the disruption of family life profoundly affected life in the nation's seventh largest state. After carefully weighing the evidence of continuity versus change, Clive came down strongly on the side of change. "In retrospect," he writes, "the Michigan and America of 1939 are clearly seen to belong to a world now vanished, while the state and nation of 1945 are more nearly recognizable." Substituting a southern state for Michigan and the South for America, could a similar claim be made for the country's most distinctive region? Did the war years in fact constitute a critical turning point in southern history?

A war and society approach necessarily focuses on change versus continuity. Only the crudest regionalist would go so far as to say that either the desire for or actuality of social change was entirely absent from the South during the fifty years prior to World War II. Although they may have offered old (and in the end not very good) wine in new bottles, such groups as New South industrialists and "business progressives" had their say and, to be sure, the region was not immune to the urbanization and industrialization that were engulfing the rest of the country. But it was not until the New Deal, or to be more precise, the period from 1936 to 1941, that a new regional consciousness began to emerge spurred on by the Depression and attempts, however inadequate, to remedy its worst effects through the actions of the federal government. If, as most historians now believe, the New Deal did not lead to significant social and economic change, the Roosevelt Administration's characterization of the South as the nation's foremost economic problem was a dramatic departure. Calling as it did for what amounted to a regional affirmative action program—to prop up the South through federal largesse—it offered an appeal that proved irresistible. As one southern newspaper editor pointed out, Franklin D. Roosevelt was not the first to say that the South was poor, but "he was the first to say with authority that its poverty should be a national economic problem and that its rank as such was Number One." Many southerners bitterly attacked some of the New Deal programs that affected the South, such as the Farm Security Administration or Tennessee Valley Authority, but the rhetoric of the South's special claim upon the American economic pie would flourish for the next thirty years. The idea that the vitality of America itself depended upon "a strong and economically prosperous South" became a staple of economic and social thought within the region. It was an article of faith among conservatives as well as liberals, blacks as well as whites.

This idea of entitlement, so crucial to the South's subsequent identification with the Sunbelt, then, had its origin not during the war but during the New Deal. Why then, one might ask, was the war so crucial?

The answer has to do with financial resources, of which the New Deal itself had relatively little. As portrayed by its opponents, the New Deal squandered public money into a sea of extravagance, waste, fraud, bureaucracy, and general misguidedness. The actual sums of money, however, spent on New Deal programs, though perhaps high by the standards of the day, were miniscule in comparison to wartime expenditures. The figures are quite staggering. Between 1940 and 1944, the ten largest corporate recipients of government war contracts received about the same amount of money as the federal government spent on *everything* from 1932 to 1939, approximately $52 billion. The top recipient, General Motors, alone received more from these war procurements during this period than the federal government had spent during the peak New Deal year of 1936. The veritable orgy of war-induced spending produced the biggest boom in American economic history. According to one scholarly estimate, the volume of American industrial output increased at an average rate of 15 percent a year; the average rate of increase for the period 1896–1939 had been 4 percent. By the end of the war, direct investment by the government in new plant and equipment had increased the productive capacity of the economy by about 50 percent.

With the Roosevelt Administration already committed to the South's economic restoration, the portion of war spending directed at the South was significant; its impact immediate and far reaching. "For the first time since the War Between the States," according to *Fortune Magazine*, "almost any native of the Deep South who wants a job can get one." By 1945 even the liberal Southern Conference for Human Welfare was referring to the South as "economic opportunity" rather than "economic problem" number one. The combination of military installations and defense plants altered the lives of southerners, white and black, in ways that would have been inconceivable to even the most visionary New Dealer. Sharecroppers and tenant farmers, who were being displaced from the land by the collapse of the South's traditional cotton economy, as well as by the New Deal's acreage reduction schemes and the introduction of more sophisticated machinery, now had an alternative, other than migration, which they had not had during the 1920s and 1930s. Thousands of new jobs appeared in the South because of the war. When compared to the sharecropper's endless cycle of indebtedness or the very low wages of the typical prewar southern industrial worker, these war-related jobs represented a genuine step forward for large numbers of southerners. It not only gave them their first taste of prosperity but began to tear apart the paternalistic patterns to which many southern whites as well as the great majority of blacks had been subjected. All the highly publicized talk among middle and upper class southerners about "how difficult it was to get good help any more" reflected not only their racism and paternalism, but also the profound social and economic transformation taking place in the South. Most of the beneficiaries of the war boom were white, and, not surprisingly, during the decade of the 1940s white migration out of the South greatly subsided. Black out-migration, on the other hand, accelerated during the war and continued for another decade. In effect this meant that for southern blacks generally a war job meant one in Detroit or Oakland rather than Mobile. Still, the overall rise in South's economic situation was such that some blacks were clearly included.

In terms of change versus continuity what seems to have happened in the South during the war was the intensification of prewar developments, which became so great that substantial change resulted. A good illustration was Mississippi's effort, beginning in 1936, to attract industries by allowing local communities to finance the construction or acquisition of industrial facilities through publicly guaranteed bonds. Known as Balance Agriculture with Industry (BAWI), the presumption of this recognizably Sunbeltish program was that, combined with give-away leases, tax exemptions, and antiunionism, these facilities would prove to be irresistible bait for industries seeking to move or expand their operations. Although debate over the plan had generated considerable political controversy in Mississippi, its actual operation was much less dramatic. By 1940 only twelve BAWI plants were either already in operation or set to begin production; merely 2,700 workers had thus far been employed. The law establishing BAWI was written off as a failure and allowed to lapse. By 1944, however, the situation had changed dramatically. The twelve plants were now all in operation and expanding rapidly. One of them, the Ingalls shipyard at Pascagoula, had become a major war production center and was providing more jobs than all the other bond-financed plants combined. Pascagoula itself grew from a town of 4,000 to one of 30,000. BAWI now appeared to be such a success that Mississippi reinstituted the public financing of industrial facilities and other southern states soon adopted similar plans, which in one form or another continue to the present.

The intensification of southern change and its implications for the future was also exemplified by the career of the region's best-known wartime industrialist, Andrew Jackson Higgins. In 1939 Higgins Industries in New Orleans consisted of one plant, which employed about 400 workers manufacturing shallow-draught boats designed primarily for use in the swampy bayous of southern Louisiana and Mississippi. Higgins's total gross sales amounted to $850,000 and rumor had it that his best customers were bootleggers. In 1941, however, Higgins's designs for landing craft and patrol torpedo boats were accepted by the U.S. Navy, and his prominence and influence, both locally and nationally, shot up like a rocket. By 1944 his operations in New Orleans consisted of eight plants that employed over 20,000 workers; his gross sales were estimated at $95–$120 million. Only Henry J. Kaiser achieved a greater reputation as a new breed of industrial genius created by the war.

Higgins should be specifically mentioned because none of the historical studies of the industrialization of the South take into account anyone quite like him. Indeed, most have emphasized two points: (1) despite southern industrialists calling for a New South that would be less reliant on agriculture, they paid homage to every racial and sectional myth about the South associated with its agrarian past; (2) they were chiefly attracted by the region's seemingly inexhaustible supply of cheap, nonunionized labor, which they sought to put into low-paying but highly profitable industries, such as textiles. Higgins was distinctly different. A dynamic and outspoken man, he was once described as a cross between Huey Long and Henry Ford. Higgins set and met production schedules that astounded military procurement officers. He accomplished this through unconventional means—walking among his employees shouting good-humored encouragement to them through a bullhorn, roping off residential streets in a fashionable uptown New Orleans neighborhood and making it part of his assembly line, and in one instance putting aboard railroad cars, along with his unfinished boats, painters who applied the final touches en route. Higgins also displayed his unconventionality in more significant ways. Not only was he willing to work with labor unions, but he was also willing, indeed anxious, to hire blacks and pay them on the same basis as whites. To be sure, he maintained segregation, but his shipyards were relatively free of the racial tensions that periodically erupted into violence elsewhere, most notably in May 1943 at the Alabama Drydock Company in Mobile. Moreover, Higgins fully complied with the directives of the Fair Employment Practices Committee, and to this day he is something of a folk hero among elderly black New Orleanians, a number of whom obtained their first decent jobs working for him. He was also a visionary who believed that his war industries could be converted to peacetime uses that would create jobs and supply consumer goods, especially low-cost housing. Its economy fueled by Higgins's operations, New Orleans, like many southern cities, grew rapidly during the war years, increasing in population from 490,000 in 1940 to 600,000 by 1944. Some of the city's well-to-do cursed Higgins and identified him with the ruin of their city. But to the great majority of middle and working class whites, not to mention blacks, he symbolized better times for themselves, their city, and the South. "This is wonderful, crowds everywhere," remarked a Higgins employee. "New Orleans and the South are really breaking through. This will be the great metropolis of the future."

Higgins's most ambitious project involved his obtaining a dollar-a-year lease on a giant federally financed industrial complex to be constructed at what then was a swampy, rather desolate location twelve miles east of downtown New Orleans. Higgins received a $200 million contract to use the site to manufacture liberty ships on an assembly line basis, which would have cut two-thirds off the time and cost of manufacturing them in drydock as was then being done. Higgins estimated that 50,000 to 60,000 workers would ultimately be needed, of whom the great majority would be women and blacks. New Orleans was astir over the plan when in July 1942, citing a shortage of steel and the possibility that the ships might not be needed, the U.S. Maritime Commission cancelled the contract. Believing the real reason for the cancellation to be a growing fear among more established corporations that his own operations threatened theirs, Higgins cried foul. In October President Roosevelt came to New Orleans and visited the site. Roosevelt assured Higgins that some use would be made of it. Within forty-eight hours, the Army informed Higgins of its intention to award him a $130 million contract to build 1,200 giant cargo planes. Construction of the plant began in January 1943. With Higgins providing the directions and the federal government the money, the plant was completed by the following October. It contained 45 acres under one roof and had cost the government $23 million to build. Known as Michoud, after the man whose sugar plantation had once occupied the site, it was the second largest industrial plant in the United States; only Ford's River Rouge complex was bigger. By early 1944 about 5,000 Higgins workers, a fifth of its capacity, were employed at Michoud.

The full story of Higgins and the Michoud plant is a fascinating one, but due to shifting military and aircraft design needs, as well as its involvement in the Manhattan Project, the plant only produced one airplane by the end of the war. Higgins's plans for its postwar use never fulfilled his expectations. In 1961, however, after President Kennedy committed the United States to putting a man on the moon before the end of the decade, the National Aeronautics and Space Administration selected Michoud as the assembly site for the giant Saturn rockets upon which the United States space program depended. At its peak in the mid-1960s, over 20,000 persons were employed there.

As Higgins represented a distinctly Sunbeltish turn in the road of southern industrial development, the very nature of American mobilization altered what C. Vann Woodward has called the "counterpoint" of "North-South dialogue." One thinks here of the twelve million Americans who entered the armed services during the war. Approximately one-third of them spent some time at military bases located in the South. Discounting the obvious fact that many of these were southerners, it is nonetheless true that a substantial number of outsiders experienced their first direct contact with the region during the war. Given the important economic, political, and cultural roles these people, as veterans, played after the war, the impression and attitudes that they carried away with them had an indelible impact upon postwar sectional issues, particularly civil rights. However much these northern GIs may have been impervious to racial injustices in their own areas, or were themselves prejudiced against blacks, given the time and place not to mention the circumstances of war, most did not find the white South's highly visible efforts to enforce segregation compatible with the democratic ideals they were ostensibly defending. For the moment, this judgment is based more on historical intuition and the experiences of members of my own family than on hard evidence. But by and large many people would agree with George Orwell's observation that "if the war didn't happen to kill you, it was bound to start you thinking." The letters home or oral histories of these northern GIs in the South for the first time would likely indicate that many of them were indeed thinking. They would also probably help to explain why so many northern states and cities adopted fair employment and civil rights laws in the immediate postwar years.

At the same time that large numbers of northerners were discovering the South, southern whites and blacks were also exposed to new locales, ideas, and influences. The former might possibly have carried away a more critical regional consciousness than white southerners who spent the war years entirely in the South. How many, for example, may have shared the sentiments of a white sergeant from Texas who in 1945 was quoted in a Fort Worth newspaper as saying that southerners could not "abuse the colored people any more." Although he specifically denied being concerned about the situation of blacks before the war, and even indicated that it might be "best" to avoid challenging school segregation, this veteran gave an otherwise impassioned plea for racial justice on the grounds that blacks as well as whites had given their lives for their country.

As for blacks, the impact of their wartime experience is less conjectural. Military service seems to have been almost a prerequisite to subsequent civil rights involvements. For instance, Medgar Evans of Decatur, Mississippi, served with U.S. Army forces in Normandy and received his college education on the GI Bill; Harry Briggs, the plaintiff in the 1949 Clarendon County, South Carolina, case that launched into the courts the issue of public school desegregation, had spent all of his thirty-four years in the county, except for the three he spent in the South Pacific with the Navy; Oliver Brown of Topeka, Kansas, who gave his name to legal history in *Brown vs. Board of Education*, was in 1951, when his case first went to court, a thirty-two-year old veteran. During the war black America saw clearly that the discrepancy between the democratic values for which the United States was fighting overseas and the realities of racially discriminatory practices at home had become intolerable. That this attitude would particularly affect blacks who experienced these discriminations first hand while in their country's uniform was hardly surprising.

The war's breakdown of the South's economic, social, and moral isolation had a demonstrable impact on one of the region's greatest natural resources—its literary imagination. For William Faulkner and Flannery O'Connor, wartime issues had a definite influence upon their work.

Although the works for which Faulkner is perhaps best noted were all written prior to World War II, his own reputation, in this country at least, was not great until after the war. Be that as it may, a sense that the war both changed the South physically and sharpened the focus of the race issue is reflected in his postwar fiction. Faulkner himself had spent most of the war years in Hollywood attempting, unsuccessfully for the most part, to bolster his financial situation by working as a screenwriter. When in September 1945 he returned to Mississippi, he had a perspective from which to observe changes that had occurred in the South during his absence. In his first postwar novel, *Intruder in the Dust* (1948), Faulkner vividly portrayed the war-induced transformation of the South reaching into Jefferson, the seat of his mythological Yoknapatawpha County. He contrasted a description of Jefferson's "old big decaying wooden houses," which had known several generations of the town's residents and the South's turmoiled history, with the Sunbeltish image of their being overburdened and set back from the very street they had once graced by

> neat small new one-story houses designed in Florida and California set with matching garages in their neat plots of clipped grass and tedious flowerbeds, three and four of them now, a subdivision now in what twenty-five years ago had been considered a little small for one decent front lawn, where the prosperous young married couples lived with two children each and (as soon as they could afford it) an automobile each and memberships in the country club and the bridge clubs and the junior rotary and the chamber of commerce and the patented electric gadgets for cooking and freezing and cleaning . . . while the wives in sandals and pants and painted toenails puffed lipstick-stained cigarettes over shopping bags in the chain groceries and drugstores.

Faulkner also used *Intruder in the Dust* to comment directly on the race issue through long digressions spoken by one of the novel's characters, the white lawyer Gavin Stevens. Stevens's distinctly southern liberal bias—something to the effect that, by recognizing blacks as fellow citizens, white southerners could both affirm their common heritage with blacks while successfully resisting the hypocritical Yankees—makes him a spokesman for Faulkner who, like Gavin Stevens, succeeded in arousing the antipathies of white racists, northern liberals, and blacks. Because of its obvious didacticism, critics have tended to dismiss *Intruder in the Dust* as one of Faulkner's lesser efforts. This may or may not be a fair judgment, but it is in any case beside the point. *Intruder in the Dust* is a richly textured novel demonstrating that even such an iconoclastic literary artist as Faulkner was not immune to the changes taking place in the South nor to their implications. In a revealing letter written in July 1943, Faulkner noted the irony as well as the significance of black political pressure, which had forced the Army to create a squadron of black pilots—the famous Tuskegee airmen—and was then being directed against the aftermath of an ugly race riot in Detroit and the second-class treatment generally accorded blacks in uniform. Sounding for all the world like Lillian Smith or Gunnar Myrdal, Faulkner claimed that the war would usher in a new era of racial justice. He wrote to his stepson who was then in military service:

> A change will come out of this war. If it doesn't if the politicians and people who run this country are not forced to make good the shibboleth they glibly talk about freedom, liberty, human rights, then you young men who have lived through it will have wasted your precious time, and those who don't live through it will have died in vain.

So moved was Faulkner by the juxtaposition of the war and the race issue that one of his recent biographers claims that it virtually destroyed his art.

If Faulkner's literary powers, brilliant as they were, were only partially successful in conveying the full sense of World War II's impact on the South, the same cannot be said of Flannery O'Connor. In her masterful story "The Displaced Person," O'Connor evoked a powerful image of the traditional world of the rural South—a world of white landowners and their poor white and black tenants—about to be torn asunder by the arrival of a Displaced Person, literally a D.P., a refugee from Poland who with his family had somehow managed to survive Hitler's death camps and had come to the South to work as a hired farmhand. A more precise representation of the consequences of World War II confronting the South could hardly be imagined. To the farm's white tenants the displaced person, whose name is Guizac, brings home all the recent horrors of Europe—"the devil's experiment station"—of which they were up to then only dimly aware. Guizac is most efficient, a much better farmhand than the existing white and black tenants. Under his disciplined hands, agricultural machinery is properly utilized and the farm, which had once belonged to the county's most influential and richest man but had grown decrepit under the management of his widow, begins to prosper. All, however, is not well. The white tenants dislike the Pole and fear, quite correctly, that his industriousness makes them expendable. Moreover, for all his lack of understanding of the social conventions of the Jim Crow South, Guizac might as well have been from Mars. He has difficulty comprehending why he should not be concerned that the blacks on the place do not seem to work very hard and occasionally steal chickens, or that the whites operate moonshine stills. His ultimate transgression, though, one that not even the relatively more sophisticated white landlady can tolerate, is to promise in marriage to one of the farm's blacks, as a way of getting her into the United States, his sixteen-year-old female cousin who was still in Poland. Like himself, the girl is a survivor of a concentration camp, and by Guizac's perfectly reasonable logic, after three years in a camp, as he puts it, "She no care black." This is too much for the social world of a southern tenant farm, and the story ends with Guizac being crushed to death by a runaway tractor as the landlady and her tenants, who could have warned the Pole to move out of the way, stand by mutely. Guizac's death, however, only hastens the breakdown of the farm, which is sold off at a loss while its inhabitants disperse.

"The Displaced Person" is a superb literary treatment of the tremendous social, economic, and moral impact of World War II on the South, or at least on the rural South as Flannery O'Connor knew it and understood it. Southern historians would do well to follow her insight in their own research and writing while keeping in mind Marc Bloch's advice against "worshipping the idol of false precision." World War II may or may not have been more important to the South than the Civil War, but it is certainly more important than has hitherto been recognized.

✝ F U R T H E R   R E A D I N G

Carl Abbott, "The Sunbelt Cities in World War II," in Abbott, *The New Urban America: Growth and Politics in Sunbelt Cities* (1981), 101–122

James A. Burran, "Urban Racial Violence in the South During World War II: A Comparative Overview," in Walter J. Fraser, Jr., and Winfred B. Moore, Jr., eds. *From the Old South to the New: Essays on the Transitional South* (1981), 167–177

Dominic J. Capeci, Jr., "The Lynching of Cleo Wright: Federal Protection of Constitutional Rights During World War II," *Journal of American History* 72 (1986), 859–887

John Temple Graves, *The Fighting South* (1943)

Howard W. Odum, "The Romance of the Eleanor Clubs," in Odum, ed., *Race and Rumors of Race: Challenge to American Crisis* (1943)

Richard Polenberg, *War and Society: The United States, 1941–1945* (1972)

Merl E. Reed, "The FEPC, the Black Worker and the Southern Shipyards," *South Atlantic Quarterly* 74 (1974), 446–467

———, "FEPC and Federal Agencies in the South," *Journal of Negro History* 66 (1980), 43–56

John R. Skates, "World War II as a Watershed in Mississippi History," *Journal of Mississippi History* 37 (1975), 131–142

Industrialization and

Urbanization

Southern writer Lillian Smith noted matter-of-factly just after World War II that *"people have moved to town."* Not only were rural southerners flocking to towns and cities, but the South appeared to be entering the industrial revolution at long last. Smith and others hoped that urbanization and industrialization would result in a new South free from the cultural shackles of the old regime.

Historians examining the growth of cities and industry, however, have discovered otherwise. The South had industries and cities long before 1945, and they seemed to have had little impact on regional culture other than to reinforce it. Most of the southern urban population after the Civil War had been born in the South, frequently in rural areas. *"Transplanted"* rather than *"uprooted"* describes the southerners' migration and life in the southern city. Often located in small communities or on the periphery of larger ones, industries such as textiles perpetuated regional racial and economic traditions.

The impact of industries and cities on the post–World War II South is more complex. The shift in the national economy to services, the rise of the Sunbelt, the changes in race relations, and the influx of northerners, especially after 1970, have altered the nature of urbanization and the regional economy.

Why and how did southern cities and industries differ from their counterparts in the North? Do these differences persist, or have the changes since World War II modified or obliterated many of the distinctions?

✛ D O C U M E N T S

The distinctive southern blend of urban with rural and agriculture with industry was especially evident in the emergence of the textile industry after 1880. The University of North Carolina at Chapel Hill has collected hundreds of interviews from former textile workers as part of its Piedmont Social History Project. The excerpts in the first document are from an interview and reflect working and living conditions in the North Carolina Piedmont mill communities during the first third of the twentieth century. Although urban boosterism is not peculiarly southern, it has attained a high art form in the South. Ironically, the results of the booster's efforts often destroy the very values he purports to represent, as the excerpt from Thomas Wolfe timelessly demonstrates in the second selection. The third document contains an excerpt from William Faulkner's chronicle of the amoral Snopes clan; it implies that the new urban-industrial order is inexorable and unyielding to traditions that have become enervated. By the 1970s, the South had blossomed into the "Sunbelt," and the national media, as the fourth document, taken from a *Time* cover story, indicates, rushed to explain the phenomenon. The 1980 census corroborated media assertions, as the five population and migration tables indicate. By the 1980s, however, more sober judgments of regional economic and urban development appeared, noting the patchy nature of Sunbelt prosperity. The Commission on the Future of the South, a nonprofit body funded by southern governors, has combined the traditional role of booster with the more modern one of thoughtful analysis to direct the South to more equitable development. In the final document, the Commission provides a profile of southern poverty in the mid-1980s and suggests some solutions.

Workers Describe Life and Labor in Early Twentieth-Century Textile Mills, 1979

James Pharis: . . . My daddy raised tobacco, his central crop was tobacco. When we come to the town he still kept his team. He done hauling around for people and done truck farming after we moved to town. He done that on up until he was able to do anything.

AT [interviewer Allan Tullos]: He would have a few acres rented around?

James Pharis: No, he just rent the land. That's what he done after he come to town.

AT: The truck farming would be different kinds of vegetables?

James Pharis: Yes, vegetables. Corn to feed his team on.

AT: He never did work in the mill, then.

James Pharis: No, he never did work in the mill.

AT: Did he talk about why they moved from the farm to town?

James Pharis: Because he kinda felt that all we had to do when we moved to town was to reach up and pull the money off of the trees. We come down and pull some off of it.

Nannie Pharis: Worked for twenty-five cents a day when we started.

James Pharis: And that was eleven hours a day, too. I went to work

---

Selected Interviews from the Piedmont Industrialization Series of the Southern Oral History Program Collection (#4007), from the Southern Historical Collection, Library of the University of North Carolina at Chapel Hill.

after I got eight or nine years old, I worked for several years there for twenty-five cents a day, eleven hours a day.

AT: When you all got paid, did you turn the money into your father?

James Pharis: Had to, it took it all to live.

AT: How did that work?

James Pharis: They'd give each kid a little allowance.

Nannie Pharis: Very little.

AT: Your parents would?

James Pharis: They'd give us so much out of what we made.

AT: Who in the family would have been the one that would have kept up with the things that had to do with keeping the money?

James Pharis: My mother, she looked after that. Weren't no money to look after much. The whole family wasn't making as much as one would make now. . . .

AT: When you started to work, what do you remember about that, the mill, working, life?

James Pharis: I don't remember too much individual things. I was about nine or ten years old when I got that hand hurt right there.

AT: How did that happen?

James Pharis: I was riding on an elevator rope in the mill. Me and another boy was getting the quills in the mill. He was on the bottom floor and I was on the top floor. We'd go to the spinning room to empty our quills out. The first one who would get up there would ride the elevator rope. He'd be down on the bottom floor. We'd ride the elevator rope up to the pulley and slide back down. I was riding one day and was looking round over the spinning room and my hand got caught under the wheel. That thing was mashed into jelly, all of it was just smashed all to pieces. They took me out. It happened pretty much after lunch one day. It started up after dinner, they gave forty-five minutes for dinner. They took me down to the company store—the drug store was in the front end of the company store—never even notified my people or nothing. Set me down in the front of that company store. There were only two doctors in town at that time, and both of them was out of town on country calls. I sat there until about four o'clock. Nobody done nothing in the world for me. My people was never notified. Nothing said about it. You tear yourself all to pieces then, nothing said about getting anything out of it. The doctor put a board on my hand there, had my fingers straight. One night the board slipped around the back and that thing crooked down. It's been that way ever since. Never even got straight.

AT: Those things happened a good deal?

James Pharis: Oh, yes, back in them days. Nothing never said about it then. . . .

AT: You said you were a leader of a band in Spray for twenty years and that you all played in two or three different towns right around there. Tell me about that.

James Pharis: We played for the fairs that come around for just about twenty years.

AT: Did you play an instrument.

James Pharis: Yes, I played a trumpet.

AT: How did you learn to play the trumpet?

James Pharis: We had an instructor the company furnished us in later years after World War I was over. They hired a man to come and teach. The whole town wanted to take part in music. . . .

Nannie Pharis: Was it 1930 when they closed the Rhode Island Mill? Then I worked some when we lived in Reidsville—I rode back and forth—1935. I would ride from Reidsville to Eden and worked. I rode with a girl. That was the last work I done.

AT: You started working in 1901 or 1902 when you were nine years old, and then worked until about 1930.

Nannie Pharis: That's right, 1930 in one place.

AT: What do you remember about the working conditions in that mill?

Nannie Pharis: They was pretty good, the overseers and supervisors. Real good, kind to you.

AT: Did you get tired working those hours?

Nannie Pharis: Sometimes. I didn't weigh but eighty-nine pounds, you see, and I could get about. I don't think I ever got very tired.

AT: Would there be ways you would rest during the day?

Nannie Pharis: Yes, if you caught up and didn't have nothing to do you could sit down a few minutes and watch your work.

AT: What would you do when you had a few minutes to sit down? Would you talk to somebody else?

Nannie Pharis: Yes, we'd talk to one another. Maybe one in the next alley to me. They wasn't very strict. They looked after us, I think, real well.

AT: Would you have a chance to eat?

Nannie Pharis: We got an hour for lunch.

AT: Where would you go for lunch?

Nannie Pharis: Go home, because we lived close enough to go to the house. Was a pink bean sandwich be all we'd have. That's the truth, I ain't lying. Sometimes something better. . . .

AT: When you had your first child, you stayed out of work for a while. Did you have somebody come look after your child or cook for you after went back to work?

Nannie Pharis: We'd hire someone. A colored woman. We'd hire her by the week. She'd stay the week and go home on Saturday afternoon, on the weekend and then come back on Monday.

AT: What kind of jobs would she do?

Nannie Pharis: She'd do everything, cook and scrub and clean and laundry. At first I did't have to pay but three dollars a week, but then it got up to five dollars a week.

AT: Would she cook some of the meals?

Nannie Pharis: She'd cook good meals. Good cooks.

AT: Which meals would she cook?

Nannie Pharis: She cooked everything but breakfast. Dinner and lunch, she did that.

AT: Did you leave that up to her, what to cook?

Nannie Pharis: She knew how to cook. I'd lay it out for her, what she was to cook during the day. . . .

AT: Did she have any unusual dishes?

Nannie Pharis: Not that I know of. Aunt Mary and Uncle Jim, he was a slave. Him and us slept in the kitchen every night.

AT: And he worked for you, too?

Nannie Pharis: No, he just stayed there for her to look after him. She couldn't leave him alone. He's a good old colored man. He was religious. You could hear him singing those old time religious songs.

AT: He was kin to her?

Nannie Pharis: He was her husband.

AT: He stayed there?

Nannie Pharis: He stayed there. And then him and her would spend Saturday night and Sunday with her son. You don't find them good old colored people any more. Uncle Jim, he had been a slave down in Georgia.

Thomas Wolfe on the Booster Spirit, 1934

During the week that followed Aunt Maw's funeral George renewed his acquaintance with his home town, and it was a disconcerting experience. The sleepy little mountain village in which he had grown up—for it had been hardly more than that then—was now changed almost beyond recognition. The very streets that he had known so well, and had remembered through the years in their familiar aspect of early-afternoon emptiness and drowsy lethargy, were now foaming with life, crowded with expensive traffic, filled with new faces he had never seen before. Occasionally he saw somebody that he knew, and in the strangeness of it all they seemed to him like lights shining in the darkness of a lonely coast.

But what he noticed chiefly—and once he observed it he began watching for it, and it was always there—was the look on the people's faces. It puzzled him, and frightened him, and when he tried to find a word to describe it, the only thing he could think of was—madness. The nervous, excited glitter in the eyes seemed to belong to nothing else but madness.

Excerpts from *You Can't Go Home Again* by Thomas Wolfe. Copyright 1934, '37, '38, '39, '40 by Maxwell Perkins as executor of the Estate of Thomas Wolfe. Reprinted by permission of Harper & Row Publishers, Inc.

The faces of natives and strangers alike appeared to be animated by some secret and unholy glee. And their bodies, as they darted, dodged, and thrust their way along, seemed to have a kind of leaping energy as if some powerful drug was driving them on. They gave him the impression of an entire population that was drunk—drunk with an intoxication which never made them weary, dead, or sodden, and which never wore off, but which incited them constantly to new efforts of leaping and thrusting exuberance.

The people he had known all his life cried out to him along the streets, seizing his hand and shaking it, and saying: "Hi, there, boy! Glad to see you home again! Going to be with us for a while now? Good! I'll be seeing you! I've got to go on now—got to meet a fellow down the street to sign some papers! Glad to see you, boy!" Then, having uttered this tempestuous greeting without a pause and without the loss of a stride, pulling and dragging him along with them as they wrung his hand, they vanished. . . .

Everyone bought real estate; and everyone was "a real estate man" either in name or practice. The barbers, the lawyers, the grocers, the butchers, the builders, the clothiers—all were engaged now in this single interest and obsession. And there seemed to be only one rule, universal and infallible—to buy, always to buy, to pay whatever price was asked, and to sell again within two days at any price one chose to fix. It was fantastic. Along all the streets in town the ownership of the land was constantly changing; and when the supply of streets was exhausted, new streets were feverishly created in the surrounding wilderness; and even before these streets were paved or a house had been built upon them, the land was being sold, and then resold, by the acre, by the lot, by the foot, for hundreds of thousands of dollars.

A spirit of drunken waste and wild destructiveness was everywhere apparent. The fairest places in the town were being mutilated at untold cost. In the center of town there had been a beautiful green hill, opulent with rich lawns and lordly trees, with beds of flowers and banks of honeysuckle, and on top of it there had been an immense, rambling, old wooden hotel. From its windows one could look out upon the vast panorama of mountain ranges in the smoky distance.

George could remember its wide porches and comfortable rockers, its innumerable eaves and gables, its labyrinth of wings and corridors, its great parlors and their thick red carpets, and the lobby with its old red leather chairs, hollowed and shaped by the backs of men, and its smell of tobacco and its iced tinkle of tall drinks. It had a splendid dining room filled with laughter and quiet voices, where expert Negroes in white jackets bent and scraped and chuckled over the jokes of the rich men from the North as with prayerful grace they served them delicious foods out of old silver dishes. George could remember, too, the smiles and the tender beauty of the rich men's wives and daughters. As a boy he had been touched with the unutterable mystery of all these things, for these wealthy travelers had come great distances and had somehow brought with them an evocation of the whole golden and unvisited world, with its fabulous cities and its promise of glory, fame, and love.

It had been one of the pleasantest places in the town, but now it was gone. An army of men and shovels had advanced upon this beautiful green hill and had <u>leveled it down to an ugly flat of clay</u>, and had paved it with a <u>desolate horror of white concrete</u>, and had built stores and garages and office buildings and parking spaces—all raw and new—and were now putting up a new hotel beneath the very spot where the old one had stood. It was to be a structure of sixteen stories, of steel and concrete and pressed brick. It was being stamped out of the same mold, as if by some <u>gigan</u>tic <u>biscuit-cutter of hote</u>ls, that had produced a thousand others like it all over the country. And, to give a sumptuous—if spurious—distinction to its patterned uniformity, it was to be called The Libya-Ritz. . . .

They had <u>squandered fabulous sums</u> in meaningless streets and bridges. They had torn down ancient buildings and erected new ones large enough to take care of a city of half a million people. They had leveled hills and bored through mountains, making magnificent tunnels paved with double roadways and glittering with shining tiles—tunnels which leaped out on the other side into Arcadian wilderness. They had flung away the earnings of a lifetime, and mortgaged those of a generation to come. <u>They had ruin</u>ed <u>their city</u>, and in doing so had ruined themselves, their children, and their children's children.

Already the town had passed from their possession. They no longer owned it. It was mortgaged under a debt of fifty million dollars, owned by bonding companies in the North. The very streets they walked on had been sold beneath their feet. They signed their names to papers calling for the payment of fabulous sums, and resold their land the next day to other madmen who signed away their lives with the same careless magnificence. On paper, their profits were enormous, but their "boom" was already over and they would not see it. They were staggering beneath obligations to pay which none of them could meet—and still they bought.

<u>And when they had exhausted all the possibilities of ruin and extrav-</u> <u>agance that the town could of</u>fer, they had rushed out into the <u>wilderness</u>, into the <u>lyrical immensities</u> of wild earth where there was land enough for all men living, and they had staked off little plots and wedges in the hills as one might try to stake a picket fence out in the middle of the ocean. They had given fancy names to all these <u>foolish enterprises</u>—"Wild Boulders"—"Shady Acres"—"Eagle's Crest." They had set prices on these sites of forest, field, and tangled undergrowth that might have bought a mountain, and made charts and drawings showing populous communities of shops, houses, streets, roads, and clubs in regions where there was no road, no street, no house, and which could not be reached in any way save by a band of resolute pioneers armed with axes. These places were to be transformed into <u>idyllic colonies</u> for artists and writers and critics; and there were colonies as well for preachers, doctors, actors, dancers, golf players,

and retired locomotive engineers. There were colonies for everyone, and, what is more, they sold the lots—to one another!

But under all this flash and play of great endeavor, the <u>paucity</u> of their designs and the <u>starved meagerness</u> of their lives were already apparent. The better life which they talked about resolved itself into a few sterile and baffled gestures. <u>All they really did for themselves was to build uglier and more expensive homes, and buy new cars, and join a country club. And they did all this with a frenzied haste, because—it seemed to George— they were looking for food to feed their hunger and had not found</u> it.

paucity-
smallness
of quantity

William Faulkner on the Snopes Clan, 1940

When he reached Frenchman's Bend in November, it had returned to normal. It had acquiesced to the clerk's presence even if it had not accepted him, though the Varners seemed to have done both. Jody had used to be in the store at some time during the day and not far from it at any time. Ratliff now discovered that for months he had been in the habit of sometimes not appearing at all, customers who had traded there for years, mostly serving themselves and putting the correct change into the cigar box inside the cheese cage, now having to deal for each trivial item with a man whose name they had not even heard two months ago, who answered Yes and No to direct questions and who apparently never looked directly or long enough at any face to remember the name which went with it, yet who never made mistakes in any matter pertaining to money. Jody Varner had made them constantly. They were usually in his own favor to be sure, letting a customer get away with a spool of thread or a tin of snuff now and then, but getting it back sooner or later. They had come to expect mistakes of him, just as they knew he would correct them when caught with a bluff, hearty amiability, making a joke of it, which sometimes left the customer wondering just a little about the rest of the bill. But they expected this too, because he would give them credit for food and plow-gear when they needed it, long credit, though they knew they would pay interest for that which on its face looked like generosity and openhandedness, whether that interest showed in the final discharge or not. But the clerk never made mistakes.

"Nonsense," Ratliff said. "Somebody's bound to catch him sooner or later. There aint a man woman or child in twenty-five miles that dont know what's in that store and what it cost as well as Will or Jody Varner either."

"Hah," the other said—a sturdy short-legged black-browed ready-faced man named Odum Bookwright. "That's it."

"You mean aint nobody ever caught him *once* even?"

"No," Bookwright said. "And folks dont like it. Otherwise, how can you tell?"

"Sho," Ratliff said. "How can you?"

"There was that credit business too," another said—a lank man with a bulging dreamy scant-haired head and pale myopic eyes named Quick, who operated a sawmill. He told about it: how they had discovered almost at once that the clerk did not want to credit anyone with anything. He finally flatly refused further credit to a man who had been into and out of the store's debt at least once a year for the last fifteen, and how that afternoon Will Varner himself came galloping up on the old fat grumble-gutted white horse and stormed into the store, shouting loud enough to be heard in the blacksmith shop across the road: "Who in hell's store do you think this is, anyway?"

"Well, we know whose store it is yet, anyway," Ratliff said.

"Or whose store some folks still thinks it is yet," Bookwright said. "Anyhow, he aint moved into Varner's house yet."

Because the clerk now lived in the village. One Saturday morning someone noticed that the saddled mule was not hitched behind the store. The store remained open until ten and later on Saturdays and there was always a crowd about it and several men saw him put out the lamps and lock the door and depart, on foot. And the next morning he who had never been seen in the village between Saturday night and Monday morning appeared at the church, and those who saw him looked at him for an instant in incredulous astonishment. In addition to the gray cloth cap and the gray trousers, he wore not only a clean white shirt but a necktie—a tiny machine-made black bow which snapped together at the back with a metal fastener. It was not two inches long and with the exception of the one which Will Varner himself wore to church it was the only tie in the whole Frenchman's Bend country, and from that Sunday morning until the day he died he wore it or one just like it (it was told of him later, after he had become president of his Jefferson bank, that he had them made for him by the gross)—a tiny viciously depthless cryptically balanced splash like an enigmatic punctuation symbol against the expanse of white shirt which gave him Jody Varner's look of ceremonial heterodoxy raised to its tenth power and which postulated to those who had been present on that day that quality of outrageous overstatement of physical displacement which the sound of his father's stiff foot made on the gallery of the store that afternoon in the spring. He departed on foot; he came to the store the next morning still walking and still wearing the tie. By nightfall the countryside knew that since the previous Saturday he had boarded and lodged in the home of a family living about a mile from the store.

Will Varner had long since returned to his old idle busy cheerful existence—if he had ever left it. The store had not seen him since the Fourth of July. And now that Jody no longer came in, during the dead slack days of August while the cotton ripened and there was nothing for anyone to do, it had actually seemed as if not only the guiding power but the proprietorial and revenue-deriving as well was concentrated in that squat reticent figure in the steadily-soiling white shirts and the minute invulnerable bow, which in those abeyant days lurked among the ultimate shadows of the deserted and rich-odored interior with a good deal of the quality of a spider of that bulbous blond omnivorous though non-poisonous species.

Then in September something happened. It began rather, though at first they did not recognise it for what it was. The cotton had opened and was being picked. One morning the first of the men to arrive found Jody Varner already there. The gin was unlocked and Trumbull, Varner's blacksmith, and his apprentice and the Negro fireman were overhauling the machinery, getting it ready for the season's run, and presently Snopes came out of the store and went across to the gin and entered it and passed from sight and so, for the moment, from remembering too. It was not until the store closed that afternoon that they realised that Jody Varner had been inside it all day. But even then they attached little importance to this. They thought that without doubt Jody himself had sent the clerk to superintend the opening of the gin, which Jody himself had used to do, out of laziness, assuming himself the temporary onus of tending store so he could sit down. It took the actual firing-up of the gin and the arrival of the first loaded wagons to disabuse them. Then they saw that it was Jody who was now tending store again, fetching and carrying for the nickels and dimes, while the clerk sat all day long on the stool behind the scale-beam as the wagons moved in turn onto it and so beneath the suction pipe. Jody had used to do both. That is, he was mostly behind the scales, letting the store take care of itself, as it always had, though now and then, just to rest himself, he would keep a wagon standing upon the scales, blocking them for fifteen minutes or even forty-five minutes, while he was in the store; maybe there would not even be any customers during that time, just loungers, listeners for him to talk to. But that was all right. Things got along just as well. And now that there were two of them, there was no reason why one should not remain in the store while the other did the weighing, and there was no reason why Jody should not have designated the weighing to the clerk. The cold surmise which now began to dawn upon them was that————

"Sho," Ratliff said. "I know. That Jody should have stayed there a-tall. Just who it was that told him to stay there." He and Bookwright looked at each other. "It wasn't Uncle Will. That store and that gin had been running themselves at the same time for nigh forty years all right, with just one fellow between them. And a fellow Uncle Will's age aint likely to change his notions. Sho now. All right. Then what?"

They could watch them both from the gallery. They would come in on their laden wagons and draw into line, mule-nose to tail gate, beside the road, waiting for their turn to move onto the scales and then under the suction pipe, and dismount and wrap the reins about a stanchion and cross to the gallery, from which they could watch the still, impenetrable, steadily-chewing face throned behind the scale-beam, the cloth cap, the minute tie, while from within the store they could hear now and then the short surly grunts with which Varner answered when his customers forced him to speak at all. Now and then they would even go in themselves and buy sacks or plugs of tobacco or tins of snuff which they did not actually need yet, or maybe just to drink from the cedar water bucket. Because there was something in Jody's eyes that had not been there before either—a shadow, something between annoyance and speculation and purest foreknowledge, which was not quite bafflement yet but was certainly sober. This was the time they referred to later, two and three years later, when they told one another: "That was when he passed Jody," though it was Ratliff who amended it: "You mean, that was when Jody begun to find it out."

Time Interprets Americans' Move to the South and the Southwest, 1976

Americans are rapidly leaving the Northern and Eastern regions, the old industrial quadrant from St. Louis and Chicago to Philadelphia and Boston, and increasingly heading toward the South and West. Between 1970 and last year [1975], 2,537,000 people migrated from the Northeastern and North Central states to the Southern and Western states. The fastest-growing states in the nation are Arizona, Florida, Nevada, Idaho and Colorado. By far the nation's fastest-developing new boom region is the Sunbelt—the lower arc of warmlands stretching from Southern California to the Carolinas.

These new migrations suggest a major change in Americans' expectations—what they want from their careers and communities and what they are willing to give up to get it. Says Pollster Louis Harris: "Most Americans don't want more quantity of anything, but more quality in what they've got."

In such impulses is a certain chastened spirit, a feeling—no doubt a residue of the manic '60s—that smaller and quieter home pleasures are more important than acquisitiveness and ambition. This is not necessarily an edifying spiritual development in America so much as a self-interested calculation that a 90-minute commute or a triple-bolted apartment door is not worth the trouble if one can escape. The ethic suggests that bigness is no longer better, that mere dollars do not mean a more satisfying life, that success is more a matter of enjoying where one is than of moving ahead. Those sentiments, of course, can carry a troubling complacency. The frankly escapist note is one theme of some of the new migrations—a kind of premature retirement, a dropping-out. That is a sweet and organically grown estimate of life, but in some cases it smacks of elitism gone to the country for the cure. Many are migrating, however, for somewhat opposite reasons. They find that in the smaller cities and towns there is more scope for their ambition, more room for competition and expansion.

"In a way it is certainly a middle-class migration," says Queens College

Political Scientist Andrew Hacker. "Those who are moving out are looking for a kind of middle-class subcountry, a place where it is safer, and where there is more predictable service, and where the school system is less problematic."

Crime is the most obsessively mentioned reason for leaving the cities. Almost all of the migrants tell horror stories of muggings just up the street, of houses burglarized, of children exposed to drugs. Overcrowded schools, pollution and noise are driving many out. So are heavy taxes and high costs of living.

Beneath the migrants' vision sometimes lurks a disturbing undercurrent of racial aversion, an unspoken desire to get away from the increasingly black urban centers. Some blacks, of course, are fleeing the cities just as fast as whites. . . . But as Rand Corp. Demographer Peter Morrison warns, there is a danger that U.S. society "is dividing into those who can buy the new life-style and those who are left. A lot of people will simply be relegated to those empty holes, the urban cores." University of Chicago Sociologist Philip Hauser says bleakly that "the country is heading toward an *apartheid* society." . . .

More typically, the migrants are looking less for a life out of Thoreau than a life out of, say, Booth Tarkington or Norman Rockwell—equidistant from the brutalities of the city and the brutalities of nature. Neil Carey, a refugee from Los Angeles, believes that he has found that golden mean in Lexington, Ky. (pop. 187,200). Lexington, with a 16% growth rate since 1971, is Kentucky's boom city—yet it is also a delightful mixture of old residential neighborhoods, a renovated downtown, a state university and a low (4.5%) unemployment rate. A clinical social worker, Carey, 37, and his wife Karen, 35, detested the rootlessness and aimless energy of Los Angeles. Says Carey: "People were always moving, moving, moving. Every promotion or raise seemed to mean a new car, new house, new friends."

The Careys, living on a much reduced income, have gladly settled for a more modest style of life—one five-year-old Dodge, a $15,000 house that they have renovated, an occasional movie and dinner out, camping, and work in the Unitarian Church. Also, says Carey, "I've been to city council meetings here. I'd never been to the city council in L.A. And here I feel as if I and my children can grow with the town and develop along with it." . . .

Industries have moved into the South and Southwest in part because taxes are relatively low, unions relatively weak, heating and other main-tenance costs modest. Three years ago Electro Corp., a manufacturer of electronic controls for industry, moved from Niles, Ill., to Sarasota, Fla. Chairman Richard Crossley found that taxes and plant costs were consid-erably lower in Sarasota, that his payroll was 15% smaller because of a lower wage scale, that the productivity of his workers was higher. Electro brought 14 key people and their families from the Chicago area and started up anew. Says Crossley: "Only one person was hesitant about moving, and he has turned out to be the biggest Chamber of Commerce man in Sarasota. There's no state income tax, no estate tax, a 4% sales tax *v.* 5%

in Illinois." Crossley now sails a 16-ft. sloop, has fewer colds and, when he consults the books, is happier still: the company has been more profitable. . . .

The number of Fortune 500 companies that are based in the South and West jumped from 75 in 1964 to 112 in 1974. Yet the movement to smaller cities takes in all regions. The Book-of-the-Month Club has relocated its operations from New York to Camp Hill, Pa.; General Electric's corporate headquarters is now in Fairfield, Conn.; the Simmons Co. moved from New York to Norcross, near Atlanta; and Greyhound changed its headquarters from Chicago to Phoenix.

Employees who made the move are usually happy with their new lives. Others who relocate on their own often have to take pay cuts, but in most cases they find that the dollar goes further. People in the South and West spend comparatively less for taxes, housing, fuel, clothing and most services. The Bureau of Labor Statistics estimates that the cost of maintaining a high standard of living for a family of four in New York City is 33% higher than in Houston or Nashville. Air conditioning has made the long, hot summers bearable. And for some people, the way of life—a moderate climate, plenty of outdoor activity, the residual Southern graces—is an attractive alternative to the iron chill of the North.

Accountant Ed Kraujalis and his wife Mildred, both 27, left New York City a year ago for Cape Coral, Fla., a community that did not exist in 1960 and still does not show on most maps. Now it has 24,000 inhabitants. The Kraujalises paid $4,500 for a lot on a canal and have started work on a $33,000 house. Terms: 20% down and a 6.5% mortgage. "It would have cost twice that to build the same house in New York City," says Kraujalis. So many other people have discovered Cape Coral and nearby communities that the Fort Myers area, of which it is a part, is the nation's fastest-rising community. Since 1970, population has grown more than 46%, and it is now 154,000. . . .

In many ways, the migrants from the North and the East are helping to alter the character of the South, which is becoming both more sophisticated and more homogenized. On the whole, Yankees who move there find themselves welcomed, mostly because they bring new money, skills and opportunity with them. At the same time, the South is changing the carpetbaggers in a number of respects. Sometimes there is no Southerner more given to Southern style and sense of place than the Confederate from, say, Chicago—the Yankee Good Ole Boy.

Whatever economic advantages they bring, however, the newcomers sometimes threaten to perpetuate in new territory many of the offenses of urban sprawl around the big cities. Especially in many communities of the Sunbelt, oldtimers have grown bitterly aware that the massive invasions have overloaded public services, overwhelmed police and fire departments, water supplies and sewage systems.

The 29 new "developer cities" just to the west of Fort Lauderdale have encountered the dark underside of extravagant growth. The recent recession slowed the boom, leaving the skeletons of half-completed communities and a number of bankrupt builders. Now, says Fort Lauderdale Mayor E. Clay Shaw, "we have gone to enforced land-use planning at the county level. We've put population caps on certain areas. We've stopped bargaining among landowners. There have been some building moratoriums because of overworked sewerage facilities." . . .

Another and in some ways more urgent problem is what the new migrations are doing to the big industrial cities, especially those of the Northeastern quadrant. They are hemorrhaging. . . .

The U.S. is more than ever a nation of immigrants, and the new, internal migration is a pursuit, as much psychological as geographical, of the remaining pockets of Frederick Jackson Turner's frontier. The migration is also the last march of a kind of expansionist privilege: the old American idea that all mistakes are canceled by the horizon, by more room, by moving out. Great population movements are hardly unique in a nation that was built by its restless energy. Never before, however, have so many Americans been able to change their lives quite so quickly, and to base their decisions about where to live on the amenities they desire. Americans undoubtedly will continue to make such choices well into the '80s. The age group that likes to move the most is between 25 and 29. Since the peak year for births in the U.S. was 1961, when 4,350,000 children were born, the biggest outward surge is yet to come.

The Making of the Sunbelt: A Statistical Profile, 1988

Table 1   Percentage Growth of Metropolitan Areas by Decade and Census Division, 1950–1984

REGION AND DIVISION	1950–1960	1960–1970	1970–1980	1980–1984
Northeast	13.7	9.6	−1.5	1.1
New England	13.0	12.8	2.6	1.6
Mid Atlantic	14.0	8.7	−2.7	0.9
Midwest	23.5	13.0	2.6	0.4
East North Central	23.4	12.7	2.0	−0.3
West North Central	23.8	13.8	5.0	2.7
South	36.2	22.0	21.5	8.0
South Atlantic	39.7	25.9	20.7	7.4
East South Central	22.6	11.6	14.4	2.8
West South Central	38.1	21.3	26.4	11.4
West	48.5	28.5	22.6	8.2
Mountain	63.9	34.6	41.4	11.4
Pacific	45.8	27.3	18.6	7.4
Total	26.5	16.8	10.3	4.4
Average annual rate	2.38	1.57	0.99	1.03

Reprinted from *Regional and Metropolitan Growth and Decline in the United States* by William H. Frey and Alden Speare, Jr. Copyright © 1988 The Russell Sage Foundation. Used with permission of the Russell Sage Foundation.

Table 2 The Biggest Gainers and Losers among MSAs [Metropolitan Statistical Area] and CMSAs [Consolidated Metropolitan Statistical Area] over 250,000 for 1970–1980 and 1980–1984

BIGGEST GAINERS

	1970–1980			1980–1984	
RANK	NAME	GAIN IN PERCENT	RANK	NAME	GAIN IN PERCENT
1	Las Vegas, NV	69.5	1	Fort Myers–Cape Coral, FL	23.2
2	West Palm Beach–Boca Raton, FL	65.3	2	Melbourne–Titusville–Palm Beach, FL	20.7
3	McAllen–Edinburg–Mission, TX	56.0	3	Austin, TX	20.3
4	Phoenix, AZ	55.4	4	West Palm Beach–Boca Raton, FL	20.0
5	Orlando, FL	54.4	5	McAllen–Edinburg–Mission, TX	19.0
6	Daytona Beach, FL	52.7	6	Orlando, FL	17.7
7	Tucson, AZ	51.1	7	Daytona Beach, FL	16.1
8	Austin, TX	48.9	8	Las Vegas, NV	15.8
9	Tampa–St. Petersburg, FL	46.0	9	Houston–Galveston–Brazoria, TX	15.0
10	Houston–Galveston–Brazoria, TX	43.0	10	Stockton, CA	14.8

BIGGEST LOSERS

	1970–1980			1980–1984	
RANK	NAME	LOSS IN PERCENT	RANK	NAME	LOSS IN PERCENT
1	Buffalo–Niagara Falls, NY CMSA	-7.9	1	Duluth, MN-WI	-4.8
2	Utica–Rome, NY	-6.0	2	Detroit–Ann Arbor, MI CMSA	-3.7
3	Cleveland–Akron–Lorain, OH CMSA	-5.5	3	Flint, MI	-3.6
4	Pittsburgh–Beaver Valley, PA CMSA	-5.2	4	Eugene–Springfield, OR	-3.2
5	New York–N. New Jersey–L.I. CMSA	-3.6	5	Buffalo–Niagara Falls, NY CMSA	-3.1
6	Dayton–Springfield, OH	-3.4	6	Peoria, IL	-2.7
7	Springfield, MA	-2.4	7	Youngstown–Warren, OH	-2.5
8	St. Louis, MO	-2.2	8	Saginaw–Bay City–Midland, MI	-2.3
9	Binghamton, NY	-1.8	9	Johnstown, PA	-2.1
10	Philadelphia–Wilm.–Trenton CMSA	-1.2	10	Pittsburgh–Beaver Valley, PA CMSA	-2.1

Reprinted from *Regional and Metropolitan Growth and Decline in the United States* by William H. Frey and Alden Speare, Jr. Copyright © 1988 The Russell Sage Foundation. Used with permission of the Russell Sage Foundation.

Table 3   Estimates of Total Net Migration, Immigration, and Internal Net Migration for Metropolitan Areas by Census Division, 1960–1980

REGION AND CENSUS DIVISION	1960–1970			1970–1980		
	TOTAL NET MIGRATION	IMMIGRATION	INTERNAL MIGRATION	TOTAL NET MIGRATION	IMMIGRATION	INTERNAL MIGRATION
Northeast	0.7	2.7	-2.0	-6.4	3.2	-9.6
New England	3.1	2.4	0.7	-2.6	2.4	-5.0
Mid Atlantic	-0.1	2.8	-2.9	-7.6	3.5	-11.1
Midwest	0.4	1.1	-0.7	-5.6	1.6	-7.2
East North Central	0.3	1.2	-1.0	-6.2	1.7	-8.0
West North Central	0.8	0.5	0.3	-3.5	1.0	-4.5
South	7.5	1.7	5.8	9.2	2.6	6.6
South Atlantic	12.2	2.5	9.6	10.2	2.7	7.5
East South Central	-1.4	0.3	-1.7	2.3	0.7	1.7
West South Central	5.0	1.2	3.8	11.0	3.5	7.5
West	14.4	3.6	10.8	12.8	7.1	5.7
Mountain	17.1	1.3	15.8	27.5	2.7	24.7
Pacific	13.9	4.1	9.9	9.8	8.1	1.7
Total	4.6	2.2	2.5	1.6	3.4	-1.8

Reprinted from *Regional and Metropolitan Growth and Decline in the United States* by William H. Frey and Alden Speare, Jr. Copyright © 1988 The Russell Sage Foundation. Used with permission of the Russell Sage Foundation.

Table 4 Net Migration by Average Income Level of Metropolitan Areas by Region (average annual rate of net migration per 1,000 persons)

MEAN HOUSEHOLD INCOME	NORTH	SOUTH	WEST	TOTAL
Net migration 1960–1970 (per 1,000 persons in 1960)				
1960 income				
Less than $6,000	− 3.2	1.6	11.5	0.9
$6,000 to $6,599	− 1.4	10.1	11.7	4.6
$6,600 to $7,249	0.7	13.0	17.3	5.0
$7,250 to $7,899	1.2	—	11.9	4.9
$7,900 or more	2.0	17.1	23.9	6.7
Net migration 1970–1980 (per 1,000 persons in 1970)				
1970 income				
Less than $9,000	2.2	10.6	18.0	10.1
$9,000 to $9,999	− 2.7	6.2	22.6	5.4
$10,000 to $10,999	− 4.7	13.4	19.9	5.9
$11,000 to $11,999	− 8.7	0.2	1.6	− 5.6
$12,000 or more	− 7.2	− 7.2	14.9	− 3.9
Net migration 1980–1984 (per 1,000 persons in 1980)				
1980 income				
Less than $18,000	− 2.8	10.8	15.9	7.0
$18,000 to $19,999	− 3.7	6.7	5.5	3.2
$20,000 to $21,999	− 3.0	11.4	14.9	2.7
$22,000 to $23,999	− 5.0	12.9	6.6	3.2
$24,000 or more	− 6.2	12.1	5.8	0.8

Table 5 Employment Growth and Net Migration, 1970–1980, by Functional Type of Metropolitan Area and Region

FUNCTIONAL TYPE	REGION			TOTAL	NUMBER OF SMSAS
	NORTH	SOUTH	WEST		
Employment growth (percent)					
Nodal (services)	11.5	43.9	41.6	27.7	101
Manufacturing	12.0	24.4	—	13.3	99
Government/military	—	28.5	46.7	34.8	36
Medical/educational	30.2	61.0	65.2	47.1	24
Resort	26.1	88.6	102.8	86.0	9
Mixed	28.8	34.4	59.7	43.7	35
Total	12.4	40.0	45.4	26.0	304
Net migration (per 1,000 population)					
Nodal	− 66.8	109.9	90.1	19.6	101
Manufacturing	− 60.0	14.7	—	− 51.9	99
Government/military	—	− 17.0	175.1	50.2	36
Medical/educational	10.5	221.2	257.0	127.0	24
Resort	93.0	630.6	558.8	569.5	9
Mixed	31.5	65.7	258.7	138.4	35
Total	− 60.1	92.1	128.4	16.2	304

A Report on Poverty and Plenty in the South, 1986

During the 1960's, poverty in the South dropped from 35 percent to 18 percent of the total population. From 1969 through 1979 the decline slowed abruptly, and during the last five years poverty in the South and the nation has generally been rising. Since 1979 when the rate was 15 percent, Southern poverty has remained above 16 percent and in 1982 was above 18 percent.

In actual numbers the pattern looks even more worrisome. Eight million persons in the South escaped poverty in the 1960s, and there was virtually no change in the numbers of poor over the next ten years. However, from 1979 through 1984, more than 2.5 million persons in the region became poor.

As in the past, blacks and children endure the highest rates of poverty. During the last five years the rate for black Southerners has increased to nearly 35 percent—a rate more than three times the poverty among whites. Based on national data, one out of every five minority children is poor, and every other black child under the age of six lives in poverty. The rates are highest in the South.

Women now constitute the largest segment of the adult population in poverty—60 percent of all poor over the age of 18. The number of women who are the sole support of poor households has almost doubled over the last twenty years. By 1984 three out of every four persons in poverty were women and their children.

In 1984, one out of every twenty families had a total income of less than $5,000. However, more than one in seven black families had an income below this substandard level. Despite an increase in the number of very poor families over the past few years, more than 1.4 million public assistance recipients in the South were removed from four government programs for the poor between 1980 and 1984 due to changes in budgets and regulations (Aid To Families with Dependent Children, Medicaid, food stamps, and Social Security Insurance). Most of the cuts came in the food stamp program, and half of all persons dropped from public assistance were children. In addition, because of program cuts and inflation, the combined value of both AFDC and food stamps in the South dropped 20 percent from 1980 through 1984.

Public assistance in the region has not reached a majority of the poor, much less the near poor. As late as 1982 none of the six major federal poverty programs provided benefits to even half the poor in the South. Only 44 percent of the poor received food stamps that year in our region; only one in three of the poor was a recipient of Medicaid; and fewer than one in six poor persons received cash payments under AFDC. The vast majority of those families receiving assistance were headed by a single parent or someone over 65 years of age.

1986 Commission on the Future of the South, "Equity: The Critical Link in Southern Economic Development" (Research Triangle Park, NC: Commission on the Future of the South, 1986), pp. 8–10.

While nothing fosters poverty as much as the absence of a job, the South's recent past reaffirms that work does not necessarily reduce poverty. Two recent trends illustrate the point. First, while the region has experienced the growth of poverty in the last five years, it also has maintained a high rate of job growth, usually outpacing most states in the other regions. Second, a relatively low rate of unemployment in some southern locations has coexisted with a high rate of poverty. In Atlanta, for instance, unemployment has been quite low for most of the last ten years especially when compared to other large urban centers. However, in 1980—the last year for a city-by-city comparison—Atlanta had the second highest rate of poverty among cities across the country.

Donald Tomaskovic-Devey, a sociologist at North Carolina State University, argues that we must expand opportunity to lessen poverty and points to some harsh realities in our economic system. "Poverty," he states, "is not exclusively defined in terms of exclusion from the labor force, but also in terms of the pattern of participation. A family of four with two wage earners at or near the minimum wage, working a combined sixty hours a week and fifty weeks a year, will still be below the poverty line." Of course, most poor people work. When the young, old, and disabled are not considered, the nationwide level of working poor among the able-bodied poor in 1984 was 60 percent—a remarkable fact for a population where almost half the poor live in families with one female parent.

Dr. Tomaskovic-Devey contends that the normal functioning of the private economy benefits from the existence of an unemployed labor force as well as the creation of an array of low quality jobs. "First, the unemployed poor provide a reserve labor force to employers. In times of employment expansion the unemployed poor can be drawn into the labor market at low wages. When the economy contracts across the business cycle, these same people are fired. In addition to providing a variable labor force for the contraction and expansion of employment in a locality, the unemployed poor by their presence in a labor market keep the wages of the employed from rising too quickly in periods of economic expansion.

"Let us pretend," he continues, "that tomorrow South Carolina's population will become all white, male, healthy, between the ages of 25 and 45, and have graduated from high school. What would happen to the amount of poverty in South Carolina? It is my contention that, at least in the short run, because the quality and quantity of jobs would be unchanged, poverty would remain. Poverty is a function of the amount of opportunity in a labor market relative to the size of the population . . . and of the quality of that opportunity." He contends that opportunity is determined by the industrial structure of a locality and the relative power of the labor force—a function of labor market "tightness" and discrimination.

E. T. Kehrer a director of the Southern Area Civil Rights Department, AFL-CIO, gives us two concrete examples of Tomaskovic-Devey's last point: "The early years of constructing the Tennessee-Tombigbee Waterway, the largest construction project ever attempted by the U.S. Army Corps of Engineers, were characterized by a virtually all white, non-union work force, and without any affirmative action plans, which at the time were required only on urban projects." Following two years of concerted pressure from community-based organizations and labor organizations (Joint Heavy and Highway Construction Committee, AFL-CIO Civil Rights Department, Southern Regional Council, Minority People's Council on the Tennessee-Tombigbee Waterway, Recruitment and Training Program and the NAACP), the Office of Federal Contract Compliance Programs (OFCCP) imposed a project-wide affirmative action plan with a five year span of goals and timetables. Although the project started 100 percent white, by June, 1983 minority work hours totaled 111,538. With an average wage of $10.00 per hour, the June, 1983 impact on the minority community in Mississippi and Alabama was roughly $1,115,380. Much of this could not have been possible without the active role of the OFCCP.

Steve Suitts, Executive Director of the Southern Regional Council, concludes that "both the South and the nation are trespassing into an era that endangers the future of many citizens. From the early signs it does not appear as a noble moment in our history nor a generous one. For the first time since the Great Depression we may be witnessing the growth of poverty and the formation of a real underclass of citizens while diminishing the government's efforts to assist the poor. It may also be an era when personal initiative and work become ineffective tools for many poor to escape their condition, when we assign a large and enlarging number of our children to live with poverty, and when the South returns to its worst tradition of ignoring the widening gap between the races.

"Yet, the real peril does not lie in the judgment of history. The South and the nation face actual and rather immediate jeopardy when so large a part of its commonwealth is divided *increasingly* unevenly among its citizens. Beyond the strains that portend the possibility of social unrest, the losses of productivity and the cost of human neglect cannot be postponed for decades and must be paid by all of society.

"If there is but one region of the country that knows the folly and tragic consequences of mortgaging the future of a large part of its people for the temporary gains of others, it should be the South. Those lessons of the recent past in race relations should be too vivid and painful to permit the current patterns of poverty in the region and nation to continue undisturbed." . . .

Suitts recommends four strategic actions at the state and federal levels to reverse the current poverty trends:

1. *Increase the minimum wage.* The minimum wage is far below any decent standard of minimum living for most families. If the minimum wage were increased by action of the federal government or the states, it could remove as many as four and a half million persons in the U.S. (and perhaps more than one million in the South) out of poverty.

2. *Strengthen the enforcement of anti-discrimination laws.* The extraordinary prevalence of poverty among blacks and women is in part a reflection of the missed opportunities in the workplace, often caused by discriminatory hiring and payment practices.

3. *Increase the availability of jobs to all poor adults who can work.*
Full employment, at decent wages, is the most sensible way to virtually
eliminate poverty. The nation has a number of important needs that should
not go unmet, and jobs should be available to carry them out. In many
areas, such as caring for the young or old, the talents required for the jobs
would not require vast training in the public or private sector. While the
task of uniting both national needs and jobs for the poor would be expensive
for the government, the costs pale in comparison to the current expenses
for the U.S. Defense Department.

4. *Provide child care for both the poor and non-poor.* With so many
women and children among the poor, nothing realistic can be done in the
private or public arena in reducing poverty without a widespread solution
to the lack of affordable child care. Five million poor children are under
the age of six and almost six million are grammar school age. The number
of single parents among the poor is rising. It makes little sense for the
mothers of poor children to take a minimum wage job when they will
accordingly spend a fourth of the income on child care. Without affordable
child care, the want ads will not (and usually should not) be answered by
many poor mothers.

ESSAYS

The textile industry demonstrates the strong link between the countryside and
southern industrialization in terms of both the work force and its culture. The
first essay, by a team of scholars from the University of North Carolina, Chapel
Hill, who use oral history, explores these links and explodes the myth of southern labor's docility. The workers emerge from these interviews much less unwitting victims than participants, however circumscribed, in their own destinies.
The second essay, by David R. Goldfield, a professor of history at the University of North Carolina, Charlotte, argues that southern urbanization has reflected
regional culture and therefore is and remains distinct from urban development in
the rest of the nation. The final essay, by historian James C. Cobb, a professor
at the University of Tennessee, Knoxville, provides a similar analysis for southern industrialization, demonstrating the persistence of historic factors that continue to set southern economic development off from other parts of the country.

The Lives and Labors of the Cotton-Mill People

JACQUELYN DOWD HALL, ROBERT KORSTAD, AND JAMES L. LELOUDIS II

Textile mills built the new South. Beginning in the 1880s, business and
professional men tied their hopes for prosperity to the whirring of spindles
and the beating of looms. Small-town boosterism supplied the rhetoric of

Jacquelyn Dowd Hall, Robert Korstad, and James L. Leloudis II, "Cotton Mill People: Work,
Community, and Protest in the Textile South, 1880–1940," *American Historical Review* 91
(April 1986), pp. 245–286. Reprinted by permission of the authors.

the mill-building campaign, but the impoverishment of farmers was industrialization's driving force. The post–Civil War rise of sharecropping, tenantry, and the crop lien ensnared freedmen, then eroded yeoman society. Farmers of both races fought for survival by clinging to subsistence strategies and habits of sharing even as they planted cash crops and succumbed to tenantry. Meanwhile, merchants who had accumulated capital through the crop lien invested in cotton mills. As the industry took off in an era of intensifying segregation, blacks were relegated to the land, and white farmers turned to yet another strategy for coping with economic change. They had sold their cotton to the merchant; now they supplied him with the human commodity needed to run his mills. This homegrown industry was soon attracting outside capital and underselling northern competitors. By the end of the Great Depression, the Southeast replaced New England as the world's leading producer of cotton cloth, and the industrializing Piedmont replaced the rural Coastal Plain as pacesetter for the region.

Despite the lasting imprint of textile manufacturing on regional development and labor relations, we have no modern survey of the industry's evolution. Nor has the outpouring of research on working-class history been much concerned with factory workers in the New South. To be sure, recent studies have uncovered sporadic, and sometimes violent, contention over the shape of the industrial South. But those findings have done little to shake the prevailing wisdom: The South's mill villages supposedly bred a "social type" compounded of irrationality, individualism, and fatalism. Unable to unite in their own interests, textile workers remained "silent, incoherent, with no agency to express their needs."

We have reached different conclusions. Our research began with a collaborative oral history project aimed at discovering how working people made sense of their own experience. We did not view memory as a direct window on the past. But we did presume the moral and intellectual value of listening to those who lacked access to power and, thus, the means of affecting historical debate. Our effort was repaid in two major ways. Oral autobiographies dissolved static images, replacing them with portrayals of mill village culture drawn by the men and women who helped create it. Workers' narratives also steered us away from psychological interpretations and toward patterns of resistance, cultural creativity, and structural evolution. Later we turned to the trade press, particularly the *Southern Textile Bulletin*. Published by David Clark in Charlotte, North Carolina, the *Bulletin* spoke for factory owners at the cutting edge of industrial innovation. Finally, from the eloquent letters textile workers wrote to Franklin D. Roosevelt and the National Recovery Administration, we gained a view of the New Deal from below. Together, retrospective and contemporary evidence revealed the social logic that underlay daily practices and suggested an analysis that distinguished one epoch from another in a broad process of technological, managerial, and cultural change.

Nothing better symbolized the new industrial order than the mill villages that dotted the Piedmont landscape. Individual families and small groups of local investors built and owned most of the early mills. Run by water wheels, factories flanked the streams that fell rapidly from the mountains toward the Coastal Plain. Of necessity, owners provided housing where none had been before. But the setting, scale, and structure of the mill village reflected rural expectations as well as practical considerations. Typically, a three-story brick mill, a company store, and a superintendent's house were clustered at one end of the village. Three- and four-room frame houses, owned by the company but built in a vernacular style familiar in the countryside, stood on lots that offered individual garden space, often supplemented by communal pastures and hog pens. A church, a company store, and a modest schoolhouse completed the scene. By 1910 steam power and electricity had freed the mills from their dependence on water power, and factories sprang up on the outskirts of towns along the route of the Southern Railway. Nevertheless, the urban mill village retained its original rural design. Company-owned villages survived in part because they fostered management control. Unincorporated "mill hills" that surrounded towns such as Charlotte and Burlington, North Carolina, and Greenville, South Carolina, enabled owners to avoid taxes and excluded workers from municipal government. But the mill village also reflected the workers' heritage and served their needs.

Like the design of the mill village, the family labor system helped smooth the path from field to factory. On farms women and children had always provided essential labor, and mill owners took advantage of these traditional roles. They promoted factory work as a refuge for impoverished women and children from the countryside, hired family units rather than individuals, and required the labor of at least one worker per room as a condition for residence in a mill-owned house. But this labor system also dovetailed with family strategies. The first to arrive in the mills were those least essential to farming and most vulnerable to the hazards of commercial agriculture: widows, female heads of households, single women, and itinerant laborers. By the turn of the century, families headed by men also lost their hold on the land. Turning to the mills, they sought not a "family wage" that would enable a man to support his dependents but an arena in which parents and children could work together as they had always done.

The deployment of family labor also helped maintain permeable boundaries between farm and mill. The people we interviewed moved with remarkable ease from farming to mill work and back again or split their family's time between the two. James Pharis's father raised tobacco in the Leaksville-Spray area of North Carolina until most of his six children were old enough to obtain mill jobs. The family moved to a mill village in the 1890s because the elder Pharis "felt that all we had to do when we come to town was to reach up and pull the money off of the trees." From the farm Pharis saved his most valuable possession: his team of horses. While the children worked in the mill, he raised vegetables on a plot of rented ground and used his team to do "hauling around for people." Betty Davidson's landowning parents came up with the novel solution of sharing a pair of looms. "My father would run the looms in the wintertime," Davidson remembered, "and go to and from work by horseback. And in the summertime, when he was farming, my mother run the looms, and she stayed in town because she couldn't ride the horse. Then, on the weekends, she would come home.''

This ability to move from farming to factory work—or combine the two—postponed a sharp break with rural life. It also gave mill workers a firm sense of alternative identity and leverage against a boss's demands. Lee Workman recalled his father's steadfast independence. In 1918 the superintendent of a nearby cotton mill came to the Workmans' farm in search of workers to help him meet the demand for cloth during World War I. The elder Workman sold his mules and cow but, contrary to the superintendent's advice, held on to his land. Each spring he returned to shoe his neighbors' horses, repair their wagons and plows, and fashion the cradles they used to harvest grain. "He'd tell the superintendent, 'You can just get somebody else, because I'm going back to make cradles for my friends.' Then he'd come back in the wintertime and work in the mill.'' This type of freedom did not sit well with the mill superintendent, but the elder Workman had the upper hand. " 'Well,' he told them, 'if you don't want to do that, I'll move back to the country and take the family.' ''

Although Lee Workman's father periodically retreated to the farm, his sons and daughters, along with thousands of others, eventually came to the mills to stay. There they confronted an authority more intrusive than anything country folk had experienced before. In Bynum, North Carolina, the mill owner supervised the Sunday School and kept tabs on residents' private lives. "If you stubbed your toe they'd fire you. They'd fire them here for not putting out the lights late at night. Old Mr. Bynum used to go around over the hill at nine o'clock and see who was up. And, if you were up, he'd knock on the door and tell you to cut the lights out and get into bed.'' Along with surveillance came entanglement with the company store. Mill hands all too familiar with the crop lien once again found themselves in endless debt. Don Faucette's father often talked about it. "Said if you worked at the mill they'd just take your wages and put it in the company store and you didn't get nothing. For years and years they didn't get no money, just working for the house they lived in and what they got at the company store. They just kept them in the hole all the time.''

The mill village undeniably served management's interests, but it also nurtured a unique workers' culture. When Piedmont farmers left the land and took a cotton mill job, they did not abandon old habits and customs. Instead, they fashioned familiar ways of thinking and acting into a distinctively new way of life. This adaptation occurred at no single moment in time; rather, it evolved, shaped and reshaped by successive waves of migrations off the farm as well as the movement of workers from mill to mill. Village life was based on family ties. Kinship networks facilitated migration to the mill and continued to play a powerful integrative role. Children of the first generation off the land married newcomers of the second and third, linking households into broad networks of obligation, responsibility, and concern. For many couples, marriage evolved out of friendships formed while growing up in the village. One married worker recalled, "We knowed each other from childhood. Just raised up together, you might say. All lived here on the hill, you see, that's how we met." As single workers arrived, they, too, were incorporated into the community. Mary Thompson explained that the boarding houses run by widowed women and older couples "were kind of family like. There ain't no place like home, but I guess that's the nearest place like home there is, a boarding house." Mill folk commonly used a family metaphor to describe village life. Hoyle McCorkle remembered the Highland Park mill village in Charlotte as a single household knit together by real and fictive kin: "It was kind of one big family; it was a 200-house family."

Mill hands also brought subsistence strategies from the countryside, modifying them to meet mill village conditions. Just as farmers had tried to bypass the furnishing merchant, mill workers struggled to avoid "living out of a tin can." Edna Hargett's father planted a large garden every spring but could not afford a mule to help till the land. He made do by putting a harness around himself and having his children "stand behind and guide the plow." . . . Self-sufficiency, however, was difficult to achieve, especially when every family member was working a ten- to twelve-hour day for combined wages that barely made ends meet. Even with their gardens, few families could sustain a varied diet through the winter months. As a result, pellagra was a scourge in the mill villages. Life was lived close to the bone.

Under these conditions, necessity and habit fostered rural traditions of mutual aid. Although each family claimed a small plot of land, villagers shared what they grew and "live[d] in common." In late summer and early fall, they gathered for the familiar rituals of harvest and hog killing. Paul and Don Faucette remembered how it was done in Glencoe, North Carolina. "We'd kill our hogs this time, and a month later we'd kill yours. Well, you can give us some, and we can give you some. They'd have women get together down in the church basement. They'd have a quilting bee, and they'd go down and they'd all quilt. They'd have a good crop of cabbage, [and] they'd get together and all make kraut." Villagers helped one another, not with an expectation of immediate return but with the assurance of community support in meeting their individual needs. "They'd just visit around and work voluntarily. They all done it, and nobody owed nobody nothing."

Cooperation provided a buffer against misery and want at a time when state welfare services were limited and industrialists often refused to assume responsibility for job-related sickness and injury. It bound people together and reduced their dependence on the mill owners' charity. When someone fell ill, neighbors were quick to give the stricken family a "pounding." "They'd all get together and help. They'd cook food and carry it to them— all kinds of food—fruits, vegetables, canned goods." Villagers also aided sick neighbors by taking up a "love offering" in the mill. . . .

Community solidarity did not come without a price. Neighborliness could shade into policing; it could repress as well as sustain. Divorced women and children born out of wedlock might be ostracized, and kinship ties could give mill supervisors an intelligence network that reached into every corner of the village. Alice Evitt of Charlotte remarked that "people then couldn't do like they do now. They was talked about. My daddy would never allow us to be with people that was talked about. This was the nicest mill hill I ever lived on. If anybody done anything wrong and you reported them, they had to move." . . .

Given such tensions, we were struck by how little ambivalence surfaced in descriptions of mill village life. Recollections of factory work were something else again, but the village—red mud and all—was remembered with affection. The reasons are not hard to find. A commitment to family and friends represented a realistic appraisal of working people's prospects in the late nineteenth- and early twentieth-century South. Only after World War II, with the expansion of service industries, did the Piedmont offer alternatives to low-wage factory work to more than a lucky few. Until then, casting one's lot with others offered more promise and certainly more security than the slim hope of individual gain. To be sure, mill people understood the power of money; they struggled against dependency and claimed an economic competence as their due. Nevertheless, they had "their own ideas . . . about what constitute[d] the 'good life.' " Communal values, embodied in everyday behavior, distanced mill folk from the acquisitiveness that characterized middle-class life in New South towns.

This is not to say that mill village culture destroyed individuality. On the contrary, it conferred status and dignity that the workplace could seldom afford. Although mill ways encouraged group welfare at the expense of personal ambition, they did support individual accomplishment of a different sort. The practice of medicine provides one example, music another.

Folk medicine formed an important part of workers' "live-at-home" culture. Until well into the twentieth century, mill hands simply could not afford medical fees; besides, they viewed doctors with distrust and fear. In emergencies, the village turned to its own specialists. Among the earliest of these in Bynum was Louise Jones's mother, Madlena Riggsbee. "She was what you'd say was a midwife. She could just hold up under anything. Unless they were bound and compelled to have the doctor, they'd usually get her to go." In the 1920s and 1930s, the company retained the services of a physician, paid for with funds withheld from workers' checks. But in the eyes of the villagers, he was a partner—indeed a junior partner—to Ida Jane Smith, a healer and midwife who was one of the most respected figures in the community. "Lord, she was a good woman," Carrie Gerringer recalled. "She knowed more about younguns than any doctor."

If the midwife was the most prestigious member of the female community, the musician held that place among men. String bands had been a mainstay of country gatherings, and they multiplied in the mill villages where musicians lived closer together and had more occasions to play. Mastery of an instrument brought a man fame as the local "banjo king" or expert guitar picker. Musicians sometimes played simply for their own enjoyment. Paul Faucette and a small group of friends and kinfolk used "to get together on the porch on Saturday night and just have a big time."

On other occasions, they performed for house dances and community celebrations. Harvey Ellington remembered that on Saturday night "you'd have a dance in somebody's house—they'd take the beds and all out, and then we'd just play." The dance might end before midnight, but the musicians' performance often continued into the morning. "We'd be going home and decide we didn't want to go to bed. So we'd take the fiddle and the guitar and the banjo and stop at the corner and harmonize—do what they call serenade. The people would raise their windows and listen. That's the best sounding music, wake up at night and hear somebody playing."

Special talents won Harvey Ellington and Madlena Riggsbee places of honor in their neighbors' memories. But most villagers never achieved such distinction. They lived in quiet anonymity, often guided and strengthened by religious faith. Most textile workers were evangelical Protestants, and many worshipped in churches built and financed by factory owners. On one level, these churches proved helpful, maybe even essential, to the mills. Like their counterparts in other industrializing societies, they inculcated the moral and social discipline demanded by factory life. Still, there was another side to evangelical religion, one that empowered the weak, bound them together, and brought them close to God. At springtime revivals, faith turned to ecstasy. "People got happy and they shouted. They'd sing and hug each other—men and women both." When the Holy Spirit moved individuals to confessions of sin, the entire body of worshippers joined in thanksgiving for God's saving grace.

The physical and social geography of the mill village, then, was less a product of owners' designs than a compromise between capitalist organization and workers' needs. For a more clear-cut embodiment of the manufacturers' will, we must look to the factory. The ornate facades of nineteenth-century textile mills reflected their builders' ambitions and the orderly world they hoped to create. The mill that still stands at Glencoe is an excellent example. Situated only a few hundred yards from the clapboard houses that make up the village, the mill is a three-story structure complete with "stair tower, corbelled cornice, quoined stucco corners, and heavily stuccoed window labels." In contrast to the vernacular form of the village, the architecture of the factory, modeled on that of New England's urban mills, was highly self-conscious, formal, and refined.

At Glencoe, and in mills throughout the Piedmont, manufacturers endeavored to shape the southern yeomanry into a tractable industrial workforce. Workers' attitudes toward factory labor, like those toward village life, owed much to the cycles and traditions of the countryside. Owners, on the other hand, sought to substitute for cooperation and task orientation a labor system controlled from the top down and paced by the regular rhythms of the machine. Barring adverse market conditions, work in the mills varied little from day to day and season to season. Workers rose early in the morning, still tired from the day before, and readied themselves for more of the same. For ten, eleven, and twelve hours they walked, stretched, leaned, and pulled at their machines. Noise, heat, and humidity engulfed them. The lint that settled on their hair and skin marked them as mill workers to the outside world. The cotton dust that silently entered their lungs could also kill them.

Owners enforced this new pattern of labor with the assistance of a small coterie of supervisors. As a rule, manufacturers delegated responsibility for organizing work and disciplining the help to a superintendent and his overseers and second hands. A second hand in a pre–World War I mill recalled, "You had the cotton, the machinery, and the people, and you were supposed to get out the production. How you did it was pretty much up to you; it was production management was interested in and not how you got it." Under these circumstances, supervision was a highly personal affair; there were as many different approaches to its problems as there were second hands and overseers. As one observer explained, "There was nothing that could be identified as a general pattern of supervisory practice."

At times, discipline could be harsh, erratic, and arbitrary. This was particularly true before 1905, when most workers in southern mills were women and children. Even supervisors writing in the *Southern Textile Bulletin* admitted that "some overseers, second hands, and section men have a disposition to abuse the help. Whoop, holler, curse, and jerk the children around." James Pharis remembered that "you used to work for the supervisor because you were scared. I seen a time when I'd walk across the road to keep from meeting my supervisor. They was the hat-stomping kind. If you done anything, they'd throw their hat on the floor and stomp it and raise hell."

In the absence of either state regulation or trade unions, management's power seemed limitless, but there were, in fact, social and structural constraints. Although manufacturers relinquished day-to-day authority to underlings, they were ever-present figures, touring the mill, making decisions on wages and production quotas, and checking up on the help. These visits were, in part, attempts to maintain the appearance of paternalism and inspire hard work and company loyalty. At the same time, they divided power in the mill. Workers had direct access to the owner and sometimes saw him as a buffer between themselves and supervisors, a "force that could bring an arbitrary and unreasonable [overseer] back into line." Mack Duncan recalled that in the early years "most all the mill owners seemed like they had a little milk of human kindness about them, but some of the people they hired didn't. Some of the managers didn't have that. They were bad to exploit people." Under these circumstances, the commands of an overseer were always subject to review. Workers felt free to complain about unjust treatment, and owners, eager to keep up production, sometimes reversed their lieutenants' orders. Federal labor investigators reported in 1910 that "when an employee is dissatisfied about mill conditions he may obtain a hearing from the chief officer of the mill . . . and present his side of the case. Not infrequently when complaints are thus made, the overseer is overruled and the operative upheld."

Authority on the shop floor was further complicated by social relations in the mill village. Before the introduction of industrial engineers and col-lege-trained foremen in the 1920s and 1930s, most supervisors worked their way up through the ranks. . . .

A personal style of labor management posed but one obstacle to the imposition of strict discipline. Mill owners also faced the limitations of existing technology. The small size of most mills before World War I made it difficult to coordinate production in a way that kept all hands constantly at work. . . .

Mill owners and workers alike had to accommodate themselves to a work environment not entirely of their own choosing. Factory labor did not allow the independence and flexibility of labor on the farm, but neither did it meet the standards of rigor and regularity desired by owners. An informal compromise governed the shop floor. "We worked longer then in the mill than they do now," explained Naomi Trammell, "and made less, too. But we didn't work hard. I done all my playing in the mill."

This tradeoff between a relatively relaxed work pace on the one hand and long hours and low wages on the other was tenuous at best. Despite man-ufacturers' efforts to create a secure world in the mill and village, there were recurrent symptoms of unrest. During the 1880s and 1890s, southern mill hands turned first to the Knights of Labor and then to the National Union of Textile Workers (NUTW) to defend their "freedom and liberty." In 1900 an intense conflict led by the NUTW flared in Alamance County, center of textile manufacturing in North Carolina, when an overseer at the Haw River Mill fired a female weaver for leaving her loom unattended. The next day, September 28, union members "threw up" their machines, defending the woman's right to "go when she pleased and where she pleased." By mid-October, workers at other mills throughout the county had joined in a sympathy strike.

The mill owners, conveniently overstocked with surplus goods, posted armed guards around their factories, declared they would employ only nonunion labor, and threatened to evict union members from company-owned houses. Undeterred, the workers resolved to stand together as "free men and free women"; five thousand strong, they brought production in Alamance mills virtually to a halt. But by the end of November evictions had overwhelmed the NUTW's relief fund, and the Alamance mill hands were forced to accept a settlement on management's terms.

The Haw River strike capped more than two decades of unrest. During those years, Populists and factory laborers challenged the power of planters, merchants, and industrialists. Between 1895 and 1902, southern Democrats turned to race baiting, fraud, and intimidation to destroy this interracial movement. The passage of state constitutional amendments disfranchising blacks and many poor whites, accompanied by a flurry of Jim Crow laws, restructured the political system, narrowing the terms of public discourse, discouraging lower-class political participation, and making it impossible for opposition movements to survive.

As prospects for collective protest diminished, Piedmont mill hands opted for a personal strategy as old as the industry itself—relocation. . . .

The decision to move was usually made by men, and it could be hard on women and children. Family ties could fray under the wear and tear of factory life. Although Edna Hargett also worked in the mills, she was evicted from her house every time her husband quit his job. "He was bad about getting mad and quitting. He was just hot-tempered and didn't like it when they wanted to take him off his job and put him on another job. When you work in the card room, you have to know how to run about every piece of machinery in there. He liked to be a slubber, and they wanted to put him on drawing or something else. Well, he didn't like to do that." Edna understood her husband's motives but finally left to settle down and rear their children on her own.

Divorce, however, was uncommon. Most families stayed together, and their moves from mill to mill were facilitated by kinship and cushioned by community. A study completed in the late 1920s revealed that 41 percent of mill families had moved less than three times in ten years. Most settled families were headed by middle-aged men and women who had "just kept the road hot" before and immediately after marriage and had then stayed in a village they liked. This relatively stable core of residents made movement possible by providing the contacts through which other workers learned of job opportunities. Established residents also mitigated the ill effects of transiency and preserved ways of life that made it easy for newcomers to feel at home. Women played central roles in this process, keeping up with the events in the village, coordinating informal acts of relief, and keeping the web of social relations intact.

In these ways, the Piedmont became what journalist Arthur W. Page described in 1907 as "one long mill village." Individual communities were woven together—through kinship, shared occupational experiences, and popular culture—into an elaborate regional fabric. According to Lacy Wright, who worked at Greensboro's White Oak Mill, "We had a pretty fair picture, generally speaking, of what you might say was a 200-mile radius of Greensboro. News traveled by word of mouth faster than any other way in those days, because that's the only way we had. In other words, if something would happen at White Oaks this week, you could go over to Danville, Virginia, by the weekend and they'd done heard about it. It looked like it always worked out that there would be somebody or another that would carry that information all around." Rooted in a regional mill village culture, workers like Wright took the entire Piedmont as their frame of reference.

Owners and workers understood that the ability to move in search of more satisfying employment could serve as a check on mill management. After a tour of North and South Carolina mills in 1906, a superintendent vented his frustrations in the pages of the *Southern and Western Textile Excelsior*. "Unfortunately," he lamented, "the help have come to think that they and not the mill owners control the situation." . . .

Through the end of World War I, mill workers' "roving disposition" not only posed serious problems for shop floor discipline but also aggravated a chronic labor shortage. As early as 1906, manufacturers worried openly that labor turnover was leaving machines idle and shrinking profits. They had unwittingly contributed to these problems by taking part in a building boom at the turn of the century that dramatically increased the demand for labor. As jobs became more plentiful, mill hands were free to move more frequently. Workers remembered that "it wasn't no job at all to get a job then." By 1907 the annual labor turnover rate in the southern textile industry had reached 176 percent, and various mill owners estimated that anywhere from 20 to 40 percent of their employees belonged to the "floating" population. Mill worker Paul Cline summed it up in one vivid image. "My daddy had an old rooster—when he seen the wagon coming, he'd just lay down and cross his legs; he knowed it was time to move."

Owners first responded to the problems of labor scarcity and control by competing more fiercely with one another. In hopes of attracting and keeping reliable workers, many mill owners raised wages. Between 1902 and 1907 the earnings of male weavers in South Carolina rose by 58 percent, those of female weavers by 65 percent, and those of spinners by 138 percent, while the cost of living increased by only 9 percent. But, if owners sought stability, they did not achieve it with wage competition. As one superintendent complained, "The more the help can earn, the less they work. . . . The prices paid at present have gotten to be so high that an average family, or individual, can make in four days what it once took a full week to earn, and the result is in most instances, such help work only four-sixths of their time. The average mill hand is inclined to care only for enough to live on and when they have made that, they rest the balance of the week."

A more drastic response to the competition for workers was labor pirating. Mill owners throughout the Piedmont hired recruiters to circulate through other mill villages and induce workers to leave their jobs. "In some instances," reported the *Southern Textile Bulletin*, "men are sent to other towns to mix with the people on Saturday night, display rolls of money, and tell remarkable stories of how much they earn at this or that mill." Owners paid moving expenses and offered free housing and groceries to lure workers into their mills. But those practices, like wage increases, only exacerbated the problems they were intended to resolve. The *Southern and Western Textile Excelsior* warned mill owners that "the scarcity of help among the cotton mills is aggravated by the pernicious practice of furnishing transportation and enticing help from one mill to another. . . . You furnish transportation from another mill to yours, and another man furnishes transportation from your mill to his, and so the game goes on and maybe there are enough operatives on the trains all the time going from place to place to operate all the idle spindles in the South."

Manufacturers took such warnings to heart, realizing that the solution to their problems lay not in fighting among themselves but in rethinking their relations to one another and the nature of mill management. Joining forces in 1908, they turned to their own advantage the efforts of overseers and second hands to organize a supervisors' union. Although uninvited, David Clark and representatives from the state's leading mills attended an overseers' meeting in Spray, North Carolina, and convinced those present that their interests would best be served by allying themselves with mill owners rather than seeking a separate voice. In October of that year, Clark presided over the formation of the Southern Textile Association, which offered membership to all superintendents, overseers, master mechanics, electricians, engineers, editors of textile publications, and instructors at textile schools. The association subsequently played a major role in the industry's development, serving as a conduit for the introduction of new theories of personnel management and industrial relations.

The manufacturers' most ambitious undertaking in the prewar years was the implementation of company-sponsored "welfare work." Taking their cue from the National Civic Federation and major northern corporations, southern mill owners embarked on a campaign to beautify their villages and provide new social services for their employees. Urged on by industry publicists such as Clark, they began substituting professional intermediaries—social workers, nurses, and teachers—for the direct surveillance of workers' lives. Welfare work was expensive and therefore gained only a limited following among small-scale manufacturers. But the Piedmont's largest mills embraced the new approach to labor-management relations with enthusiasm.

Writing in the *Southern Textile Bulletin*, manufacturers made clear the relationship between welfare work and labor mobility. One mill president explained that he and others undertook welfare work "to secure an attachment for the village to decrease the migratory tendency." W. A. Giles of Graniteville, South Carolina, advised fellow mill presidents that welfare work made employees "more loyal, better workers, better contented with their lot, and it will be found that those mills which pay more attention to work of this kind will have [the] best class of labor and more of it in times of stress." Although mill owners were no doubt sincere in their efforts to improve workers' living conditions, welfare work was "also [a] cold blooded business proposition."

But how could such mundane activities as garden clubs and organized recreation accomplish mill owners' goals? Above all, welfare programs tried to redefine the neighborhood as a physical extension of the mill rather than a network of human relations. Manufacturers awarded prizes for the best flower gardens in their villages and set aside specific plots of land for the vegetable gardens workers had always tilled. They also took over many of the activities that bound workers together. They established "domestic science" classes in which girls learned the arts of housekeeping and cooking not from their mothers and grandmothers but from a professional social worker, and company nurseries replaced informal, family-based child care. Mills financed workers' "pick-up" baseball teams and organized factory leagues in an effort to transform community games into a sport sponsored by and identified with the company. They formed brass bands to take the place of village string bands and built YMCAs to structure workers' leisure.

On occasion, owners outlawed the collection of "love offerings" and, in the 1920s, began to offer minimal insurance programs instead. Promotional literature for these programs promised to "eliminate passing the hat in the mill" and enable the employer "to assist the community in meeting some of its welfare problems."

Welfare programs also aimed at stimulating desires for consumer goods that would compel mill hands to work regularly. Here domestic science classes did double duty. As we have already seen, workers' nonacquisitiveness could decrease productivity by promoting absenteeism and "loafing." To combat the problem, professional social workers taught mill women to make fashionable clothes, cook elaborate meals, and keep neat homes furnished with upholstered sofas and chairs. The *Southern and Western Textile Excelsior* voiced owners' confidence that, if these measures did not change the present generation of mill workers, they would at least influence their children. "Their needs must be increased to equal the rise in wages to get them to work steadily," one mill president candidly explained. "The people are not sufficiently ambitious to care to work all the time, but as we are throwing about them elevating influences their needs are growing greater and the next generation will be all right."

Despite promises that welfare work would bring "the employer and the employee into closer touch and . . . eliminate industrial unrest," results were disappointing. Many workers recognized the purpose of welfare activities and refused to participate. One mill hand, writing to the Charlotte *Labor Herald*, observed that owners had substituted "cunning" for authoritarianism in their dealings with employees. "How this could best be done, was a question of much speculation, and has caused no little experimenting," he explained. "Said some, 'We will build . . . kindergartens for the tots, and Y.M.C.A.'s for the adults. . . . Thus from the cradle to the grave, we will mould their minds and formulate their convictions. . . .' To accomplish this, they learned that a good staff of social workers was as necessary as the tusks in the mouth of a vicious wild beast."

Other mill hands preserved their independence in less self-conscious ways. Mamie Shue remembered that Charlotte's Highland Park Mill "had a house fixed up for a cooking school. And we'd go down there, and they'd teach us how to cook—teach us how to make fancy meals. We just went for the fun of it. We didn't care nothing about cooking." On the whole, our interviews suggest that welfare work failed to attract workers' interest and redirect their loyalties. The carefully balanced investigations of sociologist Harriet Herring point in the same direction. North Carolina mill owners found that "the response of the villagers was so discouraging as to make the work seem not worth while." As an economic depression settled over the textile industry in the years after World War I, manufacturers became convinced that the results of welfare work did not justify the expense. Only a handful of mills initiated new programs after 1920, and many abandoned their welfare activities altogether.

World War I marked a turning point in the development of the southern textile industry. Stimulated by wartime demand, new mills sprang up, old ones operated around the clock, wages rose, and profits soared. But, when peace came, overexpanded businesses went into a tailspin. The situation worsened when tariff policies and the advent of textile manufacturing in other parts of the world cut into the southern industry's lucrative foreign markets. A sudden change in clothing styles added to manufacturers' troubles. Young women in the 1920s hiked their skirts six inches above the ankle, then all the way to the knee, causing consternation among their elders and panic in the textile industry. All in all, the depression that hit the rest of the country in 1929 began for textile manufacturers in the immediate postwar years.

Mill officials greeted the armistice with a rollback of workers' wages. But, to the owners' surprise, mill hands refused to abandon small but cherished advances in their standard of living. When wage cuts were announced in 1919, thousands of workers joined the American Federation of Labor's United Textile Workers (UTW). "They are in deadly earnest," reported the Raleigh *News and Observer*, "and almost religiously serious in their belief in the union." Manufacturers were equally determined not to employ union members, and in many cases they simply shut their factory gates to all workers. As the conflict dragged on, threats of violence mounted. Armed strikers patrolled the mill villages, intent on enforcing community and union solidarity. Manufacturers eventually agreed to a settlement but insisted that "the adjustment . . . shall not be construed as a recognition by the mills of collective bargaining." Similar confrontations occurred throughout the Piedmont until 1921, when a severe business downturn crippled union locals and gave management the upper hand. But workers had made their message clear: mill owners would no longer be able to shore up profits simply by cutting wages.

The impasse created in 1921 by hard times and workers' protests set the stage for a new era of corporate consolidation. As smaller firms went bankrupt, more aggressive competitors gobbled them up. J. Spencer Love, who took over faltering mills in Alamance County and eventually built Burlington Mills into the world's largest textile enterprise, set the pace. Love's generation led the region to ascendancy in the production of synthetics and helped effect a permanent shift of cotton manufacturing from New England to the Piedmont. These "progressive mill men" also set out to find new solutions to problems of profitability and labor control. The methods they adopted aimed at altering the structure of work and breaking the bonds between supervisors and the mill village community. But their freedom of action depended on a ballooning labor supply.

As the demand for cotton fell and an agricultural depression settled over the countryside, farmers again came to the mills—in "droves," recalled John Wesley Snipes, "all of them hunting jobs." A story that made the rounds in mill villages summed up the situation. In Snipes's version, the supervisor of the Bynum mill told a desperate applicant, " 'No, we ain't got no job for you, not unless somebody dies.' " As the man walked away, "this fellow fell out of the window and got killed." So he ran back and said, " 'How about that man; can I have his job?' " " 'No,' " replied the superintendent, " 'the man that pushed him gets his [job].' They told it as a joke,'' Snipes concluded, "but it was rough, I'm telling you." For the first time since 1900, owners could press forward with innovation, unhindered by the fear that disgruntled workers could pick up and move to another mill.

The industry looked first to simple cost-cutting measures. One approach was to run the mills around the clock. The faster old machinery could be used up and paid for, the sooner new, efficient designs could be introduced. A second strategy involved tightening operations throughout the mill. . . .

In 1924 the *Southern Textile Bulletin* announced a "Better Equipment Campaign" designed to "show the great advantage of modern machinery and methods over old style or primitive forms of machinery." Through the early 1930s, equipment manufacturers flooded the *Bulletin* and other trade journals with advertisements praising the cost effectiveness and labor-saving qualities of their machines. The Barbara-Colman Company lauded the ability of its new line of spoolers and warpers to remove "the human equation" from production by enabling mills to run with far fewer workers. Other advertisements boasted that Saco-Lowell equipment could reduce the number of men needed to run five pickers from thirteen to four: "Lost—Nine Men But They'll Never Be Missed!" . . .

General Electric and Westinghouse encouraged manufacturers to adopt "the motor way to greater production." Mill owners attached individual electric motors to their machines and abandoned older, less reliable belt-drive systems, freeing mill operation from "the whims of a river." With motor drives, the failure of a single machine no longer stopped work in other parts of the mill. Equipment also ran at more uniform speeds, reducing the number of mechanical breakdowns and damage to the goods. When combined with efficient new machinery, the turn to electricity enabled mills to "maintain maximum production speed." "That ruined our playhouse when they got power," recalled Eula Durham of Bynum. "That tore up our playhouse."

Production monitoring equipment also enforced a more rigorous pace of work. Advertisements urged owners to "use Veeder-Root 'watch-dogs of the weave room' to detect looms that steal time, operatives that waste time; loom fixers that lose time for both." Such monitors would serve as the supervisor's "all-seeing eye," putting "the screws on operating costs" by forcing every worker to "face the facts of his job." Operatives might "fool the foreman," but they could not "deceive the 'silent little superintendent' on the end of the frame."

Technological innovation alone could not solve all problems. Equally important was application of labor-saving methods in the organization of work. The weave room was the main target of reform. The Northrup loom, eagerly adopted by southern mills after the turn of the century, automated many weave-room tasks. Yet in an industry that had relentlessly stripped most jobs of initiative and skill, weavers remained more independent and better paid than most textile workers. The multiple-loom system undermined that privileged position. An adaptation of Frederick W. Taylor's scientific management, the system parceled weaving into numerous tasks performed at low pay by workers with little training. Weavers, left with the simple job of mending broken threads, could tend more looms, but at the expense of control over the pace and methods of their labor. Yoked to their work stations, they no longer moved about the mill, filling their own batteries and doffing their own cloth—and finding opportunities for conversation and companionship. Most important, the multiple-loom system brought unemployment and, when piece rates were cut, a decrease in earnings.

With this new division of labor in place, industrial engineers concentrated on maximizing each worker's productivity. Sam Finley, a loom fixer in Marion, North Carolina, remembered how it was done. "They got a stopwatch, and they followed them around. They figured out exactly how long it took you to tie that thread and start the loom up. They figured right down to the tick of that stopwatch. Then they expected you to stretch it out a little bit, to do a little more. You couldn't please them. The more you done, the more they wanted done." To Finley, the multiple-loom system was simplicity itself: "Give them more work for no more pay."

Along with new technologies and the reorganization of work came an attack on the idiosyncratic relations of the shop floor. In part because of prodding from the *Southern Textile Bulletin*, larger mills began replacing men who had come up through the ranks with young, college-trained supervisors. . . .

. . . Under this regime, overseers and second hands were less likely to ally themselves with workers by questioning company policy, and workers could no longer look to the superintendent or the owner as a mediator between themselves and their immediate supervisors.

Social critics in the 1920s were quick to point out the evils of the mill village, but few noted the extraordinary capacity for surveillance embedded in impersonal machines or imagined the psychological havoc that rationalization could bring. Workers, on the other hand, remembered conditions that "just kept getting worse and worse." The "stretch-out" was their term for the cumulative changes that set them tending machines "by the acre," filled every pore of the working day, and robbed them of control over the pace and methods of work. "There's many a times I dreamt about it," Edna Hargett recalled. "Sometimes you'd be up on your job, and other times you'd be behind. So I just sweated it out in my dreams like I did when I was there on the job, wanting to quit, but I knew I couldn't afford to."

In 1927 resistance to management tactics by individuals and small groups gave way to labor conflict on an unprecedented scale. The battle opened in Henderson, North Carolina, where workers struck for restoration of a bonus withdrawn three years before. Then on March 12, 1929, young women in a German-owned rayon plant in Elizabethton, Tennessee, touched off a strike wave that spread quickly into the Carolinas. The involvement of the communist-led National Textile Workers Union and the shooting deaths, first of the police chief and then of Ella May Wiggins, the strikers' balladeer, brought Gastonia, North Carolina, a special notoriety. But the carnage was even worse in nearby Marion, where deputies opened fire on demonstrators, wounding twenty-five and killing six. In 1930, revolt hit the massive Dan River Mill in Virginia—a model of welfare capitalism.

Responding to these workers' initiatives, the UTW tried to remedy its neglect of southern labor. Most energetic was the American Federation of Hosiery Workers, an autonomous UTW affiliate, represented by Alfred Hoffman, an intrepid organizer who popped up in virtually every trouble spot until his militancy landed him in a Marion jail. But even Hoffman usually arrived after the fact, and a number of the less well known but more successful walkouts ran their course with no official union involvement at all. In 1929, thousands of South Carolina workers formed their own relief committees, held mass meetings, and negotiated modifications in the stretch-out—all without help from the UTW. Similarly, in 1932, in High Point, North Carolina, hosiery workers sparked sympathy strikes at textile mills and furniture plants and used automobile caravans to spread walkouts to nearby towns. Fearing a "revolution on our hands," officials conceded most of the workers' demands.

Whether independently organized or union led, each walkout was shaped by local circumstances. But more important than the differences were the experiences strikers shared. In community after community, mill folk turned habits of mutuality and self-help to novel ends. Union relief funds were paltry at best, and survival depended on neighborly sharing. Many of the Marion strikers "had a good garden, and they'd divide their gardens with people that didn't have any." Those who held back found themselves donating anyway. Sam Finley remembered frying chickens for hungry picketers—supplied by a boy who could "get a chicken off the roost and leave the feathers." Baseball games, picnics, and barbecues buoyed spirits and fostered solidarity. As in the routines of daily life, women workers were essential to this mobilization of community resources. "The women done as much as the men," Lillie Price asserted. "They always do in everything."

For the most part, village churches did not support collective action. Yet evangelicalism remained a resource on which rebels could draw. Gathering in an interdenominational tabernacle built for revivals, Elizabethton workers listened to a country preacher warn that "the hand of oppression is growing on our people. . . . You women work for practically nothing. You must come together and say that such things must cease to be." Each night, another crowd "came forward" to take the union oath. Marion activists held "open air services," sang hymns on the picket line, and invited strikebreakers to join the union and be saved. At Greenville's Brandon Mill, strikers drew an analogy between "the cotton mill people" and the "children of Israel [who] were forced to work for the Egyptians," then appealed to "the good Christian people of the city to offer up prayers to God" in the textile workers' behalf.

In these ways, workers fashioned a language of resistance from established cultural forms. But the young people who led the protests had also come of age in a society different from the one their parents had known.

Most had grown up in the mill villages or moved as children from the countryside. They did not see themselves as temporary sojourners, ready to beat a retreat to the land, or as displaced farmers for whom "it was heaven to draw a payday, however small." Their identities had been formed in the mill village; they had cast their fate with the mills.

As social stratification increased, men and women who considered themselves cotton mill people traversed the psychic minefields of a changing world. Particularly in urban centers, changes in residential and unemployment patterns widened the gap between mill and town. Charlotte, for instance, acquired a large population of clerks, service workers, and professionals who settled in the suburbs of Dilworth and Myers Park—physically and socially removed from the mill communities of North and East Charlotte. Hoyle McCorkle remembered the tensions that could result. "The other children would kind of look down on you. You'd go to school and they'd call you a linthead and all that stuff. You was kind of from the wrong side of the tracks." Sam Finley had similar memories, from an adult point of view. Marion merchants "were glad to get your paycheck, glad for you to come up there and spend money in their stores, but to uptown people you were still cotton mill trash."

But such encounters do not tell the whole story. The activists of the 1920s shared a generational experience in more positive ways as well. They had entered the mills during the boom years of World War I, when rising wages and opportunities for promotion gave them reason to hope for better times ahead. Literacy increased with the decline of child labor and the spread of compulsory education; newspapers and magazines brought word of boom times in an affluent, larger world. Perhaps most important was the advent of radio. Recording studios and broadcasters discovered string-band music in the early 1920s and began transforming ballad singing, fiddle playing, and banjo picking into one of America's great popular sounds. Across the Piedmont, mill hands listened to their own music on the Grand Ole Opry and danced to the tunes of local performers playing in the studios of Charlotte's WBT. Eventually homogenized and commercialized as the Nashville sound, country music in the 1920s bolstered a sense of unique, region-wide cultural identity.

New modes of transportation forwarded the same ends, and Model T's figured prominently in the labor upheavals of the 1920s. When the Marion Manufacturing Company started "tightening down on people," Sam Finley, Lawrence Hogan, and their friends drove across the Blue Ridge Mountains to Elizabethton, "hunting somebody to organize them as a union." They brought back Alfred Hoffman, and soon twenty-five-year-old Lawrence Hogan became his right-hand man. Educating himself for "the responsibilities of class leadership," Hogan became a full-time organizer. From his base in Marion, he published *The Shuttle*, a newsletter designed to "carry the message to and fro." Hogan favored the "whirlwind system of distribution. Making about 40 [miles per hour] through a town I toss a bundle of *Shuttles* into the air, the wind whips them away, scatters them, and the mill workers, who have learned to expect them, run out and pick them up." When Hogan died—after a car wreck in 1935—he was mourned as "one of the clearest-eyed leaders of federated workingmen in this section."

Creative tactics, indigenous leaders, lessons in "the power of group action"—these were legacies of the 1920s. Still, victories were isolated and limited by external constraints. The UTW had conceded the deeper sources of workers' discontent. Its policy of "labor-management cooperation" opposed strikes and asked only that workers be made junior partners in the process of rationalization. But even a stronger and more aggressive union would have had difficulty making headway in the region. Southern mill owners monopolized social, economic, and political power. They stood united in their refusal to tolerate even the mildest form of unionism and were strengthened in their resolve by hard times. With the stock market crash of 1929 came massive lay-offs, further wage cuts, and efforts to recoup profits by "stretch[ing]-out the stretch out." The result was an atmosphere of smoldering antagonism. Lawrence Hogan described Piedmont mills in 1932 as "volcano-like. . . . Everywhere you go," he reported, "they are ready to explode."

On June 16, 1933, President Franklin D. Roosevelt signed the National Industrial Recovery Act [NIRA] into law. Introduced with much fanfare, the NIRA promised a "great cooperative movement" among business, government, and labor to bring about national recovery. It relaxed antitrust measures, permitting trade associations to control production and set prices, and encouraged manufacturers to spread employment and stimulate consumer demand by shortening hours and raising wages. Balancing the license given employers' associations was Section 7(a) endorsing workers' right to organize and bargain collectively. The Cotton Textile Institute, formed in 1926 at the instigation of southern manufacturers, welcomed the NIRA and pushed through the first Code of Fair Competition. The code called for a minimum wage of $12.00 per week ($13.00 for northern workers), a forty-hour week, and the prohibition of child labor. Mills throughout the South hoisted the National Recovery Administration's (NRA) Blue Eagle banner, proclaiming "We Do Our Part." Prices, employment, and sales climbed. The industry enjoyed its most profitable year since 1928.

Across the Piedmont, mill hands listened eagerly to Roosevelt's fireside chats and signed on as "members of the NRA." Recovery legislation seemed to place the federal government's imprimatur on ideals of equity, independence, and cooperation. Everyone, from the lowliest sweeper to the most skilled loom fixer, could join in a fervent campaign to put the industry, and the nation, back on its feet. In all this, the New Deal resonated with the past even as it spoke to present needs. But the NIRA also promised something altogether new: the intervention of a powerful third party as leverage against local elites and a guarantor of workers' rights. Within less than a month, union locals had sprung to life in 75 percent of South Carolina's mills. UTW membership jumped from an estimated forty thousand members in September 1933 to two hundred seventy thousand by August

1934. To the shock of government officials and businessmen alike, southern workers organized.

As it turned out, recovery was short-lived. It was one thing for trade associations to endorse the principle of self-regulation, quite another for individual mills to sustain the short-term losses that resulted from lower production and higher labor costs. And mill owners had no intention of joining a "great cooperative movement" with organized labor or surrendering any of their authority in the factories. By the fall of 1933, workers across the country were complaining about bosses who " 'chiseled' at the code." Skilled workers watched maximum wages sink toward the minimum, as owners reclassified jobs and cut piecework rates. The benefits of an eight-hour day evaporated, as mill hands found themselves "doing as much in 8 hours as we did in 12." Unionists summarily lost their jobs. Once more, production outran demand, warehouses bulged with unsold goods, and textile workers joined the ragged ranks of the unemployed.

Code chiseling struck hardest at the mills' most vulnerable workers. As long as they could pay low piecework rates, small firms that could not afford new machinery or efficiency experts kept less productive employees on the payroll. Children, older people, pregnant women, mothers bearing the burden of a double workday—such workers might not produce as much as young adults, but they were valued as a pool of cheap labor. Minimum-wage standards changed all that. Hoping to contain the consequent rise in labor costs, mill officials pegged the $12.00 wage to production quotas that only the fastest workers could meet. "They discharged all spinners that could not run 8 sides of spinning and that included women that was the sole dependers [supporters] of their family as bread earners," wrote one woman. "They have made work so hard [a] woman just can't hold a job," claimed another. To make matters worse, short time and hikes in the cost of living cancelled out the gains enjoyed by those who did manage to hold their jobs at the bottom of the industry's broad job pyramid. . . .

Nothing more vividly revealed the chasm opening between "the common worker and the Capitalist" than the metaphors that laced mill folks' letters to FDR. One woman reported that the superintendents were "treating the People worse than convicts." "We have been . . . treated worse than beasts," complained another. Above all, workers spoke of "bondage" and "slavery," of "release from our balls and chain." A unionist at Durham's Erwin Mill drew this parallel: "I am glad to know that Abraham Lincoln freed the negroes and am glad to know that now you are trying to free us. White slaves."

Surveillance and economic vulnerability made letter writing an act of enormous courage. In practically every case, workers closed with a plea for anonymity. It would cost them their jobs if mill officials knew what they had done. A woman with a "sick husband and children to support" mailed her letter by train because "the Washington mail is being watched here." A young girl in Whitmire, South Carolina, was also afraid. "If they thought for one instance I had written you they would fire me like lightning."

Yet, despite the risk, many offered to step forward and vouch for what they had seen. A. W. Litton from the tiny village of Glencoe wrote, "If Mr green finds out that i rote you this he will fire me and run me off this place but if you can't find out that Mr. W. G. Green is [violating] the N.R.A. law in every way call for me and i will show what is going on here."

Such men and women saw federal intervention as a two-way street. They took the law at face value and coupled petitions for help with promises of responsible citizenship and political support. "The laboring people here are trying to uphold our President and also the code. We believe in it— We talk it—And we would so love to live it," wrote Mrs. B. M. Miller from Charlotte. "Dear Demcrate Friend, I am trying to provide [abide] by the code, but our country is not. Our overseer don't want us to no anything about the NRA code . . . but I am going to provide by it even if I do loss my job," pledged a man in Bessemer City, North Carolina. "If we get fully organized we are all going to vote and elect you again," promised a Durham unionist, "for you are the only [president] that [was] ever for the working man."

This outpouring of faith, anger, and fear was shunted through a bureaucratic maze. Disputes in other industries were referred to the National Labor Board, which, despite its inability to force compliance, began hammering out enduring principles of labor law. By contrast, textile workers' complaints wound their way through local, state, and district committees until they reached the Cotton Textile National Industrial Relations Board, which followed the extraordinary procedure of forwarding them to agents of the industry's trade association, the Cotton Textile Institute. Investigators then contacted the complainant's employer. If the mill denied wrongdoing, the case was closed. Between August 8, 1933, and August 8, 1934, the Board received 3,920 complaints. It authorized ninety-six investigations and resolved only one wage and hour dispute in a worker's favor. As far as can be determined, the board never ordered reinstatement of a worker fired for union activity or even held a hearing in such a case. . . .

When help was not forthcoming, mill workers took matters into their own hands. In June 1934, the textile board ignored the suffering already caused by short time, unemployment, and rising living costs and attacked the problem of overproduction with a 25 percent cut in machine hours. Many mills simply shut down every fourth week, reducing wages accordingly. Local unionists in northern Alabama struck back on July 14, pulling twenty thousand workers out of the mills. They demanded a $12.00 minimum wage for a thirty-hour week, abolition of the stretch-out, reinstatement of workers fired for union activity, and union recognition. On August 14, a national UTW convention dominated by militant southern representatives called for a general strike of the textile industry to begin at midnight on Saturday, September 1. Union vice-president Francis Gorman took on the formidable task of organizing hundreds of walkouts in widely scattered mills. Workers organized into "flying squadrons" sped through the Carolinas, forcing plants to close "so rapidly that tabulators almost lost check."

By the end of the week some four hundred thousand employees had deserted the mills, closing down the entire industry.

Governors were immediately swamped with demands for military intervention. Twenty-two Gaston County mill executives signed a petition spelling out their fears.

> Several times daily hundreds of men, women and children parade through town yelling, screaming, threatening and intimidating citizens of the town, stating they intend confiscating automobiles and other personal property as their needs demand. . . . Our situation is desperate, much more desperate than we can express in words. Law and order no longer exists, except for the surrender of personal and property rights by a majority of the substantial citizenship and unless something is done within the next twenty-four hours no authority can be held responsible for results.

By September 7, fourteen thousand troops were on duty in the Carolinas alone. A week later, Governor Eugene Talmadge of Georgia declared martial law and interned flying squadron participants in a makeshift "Detention Camp." To panicked townsmen, the strike represented "the gravest emergency which has confronted our people since Reconstruction Days."

The depth of strike support, and the violence of repression, varied from community to community. The Chiquola Mill in Honea Path, South Carolina, was divided "about half and half" between union and nonunion workers. When flying squadrons from nearby villages encircled the plant, local authorities passed out picker sticks and deputized "just about [anybody who] could carry a gun." The result was "a regular riot" in which seven strikers died. By contrast, the General Strike in Durham, North Carolina, was peaceful, unanimous, and self-contained. Individual responses were even more complex. Some workers joined with passionate conviction. Others saw the flying squadrons as "a disorganized mob" and dreaded the divisiveness unions might bring. A Greenville woman spoke for those whose nonparticipation did not imply consent. "I like thousands of others did not strike with the union, because we knew we would lose our jobs like thousands of others have done before us. Even though we might have had faith in the union we simply couldn't afford to quit because we live right up to every penny we make. . . . It is true that every textile worker in the south would walk out of the mill to day if they were not afraid of starvation. I don't *believe* that God intended people to suffer as we have suffered. . . . The life of the average textile worker is a tragic thing."

The General Strike, whatever else it may have been, was a moment in history that laid bare longings and antagonisms ordinarily silenced, distorted, and repressed. Cotton mill people in the 1930s did not subscribe to an abstract, universalistic notion of class solidarity. If nothing else, deep racial divisions militated against such perceptions. But mill hands did see themselves as a people apart, exploited by men with interests opposed to their own and denied opportunities for progress that had seemed within their grasp. The ten thousand mourners who converged on the funeral of the strikers killed at Honea Path, the hundreds of young men and women who climbed into "Fords and rush[ed] across counties to join other familiar-unfamiliar young people in clamoring at the mesh wire of mill gates," the workers in Durham who denied executives access to their own mills—these people broke through the restraints imposed by political isolation and economic defenselessness to make their mark on the times.

Still, the opposition held all the cards. Mill owners whose warehouses were already stocked to overflowing with unsold goods simply "stopped off" and waited out the conflict. Picket lines faltered before machine guns and fixed bayonets. The UTW could not begin to provide adequate strike relief. Nor could mill folk hope for local backing in a region thoroughly dominated by conservative political elites. And Franklin Roosevelt, on whom southern workers relied, "either could not or would not grasp the critical importance" of unionization. Always more interested in agricultural policy than the problems of industry, and dependent on southern congressional support for passage of New Deal legislation, Roosevelt refused to intervene. Keeping his distance, he appointed a mediation board, headed by New Hampshire governor John G. Winant, which found merit in labor's grievances but recommended little more than further study. The president added his personal plea to the board's request that the union end the strike and that employers take back striking workers. Afraid of losing all government support, the UTW complied. The General Strike officially ended on September 22, twenty-two days after it began. . . .

Eviction was the employers' ultimate sanction. Nothing produced more terror than the prospect of being out on the road with "nowhere to go" and "cold weather . . . coming on." A man in Williamston, South Carolina, lost his job for being elected president of his union local. After the General Strike, his son and daughter were discharged as well. "Then they forced me out of the house i was living in i had no other place to go. . . . I have tried in over 300 cotton mills for work and they will not hire me because I belong to the union. . . . There is starvation ahead if i don't get work at *once*. . . . Please for God's sake help me." . . .

Mill hands learned from their history, and in 1934 the lesson for many was a deep distrust of government and trade unions alike. Above all, the General Strike drove home the cost of challenging the established order. Better the familiar securities of job and home than "air and promises," followed by exile, suffering, and defeat.

Southern workers did not abandon efforts to shift the balance of power in the mills. Their disillusionment with the NRA helped spur passage of the Wagner Act in 1935. Heartened by this restructuring of labor law, the CIO launched a southern organizing drive; by the end of World War II textile unionism had established a small but permanent beachhead in the region. Still, labor's spectacular gains in other industries bypassed the textile South. Southern legislators, unhindered by working-class bargaining power, led a postwar attack on labor's legislative gains. The unorganized South remained a mecca for runaway shops and an ongoing source of cheap labor.

Within this environment, textile leaders enlarged on the strategies developed in the 1920s and 1930s. To earlier forms of rationalization, they added destruction of the communities they had created and tried so hard to subdue. After 1938, when the Fair Labor Standards Act narrowed the wage differential between North and South, the maintenance of company housing became an economic disadvantage. Burlington Mills began selling its villages in the wake of the General Strike, and other firms followed suit. With the aid of improvements in highway transportation, which they had helped promote, southern mill owners gradually dismantled their villages, hired workers from the surrounding countryside, or relocated in rural industrial parks.

The retired workers we talked to welcomed rising wages and diminution of company control, but they reported the unraveling of social relations as a personal loss. Work was severed from community life. People "didn't visit like they once did," and neighbors seemed distant and aloof. "People misses a lot by not having community," Mary Thompson explained. "I believe it made you more secure or something. But now you're scattered. You work maybe one place, and another works way over yonder, and you don't get close to nobody."

At least some manufacturers saw the dispersion of people and the dismantling of neighborhoods in a more favorable light. A North Carolina textile promoter explained: "[Our] goal was to have one industrial employee from every farm family in [the county]. We stressed this continually until I think it got to the point that people believed it, and the employment practices of the mills we brought here confirmed it. They found that by scattering their labor they were never available in large enough numbers to attract the union. When you get a lot of people living in one community, living in one mill village, they're naturally objects of concern—and, of course, exploitation—by labor unions. But scattering these people out all over the country turned out to be a very healthy concept."

Thus was a world of cotton mill people made and unmade. Pushed off the land, white farmers created a mill village culture that sustained their personal lives and public protest. They suffered poverty and exploitation, but they did not live in a closed society that stripped them of independence, hope, and dignity. On the contrary, the manufacturers' authority was hedged about by technological and social constraints. The assault on the mill workers' world, which began with welfare work and culminated in owners' efforts to bend New Deal legislation to their own advantage, sparked the largest single strike in American history. The men and women who came forward in unparalleled numbers in 1934 did so in the belief that powerful allies were by their sides. Far from silent or incoherent, they may have misread the dynamics of national politics, but they understood the realities of power. "It is a great struggle for the people who are not so fortunate as to possess the requirements that is necessary to make Liberty," wrote a mill hand in the aftermath of the 1934 conflict. "Those who are at Liberty and Freedom *now* are those who own and possess authority and money." The defeat of the General Strike, the subsequent failure of unionization, and the breakup of the villages ended an era and reshaped the terrain of labor conflict in the postwar South.

Why Southern Urbanization Hasn't Worked That Way

DAVID R. GOLDFIELD

A short ten-minute drive from downtown Atlanta and you are no longer in the city; you are in the South. There it is still possible, journalist Pat Watters wrote, "of a late spring evening . . . to breathe the air of a small-town America (not suburbia) of the American past, suffused with the coolness and blossom fragrance of trees and bushes, roses, honeysuckle, and the wet smell of grass and weeds." The aroma had barely subsided when historians began to draw a different portrait of the urban South, demonstrating that, over the past two centuries, urban Southerners were concerned about the same issues and problems as residents in cities elsewhere and were as aggressively capitalistic in pursuing growth and prosperity. If the urban South lagged behind the urban North in population and production, the lag was of time, not of quality. Southern cities, in short, were full-fledged members of the urban nation, distinguished only by latitude and pace.

Such historical studies—and the complementary works of sociologists, geographers, and political scientists—had the beneficial effect of lifting the "cotton curtain" that had shrouded an important aspect of Southern regional development. The South could no longer be thought of simply as "the plantation, the planter, the staple crop, and the Negro, all set in a rural scene." The discovery of the Southern city, moreover, had significance beyond the academy. It provided a new perspective on an old region and portended well for its future. As early as the 1930s, Howard W. Odum and the Regionalists at Chapel Hill contended that urbanization would result in a cultural maturation that would alter the region's values. Southern political scientist V. O. Key asserted that "urbanization contained the seeds of political revolution in the South." Now cities were in a position to provide regional political leadership, which meant an end to the "tradition-bound" politics of the agrarian past.

In the 1950s, urban analyst Robert Earl Garren predicted that urbanism as a "new way of life for the South" would solve "difficulties now present in human relationships"—that is, race relations. During the 1960s and 1970s, when the sunbelt hoopla coincided with increased scholarly interest in the urban South, enthusiasm over the region's future abounded. In the mid-1960s, sociologist Edgar T. Thompson averred that "the city everywhere is the natural habitat of the liberal mind, and the southern liberal is increasing in number and making himself heard"; liberalism would bring

David R. Goldfield, "The Urban South: A Regional Framework," *American Historical Review* 86 (December 1981), pp. 1009–1012, 1015–1022, 1023–1034. Reprinted by permission of the author.

racial peace and political harmony to the region. Another sociologist, Leonard Reissman, declared at the same time that urbanization was destroying the social homogeneity of the South. The solid South was not so any longer. A decade later, sociologists Thomas H. Naylor and James Clotfelter agreed that urban growth was "undermining the unity of the region." Scholars had clearly written an epitaph for Dixie.

They had also miscalculated. These scholars assumed the existence of a community of cities—that is, American cities sharing certain characteristics that made them more like each other than like their nonurban surroundings. The assumption is based upon an urban model designed by Chicago sociologist Louis Wirth in the 1930s. In his seminal essay, "Urbanism as a Way of Life," Wirth contended that the city is a distinctive environment, set apart from the countryside and capable of altering human behavior by the very fact that it is a city. For an increasing number of social scientists, however, it is becoming evident that this model is "both time- and culture-bound to the immigrant city of North America at the turn of the twentieth century." Although the divergence of pluralistic Chicago from the homogeneous Illinois cornfields provided an empirical justification for Wirth and his followers, the dissociation of city and region has been less apparent to later scholars studying other urban settings.

Accordingly, the growing propensity in the social sciences has been to study cities in the context of regions, under the assumption that regional and urban characteristics interact, influencing the development of both. The flexibility of the regional model is one of its major advantages. It does not attribute a specific set of characteristics to either city or region but, instead, views the city as one environment among many in a given region. . . .

This essay proposes a regional framework for the study of the urban South. . . . [E]lements of regional distinction provide insights on how Southern cities differed from their counterparts elsewhere. . . . At least three general factors have characterized the South's historical development: ruralism, race, and colonialism. These elements have appeared in other American regions, but, in terms of their combination and continuity, they are distinctive to the Southern region and, therefore, to the Southern city.

The Wirthian model of urbanization established "urban" and "rural" as dichotomous environments. Contemporary scholars, however, are less certain of the differences, and a few have asserted that what distinctions exist are, in Brian J. L. Berry's word, "meaningless." Patterns of American postwar urbanization support this view. According to Oscar Handlin, "the differences between city and country have been attenuated almost to the vanishing point." But, even in the industrial era at the turn of the century when urban-rural distinctions were perhaps more obvious, social scientists groped for definitional demarcations. Pioneer urbanist Adna F. Weber complained that, in the United States, the "town" is a rural concept but that, in Europe, it is considered urban and that the numerical thresholds assigned to each concept were inadequate. Weber was most satisfied with the German subdivision of *Landstadt* (literally, "country town") as a definitional middle ground between rural and urban places that combines elements of both. . . .

Life in Southern cities in the nineteenth century remained tied to agricultural cycles. There was, as Lewis Mumford noted of Greek cities, "a tidal drifting in and out of the city with the seasons." Towns slept from late spring to early fall and awoke with the arrival of the first cotton or tobacco shipments. Even a metropolis such as New Orleans did not have a life of its own apart from the dictates of the cotton fields. "About the first of June," journalist J. D. B. De Bow wrote with some dismay, New Orleans "begins to show evidences of waste. People inquire of steam and rail routes and are buying trunks." Many were also escaping the potential of yellow fever; but, had the city been healthy, there was simply little to do while cotton was in the fields. The tempo picked up in the fall and especially in the early winter. Cities arranged their yearly social and cultural calendars around staple marketing time.

Southern urban architecture and landscape further reflected agrarian connections. Antebellum planters moved readily between country and city residences in larger cities like Charleston and established themselves more or less permanently in smaller places like Natchez and Demopolis; their presence contributed to the Southern city's hybrid appearance. Their homes, turned sideways to show narrow frontage on the street, had verandahs along the side and verdant gardens in the back to lend a country atmosphere. Travelers commenting on the distinctions between Northern and Southern cities frequently lapsed into rural metaphors. Palmettos and magnolias graced the streets of Charleston, while a walk on the Battery "to inhale the pure and cool breezes . . . and to enjoy the view" was an essential part of the itinerary of any visitor. Savannah, one visitor wrote to his Northern friends, "is a city of trees and gardens." Away from the wharf, this traveler noted an "almost rural quiet." Even on the Texas frontier, Galveston was "one of the most charming places—in appearance—that I have ever seen," one traveler exclaimed; the landscaping and the elegance of the residences along the Strand bespoke the same pastoral quietude of more civilized Natchez and Savannah.

Southern cities continued to attract notice as middle landscapes into the twentieth century. Novelist Sherwood Anderson, absorbing the exotic culture of New Orleans during the 1920s, was most impressed not by the city's urbanity but by its close relationship to nature. In a letter to his publisher concerning the impending appearance of *Dark Laughter*, a novel he wrote in New Orleans, Anderson related, "The Negro, the earth, and the river—that suggests the title." The narrator in Anderson's "A Meeting South" stated, "All good New Orleanians go to look at the Mississippi, at least once a day." This urban commune with nature, which struck Anderson as so unusual, had been the Southern urban condition for two centuries. Edd W. Parks summarized the relationship in 1934 by stating that the urban South was "governed and given character by the country immediately surrounding it."

The relatively low density of population in Southern cities complemented the rural physical appearance. Because many Southern cities experienced their most rapid growth during the twentieth century, the age of annexation and the automobile, <u>most of them remain uncluttered and sprawling</u>. But the horizontal structure of Southern urban space was evident in the nineteenth century, long before technology affected land use. Single family dwellings, no matter how modest, characterized residential areas. Blacks and poor whites on the urban periphery merely re-created their small wooden rural shacks. The ample gardens of the larger homes lent an air of spaciousness to more affluent residential districts closer to the city center. The low-rise aspect of residences persisted after local boosters began building commercial towers in refurbished downtowns at the turn of the century.

Rural elements not only permeated the physical structure of Southern cities but <u>determined the very existence of those cities as well</u>. Agriculture, especially staple agriculture, molded the region's economy and directed the size and nature of urban growth. . . .

. . . With the emergence of cotton as the region's leading staple, New Orleans developed into the South's and, for a time in the 1830s, the nation's leading export center. In the cotton belt in general, however, urban civilization barely existed. The rural quietude of Natchez was matched by dozens of other Delta towns. Except for Mobile, New Orleans seemed to enjoy an urban monopoly. Of the ten leading Southern cities in 1850, only Memphis, Mobile, and New Orleans were in the cotton belt.

Cotton, like tobacco, required relatively few concentrated services. Processing occurred elsewhere, in New England or Great Britain, so the only requisite for the crop's commercial success was an outlet to both of these locations. New Orleans merchants organized the trade by sending agents into upriver towns to collect the crop and, in turn, supply the planters with wares. The volume of cotton production and the need for quality control and price stability militated against the kind of diffuse trade that marked tobacco commerce in the early colonial era. The functions of upriver towns were limited to collection points for the staple. New Orleans's early regional dominance of cotton commerce, moreover, inhibited urban growth by restricting capital accumulation. Crescent City merchants came to control local banks as well. Finally, as the regional center for the slave trade, New Orleans had another economic monopoly to drain capital from the hinterland. So, cotton and capital flowed to the delta port.

Soil exhaustion and the limited marketing procedures surrounding tobacco cultivation restricted the development of cities similar in size to those in the North. The Chesapeake (not including Baltimore, which was tied to wheat-cultivating areas) and the North Carolina tobacco belt provided little sustenance for Richmond, Lynchburg, and Petersburg. Only in the 1850s, when these cities added processing industries, did growth occur, though on a modest scale. Thus, New Orleans was the dominant metropolis of the antebellum South; it had no rivals. Charleston, its nearest competitor in population, was one-quarter its size in 1860 and had slipped from sixth to fifteenth in national rank according to size in less than a generation.

Urbanization did indeed occur in the antebellum South. What did not, however, was the development of large cities. An urban place inhabited by fewer than four thousand persons (by 1860) was more characteristic of the antebellum South than of any other region. The urban population of the region was, therefore, more diffuse—a condition consistent with the relatively few economic functions such cities performed in support of a staple crop economy. It was urbanization without cities.

The pattern persisted for nearly another century. The development of the Southern urban system following the Civil War reflected the South's increased dependence on staple agriculture. During the period of agricultural recovery, 1865–80, urbanization came to a virtual halt. The percentage of the South's population residing in cities increased from 9.6 percent in 1860 to only 12.2 percent by 1880. In the highly urbanized Northeast, by contrast, city dwellers increased from 35.7 to 50.8 percent of the population during the same period. The ground lost by the laggard pace of Southern urbanization immediately before the Civil War was never recovered. In 1830, five Southern cities were among the nation's twenty leading cities; in 1900, only one—New Orleans—remained, and only six Southern cities were among the fifty major cities in the United States.

Changes in both marketing and processing cotton led to the even greater prevalence of smaller urban places in the Southern urban system than had existed in the antebellum period. The appearance of country stores, storehouses, and taverns around rural railroad stations signified a localization of cotton marketing. Normally, this system should have benefited Southern port cities, which could be expected to supply these merchant-crossroad settlements. The extent of the national railroad network, however, enabled these storekeepers to by-pass Southern cities in favor of connections with Northern cities. In this way, the country merchants could market the local cotton crop in exchange for goods without requiring contact with Southern ports.

The precipitous decline of New Orleans reflected the new marketing arrangements. New Orleans remained the major Southern cotton port, but only because the lower Mississippi provided easier transportation for some planters than did the railroads running eastward and westward; and not until 1883 did cotton receipts at the port attain prewar levels. Population growth, moreover, declined with commerce: in 1860, New Orleans was the sixth largest city in the nation; by 1900, it had slipped to fifteenth and was continuing to move downward.

In addition to marketing changes, the improvement of staple processing techniques in the late-nineteenth-century South induced further decline in the region's major ports. Technological innovations that enabled cotton gins to process more cotton encouraged the removal of ginning from individual plantations to nearby towns along rail routes where cotton could be cleaned more cheaply in greater volume. By the 1880s, two new processing techniques had appeared—cotton compressing, which reduced the size of the bales, and cottonseed oil mills, which extracted oil from crushed cottonseeds. Both of these techniques required relatively sophisticated machinery, which could handle the product of roughly thirty cotton gins at one time. Such industries, therefore, commanded a wider market area than the ginning enterprises and, consequently, produced urban growth. Until 1930, those communities that were able to secure all three processing services were the fastest growing cities in the cotton belt. These additional services left the planter even less reason to patronize the once-flourishing seaports.

Although the processing communities were major beneficiaries of cotton belt urban growth, they attained the limits of their expansion relatively quickly. By 1900, these towns, which were scattered remarkably evenly throughout the area of cotton cultivation from Texas to southern Georgia, had reached a population of five to ten thousand inhabitants and rarely grew beyond that. The market area required by the new procedures remained relatively stationary, and, since the processed cotton was immediately transshipped by rail to major rail centers in the South like Dallas and Atlanta or to Northern cities, the towns had little need to develop higher economic functions. Actually, those cities that were outside the cotton belt or had very little contact with the staple were most successful in generating large-scale urban growth. Cotton cultivation, as in the antebellum era, could produce a significant number of urban places, but their size was severely restricted by the limits of the marketing and processing activities imposed by the crop.

As staple cultivation came to characterize the postwar South to an even greater extent than it did in the antebellum era, the small city became even more typical of Southern urban settlement. In 1850, 68.7 percent of the South's urban population lived in cities of over twenty-five thousand inhabitants; by 1900, only 48.1 percent did, even though more Southerners lived in cities by the later date. Cities that served as major transshipment points for cotton or had little direct contact with the staple became the region's new growth centers. Among the South's five most populous cities in 1920, Atlanta possessed only a few hundred citizens in 1850, and Birmingham did not exist at that date. But Atlanta and Birmingham were only the most prominent examples of urbanization beyond simple marketing and processing. The appearance of cities like Durham, Winston-Salem, and Greenville in the Carolina Piedmont reflected a more complex industrial base than simple processing. The rise of Florida cities such as Jacksonville and Tampa, which grew from a mixture of commerce and industry, and the growth of Chattanooga, Knoxville, and Nashville, which became prominent as a result of various railroad, industrial, and educational and cultural enterprises—all within the last two decades of the nineteenth century—indicate urban economies serving other masters besides or excluding King Cotton.

These new urban centers together with the proliferating cotton marketing and processing towns represent a shift from the antebellum pattern of one primary city—New Orleans—with a few secondary seaports and a host of small urban communities. The shift did not, however, signify a change in the nature of Southern urbanization but merely a change in geography. The South remained overwhelmingly a region of the small urban settlement.

As long as staple crop cultivation, especially cotton, characterized Southern agriculture, this pattern remained. In the 1930s and 1940s, federal policy, mass migration, and mechanization diminished the significance of staple cultivation. In 1940, cities of less than ten thousand still typified the region's urban growth. In that year, one-third of the nation's population lived in cities of over one hundred thousand inhabitants; only one out of eight Southerners did. During the 1940s, small-city urbanization began to decline in importance. That this occurred simultaneously with the transformation of Southern agriculture indicates that staple marketing no longer sustained urban development. Industry and service activities became greater determinants of urbanization in the post–World War II South. For the first time in its history, the growth of cities of more than ten thousand inhabitants exceeded the rate for cities and towns of less than ten thousand. Two genuine metropolises now anchored the Southern urban system— Atlanta in the east and Dallas in the west. Both cities owed their early prosperity to cotton; but finance, diversified commerce, and industry built them into regional pacesetters. Finally, the most rapid urban growth in the region occurred in Florida, where agriculture had only an indirect impact on urbanization. Miami and Tampa–St. Petersburg counted almost one million persons between them in 1950. From the Florida panhandle to eastern Texas, however, the small city remained the characteristic urban settlement. Low in density, these communities continued to grow horizontally in the 1950s. C. Vann Woodward has called this semi-urban sprawl "rurbanization," a term that captures well the hybrid form of Southern urban settlement.

A more subtle and pervasive rural quality than size and concomitant marketing functions lingered as well: the rural values of the millions of migrants who, over the centuries, moved from the countryside to the city. The Wirthian concept of urbanization advanced two assumptions about urbanization and culture: the urban environment modified or destroyed migrant cultures, and cities functioned as disseminators of culture to the hinterland. Recent studies on ethnicity demonstrate, however, that immigrants' pre-migration cultures persisted in cities, despite the adverse impact of the city on immigrant life. As Kathleen Neils Conzen has pointed out, "considerable residues of ethnic culture can remain among socially assimilated individuals," so that the strength of these cultural values can be maintained over time. More pertinent to the Southern urban situation are studies of value persistence among native rural migrants. In 1941, anthropologist Robert Redfield discovered a broad range of values and institutions that remained intact or were only slightly modified among the rural migrants of urban Mexico; voluntary associations and kinship patterns persisted in the urban environment. More recently, African scholars have demonstrated not merely the maintenance of but the increase in tribal consciousness among transplanted rural Africans, especially in those cities where intergroup conflict is strong. This finding may have particular relevance for the persistence of rural black folk culture amid the hostile white environment of the Southern city. Not only in the Third World but in Western societies as well, the resilience of rural values in an urban setting is a prevalent phenomenon.

Anthropologists, in view of these findings on rural cultural persistence, have questioned the city's role as a disseminator of culture. Robert Redfield and Milton B. Singer have distinguished between primary and secondary urbanization. In the primary phase, cities carry the region's culture forward "into systematic and reflective dimensions." The city organizes and refines this core culture but does not alter it. During the secondary phase of urbanization—a phase induced through vast technological changes and the influx of diverse peoples—the cultural flow approaches the direction assumed by the Wirthian model. Even here, however, "the processes of cultural innovation . . . are far too complex to be handled by simple mechanical laws concerning the direction, rate, and 'flow' of cultural diffusion between 'city' and 'country.' " Redfield and Singer termed primary cities "orthogenetic" and secondary cities "heterogenetic."

Southern cities have evinced orthogenetic cultural patterns for most of the past two centuries—that is, rural folkways have persisted in Southern cities. In the nineteenth century, the roots of the Southern urban population were sunk deep in rural soil, especially in the postbellum era. As early as 1868, one-half of Atlanta's population had arrived from the countryside in the three years since the end of the war. Rural migration receded in the 1870s, but a steady stream flowed into Southern cities for the remainder of the century. Memphis, one of the region's few prosperous larger cities, was also its most rural. By 1900, 80 percent of the city's residents were from the adjacent Mississippi or Tennessee countryside. Percentages of recent rural migrants were almost as high in Jacksonville, Birmingham, and Atlanta. While rural proportions increased, the immigrant population usually declined. In Memphis, for example, 37 percent of the population was foreign-born in 1860; by 1900, only 15 percent was. Southern cities at the turn of the century were becoming both more rural and less diverse.

With the agricultural transformation during and after the Depression, migration from the farms quickened. As author Lillian Smith noted succinctly in the 1940s, "people have moved to town." While the region's farm population declined by 20 percent between 1940 and 1945, Southern cities increased by nearly 30 percent, exceeding the rate of urban growth in other regions. The acceleration of rural migration and agricultural diversification continued into the next decade. In 1950, South Carolina still produced over 700,000 bales of cotton. By 1960, cotton cultivation had virtually disappeared as the white fields receded before the green wave of pasture, soybeans, and corn. The croppers and tenants—over one hundred and fifty thousand of them—who worked those cotton fields were mostly gone, to small cities like Columbia, Spartanburg, and Greenville.

In addition to their demographic impact, the rural migrants brought their distinctive cultural baggage to the city. Although the effect of rural values on Southern urban development is not clear, several suggestions can be ventured. Family and religion were Southern rural bulwarks. "The family," Southern historian Francis Butler Simkins wrote, "was the core of Southern society; within its bounds everything worthwhile took place." The strength of family ties possibly meant the weakness of the community or collective ethic in Southern cities; kinship patterns determined social standing, and tradition counted more than novelty. Honor, vengeance, and pride, especially when women were involved, were above all family values, and they governed behavior outside the home as well. Southerners believed and practiced, as historian Gerald M. Capers has noted, "the right of private vengeance." New South urban murder rates, for example, were typically higher than for cities in other regions. During the early 1900s, the national homicide rate per one hundred thousand inhabitants was 7.2; every Southern city over twenty-five thousand exceeded that rate. Memphis, the most rural (in terms of its population) of major Southern cities, was also the nation's murder capital, with a rate of 47.1; Charleston was a distant second at 27.7.

The violence contrasted with, yet was curiously connected to, the deep religiosity of the rural migrants. The Southern church, historian George B. Tindall wrote, "is something unique in all Christendom in its single-minded focus on salvation, its sense of assurance, and its rejection . . . of other versions of Christian experience. It serves as one of the chief instruments of ethnic solidarity." As Tindall's description implies, it was not the deep religiosity of Southerners that was unique but, rather, the philosophical structure of their religious devotion. Evangelical Protestantism, which first swept over the frontier South in the 1830s, came increasingly after the Civil War to define Southern religious practices and principles and to mark religion as one of the distinctive features of Southern identity.

Specifically, this Southern religious tradition was pessimistic, emphasizing man's basic depravity, with the opportunity of individual salvation only through a conversion experience. The evangelical sects (primarily Baptists, Methodists, and Presbyterians) and their ministers were well established by 1860, but not until after the Civil War, when Southern religion became entwined with the Lost Cause, did evangelical Protestantism pervade every cultural pore of the region. The pain and the martyrdom evoked by the Lost Cause blended well with a religion obsessed with suffering and salvation. For a region wrapped in grief and defeat, where dull poverty was commonplace, evangelical ritual, liturgy, and promise filled a deep spiritual need. By 1900, a distinctive civil religion was evident, distinguishing Southern culture from the optimistic, scientific, social gospel sweeping Northern ecclesiastics and society. What began as a fervent rural pastime in the early nineteenth century became a regional hallmark by the beginning of the twentieth.

Evangelical Protestantism affected Southern culture by standing as a regional bulwark against change. The focus on individual sin and salvation and on otherworldly rewards regardless of earthly deprivations shifted attention from society to the individual and his compact with God. "Christ-centeredness," Southern theologian Samuel S. Hill, Jr., averred, "easily shades off into fearful self-centeredness." . . .

As a part—perhaps the most dominant part—of Southern culture, evangelical Protestantism invariably affected Southern urbanization, and vice versa. Although the evangelical sects first prospered on the Southern frontier, the spirit of revivalism soon penetrated the cities and towns of the antebellum South. The antebellum evangelists appealed to the "middling ranks of Southern society" and thus found numerous adherents in the urban South. Then, too, the evangelists' efforts to reach the greatest numbers for conversion and salvation meant that cities became logical centers for evangelical activity. The sheer size of the urban populations and the frequent opportunities to speak outside the church afforded the evangelist a "wider influence than he could ever hope for in the country."

After the Civil War, religion as a Southern cultural mainstay flourished in Southern cities and became inseparable from urban life. "Church was our town," author Lillian Smith recalled of her childhood during the early decades of the twentieth century. Wood planks or carpeting may have replaced the dirt floor of the forest, but the old enthusiasm and demonstrative preaching of guilt, sin, fear, and salvation persisted in the urban milieu. The evangelical church's "general spirit and outlook were transplanted to the nearby town center," Edgar T. Thompson reminisced. "Southern town and even city churches generally might almost be described as transplanted rural institutions," he concluded. Church and urban society remain closely connected. Religious affiliation is as important as lineage in describing a person today. The Southern urban church is the best place in the city to attain and maintain social and business contacts. And, even though framed by expensive architecture, the basic principles of evangelical Protestantism continue to issue forth from urban pulpits, especially in the numerous Baptist and Christian congregations.

Evangelical Protestantism and the values associated with it have maintained the orthogenetic character of Southern cities perhaps more than staple agriculture has. By blocking out ideological competitors and by supporting traditional beliefs, Southern urban religion helped make Southern cities bastions of conservatism, if not reaction, rather than of change, as in cities elsewhere in the United States. Evangelical churchmen, concerned with individual salvation or fearful of disrupting their flocks, generally either ignored or supported the biracial society—slavery in the antebellum period and segregation after the Civil War. Even so-called liberal churchmen in the twentieth century "condemned forces which they felt encouraged religious and social diversity within the city." Since evangelical precepts also divided society into absolutes of good and evil, laymen rarely questioned the status quo of urban society that the church had sanctified as the holy order. "Our first lesson about God made the deepest impression on us," Lillian Smith related. "We were told that He loved us, and then we were told that He would burn us in everlasting flames of hell if we displeased

Him." Naturally, every child hoped to avoid that fate. "The best way," Smith concluded, "was never to question anything but always accept what you were told."

The evangelical faiths facilitated the perpetuation of myths—about slavery, the Lost Cause, and the New South. The role of the church complemented that of the ubiquitous booster who, in his exaggerated rhetoric, revealed the same defensiveness, insecurity, and self-righteousness that the evangelical ecclesiastics exhibited. The "commercial-civic elite," as Blaine A. Brownell called such boosters, flourished in both the Old and the New South, but rarely as virulently as in the decades after World War I; their rhetoric adopted religious metaphors (indeed, Paul M. Gaston's New South "Creed" implies a religious connotation), and they proclaimed the ecumenicism of their policies, generally opposing change. In the early twentieth century, for example, urban leaders converted new methodologies like planning to conservative objectives designed to preserve the existing social and political structure. They dissembled to avoid pursuing policies that could threaten their hegemony. When the Memphis Chamber of Commerce boasted in early 1941 that "there is no housing shortage in Memphis. . . . Memphis is well-housed," the city had one of the worst housing shortages in the nation, and nearly four out of every five blacks and one out of three whites were living in substandard housing. Above all, like the ministers, they claimed to be the keepers of the community's welfare, creating an identity between community welfare and the leaders' policies. In this manner, as Richard Sennett has noted, "the image of community is purified of all that might convey a feeling of difference, let alone conflict, on who 'we' are." This was precisely the thrust of evangelical Protestantism, of course: purification, antipathy to change, and a sharp distinction between "we" and "them."

Although boosters and ministers occasionally clashed in the early decades of the twentieth century on, for instance, blue laws, their objectives frequently coincided. It was not unusual to see Bishop Warren A. Candler and the *Manufacturers' Record* agreeing that the Scopes trial was "one of the South's supremest advertisements." . . .

The close attention urban clerics and boosters paid to citizens' civic and spiritual ideals seems to have exhausted their communitarian spirit. Churchmen and businessmen generally neglected the social needs of their constituents. With a religious philosophy that emphasized individual sin and salvation and a booster creed that stressed public unity for economic development and racial stability, social policies were superfluous, diversionary, and potentially disruptive. Not surprisingly, from the mid-nineteenth century to the present day, per capita expenditures in Southern cities, especially for social services, have lagged far behind similar expenditures in other cities. In 1902, for example, at a time of high spiritual and civic revival, no Southern city spent the national per capita average for education ($4.37), and most educational spending was one-third to one-half less than that average. From libraries to street paving to public health services, Southern cities traditionally lagged behind cities elsewhere. As late as 1970, no Southern city matched or exceeded the national average per capita urban expenditure for public welfare ($11.98).

The urban South's dismal performance on social services restricted urban development. Nobel laureate economist Theodore W. Schultz devised the concept of human capital as an essential programming element for developing areas. "The decisive factor," Schultz declared, "is the improvement in population quality." Education, health, and housing of the poor are the most important improvements and investments in human capital. The paucity of Southern investments in these areas has reduced the quality of the regional population and, hence, its ability to contribute to the region's development.

The aversion of the civic and religious elite to such investments in human capital resulted not only from the philosophical bases of booster and evangelical ideology but also from the immense presence of a biracial society. Too much improvement in population quality implied the threat of population equality—a situation that would have eroded "civic-religious" hegemony and, therefore, the foundation of regional society. Accordingly, the region's economic and religious institutions sought to regulate, separate, isolate, and subjugate the black race. Since urban life created greater opportunities for racial interaction, urban whites were as vigilant as, if not more vigilant than, their rural counterparts in maintaining the biracial society.

The biracial society in an urban setting restricted blacks to certain low-level occupations. Agriculture and its institutions—slavery in the antebellum era and sharecropping, tenancy, crop lien, and peonage following the Civil War—restricted the free flow of black labor to the cities. This restriction provides yet another example of how agriculture controlled the economic life of the city. Migrating to the city, the blacks' primarily agrarian skills were ill suited to urban jobs and ensured black employment only in low-status occupations. The biracial system almost guaranteed that blacks stayed there. Although cities such as Charleston and New Orleans had a small black elite in the antebellum period, the black's occupational status suffered drastically with emancipation and increased migration to the cities. The existence of such a relatively large body of marginal consumers further lowered demand and capital accumulation in the urban South and provided an economic excuse for the poor, selective quality of public services.

The Civil War also produced changes in the blacks' residential status in ways that solidified the biracial society. The change from exclusion to segregation, which Howard N. Rabinowitz has advanced as the regional biracial pattern after 1865, allowed blacks access to some features of urban life that they had not enjoyed prior to the Civil War but did not, however, signify an urban departure from traditional regional racial mores. As orthogenetic entities, Southern cities "carried forward," rather than transformed, regional racial patterns. Segregation was such an adjustment, much as crop lien and peonage were racial accommodations in the rural districts. Segregation may have allowed blacks greater participation, but they could only participate on white terms. Moreover, segregation generalized blacks, ruthlessly isolating them from the mainstream of urban life; and residential patterns show most clearly the impact of segregation.

Black residential patterns in Southern cities were distinctive, resembling more the spatial characteristics of lower-caste groups in developing societies than the neighborhood arrangements of Northern cities. Some residential dispersion existed in the antebellum era due to the necessities of slavery. Rather than the single large ghetto found in Northern cities, concentrations of blacks that reflected the scattered nature of undesirable housing sites emerged in the postbellum South. In 1877, the Nashville Board of Health reported that the city's blacks "reside mainly in old stables, situated upon alleys in the midst of privy vaults, or in wooden shanties a remnant of war times, or in huts closely crowded together on the outskirts." These "neighborhoods," especially those on the periphery, presented a primitive, rural appearance: the dirt roads, outdoor facilities, poor drainage, and frame "double-pen" houses or "shotgun shacks" differed little from sharecroppers' dwellings. And, by the 1890s, the lines dividing black and white residential communities had hardened.

Housing clusters continued to characterize black residential patterns in the urban South during the twentieth century—typically, one large cluster in the most decrepit area near the center, surrounded by smaller clusters moving outward toward the periphery. The peripheral neighborhoods were frequently either the "temporary" communities that sprouted to house freedmen immediately following the Civil War or erstwhile rural areas annexed by the Southern cities' voracious appetite for land. In some of the older cities like Savannah and Charleston, reminders of the antebellum past persisted in the 1920s and 1930s, as long fingers of blacks' residences intruded into white neighborhoods on the narrow lanes behind the major residential thoroughfares. But these vestiges disappeared after World War II as whites began to abandon the centers, and residential patterns similar to those in newer Southern cities replaced such antebellum holdovers. Birmingham, for example, had a primary black neighborhood adjacent to the downtown area and several smaller clusters scattered wherever poor urban land existed.

The black isolation from white areas has increased during this century. By 1960, only 5.5 percent of the Southern urban population resided in integrated neighborhoods compared with 31.8 percent in the Northeast. Although black neighborhoods in the South were more dispersed than they were in Northern cities, they were usually more segregated. In addition, Southern urban blacks are still more likely to be peripheral and suburban residents than their Northern counterparts are, a legacy from Reconstruction and annexation. In 1970, 14 percent of the South's metropolitan black population resided on the metropolitan periphery, compared with only 3 percent in the Northeast.

Black ecological patterns in Southern cities in the last one hundred years have resembled those found in pre-industrial societies of the Third World. Peripheral settlement in poor housing is a common spatial phenom-

enon. Analysis of social areas—that is, census tracts and neighborhoods—
in cities indicates that Southern cities conform to non-Western patterns
primarily because of the presence and the character of the black population:
a separate and unequal society within the region and its cities. The virtual
identity between ethnicity and socioeconomic status—a characteristic of
social areas in underdeveloped societies—describes the separate black communities in Southern cities. Sociologist Allison Davis's description of this
convergence in 1941 could be applied to Indian or Middle Eastern outcast
groups:

> Life in the communities in the Deep South follows an orderly pattern. The
> inhabitants live in a social world clearly divided into two ranks, the white
> caste and the Negro caste. These colored castes share disproportionately
> in the privileges and obligations of labor, school, and government.

Regional biracialism has given the Southern city a non-Western character,
perhaps more than any other regional characteristic has.

In 1941, researchers undoubtedly believed that biracialism had created
a unique urban social environment that would persist as long as color
remained a decisive factor in regional life. But biracialism possessed within
it, ironically, the potential for regional and urban change. The blacks themselves, first alone and then with ouside support, produced alterations in
Southern urban society, especially following World War II. The vestiges
of biracialism, however, remain, and race continues to play its distinctive
role in the region and its cities. . . . Blacks have secured only a minimum
of white political support. In 1979, when Birmingham elected its first black
mayor, Richard Arrington, only 10 percent of the white voters supported
him. Black political strength and security depend on sheer numbers, not
on changing attitudes in the white community. Several Southern cities have
already attempted to push through reapportionment, at-large elections, annexation, and consolidation schemes under the guise of political reform,
when actually these policies have been aimed at diluting black political
strength. . . .

. . . Black political power is also circumscribed by the absence of black
economic power.

The blacks' economic deficiency is shared, in a relative sense, by the region
and its cities. Rural agricultural patterns and values (especially evangelical
Protestantism) and biracialism have limited capital accumulation and have
skewed investment patterns to labor and land, rather than to specifically
city-building enterprises. A persistent colonialism has reinforced these indigenous factors—ruralism and biracialism—to form the third major element in the region's eternal triangle.

Colonialism denotes a colonial power. In the eighteenth century, it was
the British, but, in the nineteenth and twentieth centuries, it has been—
and is—the North. The development of a national economy, centered in
New York beginning in the 1840s, fastened a type of regional specialization
upon the South that remains with it to the present day. The South as the

producer and occasionally the basic processor of raw materials has been in continuous economic servitude to the North not only for manufactured products but also for all of the financial, credit, legal, accounting, and factoring services that attend a national economy. Cities are the "instruments" of regional articulation in a national economy and set the economic tone for the region. Thus, cities were regional colonial headquarters as the South sank deeper into economic dependence. Southern cities served as collection points for and funnels to Northern centers and as distribution points for the return flow. This system limited capital accumulation in the region, which reduced the opportunities for the region to develop beyond its colonial economy. And everything limited urbanization. In fact, as the national economy grew after the Civil War, Southern cities shrunk relative to their Northern (national) counterparts.

Northern investors encouraged the economic development of the region only insofar as it enhanced their dominance in the national economy. After the Civil War, Northern control of Southern railroads, for example, ensured profitable and speedy transfers to and from the colonial region. In the antebellum era, however, local investors dominated Southern railroad directorships. The Panic of 1873 dealt struggling Southern-owned companies a financial death blow, and Northern capital willingly revived the corpse. In 1870, Northerners comprised only 19 percent of the South's railroad directors; by 1880, that percentage had reached 37. By 1900, when financial capitalists like J. P. Morgan consolidated and re-organized the nation's railroad systems, Northern financiers controlled the South's five major rail lines, and 60 percent of the directors were Northerners.

The patterns of Northern investment in the South were selective, but, even so, they restricted Southern industrial development and, hence, urbanization. The potential of Birmingham's steel production frightened, rather than attracted, Northern investors in the late 1870s. Whatever advances the city made during the next decade occurred because of local capital. Eventually, during the early years of the twentieth century, the Pittsburgh Plus system and financial control by U.S. Steel effectively limited Birmingham competition and assured Northern industrial superiority. Textile milling became a Northern investment beneficiary in the twentieth century. But, as an industrial activity that occurred in a predominantly rural setting, it generated relatively little capital for the region or its cities. Low wages coincided with low investments in human capital. The textile mill was an industrial plantation with all of the same human debilities as its agricultural counterpart.

The Great Depression revealed the shallowness of the South's economy. The region's cities were the nation's "basket cases" during the 1930s. The Depression also resulted in a modification of the national economy as the federal government became a major force for economic redistribution. Federal grants accelerated the regionalization of the national economy. Southern cities were the direct beneficiaries of this process as the federal government paid for capital facilities that Northern cities had bought for themselves in earlier decades and on which they were still paying off the debt. The almost-free modernization that Southern cities received proved to be an important economic advantage in subsequent decades.

During World War II, the redistribution of national economic advantages continued as military bases and, more significantly, industry both demonstrated the increased federal presence. Indeed, federal assistance to Southern urban industry effectively primed the pump of the regional and urban economies. The government helped stimulate new industries as, for example, in Houston and released old ones from colonial restrictions as in Birmingham. Military spending in Southern cities encouraged the development of electronics research and manufacturing firms, scientific equipment companies, and aeronautics machinery plants. The growth of high-technology industry has had a positive impact on a region traditionally burdened with low-technology, low-wage industries. Between 1940 and 1960, the high-wage industrial sector increased by 180 percent in the South (the national rate was 92 percent for the same two decades), and the industrial labor force in the region grew by more than one and a half million, with almost 90 percent of these jobs in high-wage industries. Moreover, these industries were primarily urban-based. By 1960, therefore, low-wage industries accounted for only two out of every five manufacturing jobs in the region.

The multiplier effect of federal economic policy did not ensure regional deliverance from the inequities and unbalanced development of the old ante- and postbellum industrial regime. Just as vestiges of the biracial society cling like Spanish moss to the urban South, traditional industrial patterns based on a rural, colonial economy linger on. The textile mill culture persists. In South Carolina, West German flags fly in Spartanburg, Kuwaiti money flows on Kiawah, and boosters prattle innocently, yet revealingly, saying, "What we've done here ought to be done in the underdeveloped countries. We established a good political atmosphere and showed we had a real commitment to economic growth." And, indeed, the industrialization that came in a wave during the 1960s and 1970s has transformed South Carolina from a poor agricultural state to a poor industrial state. The state ranks forty-sixth in per capita income. The average mill worker earns 20 percent less per hour than the national average. South Carolina continues to lead the nation in illiteracy and infant mortality. Manufacturing remains primarily a nonmetropolitan—that is, small-town—activity.

Colonialism persists in other areas of the Southern economy as well. While the growth of air and truck transport after World War II reduced the railroad's dominance over Southern cities, other aspects of the national economy have a distinctly northern flow. The region's cities depend upon Northern banks to finance large-scale operations. Most of Houston's corporations list a New York institution as their principal bank. Any firm in the urban South with international business connections invariably goes through New York banks. Corporations in Southern cities patronize New York and Washington law offices. They also use New York accounting firms. All of this means that Northern interests continue to control large-scale investment in Southern cities. With major banking, accounting, and legal services for the South still based in the North, capital accumulation remains a regional problem. Economist Charles F. Haywood asserted in 1978 that "the South has long been a region of capital shortage. It remains so today and will be so for some years to come." Haywood suggested that the connection of the major Southern urban corporations with the national banking network need not impede their growth. But those activities "that are heavily dependent on local sources of funds—housing, local businesses, and . . . local government"—may experience some difficulty. If this prediction is accurate, the South's traditional pattern of low services, small investments in human capital, and limited urban growth will continue.

The comparison advanced above between South Carolina and underdeveloped countries is apt because the South's subsidiary role in the national economy also corresponds in some degree to the role of underdeveloped nations in the world economy. Historian John H. Coatsworth, for example, located two major obstacles to economic development in nineteenth-century Mexico: "inadequate transport and inefficient economic organization." The South has been afflicted by both, and its cities have been similarly victimized. An over-reliance on rivers and the late development of a railroad system retarded regional economic development. The unorganized nature of the Southern economy based on the individual decisions of staple entrepreneurs, the restrictions on the mobility of capital and labor, and the low priority of innovation or of any new ideas contributed to what Coatsworth termed for Mexico "inefficient economic organization." Thus, the rural value system helped bring about the North's colonial control of the South. As historian David Bertelson has maintained, "The South was an individualistic, chaotic economy in an America whose other inhabitants held some idea of community purpose."

Mexico ultimately extricated itself from its backwardness by capitalizing on its own economic vulnerability, which provided "vast comparative advantages for foreign technology and resources." In the South, especially after the Civil War, Northern capital and expertise produced a transportation system and organized the production and processing systems to suit Northern commercial and industrial requirements. This relieved Southern backwardness to some degree—but not regional dependence. Coatsworth concluded that, although Mexico was not likely to create its own viable, self-sufficient economy, the decision to turn to foreign entrepreneurs and capital produced "a long-term dependence on foreign technology, resources, and markets." By 1865, it was obviously too late for the South to secure regional economic independence or even parity; the result was "long-term" dependence on the North. The role of Southern cities and the limits this economic system placed on their development reflected the regional situation of economic subservience. . . .

Ruralism, race, and colonialism have always characterized a distinctive region and its cities, although these factors and their impact upon urbanization have not been immutable over time. The shift to mechanized agriculture, the growth of modernism in religion, the evolution of biracialism from slavery to exclusion to segregation to integration, and the altered balance in the national economy since the Depression and World War II have affected migration patterns, ways of thought, racial interaction, and capital accumulation in the region—and, hence, urbanization. Nevertheless, these regional elements persist and have collectively produced a particular and limited urbanization that exists in the region to this day. . . .

The Southern city and the South sprang from the same soil, sheltered the same people, and suffered the same burdens—both self-inflicted and superimposed.

Why Southern Industrialization Hasn't Worked That Way

JAMES C. COBB

Industrialization has brought many changes to the South, but skyscrapers, smokestacks, and industrial parks have not destroyed the region's cultural distinctiveness, nor have they provided solutions to many of the problems traditionally associated with its historically underdeveloped economy. In fact, industrial development has not only failed to establish general prosperity but has left a large number of southerners mired in poverty.

Despite a widespread perception of the Sunbelt South as a newly prosperous paradise, in terms of absolute statistics rather than growth momentum the South of the 1980s remained the nation's number one economic problem. In 1980 only Texas had a per capita income above the national average, and the South was still home to more than 44 percent of the nation's poverty population. More than a quarter of Mississippi's population lived below the poverty level, and Virginia was the only southern state with a poverty percentage below the national average.

Impressive percentage improvements in per capita income notwithstanding, constant-dollar figures revealed that between 1960 and 1980 Mississippi and Kentucky fell more than $200 further below the national average, while Arkansas, the Carolinas, and Georgia also lost ground. Cheap nonunion labor continued to be the South's major attraction to industry, and industry seekers still took great pains to inform employers of their community's abundance of eager workers. In February 1976, for example, the Rock Hill, South Carolina, Chamber of Commerce proudly circulated statistics showing that nearly three-quarters of a 25,000 person sample of the local labor force still earned less than $5,000 per year.

Emphasis on cheap labor undermined efforts to recruit better-paying industries that would not only bid up wages but enhance the prospects for unionizing southern workers. Employers who had been lured to the South by pledges of protection from unions often forced local chambers of commerce and other booster organizations to turn a cold shoulder to firms that

From "Why the New South Never Became the North: A Summary," in *Industrialization and Southern Society, 1877–1984* by James C. Cobb, pp. 143–156. Copyright © 1984 by the University Press of Kentucky. Reprinted by permission of the publishers.

might infect the community with unions and/or higher wages. Employers in the textile belt were particularly hostile to such companies, and several cities lost large, high-paying plants because of the resistance of local industrialists.

There was little doubt that the South's nonunion climate helped to depress wages. In 1980 North Carolina was the region's most industrialized state. The Tarheel work force was also the nation's least unionized (less than 7 percent) and its workers the most poorly paid (74 percent of the national hourly wage). North Carolina's well-publicized industrial "progress" notwithstanding, average hourly manufacturing wages fell from $1.05 below the national average to $1.90 below it between 1972 and 1980.

The self-satisfaction of the Sunbelt South's boosters ignored the numerous economic disparities within the region. Some areas owed their Sunbelt prosperity to the "most favored colony" status that allowed them to receive the spinoff benefits from northern industrial progress and eventually put them in a position to attract new residents and investments when the Industrial North began to decline. On the other hand, other areas seemed to have little hope of ever transcending their quasi-colonial status, and still others lost even that. "Progress" had played a cruel joke on Appalachia, which, as much as any area in the South, met Immanuel Wallerstein's criteria for a "peripheral" region because it supplied the northern "core" states with vital but "lower ranking goods . . . whose labor is less well rewarded."

According to Ronald D. Eller, Appalachia's experience with what was supposed to be progress has actually left it "a rich land with poor people." As mountaineers became timbermen, miners, or millhands, a healthy barter economy centered around the family farm gave way to a colonial system that operated for the benefit of absentee employers and entrepreneurs whose businesses drew the mountaineer's wages out of the hills. A relatively open, informal society gave way to a more rigid social and political hierarchy presided over by the mill and mine owners. "Suspended halfway between the old and the new," Eller writes, "the mountaineers had lost the independence and self determination of their ancestors, without becoming full participants in the benefits of the modern world." When their resources were depleted, many parts of Appalachia were simply left for dead without hope for economic, environmental, or cultural resurrection. . . .

While many areas dominated by low-wage industries failed to share in the Sunbelt boom, other communities which had industrialized during the decades before and immediately after World War II became miniaturized versions of declining Frostbelt cities. The economic problems of the late 1970s and early 1980s severely injured the nation's heavy industries, and many southern towns reeled from the impact of the losses in manufacturing or manufacturing-related operations. Fayetteville, Tennessee, leaders bemoaned a long list of industrial and commercial closings that even shut down the city's "Dairy Queen" ice cream parlor. Meanwhile, as businesses collapsed or contracted, Fayetteville's abundant industrial park space failed to impress potential investors. Such towns might actually have benefited, at least temporarily, from out-migration, but instead many of them continued to absorb significant population growth. The Corinth, Mississippi, area saw its population expand at a rate of 21.5 percent during the 1970s, while the unemployment rate climbed as high as 15 percent by early 1981.

In the meantime, areas which had never attracted a significant amount of industry experienced heavy out-migration as residents fled to the region's cities, drawn by the hope of opportunities which often did not exist—at least for them. These new urbanites often found greater income disparities among city dwellers than they had encountered in rural areas. A large number of these migrants were black. In Georgia, the urban black population grew by 37 percent between 1970 and 1980. For many of them the aura of prosperity surrounding the South's larger cities was little more than a glittery veneer. For example, Mayor William B. Hartsfield's effort to blend racial moderation with headlong pursuit of growth had made Atlanta a regional model. The city's ultra-busy airport became a gateway to the South, and its downtown area dwarfed its regional counterparts with a skyline of high-rise hotels replete with their own lakes (doubling as cocktail lounges) and well-nigh stratospheric revolving restaurants from which tourists and conventioneers could simultaneously survey both Atlanta's history and its future. The underside of the Georgia capital's success story was less attractive. As blacks moved in, whites moved out, leaving the city with a two-thirds black population by 1980. Few blacks went into the high-rise hotels or other showplaces unless it was to clean them or provide services for a steady stream of conventioneers. Atlanta's ghetto was by no means the nation's worst, but as the "homicide capital" of the Deep South, the city became as well known for its broad daylight slayings as for its downtown glitter. . . .

Fast-growing Florida attracted a family of four every six minutes. Not only did this runaway growth threaten to deplete the underground water supply, it also left urban areas with major air and water pollution problems. One journalist predicted Florida was "going to die of thirst or choke to death on a glut of people, exhaust fumes, concrete and sewage."

In addition to maldistribution of income and simultaneous urban sprawl and decay, the South's leaders confronted the challenge of making the region's industrial/economic growth pay off in terms of improvements in the quality of life for all southerners. Much of the hoopla surrounding the Sunbelt phenomena had suggested that the South offered a more attractive living environment than the Industrial North. When statistical evidence was considered, however, it became apparent that the region had a long way to go before it measured up to the rest of the nation in terms of public services, equal opportunity, and overall levels of living. A major problem lay with deficiencies in institutions and services directly supported by taxation. Promises of minimal or in some cases no taxation had long been an important element in the South's appeal to new industry, but reluctance to increase taxes seemed to deny state and local governments the resources needed to cope not only with the demands created by economic growth but with the needs of those whom that growth had not touched. A 1977 analysis by the Southern Regional Education Board indicated that state and local governments in Dixie were utilizing only about 79 percent of their taxing capacity as compared to a national average of over 95 percent. The mainstay of the revenue system was the sales tax, which took a proportionately larger bite out of the incomes of the South's much greater than average share of the nation's poor. Mississippi, for example, utilized more than 160 percent of its estimated sales taxing capacity. Meanwhile, the effective business tax rate in the southern states was less than 60 percent of the nonsouthern average.

Mississippi's struggle to improve its public schools demonstrated the degree to which the traditional approach to economic progress in the South may have actually stood in the way of both human and economic progress. Mississippi's reputation as the nation's most educationally inferior state rested on the absence of even a mandatory attendance law, let alone public kindergartens. To fund a program of compulsory education with kindergartens, Governor William Winter suggested in 1981 that the legislature increase the state severance tax on oil and natural gas. Winter argued that by providing better education for its youth, Mississippi would enhance its prospects for economic growth. Not so, contended his opponents, who warned that low taxes were crucial to the state's continued economic progress, and who cited a 1980 business climate study that placed Mississippi in the number one position. When a watered-down version of Winter's program finally passed in 1982, its funding came from a modest increase in the state's income tax rate and a one-half percent increase in the already overworked sales tax, but the severance tax remained unchanged.

As the leaders of Mississippi and other southern states continued to exhibit a desperate hunger for more growth, some thoughtful writers and scholars began to question whether industrialization had been worth the cost. In the exciting first years of the Sunbelt boom many southerners had found it difficult to contain their pride in their region's economic accomplishments. Songwriter Bobby Braddock had used the traditionally uncritical medium of country music to celebrate the South's ascendance:

> I see wooded parks and big skyscrapers
> Where once stood red clay hills and cottonfields.
> I see sons and daughters of sharecroppers
> Drinking scotch and making business deals.*

By equating progress with the opportunity for young southerners to behave like Yankee capitalists, Braddock's song raised the question of whether the South had been striving all these years for nothing more than to be like the North. For some observers the growth of the 1960s and 1970s resurrected the old concerns best expressed by the Nashville Agrarians that an economic transformation would destroy the most positive aspects

---

* "I Believe the South Is Gonna Rise Again" by Bobby Braddock. © 1973 by Tree Publishing Co., Inc. International copyright secured.

of the "southern way of life." Writing in 1973 concerning the "American-ization of Dixie," John Egerton worried that "the South and the nation are not exchanging strengths as much as they are exchanging sins, more often than not, they are sharing and spreading the worst in each other, while the best languishes and withers."

Fearing that rapid growth raised the threat of a "cultural lobotomy," Marshall Frady bemoaned the fact that "for the last few decades the South has been mightily laboring to mutate itself into a tinfoil-twinkly simulation of southern California, and in the process has unwittingly worked on itself a spiritual impoverishment. Faulkner's Flem Snopes has evolved into a relentlessly bouncy and glitter-eyed neo-Babbit with an almost touching lust for new chemical plants, glassy-maized office parks and instant sub-divisions. The mischief is that, in its transfiguration into What-a-Burger drive-ins and apartment wastelands, the South is being etherized, subtly rendered pastless, memoryless and vague of identity."

The biting accuracy of Frady's descriptions and the note of concern he sounded quickly call to mind the unheeded warnings of the Agrarians, whose critique of industrialism became more meaningful in an era when the undesirable side effects of industrial growth had finally become a reality. Ironically, many of those who were once the impoverished South's sternest critics now saw in its rags-to-riches story much to lament. They appeared to have finally discovered that, just as the Agrarians had insisted, the backward South of yesteryear had possessed some redeeming qualities after all. Much of its distinctiveness had been the result of seemingly primitive attitudes and customs, but the late 1960s and 1970s had revealed these conditions as national rather than regional characteristics. For all its flaws, the South was at least a place unto itself, and all southerners, black or white, shared in a peculiar regional heritage. To paraphrase Flannery O'Connor, all southerners were at least "from somewhere." John Egerton recalled a black Chicagoan visiting relatives in Tuskegee, Alabama, who explained: "Chicago ain't where I live. It's where I stay. Chicago's *existin'*. Tuskegee is *livin'*." It was a sad paradox that the economic progress once thought necessary to solve the South's problems now threatened many of the human interactions and physical attributes that even at its most de-prived, benighted worst, had made it seem a good place to live.

Had the Agrarians been right? Was the South's birthright bartered for a mess of pottage (and thin pottage at that)? The neo-Agrarian observers of the 1970s attacked the negative results of industrialization but, like their conservative predecessors, they provided no relevant alternatives for coping with regional economic problems. Conceding that economic growth had been a mixed blessing, one southern newspaper editor quoted by Joel Garreau nonetheless reminded a visitor, "It beats the hell out of pellagra." As they lamented the urban sprawl of an Atlanta or a Houston and shud-dered as the small-town South disappeared under a tidal wave of parking lots, K-Marts, and fast food emporiums, most writers failed to realize that the people who fought over K-Mart's "blue-light specials" and wolfed down pizza and tacos viewed such opportunities as genuine examples of personal and societal progress. Imperfect as it was, the story of Dixie's industrial growth was a success story for a great many southerners, especially those who remembered the futility of tilling worn-out soil and the pain of explaining to their children why the family could not afford a decent place to live or a respectable automobile. If the factory fell far short of paradise, it nonetheless became a refuge for many southerners who felt they had no place else to go.

The South's bittersweet experience with industrialization was not atypical of a developing society. Economic gains often require cultural sacrifices, and nostalgic references to the good old days when times were bad increase in proportion to the pace of economic change. Industrialization had been so earnestly advanced as a panacea by so many scholars, politicians, and business leaders, however, that even the much ballyhooed Sunbelt South was something of a disappointment. Despite recent gains an ascendant South had yet to achieve statistical parity with a declining North, in terms of either income or the quality of public services and institutions. If an Americanized Dixie had to sacrifice some of its southern charm, should it not at least have acquired more of the positive attributes of northern industrial society? . . .

World War II set in motion a number of economic and political trends, but prior to the federal civil rights pressure of the 1960s there was little reason to conclude that the South's conservative social order was incompatible with its economic progress. By the 1970s the South was enjoying the benefits of well-publicized economic growth and extensive praise for its favorable business climate, but social and political change was hardly a regional priority. It was particularly ironic that, after decades of insistence that social and institutional progress was a prerequisite for industrial development, a 1980 business climate survey accorded Mississippi, hardly a bastion of progressivism, the distinction of having the nation's most attractive business climate. A year later, when the same survey asked respondents to consider educational factors, Mississippi, with the nation's weakest public school system, fell only to sixth place. Such surveys revealed that the political conservatism, antigovernmentalism, fiscal frugality, and hostility to organized labor so long a part of the South's overall image of backwardness were actually essential ingredients in the recipe for Sunbelt prosperity.

The tendency to equate advanced industrial capitalism with an open, democratic, progressive society stemmed from a certain degree of nationalism—pride in the fruits of the nation's economic and political development as symbolized by the Industrial North. This point of view assumed a relationship between a society's means of production and its social and political institutions, a mutually dependent relationship requiring that changes in one be accompanied by proportionate changes in the other. Theoretically, as the South moved toward economic parity with the rest of the nation, its social and political structure and the nature and quality of its institutions would keep pace. If, as Woodrow Wilson and several decades of his disciples insisted, capitalism could be counted on to spread political and social progress abroad, could any less be expected of it within the borders of the United States?

Such reasoning rested on an historical misinterpretation of the goals and actions of American corporate leaders. For example, the social and political upheaval accompanying the late nineteenth-century economic revolution in the United States had been anything but comforting to many businessmen, industrialists, and professionals, some of whom took steps to nip rambunctious pluralism in the bud, especially where labor unions and lower-class political activism were concerned. The response of corporate America to the Populist movement was particularly telling on this point. Wall Street grew apoplectic at the prospect of democratized policymaking, more equitable taxation, and greater government regulation aimed at maintaining economic competition. Only after the Populists had been crushed did economic leaders embrace the stabilizing reforms of the Progressive era, which, despite their humanitarian contributions, also included a number of measures that further insulated the electoral and governmental process from pressures from below. . . .

Many of the characteristics viewed by scholars as positive attributes of the Industrial North—worker activism, competition for labor, extensive social welfare programs, and significant government regulation—had been tolerable to the region's economic leaders largely because as a "core" area it was growing rapidly enough to provide consistently expanding profits, salaries, and wages and still meet the fiscal demands of government in a support and service society. Ironically, this society was financed to some extent by an advantageous relationship with the South, a peripheral area forced to share its economic pie with investors and financiers in the northern core. As operating efficiency decreased and overall costs mounted, locational and business climate surveys made it clear that many of the conditions that had made northern industrial society seem enlightened and progressive had actually contributed to decisions by corporate executives to forego future investments and expansions in the North. Why was it reasonable to expect that, as they transferred their operations to the South, industrial investors would insist on transplanting the social, political, and governmental conditions that had caused them to shun the North? On the contrary, the ability to avoid these conditions, to practice the "unfettered capitalism" alluded to by Harold Woodman, was a major attraction as far as many southern industrialists were concerned.

Industrialists who spurned such "fetters" as government regulation and labor activism also showed little inclination to acknowledge the responsibility for creating new jobs in areas where unemployment was high and skill levels low. Industrialization seemed to promise a chance for southern blacks to overcome the legacy of discrimination and repression that kept them at the bottom of the economic ladder, but many southbound firms deliberately avoided locations with large concentrations of blacks. In Atlanta, for example, many companies that made use of bustling Hartsfield International Airport shunned the blacker, south side of the city despite its proximity to the airport. Several industrial recruiters told a *New York*

Times reporter that some executives refused to consider locations in counties where blacks made up more than 30 percent of the population. A spokesman for Amoco Fabrics explained that his company's preference for areas with relatively few blacks reflected a simple desire for efficient, uncomplicated operation: "The lower the concentration of minorities, the better we're able to perform and get a plant started up." . . .

If the typical industrialist failed to become a major force for change in the South, what of the rest of Dixie's rapidly expanding bourgeoisie? By 1980 the South's white-collar class was growing at the rate of three to four hundred thousand a year and made up approximately 25 percent of the region's population. More affluent, better educated, less overtly racist, the new middle class had played an important role in moderating the region's social and political climate. Nonetheless, the impact of middle-class expansion on the South was hardly as explosive as had been predicted. The failure of the new middle class to revolutionize the region's sociocultural and political environment can be better understood by exploring the reasons why such a revolution was predicted in the first place. Although Leonard Reissman exaggerated the historic desire of the middle class for social and political change, particularly sweeping change, Reissman did acknowledge that a major motivation for the bourgeoisie to champion modification of the existing order was the need to win "added support from those at the bottom of the social hierarchy." According to Reissman, as in developing nations where the bourgeoisie often tried to ameliorate the conditions of the potentially restive peasants, the southern middle class might be expected to champion change in the interest of creating "as stable a social order as possible and as quickly as possible."

Although by the 1980s some political scientists saw signs of a working class coalition that promised to make southern politics more responsive to the needs of lower income voters of both races, the failure of such a coalition to emerge during the first decade and a half of two-party politics illustrated the continuing absence of pressure from below that had characterized the post-Reconstruction South. Disfranchisement, manipulation of lower-class white racial anxieties, and vigorous repression of labor activism left the South without an organized "under class" capable of forcing the creation of a more open, competitive society with services and institutions more attuned to its needs.

Liberal observers, both North and South, were continually frustrated by the reluctance of white southerners to behave in self-interested, class-conscious, "northern" fashion by joining in a color-blind labor coalition to press for better wages in the work place and more influence in the political arena. In fact, the characteristically slow pace of southern industrial growth and the traditional adherence of most industrialists to the caste system had made the dedication of white workers to the status quo eminently rational in the short run. Where, after all, was the incentive to jeopardize the creation of jobs in a labor-surplus economy or to increase the competition for these jobs by uniting with blacks or championing racial equality? The more rapid growth of the post–World War II period mitigated these anti-populist circumstances, but nearly a century of manipulated antagonism and disadvantageous labor market conditions could not be expected to disappear overnight.

Union leaders argued that decades of deprivation should be all the more reason for southern workers to engage in the collective militance needed to bring them abreast of their northern counterparts, but most southern laborers avoided this course. If anything, their acquaintance with low wages and undesirable working conditions had left them all the more grateful for their jobs, even though these jobs paid less than jobs in similar plants elsewhere. Even in the Sunbelt era southern workers continued to respond to the neopaternalism of antiunion employers such as Nissan Motors. Although one United Auto Workers leader told *Newsweek* that Nissan's desire to hire "hard working country people" really amounted to an attempt to employ "peasants," the company's guarantees of lifetime employment, its efforts to involve employees in management decisions, and its recreational and fitness programs drew 100,000 applications for 2,600 jobs at its Smyrna, Tennessee, plant. Union officials were perplexed at the attitude of one Nissan worker who insisted: "If the company treats the workers well . . . there's nothing a union can offer." Such assertions were particularly confounding in light of the fact that this worker could have earned a starting wage that was $2.50 per hour higher if he had been employed in a unionized automobile plant in the North.

In the absence of a lower-class challenge, the South's middle class was able to confine its agenda for change to those items most in line with its members' economic interests and personal concerns. Still, should not their values alone have impelled them to demand improvements in services, facilities, and institutions sufficient to bring them in line with those elsewhere in the nation? For years social scientists had insisted that members of the upper and middle classes were "future oriented" and thus always stood ready to sponsor whatever changes were necessary to insure continuing improvement in the overall quality of life in their cities and communities. At the end of the 1970s, with nearly one-fourth of the region's business leaders northern born, the progressive northern influence that had been seen as so crucial to the South's transformation should certainly have been felt. Yet, while services, facilities, and institutions appeared to be making significant progress, statistical quality-of-life surveys still put the South far behind the rest of the nation. How could so many well-educated, affluent, northern-born migrants choose to live in a region where poverty was still such a problem and public services and cultural and entertainment possibilities so limited? The resounding endorsements that these new southerners gave their states challenged the assumption that all enlightened Americans shared a set of values and preferences typically associated with the lifestyles of the northern urban bourgeoisie.

Southerners who remembered the incessant South-baiting of H. L. Mencken had the last laugh when the results of Merle Black's thirteen-state analysis of resident preferences were shown to correlate at $-.76$ with the index of "civilization" that Mencken had constructed in 1931 to damn

Mississippi as "the worst American state" and anoint Massachusetts as the best. Ironically, Massachusetts residents showed the least satisfaction with their state of any of the thirteen groups analyzed by Black in 1975.

John Shelton Reed offered the following explanation of the results of the survey: "The kind of economics and politics that can make a state healthy, wealthy and wise—civilized as Mencken would have it—can have at least short-run effects that people experience as debits in the quality of life ledger. For example, New York spends twice as much per pupil on education as North Carolina. Score one for the quality of life in New York when those pupils finish school. But North Carolina's taxes are about half of New York's, per capita. Score—how much?—for the quality of life in North Carolina right now."

Reed explained the reluctance of both native and transplanted members of the southern middle class to tamper with the status quo by arguing that "a given individual can quite rationally be unwilling to trade a clear and present good thing for a distant and hypothetical benefit." While it made sense to want to live in New York, it was not necessarily less sensible to want to live in North Carolina, or perhaps even Mississippi, without trying to transform them into New York. In the final analysis, many influential southerners had flown in the face of traditional scholarly wisdom by rejecting the short-term sacrifices necessary to achieve worthy but costly long-term societal goals.

Despite its deficiencies, statistical and otherwise, many intelligent, experienced Americans still managed to find much that was commendable about life in Dixie. If industrialization failed to cure all of the South's ills, it also failed to destroy many of its most appealing qualities. The Industrial North's long-playing role as the "state of the art" industrial society had left most social scientists, journalists, and liberal crusaders convinced that enlightened northerners, if forced to live in the South, would insist on remaking their new home in the image of their old one. Moreover, upwardly mobile native southerners were certain to cooperate by cosponsoring changes designed to revamp their region. The insistence of professional South-watchers that a more prosperous South must become a drawling version of the North resulted from a projection of their own values and prejudices on a population of executives, professionals, and workers who apparently saw life somewhat differently.

The failure of industrialization to induce greater social and political upheaval in the South may have been no more significant than the expectation that it would. This expectation reflected the extent to which the remarkable (and historically misunderstood) experience of the Industrial North had, in the minds of many Americans, become synonymous with the development of industrial capitalism regardless of the economic, cultural, or political context in which that development might occur. As American policymakers continue to intervene in the affairs of "developing" nations they would do well to study the example of the Industrial South, an example which raises some serious questions about their unfaltering conviction that economic modernization can guarantee sweeping human and institutional progress within any society.

The briefest glance at the South of 1984 with its skyscrapers, factories, and superhighways reveals that industrial development has brought significant changes to the region. Yet a closer analysis of contemporary conditions also shows that, for all its apparent impact, industrialization has not obliterated the socioeconomic and structural differences that have traditionally represented the fundamental basis of southern distinctiveness. Instead of witnessing a head-on collision between economic progress and deep-seated traditionalism, the post-Reconstruction South saw these two seemingly incompatible phenomena demonstrate a remarkable adaptability to each other. Welcomed by some and feared by others, industrialization actually served both as an agent of change and as a buttress for the status quo.

A new and truly complete perspective on the impact of industrialization on the South requires less emphasis on the region's resistance to change and more attention to the process of mutual adaptation between the influences of industrial expansion and the social, political, and cultural characteristics often associated with economic underdevelopment in Dixie. Expectations that the South's experience with industrialization would duplicate the North's ignored not only these characteristics but the structural differences between their respective economies at the time when industrialization began to accelerate in each. The historical circumstances that shaped the destiny of the agrarian South also played a major role in forging the character of an industrial South. Like the gloomy, defeated Dixie of 1877, the optimistic, skyscraper-studded Sunbelt South of the 1980s still reflected the influences of a complex heritage, a heritage whose best elements had recently become as difficult to preserve as its worst had been to overcome.

⚓ *F U R T H E R   R E A D I N G*

Carl Abbott, *The New Urban America: Growth and Politics in Sunbelt Cities* (1977)
Raymond Arsenault, "The End of the Long Hot Summer: The Air Conditioner and Southern Culture," *Journal of Southern History* 50 (1984), 597–628
Nelson M. Blake, *Land into Water—Water into Land: A History of Water Management in Florida* (1980)
Robert Emil Botsch, *We Shall Not Overcome: Populism and Southern Blue-Collar Workers* (1980)
Blaine A. Brownell, *The Urban Ethos in the South, 1920–1930* (1975)
Harry M. Caudill, *Theirs Be the Power: The Moguls of Eastern Kentucky* (1983)
James C. Cobb, *The Selling of the South: The Southern Crusade for Industrial Development, 1936–1980* (1982)
Albert E. Cowdrey, *This Land, This South: An Environmental History* (1983)
Don H. Doyle, *Nashville Since the 1920s* (1985)
Ronald D. Eller, *Miners, Millhands, and Mountaineers: Industrialization of the Appalachian South* (1982)
J. Wayne Flynt, *Dixie's Forgotten People: The South's Poor Whites* (1979)

David R. Goldfield, *Cotton Fields and Skyscrapers: Southern City and Region, 1607–1980* (1982)

Robert G. Healy, *Competition for Land in the American South: Agriculture, Human Settlement, and the Environment* (1985)

E. Blaine Liner and Lawrence K. Lynch, eds., *The Economics of Southern Growth* (1977)

Roger W. Lotchin, ed., *The Martial Metropolis: U.S. Cities in War and Peace* (1984)

Michael J. McDonald and William Bruce Wheeler, *Knoxville, Tennessee: Continuity and Change in an Appalachian City* (1983)

Randall M. Miller and George E. Pozzetta, eds., *Shades of the Sunbelt: Essays on Ethnicity, Race, and the Urban South* (1988)

Raymond A. Mohl, ed., *Searching for the Sunbelt* (1989)

Thomas H. Naylor and James Clotfelter, *Strategies for Change in the South* (1975)

William H. Nicholls, *Southern Tradition and Regional Progress* (1960)

David C. Perry and Alfred J. Watkins, eds., *The Rise of the Sunbelt Cities* (1977)

Joe Persky, "The South: A Colony at Home," *Southern Exposure* 1 (1973), 14–22

Christopher Silver, *Twentieth-Century Richmond: Planning, Politics, and Race* (1982)

George B. Tindall, "The Sunbelt Snow Job," *Houston Review* 1 (1979), 3–13

Rupert B. Vance and Nicholas J. Demerath, eds., *The Urban South* (1954)

Bernard L. Weinstein and Robert E. Firestine, *Regional Growth and Decline in the United States: The Rise of the Sunbelt and the Decline of the Northeast* (1978)

David E. Whisnant, *Modernizing the Mountaineer: People, Power, and Planning in Appalachia* (1980)

CHAPTER
13

The Civil-Rights Movement

The civil-rights movement ranks with the Civil War and World War II as a major event in southern history. Although white supremacy emerged from World War II virtually intact, blacks in southern cities quickly began to shape their destinies. The federal government also took halting steps toward addressing the more serious issues of racial inequality. Southern white resistance mounted, especially after the Supreme Court's Brown *decision in 1954. Blacks also pressed to desegregate schools and to end segregation in public accommodations through boycotts, sit-ins, and marches. Segregation fell officially with the passage of the 1964 Civil Rights Act. After a series of bloody demonstrations in Mississippi and Alabama, Congress in 1965 finally enacted the Voting Rights Act.*

The civil-rights movement was in great part a religious crusade emanating from black evangelical theology and epitomized by Martin Luther King, Jr., and the Southern Christian Leadership Conference (SCLC). The movement's grounding in regional culture accounts for its success in achieving voting rights and equal access to public accommodations. Southerners, black and white, understood each other, even if many whites did not like the words.

Historians are still sorting out the actors and events and their relative significance to the civil-rights movement. What role did the federal government play? What were the nature, source, and meaning of white resistance and black protest? What was the relationship between local protests and regional or national civil-rights organizations? Until the early 1980s, most writers concentrated on national figures and the major venues of the movement. More recent work on less publicized localities has demonstrated the rich texture of black protest, its lingering legacy (not only for blacks but for women), the various factions within the black community, and the diversity of white reactions.

✢ D O C U M E N T S

Since the 1930s, the U.S. Supreme Court had been eroding the *Plessy* v. *Ferguson* (1896) ruling that permitted separate but equal facilities in the South. In May 1954, the Court decisively overturned that precedent in *Brown* v. *Board of Education of Topeka*, declaring that segregation was itself inherently unequal. A portion of Chief Justice Earl Warren's opinion appears in the first document. The decision and subsequent protests by southern blacks provoked strong reaction in the South, fueled in part by opportunistic politicians. As white supremacy increasingly became the litmus test for officeholding and as the courts continued to rule in favor of black plaintiffs, a period of massive resistance emerged in the South. The second document, popularly known as the Southern Manifesto, marked an important stage in this resistance. Signed by almost all southern senators and congressmen, it aimed to demonstrate southern solidarity and thereby forestall Federal efforts to implement the *Brown* decision. Music was an integral part of the civil-rights movement, not surprising considering the religious backgrounds of its leaders and participants. The two songs in the third selection, one related to the sit-in demonstrations and the other to the 1961 Freedom Rides, reflect that religious base. The fourth document, written by the South's most prominent civil-rights leader, Martin Luther King, Jr., represents a clear statement of principles. The letter, which King composed in the margins of a newspaper with a stubby pencil while he was in jail for violating a court injunction during the Birmingham demonstrations of 1963, reflects well the religious and moral bases of the movement. The next excerpt by Mary King, a participant in the voting rights drive in Mississippi during the Freedom Summer of 1964, illustrates the sometimes difficult racial, gender, and class relations that characterized not only the Freedom Summer but other integrated protests as well. The memoir also shows the relationship between civil rights for blacks and the women's rights movement. The excerpt from the 1964 Civil Rights Act in the sixth selection details the heart of the act: the public accommodations provisions, as well as the Equal Employment Opportunity sections, which have continued to play a significant and sometimes controversial role. The bloody protest at Selma on March 7, 1965 led directly to the prompt passage of the other major piece of civil-rights legislation from this period, the Voting Rights Act. Roy Reed's eyewitness account of the attempted march from Selma to Montgomery, the last document, outraged a nation and provided President Lyndon Johnson with an additional argument to prod Congress to pass the measure.

Brown v. *Board of Education of Topeka, Kansas,* 1954

Mr. Chief Justice Warren delivered the opinion of the Court. . . .

Today, education is perhaps the most important function of state and local governments. Compulsory school attendance laws and the great expenditures for education both demonstrate our recognition of the importance of education to our democratic society. It is required in the performance of our most basic public responsibilities, even service in the armed forces. It is the very foundation of good citizenship. Today it is a principal instrument in awakening the child to cultural values, in preparing him for later professional training, and in helping him to adjust normally to his environment. In these days, it is doubtful that any child may reasonably be expected to succeed in life if he is denied the opportunity of an education. Such an opportunity, where the state has undertaken to provide it, is a right which must be made available to all on equal terms.

We come then to the question presented: Does segregation of children in public schools solely on the basis of race, even though the physical facilities and other "tangible" factors may be equal, deprive the children of the minority group of equal educational opportunities? We believe that it does.

In Sweatt v. Painter . . . , in finding that a segregated law school for Negroes could not provide them equal educational opportunities, this Court relied in large part on "those qualities which are incapable of objective measurement but which make for greatness in a law school." In McLaurin v. Oklahoma State Regents, . . . the Court, in requiring that a Negro admitted to a white graduate school be treated like all other students, again resorted to intangible considerations: ". . . his ability to study, to engage in discussions and exchange views with other students, and, in general, to learn his profession." Such considerations apply with added force to children in grade and high schools. To separate them from others of similar age and qualifications solely because of their race generates a feeling of inferiority as to their status in the community that may affect their hearts and minds in a way unlikely ever to be undone. The effect of this separation on their educational opportunities was well stated by a finding in the Kansas case by a court which nevertheless felt compelled to rule against the Negro plaintiffs:

> Segregation of white and colored children in public schools has a detrimental effect upon the colored children. The impact is greater when it has the sanction of the law; for the policy of separating the races is usually interpreted as denoting the inferiority of the negro group. A sense of inferiority affects the motivation of a child to learn. Segregation with the sanction of law, therefore, has a tendency to [retard] the educational and mental development of Negro children and to deprive them of some of the benefits they would receive in a racial[ly] integrated school system.

Whatever may have been the extent of psychological knowledge at the time of Plessy v. Ferguson, this finding is amply supported by modern authority. Any language in Plessy v. Ferguson contrary to this finding is rejected.

We conclude that in the field of public education the doctrine of "separate but equal" has no place. Separate educational facilities are inherently unequal. Therefore, we hold that the plaintiffs and others similarly situated for whom the actions have been brought are, by reason of the segregation complained of, deprived of the equal protection of the laws guaranteed by the Fourteenth Amendment.

The Southern Manifesto, 1956

The unwarranted decision of the Supreme Court in the public school cases is now bearing the fruit always produced when men substitute naked power for established law.

The Founding Fathers gave us a Constitution of checks and balances because they realized the inescapable lesson of history that no man or group of men can be safely entrusted with unlimited power. They framed this Constitution with its provisions for change by amendment in order to secure the fundamentals of government against the dangers of temporary popular passion or the personal predilections of public officeholders.

We regard the decision of the Supreme Court in the school cases as a clear abuse of judicial power. It climaxes a trend in the Federal Judiciary undertaking to legislate, in derogation of the authority of Congress, and to encroach upon the reserved rights of the States and the people.

The original Constitution does not mention education. Neither does the 14th amendment nor any other amendment. The debates preceding the submission of the 14th amendment clearly show that there was no intent that it should affect the system of education maintained by the States.

The very Congress which proposed the amendment subsequently provided for segregated schools in the District of Columbia.

When the amendment was adopted in 1868, there were 37 States of the Union. Every one of the 26 States that had any substantial racial differences among its people, either approved the operation of segregated schools already in existence or subsequently established such schools by action of the same law-making body which considered the 14th amendment.

As admitted by the Supreme Court in the public school case (*Brown* v. *Board of Education*), the doctrine of separate but equal schools "apparently originated in *Roberts* v. *City of Boston* (1849), upholding school segregation against attack as being violative of a State constitutional guarantee of equality." This constitutional doctrine began in the North, not in the South, and it was followed not only in Massachusetts, but in Connecticut, New York, Illinois, Indiana, Michigan, Minnesota, New Jersey, Ohio, Pennsylvania and other northern States until they, exercising their rights as States through the constitutional processes of local self-government, changed their school systems.

In the case of *Plessy* v. *Ferguson* in 1896 the Supreme Court expressly declared that under the 14th amendment no person was denied any of his rights if the States provided separate but equal public facilities. This decision has been followed in many other cases. It is notable that the Supreme Court, speaking through Chief Justice Taft, a former President of the United States, unanimously declared in 1927 in *Lum* v. *Rice* that the "separate but equal" principle is "within the discretion of the State in regulating its public schools and does not conflict with the 14th amendment."

This interpretation, restated time and again, became a part of the life of the people of many of the States and confirmed their habits, customs, traditions, and way of life. It is founded on elemental humanity and common-sense, for parents should not be deprived by Government of the right to direct the lives and education of their own children.

Though there has been no constitutional amendment or act of Congress changing this established legal principle almost a century old, the Supreme Court of the United States, with no legal basis for such action, undertook to exercise their naked judicial power and substituted their personal political and social ideas for the established law of the land.

This unwarranted exercise of power by the Court, contrary to the Constitution, is creating chaos and confusion in the States principally affected. It is destroying the amicable relations between the white and Negro races that have been created through 90 years of patient effort by the good people of both races. It has planted hatred and suspicion where there has been heretofore friendship and understanding.

Without regard to the consent of the governed, outside agitators are threatening immediate and revolutionary changes in our public-school systems. If done, this is certain to destroy the system of public education in some of the States.

With the gravest concern for the explosive and dangerous condition created by this decision and inflamed by outside meddlers:

We reaffirm our reliance on the Constitution as the fundamental law of the land.

We decry the Supreme Court's encroachments on rights reserved to the States and to the people, contrary to established law, and to the Constitution.

We commend the motives of those States which have declared the intention to resist forced integration by any lawful means.

We appeal to the States and people who are not directly affected by these decisions to consider the constitutional principles involved against the time when they too, on issues vital to them, may be the victims of judicial encroachment.

Even though we constitute a minority in the present Congress, we have full faith that a majority of the American people believe in the dual system of government which has enabled us to achieve our greatness and will in time demand that the reserved rights of the States and of the people be made secure against judicial usurpation.

We pledge ourselves to use all lawful means to bring about a reversal of this decision which is contrary to the Constitution and to prevent the use of force in its implementation.

In this trying period, as we all seek to right this wrong, we appeal to our people not to be provoked by the agitators and troublemakers invading our States and to scrupulously refrain from disorder and lawless acts.

Two Civil-Rights Songs

"I'm Gonna Sit at the Welcome Table One of These Days," 1960

I'm gonna sit at the welcome table,
I'm gonna sit at the welcome table
one of these days, hallelujah,
I'm gonna sit at the welcome table,
I'm gonna sit at the welcome table
one of these days.

I'm gonna walk the streets of glory,
I'm gonna walk the streets of glory
   one of these days, hallelujah,
I'm gonna walk the streets of glory,
I'm gonna walk the streets of glory
   one of these days.

I'm gonna tell God how you treat me . . .

I'm gonna sit at Woolworth's lunch
   counter . . .

I'm gonna get my civil rights . . .

I'm gonna walk this ole picket line . . .

"Hallelujah I'm A-Travelin'," 1961

Stand up and rejoice, a great day is here
We're riding for freedom and the victory is near.
Chorus
Hallelujah I'm a travelin', hallelujah ain't it fine,
Hallelujah I'm a travelin' down freedom's main line.

In 1954 our Supreme Court said, "Look a here
   Mr. Jim Crow,
It's time you were dead."

I'm paying my fare on the Greyhound Bus line
I'm riding the front seat to Montgomery this time.

In Nashville, Tennessee, I can order a coke
And the waitress at Woolworth's knows it's no joke.

I'm travelin' to Mississippi on the Greyhound Bus line
Hallelujah I'm ridin' the front seat this time.

Martin Luther King, Jr.'s Letter from Birmingham Jail, 1963

My dear Fellow Clergymen,

   While confined here in the Birmingham city jail, I came across your recent statement calling our present activities "unwise and untimely." Seldom, if ever, do I pause to answer criticism of my work and ideas. If I sought to answer all of the criticisms that cross my desk, my secretaries would be engaged in little else in the course of the day, and I would have no time for constructive work. But since I feel that you are men of genuine good will and your criticisms are sincerely set forth, I would like to answer your statement in what I hope will be patient and reasonable terms.

   I think I should give the reason for my being in Birmingham, since you have been influenced by the argument of "outsiders coming in." I have the honor of serving as president of the Southern Christian Leadership Conference, an organization operating in every southern state, with headquarters in Atlanta, Georgia. We have some eighty-five affiliate organizations all across the South—one being the Alabama Christian Movement for Human Rights. Whenever necessary and possible we share staff, educational and financial resources with our affiliates. Several months ago our local affiliate here in Birmingham invited us to be on call to engage in a nonviolent direct-action program if such were deemed necessary. We readily consented and when the hour came we lived up to our promises. So I am here, along with several members of my staff, because we were invited here. I am here because I have basic organizational ties here.

Beyond this, I am in Birmingham because injustice is here. Just as the eighth century prophets left their little villages and carried their "thus saith the Lord" far beyond the boundaries of their hometowns; and just as the Apostle Paul left his little village of Tarsus and carried the gospel of Jesus Christ to practically every hamlet and city of the Graeco-Roman world, I too am compelled to carry the gospel of freedom beyond my particular hometown. Like Paul, I must constantly respond to the Macedonian call for aid.

Moreover, I am cognizant of the interrelatedness of all communities and states. I cannot sit idly by in Atlanta and not be concerned about what happens in Birmingham. Injustice anywhere is a threat to justice everywhere. We are caught in an inescapable network of mutuality, tied in a single garment of destiny. Whatever affects one directly affects all indirectly. Never again can we afford to live with the narrow, provincial "outside agitator" idea. Anyone who lives in the United States can never be considered an outsider anywhere in this country.

You deplore the demonstrations that are presently taking place in Birmingham. But I am sorry that your statement did not express a similar concern for the conditions that brought the demonstrations into being. I am sure that each of you would want to go beyond the superficial social analyst who looks merely at effects, and does not grapple with underlying causes. I would not hesitate to say that it is unfortunate that so-called demonstrations are taking place in Birmingham at this time, but I would say in more emphatic terms that it is even more unfortunate that the white power structure of this city left the Negro community with no other alternative.

In any nonviolent campaign there are four basic steps: (1) collection of the facts to determine whether injustices are alive, (2) negotiation, (3), self-purification, and (4) direct action. We have gone through all of these steps in Birmingham. There can be no gainsaying of the fact that racial injustice engulfs this community.

Birmingham is probably the most thoroughly segregated city in the United States. Its ugly record of police brutality is known in every section of this country. Its injust treatment of Negroes in the courts is a notorious reality. There have been more unsolved bombings of Negro homes and churches in Birmingham than any city in this nation. These are the hard, brutal and unbelievable facts. On the basis of these conditions Negro leaders sought to negotiate with the city fathers. But the political leaders consistently refused to engage in good faith negotiation.

Then came the opportunity last September to talk with some of the leaders of the economic community. In these negotiating sessions certain promises were made by the merchants—such as the promise to remove the humiliating racial signs from the stores. On the basis of these promises Rev. [Fred] Shuttlesworth and the leaders of the Alabama Christian Movement for Human Rights agreed to call a moratorium on any type of demonstrations. As the weeks and months unfolded we realized that we were the victims of a broken promise. The signs remained. Like so many experiences of the past we were confronted with blasted hopes, and the dark shadow of a deep disappointment settled upon us. So we had no alternative except that of preparing for direct action, whereby we would present our very bodies as a means of laying our case before the conscience of the local and national community. We were not unmindful of the difficulties involved. So we decided to go through a process of self-purification. We started having workshops on nonviolence and repeatedly asked ourselves the questions, "Are you able to accept blows without retaliating?" "Are you able to endure the ordeals of jail?" We decided to set our direct-action program around the Easter season, realizing that with the exception of Christmas, this was the largest shopping period of the year. Knowing that a strong economic withdrawal program would be the by-product of direct action, we felt that this was the best time to bring pressure on the merchants for the needed changes. Then it occurred to us that the March election was ahead and so we speedily decided to postpone action until after election day. When we discovered that Mr. [Eugene "Bull"] Connor [Birmingham's Public Safety Commissioner] was in the run-off, we decided again to postpone action so that the demonstrations could not be used to cloud the issues. At this time we agreed to begin our nonviolent witness the day after the run-off.

This reveals that we did not move irresponsibly into direct action. We too wanted to see Mr. Connor defeated; so we went through postponement after postponement to aid in this community need. After this we felt that direct action could be delayed no longer.

You may well ask, "Why direct action? Why sit-ins, marches, etc.? Isn't negotiation a better path?" You are exactly right in your call for negotiation. Indeed, this is the purpose of direct action. Nonviolent direct action seeks to create such a crisis and establish such creative tension that a community that has constantly refused to negotiate is forced to confront the issue. It seeks so to dramatize the issue that it can no longer be ignored. I just referred to the creation of tension as a part of the work of the nonviolent resister. This may sound rather shocking. But I must confess that I am not afraid of the word tension. I have earnestly worked and preached against violent tension, but there is a type of constructive nonviolent tension that is necessary for growth. Just as Socrates felt that it was necessary to create a tension in the mind so that individuals could rise from the bondage of myths and half-truths to the unfettered realm of creative analysis and objective appraisal, we must see the need of having nonviolent gadflies to create the kind of tension in society that will help men to rise from the dark depths of prejudice and racism to the majestic heights of understanding and brotherhood. So the purpose of the direct action is to create a situation so crisis-packed that it will inevitably open the door to negotiation. We, therefore, concur with you in your call for negotiation. Too long has our beloved Southland been bogged down in the tragic attempt to live in monologue rather than dialogue.

One of the basic points in your statement is that our acts are untimely. Some have asked, "Why didn't you give the new administration time to act?" The only answer that I can give to this inquiry is that the new administration must be prodded about as much as the outgoing one before it acts. We will be sadly mistaken if we feel that the election of Mr. Boutwell will bring the millennium to Birmingham. While Mr. Boutwell is much more articulate and gentle than Mr. Connor, they are both segregationists, dedicated to the task of maintaining the status quo. The hope I see in Mr. Boutwell is that he will be reasonable enough to see the futility of massive resistance to desegregation. But he will not see this without pressure from the devotees of civil rights. My friends, I must say to you that we have not made a single gain in civil rights without determined legal and nonviolent pressure. History is the long and tragic story of the fact that privileged groups seldom give up their privileges voluntarily. Individuals may see the moral light and voluntarily give up their unjust posture; but as Reinhold Niebuhr has reminded us, groups are more immoral than individuals.

We know through painful experience that freedom is never voluntarily given by the oppressor; it must be demanded by the oppressed. Frankly, I have never yet engaged in a direct action movement that was "well-timed," according to the timetable of those who have not suffered unduly from the disease of segregation. For years now I have heard the words "Wait!" It rings in the ear of every Negro with a piercing familiarity. This "Wait" has almost always meant "Never." It has been a tranquilizing thalidomide [a drug that caused birth defects], relieving the emotional stress for a moment, only to give birth to an ill-formed infant of frustration. We must come to see with the distinguished jurist of yesterday that "justice too long delayed is justice denied." We have waited for more than 340 years for our constitutional and God-given rights. The nations of Asia and Africa are moving with jetlike speed toward the goal of political independence, and we still creep at horse and buggy pace toward the gaining of a cup of coffee at a lunch counter. I guess it is easy for those who have never felt the stinging darts of segregation to say, "Wait." But when you have seen vicious mobs lynch your mothers and fathers at will and drown your sisters and brothers at whim; when you have seen hate-filled policemen curse, kick, brutalize and even kill your black brothers and sisters with impunity; when you see the vast majority of your twenty million Negro brothers smothering in an airtight cage of poverty in the midst of an affluent society; when you suddenly find your tongue twisted and your speech stammering as you seek to explain to your six-year-old daughter why she can't go to the public amusement park that has just been advertised on television, and see tears welling up in her little eyes when she is told that Funtown is closed to colored children, and see the depressing clouds of inferiority begin to form in her little mental sky, and see her begin to distort her little personality by unconsciously developing a bitterness toward white people; when you have to concoct an answer for a five-year-old son asking in agonizing pathos: "Daddy, why do white people treat colored people so mean?"; when you take a cross-country drive and find it necessary to sleep night after night in the uncomfortable corners of your automobile because no motel will accept you; when you are humiliated day in and day out by nagging signs reading "white" and "colored"; when your first name becomes "nigger" and your middle name becomes "boy" (however old you are) and your last name becomes "John," and when your wife and mother are never given the respected title "Mrs."; when you are harried by day and haunted by night by the fact that you are a Negro, living constantly at tiptoe stance never quite knowing what to expect next, and plagued with inner fears and outer resentments; when you are forever fighting a degenerating sense of "nobodiness"; then you will understand why we find it difficult to wait. There comes a time when the cup of endurance runs over, and men are no longer willing to be plunged into an abyss of injustice where they experience the blackness of corroding despair. I hope, sirs, you can understand our legitimate and unavoidable impatience.

You express a great deal of anxiety over our willingness to break laws. This is certainly a legitimate concern. Since we so diligently urge people to obey the Supreme Court's decision of 1954 outlawing segregation in the public schools, it is rather strange and paradoxical to find us consciously breaking laws. One may well ask, "How can you advocate breaking some laws and obeying others?" The answer is found in the fact that there are two types of laws: there are *just* and there are *unjust* laws. I would agree with Saint Augustine that "An unjust law is no law at all."

Now what is the difference between the two? How does one determine when a law is just or unjust? A just law is a man-made code that squares with the moral law or the law of God. An unjust law is a code that is out of harmony with the moral law. To put it in the terms of Saint Thomas Aquinas, an unjust law is a human law that is not rooted in eternal and natural law. Any law that uplifts human personality is just. Any law that degrades human personality is unjust. All segregation statutes are unjust because segregation distorts the soul and damages the personality. It gives the segregator a false sense of superiority, and the segregated a false sense of inferiority. To use the words of Martin Buber, the great Jewish philosopher, segregation substitutes an "I-it" relationship for the "I-thou" relationship, and ends up relegating persons to the status of things. So segregation is not only politically, economically and sociologically unsound, but it is morally wrong and sinful. Paul Tillich has said that sin is separation. Isn't segregation an existential expression of man's tragic separation, an expression of his awful estrangement, his terrible sinfulness? So I can urge men to disobey segregation ordinances because they are morally wrong.

Let us turn to a more concrete example of just and unjust laws. An unjust law is a code that a majority inflicts on a minority that is not binding on itself. This is difference made legal. On the other hand a just law is a code that a majority compels a minority to follow that it is willing to follow itself. This is sameness made legal.

Let me give another explanation. An unjust law is a code inflicted upon a minority which that minority had no part in enacting or creating because they did not have the unhampered right to vote. Who can say that the legislature of Alabama which set up the segregation laws was democratically elected? Throughout the state of Alabama all types of conniving methods are used to prevent Negroes from becoming registered voters and there are some counties without a single Negro registered to vote despite the fact that the Negro constitutes a majority of the population. Can any law set up in such a state be considered democratically structured?

These are just a few examples of unjust and just laws. There are some instances when a law is just on its face and unjust in its application. For instance, I was arrested Friday on a charge of parading without a permit. Now there is nothing wrong with an ordinance which requires a permit for a parade, but when the ordinance is used to preserve segregation and to deny citizens the First Amendment privilege of peaceful assembly and peaceful protest, then it becomes unjust.

I hope you can see the distinction I am trying to point out. In no sense do I advocate evading or defying the law as the rabid segregationist would do. This would lead to anarchy. One who breaks an unjust law must do it *openly, lovingly* (not hatefully as the white mothers did in New Orleans when they were seen on television screaming, "nigger, nigger, nigger"), and with a willingness to accept the penalty. I submit that an individual who breaks a law that conscience tells him is unjust, and willingly accepts the penalty by staying in jail to arouse the conscience of the community over its injustice, is in reality expressing the very highest respect for law.

Of course, there is nothing new about this kind of civil disobedience. It was seen sublimely in the refusal of Shadrach, Meshach and Abednego to obey the laws of Nebuchadnezzar because a higher moral law was involved. It was practiced superbly by the early Christians who were willing to face hungry lions and the excruciating pain of chopping blocks, before submitting to certain unjust laws of the Roman Empire. To a degree academic freedom is a reality today because Socrates practiced civil disobedience.

We can never forget that everything Hitler did in Germany was "legal" and everything the Hungarian freedom fighters did in Hungary was "illegal." It was "illegal" to aid and comfort a Jew in Hitler's Germany. But I am sure that if I had lived in Germany during that time I would have aided and comforted my Jewish brothers even though it was illegal. If I lived in a Communist country today where certain principles dear to the Christian faith are suppressed, I believe I would openly advocate disobeying these anti-religious laws. I must make two honest confessions to you, my Christian and Jewish brothers. First, I must confess that over the last few years I have been gravely disappointed with the white moderate. I have almost reached the regrettable conclusion that the Negro's great stumbling block in the stride toward freedom is not the White Citizen's Counciler or the Ku Klux Klanner, but the white moderate who is more devoted to "order" than to justice; who prefers a negative peace which is the absence of tension to a positive peace which is the presence of justice; who constantly says, "I agree with you in the goal you seek, but I can't agree with your methods of direct action"; who paternalistically feels that he can set the timetable for another man's freedom; who lives by the myth of time and who constantly advised the Negro to wait until a "more convenient season." Shallow understanding from people of good will is more frustrating than absolute misunderstanding from people of ill will. Lukewarm acceptance is much more bewildering than outright rejection.

I had hoped that the white moderate would understand that law and order exist for the purpose of establishing justice, and that when they fail to do this they become dangerously structured dams that block the flow of social progress. I had hoped that the white moderate would understand that the present tension of the South is merely a necessary phase of the transition from an obnoxious negative peace, where the Negro passively accepted his unjust plight, to a substance-filled positive peace, where all men will respect the dignity and worth of human personality. Actually, we who engage in nonviolent direct action are not the creators of tension. We merely bring to the surface the hidden tension that is already alive. We bring it out in the open where it can be seen and dealt with. Like a boil that can never be cured as long as it is covered up but must be opened with all its pus-flowing ugliness to the natural medicines of air and light, injustice must likewise be exposed, with all of the tension its exposing creates, to the light of human conscience and the air of national opinion before it can be cured.

In your statement you asserted that our actions, even though peaceful, must be condemned because they precipitate violence. But can this assertion be logically made? Isn't this like condemning the robbed man because his possession of money precipitated the evil act of robbery? Isn't this like condemning Socrates because his unswerving commitment to truth and his philosophical delvings precipitated the misguided popular mind to make him drink the hemlock? Isn't this like condemning Jesus because His unique God-consciousness and never-ceasing devotion to his will precipitated the evil act of crucifixion? We must come to see, as federal courts have consistently affirmed, that it is immoral to urge an individual to withdraw his efforts to gain his basic constitutional rights because the quest precipitates violence. Society must protect the robbed and punish the robber.

I had also hoped that the white moderate would reject the myth of time. I received a letter this morning from a white brother in Texas which said: "All Christians know that the colored people will receive equal rights eventually, but it is possible that you are in too great of a religious hurry. It has taken Christianity almost two thousand years to accomplish what it has. The teachings of Christ take time to come to earth." All that is said here grows out of a tragic misconception of time. It is the strangely irrational notion that there is something in the very flow of time that will inevitably cure all ills. Actually time is neutral. It can be used either destructively or constructively. I am coming to feel that the people of ill will have used time much more effectively than the people of good will. We will have to repent in this generation not merely for the vitriolic words and actions of the bad people, but for the appalling silence of the good people. We must come to see that human progress never rolls in on wheels of inevitability. It comes through the tireless efforts and persistent work of men willing to be co-workers with God, and without this hard work time itself becomes an ally of the forces of social stagnation. We must use time creatively, and forever realize that the time is always ripe to do right. Now is the time to make real the promise of democracy, and transform our pending national elegy into a creative psalm of brotherhood. Now is the time to lift our national policy from the quicksand of racial injustice to the solid rock of human dignity.

You spoke of our activity in Birmingham as extreme. At first I was rather disappointed that fellow clergymen would see my nonviolent efforts as those of the extremist. I started thinking about the fact that I stand in the middle of two opposing forces in the Negro community. One is a force of complacency made up of Negroes who, as a result of long years of oppression, have been so completely drained of self-respect and a sense of "somebodiness" that they have adjusted to segregation, and, of a few Negroes in the middle class who, because of a degree of academic and economic security, and because at points they profit by segregation, have unconsciously become insensitive to the problems of the masses. The other force is one of bitterness and hatred, and comes perilously close to advocating violence. It is expressed in the various black nationalist groups that are springing up over the nation, the largest and best known being Elijah Muhammad's Muslim movement. This movement is nourished by the contemporary frustration over the continued existence of racial discrimination. It is made up of people who have lost faith in America, who have absolutely repudiated Christianity, and who have concluded that the white man is an incurable "devil." I have tried to stand between these two forces, saying that we need not follow the "do-nothingism" of the complacent or the hatred and despair of the black nationalist. There is the more excellent way of love and nonviolent protest. I'm grateful to God that, through the Negro church, the dimension of nonviolence entered our struggle. If this philosophy had not emerged, I am convinced that by now many streets of the South would be flowing with floods of blood. And I am further convinced that if our white brothers dismiss us as "rabble-rousers" and "outside agitators" those of us who are working through the channels of nonviolent direct action and refuse to support our nonviolent efforts, millions of Negroes, out of frustration and despair, will seek solace and security in black nationalist ideologies, a development that will lead inevitably to a frightening racial nightmare.

Oppressed people cannot remain oppressed forever. The urge for freedom will eventually come. This is what happened to the American Negro. Something within has reminded him of his birthright of freedom; something without has reminded him that he can gain it. Consciously and unconsciously, he has been swept in by what the Germans call the *Zeitgeist,* and with his black brothers of Africa, and his brown and yellow brothers of Asia, South America and the Caribbean, he is moving with a sense of cosmic urgency toward the promised land of racial justice. Recognizing this vital urge that has engulfed the Negro community, one should readily understand public demonstrations. The Negro has many pent-up resentments and latent frustrations. He has to get them out. So let him march sometime; let him have his prayer pilgrimages to the city hall; understand why he must have sit-ins and freedom rides. If his repressed emotions do not come out in these nonviolent ways, they will come out in ominous expressions of violence. This is not a threat; it is a fact of history. So I have not said to my people "get rid of your discontent." But I have tried to say that this normal and healthy discontent can be channelized through the creative outlet of nonviolent direct action. Now this approach is being dismissed as extremist. I must admit that I was initially disappointed in being so categorized.

But as I continued to think about the matter I gradually gained a bit of satisfaction from being considered an extremist. Was not Jesus an extremist in love—"Love your enemies, bless them that curse you, pray for them that despitefully use you." Was not Amos an extremist for justice—"Let justice roll down like waters and righteousness like a mighty stream." Was not Paul an extremist for the gospel of Jesus Christ—"I bear in my body the marks of the Lord Jesus." Was not Martin Luther an extremist—"Here I stand; I can do none other so help me God." Was not John Bunyan an extremist—"I will stay in jail to the end of my days before I make a butchery of my conscience." Was not Abraham Lincoln an extremist—"This nation cannot survive half slave and half free." Was not Thomas Jefferson an extremist—"We hold these truths to be self-evident, that all men are created equal." So the question is not whether we will be extremist but what kind of extremist will we be. Will we be extremists for hate or will we be extremists for love? Will we be extremists for the preservation of injustice—or will we be extremists for the cause of justice? In that dramatic scene on Calvary's hill, three men were crucified. We must not forget that all three were crucified for the same crime—the crime of extremism. Two were extremists for immorality, and thusly fell below their environment. The other, Jesus Christ, was an extremist for love, truth and goodness, and thereby rose above his environment. So, after all, maybe the South, the nation and the world are in dire need of creative extremists.

I had hoped that the white moderate would see this. Maybe I was too optimistic. Maybe I expected too much. I guess I should have realized that few members of a race that has oppressed another race can understand or appreciate the deep groans and passionate yearnings of those that have been oppressed and still fewer have the vision to see that injustice must be rooted out by strong, persistent and determined action. I am thankful, however, that some of our white brothers have grasped the meaning of this social revolution and committed themselves to it. They are still all too small in quantity, but they are big in quality. Some like Ralph McGill, Lillian Smith, Harry Golden and James Dabbs have written about our struggle in eloquent, prophetic and understanding terms. Others have marched with us down nameless streets of the South. They have languished in filthy roach-infested jails, suffering the abuse and brutality of angry policemen who see them as "dirty nigger-lovers." They, unlike so many of their moderate brothers and sisters, have recognized the urgency of the moment and sensed the need for powerful "action" antidotes to combat the disease of segregation.

Let me rush on to mention my other disappointment. I have been so greatly disappointed with the white church and its leadership. Of course, there are some notable exceptions. I am not unmindful of the fact that each of you has taken some significant stands on this issue. I commend you, Rev. Stallings, for your Christian stance on this past Sunday, in welcoming Negroes to your worship service on a non-segregated basis. I commend the Catholic leaders of this state for integrating Springhill College several years ago.

But despite these notable exceptions I must honestly reiterate that I have been disappointed with the church. I do not say that as one of the negative critics who can always find something wrong with the church. I say it as a minister of the gospel, who loves the church; who was nurtured in its bosom; who has been sustained by its spiritual blessings and who will remain true to it as long as the cord of life shall lengthen.

I had the strange feeling when I was suddenly catapulted into the leadership of the bus protest in Montgomery several years ago that we would have the support of the white church. I felt that the white ministers, priests and rabbis of the South would be some of our strongest allies. Instead, some have been outright opponents, refusing to understand the freedom movement and misrepresenting its leaders; all too many others have been more cautious than courageous and have remained silent behind the anesthetizing security of the stained-glass windows.

In spite of my shattered dreams of the past, I came to Birmingham with the hope that the white religious leadership of this community would see the justice of our cause, and with deep moral concern, serve as the channel through which our just grievances would get to the power structure. I had hoped that each of you would understand. But again I have been disappointed. I have heard numerous religious leaders of the South call upon their worshippers to comply with a desegregation decision because it is the *law,* but I have longed to hear white ministers say, "Follow this decree because integration is morally *right* and the Negro is your brother." In the midst of blatant injustices inflicted upon the Negro, I have watched white churches stand on the sideline and merely mouth pious irrelevancies and sanctimonious trivialities. In the midst of a mighty struggle to rid our nation of racial and economic injustice, I have heard so many ministers say, "Those are social issues with which the gospel has no real concern," and I have watched so many churches commit themselves to a completely otherworldly religion which made a strange distinction between body and soul, the sacred and the secular.

So here we are moving toward the exit of the twentieth century with a religious community largely adjusted to the status quo, standing as a taillight behind other community agencies rather than a headlight leading men to higher levels of justice.

I have traveled the length and breadth of Alabama, Mississippi and all the other southern states. On sweltering summer days and crisp autumn mornings I have looked at her beautiful churches with their lofty spires pointing heavenward. I have beheld the impressive outlay of her massive religious education buildings. Over and over again I have found myself asking: "What kind of people worship here? Who is their God? Where were their voices when the lips of [Mississippi] Governor [Ross] Barnett dripped with words of interposition and nullification? Where were they when [Alabama] Governor [George] Wallace gave the clarion call for defiance and hatred? Where were their voices of support when tired, bruised and weary Negro men and women decided to rise from the dark dungeons of complacency to the bright hills of creative protest?"

Yes, these questions are still in my mind. In deep disappointment, I have wept over the laxity of the church. But be assured that my tears have been tears of love. There can be no deep disappointment where there is not deep love. Yes, I love the church; I love her sacred walls. How could I do otherwise? I am in the rather unique position of being the son, the grandson and the great-grandson of preachers. Yes, I see the church as the body of Christ. But, oh! How we have blemished and scarred that body through social neglect and fear of being nonconformists.

There was a time when the church was very powerful. It was during that period when the early Christians rejoiced when they were deemed worthy to suffer for what they believed. In those days the church was not merely a thermometer that recorded the ideas and principles of popular opinion; it was a thermostat that transformed the mores of society. Wherever the early Christians entered a town the power structure got disturbed and immediately sought to convict them for being "disturbers of the peace" and "outside agitators." But they went on with the conviction that they were "a colony of heaven," and had to obey God rather than man. They were small in number but big in commitment. They were too God-intoxicated to be "astronomically intimidated." They brought an end to such ancient evils as infanticide and gladiatorial contest.

Things are different now. The contemporary church is often a weak, ineffectual voice with an uncertain sound. It is so often the arch-supporter of the status quo. Far from being disturbed by the presence of the church, the power structure of the average community is consoled by the church's silent and often vocal sanction of things as they are.

But the judgment of God is upon the church as never before. If the church of today does not recapture the sacrificial spirit of the early church, it will lose its authentic ring, forfeit the loyalty of millions, and be dismissed as an irrelevant social club with no meaning for the twentieth century. I am meeting young people every day whose disappointment with the church has risen to outright disgust.

Maybe again, I have been too optimistic. Is organized religion too inextricably bound to the status quo to save our nation and the world? Maybe I must turn my faith to the inner spiritual church, the church within the church, as the true *ecclesia* and the hope of the world. But again I am thankful to God that some noble souls from the ranks of organized religion have broken loose from the paralyzing chains of conformity and joined us as active partners in the struggle for freedom. They have left their secure congregations and walked the streets of Albany,. Georgia, with us. They have gone through the highways of the South on tortuous rides for freedom. Yes, they have gone to jail with us. Some have been kicked out of their churches, and lost support of their bishops and fellow ministers. But they have gone with the faith that right defeated is stronger than evil triumphant. These men have been the leaven in the lump of the race. Their witness has been the spiritual salt that has preserved the true meaning of the gospel in these troubled times. They have carved a tunnel of hope through the dark mountain of disappointment.

I hope the church as a whole will meet the challenge of this decisive hour. But even if the church does not come to the aid of justice, I have no despair about the future. I have no fear about the outcome of our struggle in Birmingham, even if our motives are presently misunderstood. We will reach the goal of freedom in Birmingham and all over the nation, because the goal of America is freedom. Abused and scorned though we may be, our destiny is tied up with the destiny of America. Before the Pilgrims landed at Plymouth we were here. Before the pen of Jefferson etched across the pages of history the majestic words of the Declaration of Independence, we were here. For more than two centuries our foreparents labored in this country without wages; they made cotton king; and they built the homes of their masters in the midst of brutal injustice and shameful humiliation— and yet out of a bottomless vitality they continued to thrive and develop. If the inexpressible cruelties of slavery could not stop us, the opposition we now face will surely fail. We will win our freedom because the sacred heritage of our nation and the eternal will of God are embodied in our echoing demands.

I must close now. But before closing I am impelled to mention one other point in your statement that troubled me profoundly. You warmly commended the Birmingham police force for keeping "order" and "preventing violence." I don't believe you would have so warmly commended the police force if you had seen its angry violent dogs literally biting six unarmed, nonviolent Negroes. I don't believe you would so quickly commend the policemen if you would observe their ugly and inhuman treatment of Negroes here in the city jail; if you would watch them push and curse old Negro women and young Negro girls; if you would see them slap and kick old Negro men and young boys; if you will observe them, as they did on two occasions, refuse to give us food because we wanted to sing our grace together. I'm sorry that I can't join you in your praise for the police department.

It is true that they have been rather disciplined in their public handling of the demonstrators. In this sense they have been rather publicly "non-violent." But for what purpose? To preserve the evil system of segregation. Over the last few years I have consistently preached that nonviolence demands that the means we use must be as pure as the ends we seek. So I have tried to make it clear that it is wrong to use immoral means to attain moral ends. But now I must affirm that it is just as wrong, or even more so, to use moral means to preserve immoral ends. Maybe Mr. Connor and his policemen have been rather publicly nonviolent, as Chief Pritchett was in Albany, Georgia, but they have used the moral means of nonviolence to maintain the immoral end of flagrant racial injustice. T. S. Eliot has said that there is no greater treason than to do the right deed for the wrong reason.

I wish you had commended the Negro sit-inners and demonstrators of Birmingham for their sublime courage, their willingness to suffer and their amazing discipline in the midst of the most inhuman provocation. One day the South will recognize its real heroes. They will be the James Merediths, courageously and with a majestic sense of purpose facing jeering and hostile mobs and the agonizing loneliness that characterizes the life of the pioneer. They will be old, oppressed, battered Negro women, symbolized in a seventy-two-year-old woman of Montgomery, Alabama, who rose up with a sense of dignity and with her people decided not to ride the segregated buses, and responded to one who inquired about her tiredness with ungrammatical profundity: "My feet is tired, but my soul is rested." They will be the young high school and college students, young ministers of the gospel and a host of their elders courageously and nonviolently sitting-in at lunch counters and willingly going to jail for conscience's sake. One day the South will know that when these disinherited children of God sat down at lunch counters they were in reality standing up for the best in the American dream and the most sacred values in our Judeo-Christian heritage, and thusly, carrying our whole nation back to those great wells of democracy which were dug deep by the Founding Fathers in the formulation of the Constitution and the Declaration of Independence.

Never before have I written a letter this long (or should I say a book?). I'm afraid that it is much too long to take your precious time. I can assure you that it would have been much shorter if I had been writing from a comfortable desk, but what else is there to do when you are alone for days in the dull monotony of a narrow jail cell other than write long letters, think strange thoughts, and pray long prayers?

If I have said anything in this letter that is an overstatement of the truth and is indicative of an unreasonable impatience, I beg you to forgive me. If I have said anything in this letter that is an understatement of the truth and is indicative of my having a patience that makes me patient with anything less than brotherhood, I beg God to forgive me.

I hope this letter finds you strong in the faith. I also hope that circumstances will soon make it possible for me to meet each of you, not as an integrationist or a civil rights leader, but as a fellow clergyman and a Christian brother. Let us all hope that the dark clouds of racial prejudice will soon pass away and the deep fog of misunderstanding will be lifted from our fear-drenched communities and in some not too distant tomorrow the radiant stars of love and brotherhood will shine over our great nation with all of their scintillating beauty.

Yours for the cause of Peace and Brotherhood,

Martin Luther King, Jr.

Mary King on Women in the Civil-Rights Movement (1964), 1987

Our second document [on women's rights] was written when Casey [Hayden, a white SNCC civil-rights worker] and I were spending a few days at my family's cottage in a remote tract of woods in Spotsylvania County, Virginia. There, in the quiet isolation of a forest, and with woodsmoke from the cottage fire scenting our walks, on November 18, 1965, Casey wrote the first draft and then together we polished our challenge to women who were involved across the spectrum of progressive organizing. This call would go out to women in Students for a Democratic Society, the National Student Association, the Northern Student Movement, and the Student Peace Union as well as SNCC [Student Nonviolent Coordinating Committee]. Working from notes from conversations we had had with Dona Richards [black SNCC worker and wife of SNCC official, Bob Moses], we composed our message and mailed it to forty women activists across the country. We wrote:

> We've talked a lot to each other and to some of you, about our own and other women's problems in trying to live in our personal lives and in our work as independent and creative people. . . . In particular, women we've talked to who work in the movement seem to be caught up in a common-law caste system that operates, sometimes subtly, forcing them to work around or outside hierarchical structures of power which may exclude them. Women seem to be placed in the same positions of assumed subordination in personal relationships too. It is a caste system which, at its worst, uses and exploits women. . . .

A very few men seem to feel, when they hear conversations involving these problems, that they have a right to be present and participate in them since they are so deeply involved. At the same time, very few men can respond nondefensively since the whole idea is either beyond their comprehension or threatens to expose them. The usual response is laughter. That inability to see the issue as serious, as the straitjacketing of both sexes, and as societally determined, often shapes our own response so that we learn to think in their terms about ourselves and to feel silly rather than to trust our inner feelings. . . .

The reason we want to try to open up dialogue is mostly subjective. Working in the movement often intensifies personal problems, especially if we start trying to apply things we're learning to our personal lives. Perhaps we can start to talk with each other more openly than in the past and create a community of support for each other so we can deal with ourselves and others with integrity. . . .

All the problems between men and women functioning in society as equal human beings are among the most basic that people face. We've talked in the movement about trying to build a society which would see basic human problems (which are now seen as private troubles) as public problems and would try to shape institutions to meet human needs rather than shaping people to meet the needs of those with power. . . .

Even in our fantasies, we had no hope that a movement would develop. "Objectively the chances seem nil that we could start a movement based on anything as distant to general American thought as a sex-caste system," we wrote. Instead, we wanted to provoke the reaction of a selected group of women including some of the black women in SNCC to whom we felt drawn. We wanted the support of other women who were politically involved with civil rights and antiwar issues, women who were risk takers and who shared a commitment to fostering social change. We hoped that a network would evolve. What developed was far beyond our expectations. . . .

Misconceptions have developed along the way, perhaps because so few books have been written by direct participants in the civil rights movement. One damaging notion implanted in the literature, even by such pathfinding authors as history professor Sara M. Evans of the University of Minnesota and author of *Personal Politics*, was that in the years after 1965 the movement became increasingly alienating for women. This was true for me, but *not* for the reasons given. As this story goes, women in the movement were relegated to typing, running mimeograph machines, preparing and serving coffee, washing dishes, and being available for sex. This is not correct and is not an explanation of Casey's and my protests. Our status in the movement was never the issue. Furthermore, this distortion overlooks the truly significant roles women played, the responsiveness of SNCC to women leaders before such an issue had been articulated, and the fact that, by and large, the movement was peopled by women; worst of all, it belies the seriousness and earnestness with which women in SNCC were involved and denies the important debate within SNCC that gave rise to our two documents.

This distorted characterization represents an imposition of a later feminist construction on a period of ferment. While the civil rights movement and the people in it mirrored the conventions and stereotypes of the larger society, that movement was at the same time giving rise to a challenge from within it that would contribute to producing a successor movement. . . .

Our manifesto that was sent to the forty activists came from the heart of the civil rights movement and may, in its own way, have helped to redress an imbalance that had dated back to the period of abolition. The constitutional exclusion of women from suffrage and other rights, despite the visible and significant leadership of women of both races in the effort to end slavery, has been a travesty to women who are aware of the history. After the Civil War, former male slaves were given the vote, in statute if not in practice, while both white women and black women were legally excluded. This inequity, in which black men got the vote several decades before white women—so many of whom had been active in the abolition movement—had continued to fester.

Healing a rift that was developing between black and white women was an important objective for Casey and me. . . .

The black women of SNCC were slow to respond to our missives. . . .

. . . [W]ithin the black community, women since the days of slavery had often been the primary responsible person in many families and were not constrained by the harsh gender-stereotyping of middle-class white women. Although formal leadership roles might go to men, and the most prestigious professions such as those held by the clergy and morticians were for males only, there was no question about the authority or clout of women in the family and community. If any generalization can be made, it is that black women had too little support for the responsibility they carried. . . .

Sexually aggressive styles of behavior are more acceptable in some strata of the black community than in the white. Most of the handful of white women who were members of the SNCC staff understood this. But for the several hundred white women who came as volunteers during the summer of 1964—in their newness and also because they did not have to work their way laboriously into the movement to gain trust, having been recruited—they sometimes found themselves the focus of blandishments. Wittingly or unwittingly, a number of them found themselves attracted by the sexually explicit manner of certain black men in the local community and also on the SNCC staff. Many wore décolleté necklines and dangling earrings, not realizing that these would be provocative in southern rural communities, and seemed sometimes to strike an incautious pose. In contrast, women on the SNCC staff were plain; we wore little or no makeup, cut one another's hair, and had no possessions or clothing worth mentioning. Lack of awareness coupled with sudden exposure to the sexual frankness of some of the black men meant that a few of them fluttered like butterflies from one tryst to another. Sexual dalliances were one way for a volunteer to prove she was not racist and I'm certain any number of black men manipulated this anxiety.

This complex dynamic created stress between the veteran black women and white women on the SNCC staff, because the black women could see the allure of the white women volunteers to black male staff. Such desire was unacceptable intellectually, but, psychologically, for some men, it was compelling. I have often wondered whether resistance to this pattern might not have contributed to the surge toward black nationalism that showed itself in SNCC after the November 1964 Waveland meeting. Black men, suddenly exposed to large numbers of white women volunteers—with many of the local men talking to a white woman for the first time in their lives as an equal—suddenly had the real or hypothetical opportunity to break an old taboo. Black women who were field secretaries and project directors, working side by side with black male colleagues all day, found that after hours some of the latter sought the company of the white women volunteers.

This behavior was denounced and bitterly attacked during tormented sessions in a second meeting at Waveland in May of 1965. It was termed "backsliding," because the rhetoric of black pride seemed inconsistent with the reality for some black men. Insofar as I know, this was the only time that sex and politics affected each other during the civil rights movement.

This tension inevitably spilled over and affected Casey's and my relationships with treasured black women friends; nevertheless, we included some of them among the forty activists to whom we sent our second document at the end of 1965.

In my case, there was no undercurrent of sex affecting my experiences in the civil rights movement. Not one of the black men and only one of the white men that I have written about in this book—all the men who were central to SNCC—ever made an explicit sexual advance to me during the years I was involved in the civil rights movement.

Yet, our lives defied conventional morality. For the most part in our twenties and unmarried, peripatetically moving from one crisis to another, from one meeting to another, from one county to another, our toothbrushes in our pockets because of the possibility of being locked up, survival required that we be flexible, sleep anywhere, and made do.

Of course there was flirtation and repartee. This created play in the middle of unrest and provided the gaiety of comic relief. The ebullient field secretary from Baltimore with a cherubic face, Reggie Robinson, constantly flirted with me, but this was part of his exuberance and he still flirts with me. When Reggie stops flirting with me, I will be upset. James Jones, a strikingly handsome and quietly tenacious black field secretary from the Arkansas project, arrived at a staff meeting in Atlanta and shyly came to tell me that he and William Hansen, our white Arkansas state director, had a competition going. The purpose of the contest was to see which of them was the more attractive to me! Yet those with whom I worked the longest, and in some cases the closest, never asked to become sexually intimate, and these were men for whom I felt, and still feel, love—Julian Bond, Jim Forman, Bob Moses, Stokely Carmichael, Bob Zellner, Ivanhoe Donaldson, and many more.

The Civil Rights Act of 1964

An Act

To enforce the constitutional right to vote, to confer jurisdiction upon the district courts of the United States to provide injunctive relief against discrimination in public accommodations, to authorize the Attorney General to institute suits to protect constitutional rights in public facilities and public education, to extend the Commission on Civil Rights, to prevent discrimination in federally assisted programs, to establish a Commission on Equal Employment Opportunity, and for other purposes. . . .

Title II—Injunctive Relief against Discrimination in Places of Public Accommodation

Sec. 201. (a) All persons shall be entitled to the full and equal enjoyment of the goods, services, facilities, privileges, advantages, and accommodations of any place of public accommodation, as defined in this section, without discrimination or segregation on the ground of race, color, religion, or national origin.

(b) Each of the following establishments which serves the public is a place of public accommodation within the meaning of this title if its operations affect commerce, or if discrimination or segregation by it is supported by State action:

(1) any inn, hotel, motel, or other establishment which provides lodging to transient guests, other than an establishment located within a building which contains not more than five rooms for rent or hire and which is actually occupied by the proprietor of such establishment as his residence;

(2) any restaurant, cafeteria, lunchroom, lunch counter, soda fountain, or other facility principally engaged in selling food for consumption on the premises, including, but not limited to, any such facility located on the premises of any retail establishment; or any gasoline station;

(3) any motion picture house, theater, concert hall, sports arena, stadium or other place of exhibition or entertainment; and

(4) any establishment (A)(i) which is physically located within the premises of any establishment otherwise covered by this subsection, or (ii) within the premises of which is physically located any such covered establishment, and (B) which holds itself out as serving patrons of such covered establishment.

(c) The operations of an establishment affect commerce within the meaning of this title if (1) it is one of the establishments described in paragraph (1) of subsection (b); (2) in the case of an establishment described in paragraph (2) of subsection (b), it serves or offers to serve interstate travelers or a substantial portion of the food which it serves, or gasoline or other products which it sells, has moved in commerce; (3) in the case of an establishment described in paragraph (3) of subsection (b), it customarily presents films, performances, athletic teams, exhibitions, or other sources of entertainment which move in commerce; and (4) in the case of an establishment described in paragraph (4) of subsection (b), it is physically located within the premises of, or there is physically located within its premises, an establishment the operations of which affect commerce within the meaning of this subsection. For purposes of this section, "commerce" means travel, trade, traffic, commerce, transportation, or communication among the several States, or between the District of Columbia and any State, or between any foreign country or any territory or possession and any State or the District of Columbia, or between points in the same State but through any other State or the District of Columbia or a foreign country. . . .

Title VII—Equal Employment Opportunity

Discrimination Because of Race, Color, Religion, Sex, or National Origin
Sec. 703. (a) It shall be an unlawful employment practice for an employer—

(1) to fail or refuse to hire or to discharge any individual, or otherwise to discriminate against any individual with respect to his compensation, terms, conditions, or privileges of employment, because of such individual's race, color, religion, sex, or national origin; or
(2) to limit, segregate, or classify his employees in any way which would deprive or tend to deprive any individual of employment opportunities or otherwise adversely affect his status as an employee, because of such individual's race, color, religion, sex, or national origin.

(b) It shall be an unlawful employment practice for an employment agency to fail or refuse to refer for employment, or otherwise to discriminate against, any individual because of his race, color, religion, sex, or national origin, or to classify or refer for employment any individual on the basis of his race, color, religion, sex, or national origin.

(c) It shall be an unlawful employment practice for a labor organization—

(1) to exclude or to expel from its membership, or otherwise to discriminate against, any individual because of his race, color, religion, sex, or national origin;
(2) to limit, segregate, or to classify its membership, or to classify or fail or refuse to refer for employment any individual, in any way which would deprive or tend to deprive any individual of employment opportunities, or would limit such employment opportunities or otherwise adversely affect his status as an employee or as an applicant for em-

ployment, because of such individual's race, color, religion, sex, or national origin; or

(3) to cause or attempt to cause an employer to discriminate against an individual in violation of this section.

(d) It shall be an unlawful employment practice for any employer, labor organization, or joint labor-management committee controlling apprenticeship or other training or retraining, including on-the-job training programs to discriminate against any individual because of his race, color, religion, sex, or national origin in admission to, or employment in, any program established to provide apprenticeship or other training. . . .

Equal Employment Opportunity Commission Sec. 705. (a) There is hereby created a Commission to be known as the Equal Employment Opportunity Commission, which shall be composed of five members, not more than three of whom shall be members of the same political party, who shall be appointed by the President by and with the advice and consent of the Senate. . . .

The *New York Times* Reports on the Protest at Selma, 1965

SELMA, Ala., March 7—Alabama state troopers and volunteer officers of the Dallas County sheriff's office tore through a column of Negro demonstrators with tear gas, nightsticks and whips here today to enforce Gov. George C. Wallace's order against a protest march from Selma to Montgomery.

At least 17 Negroes were hospitalized with injuries and about 40 more were given emergency treatment for minor injuries and tear gas effects. . . .

The suppression of the march, which was called to dramatize the Negroes' voter-registration drive, was swift and thorough.

About 525 Negroes had left Browns Chapel and walked six blocks to Broad Street, then across Pettus Bridge and the Alabama River, where a cold wind cut at their faces and whipped their coats. They were young and old and they carried an assortment of packs, bedrolls and lunch sacks.

The troopers, more than 50 of them, were waiting 300 yards beyond the end of the bridge.

Behind and around the troopers were a few dozen possemen, 15 of them on horses, and perhaps 100 white spectators. About 50 Negroes stood watching beside a yellow school bus well away from the troopers. The marchers had passed about three dozen more possemen at the other end of the bridge. They were to see more of that group.

The troopers stood shoulder to shoulder in a line across both sides of the divided four-lane highway.

They put on gas masks and held their night sticks ready as the Negroes approached, marching two abreast, slowly and silently.

When the Negroes were 50 feet away, a voice came over an amplifying system commanding them to stop. They stopped.

The leader of the troopers, who identified himself as Maj. John Cloud said, "This is an unlawful assembly. Your march is not conducive to the public safety. You are ordered to disperse and go back to your church or to your homes."

Mr. [Hosea] Williams answered from the head of the column.

"May we have a word with the major?" he asked.

"There is no word to be had," the major replied. . . .

The two men went through the same exchange twice more, then the major said, "You have two minutes to turn around and go back to your church."

Several seconds went by silently. The Negroes stood unmoving.

The next sound was the major's voice. "Troopers, advance." he commanded.

The troopers rushed forward, their blue uniforms and white helmets blurring into a flying wedge as they moved.

The wedge moved with such force that it seemed almost to pass over the waiting column instead of through it.

The first 10 or 20 Negroes were swept to the ground screaming, arms and legs flying, and packs and bags went skittering across the grassy divider strip and on to the pavement on both sides.

Those still on their feet retreated. . . .

The troopers continued pushing, using both the force of their bodies and the prodding of their nightsticks.

A cheer went up from the white spectators lining the south side of the highway.

The mounted possemen spurred their horses and rode at a run into the retreating mass. The Negroes cried out as they crowded together for protection, and the whites on the sideline whooped and cheered.

The Negroes paused in their retreat for perhaps a minute, still screaming and huddling together.

Suddenly there was a report, like a gunshot, and a gray cloud spewed over the troopers and the Negroes.

"Tear gas!" someone yelled.

The cloud began covering the highway. Newsmen, who were confined by four troopers to a corner 100 yards away, began to lose sight of the action.

But before the cloud finally hid it all, there were several seconds of unobstructed view. Fifteen or twenty nightsticks could be seen through the gas, flailing at the heads of the marchers. . . .

The Negroes broke and ran. Scores of them streamed across the parking lot of the Selma Tractor Company. Troopers and possemen, mounted and unmounted, went after them.

Several more tear gas bombs were set off. One report was heard that sounded different. A white civil rights worker said later that it was a shotgun blast and that the pellets tore a hole in the brick wall of a hamburger stand five feet from him.

After about 10 minutes, most of the Negroes were rounded up. They began to move toward the city through the smell of the tear gas, coughing and crying as they stumbled onto Pettus Bridge.

Four or five women still lay on the grass strip where the troopers had knocked them down. Two troopers passed among them and ordered them to get up and join the others. The women lay still.

The two men then set off another barrage of tear gas and the women struggled to their feet, blinded and gasping, and limped across the road. One was Mrs. Amelia Boynton, one of the Selma leaders of the Negro movement. She was treated later at the hospital.

Lloyd Russell of Atlanta, a white photographer who had stayed at the other end of the bridge, said he saw at least four carloads of possemen overtake the marchers as they re-entered Broad Street. He said the possemen jumped from the cars and began beating the Negroes with nightsticks.

Two other witnesses said they saw possemen using whips on the fleeing Negroes as they re-crossed the bridge.

The other newsmen were finally allowed to follow the retreat.

Ron Gibson, a reporter for The Birmingham News, reached Browns Chapel ahead of the other newsmen. He said later that he had seen Sheriff Clark lead a charge with about half a dozen possemen to try to force the Negroes from Sylvan Street into the church.

Mr. Gibson said the Negroes fell back momentarily, then surged forward and began throwing bricks and bottles. He said the officers had to retreat until reinforcements arrived. One posseman was cut under the eye with a brick, he said.

Mr. Gibson said that Wilson Baker, Selma's Commissioner of Public Safety, intervened and persuaded the Negroes to enter the church. He said Captain Baker held back Sheriff Clark and his possemen, who were regrouping for another assault.

Mr. Gibson said that Sheriff Clark was struck on the face by a piece of brick but was not injured.

When the other newsmen arrived, more than 100 possemen were packed into Sylvan Street a block from the church. They were joined shortly by the 50 troopers, who had been called back to regroup after turning back the marchers.

The ground floor of the two-story parsonage next to the church was turned into an emergency hospital for an hour and a half.

Negroes lay on the floors and chairs, many weeping and moaning. A girl in red slacks was carried from the house screaming. Mrs. Boynton lay semiconscious on a table. Doctors and nurses threaded feverishly through the crowd administering first aid and daubing a solution of water and baking soda on the eyes of those who had been in the worst of the gas.

From the hospital came a report that the victims had suffered fractures of ribs, heads, arms and legs, in addition to cuts and bruises.

Hundreds of Negroes, including many who had not been on the march, milled angrily in front of the church.

An old Negro who had just heard that officers had beaten a Negro on his own porch said to a friend, "I wish the bastard would try to come in my house."

The Negro leaders worked through the crowd urging calm and nonviolence.

At the end of the street the possemen and troopers could be seen grouping into a formation. The officers left after an hour, and tonight the Negroes emerged from their houses and poured into Browns Chapel for a mass meeting.

At the meeting Mr. Williams, who was not injured, told the 700 Negroes present about the plans for the Tuesday march.

"I fought in World War II," Mr. Williams said, "and I once was captured by the German army, and I want to tell you that the Germans never were as inhuman as the state troopers of Alabama."

⚓ *E S S A Y S*

David Garrow, a political science professor at the City College of New York, wrote a Pulitzer Prize–winning biography of Martin Luther King, Jr., that emphasizes the religious base of King's nonviolent philosophy. In this excerpt in the first essay, Garrow recounts the Birmingham campaign, the disagreements within the black community, the debate over tactics, the role of the federal government, and the leadership of King. Less-publicized locales, such as Tuskegee, Alabama, were similarly embroiled in the conflicts of the times. Tuskegee spent the civil-rights era removed from the national spotlight. Robert J. Norrell's account of the movement there demonstrates the potential of such relatively hidden places for providing insights into the period. In this excerpt, Norrell, a historian teaching at the University of Alabama, Tuscaloosa, discusses voting-rights protests in the community, the influence of Selma, and the growing generational divisions within the black community that would ultimately result in new leadership in the period after the Voting Rights Act.

Martin Luther King, Jr. and the Fall of Birmingham

DAVID GARROW

On January 23, SCLC's executive staff met to discuss Birmingham in detail. The city election was scheduled for March 5, and King knew that Birmingham's black leaders wanted no protests before that time. SCLC settled

Excerpts from pp. 231–232, 234–264 of *Bearing the Cross: Martin Luther King, Jr., and the Southern Christian Leadership Conference*, a personal portrait by David J. Garrow. Copyright © 1986 by David J. Garrow. Reprinted by permission of William Morrow & Co., Inc.

on a target date of March 14. King said that jail going would be a necessary part of the campaign and that as many SCLC board members as possible should be recruited to join the effort. Wyatt Walker [SCLC Executive Director] described how he would proceed with reconnoitering Birmingham's segregated facilities, especially the lunch counters and other whites-only facilities in the downtown department stores that had reneged on their fall agreement with Shuttlesworth. King said that a larger session with Shuttlesworth and his Birmingham associates would be scheduled for early February.

In Birmingham word of the planned protest was very tightly held, although the principal black leaders and white liberals associated with the Alabama Council on Human Relations understood that something was in the offing. Few if any knew the target date King had selected. There was considerable concern that no protests be launched prior to the crucial mayoral election in which Connor [Eugene "Bull" Connor, Birmingham Public Safety Commissioner] would oppose two relative moderates, former Lieutenant Governor Albert Boutwell and the somewhat more liberal Tom King. The city's business leadership rallied behind Boutwell as the strongest alternative to the dangerous Connor. They hoped that a Boutwell victory would lead to some agreement that would end the boycott, which continued to exact a high toll from the white stores.

To many Birmingham residents, black and white, expelling Connor from public office represented an opportunity to eliminate the segregationist violence that had long troubled Birmingham and stained its national reputation. In 1960 *The New York Times* had created a municipal furor by detailing how extremist white violence against anyone who spoke up for desegregation had frightened virtually every white, and most blacks, into timid silence. By early 1963 the climate had changed little. One national magazine article, written by a native Birmingham white, labeled it "A City in Fear." Years of unsolved bombings had led to one neighborhood of upper-class black homes being called "Dynamite Hill," and jokes about "Bombingham" abounded. Well-informed observers decried the lack of moderate and courageous white leaders. Only a defeat of Connor would allow some official dialogue to begin between blacks and whites. Leaders of both races hoped that SCLC would not complicate their task. . . .

Two days before the mayoral election, King slipped into Birmingham to speak with several young ministers whom Wyatt Walker had contacted during trips back and forth from Atlanta. Walker had selected three downtown stores—Loveman's, Pizitz's, and Britt's—as primary targets for direct action. A group of federal buildings near the post office was a secondary target, and a suburban shopping center, Atlantic Mills, was a third possibility. Once the election was over, training of prospective demonstrators could begin. Tuesday night's election results, however, threw a sudden obstacle in SCLC's path. None of the three candidates won a majority, and a runoff between the two top finishers, Boutwell and Connor, would be held on April 2.

King and Walker wondered whether the protests should be postponed until after the runoff. Birmingham's black leaders advised them to wait, and King agreed. The local leaders breathed a sigh of relief. They worried that Connor might arrange a staged racial incident in advance of the runoff in order to stimulate segregationist voters. Shuttlesworth publicly announced that the ACMHR [Alabama Christian Movement for Human Rights] would undertake no demonstrations prior to the contest. . . .

On April 2, Birmingham's voters went to the polls and gave Albert Boutwell a decisive eight thousand-vote victory over Bull Connor. Walker and Shuttlesworth made final plans for launching the first department store sit-ins the next morning, and King, busy in Atlanta with meetings about SCLC's voter registration troubles, planned to fly in the next afternoon. While Wednesday's *Birmingham News* celebrated Boutwell's win with a huge headline proclaiming NEW DAY DAWNS FOR BIRMINGHAM, two dozen protesters, many of them students from Miles College, initiated lunch-counter sit-ins at four stores. Bull Connor, still the public safety commissioner, announced that the demonstrators would be arrested only upon complaints by store managers, and by the end of the afternoon, over twenty had been taken into custody. That evening King and Ralph Abernathy joined Shuttlesworth at a mass meeting, where they told the crowd that it was the merchants' failure to keep their fall promises that necessitated protests now. "If you create enough tension you attract attention to your cause" and "get to the conscience of the white man," King explained. About seventy-five members of the audience volunteered to join future demonstrations. The volunteers then went into a back room with Walker, A. D. King, and James Lawson for training in nonviolence. The next morning another group of demonstrators descended on the downtown stores, and a handful were arrested. Puzzled reporters wondered why the protests were getting off to such a quiet start.

King asserted at a press conference that the small scale of activity had been planned. He denied rumors that the lack of larger demonstrations was because few Birmingham blacks wanted to join a jail-going protest. The key element in the movement's effort, he said, was a tight boycott of the white downtown stores, whose traditionally strong sales during the Easter season depended in good part upon black consumers. "The Negro has enough buying power in Birmingham," King stated, "to make the difference between profit and loss in a business." . . . The boycott would be an inducement to Birmingham to grant the movement's six specific goals: desegregation of the store facilities; adoption of fair hiring practices by those stores; dismissal of all charges from previous protests; equal employment opportunities for blacks with the city government; reopening on a desegregated basis of Birmingham's closed municipal recreation facilities; and establishment of a biracial committee to pursue further desegregation. Although those goals received little coverage in news accounts of the campaign's debut, King emphasized the importance of the boycott at that evening's mass rally. Fifty more volunteers came forward, and ten were arrested during sit-ins the next morning. King stressed the boycott again at Friday's mass meeting, and thirty people agreed to join Shuttlesworth in a Saturday morning march to City Hall. To no one's surprise, the small band was arrested after moving only a few blocks.

By that time it was clear to King that he had made several miscalculations about Birmingham. Despite public statements to the contrary, SCLC was finding it difficult to recruit the large number of potential demonstrators it had anticipated. The problem was rooted in Fred Shuttlesworth's controversial stature among Birmingham blacks, and the reluctance of many black citizens to help launch protests in the immediate wake of Boutwell's victory over Connor.

King had long known that many people found Shuttlesworth excessively autocratic. Some cited his often-expressed conviction that his civil rights activism was a mission given to him directly by God. As one sympathetic friend described him then, "Shuttlesworth sees himself as taking orders only from God who speaks to him and through him." Hence, he was "difficult for more sophisticated people to appreciate." Among Birmingham's black leaders, respect for Shuttlesworth's courage was universal, but respect for his judgment and emotional stability was not. . . .

Black antipathy toward Shuttlesworth was not the only problem King had failed to anticipate. Even more pressing was the feeling among several important constituencies—the black ministers, some of the professional people, the most sympathetic local whites, and the Kennedy administration—that Boutwell's victory was a compelling reason to delay the protests. These groups shared the hope that once a moderate administration took office, both the merchants and the city government would grant some of the movement's requests without demonstrations being necessary. A further consideration was that Birmingham momentarily was in the odd situation of having two competing city governments. Connor and his two fellow commissioners vowed that they would not surrender control until the terms to which they had been elected prior to the change of government plebiscite expired several years hence. It would take at least a month for the Alabama Supreme Court to resolve that claim, and until a decision was rendered, lame-duck Connor would remain in day-to-day control of the police. [Birmingham citizens had voted earlier in the year to change from a commission to a mayor-council form of government.]

While local blacks made that case to King in private, some ostensibly moderate Alabama whites were less circumspect. Father Albert S. Foley, chairman of the U.S. Civil Rights Commission's Alabama advisory committee, publicly criticized King's entry into Birmingham, asserting that voluntary desegregation of downtown facilities would have taken place shortly if blacks had been willing to wait. *Birmingham News* publisher Vincent Townsend phoned Burke Marshall to ask that federal officials intercede with King and request a postponement. Marshall reluctantly made the call, repeating to King the argument that Boutwell's election eliminated the need for protests. To Marshall, and to others who voiced similar contentions, King replied that he failed to see what there was to welcome about the polite advocacy of continued segregation that Boutwell had offered during his campaign. "We feel Mr. Boutwell will never desegregate Birmingham voluntarily," King said at his Thursday news conference, and

Boutwell's victory "does not appear to materially affect the life of the Negro."

Vowing to remedy what he admitted was the "tremendous resistance" of many local black leaders to mass demonstrations, King made personal pleas to influential figures. He also organized two important meetings for Monday and Tuesday, April 8 and 9, the first with more than one hundred of the city's black pastors and the second with a number of black business and professional leaders. In the meantime, the nightly mass rallies and SCLC's efforts to recruit additional demonstrators continued. King appeared at Saturday evening's mass meeting dressed in a pair of overalls, announced another march for Sunday, and vowed that he would be going to jail in the near future. The next day his brother A.D., led a small march, and for the first time, Bull Connor displayed one of the weapons that Walker had been hoping for: a squad of snarling police dogs. A large crowd gathered as police arrested the two dozen marchers. One black bystander lunged at a dog with a large knife. As *The New York Times* described it, "The dog immediately attacked and there was a rush of other Negroes toward the spot where the dog had pinned the man to the ground. Policemen with two more dogs and other policemen who were congregated in the area quickly rushed against the crowd, swinging clubs." The black onlookers dispersed, but the crowd's presence and the officers' use of the dogs and clubs had given Walker the sort of incident he had been looking for. Just a day or two earlier, King had said to him, "Wyatt, you've got to find some way to make Bull Connor tip his hand" and show the movement and the press the kind of brutal tactics local blacks knew he was capable of. Although Walker had taken to calling the Birmingham campaign "Project C," for "confrontation," he had told King, "I haven't found the key yet, but I'm going to." Now, the chance gathering of that late-afternoon crowd, and one man's unrestrainable anger toward the police dogs, had suddenly given the movement the national coverage King and Walker had been seeking. Walker thought that their problems in recruiting demonstrators were solved, that crowds of black bystanders could give the protests the "mass" quality that staff recruiters had not yet been able to produce. He reached King by phone, and informed him excitedly, "I've got it. I've got it." From now on, if demonstrations took place when the black populace was present and ready to look on, press reports would portray mass community support for the protests even if no more than a few dozen marchers had been recruited. SNCC's James Forman encountered Walker and Dorothy Cotton at the SCLC headquarters, the Gaston Motel, soon after Walker made that realization, and was appalled at their joy over the day's events. They "were jumping up and down, elated," Forman later wrote. "They said over and over again, 'We've got a movement. We've got a movement. We had some police brutality. They brought out the dogs. We've got a movement.' " To Forman, this celebration "was a disgusting moment . . . for it seemed very cold, cruel and calculating to be happy about police brutality coming down on innocent people, bystanders, no matter what purpose it served." Walker's enthusiasm was soon tempered, however, when he realized that these "helpful" events were dependent upon the movement having at least some protesters, a problem made no less pressing by Sunday's violent clash.

King took a major step toward surmounting that obstacle with a persuasive appearance before the large group of black ministers on Monday. He apologized for not having consulted with them earlier about the protests, but explained that the need for secrecy had been paramount. He argued that the time for protests had come, and that the black community should not allow internal disunity to halt the movement. He repeated those contentions the next day to the gathering of black professionals, who also responded positively. The crowds at both the Monday and Tuesday night mass meetings were larger and more enthusiastic. Late Tuesday, following the arrest of another small group of protesters, word spread that Reverend Ware's Baptist Ministers' Conference had voted unanimously to support the protests and that wealthy businessman A. G. Gaston also was ready to declare his support.

King's ability to bring the black leadership to his side, and his declarations at the evening rallies that he intended to get arrested, led the white business community to launch one more effort to forestall large-scale protests. Sidney Smyer, the key white negotiator, arranged to meet secretly with Shuttlesworth, who had been released from jail the day before. Believing he was in a position of strength, Shuttlesworth told Smyer that whites would have to grant all of the movement's requests, plus commit themselves to prompt school desegregation, in order to avoid mass demonstrations. Smyer demurred and emphasized that the merchants could not speak for Boutwell or the city. Given the governmental confusion, there was no way that any official negotiations could be undertaken, he explained.

Although the Wednesday issue of Birmingham's black newspaper, the *World*, decried direct action as "both wasteful and worthless," that editorial evaluation was outweighed by Gaston's declaration of support. King told the Wednesday night mass meeting that on Friday, "Ralph Abernathy and I will make our move. I can't think of a better day than Good Friday for a move for freedom," and a move toward jail. At virtually the same moment, two city attorneys asked State Circuit Court Judge William A. Jenkins, Jr., to issue a temporary injunction against King and other movement leaders barring all marches or other protests. Jenkins signed the request at 9:00 P.M., and four hours later the court order was served on King, Abernathy, and Shuttlesworth.

. . . At 8:30 A.M. Friday, some two dozen people gathered in King's room. King sat at the head of the bed and outlined the problem to his colleagues. There were protesters in jail who had been promised they would be bailed out in less than a week, and for whom there were no monies to secure their release. Anyone else arrested would be in a similar fix. King felt he had a responsibility to keep the promises the movement had made to these people. However, there were other considerations. He had been telling everyone for a week now that he would be arrested. The campaign had not caught fire, and King hoped that his arrest would inspire black citizens who had not yet made a commitment to the movement. Then King sat back to listen to his colleagues' opinions. As the discussion progressed, a consensus emerged: No matter whether King got arrested or stayed out, the movement was in trouble. If he backed off, it would look like Albany. Any judge willing to sign an order could stop King in his tracks and immobilize the campaign. Perhaps that would allow him to raise the funds, but there might not be a Birmingham movement left in which to use them if the protests came to an end because of Jenkins. Alternatively, if King did submit to arrest, there was no guaranteeing when he would be released, and he would be cut off from contact with movement colleagues. Either way, his choice might result in disaster. He was uncertain what to do, and later remarked that "a sense of doom began to pervade the room."

Deeply troubled, King told his colleagues he would pray over the decision alone in another room. He left, and the others waited for his return. Thirty minutes later, King reappeared wearing a new pair of blue-denim overalls. The group quieted, and King spoke with firmness. "The path is clear to me. I've got to march. I've got so many people depending on me. I've got to march." The injunction would have to be disobeyed. "If we obey it, then we are out of business." As some remembered it, Daddy King was one of the first to speak up. "Son, I've never interfered with any of your civil rights activities, but I think at this time my advice would be to you to not violate the injunction." King let his father finish, then said no, there were other things more important than the injunction. With a downcast look, Dad acquiesced.

It was well past noon, and King and Abernathy hurried to Sixth Avenue Zion Hill Baptist Church, where the march would begin. Only fifty movement supporters stood ready to join the Good Friday pilgrimage. The group set out for City Hall in a double-file column, the two SCLC leaders at the front. They moved at a moderate pace, with curious onlookers bringing up the rear and Wyatt Walker striding alongside, camera in hand, ready to photograph whatever transpired. Four and a half blocks from their starting point they met a squad of Connor's officers ready to block their advance. A paddy wagon pulled up, the marchers were placed under arrest, and within moments they were on their way to the downtown city jail. Photos showing an apprehensive-looking King, clad in his blue overalls and being led to the wagon, were flashed around the world.

At that evening's mass meeting, Wyatt Walker called for student supporters to rally on Saturday morning and for volunteers to "test" segregated white churches on Sunday. Earlier that day, he noted, just hours before King's arrest, some of Birmingham's most liberal white churchmen had condemned the protests as "unwise and untimely" and had urged "our own Negro community to withdraw support from these demonstrations." They had lashed out at "outsiders," and had asserted that black demands "should be pressed in the courts and in negotiations among local leaders, and not in the street." The ministers failed to mention that almost every white church in Birmingham refused to admit black worshipers, and also omitted any reference to the undependable track record of white negotiators over the past year. It was hard to believe that the white churchmen were being anything other than disingenuous by publicly reprimanding the *black* leadership for Birmingham's lack of biracial negotiations.

At the city jail, King was placed in solitary confinement, cut off from contact even with Abernathy. He expected some word from the movement's lawyers, but the long night passed without news from anyone on the outside. Jail going had always been extremely difficult for King, even when Abernathy accompanied him, but the loneliness of solitary confinement and absence of outside contact made it considerably more painful. King said later that first night in the Birmingham jail represented some of "the longest, most frustrating and bewildering hours I have lived . . . I was besieged with worry."

Unbeknownst to King, movement attorney Norman Amaker tried to see him at the jail Friday evening. The jailers told Amaker he could meet with King only with guards present. Amaker had protested this denial of a private conversation and refused to accept a monitored one. At about 11:00 P.M., Amaker told Wyatt Walker what had transpired, and Walker was infuriated. Near midnight, Walker called Burke Marshall at home to ask for federal help. Marshall promised to make inquiries, and later in the morning Walker sent a telegram to President Kennedy: WE ASK THAT YOU USE THE INFLUENCE OF YOUR HIGH OFFICE TO PERSUADE THE CITY OFFICIALS OF BIRMINGHAM TO AFFORD AT LEAST A MODICUM OF HUMAN TREATMENT to King and Abernathy. John Kennedy had heard news reports of King's imprisonment and called Marshall to inquire about the Birmingham situation. Marshall explained to the president, as he had to reporters, that no grounds existed for federal action. By late Saturday afternoon, movement attorneys made contact with King, but questions of further access and of King's opportunity to speak by phone with people on the outside remained unresolved. Wyatt Walker knew a good issue when it was placed in his lap, so on Sunday morning he told a concerned Coretta King that they should take additional steps to draw attention to the troubling conditions under which her husband was being held. Coretta suggested she issue a statement, but Walker recommended that she call President Kennedy instead. Mrs. King demurred, saying they should get a note to her husband asking his judgment before they tried that. Walker consented but had no success in getting the message through. Later in the day he called Coretta back, reported that he had been unable to make any contact with King, and encouraged her to phone the White House. She agreed, calling both there and at Vice-President Lyndon Johnson's office without getting through to anyone. Finally, an operator connected her with presidential press secretary Pierre Salinger, who was in Florida with his boss. Salinger promised to pass along her message, and forty-five minutes later Attorney General Robert Kennedy phoned Mrs. King. He expressed the administration's concern and said that the Justice Department would make inquiries in Birmingham about the conditions of her husband's imprisonment.

At the time those phone calls were taking place, King's brother, A.D., tried to lead a small march from Sixteenth Street Baptist Church to the jail. The thirty participants were arrested before getting very far, but just like one week earlier, an angry crowd gathered while the police were waiting for their paddy wagons to arrive. Officers arrested one onlooker, and were showered with rocks by other bystanders. The police moved in with clubs, and the crowd dispersed. Once again those police tactics received prominent coverage in Monday's national newspapers.

Although Bull Connor personally blocked movement attorneys from seeing King at midafternoon Sunday, by the end of the day lawyers Arthur Shores and Orzell Billingsley were allowed to meet with him. They told King that there was no good news yet on the financial front, but that Clarence Jones would be arriving from New York on Monday. King was worried about the movement's lack of bail money when he was arraigned in court the next morning but later that afternoon Jones arrived at the jail to report that [entertainer Harry] Belafonte and other supporters had obtained sufficient funds for SCLC to meet all the bail costs. King was relieved, and relaxed for the first time since his arrest. His faith that Friday's decision would somehow prove correct had been justified. Meanwhile, movement attorneys filed an application to dissolve Jenkins's injunction banning all protests, and the city's lawyers petitioned the judge to hold King and his colleagues in contempt for defying that edict.

On Monday afternoon, without warning, came just the event Walker had been hoping for ever since Friday's arrests: John Kennedy phoned Coretta King to express his concern about her husband's imprisonment and to assure her that FBI agents had ascertained he was safe. Furthermore, Kennedy said, it had been arranged for King to phone her, and she should await his call. Thirty minutes later, a somewhat puzzled King was told by his jailers that he could call home. He was pleased, but surmised correctly that the phone was tapped and that whatever he and his wife said would not be private. After initial greetings, he assured Coretta that he was doing "pretty good," and she eagerly told him what had transpired. "I just got a call from the President and he told me you were going to call me in a few minutes." Yoki and Marty [the Kings' children] came on the line . . . and King spoke with them before asking Coretta about her earlier comment.

"Who did you say called you?"

"Kennedy, the president."

"Did he call you direct?"

"Yes, and he told me you were going to call in a few minutes. It was about thirty minutes ago. He called from Palm Beach. I tried to phone him yesterday."

"Is that known?"

"It's known here; I just got it."

"Let Wyatt know."

"The executive in Birmingham?"

"Yes, do that right now."

King was elated at John Kennedy's gesture and wanted to be certain that news of it was disseminated quickly. He asked his wife about their new baby, Bernice, and reassured her that his own spirit was "all right." Coretta told him of the FBI inquiries, which King had not heard about, and mentioned her phone conversation with Robert Kennedy the night before. She thought he might call back today, but instead "it was the President himself, and he assured me of his concern. He asked if we had any complaints and said if we did to be sure and let them know." King responded:

"Be sure and get that to the Reverend. I think it will make a very good statement."

"He's very sympathetic and kept saying, 'How are you, I understand you have a little baby.' He said things might get better with the new [city] administration. This is a problem."

"Is it being carried well [by the press]?"

"Not too well here, still not too well. There was a good program today with Dick Arnell."

"What about the *Constitution*? . . ."

"They have been carrying articles. Yesterday they had something. . . . The *[Atlanta Daily] World* has had front page about every day recently, but it was not accurate. They said the boycott was not effective. There was something this morning about yesterday. It's been carried pretty good. They had a picture last night of A.D. [King]. I think with the national it's been pretty good; it's been pretty good today."

"When you get this over it will help."

Coretta explained she would travel to Birmingham on Thursday, and King asked her to give his greetings to his parents. He assured his wife that the jail food was "all right," and told her there was nothing she needed to bring him. "I'll probably come out in the next day or so. Be sure to get in touch with the Reverend. I think this gives it a new dimension."

Coretta notified Wyatt Walker of these developments, and Walker announced the news of John Kennedy's phone call to that evening's mass rally. Newsmen reported it, and Birmingham police officials denied there had been federal pressure to allow King to make his call. The decision, they claimed, had been entirely their own. Walker also announced that the Birmingham campaign would move into its second phase, with primary efforts being directed toward voter registration. Asked by reporters to explain the shift from integrating lunch counters to voting, Andrew Young said that "this is the only way we can get the Justice Department in on this."

On Thursday afternoon Coretta King and Juanita Abernathy visited their husbands. They found them in good spirits. King explained he had been spending much of his time composing a response to the criticisms of the protests voiced by local white religious leaders a week earlier. Attorneys Shores, Billingsley, and Jones had been visiting King daily, and had been passing the handwritten sheets to Walker, who would go over them each evening and then have them typed up by his secretary, Willie Pearl Mackey. The typescripts would be sent back to King for editing. Shortly after Coretta's visit, Walker phoned Burke Marshall to say that the black leadership would like him to meet with Fred Shuttlesworth the next morning in Washington. Marshall granted the appointment but reiterated both to Shuttlesworth and SCLC's Walter Fauntroy that no grounds for federal action existed. Shuttlesworth returned to Birmingham in time for Friday night's mass meeting, and announced to the crowd that King and Abernathy would be leaving jail voluntarily on Saturday. When they were released, the two men were blocked from holding an impromptu press conference at the jail, but told reporters afterward that although they would be heading to Atlanta that night in order to preach at their respective churches the next morning, they would return to Birmingham almost immediately and the protest campaign would go forward.

Monday morning, April 22, King and fourteen others went on trial before Judge Jenkins on the charge of violating his injunction. The proceedings continued through Wednesday afternoon, with defense attorneys winning dismissal of the charges against four defendants on the grounds that they had never been served with the order. Otherwise, Jenkins gave short shrift to the lawyers' efforts to set forth the constitutional infirmities of his injunction. When not in court, King and his colleagues spent much of their time discussing the best avenues for appealing Jenkins's decision once the expected guilty verdicts were announced, and how to continue the protests in the wake of that outcome. King told one midweek mass meeting that he expected to be sent back to jail, and that he was prepared for that burden. ''I would rather stay in jail the rest of my days than make a butchery of my conscience. . . . I'm ready to go to jail with my colleagues; I will die there if necessary.'' James Bevel of SCLC and Isaac ''Ike'' Reynolds from CORE [Congress of Racial Equality] were training youths for future demonstrations, and on Thursday, white intermediary Sidney Smyer and two young lawyers, David Vann and Erskine Smith, indicated to the local black leadership that meaningful biracial negotiations might soon be in the offing. That same day, King had an unsatisfactory meeting with several local white ministers. He felt that their criticism of the movement was one more indication of the southwide failure of white clergy to play a positive role in reforming the region's morally repulsive racial practices. These Birmingham clergy had asserted that black leaders were not interested in negotiating, but King pointed out that the disinterest in meaningful talks lay with the whites. ''The purpose of . . . direct action is to create a situation so crisis-packed that it will inevitably open the door to negotiation. . . . We who engage in nonviolent direct action are not the creators of tension. We merely bring to the surface the hidden tension that is already alive. We bring it out in the open where it can be seen and dealt with.'' The movement's efforts to do just that, King made clear at that Thursday session, would go forward aggressively.

On Friday morning, Judge Jenkins announced that all eleven defendants were guilty of criminal contempt. He sentenced each of them to five days in jail and a $50 fine. The sentences would be held in abeyance while appeals were pursued. King told the crowd at that evening's mass meeting that they must continue the boycott of the downtown stores and expand their efforts to integrate worship services at Birmingham's white churches. King had a Sunday preaching engagement in Little Rock, Arkansas, but

Walker and Bevel continued to recruit more young demonstrators for future protests. Saturday's rally marked the twenty-fifth consecutive night on which the movement had held a mass meeting, but this time the crowd was small and showed little promise of furnishing the numbers of protesters Walker had hoped for. Black "testers" were admitted to nine of thirty-eight white churches on Sunday morning, and King canceled a speech in Houston to return to Birmingham on Monday. Movement leaders met that day to discuss their next steps, and to hear Bevel and Reynolds argue that the movement's shortage of demonstrators could be remedied if organizers enlisted the hundreds of black high school students who were eager to participate in direct-action protests. Several local black adults who sat on the advisory board, or "central committee," that had been set up as part of King's entreaties earlier in the month opposed the use of teenagers, but Bevel was more persuasive. National news coverage of Birmingham had all but vanished over the past few days, and King was worried that national newsmen would leave town. "You know, we've got to get something going. The press is leaving, we've got to get going," King told John Thomas Porter, who was astounded by King's emphasis on pragmatic rather than spiritual considerations. " 'We've got to pick up everything, because the press is leaving.' And I looked at him," Porter recalled, "and really couldn't believe my ears to hear him say that we need the press." King spoke with some urgency, and his SCLC associates agreed that "the press is losing interest. We've got to do something to get their attention again." Bevel's plan for using the high school students would do just that, and Walker endorsed it enthusiastically. "We needed more troops. We had run out of troops. We had scraped the bottom of the barrel of adults who could go," Walker later explained. "We needed something new," and Bevel's proposal fit the bill. Though King held back from giving authorization for the use of student demonstrators, he endorsed the suggestion that interested students be told to gather at Sixteenth Street church at noon Thursday.

By midday Tuesday, scores of leaflets were circulating in Birmingham's black high schools urging students to join Thursday's gathering. Worried local FBI agents warned the city's police intelligence squad commander, Maurice House, and two white detectives who attended that evening's mass rally reported that Bevel had given clear indications that some big plans were on tap for Thursday. Although King, Walker, Shuttlesworth, and Abernathy left town overnight for a fund-raising rally in Memphis, Bevel, Reynolds, Dorothy Cotton, and Andrew Young spent all of Tuesday and Wednesday spreading the word about the Thursday action. Shortly before noon on Thursday the leaders gathered. Sixteenth Street church was packed with hundreds of eager youngsters. Connor's forces were deployed alongside Kelly Ingram Park, a square-block expanse of greenery marking the symbolic dividing line between the black district and white downtown. An effort by officials at Parker High School to detain their pupils backfired as scores jumped over fences to head for Sixteenth Street. Although King was hesitant about unleashing the untrained teenagers, especially when black adults were arguing that children should not be used as the shock troops of the movement, Bevel and Walker knew it was no time for hesitation. Shortly after noon, while King remained closeted at the Gaston Motel, the first wave of youngsters headed out the door of Sixteenth Street church in a brave pilgrimage to City Hall. Singing and laughing, the several hundred teenagers willingly submitted to arrest at the hands of Birmingham's police. After the first wave of students had been taken into custody and driven away, a second group marched out of Sixteenth Street church, and then a third. James Bevel was in direct command of the young troops, although Wyatt Walker served as overall field general, coordinating tactical moves with Bevel, Young, and others through a system of walkie-talkies. Walker was optimistic that the young masses, and the attendant interest of black adults, would be just what was needed to evoke segregationist brutality from the trigger-tempered Connor. Walker wanted to mount as strong an effort as possible, and did not shy from employing a wide variety of tactics, some of which he did not reveal to King. One example, Walker said later, was dispatching "eight or ten guys to different quarters of the town to turn in false alarms." Connor was trying to mass both the police and the hoses of the city's fire companies in the area between the protesters and downtown, and Walker's tactics were aimed at depleting Connor's forces. Very few had knowledge of such efforts, but in subsequent years Walker made no apologies for employing tactics he felt would be effective for revealing to the entire nation the racist brutality of Connor and the system he represented. "I had to do what had to be done," Walker explained. "At times I would accommodate or alter my morality for the sake of getting a job done . . . I did it consciously. I felt I had no choice. I wasn't dealing with a moral situation when I dealt with a Bull Connor. We did with design precipitate crises, crucial crises in order to expose what the black community was up against," Walker said. "There was premeditation and calculated design in that for which I don't think we ever made any apologies." King and Walker were reticent about their pragmatism, even in private, and Walker purposely kept some of the specifics from his boss. "Dr. King never knew that I sent people to turn in false alarms . . . that's one thing I was very guarded about, because I knew he would not want to do that." Thursday afternoon, while King continued to ponder using the children, Walker and Bevel proved within several hours that the decision had been one of the wisest SCLC had made.

By Thursday night more than five hundred marchers had been taken into custody, and Birmingham was again in the headlines. More than two thousand people crowded into that evening's mass meeting. King and his colleagues met late into the night discussing more youth marches for Friday. The next morning King told reporters that Friday afternoon's demonstrations would be even more massive than Thursday's. "We intend to negotiate from strength. If the white power structure of this city will meet some of our minimum demands, then we will consider calling off the demonstrations, but we want promises, plus action." In midafternoon, another column of young demonstrators marched out of Sixteenth Street church and headed east toward Connor's officers. At the front of the ranks stood fire fighters equipped with high-pressure hoses, ready to repulse any protesters who attempted to evade the blockade. Black onlookers gathered along the fringes of Kelly Ingram Park, and some hurled verbal taunts at the white officers. Connor was on the scene, and ordered six police dogs deployed to force the crowd back. The sight of the snarling dogs further roused the hostility of the onlookers, and rocks and bottles began to sail out of the crowd toward the police and firemen. Then Connor ordered the dogs into action, and instructed that the powerful hoses be used to drive the demonstrators and bystanders from the park. "I want to see the dogs work. Look at those niggers run," one newsman quoted Connor as yelling. Firemen used the hoses to chase protesters out of the park and away from nearby buildings; the high-pressure water literally tore the clothes off some victims' backs. After a half hour of this brutal and uneven combat, no black faces remained in Ingram Park. The movement's foot soldiers retreated to the church, and the hundreds of onlookers scattered.

Even before the ground in Ingram Park was dry, Burke Marshall was on the phone to King and others in Birmingham. He had called King that morning to question the wisdom of any further mass demonstrations, and now he remonstrated over the disorder that had erupted that afternoon. Marshall spoke also with *Birmingham News* publisher Vincent Townsend, black businessman A. G. Gaston, and Jefferson County Sheriff Mel Bailey. From all of them he heard that there were no ongoing biracial discussions, and that Birmingham's white leadership had no idea what concessions the blacks would require in order to halt the protests. Marshall later said he had found King rather vague on the movement's precise goals, but in addressing that evening's mass meeting, King stressed to the crowd and the many reporters present the protests' four principal aims: desegregation of the downtown stores, better job opportunities for blacks in those stores, dismissal of all charges against demonstrators, and establishment of a biracial negotiating committee to discuss school desegregation and other aspects of Birmingham life. King also announced that new demonstrations would take place on Saturday, and noted that Connor had one weapon in reserve behind his dogs and hoses: an armored military vehicle called the "tank," which appropriately was painted white.

Friday's clash made Saturday headlines across the country. Striking photographs of the snarling dogs and the high-pressure hoses appeared everywhere. One popular picture depicted a Birmingham officer holding a black citizen with one hand and a police dog's leash in the other while the dog attempted to sink it's teeth into the man's stomach. News reports stated that three people had been treated at hospitals for dog bites, that five black children had been injured by the fire hoses or police clubs, and that one black woman bystander had accused police of knocking her down and kicking her in the stomach intentionally. Reactions to such images were strong, and members of one group that visited President Kennedy Saturday morning stated that the chief executive had said the photos made him "sick." Kennedy also mentioned that although he had no power to intervene, Burke Marshall and Assistant Deputy Attorney General Joseph Dolan were on their way to Birmingham to mediate.

King was leery about Marshall coming to Birmingham. Perhaps, as in Albany, the Kennedy administration was interested not in winning greater racial justice, but in quieting racial trouble and getting those scenes of violence out of the national and international media. When Marshall arrived, however, King's worries dissipated. Marshall immediately met with Smyer, David Vann, Erskine Smith, and several of the downtown merchants to press for biracial talks and meaningful concessions. He told them he would not advise them what to do but would endeavor to be helpful. Marshall believed the black leadership would settle for less than it was demanding. He also understood that there was no possibility of persuading the local black leadership to break away from King and Shuttlesworth, as the whites hoped. Reputable lawmen explained that the involvement of black bystanders meant that the demonstrations were only loosely under SCLC's control, and that unrestrained combat could break out at any time. Additionally, the city's jails were full and it appeared likely that Connor would pursue a policy of violently dispersing the demonstrators rather than arrest people he could not imprison. The movement's long-proclaimed desire to "fill the jails" had become a reality. Faced with those circumstances, the white representatives felt that they had little choice but to take a step forward. They agreed that a larger, more representative group would meet with Marshall on Sunday to consider new negotiations with black representatives.

While Marshall had been prodding those moderate whites, James Bevel brought another column of young protesters up against Bull Connor's men on Saturday afternoon. The atmosphere was even tenser than on Friday, and a large crowd of onlookers taunted the police. Connor kept the police dogs in their kennel trucks, but the high-pressure fire hoses drove the throng out of Kelly Ingram Park. Angry members of the crowd threw rocks, and Bevel and other organizers used bullhorns to ask the black citizenry to disperse before further violence erupted. Photographs in Sunday papers across the country showed club-wielding officers pursuing drenched black citizens as they fled the scene.

King and Walker were overjoyed at Connor's tactical stupidity and hoped it would continue. As Walker commented later:

> Bull Connor had something in his mind about not letting these niggers get to City Hall. I prayed that he'd keep trying to stop us. . . . Birmingham would have been lost if Bull had let us go down to the City Hall and pray; if he had let us do that and stepped aside, what else would be new? There would be no movement, no publicity. But all he could see was stopping us before we got there. We had calculated for the stupidity of a Bull Connor.

While Connor's allies in city government, outgoing Mayor Arthur Hanes and Police Chief Jamie Moore, thought he had lost his head, movement strategists such as Walker wondered if Connor was intentionally using such tactics to bolster his reputation with segregationist voters in preparation for a statewide political race. Chief Moore thought Connor did not care if his actions were winning sympathy and support around the globe for Birmingham's protesters. Connor's only priority was teaching those good-for-nothing agitators who was boss. Walker, on the other hand, presumed that Connor, like the movement's leaders, was more calculating than his public image indicated:

> He was a perfect adversary. Connor wanted publicity, he wanted his name in the paper. He believed that he would be the state's most popular politician if he treated the black violently, bloodily, and sternly. We knew that the psyche of the white redneck was such that he would inevitably do something to help our cause.

. . . Birmingham's merchants spent much of Sunday discussing how to resolve the crisis. At an afternoon meeting, the entire group reluctantly agreed that they had no choice but to make contact with the black leadership and try to halt the protests. "The idea of negotiation," one participant indicated, "was offensive to all present," but "the prospect of continued violence" was "an unpleasant and even more disastrous alternative." They emphasized to each other that they could negotiate only matters involving their own stores, and not city government issues, but they instructed Smyer and Vann to contact black businessman A. G. Gaston and ask for a meeting that night with black representatives. Gaston assented and the session was arranged. It began, one participant said, with "a free interchange of counter accusations of bad faith" between the two sides. Then the black representatives presented a brief document entitled "Points for Progress," which specified the movement's minimum demands. These were:

1. Immediate desegregation of all store facilities including lunch counters, rest rooms, and fitting rooms.
2. Immediate upgrading of store employees and a program of nondiscriminatory hiring.
3. Merchant pressure on city government to drop all charges against arrested demonstrators.
4. Merchant pressure on city government to establish [a] biracial committee to deal with future problems and to develop specific programs for the hiring of Negro policemen, removal of voter registration obstacles, school desegregation, reopening of all municipal facilities, and the desegregation of movies and hotels.

The white representatives declared that points three and four were not negotiable. They "absolutely refused to deal in any way with matters before the courts, or prerogatives of city government." Additionally, the representatives of some stores claimed they had already removed some segregation signs and begun upgrading their black employees. Furthermore, the whites said they could do nothing until the question of which administration was the real city government had been settled. On that negative note the session ended.

Monday morning, Burke Marshall met with King for two hours to discuss the whites' position. Further conversations between the various parties continued throughout the day, and early in the afternoon more protesters confronted Connor's forces at the edge of Kelly Ingram Park. The police and firemen used neither dogs nor hoses, but arrested all the marchers. Wave after wave of young protesters willingly submitted to arrest, and by the end of the afternoon more than one thousand had been taken into custody. Birmingham no longer had any facilities in which to house them, so hundreds were placed into an uncovered outdoor pen with no protection from a chilly rain. SNCC's James Forman, trying to assume a role in the protests despite SCLC's hostility, argued to King that the leadership had to do something about that. After some angry words, King, Forman, and Bevel went to the stockade, after which King called Marshall to complain. Later, at the mass meeting, he reassured the crowd that the prisoners were being moved indoors.

The black and white negotiators met again Monday night. The merchants said they had five or six black employees who could be promoted to sales jobs immediately, and that stores with fitting rooms would integrate them. The whites wanted to delay desegregation of lunch counters and rest rooms until the federal courts compelled the city to begin desegregating its schools, but the blacks rejected this suggestion and argued that the counters be integrated right away *if* Boutwell's administration won the legal battle over which was the true city government. The discussion bogged down at that point, and both sides agreed to talk further on Tuesday.

Late Monday evening, after the black negotiators reported back, the movement's leaders began making plans for an intensification of demonstrations on Tuesday morning. Walker, Bevel, Dorothy Cotton, and Forman developed a scenario for replacing the standard pattern of several sequential waves of afternoon marchers with fifteen separate groups of protesters who would strike simultaneously at noontime, when most of the police were on their lunch break, in an effort to get a substantial number of young demonstrators into the heart of downtown Birmingham. With so many different groups heading downtown by a variety of routes, some no doubt would succeed in getting there.

Tuesday morning, May 7, the white merchants met with Smyer, Vann, and Erskine Smith to mull over where they stood in the negotiations. The merchants believed they could satisfy the demand for upgraded jobs in the stores, but most remained opposed to lunch-counter integration before school desegregation began. More important, they felt that they could do nothing concerning the arrest charges or further biracial discussions about city government policies unless a larger group of white notables was drawn into the negotiations. If the merchants could offer nothing on those latter points to the black representatives, it was clear that no hope existed of ending the protests through negotiations. If there was no settlement, no one could predict what might happen. "Continued use of force on the demonstrators" would "aggravate the situation further," but the police could not make more arrests, for "there was no room in the jails," as one white negotiator explained. With considerable exasperation, the store owners agreed that they would have to ask all seventy-odd members of the "Senior Citizens Committee," a Chamber of Commerce-sponsored group established eight months earlier to push the change of government referendum, to meet that afternoon to discuss what to do. Sidney Smyer informed Burke Marshall, who immediately got on the phone to Washington to be certain that Kennedy officials would contact their acquaintances among Birmingham's Senior Citizens to urge that the white leadership authorize a comprehensive settlement.

By noontime Tuesday, movement staffers had six hundred young demonstrators ready to invade downtown Birmingham. King told newsmen that "demonstrations will go on until some progress has been made," and when the noon hour came, SCLC made good on King's promise. Catching the police off guard, the groups of protesters made it into the heart of the city without one person being arrested. Dozens of youngsters scampered through the business district, causing no damage but shattering whites' presumption that the protesters were not their problem and could be kept in check by lawmen. NEGRO MOBS BREAK THROUGH POLICE screamed that afternoon's edition of the *Birmingham News*. Anxious members of the Senior Citizens Committee worried what would come next as they assembled for the early-afternoon meeting. Sidney Smyer introduced Jefferson County Sheriff Mel Bailey, who explained that the day's events were evidence that the police had been stretched to the breaking point. He told them that another clash was now under way in Kelly Ingram Park between Connor's men and a second wave of protesters whom SCLC had attempted to send downtown. Smyer also introduced Burke Marshall, who recommended a negotiated peace. Several men spoke in favor of pursuing an agreement, and a reluctant consensus emerged that a settlement would have to be negotiated unless the city wanted to bring in state troopers or national guardsmen. "None of the Senior Citizens were anxious to urge a settlement," one participant later indicated, "but only a few preferred an apparently imminent declaration of martial law." The merchants asked that the larger body vote its consent for their negotiators to pursue a comprehensive settlement with the black leaders, and the eighty people did so with only two or three dissents. Everyone present understood that they were committing themselves to the desegregation of downtown facilities as soon as Boutwell's administration was victorious in the courts, and to support ongoing biracial discussions.

Burke Marshall left the meeting extremely pleased. He called the White House to report that he expected a settlement could be won in a day or so's time. That sounded all the better in light of the continuing brutality Connor's forces had demonstrated that afternoon. After the successful noontime breakthrough into downtown Birmingham, King and Walker ordered a second attempt several hours later. This time, however, the police and firemen were waiting. An angry James Forman went to the Gaston Motel to ask King to call it off, since serious injuries seemed certain to result. King was on the phone; he had changed into his pajamas and was eating a steak for lunch. Forman took one look and gave up. He felt again how wide the gap had grown between the style of the SNCC's field-workers and that of King's SLC.

When the young demonstrators ventured toward Connor's men, the hoses were unleashed and black onlookers began to pelt the officers with bricks and bottles. The firemen used the high-powered water to drive the blacks back toward Sixteenth Street church, and movement staffers asked their troops to pull back. Fred Shuttlesworth was slammed against a wall by a blast from one hose and was carried away on a stretcher. Newsmen quoted Bull Connor expressing regret that Shuttlesworth had left in an ambulance and not a hearse. While many reporters distinguished between the movement's peaceful protesters and the violent bystanders, almost all observers could see that SLC's staff had no way of maintaining control of the situation. Some accounts of the Tuesday afternoon clash bore headlines such as RIOTING NEGROES ROUTED BY POLICE, and King and his aides knew that that sort of national portrayal could harm the movement's cause.

Tuesday evening four white negotiators—Smyer, Vann, Edward Norton of Royal Crown Cola, and Roper Dial of Sears—met privately with L. H. Pitts, Arthur Shores, and SLC's Andrew Young. Burke Marshall and Billy Hamilton, Boutwell's chief aide, also were present. In several hours time the small group reached agreement on the desegregation of the downtown stores, the upgrading of black employment opportunities, and the establishment of a committee for ongoing biracial discussions. Although total accord was not reached on the precise wording with which to announce those points, a fourth topic remained a serious obstacle: By what means would the hundreds of arrested demonstrators be released and the charges against them dropped? The whites were adamant that they could not arrange an amnesty, and the blacks were reluctant to concede this point and be faced with the massive financial obligations that the bonding and defense of some 2,600 people would entail. Though everyone present felt that the group was close to a settlement, the session broke up with no firm commitment except a promise to talk again on Wednesday.

. . . King believed that the progress in the negotiations, and Tuesday's near riot, argued for a one-day truce in demonstrations. Such a halt would signify the blacks' good faith to the white negotiators, and perhaps hasten a settlement. If an agreement was not won, demonstrations could resume Thursday, with movement staffers better prepared to keep a tight rein on them. . . .

One person who was not pleased by the truce was Fred Shuttlesworth, who had left the hospital but remained under sedation at the Gaston Motel. Early Wednesday afternoon, Shuttlesworth went to meet King at the home of John and Addine Drew. Shuttlesworth was livid because King had halted the demonstrations without notifying him. ACMHR's fiery leader had always been more suspicious of Marshall's and the Kennedys' priorities than was his SLC colleague. Now it appeared that while Shuttlesworth had been hospitalized, King had caved in to pressure from Marshall to accept dubious promises from the white negotiators. Already unhappy with Marshall's role, and irritated that King had not visited him in the hospital, Shuttlesworth erupted when King told him that Wednesday's demonstrations had been called off. " 'Say that again, Martin,' " Shuttlesworth later recalled asking.

> "Did I hear you right?" He said, "We have decided to call off the demonstrations." I said, "Well, Martin, *who* decided?" He said, "Well, we just decided that we can't have negotiations with all this going on." I said, "Well, Martin, it's hard for me to see . . . how anybody could decide that without me. . . . We're not calling anything off. . . ." And he said, "Well, uh—" And I said, "Well, Martin, you know they *said* in Albany that you come in, get people excited and started, and you leave town." I said, "But I live here, the people trust me, and I have the responsibility after SCLC is gone, and I'm telling you it will not be called off."

. . . Another important figure who was not pleased with the truce was Bull Connor. Faced now with the likely loss of both his city post and his personal crusade to keep Birmingham segregated, Connor struck hard in a last-ditch effort to derail the talks. Late Wednesday afternoon, with no warning, Connor's officers confronted King and Abernathy with the news that the required value of the bonds on which they had been released three weeks earlier had been increased to $2,500 per person. The two men could pay up or return to custody. King and Abernathy declined to comply, and were taken to jail. That further enraged Fred Shuttlesworth. He announced that protests would resume immediately, and headed for Sixteenth Street church. Burke Marshall's subordinate, Joseph Dolan, physically waylaid the Birmingham leader and persuaded him to speak by phone with Robert Kennedy before returning to the streets. Meanwhile, Marshall and local black leaders quickly decided that the best way to blunt Connor's thrust was to post the money for King's and Abernathy's release. Within minutes businessman A. G. Gaston wrote out the checks, and King and Abernathy returned to the motel.

While the negotiations continued into Wednesday evening, King, under pressure from Shuttlesworth, told reporters that demonstrations would resume on Thursday if an agreement was not reached by 11:00 A.M. Thursday morning. The hour came and passed with no settlement and no marches. King told the news media that the truce had been extended while the talks continued. He acknowledged that tentative agreement had been reached on desegregating the stores and continuing the biracial discussions, but that neither the details of the employment accord nor the terms for the release of the jailed protesters had been finalized. The major obstacle was securing the several hundred thousand dollars that would be necessary to meet bail costs for the jailed demonstrators. The white representatives refused to budge on this point, and by midday Thursday both the black negotiators and Marshall realized that the movement would have to come up with the money. Gaston was willing to guarantee some of it, but Marshall and Robert Kennedy had to lend their assistance to secure the remainder. Contact was made with United Auto Workers President Walter Reuther and with the UAW's Washington attorney, Joseph L. Rauh, and four different labor organizations promised to supply $40,000 each to help meet the costs. With those commitments in hand, Rauh wired a guarantee for $160,000 to white Birmingham attorney Erskine Smith. That settled, David Vann, Andrew Young, and several others worked late into Thursday night finalizing the text of a "Birmingham Truce Agreement." The whites' fears dictated that the document not be released publicly, but all agreed that King could announce the general terms of the settlement sometime Friday.

The completed document intentionally papered over one specific demand that the negotiators had not resolved: the number of black sales clerks to be hired by the downtown stores. In their effort to reach an agreement, both sides had chosen to ignore that particular problem. However, the agreement did give the movement some of what it had been seeking on three of the four principal points: store desegregation, upgraded employment, and ongoing biracial talks. The movement's concession to pay the bail costs to secure the release of its protesters was not a part of the formal text. . . .

[Saturday] evening, while the movement's regular rally was taking place at A. D. King's First Baptist Church in suburban Ensley, the Ku Klux Klan gathered outside the city. Some conscientious city and state police investigators were thankful that the Klan had kept its distance from the daily demonstrations. Some of the investigators, aware of Bull Connor's close personal ties with several Klan activists, believed the Klan's restraint was not accidental, and that word had gone out to the white terrorists in April that they should stay clear of local racial events. Unlike previous periods of racial tension in Birmingham, the past six weeks had witnessed no terror bombings.

Late Saturday night, after Connor's earlier efforts to derail a settlement had failed, the terrorist lull suddenly ended. Shortly before midnight, a powerful bomb destroyed the front portion of A. D. King's home in Ensley. Luckily, the family was in the rear of the house and no one was injured. Friends had gathered on the Kings' lawn when a second loud explosion sounded from the direction of downtown. Immediately members of the crowd guessed the second target: the Gaston Motel. A powerful explosive had been detonated directly under and outside of King's room. In another stroke of good fortune, no one was injured by the motel blast. Joseph Lowery had changed his mind and decided to take the night train home to Nashville rather than stay over in King's room.

Police and firemen hurried to the motel, as a large crowd of angry black citizens gathered. Wyatt Walker and other activists moved through the crowd urging calm and reassuring everyone that there had been no injuries. Among themselves, however, the movement staffers were furious at what they perceived as an intentional setup. Until just hours earlier, the area around the motel and Ingram Park had been heavily patrolled by Alabama state troopers under the command of Colonel Al Lingo, a close ally of Connor's and a trusted confidant of Governor George C. Wallace. Then, as suddenly as they had withdrawn, Lingo's troopers returned to downtown Birmingham after the bombings. Some bystanders threw bricks and bottles at the officers, and the call went out for Connor's dogs and the white armored car. A full-scale riot was soon under way. Angry blacks overturned a passing car and set it afire, and brutal state troopers used their billy clubs on anyone within reach. Movement staffers had little success trying to halt the growing disorder. Violence flared in the area until after dawn. News stories the next day reported that one policeman had been stabbed during the lengthy melee, and many papers featured a photo of a heavily bloodied Birmingham police inspector who had been brained by a rock.

Martin King preached his Sunday morning sermon in Atlanta before hurrying back to Birmingham. He told his congregation that he had had no more than two hours sleep in one night for almost a week, but that he was happy with the accord and that the movement would not allow Saturday night's violence to destroy it. After church he spoke by phone with Robert Kennedy, whose Justice Department aides were pondering what federal action might be appropriate. While King flew into Birmingham and huddled with Joseph Dolan, Kennedy, Burke Marshall, and other administration strategists discussed whether federal troops should be sent into the city to restrain both potential black rioters and the state troopers. Kennedy was especially worried that any more white bombings might beget a black response of greater magnitude than Saturday night's clash. Kennedy dispatched two more assistants, Ramsey Clark and John Nolan, to Birmingham, and early that evening he and Marshall went to the White House to discuss the Birmingham situation with the president.

John Kennedy shared his brother's concerns about the provocative conduct of the Alabama state troopers and the black violence the lawmen might provoke. "This could trigger off a good deal of violence around the country" by blacks in other cities, the attorney general warned, and recommended the president act strongly to show blacks "that the federal government is their friend." John Kennedy agreed, emphasizing that everything should be done to save the Birmingham accord. "If the agreement blows up, the other remedy that we have . . . is to send legislation up to the Congress this week as our response to that action. . . . We may have to do that anyway, but at least that would be our public response . . . if the agreement blows up." The men discussed the possible use of soldiers in Birmingham, and Marshall stepped out to phone King to get his opinion of the situation. "He says he thinks that if there are no other incidents, like no other bombings, that he can control his people," Marshall reported back to Kennedy. The president decided he would federalize the Alabama National Guard to block any use of it by Governor Wallace, and would also move regular federal troops into position near Birmingham so that they would be available if needed. Later that night John Kennedy appeared on nationwide television to announce those steps and to pledge that violence would not be allowed to sabotage the Birmingham settlement. King spoke to a Sunday night meeting at one Birmingham church and tried to calm the volatile black community. Local white moderates lobbied hard to get Lingo's troopers withdrawn from town. On Monday, Sidney Smyer held a press conference to reiterate the business community's support for Friday's agreement. He noted pointedly that he had never met Martin Luther King during the negotiations, and that he understood the settlement would require only one black sales clerk somewhere among the downtown stores. Early in the afternoon King and a sizable press contingent took to the sidewalks for a pool-hall-by-pool-hall effort to sell nonviolence to black Birmingham. At the New Home Billiard Parlor, Ralph Abernathy quieted the players and introduced King to the ambivalent crowd. King spoke briefly, emphasizing that black violence hurt the movement's cause. "Bull Connor is happy when we use force." After a rendition of "We Shall Overcome," the group moved on to a similar establishment and repeated the procedure. Then Lingo's troopers moved in and halted the procession on the grounds that the walking tour obstructed Birmingham's sidewalks. A disappointed King retreated to the Gaston Motel. . . .

While Birmingham remained quiet throughout the week, pressure grew within the white community for a full airing of just who had agreed to the settlement, which so far had only Sidney Smyer's name publicly attached to it. On Thursday, May 16, Smyer finally released a list of the seventy-seven men who had authorized the white negotiators to proceed at the crucial session on May 7. Smyer again stated, with only a little stretching of the truth, that the white representatives had never dealt with any SCLC officials or out-of-towners, and stressed that the accord called only for one black salesclerk to be employed in a downtown store.

Smyer's statement led to new media reports that "King won little or nothing" in the settlement. The stories also harped on what one reporter called "King's exaggerated version of the concessions." Thursday afternoon King held a press conference to rebut those assertions and to repeat that the movement expected one black clerk to be hired in each of seven different downtown stores. King also, mistakenly, stated that Smyer had erred in saying lunch-counter and rest-room desegregation was pegged to the legal vindication of Boutwell's election rather than to the date of the agreement itself. He added that he had faith in the whites, but that the employment problem had to be resolved. The next morning a letter was dispatched over Shuttlesworth's signature to the white negotiators stating that "it is our understanding that at least one clerk in each of the major stores was the point of agreement." The letter made no reference to the purposely vague text of the agreement, and there was no response from the whites before King flew to Chicago for a weekend speech.

The first week's anniversary of the two bombings passed without incident, but at midday Monday, another conservative white effort to derail the settlement occurred. Birmingham school authorities expelled 1,100 students for having skipped classes to demonstrate. Local black leaders were outraged and issued an immediate call for a total boycott of all schools and white businesses. King was notified of this new problem and hurried back to Alabama. In a hastily called strategy meeting, he argued that the expulsions were simply one more Connor-style effort to destroy the agreement, and that the black leadership should go to court to win the students' reinstatement rather than react in a way that hostile whites would welcome.

On reflection, the black leaders agreed, and at that night's meeting King announced that the boycott call had been scrapped. The next morning, movement attorneys went into federal court seeking an order reinstating the pupils, and within thirty-six hours, Chief Judge Elbert P. Tuttle of the Fifth Circuit Court of Appeals issued the necessary command. One day later the finishing touch was placed upon the Birmingham accord when the Alabama Supreme Court ruled in Boutwell's favor and ordered Connor and his fellow commissioners to surrender their offices posthaste.

The apparent resolution of the many successive crises threatening the Birmingham accord gave King and his assistants their first real opportunity to reflect upon the events of the last seven weeks. In retrospect, they could see that they had prevailed despite their having begun with several misconceptions. First, they had not appreciated the depth of the split that existed within the Birmingham white community. Their expectations of how Bull Connor would react to mass protests had been fulfilled, and they had also correctly assumed that the segregationist preferences of the white business leadership would buckle under the economic pressure of a boycott. As Walker put it, "what I did in Birmingham I learned in Albany." SCLC had not fully understood, however, that white Birmingham lacked an effective civic leadership when the demonstrations began. Everyone appreciated the legal complexities arising from the two competing city administrations, but the movement had not perceived the deep-seated fear that kept Birmingham's economic elite impassive until the threat of citywide turmoil forced them into action on May 7. No matter how great an economic price the movement exacted from the downtown merchants, that price would seem insignificant if those merchants refused to follow their self-interest or if they were unable to influence the wielders of official power. Although the boycott had been effective, only the widespread disorder of that Tuesday afternoon had convinced the city's business leadership to settle. Masses of unrestrained black teenagers had convinced the downtown businessmen in a way that peaceful picketing or sit-ins never had that segregation was not worth the price they would have to pay.

At the outset King had misjudged the black community as well as the white. Fred Shuttlesworth had had neither the troops nor the adult peer support that SCLC had anticipated. Neither ACMHR nor the Miles College student body had been able to supply enough demonstrators, and only the recruitment of the eager high school students had given SCLC the foot soldiers it needed to reveal Connor's true colors to the nation. King's decision to go to jail despite the financial crisis had been the emotional high point of the campaign, but Walker's accidental discovery of how black bystanders could contribute to the movement's cause had been the principal strategic breakthrough. The teenagers and onlookers could not have contributed so well had it not been for Connor's tactical stupidity in repeatedly using police dogs and fire hoses. Walker had been sagacious and pragmatic in his efforts to use the protests to evoke those reactions from Connor's men. Walker appreciated the huge amount of sympathetic national news coverage those police excesses had garnered for the civil rights cause, and in private he made no excuse for his tactics. "I didn't believe in provo-cation—unless the stakes were right." In Birmingham the stakes had been right, and Connor had complied perfectly by attempting to keep the protes-ters from reaching City Hall. "We didn't really want to get down there," Walker admitted; the news coverage of Connor's efforts to block them was far more valuable. "In essence," Andrew Young commented, "we were consciously using the mass media to try to get across to the nation what our message was," that southern segregation was far more vicious than most white Americans had ever realized. "The movement was really about getting publicity for injustice . . . the injustice was there under the surface and as long as it stayed below the surface, nobody was concerned about it. You had to bring it out in the open." As Walker later boasted, "There never was any more skillful manipulation of the news media than there was in Birmingham." SCLC had succeeded in bringing the civil rights struggle to the forefront of the national consciousness. This success far outweighed the narrower question of whether the settlement provided for speedy enough desegregation of Birmingham's stores or an acceptable number of black sales clerks.

A New Generation of Black Leaders in Tuskegee

ROBERT J. NORRELL

The Macon County [Alabama] Democratic Club approached the Democratic primary in May 1964 with great anticipation. The TCA [Tuskegee Civic Association] leadership had formed the Democratic Club in 1954 to support the unsuccessful candidacy of Jessie P. Guzman for the Board of Education. Ten years of conflict had made club members more realistic about politics than they had been in 1954, but they now had good reason for optimism: blacks composed a majority of voters in the county. Under Gomillion's [C. G. Gomillion, head of TCA] direction, the Democratic Club had made preparations to see that black voting strength was felt fully in the coming election. It organized the county by precincts and chose men like Hosea Guice of Shorter to lead the voters of the rural beats. It arranged the appointment of blacks to work at the polls, an effort to counter possible intimidation of new voters. It held a series of candidates' forums throughout the county where, for the first time since Reconstruction, white candidates appeared in public to ask for black votes.

The Democratic Club endorsed candidates in seven local races. It rec-ommended three whites, including Sheriff Hornsby, who was running for the probate judgeship (because of poor health, Judge Varner had resigned that office in 1963), and candidates for positions on the county commission

From *Reaping the Whirlwind: The Civil Rights Movement in Tuskegee* by Robert J. Norrell. Copyright © 1985 by Robert Jefferson Norrell II, pp. 164–186. Reprinted by permission of Alfred A. Knopf, Inc.

and the county school board. The club supported four blacks: William C. Allen, the proprietor of a general store, and William J. Childs, the owner of a service station, received endorsements for justice of the peace, the lowest level of county magistrate; V. A. Edwards, a retired religion professor at the [Tuskegee] Institute, for a second seat open on the county commission; and Gomillion for a second position on the Board of Education. These endorsements bore the distinct markings of Gomillion's gradualist, interracial approach: he wanted blacks to move into officeholding slowly.

Gomillion chose a gradualist course because he believed that the Tuskegee example would influence the way other Alabamians and southerners viewed black political participation. He was determined not to fulfill conservatives' prediction that Tuskegee would reenact the worst horror of the Reconstruction myth—a political takeover by ignorant and unscrupulous blacks. Tuskegee would demonstrate that blacks and whites could govern a southern community as equal partners. The Tuskegee model would "encourage whites elsewhere to be willing to appoint or elect qualified Negroes, even in places where Negroes were less numerous than in Macon County." Gomillion hoped to show that blacks would not do to whites what had been done to them. Blacks in Tuskegee would abide by "principles that we had accused the white power structure of failing to honor in the past. . . . We were not interested in replacing white demagoguery with black demagoguery." A black takeover, Gomillion feared, might inspire spiteful whites, especially outgoing officeholders, to try to make new black politicians look inept or dishonest. "And then we would have been saddled with the blame," Gomillion said. Blacks' lack of experience in government made patience the practical course. "The truth is we *are* just beginners at this, by virtue of having been kept on the sidelines so long, and we *do* have much to learn." Gomillion's strategy prevailed in the primary: all seven local candidates endorsed by the Democratic Club won their races.

The city election on August 11 promised to be even more interesting than the county races had been. Blacks made up only about 900 of the 1,900 city voters—on a strictly racial vote, whites could still prevail. The Macon County Democratic Club again endorsed an interracial slate. It picked the incumbent white councilmen L. M. Gregg and John Sides, who had proved to be friendly and cooperative with black Tuskegee. It endorsed Allan Parker for another council position and Alton B. Taylor, a white retired army sergeant, for mayor. The club gave its strongest support to two black council candidates: Kenneth L. Buford and Stanley Smith. Smith was a young sociologist who had also been active in the TCA.

The three white council candidates endorsed by the club won in the first election. Buford and Smith each faced white incumbent councilmen in the runoff. Black voters defected in large numbers from Taylor, the club's white mayoral candidate; most of them instead supported Charles Keever, a local white businessman and political liberal who had campaigned vigorously among blacks. Keever and incumbent mayor Howard Rutherford, whose support for the private school had damaged his initially good reputation among the black leadership, were forced into a runoff.

Buford and Smith would probably have won in the first election except for the presence of other black candidates in their races. Council candidates supported by the Non-Partisan Voters League of Macon County, an independent political group formed in early 1964, drew about twenty percent of the black vote. Led by Paul Puryear, a young Institute political scientist, the Non-Partisan League supported five black candidates. Unlike the Democratic Club, which attempted only "to educate" its members about school candidates and issues, the league put forth a specific platform calling for better city services, more low-income housing, vocational education for the unemployed, and more federal assistance to city government. The league geared its concerns to the interests of lower-income blacks, though its candidates, including Puryear, were solidly middle class. None, however, had been part of the TCA leadership.

The Non-Partisan League directly challenged Gomillion's gradualist strategy. Puryear assailed the assumption that blacks' lack of experience in government necessitated a deliberate entry into politics. That thinking, Puryear wrote to the *Advertiser* a few days after the election, assumed that blacks were a " 'child-race' unable to cope with the complexities of modern life." Puryear and a significant minority of Macon County blacks believed that the newly acquired political power should be used to put as many blacks as possible into positions of authority. Several black citizens had begun to see themselves as political candidates. Detroit Lee had told the Democratic Club in early 1964 that he wanted to run for probate judge that year. "Don't rock the boat, Mr. Lee," Beulah Johnson, a longtime TCA activist and staunch Gomillion loyalist, had responded, knowing that Gomillion did not believe a black ought to run for probate judge at this time. "I may turn the damn boat over," Lee replied. He soon approached Puryear about forming a new political organization. Thus, the Non-Partisan League was born.

Gomillion and the Democratic Club leadership viewed the runoff election on September 15 as a critical moment for Macon County. In August Gomillion wrote to Neil Davis, the new editor of the Tuskegee *News*, expressing his fear that "even among the most 'liberal' white citizens there is not now the readiness to act courageously in moving toward more responsible civic behavior." The consequences of a failure to act "responsibly" could be serious, Gomillion suggested. "If white citizens do not cooperate with Negro citizens on September 15 in the election of Reverend Buford and Dr. Smith, in view of what Negro voters did on August 11, white officials and white citizens might as well expect on September 16 the beginning of an all-out effort to take over the government of the city and the county, in which Negroes are now willing to share." Gomillion called for whites to make "a noticeable demonstration of democratic behavior," which he defined as one hundred white votes for Buford and Smith.

The white liberals had already surmised what Gomillion made explicit. The Non-Partisan League's presence showed them what the future might hold if Gomillion's leadership were undermined. The liberals mustered, if only barely, the requisite white support for the two black candidates. According to the Democratic Club's calculations, Smith received at least 120 white votes and Buford 89 in winning their races. With solid black support, Charles Keever defeated Howard Rutherford for the mayoralty.

The results of the city election sparked new optimism among blacks and liberal whites. The idea of Tuskegee as a model community reemerged, and liberal whites grasped the notion with enthusiasm. Indeed, Charles Keever had used the idea in his campaign literature: "This is our opportunity to establish with certainty that Southern civic government can function with the good of *all of its people* in mind." The new City Council announced at its first meeting that it was consciously breaking with the past and would henceforth base its policies on justice and fairness to all Tuskegeeans. "We shall work for a community composed of citizens whose hearts are united in brotherly love," the councilmen said. "I believe that this little community can become the showplace of the world," Neil Davis said a few months later. The white liberals now publicly espoused the goal toward which Gomillion had been working for twenty-five years: a community in which blacks and whites shared political power and worked together for common ends.

The new city government succeeded in becoming thoroughly interracial. Blacks were appointed to municipal boards and committees. Allan Parker, now a leader of the city council, formed a Community Action Committee to seek and administer federal poverty program funds. The council named twelve blacks and nine whites to an official interracial committee to advise the city on racial matters. Formed at about the same time was an unofficial interracial group, the Committee for a Greater Tuskegee, to which all elected officials, most leading blacks, and the white liberals belonged. This committee worked for economic development in Tuskegee and supported the public-school system.

White liberals reasserted their support for the public schools in the summer of 1964. They resolved to reenroll their children in Tuskegee High and expressed the hope that other whites, perhaps overburdened by the private-school tuition, would do the same. They were reasonably certain that the state would not interfere again. In July a three-judge panel ordered Governor Wallace and the state Board of Education to stay out of local desegregation efforts, and particularly to let Macon County alone. Only "through the exercise of considerable judicial restraint" were they not issuing a statewide school desegregation order, the judges warned Wallace. The local school board, which had given in to Wallace's demands for more defiance the previous February, once again supported compliance. The appointment of Frances Rush, a staunch public-school supporter, to the board in June had strengthened its resolve. Superintendent Pruitt, however, wanted no part of another desegregation try; he retired on July 1, 1964, to be replaced by Joe Wilson, a younger man who also favored compliance. Tuskegee High had fifty-nine white students and fourteen blacks when it opened in September 1964. The number of whites would grow to 133 by the end of the school year.

Nonetheless, white support for Tuskegee High did not inhibit the growth of Macon Academy. The private institution added a grammar school, new classrooms, more books to its library, Latin and Spanish to its curriculum, and basketball and football teams to its athletic program in 1964 and 1965. The school continued to be the focus of conservative energy and hopes. With the liberals now rallied around Tuskegee High, the division among whites over the schools looked to be a long-term reality.

But by the fall of 1964 a schism in the black community began to overshadow the white division. The Non-Partisan League nominated Detroit Lee to run against Preston Hornsby for probate judge in the November general election. Lee believed that he was as well qualified as Hornsby for the office and that his years of activism had earned him a political reward. The probate office had a special attraction for him: as a boy growing up in Mt. Pleasant, Texas, Lee had been friendly with the local probate judge and his family. He had spent many hours in the Mt. Pleasant probate office, and he believed that he knew well the functions of the probate court.

Gomillion respected Detroit Lee's integrity and commitment to the civil rights cause, but he doubted that Lee would make a good judge. The probate judgeship should go only to an eminently qualified black, Gomillion felt. He also thought it was too early to run a black for that office. Although Gomillion was not personally close to Preston Hornsby, the sheriff had been a friend to the black community when it had had few white friends. Gomillion also believed that support for the Democratic party would best serve black interests in the long run. In a letter to the Democratic Club precinct leaders encouraging their backing of the entire Democratic ticket, Gomillion used only the last reason to explain the club's endorsement of Hornsby. "The important issue here is whether or not we want to continue to act and be treated as Negroes, or move into the larger area of politics and act as Democrats who *happen* to be Negroes."

In case the appeal to assimilationist values was not fully persuasive, Gomillion enclosed a copy of a White Citizens Council leaflet promoting a write-in strategy to elect to the probate judgeship James N. "Kayo" Rea, the Notasulga mayor who had blocked the door at the high school the previous February. "If the negro block [*sic*] splits between the negro candidate and Sheriff Hornsby," the Citizens Council strategist explained, "its [*sic*] possible for the white people of Macon County to elect a real white man to this office." Most black voters again followed Gomillion's advice, and Hornsby won easily.

After the election Paul Puryear denounced the Democratic Club's support of Hornsby. "While many of the nation were exercising discriminating judgment by voting for the candidates deemed most fit," he wrote to the *Advertiser*, "the Negro leaders of Macon County continued to adhere slavishly to the notion that the viability of the Alabama Democratic Party must be maintained at all cost." Puryear hoped that as Macon County blacks became "more sophisticated in the use of the ballot" they would vote independently "without regard to race, party, or organizational affiliation." The Democratic Club's political strategy retarded progress for Tuskegee blacks, Puryear believed. "The pace of social change in Tuskegee is unconscionably slow."

Puryear accused Gomillion and the TCA leadership of exercising an oligarchical control over Macon County blacks. The Non-Partisan League, he explained to a reporter, was concerned "with what is going to emerge as one of the key political issues of the time . . . that of democratizing the Negro leadership." In Tuskegee and other places in the South "everybody has been so busy obtaining the right to vote that we've all neglected to notice that time and again the drive for freedom has resulted in the establishment of a black oligarchy—a narrow leadership that presumes to speak for the mass of Negroes and to treat with the white power structure in the manner of an ambassador." While acknowledging "the heroic way" Gomillion had worked for so many years, Puryear said that the TCA leadership "has become sterile and limited in its approach, and perhaps satisfied that it knows all the answers."

Puryear and Gomillion viewed the Tuskegee situation from widely different perspectives. Age accounted for many of their differences. Gomillion, now approaching sixty-five, had matured during the 1920s and 1930s, a time of relatively little progress for blacks. For most of his adult life he had worked to make small gains for black rights; only in the previous five years had the pace of change accelerated significantly. Puryear was twenty-eight. He had matured during the 1950s, when blacks had much higher expectations, and realizations, of change. So much change in race relations had taken place since 1960—national civil rights legislation, the virtual end of segregation in public accommodations, real progress in getting blacks the right to vote—that men and women of Puryear's generation began to look on rapid change as the norm. They tended to assume that change had come easily. Gomillion knew it had not. . . .

. . . Among those likely to rebel against gradualism were persons who were younger than the TCA leadership; who considered themselves capable of leadership; and who were in touch with the shift to a more aggressive, militant approach among civil rights activists outside Tuskegee. Many such people lived within the boundaries of Macon County by 1965.

After five years of quietude, the Institute students suddenly awakened in early 1965. The Student Nonviolent Coordinating Committee had sent organizers to the campus in the winter of 1964–65 to recruit participants for voting rights campaigns in the Alabama Black Belt. The Tuskegee students were a large pool of potential activists to help with SNCC's Selma campaign in Dallas County. SNCC workers visited the Institute dormitories and taught students "freedom songs," the protest music of the civil rights movement. James Forman, SNCC executive director, persuaded several talented students to join the SNCC cause. George Ware, a graduate student in chemistry from Birmingham, became a leader in the Tuskegee SNCC contingent. Forman, who had become highly disaffected from the leadership of Dr. Martin Luther King, Jr., and the Southern Christian Leadership Conference, brought to Tuskegee a militant strategy for the civil rights cause. "If we can't sit at the table of democracy," Forman said in March 1965, "then we'll knock the fucking legs off."

The students formed the Tuskegee Institute Advancement League [TIAL] in February 1965 to support the Selma movement, which SNCC and SCLC had escalated into a major protest against voting discrimination. King and other protesters had marched on the Dallas County Courthouse many days during January and February. TIAL planned a march of Tuskegee students on the state capitol for March 10 to show their sympathy with the Selma protest. After state troopers and Jim Clark's posse bludgeoned the Selma protesters on the Edmund Pettus Bridge on Sunday, March 7, Judge Johnson issued a temporary restraining order against more marches. Confident that Johnson would allow the march to proceed once protection for participants was secured, King sent a telegram to the Tuskegee Institute campus asking the students to postpone their Montgomery protest. Institute administrators put a copy of King's telegram at each student's place in the dining hall the night before the march was to take place. But the students' loyalty was to SNCC. They began a rhythmic tapping on the dining hall tables as they read the telegram. "March, march, march," they chanted in response.

March 10 proved to be a chaotic day for the seven hundred students and faculty members who rode chartered buses to Montgomery. Upon their arrival, a debate developed between student leaders and several local clergymen about who would lead the protest. This is a *student* protest, George Ware insisted, and students will lead it. At the state capitol, the protesters encountered a state trooper contingent and more than a hundred Montgomery city policemen. Ware and another student leader attempted to read a petition demanding voting rights for black people, but a city detective arrested them. The local ministers and Dr. P. B. Phillips, the Institute dean of students, then attempted to persuade the students to give up the protest and return to Tuskegee. Frustrated by the result of their efforts, the students refused to leave. They sat down on the sidewalk in front of the state capitol. City policemen encircled the students and did not allow any protester to reenter the circle once he had left. The number began to dwindle, but most students were adamant. After several hours of confinement, some urinated within the circle, albeit as modestly as possible. Finally at nightfall half the students gave up. The others remained for several hours and then retired to a local black church, where they spent the night. The next morning they returned to Tuskegee.

The Montgomery protest profoundly affected many Tuskegee students. "After the march, a lot of people couldn't take Tuskegee any more," said Gwen Patton, a junior from Montgomery who joined SNCC after the protest. Students began to object to compulsory class attendance and to accuse the administration of treating them like "babies." In April Patton ran successfully for president of the Institute Student Council on a student rights platform. Several TIAL members left school to work on SNCC projects away from Tuskegee. Among the students most affected by the Montgomery protest were several descendants of prominent black families in Tuskegee.

Wendell Paris, Simuel Schutz, Eldridge Burns, and Sammy Younge had grown up in the affluent, insulated environment of the Institute community. All began to reject many of the values and attitudes of the black middle class and to identify consciously with poor blacks. Younge and Burns, who had attended prep schools in the East, "had some sense of guilt for having been separated from other blacks," Patton later said. They responded to these feelings by plunging into civil rights work in the spring and summer of 1965.

In April and May the students organized a protest against the hiring practices of white Tuskegee merchants. They picketed a grocery store and succeeded in preventing most blacks from shopping there. The store soon put a black on its staff. They picketed the Alabama Exchange Bank, of which Allan Parker was president. The students had singled out Parker's bank because they believed the city council president had the power to implement the changes they demanded. Parker announced that, although no blacks were now employed at the bank, all blacks would be given an equal opportunity in future hiring. When the picket did not result in immediate hirings, the students bitterly blamed their failure on Parker's power. "Parker really screwed the whole county," Wendell Paris said later. "He controlled all the Negroes." In fact, the protests did soon elicit promises of fair hiring practices from many Tuskegee merchants.

Twenty-five TIAL members desegregated the formerly all-white Tuskegee city swimming pool on May 31. The next day fifty students swam in the pool, but when they returned on the third day the pool was closed because white vandals had dumped garbage into it. Acid and a baby alligator were thrown into the pool on subsequent days. City officials chose not to reopen it, citing a current water shortage. Actually, they feared the outcome of more protests. In the view of the city fathers, the picketing at the stores and the swimming pool incidents were threatening to destroy the interracial harmony engendered by the previous year's elections.

Luther Foster summoned Gwen Patton to his office in early June and asked her to stop the protests in downtown Tuskegee. The town was approaching model race relations, Patton later said Foster told her, and the students' activities were threatening further progress. Patton reported Dr. Foster's request to the other student activists. "If this is such a model city," George Ware replied, "if blacks and whites get along so well, then let's go to the churches." The students then planned a series of protests designed specifically to polarize the black and white communities, which they deemed the best way to achieve more rapid change in the status of blacks. "We figured that if there was one point on which white people in [Tuskegee] would not relent, it would be the church," Ware said later. But the students did not announce their real intent. At the first desegregation effort at the Methodist Church on June 26, a church usher denied the students entry and told Ware that the presence of blacks would "break up" the congregation. "If as Christians you deny other Christians the right to enter the house of God, then your congregation is already broken up," Ware responded. The students understood that the denial of their entry into the church, whatever their own real motives, offered a powerful symbol of white bigotry.

The students returned to the Methodist Church the following Sunday, but were again turned away. On Saturday, July 10, three hundred students and several newly arrived SNCC workers met around the Confederate monument on the Tuskegee town square. They sang freedom songs and made speeches. Charles Sherrod, a SNCC field worker, told the group that there should be more black candidates for town offices. "Those white people don't believe us," Sherrod said sarcastically. "They think we want to get into office and do the same things they done to us." The students continued their church protest the next day. Approximately five hundred persons, including a few whites, went to the Methodist Church, but for the third consecutive Sunday they were denied entrance. Some protesters managed to slip inside but were quickly ejected. White bystanders attacked several protesters. Former mayor Howard Rutherford and another white resident were arrested for beating a news photographer.

The scene was re-created the following Sunday, only with a larger group of unruly whites. After the students were denied entrance for the fourth straight time, the whites set upon them. Simuel Schutz, Wendell Paris, and Sammy Younge were beaten. The students later charged that the Tuskegee police had vacated the area just before the attack. Afterward several whites were arrested for the beatings. They included the proprietor of a gas station; a mechanic; the owner of a small grocery store; a bread salesman; the proprietor of a cafe; and a clerk in the local state-controlled liquor store. All were apparently part of a small group of lower-middle-class vigilantes who had coalesced during the school desegregation crisis. They now had a new cause.

The students again appeared on the steps of the Methodist church on July 25, the fifth consecutive Sunday. "Your attendance here at this time will harm human relations in this city," Max Smith, a church steward, told approximately one hundred demonstrators. He denied them entrance and asked them to leave church property. "We will remain here until we are arrested or until the service is over," Sammy Younge responded. "We are aware we have no legal right to attend the church, but we will continue to demand our moral right," George Ware announced. Milling around the front of the church were dozens of blacks and whites, all apparently waiting for trouble to develop. No doubt embarrassed by the recent incidents, Tuskegee policemen patrolled the area in full force and went through the crowd collecting bottles and other weapons. The demonstration finally ended without incident.

The church protests, and the resulting violence, raised the level of racial tension in Tuskegee to a new height. The students had quickly achieved the polarization they wanted. To many whites, the churches were the only institutions that blacks had not yet invaded. They were the last bastion of white power and control. Even the white liberals who believed the churches ought to be open to all took a dim view of the demonstrations, regarding them as needless, destructive incidents which undid the recent progress toward interracial harmony. The protests frightened whites already insecure about their future in Tuskegee. "The cause of civil rights, of equal opportunity," Neil Davis wrote in the *News*, "was not well served by the church integration attempts. The cause of Christian religion was not well served by the unfortunate display of ugly spiritedness which resulted." Davis posed a question to local blacks: "Would not the wiser course for civil rights proponents be to look to the proven leadership of such groups as the Tuskegee Civic Association?"

Gomillion also strongly disapproved of the church demonstrations. He believed that enough distrust already existed between blacks and whites without injecting a highly emotional issue like church integration. He viewed churches as private institutions that should be controlled entirely by their members, and later suggested that if whites had been trying to force their way into his church, he would have resisted that intrusion. To him, the church protests were an immature and unfocused rebellion that damaged the already precarious race relations in Tuskegee.

Still, he had not tried to stop them. He doubted that he could thwart the students' impulse to create conflict. He later observed that in 1965 many black adults in Tuskegee believed that they ought to "let the children lead." Many of the "children" involved were well known locally and no doubt had widespread support for their activities. They represented the growing national militance among young activists. Gomillion was not willing to fight for control of a community that he had led for twenty-five years. His wife was ill. At sixty-five, he recognized that younger men and women had more energy and enthusiasm for leadership. A man who had had too much pride and self-respect to suffer quietly the indignities of the Jim Crow system, Gomillion perhaps also felt that he should not have to fight to retain his power.

He certainly did not want to endure the acrimony that a challenge to the students would cause. He had seen what such a fight might involve when several TIAL members appeared at a Tuskegee City Council meeting in July. Sammy Younge, who was emerging as the most militant student leader, argued with Mayor Charles Keever about the city's commitment to fairness for blacks. Younge directed several questions to Gomillion, who ignored him. Angered by Gomillion's refusal to acknowledge his question, Younge shouted, "Gomillion, you're supposed to be the leader of the Negro people. What are you doing?" Again Gomillion made no response, but he had witnessed what might happen if he publicly denounced the students.

He would acknowledge later that his unwillingness to try to counter the students' demonstrations amounted to an abdication of responsibility. He had worked for many years against seemingly more formidable opponents—Judge Varner and Sam Engelhardt, for example—to try to make Tuskegee and Macon County an interracial community. Now he failed to oppose persons who presented a different but nevertheless destructive challenge to his ideal. Coming at this time in his life, presenting opponents who should have been allies, that fight was simply too distasteful.

The mood of protest among the young people continued into the fall.

Institute students voted in November not to allow their annual Homecoming parade to go through downtown Tuskegee. The editor of the student newspaper, *Campus Digest*, believed that the city's invitation to have the parade come through town was "politically based." It had not been "a sincere plea for understanding and unity," the editor wrote. In making the request, Mayor Keever had said that routing the parade through town might "contribute very much to a better understanding and unity of everyone. . . . As long as people never get together, they don't know much about each other or have much interest in each other." If the city wanted to improve race relations, the editor retorted, it could prosecute the men who had beaten up the protesters at the Methodist church the previous summer. Most blacks had been angered recently when a grand jury composed largely of local whites had failed to indict any of the men charged with assaulting the demonstrators. Gwen Patton announced that she refused "to let the Tuskegee Institute student body be used as some sort of public relations group to mend differences." . . .

The student activists turned their attention to voter registration during the winter of 1965–66. Some had in mind building an all-black political organization like the Black Panther Party, which SNCC workers had formed in Lowndes County, Alabama. The students worked primarily in rural Macon County where most unregistered blacks were. The TCA had increased its efforts to register rural blacks after the 1961 court decision, but they had been only minimally successful. Illiteracy, fear of economic coercion, and poor community leadership hampered the TCA's efforts to get large numbers of rural blacks to try to register.

The Tuskegee students helped many rural blacks overcome the obstacles. They sometimes lived in the rural communities and provided a daily source of assistance and leadership. Whereas the TCA had always stressed the numerous responsibilities connected with full citizenship rights, the young activists emphasized what blacks might gain by controlling county government. The Voting Rights Act of 1965, which was passed in the aftermath of the Selma march, aided the registration effort. It forbade the state to require that voters be literate. Instead of a grueling examination before harsh white registrars intent on embarrassing them, rural blacks now had to answer only a few questions, which they could do orally if they were illiterate. The number of black voters in Macon County began to increase sharply after the voting rights bill was enacted in July. The following January, when the students' registration effort reached its zenith, more than sixteen hundred blacks added their names to the voting rolls. The students, with the help of the new federal guarantee of the right to vote, were completing work that Gomillion and the TCA had begun twenty-five years earlier.

The students' success would, however, be virtually overlooked because of what happened on Monday night, January 3, 1966. After working in the registration effort that day, several student activists organized a small party at the SNCC "freedom house." Sammy Younge left the party at about ten o'clock to go to a grocery store for a jar of mayonnaise. On his way Younge stopped at a Standard Oil service station in downtown Tuskegee and asked the whereabouts of "the damn bathroom." Marvin Segrest, the sixty-seven-year-old service station attendant, directed Younge to the rear of the station. Apparently believing that he was being sent to the Jim Crow toilet, Younge swore at Segrest and demanded to use the "public restroom." Segrest then drew a gun and ordered Younge off the service station property. The student left, but, according to Segrest, he made a threat. "I'm going to get you," Younge reportedly said to Segrest. The old man dared Younge to "come back on my property." Segrest would later testify that Younge had harassed him for four or five months before this night. Younge had once tried to leave the station without paying for gasoline purchased, Segrest said. Another time he had become impatient with Segrest's service and had said, "Put some goddamn gas in the car or I'll hurt you." Segrest also said Younge had "tried to run me down with the car."

After Segrest pulled the gun, Younge went next door to the Greyhound bus station and asked Joseph Morris, a Tuskegee Institute student, if he had a gun. Morris replied that he did not. Facing the service station, Younge bobbed up and down behind his car and called out to Segrest, "Go ahead and shoot me." Segrest stepped toward the bus station with his gun. Younge ran to a bag of golf clubs belonging to a student waiting for a bus and took out a single club. Younge then began to run—toward Segrest, the old man later testified. Morris stated that Younge had run away from Segrest. Segrest fired a shot, missing Younge, who then ran across the street to where Morris had now moved. Younge said to Morris, "Don't leave. . . . I want you to witness this." Younge ran back across the street to the bus station and stepped on and off a parked bus. He ran around the bus into the open, still holding the golf club, when Segrest fired again. Segrest later claimed that Younge had come toward him, but Morris stated unequivocally that Younge had been moving away from Segrest. A few minutes later, Younge's body was discovered in an alley on the side of the bus terminal away from Segrest's station, a fact which supports Morris's version of the events. The second shot had hit Younge in the head, killing him instantly.

The death of Sammy Younge led to an examination of the lives of two men who might otherwise have remained almost anonymous. Marvin Segrest was one of the lesser members of the large Segrest clan of Macon County. Neither well educated nor economically successful, he was known to be law-abiding. He had attended White Citizens Council meetings, but he would not have been included among Macon County's likely candidates to murder a civil rights worker. Indeed, Segrest and his supporters maintained that the incident resulted from a personal conflict, not racial hatred.

Sammy Younge was descended from an old and prominent Tuskegee Institute family. His father had held administrative positions at the VA hospital and in other federal agencies. His mother was a grammar-school teacher active in social and cultural affairs in the Institute community. Sammy attended Children's House, the grammar school for the Institute children, and Cornwall Academy in Massachusetts before returning to Tuskegee to finish high school. He was a handsome boy with very light skin, blue eyes, and curly black hair who easily "passed" as white. He had good manners, many girlfriends, and a talent for singing. After high school, he joined the United States Navy, but his tour of duty was foreshortened by two serious operations, which resulted in the loss of one kidney. According to friends, he was later haunted by the memory of these operations.

After the navy stint, Sammy enrolled at the Institute for the spring semester of 1965, but his civil rights activity immediately crowded out his educational interests. He went to Mississippi to work on SNCC projects after the Montgomery demonstration, but soon returned to Tuskegee to help lead the swimming pool and church protests. After the church demonstrations ended in July, Younge resigned from TIAL and withdrew from civil rights activities. He reportedly was very upset over the murder of Jonathan Daniels, a white ministerial student, in Lowndes County in the late summer of 1965. Gwen Patton also believed he was disappointed that many older blacks disapproved of the student protests. Other friends interpreted his action as an effort to conform to Tuskegee's middle-class values, of which he had recently been extremely critical. They noted that he began to drink heavily, despite doctors' orders against any alcoholic consumption. He suddenly decided to return to the movement in December, planning to form an all-black political party. His renewed civil rights involvement apparently did not change Sammy Younge's drinking habits. On the night of his death he had drunk enough to be under "the early influence of alcohol" and to experience some "impairment in judgment and reasoning," the investigating toxicologist would later testify.

On Tuesday morning all that mattered in Tuskegee was the reality of Sammy Younge's death. Three thousand Tuskegee Institute students marched in the rain from the campus to downtown Tuskegee. They demanded an audience with the mayor and the City Council, who soon appeared. "You have told us this is a model city where whites and Negroes get along together," Gwen Patton said to the city fathers. "You have told us how good the Tuskegee image is. . . . You have invited us downtown for a homecoming football parade. . . . Yet, you closed the city swimming pool and barred us from your churches . . . now, we want to know what you are going to do." Mayor Charles Keever deplored the killing and promised to do all in his power to see that justice was rendered. "Regret will not bring Sammy back!" a student shouted to Keever. "That's good, but what are you going to do?" another asked. More questions followed, and then the mayor and the councilmen joined the students in prayer. They all stood in the rain and sang "We Shall Overcome," after which the students returned to the campus.

One march did not vent the anger released by Sammy Younge's death. Students marched again the next day. There was no march on Thursday, the day of Younge's funeral, but President Foster called a meeting of students and faculty for that evening. Foster affirmed the right of all members of the Institute community to participate in civil rights activity and stated that he expected that "people will so involve themselves." Speaking on behalf of the just-formed Ad Hoc Committee for Justice in Macon

County, Paul Puryear announced a series of demands for equal access to public accommodations in Tuskegee. Gwen Patton read a letter that she had sent to Lyndon Johnson about Younge's death. "Sir, to be honest with you," she wrote to the president, "the students of Tuskegee Institute are not planning to follow the course of nonviolence if justice is not done in this case."

The students marched again on Friday morning. Patton called another meeting for that evening, but this one lacked the unity of feeling at the previous night's convocation. Luther Foster listed the actions taken in response to Younge's death. Both federal and state agents were investigating the killing. The Justice Department had filed discrimination suits against two Tuskegee restaurants. The Tuskegee City Council had already considered Puryear's proposed antidiscrimination ordinances and promised to act on them the following Tuesday. Foster ended on a cautionary note: local authorities believe that more marches would present "grave dangers" to everyone involved.

Gwen Patton responded to the warning with vehemence. "Ain't no guns or rifles gonna turn us around. We realize the danger, but Sammy Younge did it by himself. So what difference does it make whether it's one or a million?" After her remarks, the group voted to march the next day. But not every one of the fifteen hundred students present agreed with the militant position. One student objected to any further marches, saying that the first one had been constructive but the others had only served to "rile people up." After this student received catcalls, P. B. Phillips, the dean of students, complained that "the rudeness tonight is certainly not civil, and if we're going to have civil rights then we have to be civil right down the line."

But the militants clearly had the upper hand. If the students backed down from their demands, then they would be responsible for the next black who was murdered, George Ware warned. Wendell Paris argued against any moderation of demands by condemning Booker Washington. Referring to the famous sculpture on the Institute campus which depicts Washington lifting the veil of ignorance from a kneeling Negro, Paris said, "We got this statue out here of that man who's suppose to be lifting up the veil. Man, he's putting it back on." Here Paris was paraphrasing the author Ralph Ellison, a former Tuskegee student, who had stressed the ambiguity of the sculpture in *Invisible Man*, a novel which harshly characterized Tuskegee Institute and its leadership. Washington was a convenient and powerful symbol of gradualism on which young militants could focus their anger.

Perhaps the most effective speech of the meeting was made by James Forman, who had come to Tuskegee for Younge's funeral. When will the terrorism against civil rights workers end? Forman asked. He alluded to an answer by saying that he knew his own days were numbered. He challenged the students: "What do you live for? That's the basic question, baby." He described a paradise of luxury items but asked, "Is that enough? Is that enough? Or are you going to take the education you get and give it back to the people?'' Closing with a call for more action, Forman paraphrased Frederick Douglass's famous statement: ''A man who won't agitate for his rights don't need no rights.''

One thousand students began another march toward downtown Tuskegee the next day. City policemen stopped the marchers and informed them that they could not continue without a parade permit. The marchers insisted that they would continue, and the policemen relented. When they reached the town square, the marchers sat on the sidewalk and obstructed the entry to one block of stores. Willie Ricks, a SNCC worker, pleaded with townspeople to join the protest. ''When they killed Sammy, they killed all of us.'' Younge's death had been planned in the chambers of the Tuskegee City Council, Ricks announced to onlookers. But the inflammatory rhetoric did not spark more protest; the marchers returned peacefully to Tuskegee Institute.

The City Council faced the militance on January 10 and 11 when it attempted to respond to the students' call for action. ''Tuskegee is far from the model community that some insist that it is,'' Puryear told the councilmen. He demanded a public accommodations ordinance, the firing of the Tuskegee public safety director, and a civilian review board for the police department. Ben-Zion Wardy, an Israeli citizen teaching political science at the Institute and a participant in the church protests the previous summer, warned the council that ''people will take steps to obtain these substantial demands by using other means'' if the public accommodations ordinance was not passed. Wardy gave the council one day to enact the measure. He further urged it to remove the Confederate monument from the town square and rename the area ''Samuel Younge, Jr., Park.'' Gwen Patton asked that the city boycott the service station at which Marvin Segrest was employed. Puryear told the council that Younge's death was not the result of a ''personal feud,'' as some city officials had claimed. ''We . . . do not share the view that the killing of Samuel Younge was the isolated act of one individual. . . . Mr. Younge's murder is symptomatic of much deeper and pervasive evils in our community.''

A small group of SNCC workers and Institute students marched every day that week. The demonstrations were peaceful until Saturday, January 15, when one of the marchers struck a deputy sheriff who was attempting to arrest him. A local merchant had charged that the demonstrator, William Scott, had bumped and kicked him as the merchant tried to enter his store. The students later said that the police had initiated the fighting. After Scott was arrested, the other demonstrators began throwing rocks and bottles at some white men who had taunted them from an automobile. Several store windows were broken.

The aftermath of Younge's death worried Tuskegee whites. The liberals' regret about the killing soon gave way to concern about the impact of the protests that followed. ''Those students are just a liability to this town,'' one liberal told a reporter. ''They don't live here, they don't spend money here, they got no real stake in what happens to this town.'' He was frightened and pessimistic. ''Tuskegee's burning down around our ears and there ain't no way out." The liberals knew that the harsh antiwhite feelings unleashed by Younge's death had damaged their efforts for interracial understanding and community peace. The dire predictions of conservative whites that racial change would result in violence, hatred, and death now seemed all too close to reality.

The TCA leadership also objected to what the students were doing. Beulah Johnson, a longtime TCA activist, expressed her concerns about the effect of the student demonstrations in a letter to the *News*. "Those of us who live here and love this community have much at stake. The SNCC-type from outside and the handful who are persuaded to act outside the law do not understand this." She criticized a recent *Time* magazine article which stated that the Younge murder had removed the "façade" of racial progress. Anyone familiar with the voting situation just a few years ago knew how much progress had been made, she wrote. Councilman Buford complained to the *News* that "an idiotic climate has been created in this community by mob activities of college students and their associates which, from a behavioral point of view, cannot be differentiated from those same activities by misguided hoodlums, color notwithstanding." Another TCA member contended that "the students are downtown destroying things we worked years to get. They're emotional and immature. They don't know what they're doing."

The divisions in the Tuskegee black community were dramatized at a conference on "Alabama Justice" held at the Institute in early February. Sponsored by the Ad Hoc Committee for Justice in Macon County, the conference precipitated a full public debate about civil rights strategy. Floyd McKissick, soon to become head of the Congress of Racial Equality, advanced a militant position. "If the black man is ever going to be free," McKissick said, "he's going to have to free himself. No one ever gave away power. That just ain't politics. We're going to the polls and take that power." Fred Gray, the black attorney who had represented the TCA in both the gerrymander and the school desegregation cases, agreed with McKissick and argued that blacks could best attain that power within the Democratic party. Several students roared objections to that. Referring to the Alabama Democratic party's emblem, the bantam rooster, Wendell Paris responded, "People ain't going to vote for that white rooster no more. The whole thing is corrupt."

The students' vehemence evoked criticism from older black residents. "I'm disturbed by this uncontrolled hostility," Lawrence Haygood, a local minister, said. "Whites have played a magnificent role in the civil rights movement, especially in their financial support." When several TCA members defended their past record of activism, Wendell Wilkerson, a TIAL member, retorted: "I ain't interested in what you did. I'm interested in what you're going to do." The young militants accused middle-class Tuskegee blacks of not caring about poor people. One such middle-class person objected: "You're creating animosity—setting the middle class against the lower class. Where are you going to get money? How are you going to unite us?" That is not our concern, said Michele Moreland, a SNCC worker.

"The question of how to unite is your problem. There are more of the poor people than of you."

Deeply troubled by the open hostility of the young militants, the older activists asked for guidance from the man who had led them for twenty-five years. Gomillion's unwillingness to compete with the students for the leadership of the black community had kept him publicly silent during 1965 and through the recent weeks of turmoil. But on February 13, Race Relations Sunday, the day that he traditionally called for unity and brotherhood with white Tuskegeeans, Gomillion announced that he would make a statement. He hoped that it would not be "taken as an attempt to justify what we have done or an apology for what we have not done." He noted that the TCA as an organization had tried to refrain from telling other groups what they should do, implying that he hoped that the courtesy would be returned. "Our way is not the only way, but we have been able to accomplish many of our goals." He denied that he or the TCA had ever called Tuskegee a model community. "I have said it could become one. I still think it could. If I didn't, I wouldn't have stayed here." He defended the TCA's approach to civil rights work. "Maybe our goals haven't been high enough or comprehensive enough. But there are many of us who believe that by working together, by making necessary compromises, we can make Tuskegee a better place to live."

Gomillion had accepted the fact that his leadership now seemed anachronistic to many blacks. But he was not willing to adjust his style to meet the dictates of a more militant age. If his kind of leadership was no longer popular, then he would simply step aside. Although he considered the violent, profane rhetoric of the students altogether distasteful and doubted that their militance would produce real progress, he understood that they were a young generation intent on advancing the cause of black people further than their elders had. Indeed, he had felt the same impulse in the 1930s and had begun working for change. The change he set in motion had led to greater expectations and strident demands for more change. Now, thirty years later, the mounting force of change was bringing an end to his leadership. Charles Gomillion was caught in a whirlwind that he had sown. Fortunately for him, he knew that.

✣ F U R T H E R   R E A D I N G

Numan V. Bartley, *The Rise of Massive Resistance: Race and Politics in the South in the 1960s* (1969)

Jack Bass, *Unlikely Heroes: The Southern Judges Who Made the Civil Rights Revolution* (1981)

Robert Frederick Burk, *The Eisenhower Administration and Black Civil Rights* (1984)

Clayborne Carson, *In Struggle: SNCC and the Black Awakening of the 1960s* (1981)

William Chafe, *Civilities and Civil Rights: Greensboro, NC, and the Black Struggle for Freedom* (1980)

Robert Coles, *Children of Crisis: A Study in Courage and Fear* (1964)

Sara Evans, "Women's Consciousness and the Southern Black Movement," *Southern Exposure* 4 (1976), 10–17

Adam Fairclough, *"To Redeem the Soul of America": The SCLC and Martin Luther King, Jr.* (1987)

Tony Freyer, *The Little Rock Crisis: A Constitutional Interpretation* (1984)

David Garrow, *Protest at Selma: Martin Luther King, Jr., and the Voting Rights Act of 1965* (1978)

David R. Goldfield, *Black, White, and Southern: Race Relations and Southern Culture, 1940 to the Present* (1990)

Elizabeth Jacoway and David R. Colburn, eds., *Southern Businessmen and Desegregation* (1982)

Martin Luther King, Jr., *Stride Toward Freedom: The Montgomery Story* (1958)

Richard Kluger, *Simple Justice: The History of* Brown *v.* Board of Education *and Black America's Struggle for Equality* (1976)

Steven F. Lawson, *Black Ballots: Voting Rights in the South, 1944–1969* (1976)

Neil R. McMillan, *The Citizens' Council: Organized Resistance to the Second Reconstruction* (1971)

Anne Moody, *Coming of Age in Mississippi* (1968)

Aldon D. Morris, *The Origins of the Civil Rights Movement: Black Communities Organizing for Change* (1984)

Gunnar Myrdal, *An American Dilemma* (1944)

Howell Raines, *My Soul Is Rested: Movement Days in the Deep South Remembered* (1977)

James Silver, *Mississippi: The Closed Society* (1964)

Harvard Sitkoff, "Harry Truman and the Election of 1948: The Coming of Age of Civil Rights in American Politics," *Journal of Southern History* 37 (1971), 597–616

——, *The Struggle for Black Equality, 1954–1980* (1980)

J. Mills Thornton III, "Challenge and Response in the Montgomery Bus Boycott of 1955–1956," *Alabama Review* 33 (1980), 163–235

CHAPTER
14

Race and Politics in the

Recent South

In the years after the 1965 Voting Rights Act, the major civil-rights organizations disintegrated into warring factions, the Vietnam War consumed the domestic mission of the Johnson administration, and the succeeding Nixon administration was more interested in appealing to southern whites than in maintaining the gains of the 1960s. In the South, the annealing had occurred, and the healing was beginning. The southern caterpillar was transformed into the Sunbelt butterfly, and the business of business soon overshadowed lingering racial tensions. However, the South had hardly become a national model for race relations. Still, at a time when race riots were scorching cities in other regions, the relative calm in the South implied that relations were good.

Gains for blacks were most visible in southern politics. By 1975, blacks held more political offices in the South than any other region. Race baiting virtually disappeared from campaigns, and many leaders who emerged during the 1970s owed their election in great part to the expanding black electorate. The Democratic party that once based its power on white supremacy came to rely heavily on black votes. And the Republican party gained converts among southern white conservatives and retained the allegiance of migrating northerners. As a result, in many parts of the South, the era of one-party politics was over.

In employment the advances for southern blacks were less noticeable than in politics. Though the urban black middle class grew, subtle barriers remained: and a black underclass, increasingly estranged from the metropolitan economy and from middle-class blacks, expanded.

Historians are beginning to answer the question, "What happened to the civil-rights movement?" They are also probing the extent of black political and economic advances. How significant is black political power? Does black office-holding translate into policy changes? How does two-party politics affect race relations? What is the relative importance of race and class in accounting for the extent and persistence of black poverty?

Southern politics today is relatively dull compared to an earlier era when race and class issues dominated. Modern campaigns are more often run from Madison Avenue than from the back porch. In the first excerpt, from a Robert Penn Warren novel, a campaign manager in Louisiana during the late 1920s, Jack Burden, offers some good advice to a novice candidate, Willie Stark, evoking the substance of old-style southern political campaigns. More than any other measure, the Voting Rights Act of 1965, reprinted in part in the second selection, changed the southern political process. It established the framework for black political equality in the South for the next generation. Although initially designed to ensure fair registration and voting procedures, the act has become a means to limit black vote dilution and improve the chances of black candidates. Jimmy Carter represented the new southern politics. The unmistakable message of his 1971 inaugural speech as governor of Georgia, the third document, was that the good old days of white supremacy and business as usual were over. President Lyndon B. Johnson set the agenda for the next major step in the struggle for black civil rights in a speech at Howard University in June 1965, reprinted in part in the fourth selection, where he declared that the nation must work to remove the shackles of history from blacks to enable them to enjoy the benefits of the new civil rights legislation. How difficult that would be in at least one part of the South was demonstrated at Jackson State College [now University] in Mississippi in 1970. The fifth document contains excerpts from the report investigating the deaths of two students there; it reflects the persistence of serious racial problems in that state. The racial bifurcation of southern political parties implies a more subtle but nonetheless important indication of the persistence of race in regional life and politics as the next documents—first, two interviews of a southern Republican and Democratic official respectively, conducted by Case Western Reserve political scientist Alexander Lamis, and second, a political cartoon from the pen of *Charlotte Observer* (and now *New York Newsday*) cartoonist Doug Marlette—demonstrate. Andrew Young has been one of the nation's most prominent black officials during the past two decades. As he began his final year as mayor of Atlanta in January 1989, he took a retrospective view of Atlanta politics. His address, the eighth selection, drew upon the booster spirit of the old politics with some reference to the social conscience of the new. It was a valedictory that any of his recent white predecessors could have delivered. This may indicate a convergence of political styles and priorities among southern black and white politicians that may not be good news for the persistent black underclass. Still, the gains of southern blacks, at least in politics, have many southern whites believing that something significant has occurred and that now that blacks and whites have accommodated their racial differences, the South can accomplish anything, as the last document, the country song, "I Believe the South Is Gonna Rise Again," indicates.

Robert Penn Warren's Advice to a Candidate, 1946

He couldn't figure out what was wrong. He was like a man with a chill who simply reckons that the climate is changing all of a sudden, and wonders why everybody else isn't shivering too. Perhaps it was a desire for just a little human warmth that got him in the habit of dropping into my room late at night, after the speaking and the handshaking were over. He would sit for a spell, while I drank off my nightcap, and not talk much, but one time, at Morristown, where the occasion had sure-God been a black frost, he did, after sitting quiet, suddenly say, "How you think it's going, Jack?"

It was one of those embarrassing questions like "Do you think my wife is virtuous?" or "Did you know I am a Jew?" which are embarrassing, not because of anything you might say for an answer, the truth or a lie, but because the fellow asked the question at all. But I said to him, "Fine, I reckon it's going fine."

"You think so, for a fact?" he asked.

"Sure," I said.

He chewed that for about a minute and then swallowed it. Then he said, "They didn't seem to be paying attention much tonight. Not while I was trying to explain about my tax program."

"Maybe you try to tell 'em too much. It breaks down their brain cells."

"Looks like they'd want to hear about taxes, though," he said.

"You tell 'em too much. Just tell 'em you're gonna soak the fat boys, and forget the rest of the tax stuff."

"What we need is a balanced tax program. Right now the ratio between income tax and total income for the state gives an index that—"

"Yeah," I said, "I heard the speech. But they don't give a damn about that. Hell, make 'em cry, or make 'em laugh, make 'em think you're their weak and erring pal, or make 'em think you're God Almighty. Or make 'em mad. Even mad at you. Just stir 'em up; it doesn't matter how or why, and they'll love you and come back for more. Pinch 'em in the soft place. They aren't alive, most of 'em, and haven't been alive in twenty years. Hell, their wives have lost their teeth and their shape, and likker won't set on their stomachs, and they don't believe in God, so it's up to you to give 'em something to stir 'em up and make 'em feel alive again. Just for half an hour. That's what they come for. Tell 'em anything. But for Sweet Jesus' sake don't try to improve their minds."

The Voting Rights Act of 1965

Sec. 2. No voting qualification or prerequisite to voting, or standard, practice, or procedure shall be imposed or applied by any State or political subdivision to deny or abridge the right of any citizen of the United States to vote on account of race or color. . . .

Sec. 4. (a) To assure that the right of citizens of the United States to vote is not denied or abridged on account of race or color, no citizen shall be denied the right to vote in any Federal, State, or local election because of his failure to comply with any test or device in any State. . . .

(c) The phrase "test or device" shall mean any requirement that a person as a prerequisite for voting or registration for voting (1) demonstrate the ability to read, write, understand, or interpret any matter, (2) demonstrate any educational achievement or his knowledge of any particular subject, (3) possess good moral character, or (4) prove his qualifications by the voucher of registered voters or members of any other class. . . .

Sec. 5. Whenever a State or political subdivision with respect to which the prohibitions set forth in section (4)(a) are in effect shall enact or seek to administer any voting qualification or prerequisite to voting, or standard, practice, or procedure with respect to voting different from that in force or effect on November 1, 1964, such State or subdivision may institute an action in the United States District Court for the District of Columbia for a declaratory judgment that such qualification, prerequisite, standard, practice, or procedure does not have the purpose and will not have the effect of denying or abridging the right to vote on account of race or color, and unless and until the court enters such judgment no person shall be denied the right to vote for failure to comply with such qualification, prerequisite, standard, practice, or procedure: *Provided*, That such qualification, prerequisite, standard, practice, or procedure may be enforced without such proceeding if the qualification, prerequisite, standard, practice, or procedure has been submitted by the chief legal officer or other appropriate official of such State or subdivision to the Attorney General and the Attorney General has not interposed an objection within sixty days after such submission, except that neither the Attorney General's failure to object nor a declaratory judgment entered under this section shall bar a subsequent action to enjoin enforcement of such qualification, prerequisite, standard, practice, or procedure. Any action under this section shall be heard and determined by a court of three judges in accordance with the provisions of section 2284 of title 28 of the United States Code and any appeal shall lie to the Supreme Court.

Sec. 6. Whenever (a) a court has authorized the appointment of examiners pursuant to the provisions of section 3(a), or (b) unless a declaratory judgment has been rendered under section 4(a), the Attorney General certifies with respect to any political subdivision named in, or included within the scope of, determinations made under section 4(b) that (1) he has received complaints in writing from twenty or more residents of such political subdivision alleging that they have been denied the right to vote under color of law on account of race or color, and that he believes such complaints to be meritorious, or (2) that in his judgment (considering, among other factors, whether the ratio of nonwhite persons to white persons registered to vote within such subdivision appears to him to be reasonably attributable to violations of the fifteenth amendment or whether substantial evidence exists that bona fide efforts are being made within such subdivision to comply with the fifteenth amendment), the appointment of examiners is otherwise necessary to enforce the guarantees of the fifteenth amendment, the Civil Service Commission shall appoint as many examiners for such subdivision as it may deem appropriate to prepare and maintain lists of persons eligible to vote in Federal, State, and local elections. . . .

Jimmy Carter's Gubernatorial Inaugural Address, 1971

This is a time for truth and frankness. The next four years will not be easy ones. The problems we face will not solve themselves. They demand from us the utmost in dedication and unselfishness from each of us. But this is also a time for greatness. Our people are determined to overcome the handicaps of the past and to meet the opportunities of the future with confidence and with courage.

Our people are our most precious possession and we cannot afford to waste the talents and abilities given by God to one single Georgian. Every adult illiterate, every school dropout, every untrained retarded child is an indictment of us all. Our state pays a terrible and continuing human financial price for these failures. It is time to end this waste. If Switzerland and Israel and other people can eliminate illiteracy, then so can we. The responsibility is our own, and as Governor, I will not shirk this responsibility.

At the end of a long campaign, I believe I know our people as well as anyone. Based on this knowledge of Georgians North and South, Rural and Urban, liberal and conservative, I say to you quite frankly that the time for racial discrimination is over. Our people have already made this major and difficult decision, but we cannot underestimate the challenge of hundreds of minor decisions yet to be made. Our inherent human charity and our religious beliefs will be taxed to the limit. No poor, rural, weak, or black person should ever have to bear the additional burden of being deprived of the opportunity of an education, a job or simple justice. We Georgians are fully capable of making our judgments and managing our own affairs. We who are strong or in positions of leadership must realize that the responsibility for making correct decisions in the future is ours. As Governor, I will never shirk this responsibility.

Georgia is a state of great natural beauty and promise, but the quality of our natural surroundings is threatened because of avarice, selfishness, procrastination and neglect. Change and development are necessary for the growth of our population and for the progress of our agricultural, recreational, and industrial life. Our challenge is to insure that such activities avoid destruction and dereliction of our environment. The responsibility for meeting this challenge is our own. As Governor, I will not shirk this responsibility.

In Georgia, we are determined that the law shall be enforced. Peace officers must have our appreciation and complete support. We cannot educate a child, build a highway, equalize tax burdens, create harmony among our people, or preserve basic human freedom unless we have an orderly society. Crime and lack of justice are especially cruel to those who are least able to protect themselves. Swift arrest and trial and fair punishment should be expected by those who would break our laws. It is equally important to us that every effort be made to rehabilitate law breakers into useful and productive members of society. We have not yet attained these goals in Georgia, but now we must. The proper function of a government is to make it easy for man to do good and difficult for him to do evil. This responsibility is our own. I will not shirk this responsibility.

Like thousands of other businessmen in Georgia, I have always attempted to conduct my business in an honest and efficient manner. Like thousands of other citizens, I expect no less of government.

The functions of government should be administered so as to justify confidence and pride.

Taxes should be minimal and fair.

Rural and urban people should easily discern the mutuality of their goals and opportunities.

We should make our major investments in people, not buildings.

With wisdom and judgment we should take future actions according to carefully considered long-range plans and priorities.

Governments closest to the people should be strengthened, and the efforts of our local, state and national governments need to be thoroughly coordinated.

We should remember that our state can best be served by a strong and independent governor, working with a strong and independent legislature.

Government is a contrivance of human wisdom to provide for human wants. Men have a right to expect that these wants will be provided by this wisdom.

The test of a government is not how popular it is with the powerful and privileged few, but how honestly and fairly it deals with the many who must depend upon it.

William Jennings Bryan said, "Destiny is not a matter of change, it is a matter of choice. Destiny is not a thing to be waited for, it is a thing to be achieved."

Here around me are seated the members of the Georgia Legislature and other State Officials. They are dedicated and honest men and women. They love this state as you love it and I love it. But no group of elected officers, no matter how dedicated or enlightened, can control the destiny of a great state like ours. What officials can solve alone the problems of crime, welfare, illiteracy, disease, injustice, pollution, and waste? This control rests in *your* hands, the people of Georgia.

In a democracy, no government can be stronger, or wiser, or more just than its people. The idealism of the college student, the compassion of a woman, the common sense of the businessman, the time and experience of a retired couple, and the vision of political leaders must all be harnessed to bring out the best in our State.

As I have said many times during the last few years, I am determined that at the end of this administration we shall be able to stand up anywhere in the world—in New York, California, or Florida and say "I'm a Georgian"—and be proud of it.

I welcome the challenge and the opportunity of serving as Governor of our State during the next four years. I promise you my best. I ask you for your best.

Lyndon B. Johnson's Commencement Address at Howard University, 1965

Legal Protection for Human Rights

Thus we have seen the high court of the country declare that discrimination based on race was repugnant to the Constitution, and therefore void. We have seen in 1957, and 1960, and again in 1964, the first civil rights legislation in this Nation in almost an entire century. . . .

The voting rights bill will be the latest, and among the most important, in a long series of victories. But this victory—as Winston Churchill said of another triumph for freedom—"is not the end. It is not even the beginning of the end. But it is, perhaps, the end of the beginning."

That beginning is freedom; and the barriers to that freedom are tumbling down. Freedom is the right to share, share fully and equally, in American society—to vote, to hold a job, to enter a public place, to go to school. It is the right to be treated in every part of our national life as a person equal in dignity and promise to all others.

Freedom Is Not Enough

But freedom is not enough. You do not wipe away the scars of centuries by saying: Now you are free to go where you want, and do as you desire, and choose the leaders you please.

You do not take a person who, for years, has been hobbled by chains and liberate him, bring him up to the starting line of a race and then say, "you are free to compete with all the others," and still justly believe that you have been completely fair.

Thus it is not enough just to open the gates of opportunity. All our citizens must have the ability to walk through those gates.

This is the next and the more profound stage of the battle for civil rights. We seek not just freedom but opportunity. We seek not just legal equity but human ability, not just equality as a right and a theory but equality as a fact and equality as a result.

For the task is to give 20 million Negroes the same chance as every other American to learn and grow, to work and share in society, to develop their abilities—physical, mental and spiritual, and to pursue their individual happiness.

To this end equal opportunity is essential, but not enough, not enough. Men and women of all races are born with the same range of abilities. But ability is not just the product of birth. Ability is stretched or stunted by the family that you live with, and the neighborhood you live in—by the school you go to and the poverty or the richness of your surroundings. It is the product of a hundred unseen forces playing upon the little infant, the child, and finally the man. . . .

To Fulfill These Rights

There is no single easy answer to all of these problems.

Jobs are part of the answer. They bring the income which permits a man to provide for his family.

Decent homes in decent surroundings and a chance to learn—an equal chance to learn—are part of the answer.

Welfare and social programs better designed to hold families together are part of the answer.

Care for the sick is part of the answer.

An understanding heart by all Americans is another big part of the answer.

And to all of these fronts—and a dozen more—I will dedicate the expanding efforts of the Johnson administration. . . .

The Presidential Commission's Conclusions on the Killings at Jackson State, 1970

Two nights of campus demonstrations at Jackson State College in May 1970 ended in violent confrontation and tragedy. After 28 seconds of gunfire by Mississippi Highway Safety Patrolmen and Jackson city policemen, two black youths lay dying and 12 others were wounded. . . .

Causes of Student Conduct

Jackson State College is a black school situated in a white-dominated state. This is the starting point for analyzing the causes of the student disorders of May 13 and 14, 1970.

The stark fact underlying all other causes of student unrest at Jackson State is the historic pattern of racism that substantially affects daily life in Mississippi. . . .

It is important to emphasize that in any normal sense of the term, "student unrest" does not exist on the Jackson State campus. There is virtually no student movement as such and no deep or serious grievance expressed by students with respect to the administration of the school. . . .

The students perceive that years of protest—by turns vigorous and muted—have not brought white Mississippians to respect the full human dignity of black people. It is a fact, for example, that Jackson State College remains a separate, black state school. To be sure, Jackson State is a source of pride, and it offers a possibility of restructuring education in terms relevant to Blacks. But its existence is also a reminder that the "separate but equal" spirit of 1896 is still a Mississippi reality.

Second, Jackson State students do not readily engage in protest activities because they cannot afford to, especially given their belief that the utility of such action is marginal at best. In their daily life in Mississippi, Jackson State students are too busy fighting for their physical, economic, social, and psychological lives to engage in protests. Many adopt a posture of apathy in an attempt to insulate themselves from the oppressiveness of daily life. Others have a singleminded purpose, often drummed into them from an early age by weary and all but hopeless parents: Get an education, learn a profession, and get out of Mississippi. An increasing number pursue that goal, but with a different purpose: Get an education and use it to serve the needs of the Black community today.

There is a third reason why Jackson State students do not readily protest: Southern black people as a group still believe that the American system will respond to their legitimate demands without the necessity of bringing to bear the pressure of protest activities. . . .

While the decline in hope and the rise in frustration help to explain why some students condoned or participated in the violent actions that occurred on the Jackson State College campus, they do not provide sufficient explanation. . . .

It does appear that some people wanted to exacerbate the trouble once it had started. On May 14, a black man, about 45 years old, drove through campus spreading the false rumor that Charles Evers had been assassinated as his brother Medgar Evers had been several years ago. The same false rumor was telephoned to several bars frequented by corner boys. Both nonstudents and some students responded to the rumor.

A small group of students believed that it would help focus attention on student concerns to engage in violent action that would bring the National Guard onto the campus. . . .

One student, asked at the Commission [President's Commission on Campus Unrest] hearings why the rock-throwing started, gave this response: . . .

> When you go to class every day and in overcrowded classrooms and it is hot and sweaty in there, you just get fed up with it and, you know, you should have had more classrooms and your classrooms should have been cool and you are sitting in a hundred degree classroom and that night it is the same thing, and you ain't got nothing to do. You just got to do something, and it is just one thing led to another, so that is the way it was.

Another student said:

> They throw rocks because they are angry. And they throw rocks at cars passing on Lynch Street, those cars carrying whites. Because, I guess, always in the back of your head you are thinking that somebody hasn't been doing something right all along and if you can't get to the source, get to the next best thing. . . . If you are angry about anything that has political or social overtones, and if you can't get to the politicians and the government officials that are white here, and get them to do a little better, then you go to the next best thing; you get something that looks a little like them, I guess.

Causes of Police Conduct

. . . Many white Mississippi law enforcement officers—and all officers who fired were white—are afraid of what black men may do to them in hostile surroundings. Whether that fear is justified is of little consequence; the fear exists. That fear is intensified enormously in a violent confrontation—one in which foul language is made more threatening by thrown bricks and bottles and by the knowledge that there are Blacks with guns in the immediate area.

Moreover, many white police officers are influenced by their disdain or hatred of Blacks. One officer characterized the rock-throwing on Wednesday night as follows: "It's just a bunch of damn niggers." . . .

[A highway patrolman radioed a] . . . catalog of injuries shortly after the shooting. The attitude reflected in a statement of that type—"I think there are about three more nigger males over there, one of 'em shot in the arm, one of 'em shot in the leg, and one of 'em somewhere else"—is an attitude that Blacks are not fully human.

Racial antagonism is aggravated by the all-white makeup of the Mississippi Highway Patrol and the nearly all-white makeup of the Jackson City Police Department. The highway patrol's director of personnel testified there has never been a black highway patrolman. The Jackson City Police Department has 19 uniformed black policemen on a force of 279 members. No black policeman holds an officer rank. Of the 65 law enforcement officers in front of Alexander Hall [a dorm on the Jackson State campus], two were black; they did not shoot.

The Commission concludes that racial animosity on the part of white police officers was a substantial contributing factor in the deaths of two black youths and the gunshot injuries of twelve more.

One of the most tragic aspects of the Jackson State College deaths, however, is that—despite the obvious existence of racial antagonisms—the confrontation itself could have been avoided.

The Commission concludes that the 28-second fusillade from police officers was an unreasonable, unjustified overreaction. Even if we were to assume that two shots were fired from a window in the west wing of Alexander Hall, the 28-second fusillade in response was clearly unwarranted. Peace officers should respond to sniper fire by taking cover and holding their fire. The Jackson City Police sniper team on the scene should have been used to deal with reported sniper fire. A broad barrage of gunfire in response to reported and unconfirmed sniper fire is never warranted.

Moreover, the Jackson City Police and Mississippi Highway Patrol lacked adequate planning, communications, training, and discipline—but not weapons—as they entered the Jackson State campus on May 14. . . .

Law enforcement officers stated that they did not fire to disperse the crowd in front of Alexander Hall, but rather were responding to what they believed was a sniper located in the west wing. Every officer who admits firing stated that he fired either into the west wing or into the air. The physical evidence and the positions of the victims, however, indicate that the officers were firing indiscriminately into the crowd, at ground level, on both sides of Lynch Street.

Even though the officers did fire into the crowd, it appears that no one would have been killed if birdshot had been used rather than buckshot. The highway patrol was using buckshot because of a change in its policy concerning ammunition. . . .

This change in policy lends some support to the view, widespread among Jackson State students, that police, particularly highway patrolmen, have become more hostile in recent years to Blacks and more inclined to deal harshly with black protestors. Some students say that national, state, and local officials have created a favorable climate for such police attitudes.

Finally, the Commission concludes that a significant cause of the deaths and injuries at Jackson State College is the confidence of white officers that if they fire weapons during a black campus disturbance they will face neither stern departmental discipline nor criminal prosecution or conviction.

This view received confirmation by the Mississippi Highway Safety Patrol investigation and by the report of the Hinds County grand jury. . . .

We offer one final observation on the grand jury report. Its underlying philosophy is summarized in the following passage from the report: "When people . . . engage in civil disorders and riots, they must expect to be injured or killed when law enforcement officers are required to reestablish order."

That position, which the grand jury drew almost verbatim from grand jury charges by Federal District Judge Harold Cox and State Circuit Judge Russell Moore, may reflect the views of many Americans today. It is a view which this Commission urges Americans to reject.

The Commission categorically rejects rhetorical statements that students must "expect" injury or death during civil disorders. Such statements make no distinction between legitimate dissent and violent protest. It is the duty of public officials to protect human life and to safeguard peaceful, orderly, and lawful protest. When disorderly protest exists, it is their duty to deal with it firmly, justly, and with the minimum force necessary; lethal force should be used only to protect the lives of officers or citizens and only when the danger to innocent persons is not increased by the use of such force.

Interviews with a Republican and a Democratic Leader, 1981, 1982

Interview with Unidentified Republican Official, 1981

Official. As to the whole Southern strategy that Harry Dent [Republican strategist from South Carolina] and others put together in 1968, opposition to the Voting Rights Act would have been a central part of keeping the South. Now [the new Southern strategy] doesn't have to do that. All you have to do to keep the South is for Reagan to run in place on the issues he's campaigned on since 1964 . . . and that's fiscal conservatism, balancing the budget, cut taxes, you know, the whole cluster. . . .

Questioner: But the fact is, isn't it, that Reagan does get to the [George] Wallace voter and to the racist side of the Wallace voter by doing away with Legal Services, by cutting down on food stamps . . . ?

[The official answered by pointing to what he said was the abstract nature of the race issue today.]

Official: You start out in 1954 by saying "Nigger, nigger, nigger." By 1968 you can't say "nigger"—that hurts you. Backfires. So you say stuff like forced busing, states' rights, and all that stuff. You're getting so abstract now [that] you're talking about cutting taxes, and all these things you're talking about are totally economic things and a by-product of them is [that] blacks get hurt worse than whites. And subconsciously maybe that is part of it. I'm not saying that. But I'm saying that if it is getting that abstract, and that coded, that we are doing away with the racial problem one way or the other. You follow me—because obviously sitting around saying, "We want to cut this," is much more abstract than even the busing thing *and* a hell of a lot more abstract than "Nigger, nigger." . . .

Interview with U.S. Representative David R. Bowen (D-Miss.), 1982

Yes, it was a little bit [like walking a tightrope]. Of course, I had a lot of very conservative white people supporting me, a lot of conservative farmers and businessmen, people like that. And at the same time a large bloc of the black community. I think if you don't have a hard-core doctrinaire position on something in which you lock yourself in by saying, "I am a liberal and I believe in a liberal program, which is the following," and therefore you sort of announce that "I am going after labor votes and black votes and that's that and if I can pick up any more on friendship or personal charm or on whatever, well, I'll get a few more someplace else." That's one way.

Or you can go to the other side and say, "I am a conservative and I am going to get business votes and wealthy farmer votes and I am going to pick up any others wherever I can." Obviously, I was not either of those two extremes. . . . And I had no particular reason to be. . . .

It's easy enough when you are in [the first] campaign to make everybody happy because you never had to vote on anything . . . but how'd you stay in office for ten years? I think I just didn't do anything to alienate either of those two blocs that I had put together. Obviously, there were a lot of white votes I didn't get. Because if my high-water mark was 70 percent of the votes and I was getting maybe 90 percent of the black votes, there were a lot of white votes I was not getting. But my voting record was often on the conservative side, but it varied across the middle of the board. It was not far right or far left. In all these national organizations that rate you, I might range from 35 to 85. . . . My ADA [Americans for Democratic Action] and liberal-type votes were usually in the low numbers. The conservative organizations were more often in the high numbers, but usually in the middle ranges somewhere.

So it was not a very doctrinaire sort of pattern. You could look at it and you could say, "I don't know whether it falls under liberal or conservative." That's pretty much the way it was. No one could really stamp me as a liberal or a conservative. I never did anything to alienate the black support that I had. I never did anything to alienate the business support that I had. There were never very many issues that came along which were kind of no-win issues where you would totally outrage half the people whatever you did. . . .

Take things like food stamps. . . . Theoretically, a lot of the people who do not receive food stamps are against them. Of course, almost all the black community is for them as well as a lot of the whites. I'm on the Ag[riculture] Committee and I have to write food stamp legislation. Of course, blacks stayed with me because I voted for food stamps. And [to] the whites, I was able to explain that I was tightening up the legislation, improving it. And it would have been a lot more costly and a lot less efficient if I were not in there trying to put amendments in there to improve it—conditions that require recipients to register for work and accept work if it is offered and to make sure that people don't draw food stamps who are able-bodied and unwilling to work. So, generally those conservatives who would cuss and holler about food stamps all the time would say, "Well, David's doing a good job trying to improve the program. They are going to pass the thing . . . anyhow. He's in there trying to improve it, trying to tighten it up, trying to cut out the fraud, the waste." But I would certainly vote for the program after I got through tightening it up.

So, . . . what makes good politicians, I guess, is someone who can take whatever his vote is and do a good job of explaining it. . . . If you can explain it to those who are against it and make them like it, even though you voted for it, and then, of course, let the ones who are for it know that you voted for it . . . then you are in good shape. And I think that is probably what I did. . . . It's just kind of a matter of personal skill and packaging what you do and explaining it.

Cartoonist Doug Marlette's View of Political Segregation, 1985

Political cartoon by Doug Marlette, New York Newsday Creators Syndicate. Reprinted by permission of Doug Marlette.

Andrew Young's State of the City Address, 1989

The past seven years have been among the most exciting of my life. The opportunity to serve the citizens of this city during what I believe is truly the golden age of growth and development in Atlanta has been perhaps the most rewarding chapter to date in my more than three decades of public service. I cannot claim sole credit for the advances we have made in this city during the 1980's, instead I must look to the past and recognize the business, government and religious leaders who laid the foundation for the rewards which we currently reap.

A Tribute to Past Leadership

It was Mayor William B. Hartsfield in partnership with J. Paul Austin, then president and chief executive officer of Coca-Cola, who confronted the race question in the late 1950's by proclaiming Atlanta, "A City Too Busy to Hate." It was also Bill Hartsfield who began to make Atlanta an international city by paying $90,000 for the land for the Atlanta airport and luring Delta Airlines out of Louisiana by leasing the land to that fledgling company for $1 per year.

It was early members of the Atlanta Action Forum like Billy Stern, Herman Russell, Mills B. Lane and Bill Calloway, and civic, political and religious leaders like Mayor Ivan Allen, Dr. Martin Luther King, Jr., Daddy King, Robert W. Woodruff, Jesse Hill and Ralph McGill who safeguarded this city from the racial strife which ripped across the southland in the early 1960's. It was also Mayor Allen and C&S president Mills Lane who first realized that Atlanta could and should be a Big League city, and who then proceeded to build a home for professional sports in Atlanta and bring in the Falcons and the Braves.

Later in the 1960's, it was Mayor Sam Massell who utilized the type of communication developed in the Action Forum to fashion a compromise which allowed Atlanta to build a modern mass transit system long before our sister cities in the South. After failing in his first attempt to pass the Marta referendum, Mayor Massell joined forces with Jesse Hill and realized that the key to voter approval was an agreement which would afford black businesses a 20% share of the design and construction contracts on the new system, ensure that 30% of the new jobs created would be held by minorities and guarantee a fare of 15 cents during the first seven years of construction.

Mayor Maynard Jackson institutionalized Mayor Massell's recipe for affirmative action in a minority business enterprise program and then proceeded to build the largest economic generator in the southeastern United States, on time and under budget, with 25% participation from minority contractors. Besides being perhaps the single greatest asset to the growth and development of this city, the new Hartsfield Atlanta International Airport is another concrete example of what makes Atlanta work. It is a public-private partnership, a tribute to the notion of full and fair participation by all segments of a diverse society, and the crown jewel in a system of rail, interstate and air transportation which, I believe, is unparalleled in the world.

A Philosophy for Governing

In 1982, as I took the oath of office from Judge Osgood Williams and became Atlanta's 55th mayor, the example of leadership set by this community gave me the confidence to say that, "*Atlanta is not now rising from the ashes. It is rocketing into orbit from a solid foundation.*"

On that cold and sunny day in January, as over 8,000 Atlantans joined me in a candle-lit inaugural ceremony at the Omni, I knew that the challenges which awaited this city were great. I also knew that, "*the American southland has been at the forefront of the struggle against poverty and racism, and Atlanta has always led the way in the South.*"

With that knowledge—and with the lessons which I learned by serving the citizens of this city, this region and this nation, in the civil rights movement, the United States Congress, and at the United Nations—I was confident in 1982 that all the ingredients existed here for propelling Atlanta into the 1990's as a true economic, social and cultural leader among the cities of the world.

When I was elected mayor, I felt as though an era was coming to an end. In fact, the banks in this city were all in a state of shock, there was anxiety about the investment climate and a fear that investment was moving out of our city. There was, at the same time, a concern and a fear that the government funds upon which we had depended so much in the 1950's, 1960's and 1970's were not going to be present for us in the 1980's.

It was with some fear and trembling that I declared my candidacy for mayor, but it was also in a hope that we might find new, alternative sources of revenue. I knew that together we might chart a course that would continue our city's growth and development in spite of the private sector decline that was characteristic of the moment and the decline in government funds which was foreshadowed by a rising government debt burden.

We have seen a diminishing of government funds. We have almost seen the end of revenue sharing. We have seen some $30–$40 million in government funds that used to come into the city now dwindle to less than $10 million, and yet we have been able to find a way to help our city grow.

I contend that that was not just an accident. I contend that as we began to look around us and as we began to decide how we would meet the shortfall, we determined that only through attracting private capital could we continue to meet the needs of our citizens. Indeed, I think we have developed something which I call **Public Purpose Capitalism,** a pragmatic philosophy in which we have attempted to attract private capital for public purposes.

Quite different from anything that had happened in the 1950's and 1960's, when it was largely government money that drove our growth and development, we knew that in the 1980's more and more of our development had to come from the private sector. Immediately, we embarked upon a strategy which I think is going to be even more important in the years to come, because even though we have tapped private sources of capital, government sources of capital continue to dry up and there seems to be little or no hope of getting more funds from the federal or the state government. What we are going to have to do is to continue to evolve this system of public purpose capitalism, to attract private capital to public purposes which are beneficial to the total growth of our community.

I knew in 1982 that America cried out for answers to a worldwide economic crisis, and that these answers would not come simply by debating the supply-side theories of Reaganomics. I knew that the answers would come only as new economic development projects emerged which would actually demonstrate that it was possible, through new joint ventures between U.S. business and the demand of world markets, to create jobs right here at home. I knew that the challenge of the '80's was economic—jobs— and that Atlanta had to once again point the way in the economic arena just as we had in the social and political spheres.

In order to meet that challenge, I outlined several areas which would receive top priority and emphasis during my administration. They included developing a close working relationship between city hall and the business community, encouraging business investment and expansion, ensuring the public safety of all our citizens, creating downtown entertainment and housing opportunities, promoting Atlanta as a regional center for international finance and export trade, developing a genuine partnership with our state government and the governments of surrounding counties, safeguarding our reputation for minority participation and civil rights, and demanding honest and efficient government at the lowest possible cost to the taxpayer.

Country Song, "I Believe the South Is Gonna Rise Again," 1973

Mama never had a flower garden
'Cause cotton grew right up to our front
   door
Daddy never went on a vacation
He died a tired old man at forty-four.
Our neighbors in the big house called us
   "Redneck"
'Cause we lived in a poor share-cropper
   shack
The Jacksons down the road were poor
   like we were
But our skin was white and theirs was
   black.

Bobby Braddock, "I Believe the South Is Gonna Rise Again" (Nashville: Tree Publishing Co., 1973).

But I believe the south is gonna rise
  again
But not the way we thought it would
  back then
I mean ev'rybody hand in hand
I believe the south is gonna rise again.

I see wooded parks and big skyscrapers
Where once stood red clay hills and cot-
  ton fields
I see sons and daughters of
  sharecroppers
Drinking scotch and making business deals.

But more important I see human
  progress
As we forget the bad and keep the good
A brand new breeze is blowing 'cross
  the southland
And I see a brand new kind of
  brotherhood.

Yes, I believe the south is gonna rise
  again
But not the way we thought it would
  back then
I mean ev'rybody hand in hand
I believe the south is gonna rise again.

⚓ E S S A Y S

V. O. Key, Jr.'s *Southern Politics in State and Nation* remains the classic work on southern politics prior to the upheaval of the 1960s. The centrality of race in politics and the dominance of the black belt are two of the book's major themes. As the excerpt in the first essay indicates, Key, a political science professor at the University of Alabama at the time he wrote the book, was optimistic that urbanization, changing attitudes, a declining agricultural economy, and blacks' migration to other parts of the country would eventually open up southern politics, though admittedly this would take some time. Little did Key realize that within somewhat more than a decade after the publication of *Southern Politics*, the civil-rights movement would appreciably accelerate that process. The next essay, by brothers Earl Black and Merle Black, political science professors, respectively, at the University of South Carolina and the University of North Carolina, Chapel Hill, notes the stubborn persistence of some forms of racial inequality in southern politics. This inequality perseveres, they argue, not despite, but perhaps because of, the factors Key touted as tempering the influence of race on politics—most notably urbanization and black outmigration. In the third selection, Joel Williamson, professor of history at the University of North Carolina, Chapel Hill, argues that the advances in southern race relations over the past two decades have been superficial and that the southern white elite has skillfully maintained its power in the process. Hugh Davis Graham, professor of history at the University of Maryland, Baltimore County, in the last essay assesses why economic inequality represents such a difficult problem from a policy perspective. Graham contends that the shift toward compensatory justice—that is, "the unequal treatment of citizens by race"—created sufficient ironies and contradictions that it shattered the political consensus of an earlier era but has nonetheless produced an important legacy.

The Prospects for Breaking the Solid South

V. O. KEY, JR.

The Solid South

Southern political regionalism derives basically from the influence of the Negro. Other factors, to be sure, contribute to sectional character, but in the final analysis the peculiarities of southern white politics come from the impact of the black race. Common concern with the problems of a cotton economy forms a foundation for regional unity, although perhaps to a lesser extent than several decades ago. A white population that is predominantly native-born, Anglo-Saxon is bound together by a sentiment of unity against those sections whose people include many recent immigrants. A rural, agricultural people views with distrust the urban, laboring classes of the North. The almost indelible memories of occupation by a conqueror create a sense of hostility toward the outsider. Yet most of these nonracial bonds of unity differ little from those factors that lend political cohesion, for example, to the wheat states or to the corn belt.

Southern sectionalism and the special character of southern political institutions have to be attributed in the main to the Negro. The one-party system, suffrage restrictions departing from democratic norms, low levels of voting and of political interest, and all the consequences of these political arrangements and practices must be traced ultimately to this one factor. All of which amounts to saying that the predominant consideration in the architecture of southern political institutions has been to assure locally a subordination of the Negro population and, externally, to block threatened interferences from the ouside with these local arrangements.

While these objectives have molded southern political institutions, it would be incorrect to say that the problem of race relations is a constant preoccupation of politicians or a matter of continuous debate. Campaign after campaign is waged in which the question of race is not raised; in campaign after campaign candidates most unrestrained in Negro baiting find themselves defeated when the votes are counted. The situation is, rather, that the struggles of politics take place within an institutional framework fixed by considerations of race relations, a framework on the order of a mold which gives shape and form to that which it contains. It is chiefly

---

V. O. Key, Jr., "Is There a Way Out?" from *Southern Politics in State and Nation*, Knopf, 1949, Vintage Edition, 1963, pp. 665–675. Reprinted by permission of Marion T. Key.

when the equilibrium in race relations is threatened that the issue of the Negro comes to the fore in political discussion.

It is, of course, no news to conclude that the Negro gives the South its special political color. Yet our analyses indicate that the influence of race is more complex than might be supposed from the usual notions derived from white-supremacy oratory and from fictional pictures of the South. In fact, the effects of race are such that the participants in politics are not always conscious of them. Much less are outside observers aware of the precise nature of the consequences of race and, indeed, in many instances it is most difficult to estimate their significance although their general nature may be divined.

The mechanisms of race and regionalism are identified if attention is focused on those counties of the South with large proportions of Negroes in their population. With almost monotonous regularity, no matter from what angle the politics of the South is approached, the black belt stands out as the hard core of the political South. It is in this relatively small part of the South that attitudes thought to be universal in the South occur with highest intensity. The black-belt counties can be regarded as a skeleton holding together the South. They have, in a sense, managed to subordinate the entire South to the service of their peculiar local needs.

. . . In the period of the disfranchisement movement, the black-belt counties, with a relatively high degree of uniformity, turned in by far the highest popular majorities in favor of proposals to tighten suffrage restrictions for the purpose of excluding the Negro from the suffrage and perhaps also incidentally to make it inconvenient for lesser whites to vote. This cleavage between the white and the black counties had appeared even earlier, with varying degrees of sharpness, in the return to power of the old Whigs who were reincarnated as Conservative Democrats and gradually became the exclusive bearers of the true Democratic faith. By the time of the Populist revolt, in state after state the lines were fairly clearly drawn between the black belts and the white areas. The black belts allied themselves with the conservative forces of the cities and towns to beat down the radicals who flourished in the hills where there were few Negroes. The division was not, of course, governed solely by the distribution of Negroes; the areas of heavy Negro concentrations have tended to possess a peculiar economic structure based on large-scale agricultural operations.

Although the differences between the lowlands and the uplands, between the delta and the hills, and between other such regions have become less, far less, bitter with the passage of time, in several states the black belt continues to play a major role in state politics. By the overrepresentation of rural counties in state legislatures, the whites of the black belts gain an extremely disproportionate strength in state law making. By the political alertness of their people, an alertness growing perhaps out of necessity, they also gain strength. While the black belts have a significant place in state politics, the lines are often blurred and in some states the black belts are too small to exert a controlling influence.

The role of the black belts in giving cohesion to the South appears with most clarity in national politics. At times when the unity of the South is strained the black belts are etched out sharply as the backbone of the South. In the presidential election of 1928 by and large the voters of the black-belt counties showed greatest resistance to the appeal of the Republican candidate. In the white counties Democratic loyalties were not nearly so strong. The whites in these counties could vote their convictions on prohibition and religion. They had far less concern about the maintenance of a solid Democratic front as a means for the long-run preservation of the racial equilibrium. The black-belt counties may have been immediately governed by a more potent partisan tradition than by conscious calculations about party and race, yet that tradition itself rested ultimately on such considerations. In the Dixiecrat revolt of 1948, on the other hand, the most serious defections from the Democracy occurred in the black-belt counties. In the white counties the traditional attachment to the Democratic party coincided with a generally liberal viewpoint and Mr. Truman polled his strongest vote in these counties. The black-belt counties, most immediately and most deeply concerned about civil rights proposals, had most reason to support the Dixiecratic candidates. In both 1928 and 1948 there were many departures in individual localities from the cleavage along white-black lines, yet in general divisions fell along those lines.

In presidential voting at moments of strain the roots of southern solidarity are defined by the split in the popular vote. In the South's representation in Congress, however, no such split occurs, at least on the race issue. The solidarity of southern spokesmen in Congress reflects in part the success of the black belts in converting the entire South to their will and in part a regional aversion to external interference on any question. Yet it is only on the race question that the South presents a solid front in Congress. In the Senate to a relatively greater extent than in the House the factional differences within the Democratic party of each southern state are projected into the voting on nonracial matters. In the House, however, it appears that one of the serious consequences of the one-party system is a much higher degree of solidarity on all kinds of questions than in the Senate. Yet in both House and Senate it is the race issue that evokes the highest degree of southern solidarity. This phenomenon contributes additional support to the proposition that the Negro gives the South its peculiar political characteristics.

This summary may seem to overstate the role of the black belts. . . . Nevertheless, the general point is valid that the most profound conditioning of white political behavior by the Negro occurs in the areas of heavy Negro population concentrations. . . .

The South Divided

In congressional politics, southern cohesiveness in the resistance of proposals to repeal the poll tax, to punish lynching, and to enact other race legislation conveys a false impression about the political homogeneity of the South. There is, to be sure, a high degree of solidarity in congressional politics on a limited range of issues. The black belts manage to control almost the entire southern congressional delegation in opposition to proposals of external interference. Yet in intrastate politics, even on issues of race, uniformity of attitude by no means prevails. Departures from the supposed uniformity of southern politics occur most notably in those states with fewest Negroes and in those sections that are predominantly white. The unknown political South is in a sense the obverse of the Solid South; it consists in the main of those areas outside the black belt.

Outside the black belts southern political behavior often takes on a tone distinctly at odds with the planter-financier stereotype. The area outside the black belt in several states consists largely of the highlands which have been marked by an unbroken strain of political rebelliousness. Opposition to The War was most intense in the uplands. Afterwards the Republican party won strength in the hills as did the Populists. In the disfranchisement movement the people of the piedmont and the hills manifested a coolness toward schemes to restrict the suffrage. Through the years in state campaigns radical or progressive candidates generally have been accorded their most enthusiastic support in these regions. In Alabama, Hugo Black and Jim Folsom came out of the hills to harry the "big mules." Louisiana's northwestern red hills gave Huey Long to the world, and Mississippi's hills unwaveringly supported Bilbo. Virginia's southwestern uplands nurtured John Flannagan, a thorn in the side of the Byrd machine. Tennessee's mountain country sent Estes Kefauver to Congress, while Ellis Arnall came from the Georgia piedmont. Olin Johnston built on a mill following in South Carolina's piedmont, while North Carolina's progressivism must be attributed in considerable measure to the spirit of the uplands. Throughout the South in the presidential campaign of 1948 it was in the hills that Truman's support tended to be strongest. Although the uplands constitute the area of most striking deviate political behavior, similar departures from the supposed southern norm occur in other areas with few Negroes. Along the coast in almost every state there are tidewater counties, too poor in soil to develop a plantation agriculture, that often join hands with the hills against the black belt.

Within individual states the areas predominantly white stand out as centers of political ferment. Similarly among the states those with fewest Negroes seem most disposed toward deviation from the popular supposition of how the South behaves politically. It is the custom to speak of the border states. It is more accurate to speak of the states around the rim of the South. Texas, Arkansas, and Florida seem destined to develop in the long run a nonsouthern sort of politics. The extraordinary growth of industry and trade in Texas and the decline in the proportion of Negro population conspire to create a new variety of politics not much concerned about the Negro. Florida similarly has enjoyed a tremendous population growth. While the state has a relatively large number of Negroes, the whites of the newly settled areas do not seem to be governed by a Negrophobia to the same extent as the long settled agricultural areas of the Old South. To a less marked degree Arkansas politics seems to be moving toward an emancipation from the Negro question; large areas with few Negroes are gaining rapidly in population and shifting the balance of power away from the plantation principalities of the eastern part of the state. Tennessee, Virginia, and North Carolina are other states of the southern rim, and all of them manifest a considerably higher degree of freedom from preoccupation with the race question than do the states of the Deep South.

Although there can be no exact measure, the apparent variations in intensity of reaction to the Supreme Court decision outlawing the white primary [*Smith* v. *Allwright*] define the rim of the South. Texas, Arkansas, Tennessee, Virginia, North Carolina, and Florida seemed to accept the new state of affairs with the least effect on their political temperatures. There were, to be sure, outbursts here and there . . . yet on the whole political leaders in these states did not exhibit the irreconcilability so manifest in South Carolina, Georgia, Alabama, Mississippi, and, to a lesser extent, in Louisiana. Indeed, around the rim of the South there was less reason for concern, for there were fewer Negroes.

By the types of analysis employed in this study the people of the areas with few Negroes show striking departure from the political attitudes of the black belt. Perhaps more significant for the long pull is the differential in attitudes of the larger urban centers. In many ways the cities differ from rural areas with like proportions of Negro population. It is in the cities that the obstacles to Negro political participation are least formidable. It is mainly in the cities that a Negro is now and then elected to a minor office. In the cities, too, the white vote is conditioned to a much less degree by the Negro than in the rural counties. Urban Representatives in Congress free themselves to a much higher degree from the black-belt-conservative coalition than even Representatives from white rural districts. In the cities there is, to be sure, gross discrimination in public services, but the conditions of city life compel a much greater concern for the colored population than generally prevails in rural counties. The causes of the different racial equilibrium of the cities are difficult to discern. Perhaps the physical conditions of urban life permit the development of more or less autonomous, parallel communities. The organization of authority is more institutionalized, less personal, and the Negro may exercise, for example, the right of petition without great fear of illegal or extralegal retaliation against him as an individual. It should be remembered, however, that the institutional arrangements of the South prevent the exertion of the full strength of the cities in politics. Gerrymandering against the urban centers takes on special significance in that it gives heavy weight to those areas in general the most conservative and in particular the most irreconcilable on the Negro issue. And in Georgia, of course, even in gubernatorial politics the cities are practically disfranchised.

The prominent place of the plantation counties in the conservative wing of the southern Democratic party makes it almost impossible for the conservative wing to take the leadership in moves to ameliorate race problems. That leadership goes to the liberal wing which draws its heaviest popular support ordinarily from the areas of white dominance and from the cities.

And southern liberalism is not to be underestimated. Though southern conservatism is not entirely a myth, as W. G. Carleton has argued, fundamentally within southern politics there is a powerful strain of agrarian liberalism, now re-enforced by the growing unions of the cities. It is not always perceptible to the outsider—or even to the southerner—because of the capacity of the one-party system to conceal factional differences. Yet an underlying liberal drive permeates southern politics. It is held in check in part by the one-party system which almost inevitably operates to weaken the political strength of those disposed by temperament and interest to follow a progressive line. Moreover, if the Negro is gradually assimilated into political life, the underlying southern liberalism will undoubtedly be mightily strengthened, for the Negro, recent experience indicates, allies himself with liberal factions whenever they exist. The potentialities in national politics of a South freed from the restraint of the Negro and of the one-party system are extremely great. On the contrary, the maintenance of the degree of conservatism that prevails depends ultimately on ability to frighten the masses with the Negro question or the winning over of the growing Negro vote to the conservative wing of the Democratic party. The latter alternative is not open; hence, the long-run prospect for southern reaction can be considered only as dark unless the Negro issue can be raised in a compelling manner. The Dixiecrats beat the drums of racial reaction in 1948 without impressive results; the Dixiecratic movement may turn out to have been the dying gasp of the Old South.

In the combination of economic conservative and Negro baiter against economic liberal and Negro there occurs a coalition at odds with political folklore about the South. Upper bracket southerners habitually attribute all the trouble with the Negro to the poorer whites. Yet it is the poorer whites who support candidates favoring governmental policies for the reduction of racial discriminations and for the alleviation of racial tensions. The line is by no means, of course, sharply drawn between rich and poor, but the economic conservatives are by interest thrown on the side of those who wish to maintain discrimination, to keep alive racial antagonisms. Such policies accrue to the short-term advantage of the economic conservatives.

Portent of Trends

Not of the least significance in altering the conditions of southern politics is the gradual decline of the relative position of the Negro population. Since 1900 the colored proportion of the population has decreased in each state. In several states the Negro population percentage dropped sharply from 1900 to 1940. In Florida the percentage fell from 44 to 27; in Louisiana, from 47 to 36; in South Carolina, from 58 to 43. Of equal or greater importance is the fact that over the same period the areas with high proportions of Negro population contracted, again sharply in some states. It is these areas that constitute the backbone of southern intransigence on the race question. In Virginia, for example, the number of counties over 50 per cent Negro dropped from 36 to 18; in Louisiana the decline was from 31 to 15.

The shrinkage of the black belt is probably of greater importance than the simple decline in Negro population percentages for entire states. It is not to be supposed, of course, that a reduction in the Negro population ratio brings with it immediately a shift in white political attitudes. That change comes only gradually; an alteration of population composition, however, creates a new political setting that will eventually make itself felt.

The growth of cities contains the seeds of political change for the South. In almost every type of analysis urban political behavior differs significantly from that of the rural areas. Apart from other political consequences of urbanism, cities seem to be less dominated in their political behavior than rural areas by consideration of the race question. The Negro himself meets less rigid obstacles to political participation in the cities; the whites, in turn, appear to be less bound by Reconstruction tradition and free to vote without the same regard for the maintenance of the racial system that governs the whites of the rural counties with high proportions of Negro population. If the consequences of urbanization are conceded, the important question then is whether the extent and rate of city growth are great enough to be of significant effect. The South has lagged behind the remainder of the nation in urbanization, and the chances are that urban-rural population readjustment will continue to occur in the region. Nevertheless, striking shifts in population have already taken place. In 1900 the 11 southern states had only seven cities with over 50,000 population; by 1940, this number had grown to 41. Doubtless the 1950 census will show a larger number of cities within the category of 50,000 and over. Another measure of the magnitude of population redistribution is provided by the urban-rural division of the Negro population. In 1900, 14.7 per cent of the Negro population of the South was urban; in 1940, 33.7 per cent. The southern Negro may migrate to Detroit and Chicago but he also moves to Houston, Atlanta, and Birmingham, and migration internal to the South has somewhat the same political effect as movement to points outside the South. With a continuation of improvement of agricultural technology, an acceleration of population shifts may be expected.

Apart from its effects on the race question, urbanization is, of course, an accompaniment of other changes of profound consequence for political behavior. The development of industry and trade in a region hitherto more completely dedicated to agriculture has had and will continue to have far reaching influences in several directions. The growth of urban labor already has had considerable effect and will undoubtedly have further consequences. In all the recent movements for the abolition of the poll tax and for the mitigation of other suffrage restrictions labor unions have played a prominent role. In the factional struggles of particular states organized labor has come to play a controlling role at times. In states such as Texas and Florida, for example, labor organizations in recent years have exerted a rapidly increasing influence. The political activation of urban labor has proceeded less rapidly than the growth of the laboring population. As obstructions to urban political activity are overcome, a significant expansion of labor influence may be expected. Nor must the South become completely urbanized or industrialized to a high degree for union political strength to become formidable. It is virtually a law of our politics that any considerable minority, if it becomes highly vocal, can command a remarkable deference from political leaders. The southern urban dweller has scarcely begun to speak politically.

Concurrently with the growth of the number of urban workers there are coming into being, of course, industrial and financial interests that have a fellow feeling with northern Republicanism. A continuing growth of industry and a continued leftward veering of the Democratic party nationally would place a greater and greater strain on the Democratic loyalties of rising southern big business. At each recent presidential election the results of that strain have been perceptible in the open support of Republican presidential candidates by southern personages formerly of prominence in Democratic councils. In the building of a party within most southern states the Republicans work under the handicap that a large proportion of their existing popular following has little reason to be enthusiastic about Republican policies nationally. The Dixiecrats rather than the hill Republicans are the natural allies of northern Republicanism. Moreover, the strength of the Democratic loyalties of most southern voters is not to be underestimated. In fact, partisan loyalties of Americans wherever they live have an extraordinary persistence. Southerners are no exception to the rule and Republicans have no easy task in making converts among the mass of southern voters. Of course, Republicans make little effort over most of the South to win votes. The development of an opposition party in the South will probably depend more on events outside the South than on the exertions of native Republicans. If the balance of power becomes one that clearly requires a Republican fight for southern votes to win the Presidency, presumably the national party could no longer tolerate its ineffective southern leadership. If and when Republicans make a real drive to gain strength in the South, they will find, if present trends continue, a larger and larger group of prospects susceptible to their appeal.

The decline in the Negro population, the growth of cities, and the dilution of an agricultural economy by the rise of industry and trade occur only slowly and their influences on the political system occur even more slowly. Moreover, it is not to be supposed that these fundamental trends automatically bring political change. They only create conditions favorable to change that must be wrought by men and women disposed to take advantage of the opportunity to accelerate the inevitable. In every state of the South there are many such persons and their efforts are bringing results to an extent not commonly appreciated outside the South. Yet the hard fact has to be recognized that their labors bear fruit most readily in those localities where the underlying population movements and economic developments create the most favorable surrounding circumstances. The way is hard and progress is slow. Yet until greater emancipation of the white from the Negro is achieved, the southern political and economic system will labor under formidable handicaps. The race issue broadly defined thus must be considered as the number one problem on the southern agenda. Lacking a solution for it, all else fails.

Old Themes for the New Southern Politics

EARL BLACK AND MERLE BLACK

Immense socioeconomic, demographic, and political forces have reshaped the South in the twentieth century, sometimes shattering, sometimes simply modifying traditional institutions, practices, and beliefs. We shall . . . [develop] several themes that link the past with the future of southern politics: the strikingly different but still tangential position of blacks; the increasing prominence of middle-class southerners embracing entrepreneurial individualism as their political creed; the diminished presence of black belt whites in leadership roles; the rise of urban leaders; changing elite perspectives on race and economic development; the gradual modification of one-party Democratic rule; and, in a growing number of states, the establishment of sustained two-party competition for major offices.

The Politics of Race

Key concluded *Southern Politics* by urging the necessity of resolving the South's racial dilemma. "The way is hard and progress is slow," he conceded. "Yet until greater emancipation of the white from the Negro is achieved, the southern political and economic system will labor under formidable handicaps." Prospects for immediate reform were so bleak and unpromising that Key could imagine such an "emancipation" occurring only after secular socioeconomic forces (withdrawal from the region by dissatisfied black southerners, as well as huge increases in urbanization and industrialization) had fashioned a more permissive environment, one in which "progressive" white southerners could slowly assimilate "qualified" blacks into active political involvement.

   Although these trends certainly contributed to the eventual dissolution of the Jim Crow South, Key's scenario for racial change profoundly underestimated political developments. Key failed to anticipate the civil rights movement, the "revolt from below" by black southerners, and he largely discounted the possibility of effective national intervention to reform southern race relations. Much of the fierce racial conflict that suffused southern politics from the *Brown* decision and the Montgomery bus boycott through the heyday of George Wallace and the black power movement—conflict that in the broadest sense represented an historical reckoning with the traditional caste system—was initiated by small numbers of black southerners determined to protest the injustices and irrationalities of southern racism. Southern race relations now lies somewhere between old-fashioned strict segregation, on the one hand, and complete racial integration, on the other. The entrenched and pervasive racism that victimized practically all black southerners through the early 1960s has been ameliorated, and many white southerners have been released from the obligation to practice white supremacy. No longer does the white South differ radically from the rest of the nation in its treatment of black people.

. . . From a vantage point two decades removed from the climactic period of federal intervention, the southern political system is considerably more democratic, considerably more open to minority involvement and participation, than it was during the first six decades of this century.

Yet even these obvious improvements warrant qualification and perspective. In terms of the leverage that they can realistically expect to exert in southern politics, blacks have made substantial gains but still face enduring limitations. If systematic black disfranchisement magnified the numerical advantage of the South's large white majority in the past, to what extent have white advantages diminished in recent decades? Ratios of white voter registration rates to black voter registration rates indicate how evenly or unevenly the races are mobilized, and the results show that traditional white advantages in relative mobilization diminished considerably—due to federal intervention and extensive organization within black communities— between 1960 and 1970 and hovered around unity in 1980. Thus the long-standing white superiority in rates of voter registration, an area where rapid change *was* possible, has essentially vanished.

The more fundamental and permanent white advantage, however, flows from the vastly different sizes of the white and black populations. Because blacks are nowhere near a majority of any state's population, whites invariably cast most of the votes in general elections. Although ratios of white registered voters to black registered voters have declined, once blacks became effectively mobilized these ratios have been inherently much more resistant to rapid change. When white registrants outnumber black registrants by two to one or three to one in the Deep South states with the largest black populations (South Carolina, Mississippi, Louisiana, and Alabama) and hold an advantage of more than six to one in the Peripheral South states with the smallest black populations (Texas, Arkansas, Florida, and Virginia), the population-based limitations on black political leverage are manifest. Minority status ineluctably constrains and limits black political influence in the modern South.

. . . The enormous historical disparities between the races in jobs, schooling, and housing could hardly be overcome in less than a generation. It is not surprising, therefore, that in the 1980s, despite progress, whites are more educated, are more likely to work in middle-class employment, and earn substantially higher incomes than blacks as a group. Only recently have southern schools even attempted to provide equal educational opportunities for blacks. Future generations of black southerners will be better educated than their predecessors, and gains in formal education will be translated into an expanded black middle class.

Nearly one-quarter of southern black families already have incomes higher than the median southern white family. At the same time, a large fraction of black families possess incomes that are above poverty but well below affluence, and a considerable minority remain trapped in poverty. Until very recently impoverishment was the central tendency of the black experience in the South, and nearly one-third of the South's black families, versus only one-fourteenth of its white families, continued to experience poverty in the late 1970s. Egregious differences in rates of poverty not only illustrate a broad range of racially based socioeconomic disparities but powerfully reinforce political cleavages—cleavages appearing more distinctly in national than in state elections—between most blacks and most whites.

Because poverty and marginal economic status affect the two racial groups so differently, the economic priorities of most southern whites and most southern blacks commonly diverge rather than converge. Most whites believe in the primacy of individual rather than governmental responsibility for family economic well-being; nearly half of southern blacks, according to the opinion surveys, place central reliance upon government rather than upon themselves for good jobs and wages. Politicians who advocate massive governmental assistance programs for the impoverished are viewed as radical by most southern whites, who perceive themselves as being overtaxed to pay for programs they detest on behalf of recipients whom they do not esteem. Furthermore, blacks and whites usually differ strongly on most current civil rights controversies, especially on matters involving affirmative action to compensate for past discrimination.

When persistent interracial differences on these types of issues are combined with the whites' vastly superior political leverage, the inescapable conclusion for southern politics is that, even under the most favorable circumstances imaginable, black political influence will operate at the margins rather than the center of decisionmaking. Only when whites sharply divide will blacks be positioned to affect electoral outcomes, and then the result will be more to assist the winning white group than to secure immediate, substantial benefits for blacks. . . .

Whites totally monopolized the electorate of the old southern politics, and they remain predominant in the electorate underlying the new southern politics. This is especially true in the Peripheral South, where whites contributed 85 percent of the registered voters in 1984, and it is still the case in the Deep South, where the majority group formed 76 percent of the electorate. On matters involving the races, outcomes in modern southern politics depend more upon the whites' continuing numerical supremacy in the electorate than upon the significant increases that blacks have achieved in their proportion of the total electorate.

White priorities and preferences still fundamentally define southern political agendas, and blacks are usually placed in the position of reacting to the prevailing white views. To understand why biracial politics directed toward liberal goals faces long odds, why most Democratic officeholders blend conservative and progressive themes, and why conservative Republicanism is on the rise, it is crucial to focus on the values, beliefs, and predilections of the white majority, and particularly on the urban middle-class sector of white opinion.

The Political Leverage of the Growing Middle Class

Since World War II the southern social order has been remarkably transformed. Like Americans generally, practically all employed southerners inhabit the new middle class or the working class, and, even more important, by 1980 the South's new middle class outnumbered its working class. The contrast between 1940, when less than a quarter of southern jobholders performed white-collar duties, and 1980, when a majority of them did so, points to the establishment of a far more complex and diversified socio-economic setting than ever before. It also signifies the replacement of the agrarian middle class's traditionalists by the entrepreneurial individualists of the new middle class as the central source of regional leadership. Significant features of the old South persist, of course, as illustrated by the heavy concentration of blacks (especially men) in the working class and the prominence of whites (particularly women) in the new middle class.

The reigning political philosophy of the new southern middle class is the entrepreneurial version of the individualistic political culture, a blend of conservative and progressive themes. In its emphasis on low rates of taxation, minimal regulation of business, and resolute opposition to unions and redistributive welfare programs for have-nots and have-littles, the current political ideology retains important continuities with the traditionalistic political culture. Its progressive element consists in its willingness to use governmental resources to construct the public infrastructure—highways, airports, harbors, colleges and universities, research parks, health complexes—that in turn stimulates and makes possible additional economic growth. The critical transition occurred in the aftermath of federal intervention, as southern states began to spend much larger amounts of money on public education. In due course the social payoff will be a significant reduction in the waste of human talent that had been one of the worst outcomes of traditional southern politics.

For a region accustomed to economic stagnation, the prospect of actually making and keeping big money is an incredibly powerful stimulant. Visions of material abundance obviously excite those with realistic prospects of achieving wealth, and a growing economy at least offers steady employment for the vast majority of southerners who will never attain affluence. Furthermore, because southern state governments collect lower taxes, wealthy southerners can keep more of their earnings than is possible elsewhere, and those with smaller incomes pay less tax than their non-southern counterparts. The southern business creed, which has reminded more than one observer of a new "McKinley era," exerts a compelling popular appeal extending far beyond its direct and most obvious beneficiaries.

In the evolving struggle for power and advantage in southern politics, the new middle class enjoys impressive advantages. It is the most conspicuously successful segment of the society, and its numbers expand yearly. Through personal ownership or institutional control, its members command far more financial resources than any other part of the society, and the new middle class furnishes almost all of the region's managerial and entrepreneurial leadership. Yet the political domination of the middle class occurs also because many of its core values and beliefs are widely shared elsewhere in the society. Though most southerners are not militant conservatives, conservatism's attraction far outstrips liberalism's appeal among the region's working class as well as its middle class. The South has many uncritical loyalists but few loyal critics, and southern politics generally involves narrow ranges of public controversies. Whatever their educational achievement or social position, most white southerners appear satisfied with the region's quality of life and hostile to movements advocating or implying radical political changes.

Not the least of the middle class's assets is the common ground it shares with the white working class and (to a lesser extent) with blacks in terms of emotional predispositions to particular political symbols. When the reactions of middle-class whites, working-class whites, and blacks to relevant political terms are divided into three categories—symbols toward which a majority of a given group felt "warm," those toward which a majority of a particular group felt "cold," and those toward which no majority sentiment existed—the results help explain the persistent absence of effective have-not coalitions and the enduring success of middle-class whites.

Successful campaigns against the haves (the upper-middle class) presuppose this group's isolation, an isolation not at all supported by the facts. To the contrary, the evidence of political symbols suggests numerous ties binding the white middle class and white working class (for example, warmth toward conservatives and Republicans and coldness toward radical students and black militants), as well as important opinions shared by both of the white classes and the blacks, including attitudes toward southerners, police, whites, military, Democrats, blacks, marijuana users, and gays/lesbians.

In contrast, black southerners were completely distinct, completely separated from white workers and the white middle class. Nothing unites blacks and working-class whites that is not equally approved and disapproved by the white middle class. Many realities—white middle-class invulnerability compared with multiple black vulnerabilities, the absence of symbols uniquely joining blacks to working-class whites versus the many commonalities uniting the white middle and working classes, and the conservative nature of the views shared by all three groups—contribute significantly to the thoroughly middle-class orientation of electoral politics in the region.

Beyond Black Belt Control

The predominance of the middle class also influences the types of politicians who can prevail in statewide races and the policies they pursue once elected. One of the most crucial differences between the old and new southern politics is the collapse of the black belt as a central source of leadership in state and national politics. In every southern state long-term population shifts have reduced substantially the proportion of whites residing in high-black rural counties. This secular change has loosened the grip of tradition upon southern politics, for it has undermined the prospects of most politicians currently residing in black belt areas to create followings capable of winning either U.S. Senate seats or governorships.

Over the decades precipitous losses have occurred in the de facto representation of the black belt in the U.S. Senate. In the 1920s nearly three-fourths of all southern senators had been born in a high-black rural county, and two-fifths of them still resided there when elected (or reelected) to the Senate. Even if most senators no longer lived in the black belt, all could be depended upon to support the racial policies espoused by their colleagues from the most conservative part of the region. When the civil rights movement commenced its offensive against southern racism in the 1960s, almost 90 percent of the region's population resided outside the high-black rural counties, and only three of the South's twenty-two senators still lived in a high-black rural county. Though nearly all southern senators voted against the major civil rights legislation, the hard-core southerners were so isolated from the rest of the Senate that they were unable to sustain filibusters against the Civil Rights Act and Voting Rights Act.

The decline and fall of black belt influence has meant the end of the most transparent forms of southern racism in the U.S. Senate. Because most southern senators take conservative positions on many controversies of the intermediate color line, however, the demise of the black belt has by no means resulted in the triumph of racial liberalism within the delegation. To the contrary, a few southerners still vote as though they were living in the 1920s and a smaller number sometimes talk that way for the record. On the whole, though, the region's senatorial delegation has been emancipated from its former unquestioning subservience to the racial views of the black belt whites.

Diminishing black belt control over southern governorships also represents a major change in *state* racial policies. Unlike the situation around the turn of the century, in most states unregenerate black belt conservatives failed to dominate the governorship during the racial crises of the 1950s and 1960s. After the *Brown* decision black belt whites again succeeded for a time in rallying non–black belt whites to the common cause of massive resistance. Nonetheless, despite the fact that most white southerners vastly preferred segregation to integration, they did not usually elect totally unreconstructed black belt politicians to implement segregationist policies. No more than nine of the fifty-four governors elected (or reelected) between 1950 and 1965 had been born and were still living in high-black rural counties when chosen governor. . . .

   Militant support for segregation, the stance typical of black belt governors, was *not* the central tendency among governors who resided outside
the high-black rural section. Unqualified support for segregation was advocated by only 45 percent of the successful candidates who were born in
the black belt but resided elsewhere at the time of their election, and by
merely one-third of the governors who had no ties to the most conservative
part of the region.
   Black protest and federal intervention, not any gradual tendency toward
racial liberalism among southern politicians themselves, liberated white
politicians from the explicit defense of Jim Crow. Following federal intervention, most successful southern politicians finally abandoned segregationist postures. Politicians with interests and constituencies outside the
high-black rural counties began to run as nonsegregationists, and, after a
flurry of last-ditch resistance, even candidates with ties to the black belt
jettisoned segregation. No better symbol of the change exists than George
Wallace, who did so much to obstruct the civil rights movement (in his
come-from-behind victory in 1970, Wallace galvanized white voters by
warning, "If I don't win, them niggers are going to control this state"),
but who began to solicit black votes in 1974 in order to fashion "a new
image to improve his national standing." When Wallace returned to campaigning in 1982 after four years of retirement, he apologized to black
Alabamians for his past behavior and asked for their support in another
successful gubernatorial campaign. As a result of federal intervention, state
racial policies were no longer held hostage to the obsessive concerns of
conservative black belt whites. . . .
   The traditionalistic state policies fashioned and maintained by the black
belt elite included not only the preservation of white supremacy in all forms
and the constriction of state electorates to safe and sound voters, but also
antipathy to taxation, very limited notions of state responsibility for public
services, the primacy of local elite control over economic development at
the expense of more rapid growth, and firm reliance upon the Democratic
party as the only legitimate instrument for the control of state government.
In light of the black belt elite's historical success in shaping public policy,
the waning of black belt governors has been of no small consequence in
shifting the region away from policies and practices that failed to nurture
and encourage the talents and skills of colossal numbers of its citizens. . . .

The Rise of Urban Leaders

   . . . The broader transformation of southern politics involves a shift from
an almost completely rural politics in the 1920s to a mixed urban and rural
politics in the 1970s and 1980s. Most southern governors in the 1920s were
unmistakable products of rural culture, individuals who had been born in
the country or in small towns and who were still living in similar settings
when elected to high office. Even in the 1970s, the rural and small town
origins of most of the region's political elite were still plainly visible.
   . . . [I]n the 1970s majorities of southern senators and governors claimed
either a medium-sized city or a large metropolitan area as their place of

residence. The combination of a rural or small-town childhood with adult experiences in larger cities has become advantageous in statewide campaigns, allowing candidates to bridge different sectors of the electorate. Though southern politicians with exclusively big city backgrounds have occasionally won their states' highest offices, complete identification with a large metropolitan area is generally a liability in statewide contests.

The main political significance of these secular changes again consists in the weakening of the traditionalistic political culture, for the admixture of politicians from medium-urban and large metropolitan areas frequently produces governors and senators whose connections, interests, and priorities differ from those characteristic of purely rural politicians. During this transformation the values associated with entrepreneurial individualism have gained strength, though it helps a politician to be perceived as someone who can simultaneously appeal to the "dynamic" *and* the "static" South, someone who stands both for "progress" (usually understood as economic growth) and for preserving some of the more civilizing norms of the older rural culture. . . .

Beyond Pure One-Party Politics

The traditional hegemony of southern Democracy has ended. Millions of southerners, of course, still think of themselves as Democrats, and many of them continue to vote for their party's candidates. In the past two decades, however, millions of other southerners have come to feel that the policies and candidates associated with the national Democratic party serve neither their interests nor their ambitions, and these negative perceptions have begun to affect many state and local candidates of southern Democracy. As yet many of the Democrats who have lost their political faith have not fully converted to Republicanism. But even though self-identified Republicans remain a minority of the electorate, the region now contains so many independents that Democratic candidates can be defeated whenever non-Democrats (Republicans and independents) join forces.

. . . Though the rise of an urban new middle class provides a firm social grounding for the diffusion of Republican loyalties across the South, the size of that white middle class varies considerably from one state to another. Disregarding other factors, the larger the white urbanized new middle class, the greater the potential for Republican advances. . . .

Future Partisan Balance

The Democratic party in the South is now composed of whites and blacks, and in some quarters it is doubtless perceived as a "black" political party. In fact, although most politically active blacks are Democrats, most southern Democrats are whites. Indeed, a majority of the modern Democratic party's southern identifiers are whites born and raised in the region. The racial, social, and ideological diversity of the Democratic party explains both its strengths and its weaknesses. Though much of the party's leadership and financial support derives from affluent whites, the vast majority of white and black southern Democrats did not attend college, belong to the working class, and are modestly housed. Robust differences in political philosophy further complicate the party's racial and socioeconomic diversity.

Under imaginative and skillful leadership, it is still possible for liberals, moderates, and conservatives to unite in the task of electing Democrats. Most Democratic candidates for state office prevail by assembling virtually all of the black vote and a sufficiently large minority of the white vote. Whenever party unity *is* achieved, Democratic nominees can be truly formidable in most of the Deep South and truly competitive in most of the Peripheral South. Because Democrats still constitute majorities of the electorate in the Deep South, party unity is usually sufficient for victory. In much of the Peripheral South, though, even a united Democratic party may no longer be large enough to win general elections. To achieve victory Democrats have to appeal to many political independents as well.

Nevertheless, the Democratic party is acutely vulnerable to racial, social, and ideological cleavages that have no easy solutions; and it is not always possible to present a cohesive party in general elections. When Democrats divide, whether over critical issues of public policy or simply over the conflicting ambitions of rival politicians, Republicans are strategically positioned to construct winning ad hoc coalitions of real Republicans, independents, and disaffected Democrats. Unless there is a profound revitalization and remobilization of Democratic support in the lower two-thirds of the South's social structure, as time goes on Democratic majorities will become even harder to achieve in statewide elections.

Southern Republicanism increasingly epitomizes the values and beliefs of the most affluent white southerners, as well as those who aspire to such status and rewards. Though its mass base includes some working-class southerners, in terms of real influence and control the GOP is preeminently the vehicle of upper-middle-class, well-educated, conservative whites. Southern Republicanism is the party of *Southern Living*, if that magazine could be imagined to possess an explicit political philosophy. The appeal of the southern version of the American Dream is palpable, but the party's firm grounding in the upper middle class also entails serious risks and liabilities for southern Republicanism as a potential majority party.

The Republican party has practically no attraction, of course, to the region's black voters. Although some white southerners find the absence of blacks a compelling argument in favor of Republicanism ("Why don't you leave the niggers behind and come join us?" was the friendly invitation to one of the authors after he had addressed a gathering of South Carolina Republicans), others decry the party's limited appeal to blacks and rationalize it as the regrettable but predictable consequence of a misguided and underdeveloped black middle class. The practical effect of microscopic black support is that Republicans can win two-candidate elections only by capturing landslide majorities of the white vote.

Unlike the case with the Democrats, substantial portions of the mass base of many southern Republican parties consist of transplanted Yankees and midwesterners. Migration gives the GOP an expanding membership, yet makes some state Republican parties appear "foreign" to many native southerners. Furthermore, while the Democratic party's roots lie in the middle and lower portions of the South's social structure, southern Republicans look upward for their core support. The apex of the social order is a better place to acquire leaders, ideology, and finance than to find votes. If the Republican party is ever to capture the partisan loyalties of a majority of all southerners, its working vision of who is politically important, who really counts in the society, will have to be dramatically broadened. Country clubs and magnificent resorts, the natural habitats of the Republican elite, do not provide the best vantage points for "seeing" the millions of southerners in the lower-middle and working classes.

Democrats will probably continue to win most southern state and local offices for some time to come. But the shift of conservatives from the Democratic to the Republican party and the GOP's popularity among college-educated whites portend a brighter Republican future. Educated white conservatives have already realigned their party identifications. Including the partisan leanings of independents, 65 percent of educated conservatives were sympathetic to the Republicans, while merely 28 percent found the Democrats attractive in 1980. On the eve of Ronald Reagan's first term, highly educated white conservatives were clearly embracing Republicanism. Reagan's performance in office presumably accelerated the realignment: by 1984, 75 percent of the white conservatives with some exposure to college leaned toward or identified with the Republicans, compared with only 18 percent who favored the Democrats. This stratum of southern society contributes most of the Republican party's officeholders, candidates, organizers, and fund raisers.

Throughout southern history economic achievement and political conservatism have not ordinarily been long separated from actual political power. As a group, conservatives—educated and uneducated—used the Democratic party as their main political instrument in the past. Partisan realignment of the most highly educated sector of southern conservatives probably signifies a fundamental shift in the party affiliations of conservative southerners generally, a shift that may eventually make the Republicans the South's leading party.

Nonetheless, despite the obvious political assets enjoyed by educated white conservatives, a comprehensive Republican realignment in southern politics is not inevitable. In the dealigned electorate Republican success depends upon creating *and* sustaining favorable impressions of the GOP as well as negative images of the Democrats among white voters, perceptions that are influenced by the performance of Republican and Democratic officeholders in the South and also by the tides of national partisan politics, which cannot always favor the GOP. Continued economic growth is crucial to Republican success, for it is through the expansion of jobs that Republicans can appeal to the region's common whites. Fluctuations in the business cycle will doubtless provide political opportunities for the Democrats in the future.

Shifts in party strength since the Great Society have been most convincingly expressed in the outcomes of presidential elections. The symbols and issues associated with Republican presidential candidates have generally been far closer to the interests, beliefs, wishes, and expectations of the white middle class than have those identified with Democratic presidential candidates. In recent times no politician has exploited the mismatch in party symbols more skillfully than Ronald Reagan, who is much more conventionally "southern" in his style and practice of politics than either Lyndon Johnson or Jimmy Carter. Shrewdly blending themes from the entrepreneurial individualistic culture and the traditionalist heritage, Reagan's positions on most issues—with the glaring exception of his administration's massive federal deficits—appear eminently reasonable to most middle-class southern whites. . . .

The Democrats who have won office since federal intervention have usually done so by deliberately mixing presentable features of the traditionalistic culture with dynamic aspects of the entrepreneurial culture. A judicious fusion of conservative and progressive themes expresses the essence of modern southern Democracy and constitutes an operational definition of political "moderation" in the South. At best it is a winning formula; at worst it allows most Democrats to remain competitive. Democratic nominees are unlikely to abandon this style of campaigning.

All southern Republicans embrace conservatism, but some are more militantly right-wing than others. Because the national political agenda provides the Republican far right with more targets and symbols to deploy against their opponents than do the more mundane and practical agendas of state politics, the far right has done much better in contests for the U.S. Senate than for the governorships. Senate races are more likely to involve distinct ideological contrasts than are gubernatorial campaigns. In Senate contests "progressive-conservative" Democrats will sometimes fight conservative or right-wing Republicans, and voters may find it fairly easy to pick the candidate nearest to their own views.

The situation will be somewhat different in most gubernatorial contests. In state politics there is no reliable demand for an unadulterated conservative Republicanism. Although most Republican gubernatorial candidates will emphasize conservative themes more than their Democratic opponents, they will not ordinarily win southern governorships by marketing themselves as uptown Dixiecrats. Far more likely to succeed are those Republican contenders who imitate the winning Democrats by combining elements of conservatism with dynamic, progressive appeals. Voters in future elections for governor may have difficulty perceiving striking issue differences between Democratic and Republican nominees. Frequently their effective choices will lie between the "progressive conservatives" or "conservative progressives" of the Democratic party and the "conservatives" or "moderate conservatives" of the Republican party.

Statewide elections in the new southern politics will typically determine which segments of the white middle class will rule, that is, whether the self-described "moderates" or the "conservatives" of the educated middle class will hold the key offices, command the public institutions, make the policies, and distribute the patronage and perquisites of a rapidly growing region. Though elected officials will differ in agendas, priorities, and style, the middle-class politicians of both parties will normally strive to maintain a friendly climate for economic development, will tax individuals and corporations at comparatively low rates, will spend substantial sums only for purposes that unmistakably serve the self-interest of the expanding middle class, and will generally minimize transfer payments that would mainly benefit have-not and have-little southerners. Southern elections will not ordinarily focus on explicit differences between whites and blacks, nor will they usually feature overt conflicts between middle-class and working-class southerners. By and large, open political conflict will involve differences within the white middle class itself. Whether the moderates rule through the Democratic party or the conservatives govern through the Republican party, southern politics can be expected to perpetuate much of the past even as a different future beckons.

The South Has Not Yet Overcome

JOEL WILLIAMSON

Race relations in the South over the last century and a half have not been purely a Southern matter; they have also steadily involved the North and the nation at large. At the same time that it undertook to adjust race relations at home, the white elite has been forced to adjust relations between North and South. In that process it moved the South from a position of increasing antagonism toward the North during the last generation of slavery to one of accommodation in the twentieth century.

In pressing that early antagonism to the extreme of war, they overplayed their hand and lost. Southern leadership lost power in the nation, and they lived for a time in an economic and political colony, a South nearly totally at the mercy of the imperial nation. They were forced to negotiate successive settlements from weakness rather than strength. By the early years of the new century, however, they had brokered out an arrangement in which they settled for markedly less wealth in the South and less power in the nation in return for a high level of power for themselves at home. Because politics both at home and away no longer carried great power, politics and politicians became less important. Southern politics rapidly degenerated into something very close to entertainment, and politicians often became more showmen than statesmen. They were, figuratively, the new minstrels, white men in white face displacing white men in black face, each attesting in very different ways to the same fact that black men were powerless. By the second quarter of the century, remnants of the slave-holding elite had passed away, and the white elite, no longer based on a single institution, would be found somewhere among the array of lawyers, businessmen, bankers, industrialists, ministers, newspaper editors, profes-sors, educators, writers, intellectuals, dentists, and physicians, as well as large farmers and locally powered politicians, and the wives, mothers, and daughters of all these. The white elite varied widely in its constituency from one community to the next. In one it might center in the Men's Bible class in the First Baptist Church, in another the country club. In the Old South, the ruling element in the white elite had been powered by slavery; in the twentieth century they were powered by a capacity to organize and stabilize the white community, and either to exclude alien influences or tame them.

In the last quarter of the twentieth century it appears that the Southern white elite has managed superbly its campaign to retain local power. The all-white alliance in the South—in spite of the civil-rights movement, in spite of the drive by blacks for a fully equal participation in education, politics, and economics and the successes that they have achieved—re-mains in place and secure. Moreover, with well over fifty million people, the white South is gaining power in the nation, slowly and subtly in eco-nomics and politics, but rapidly and markedly in religion and race.

The Southern share of religious power in America is on the rise and already no less than astounding in its magnitude. On Sunday mornings from Castine, Maine, to Coos Bay, Oregon, it is easily possible to tune one's television set to a Southern evangelist. Indeed, in those still most segregated hours in America, if the set is on and the dials are turned, it is almost impossible not to hear Jerry Falwell from Lynchburg, Virginia, the Louis-ianian Jimmy Swaggart, Jim Bakker from Charlotte, or Oral Roberts from Oklahoma. Billy Graham, first and most famous, has achieved invasions of the North that Robert E. Lee might well envy, having stormed Wash-ington several times and occupied the White House once or twice. The power of Southern evangelists in national religion is vast, not always rec-ognized, and when it is recognized not usually welcomed. It smacks too much, for instance in the "Moral Majority," of St. Augustine presuming after all to bring the City of God down to Rome.

On the other hand, the rise of the South again to leadership in matters of race is recognized and, nearly universally, approved. In the twentieth century, it seems clear that the white South and the white North, in spite of their real cultural differences, have reached a practical congruence in their behavior in regard to black people. In all regions, when black people in large numbers have become relatively assertive in their pursuit of a fair share of the good things in life, white people have proved themselves ready for violence. Racially speaking, Chelsea [Massachusetts] in 1975 was not many miles from Birmingham in 1963. In a dozen years, the North had clearly lost legitimate claim to moral superiority in passing judgment on race relations in the South. Thereafter, an embarrassed North virtually ceased to shout "racist" at the South. By the time Alex Haley's *Roots* as book and film had run its course in 1976 and 1977, the North seemed to lose any inclination to pass judgment at all. There had been a horrible racism down there in the South back then, ran the response to that work, but there was none in the nation now and hence no reason why white people should feel guilty. The racist South had been cursed, whipped, and cured, and white America thereby cleansed and forgiven. In the new dispensation, Southern white leaders were seen to have some special affinity for dealing with black people, and it seemed best to leave local racial matters again in their hands. Most recently, one hears much about how the South has better relations between the races and hence should point the way to national progress in the future. Thus, within the twentieth century, the needle of leadership in matters racial in the nation has swung full compass and found no solution. The *style* of race relations in the South is certainly different from that of the North, but it is not at all clear that it is better.

Economic power, also, is moving southward—to centers such as Atlanta, Miami, Houston, and Dallas, not only in the form of sophisticated new factories, but even in the more vital spheres of communications, image-making, money, banking, and credit. That power is national, but it is also distinctly international and promises, vaguely, therein to bypass the North and West. The "Sunbelt" phenomenon as economics is new and real, and the end effect seems to be an evolving Southernization of national business as it operates in the South rather than a nationalization of Southern culture by way of business.

In politics, the South has recently produced a President who took office from the South and returned to the South when he had served his term. Even with that President's defeat in his bid for re-election, the South switched parties and maintained a measure of power in Washington. The most conspicuous new ambassadors of the region in the nation's capital are Republicans, and, at least presently, they are generally in tune with the rest of the country. These Republicans pose no threat to the traditional balance in the South; there is virtually no reason to expect that they will attempt to bring black power into play again. On the contrary, there is no history among the best known and most powerful of Southern Republicans in Congress that would lead one to suspect that they might favor black people in any substantial way. The long-sought two-party South has arrived, but it promises no revolution in either race relations or Southern culture, and it offers no invitation to the North to attempt again to reconstruct the South in its own image.

As the Southern white elite works to accommodate itself to Northern desires at the national and international level, local power is more assuredly in their hands. They can yield or not yield, as they choose, a great deal to black people without significantly threatening their power at home. After their momentary fright in the 1950s and 1960s, the Conservative elite in the South has come to realize that the civil-rights movement has resulted in no great revolution in race relations. In spite of strenuous efforts to do so, it has not pushed the power line back again toward an alliance between the white elite and the black mass, and there is no compelling evidence that the white mass and the black mass might soon combine against the white elite. The revolutionary but tentative experiments of Reconstruction and the Populist era on that bottom line were repeated with much the same result. Things are better, and blacks are more free in the last quarter of this twentieth century; but while the white elite might not have everything just the way they want it all the time in relations with black people, they generally have them so. On the other hand, over time they virtually always get exactly what they want from the mass of white people. The self-conscious all-white communion is still in place in the South, and, sadly, it is spreading to cover the nation. The Black Revolution appears to have been literally that, a revolution of awareness on the black side of the line not the white. Indeed, the Black Revolution seems, in a very large way, a reflection of the realization by black people that the all-white system still lives and grows and that the heartland of white exclusiveness remains intact. . . .

The Shifting Civil-Rights Battleground: From Equal Treatment to Equal Results

HUGH DAVIS GRAHAM

The Watershed of 1965: Two Phases of the Civil Rights Era

It is this policy watershed, between classic liberalism's core command against discrimination on the one hand, and the new theory of compensatory justice on the other, that was crossed during 1966–68. After 1965 the civil rights era moved from Phase I, when antidiscrimination policy was enacted into federal law, to Phase II, when the problems and politics of implementation produced a shift of administrative and judicial enforcement from a goal of equal treatment to one of equal results. The Phase II shift from nondiscrimination to preferential treatment for minorities produced a stiffening of white resistance that was reflected in the public opinion polls. In 1978 Seymour Martin Lipset and William Schneider reviewed nearly a hundred opinion polls taken over the previous 40 years. They concluded that a large majority of white Americans continued to support not only nondiscrimination, but also positive programs to compensate for past discrimination—such as special training programs, head start efforts, financial aid, and community development funds. These majorities continued to support "soft" affirmative action in the sense of President Kennedy's original executive order of 1961. This required special recruiting efforts for minorities but it also included compensatory programs that were positive-sum and not driven by an equal results test. But when compensatory efforts moved in Phase II into the zero-sum game of preferential treatment or racial quotas that would predetermine the results of competition, most Americans drew the line—including majorities of blacks in some polls.

The fundamental shift of goals and means that distinguished Phase I from Phase II, then, was the shift from "soft" to "hard" or from positive-sum to zero-sum affirmative action. The shift was from a goal of equal treatment with positive assistance, such as special recruitment and training efforts, to a goal of equal results or a proportional distribution of benefits among groups. This shift created the tension, captured by the polls, between Phase II's preferential treatment and the American consensus for equal opportunity and against equal results through minority preferences. Historian J. Mills Thornton has emphasized this distinction between the individualist ideal of personal liberty which dominated the civil rights movement through 1968, and the collectivist ideal of material equality that transformed the post-1968 phase. "From the perspective of the ideal of individual liberty," Thornton said, "the Civil Rights Movement ended because, with the Civil Rights Act of 1964, the Voting Rights Act of 1965 and finally the Fair Housing Act of 1968, the movement had achieved its goals." "In these terms," he concluded, "the movement ended for the same reason that World War II ended: the enemies had been defeated." But if the enemy was defeated, what accounts for the turmoil and disarray in Phase II, when the liberal coalition, having at last triumphed over the conservatives on the battlefield, fell to bickering over the terms of the new order?

The answer, voiced by a growing chorus of contemporary critics from within the liberal reform tradition itself, was that in the process of implementing the victories of the antidiscrimination laws of 1964–65, the enforcement agencies and courts and the civil rights coalition behind them fundamentally transformed the original goals themselves. During the 1970s students of public policy built a substantial literature studying the obscure but crucial process of policy implementation. They concluded that the politics of implementation often transform the original policy goals, sometimes deflecting them in novel and occasionally even contradictory directions. Thus in the process of implementing the antidiscriminatory commands of Phase I of the civil rights reforms of 1964–65, the EEOC [Equal Employment Opportunity Commission] and the OFCC [Office of Federal Contract Compliance], together with their allies in the civil rights coalition and in the agencies and Congress and also increasingly in the federal courts, fundamentally transformed the Phase I goal of equal treatment into the Phase II goal of equal results. This, however, created an internal contradiction because it required the unequal treatment of citizens by race and

minority status so as to compensate for the results of past discrimination. . . .

The War over Reverse Discrimination

. . . Why was it that by the early 1970s the legal majesty of the American
state once again, as it had in the segregationist era between *Plessy* and
Brown, ordained that citizens who had wronged no one must be denied
important rights and benefits because of genetic attributes like the color of
their skin? . . . From its origin in the Wagner Act to President Kennedy's
borrowing for his executive order of 1961, the term "affirmative action"
had always required something more than mere even-handedness or nondiscrimination. The "something" remained ambiguous, to be sure. But it
ranged from the NLRB's [National Labor Relation Board] opposition to
unfair labor practices within a larger presumption that labor unions were
a desirable norm in modern industrial society, to the PCEEO's [President's
Committee on Equal Employment Opportunity] insistence that employers
make special recruiting efforts to hire "underrepresented" minorities. The
notion of underrepresentation, with its implicit, ethno-racial standard of
proportional distribution, provided the key for the transition from the soft
affirmative action of the Kennedy approach to the hard or equal-results
affirmative action developed under Nixon. In between, the Johnson administration courageously won the great campaigns of the Second Reconstruction, then struggled inconclusively with the complexities of implementation while the Vietnam War consumed its energy and its future.

Johnson's footrace metaphor in the Howard University speech of 1965
captured allegorically the historical core of the compensatory approach:
innocent minorities had inherited a crippling legacy, and social justice therefore required a period of preferential discrimination. Johnson never followed
through on his speechwriter's rhetoric. But the non-labor wing of the civil
rights coalition rather quietly fashioned a results-centered rationale that
countered the equal-treatment creed with an essentially historical argument
about institutions and culture. Equality must mean more than the equal
right of the rich and the poor to sleep under the public bridges, they insisted.
Liberalism's historic command not to discriminate could not achieve its
goal of a color-blind society because the racism of the past had become
institutionalized. Current institutions thus might perpetuate discrimination
even though no one in those institutions remained personally prejudiced. . . .

In *Contractor's Association, Allen, Gaston, Swann, Griggs* and similar
test cases, the federal courts embraced the compensatory argument to
justify as equitable relief a preferential treatment for minorities in fields as
varying as voting, employee and union seniority, education, hiring and
promotions, and job testing. Increasingly the judicial decree sought less to
judge past behavior than to adjust future behavior. As the courts declared

that Congress's overarching substantive purpose (more jobs for minorities) was more compelling than its specific procedural prohibitions (no discrimination in a color-blind society), sympathetic legal scholars argued that the Warren-era judges were correcting a formalist bias of the late 19th century. Anglo-American law had then defined punitive damages in tort and criminal prohibition in terms of malicious "intent," and held that courts properly interpreted statutes only by divining and applying their legislative intentions. Thus in Phase II the intent test in statutory interpretation was replaced by statistical demonstrations of disparate impact or disproportionate results. Hard affirmative action through preferential remedies was transforming nondiscrimination into modern, no-fault civil rights. . . .

The continuing debate over the effectiveness of affirmative action programs finds its origins in the civil rights era of 1960–1972, but not its resolution. Its ironies abound. But ironists flirt dangerously with cynicism, because the ironic stance allows us to comment coyly, armed by hindsight, on the paradoxical contradictions that entrap historical actors and confound their best-laid plans. It is the *intended* consequences of the civil rights era's great social reforms, however, that mark its most fundamental and promising breaks with the continuities of history. In 1960, most American blacks still confronted the formal as well as informal symbols of daily humiliation that marked a caste society. Southern whites, the chief but not the exclusive offenders, were also—but unknowingly—victimized economically and brutalized psychologically by the daily corruptions of caste dominance.

Similarly in the America of 1960, males dominated the worlds of power and status so overwhelmingly that most women and girls could realistically aspire to an independent status and achievement, beyond the rewards of housewifery and motherhood, little loftier than that of airline stewardess. Even that was reserved for white women only. While the percentage of women who worked outside the home continued to rise in 1960, their horizons for reward in income and status had in many ways declined from levels reached earlier in the century. Most American men and boys took for granted a world of male norms in which women were auxiliaries, and in which the creative talents, beyond the acknowledged procreative capacities, of half of humankind remained largely untapped. Feminism was at bottom about gender freedom, and everybody had a gender. Martin Luther King understood that the same principle obtained about racial freedom for all of God's children.

The civil rights era was a rare American epiphany, covering a dozen years of astonishing achievement against the most formidable odds. By 1972, we were by no means all "Free at Last"—the imminent goal that King had lyrically proclaimed at the Lincoln Memorial in 1963. In our more sober era, we know that total freedom must elude us until we have seen the mountaintop. But as a more cautious yet still inspired King had so frequently explained, exhorting his legions to greater efforts by reminding them of how far they had already come: "We ain't what we want'a be, and we ain't what we ought'a be, but thank God, we ain't what we was!"

⚓ *F U R T H E R   R E A D I N G*

Carl Abbott, *The New Urban America: Growth and Politics in Sunbelt Cities* (1981)

Howard Ball et al., *Compromised Compliance: Implementation of the 1965 Voting Rights Act* (1982)

Numan V. Bartley, "Another New South?" *Georgia Historical Quarterly* 65 (1981), 119–137

——— and Hugh D. Graham, *Southern Politics and the Second Reconstruction* (1975)

Jack Bass and Walter De Vries, *The Transformation of Southern Politics: Social Change and Political Consequences Since 1945* (1976)

Joan Turner Beifuss, *At the River I Stand: Memphis, the 1968 Strike, and Martin Luther King* (1985)

Earl Black, *Southern Governors and Civil Rights: Racial Segregation as a Campaign Issue in the Second Reconstruction* (1976)

Chandler Davidson, ed., *Minority Vote Dilution* (1984)

Paul Delaney, "A New South for Blacks?" in John B. Boles, ed., *Dixie Dateline: A Journalistic Portrait of the Contemporary South* (1983)

Gary M. Fink, *Prelude to the Presidency: The Political Career and Legislative Leadership Style of Governor Jimmy Carter* (1980)

Frye Gaillard, *The Dream Long Deferred* (1988)

Carl Grafton and Anne Permaloff, *Big Mules and Branchheads: James E. Folsom and Political Power in Alabama* (1985)

Dewey W. Grantham, *The Life and Death of the Solid South: A Political History* (1988)

Edward R. Haas, *De Lesseps S. Morrison and the Image of Reform: New Orleans Politics, 1946–1961* (1974)

William C. Havard, ed., *The Changing Politics of the South* (1972)

———, "Intransigence to Transition: Thirty Years of Southern Politics," *Virginia Quarterly Review* 51 (1975), 497–521

Alexander Heard, *A Two-Party South?* (1952)

Martin Luther King, Jr., *Where Do We Go from Here: Chaos or Community* (1967)

Alexander P. Lamis, *The Two-Party South* (1984)

Kevin E. McHigh, "Black Migration Reversal in the United States," *Geographical Review* 77 (1987), 171–182

Harold H. Martin, *William Berry Hartsfield: Mayor of Atlanta* (1978)

Richard A. Pride and J. David Woodard, *The Burden of Busing: The Politics of Desegregation in Nashville, Tennessee* (1985)

John Shelton Reed, "Up from Segregation," *Virginia Quarterly Review* 60 (1984), 377–393

John Rozier, *Black Boss: Political Revolution in a Georgia County* (1982)

Robert Sherrill, *Gothic Politics in the Deep South* (1968)

David M. Tucker, *Memphis Since Crump: Bossism, Blacks, and Civic Reformers, 1948–1968* (1980)

William Julius Wilson, *The Declining Significance of Race: Blacks and Changing American Institutions* (1978)

Raymond Wolters, *The Burden of Brown: Thirty Years of School Desegregation* (1984)

CHAPTER
15

An Enduring Culture?

To paraphrase historian George B. Tindall, the South has had more lives than a cat. Some writers have argued that despite momentous changes in the South since World War II, many elements of southern culture persist. Surely, they admit, the South is the bursting buckle on the Sunbelt, but its cities and industries, for all their superficial resemblance to their counterparts elsewhere, reflect some enduring traditions. Two-party politics may imply that the South has rejoined the Union, but labels still matter more than ideology in certain places. And while the South has unquestionably dispatched its peculiar racial customs such as segregation and disfranchisement, it is not yet clear whether the region is settling into the racial patterns of the rest of the nation or, influenced by its ordeal by fire, is in the process of charting totally new directions in race relations. Then, of course, there are the music, the food, the idioms and patterns of speech, and above all the history.

Other writers, however, citing statistics and behavioral patterns, point out that while some aspects of regional life remain different, the South as a distinctive entity has vanished. The South and the rest of the nation have at last reached a compromise. With so many Yankees coming down and so many shopping malls and skyscrapers going up, southern metropolitan areas could be mistaken for any other place. In education, per capita income, boutiques, and nouvelle cuisine, the South is approaching the national average.

Is it time, at long last, to write an epitaph for Dixie? Or is the South still alive and distinctively well?

✛ D O C U M E N T S

Polls continue to support the existence of a southern distinctiveness. The data in the first document, from a 1980 survey undertaken by the Center for Political Studies at the University of Michigan, indicate that regional differences on prayer in the schools and abortion can be greater than racial and political divisions. Country music is an indigenous southern art form. Although it is often a medium to express the trials of ordinary people in and out of money, love, and faith, it also provides insight into the important and distinctive elements of an ethnic culture. In the second selection, the lyrics from a song recorded by Don Williams evoke past and place with sensitivity. A distinctive cuisine is another important index of persisting ethnicity. Perhaps "cuisine" is too highfalutin to describe southern food, but distinctive it is, as the recipes in the third selection demonstrate. In the last selection, a sampling of articles from the *Charlotte Observer*, 1983–1984, on religion and regional patriotism shows that some southerners, even in the metropolitan areas, still hold provincial views on these subjects. The fact that a majority of southerners would cringe at certain of these views does not necessarily mean that faith, past, and place are fading—just that these latter-day southerners interpret their heritage more broadly.

Polling Data on School Prayer and Abortion, 1980

Attitudes on Prayer in the Public Schools

| | SOUTHERN WHITES [FOR] | | SO. BLACKS | NORTHERN WHITES | |
	REAGAN	CARTER	CARTER	REAGAN	CARTER
Allow prayer in schools	86%	91%	91%	76%	58%
Religion does not belong in schools	14	9	9	24	42
	100%	100%	100%	100%	100%
N	136	80	45	254	165

Question: "Some people think it is all right for the public schools to start each day with a prayer. Others feel that religion does not belong in the public schools but should be taken care of by the family and the church. Which do you think—schools should be allowed to start each day with a prayer *or* religion does not belong in the schools?" CPS, 1980 National Election Study.

Attitudes on Abortion

| | SOUTHERN WHITES [FOR] | | SO. BLACKS | NORTHERN WHITES | |
	REAGAN	CARTER	CARTER	REAGAN	CARTER
Never permit abortion	13%	10%	28%	10%	8%
Allow only in case of rape, etc.	31	49	26	35	34
Allow when need is clearly established	22	16	16	23	13
Always allow woman choice of abortion	34	26	30	32	46
	100%	101%	100%	100%	101%
N	156	94	50	306	179

Question: "There has been some discussion about abortion during recent years. Which one of the opinions on this page best agrees with your view?
1. By law, abortion should never be permitted.
2. The law should permit abortion *only* in case of rape, incest or when the woman's life is in danger.
3. The law should permit abortion for reasons *other than* rape, incest, or danger to the woman's life, but only after the need for the abortion has been clearly established.
4. By law, a woman should always be able to obtain an abortion as a matter of personal choice."

Supplied by the SRC/CPS American National Election Studies, University of Michigan.

Country Song, "Good Ole Boys Like Me," 1979

BOB MCDILL

When I was a kid Uncle Remus would put me to bed
With a picture of Stonewall Jackson above my head
Then Daddy came in to kiss his little man
With gin on his breath and a Bible in his hand;
And he talked about honor and things I should know
Then he staggered a little as he went out the door.

> I can still hear the soft southern winds in the live oak trees
> And those Williams boys they still mean a lot to me
> Hank and Tennessee
> I guess we're all gonna be what we're gonna be
> So what do you do with good ole boys like me.

Well nothing makes a sound in the night like the wind does
But you ain't afraid if you're washed in the blood like I was
The smell of cape jasmine through the window screen
John R. and the Wolfman kept me company
By the light of the radio by my bed
With Thomas Wolfe whisperin' in my head.

When I was in school I ran with a kid down the street
And I watched him burn himself up on bourbon and speed
But I was smarter than most and I could choose
Learned to talk like the man on the six o'clock news
When I was 18, Lord, I hit the road,
But it really didn't matter how far I'd go.

Southern Cooking, 1988

Sweet Potato Pudding

This recipe has been handed down from mother to daughter for generations
of the Crim family in Winston-Salem, NC

Grate one large sweet potato
Add enough canned Pet milk to the grated sweet potato to make a thin
   batter
Add brown sugar to taste
Add cinnamon and nutmeg (a little of each)
Add 1/2 stick melted butter or margarine

Add two beaten eggs
Add vanilla to taste
Raisins may be added if desired

Grease a black frying pan and pour the mixture into the pan and bake at 350 degrees until firm (about one hour)

Mary Ruth Crim, Winston-Salem, NC

Fried Hog Chitterlings (five pounds)

Clean and remove fat from the intestines
Wash thoroughly
Boil for two to three hours until done (be sure to keep the water above
   the meat for the first hour; then reduce the heat to moderate)
Add one or two small onions to the pot
When the meat is done, cut it into bite-size pieces

Make a batter using flour, water, salt, and pepper
Dip the meat and fry in hot grease until brown
Eat

Walter Dumas, Charlotte, NC

Country Stew

2 cans tomatoes
2 cans corn (cream-style corn)
3 cans chicken (or one whole chicken, boiled and picked off the bone)
3 or 4 pounds stew beef (cooked)
1 pack of crackers
2 tsp. sugar
salt and pepper to taste
2 tbsp. hot pepper (red pepper or Texas Pete)
Vinegar
4 medium-sized onions

Grind in a sausage mill
Put in chicken broth and bring to a boil
Add 2 sticks of margarine
Cook on low, 2 to 3 hours

Dionna Woodward, Kannapolis, NC

Only in the South: Southerners' Comments on History and Religion, 1983–1984

"Religious Dispute Stops Play," *Charlotte Observer*, March 31, 1983

A Carteret County [North Carolina] softball league has struck out with local parks officials in a dispute over the religious beliefs of one of the teams. The league, which voted to exclude Mormons on grounds that they "do not believe in the same Jesus Christ," has been barred from playing in Carteret County parks.

"Some See Jesus' Image on Door," *Charlotte Observer*, April 17, 1983

For a week, crowds have been jamming the third floor of a hospital [in Jasper, Alabama] where Joel Naramore said he saw a likeness of Jesus on the wooden door of a recovery room. Some say the image is that of a face. Others say it is nothing more than the wood grain.

"I see a face and under one eye I see a tear," said one visitor, Pam Boyer. "I think it bears a resemblance to the pictures I've seen of Jesus Christ."

Whatever, the crowds are posing a problem for the Walker County Medical Center which has limited the viewing to three hours at night. More than 750 people showed up Thursday. . . .

A week ago Saturday night, Naramore was standing outside the room, praying for his critically ill 16-year old son, Charles Ray, who had been injured in a motorcycle accident and had an adverse reaction to anesthesia. A hospital employee, Shirley McGough, said she watched Naramore praying. "When he looked up, he saw the face and he said, 'My son is going to be all right now,'" she said. The son's condition later stabilized.

"Church Trial Bares Unholy Share of Steamy Accusations," *Charlotte Observer*, April 21, 1983

Rev. Thomas Butts, pastor of First United Methodist Church in Montgomery [Alabama] is on trial in the first public church trial in Alabama of a Methodist minister in at least 100 years. . . . A bishop is the judge, and 13 Methodist ministers are the jury. If Butts is found guilty, the penalty is either a reprimand or loss of his ministerial credentials.

Butts, 53, is well known and well regarded in Montgomery. His 2,000-member church is the largest Methodist church in the city and includes powerful political figures.

"Only in the South," a compilation of articles and letters from the *Charlotte Observer*, March 31, 1983, to May 2, 1984, on persisting religious and historical perspectives among southerners.

Butts stands accused of having sexual affairs with at least 3 married women in his church, of getting drunk at a church camp and at a church picnic, and of denying due process to his former associate minister, the Rev. Al Norris, when he learned Norris was having an affair with the married daughter of a politically powerful church member.

Norris, 40, who is one of Butts's chief accusers, has not denied having an affair with the women or with several others. He has testified, essentially, that Butts was more immoral than he was.

Norris and his supporters say he and Claudia Pike, a church member who testified she had had an affair with Butts, came forward with their accusations against Butts because they wanted the truth to be known. The defense put on many witnesses to attempt to discredit Norris and Pike, portraying him as a marijuana-smoking Svengali and her as an emotionally unstable kleptomaniac. . . .

Norris charged Butts with keeping liquor in his file cabinet, with getting so drunk at a church picnic that he tripped and almost fell into a barbecue pit and with having a menage a trois with him and a woman employee in his office.

"Youths Burn 'Satanic' Music," *Charlotte Observer*, May 27, 1983

Stacks of records, shopping bags of tapes and some books went up in flames at Faith Presbyterian Church in Mount Mourne [North Carolina], as about 15 young people disposed of what they called "satanic" music.

"Music that doesn't praise the Lord, depreciates humans and invokes our lower nature should be burned," said the Rev. Robert Brawley, who endorsed Wednesday night's bonfire.

"Anti-Catholic Pamphlets Distributed," *Charlotte Observer*, May 2, 1984

Anti–Roman Catholic pamphlets entitled "The Pope's Secrets" are being handed out in the Charlotte area. The pamphlets are [from] the Tony and Susan Alamo Christian Foundation of Alma, Arkansas.

"It's not a church, you know," Alamo said in a telephone interview. "Never has been, never will be. It's totally opposed to anything that's Christian."

"The Pope's Secrets" is 8 pages long and calls the Vatican a "satanic whore." The Pamphlet claims Catholic leaders ordered the assassination of President Kennedy because he pledged his loyalty to the U.S. Constitution instead of Catholic Canon Law. The Vatican is also blamed for the death of Lincoln and for World War II, conflict in Central America, communism, the Jonestown suicides and murders, Cuba's Fidel Castro ("Jesuit trained"), drug abuse, homosexuality, the Internal Revenue Service ("which answers only to Rome"), labor unions and government regulatory agencies.

Charlotte Observer, December 31, 1983

"We thought they were merely a private school. We didn't know they were Catholic. We played them when we had a broader philosophy." Stan Kiefer, basketball coach at Longview [Texas] Christian Academy, which canceled a basketball game with Cistercian Preparatory School in Irving, Texas, because the school is Catholic.

Letter to the Editor of the *Charlotte Observer*, August 3, 1983

You people who aren't Christians should think about what you're saying when you criticize Jim Bakker. After all, the Lord does answer prayers to all his followers, and if Jim Bakker is what you call a fake or briber, the Lord sure wouldn't have let him come this far in his godly works.

Sherri Wallace, Charlotte

Letters to *Charlotte Observer* Editor Rich Oppel Who Objected to Standing While Dixie Was Played, June 12, 1983

How does he expect to sell advertising space to Southerners whose blood kin gave their life on the battlefield for the Confederacy? I had 28 ancestors who fought for the South during the War Between the States. They sang "Dixie" and they carried the Confederate flag. . . . I love all black people. I would fight to uphold their freedom. I respect their heritage, and will support their efforts to show pride in it. I am a white man. I also have my heritage. . . . My suggestion to Mr. Oppel is that he pack his intelligence in an aspirin box and buy a one-way bus ticket that would take him on a perpetual bus trip around the world, because I personally don't think the idiotic Neanderthal has a place he can call home.

William Ferguson, Rock Hill, SC

Those of us who are Southerners are proud to be Southerners; we don't need carpetbaggers [Oppel grew up in St. Petersburg, Florida] like him coming into our area telling us what he thinks is proper. The same road that brought him into the South will take him out. I hope he uses it soon.

Godfrey G. Bennett Jr., Matthews, NC

If Mr. Oppel doesn't like the Southern traditions, let him go north past the Mason-Dixon line.

Mrs. Brenda Bean, Charlotte

Gladstone said: "Show me the manner in which a nation cares for its dead, and I will measure with mathematical exactness the tender mercies of its

people, their respect for the laws of the land and their loyalty to high
ideals." It is in this spirit that we of the South honor the memory of our
ancestors. Despite the war's bitter disappointments and sorrows, we are
proud that we came through years of trial and struggle with our battered
shields pure, our character as a patriotic and courageous people untar-
nished, and nothing to regret in defense of the rights and the honor of our
Southland.

Martha H. Washam, Charlotte

✠ *E S S A Y S*

George B. Tindall suggests in the opening selection that perceiving and studying
black and white southerners as a distinctive ethnic group could provide some
valuable insights into southern and national history. As with other ethnic groups,
urbanization, migration, and affluence have changed the nature of ethnicity, but
an identifiable ethnic culture persists. John Egerton, a Nashville journalist writing in the same year as Tindall (1974), dissents from this view and contends with
regret in the second essay that the South and the rest of the nation are merging
into a homogeneous mass, keeping the worst of each. Sociologist John Shelton
Reed of the University of North Carolina, Chapel Hill, has made a career of
demonstrating southern distinctiveness. While he concedes in the last essay that
certain regional differences have disappeared, these very changes have served to
heighten the sense of distinction southerners feel today, even as they become
assimilated into American society at large.

Southerners: America's Unmeltable Ethnics

GEORGE B. TINDALL

About two years ago a newsman based in Atlanta sent forth to the readers
of *Esquire* the good news that "the South is over" and then proceeded to
elaborate "some of the ways the cracker crumbled." His findings were
hardly without precedent, although expressed with more wit than we have
come to expect in such write-ups. The Vanishing South has long been staple
fare at regional symposia—just as surely as the rubber chickens and pet-
rified peas. Looking back sixteen years we can find Harry S. Ashmore
carving out an epitaph for Dixie, and John T. Westbrook heralding "The
happy truth that the South . . . [had] lost its 'regional integrity' " and grown
"rich . . . , urban, industrialized, and no longer 'Southern,' but rather
northernized, Europeanized, cosmopolitan." Ten years before Ashmore
and Westbrook, Charles S. Johnson published a study of changing race
relations which he called *Into the Main Stream.* For a generation now the

From "Beyond the Mainstream: The Ethnic Southerners" by George B. Tindall, *Journal of
Southern History* XL (February 1974), pp. 3–14, 16–18. Copyright © 1974 by the Southern
Historical Association. Reprinted by permission of the Managing Editor.

metaphor has been so often applied to the South, black and white, and so often repeated that there has been little reason to doubt the conventional wisdom that the benighted South was beginning to see the light, that it was getting right with God and was gathering down by the mainstream of American life for baptism by total immersion.

The belief that the South is forever disappearing has a long and honored tradition. It has affected southerners of every walk and every faith, including those who resisted the thought that the distinctive region might become one with Nineveh and Tyre. The New South creed of the nineteenth century, according to Paul M. Gaston, promised to make the South, like the nation, "rich, triumphant, and morally innocent." New South liberals looked forward to a region absorbed into the national abundance of both progress and equality. Assimilation seemed most of all the goal of black southerners, who became in many ways the most nationalistic of all Americans. Even after repeated betrayals, their faith in the nation, in its promise and its Constitution, continued to flicker and sometimes to flame.

But the white South, too, had a claim on nationalism. In the beginning a white southerner had defined the American Creed. Much later, the prophets of a New South looked upon the sectional conflict as the Great Aberration; they sought the true South in the world of the Founding Fathers and once again embraced the national myths. In the Spanish-American War, and more intensely in the First World War, the South went through its own peculiar "Americanization" in the melting pot of patriotism. The idea that the South embodied the purest Americanism (with overtones of nativism and Fundamentalism) grew into an established article of the regional faith. And during the years of the New Deal and the Second World War the South entered still more fully into the orbit of national affairs.

By the 1950s and 1960s southern distinctiveness appeared to be doomed. In quick sequence the region encountered the Bulldozer Revolution, the Urban Breakthrough, the Civil Rights Movement, the Black Revolt, and the Disruption of the Solid South. Socioeconomic change fast eroded old landmarks, and sociologists took to listing the indices of a Vanishing South as eagerly as they had once enumerated the indices of a Deficient South. In a presidential address to the Southern Sociological Society nine years ago Selz C. Mayo chose to speak on "the Disappearing Sectional South" and quoted George L. Simpson on the facts of change: ". . . the movement from rural to urban; from one crop to diversification . . . ; from bad health to good health; from about one-half the national per capita income to nearly three-fourths; from some 1,280,000 to nearly 2,500,000 industrial workers; from the kerosene lamp to universal electricity and the winking eye of television; from one world of race relations to another." Just two years ago in the *American Sociological Review* John C. McKinney and Linda Brookover Bourque discounted as illusory the "Southern mystique," "the belletristic tradition [of] . . . local color," and the mass media's fascination with southern idiosyncrasy. They dwelt instead on solid evidence that confirmed an "increasing similarity between the South and non-South" in the realms of urbanization, industry, occupations, income, and education.

Yet since the mid-1960s the existence, certainly the appearance, of consensus in American life has been visibly shaken. The suspicion grows that the legend of a homogenized American culture had all along the shimmering quality of mirage, like those situation comedies where people live in boxes made of ticky-tacky and all look the same. It is not the South that has vanished but the mainstream, like one of those desert rivers that run out into the sand, consumed by the heat.

The convulsions of recent years have made manifest what David M. Potter called "the unseen revolution of the 1920's and 1930's." In a posthumous essay published this year Potter suggested that conformity rather than compulsion had long provided the chief sanction against disruption in American life and that this meant conformity mainly to the values of a dominant white Anglo-Saxon Protestant culture. By the 1920s and 1930s, however, those values had suffered crippling blows, most conspicuously in the failure of prohibition and the social trauma of the Great Depression. Perhaps most crippling of all had been the rise of a new class, the academic intellectuals, who "set busily about laying their axes to the mythic underpinnings of the American identity."

By the 1960s, therefore, defenders of the society had become guiltily aware of its failure to fulfill its own promises and "disarmed also by their broad, absolutist, and somewhat indiscriminate ideas of the right to dissent." The almost simultaneous disintegration of the civil rights movement and of the Vietnam situation gave rise to a major crisis of confidence. A severe case of war weariness—involving wars foreign and domestic—seized the nation. Amid the tumult, the mass media, often thought to be agents for conformity, fostered counterforces instead: black revolt, student rebellion, fem lib, food fads, hard rock, the cult of slovenliness, raw incivility and violence, pornography, and the occult—and the more bizarre the better.

Then came the backlash. Its source was said to be the Silent Majority, the Middle American. "There is hardly a language to describe him," Peter Schrag wrote in *Harper's*, "or even a set of social statistics. Just names: racist-bigot-redneck-ethnic-Irish-Italian-Pole-Hunkie-Yahoo. The lower middle class. A blank. The man under whose hat lies the great American desert. Who watches the tube, plays the horses, and keeps the niggers out of his union and his neighborhood. Who might vote for Wallace (but didn't). Who cheers when the cops beat up on demonstrators. Who is free, white, and twenty-one, has a job, a home, a family, and is up to his eyeballs in credit. In the guise of the working class . . . he was once the hero of the civics book. . . . Now he is 'the forgotten man,' perhaps the most alienated person in America." The description, it should be noted, was ironic, a parody of the respectable bigotry that had infected a fashionable elite.

In the strange new world of the 1960s history manifested some further ironies. The "most alienated person" was the one who flew the flag and invented a new symbol of loyalty, the hard hat. To be a worker or a *petit bourgeois* was no longer to command the respect of the media. What was in some ways a display of class consciousness, therefore, turned into a display of ethnic identity, for it was among the workers and lower middle class that large, perhaps the largest, portions of second- and third-generation immigrant stock had found lodgment. And their behavior followed in spirit, if not in mathematical fidelity, Marcus Lee Hansen's law that the second generation embraced Americanism and the third generation rediscovered its heritage. Something like this had happened in the progression from civil rights and Americanism to black power and the Afro-American identity. Now the new ethnicity manifested striking parallels. Indeed, it conferred on black power the sincerest form of flattery, imitation. . . .

The first reaction of a southerner to all this is apt to be that it has little to do with him. It may be true that back in 1809 David Ramsay could write in his *History of South Carolina*: "So many and so various have been the sources from which Carolina has derived her population, that a considerable period must elapse, before the people amalgamate into a mass possessing an uniform national character." But a considerable period *has* elapsed. Perhaps, to be sure, there are still those exceptions which prove the rule: a few reminders of forgotten Spaniards and Frenchmen, some Mexican-Americans renamed Chicanos, some Cuban cigar-makers and the more recent Cuban refugees, some German counties out in Texas, Cajuns up the bayous, Italians in New Orleans, Hungarians over in Tangipahoa Parish, a scattering of Czechs, Dutch, Ukrainians, and in Mississippi, even Chinese. Jews are visible, if scarce, in most localities; politicians in Charleston used to reckon with the Irish and Germans; and there are those enclaves of mixed-blood Lumbees, Tuscaroras, "Brass Ankles," Melungeons, and Turks, not to mention remnants of Cherokees, Catawbas, Creeks, and Seminoles. One might even have to throw in those quaint hillbillies, who have achieved ethnic identity as "Yesterday's People" by strumming dulcimers and singing Elizabethan ballads when not employed in shooting their neighbors or distilling forty-rod bug juice back in the coves.

And if, out in the boondocks of the North, hillbilly has become a synonym for southerner, the perception may be more acute than one might think. For the South *is* the habitat of the quintessential WASP. Is it not, in fact, the biggest single WASP nest this side of the Atlantic? Is it not, perhaps, the one part of the country where the melting pot really worked, because so few ingredients were added after independence? Over the years all those southerners with names like Kruttschnitt, Kolb, DeBardeleben, Huger, Lanneau, Toledano, Moise, Jastremski, or Cheros got melted down and poured back out in the mold of good old boys and girls, if not of the gentry. Who, for example, could be more WASPish than Scarlett O'Hara, in more ways than one?

At the same time, and too often forgotten, a separate and unequal melting pot bubbled away all the more furiously. Is there not "a sense," Michael G. Kammen has asked, "in which the melting pot notion is more applicable within the black American nation than within the white? There was great diversity in the African origins of American Negroes: regional, linguistic, and tribal differences, as well as in their prior condition of freedom. . . . Despite this diversity, however, Africans were forcibly homogenized after several generations into a fairly singular Afro-American mold with common folkways. Thus, the only American melting pot has perhaps been a black one, though in this case the putative pot has been reluctant to call the kettle black.''

However surprising it may sound at first, the function of melting pots is to create new ethnic groups. Everybody has a melting pot in his past, and two of them have been located down home, with some of the same ingredients going into both. The two ethnic groups, black and white, which have emerged from the crucibles of the South, have been reluctant to acknowledge kinship, but each has been keenly aware of its separate identity in the nation.

The North, that "significant other," has been equally aware, most acutely when southerners move into the hillbilly or black ghettos of Chicago or New York—or conversely, when Yankees populate Houston or Hunts-ville. A few years ago Flannery O'Connor told of a friend from Wisconsin who came to Atlanta and bought a house in the suburbs. The man who sold it was from Massachusetts and recommended the property by saying: " 'You'll like this neighborhood. There's not a Southerner for two miles.' At least," Miss O'Connor added, "we can be identified when we do occur."

For more than a century the South has been a seedbed of population and cultural styles for the rest of the country. We have progressed (or receded) from things like minstrel shows, cavalier romances, and bourbon whiskey to things like Coca-Cola, *Gone with the Wind*, and the latter-day Ku Klux Klan, each of which was first bottled in Atlanta. Southern styles have threatened to conquer the fields of writing and pop culture. Blacks exported spirituals, jazz, blues, slang, and southern cuisine in the guise of "soul food." The good old boys finally arrived with "countrypolitan" mu-sic, bluegrass, and stock-car racing. One of those stock-car racers was Junior Johnson, who learned the trade running his daddy's moonshine out of Ingle Hollow. And in one of Tom Wolfe's hopped-up essays Johnson was anointed the Last American Hero. But at the time, like most of us, Wolfe overlooked the potential of an old country lawyer named Samuel James Ervin, Jr., who lived just down the mountains a piece and still harbored a quaint faith in the Bill of Rights.

At times the South appears to have a premonitory sense of coming styles. For instance, two salient styles of the 1960s, public demonstrations and the generation gap, arrived simultaneously with the student sit-ins at Greensboro, which started one month after the decade began. The lazy South cultivated the art of relaxation long before the greening of America, and the fashion of "overhauls" long before the jeaning of America. When the cult of outward poverty became the in-thing, the profits accrued to southern textile and garment mills, not to mention the few cotton farmers who are still around. The makers even learned to fade, fray, and patch the fabric in advance, thus sparing consumers the trouble of what southerners once had to do for themselves. Now the youth cult has discovered Pentecost and gospel songs. Other rebels, preaching participatory democracy, have joined the revolt against Leviathan which southerners kept up throughout the whole descent from Williamsburg to Watergate.

Some educational work remains to be done, however. Only a tin ear, or an unaccountable deafness to regional intonations, can explain the current fashion of omitting the "r" when spelling "Miz." Anybody who had been properly raised would know better than that. Perhaps the northern culture lag can be fully corrected only when the South can export some real educators like Al Capp's fictional Earthquake McGoon, who was rescued from a lynch mob in Dogpatch so that he might accept tenure as the first professor of redneck studies at Harvard University, where he introduced the elite to the fundamentals of hillbilly logic.

The average inhabitant of the non-South, however, has trouble getting the hang of it. Like members of other tribes, he is apt to resist the intrusion of exotic cultures and apt to view them as hostile and threatening. One septentrional professor explains, for example, that "high homicide rates in the United States today are related primarily to the persistence of Southern cultural traditions developed before the Civil War and subsequently spreading over much of the country." Another notes that the South "is a distillation of those traits which are the worst (and a few which are the best) in the national character. . . . and the nation reacts emotionally to the South precisely because it subconsciously recognizes itself there." Nor has the South been blameless in the search for scapegoats (New England slave traders, for instance) or for the Great Alibi (the Civil War). At the same time southerners, black and white, have made each other into scapegoats and alibis. Both have done the same with immigrant groups of the motley North—and have seen the practice reciprocated.

In the polemics of the new ethnicity Yankeefied images of the South persist, and there is little recognition of kinship on either side. Yet, Jonathan Daniels wrote years ago, "For good or for ill, being a Southerner is like being a Jew. And, indeed, more needs to be written about the similarity of the minds and the emotions of the Jew, the Irishman, the Southerner, and, perhaps, the Pole, as a basis for the better understanding of each of them and of them all. Their common experience has been migration from a peasant background into the mills and towns. It has been to bear a common stigma as the perpetual outsiders, yet for that reason to be fascinating to other folk. In recent years southerners (white southerners, at least), like other ethnic groups, have rallied to the flag—somehow the Stars and Stripes quickly replaced the Stars and Bars as a symbol of resentment and defiance. And southerners betray a human tenacity in clinging to their heritage. Still, as William Appleman Williams has said, "The visceral essay on the white southerner as a second-class citizen has yet to be written. C. Van Woodward is just too damn polite. And Norman Mailer has not considered it important enough."

Southern historians all more or less share the rustic urbanity of Woodward, and lack the urban vulgarity of Mailer, but whether they chronicle the Vanishing South or the Southerner as American, they all share that instinct which Hansen ascribed to the third generation: the need for roots, for a usable past. They are not given to speaking or writing about ethnic identity, but they have somehow felt the regional differences in their bones. Some would call this feeling "impressionistic." David Potter, I think, more aptly spoke of "an awareness of the historical process." But the awareness is overpowered by the ready assumption that socioeconomic change will quickly erase the differences, although the South has gone through nearly four centuries of change without disappearing.

Sociologists have reinforced such attitudes both theoretically and empirically. They have written copiously about the transition from folk community to modernization or from what Howard W. Odum called "folkways" to "stateways" and "technicways," or from what classical sociology called *Gemeinschaft* to *Gesellschaft*. Sociologists further reinforced the idea by their methods. They focused on those things which could be enumerated, and those were the very things which registered the most visible changes: population, industry, occupations, income, and schooling.

In the last few years, however, a few sociologists have turned their attention toward a different kind of data, the opinion polls. As a result, computers have begun to print out quantitative findings which support the "impressionistic" sense of things, and scattered reports on persisting regional differences have begun to surface in the journals. A belief in cultural convergence, to quote one article, seems "based upon little more than the belief that common influences *should* produce greater uniformity. . . ." Another piece reports that "In general, Negro-white differences are smaller than the differences between Southern and non-Southern whites. . . . In other words, . . . the population of the United States is apparently somewhat more [culturally] divided along regional than along racial lines." If the country is divided into two societies, therefore, as the Kerner Commission asserted, could the two societies be North and South rather than black and white?

The findings so far rest on limited evidence. The reports focus mainly on whites, and all rely on surveys conducted for other purposes, but they have now been summarized and extended in two useful books. Lewis M. Killian, whose perceptions had been heightened by an earlier study of hillbillies in Chicago, recently brought out a book entitled *White Southerners*, which appeared in a series devoted to American ethnic groups. More recently John Shelton Reed published *The Enduring South: Subcultural Persistence in Mass Society*. Both books demonstrate by their vigorous prose that the English language remains in style with sociologists despite rumors to the contrary. Both are relatively short and will repay the time spent with them, although I propose here to focus on the findings of John Reed.

In *The Enduring South* Reed asserts "that regional cultural differences have existed and still exist, and that they correspond at least roughly to Americans' perceptions of them. These differences are substantial, and larger than most differences which are thought to be important in the United States." Using opinion polls Reed systematically investigates three broad cultural areas: attitudes toward religion, violence, and localism. He finds that "Southerners . . . are more likely than non-Southerners to be conventionally religious, to accept the private use of force (or the potential for it), and to be anchored in their homeplace." Little of the difference seems to result from differences in urbanization, occupation, or education. And, surprisingly, the differences have not decreased in recent years; in some cases they have actually increased.

In a concluding chapter Reed seeks to explain the sources of continued distinctiveness. Two institutions, the family and the church, are found to be more important in the South than in other regions. Two other institutions, the schools and the mass media, appear to be less influential; both are staffed by southerners who affect the tone and content of the messages transmitted, and both impart information to southerners who are conditioned to receive some messages better than others. In seeking the ultimate explanation Reed follows the reasoning of Sheldon Hackney: "Localism, violence, and a conservative religion are all plausible responses for a minority group, surrounded by a culture which is viewed as powerful, hostile, and unresponsive; all can be seen as adaptive reactions to the situation in which Southerners have, time and again, found themselves." Throughout the book Reed consistently pursues an ethnic analogy. "Southerners' differences from the American mainstream," he writes, "have been similar in kind, if not degree, to those of the immigrant ethnic groups."

There are some lessons for historians in these findings. One of the first is that we have been so caught up in deriving lessons from history and in searching for a usable past that we have neglected the living past of the community. The lessons which southerners in the large have derived from their history—or rather from their communal heritage—are not, properly speaking, lessons at all so much as formative influences which have shaped their identity. The current signposts, therefore, would seem to be pointing southern historians toward those areas in which their contributions have been least developed—the cultural and social history of the region, the study of the South as an American subculture. . . .

Most of what I have said so far applies equally to the white South and the black South, for the cultural affinities are great. The renewed interest in African culture and history may eventually trace more transatlantic legacies than we have suspected. One expression of that interest will be the formation at this convention [annual meeting of the Southern Historical Association, 1973] of a Southern Association of Africanists. One of its goals, we may hope, will be the exploration of cultural ties between Africa and the South. So far, however, little has been found to equal the visible African influences in Latin America and the West Indies or to equal the continuing identification with black Africa which has nourished the social myth of *négritude*. Whatever African traits endure, black Americans like other ethnic groups have an American experience and an American identity not shared by their cousins who were left behind. *Négritude* may evoke echoes of Africa, but "soul" evokes echoes of the South.

Ralph W. Ellison once wrote, moreover, that "Southern whites cannot walk, talk, sing, conceive of laws or justice, think of sex, love, the family or freedom without responding to the presence of Negroes.'' Three and a half centuries of confrontation upon the southern soil have marked the culture of both black and white. The experience of each, while different, has touched the experience of the other. Like other aspects of ethnicity, this becomes most apparent when either group moves North and encounters the selfsame response that greeted earlier migrants from the Habsburg and Romanov empires. For both groups bring in their train that final indignity, that ultimate doom—the ''southernization'' of the North.

When black militants begin to put on dark glasses and menacing mannerisms, therefore, Glazer and Moynihan take notice that ''the Southern style is now being brought into the North. . . . Violence is beginning to play a frightening role in politics. The demand for a rigid line between the races is now raised again, more strongly from the black side, this time.'' There had occurred a curious inversion, they said. The new practice of ''mau-mauing the flak catchers'' simply inverted an old southern habit of bulldozing the darkies. ''The 'nigger' speech of the Georgia legislature became the 'honky' speech of the Harlem street corner, or the national television studio, complete with threats of violence.''

To press the analogy further, the quest for ''black power'' might evoke memories of another quest for minority power: for local self-determination, for the concurrent majority, for constitutional guarantees—and the final desperate plunge into secession (the operative word now being separatism). The parallels, if not exact, are at least suggestive. '' 'Black pride,' '' John Reed has suggested, ''translates as the opposition that a man should be proud of what he is—which might appeal to a people as idiosyncratic, and proud of it, as white Southerners. 'Black power' can mean simply self-determination and freedom from outside meddling—another down home note. And the abandonment of nonviolence seems to mean that if someone is pushing you around, you hit him—the time-honored Southern white response, and one that may strain . . . empathic powers less than did saintly self-restraint.''

It is scarcely a new finding that southerners white and black share the bonds of a common heritage, indeed a common tragedy, and often speak a common language, however seldom they may acknowledge it. But in this connection and countless others the idea of ethnicity affords historians a strategic vantage point from which to reassess the southern past. If we accept the ethnic analogy as a device serving to stimulate investigation and discovery, we can probably discount the danger that southern historians will be overwhelmed by the marvelous discovery that their field of study is nothing more or less than the formation of ethnic groups.

If we can remember that all humans are finite and different, but alike in having limitations, we can perhaps also discount the danger that the ethnic analogy will only reinforce old habits of seeking scapegoats and finding motes in the eyes of others. We cannot discount the possibility, however, that, like Frederick Jackson Turner writing about the frontier or Vann Woodward writing about Jim Crow, we have a heightened awareness of something that is passing away. Change is manifest and undeniable—certainly here in Babylon on the Chattahoochee [Atlanta], the "city too busy to hate"—and our whole ethnic life may be flashing in front of our eyes just before we sink finally into the mainstream, never to rise again. Yet we learn time and again from the southern past and the history of others that to change is not necessarily to disappear. And we learn from modern psychology that to change is not necessarily to lose one's identity; to change, sometimes, is to find it.

Americanization of Dixie

JOHN EGERTON

"Am I a Southerner, Dad?"

The question is put by an eight-year-old boy to his father, a white, Anglo-Saxon, Protestant, middle-class, over-thirty, liberal, Southern writer who hunches agonizingly over the bloodless turnips on his typewriter keyboard, trying to write something about the Americanization of Dixie and the Southernization of America.

There is invitation in the question, and challenge, and threat; it can't be turned away. The man's answer is studied, thoughtful, tinged with a trace of pride and a hint of shame. It comes out . . . yes . . . and no.

The boy's face masks whatever impression the answer has made, if any. "I think I'll go see what's for supper," he says.

Every year, one of every five Americans changes addresses. The White House has annexes in San Clemente and Key Biscayne. The Miami Dolphins are the champions of professional football. Thurgood Marshall is on the Supreme Court. Robert Kennedy has been murdered in Los Angeles by a man from the Middle East, Martin Luther King has been killed in Memphis by an escaped convict from Missouri, and George Wallace has been shot in a Washington suburb by a man from Michigan. Richard Nixon has been elected President, reelected almost by national acclaim, and then disgraced by revelations of high crimes and misdemeanors in the White House. Two black Southerners, Barbara Jordan and Andrew Young, have been elected to Congress from districts in which blacks are a minority. Billy Graham is the unofficial high priest and chaplain of America. School buses have been bombed in Denver and Pontiac, white parents have vented their wrath on black children at a school in Brooklyn, and Chinese Americans in San Francisco have boycotted schools to protest integration. Country music is all the rage in London and Tokyo, and even in New York it is finding a following. There are 1,500 Holiday Inns in the fifty states and in twenty foreign countries, and there are about 4,000 Kentucky Fried Chicken stands and 5,000 Hertz Rent-a-Car outlets. You can buy a mobile

John Egerton, "Prologue" In *The Americanization of Dixie: The Southernization of America* (New York: Harpers Magazine Press, 1974), pp. xvii–xx.

home with a porch and white columns—Tara on wheels—in Montgomery or Baton Rouge (or Detroit), and you can get Confederate money from a motel vending machine in Meridian, Mississippi. Men have gone to the moon, women have gone to work, kids have gone to Vietnam and Canada and communes. There is a black mayor in Tuskegee, Alabama, and he has a white wife, and he campaigned for Richard Nixon. Half of the inmates in California prisons are black or Chicano, and two-thirds of the prisoners in New York state are black or Puerto Rican. Litton Industries is the biggest employer in Mississippi, ITT has entered the political arena in the United States and Chile, IBM is everywhere, and Macy's is on Miami Beach. Birmingham's air pollution rivals the smog in Los Angeles. The South has more school desegregation, more black elected officials, and less unemployment than any other region of the country—and also lower wages, more poverty, and more murders per capita. You can go from Tampa to Detroit in about eighteen hours via interstate highway, from Atlanta to San Francisco in about four hours via jet, and from New York to a tarpaper shack in Louisiana in a split second via television.

With all that going on, it is hard to make sense to an eight-year-old who wants to know if he is a Southerner. The South is no longer simply a colony of the nation, an inferior region, a stepchild; it is now rushing to rejoin the Union, and in the process it is becoming indistinguishable from the North and East and West. The Union is meeting the South at the front door with overtures of welcome. It, too, is changing: Having failed for the first time to win at war, having found poverty and racism alive and menacing in its own house, the North (that is to say, all of the non-Southern states) has lately shown itself to be more and more like the South in the political, racial, social, and religious inclinations of its collective majority.

A friend of mine, a fellow Southerner who tends in his more optimistic moments to see the good side of this phenomenon of Americanization, is both weary and wary of the perennial attempts of some Southerners to keep alive the distinctive characteristics of the region. Old South nostalgia and New South narcissism are beginning to bore him excessively. Recalling that he has heard the South described as a history without a country, my friend says: "Now we have a country, and we are free to start a new history. It could be something special."

I want very much to believe that. It could indeed be something special. But the evidence that it is going to be is difficult to find. Far more visible and conspicuous are the examples of mistakes being repeated, of warnings being ignored, of opportunities being missed. Excessive preoccupation with the South as a separate entity *is* a bore and a diversion; but the opposite danger is in assimilation, in an amalgamation of regions that spreads and perpetuates the banal and the venal while it melts the great and valuable diversity of America into a homogenized purée. . . .

. . . The South and the nation are not exchanging strengths as much as they are exchanging sins; more often than not, they are sharing and spreading the worst in each other, while the best languishes and withers. There are exceptions, of course. . . . But the dominant trends are unmistakable: deep divisions along race and class lines, an obsession with growth and acquisition and consumption, a headlong rush to the cities and the suburbs, diminution and waste of natural resources, institutional malfunctioning, abuse of political and economic power, increasing depersonalization, and a steady erosion of the sense of place, of community, of belonging.

Why the Changing South Remains the South

JOHN SHELTON REED

The economic and demographic changes that have swept across the region have clearly *not* rendered Southern identity useless and irrelevant, nor have they doomed it to early extinction.

To be sure, these changes have had momentous consequences for Southerners: not just for their standard of living and for the settings in which they make and do that living, but for the South's culture, for its politics, its patterns of race relations and family life, the nature of its towns and cities, and much else besides. Some of these changes, nearly everyone would agree, have been improvements; others, in my view at least, have been regrettable; perhaps most have simply been changes. But, for better or for worse, Southerners are becoming more "modern"—that is to say, more "American"—in many respects, particularly those that are linked to urban life, education, and exposure to the "outside world."

The question of regional differences may be another matter. In certain areas, limits to this process of change may preserve some residual differences between the South and the rest of the United States; in others, the South may be aiming at a moving target; in still other areas—in some aspects of religion and politics, for example—the South does not seem to be changing at all or seems to be changing *away* from the national norm.

In one respect, however, there seems little question that regional differences are evaporating: the traditional value orientation that has served as an ethnic marker, distinguishing Southerners, in the aggregate, from other Americans, is on the wane. I once saw one of those sappy posters, probably mass-produced in California, with a yellow "Happy Face" and the legend "Today is the first day of the rest of your life." Some philosopher had altered it to read "Today is the last day of the first part of your life." This elegiac posture may be a characteristically Southern stance, but the revised statement is certainly as accurate. As new things begin, old ones end. Southernness as we have known it is almost over. It seems to have a future, but in some new form, as yet indistinct.

Perhaps, in some sense, the regional differences that are going away are "the important ones" and may somehow *count* more than the ones that remain. Certainly those—on both political right and left—who feel

From "The End of the Beginning" by John Shelton Reed, in *Southerners: The Social Psychology of Sectionalism*, by John Shelton Reed. © 1983 The University of North Carolina Press. Reprinted by permission.

that racism is central to Southern culture will find the decreasing differences in that respect of tremendous and perhaps decisive importance. But that judgment is imposed from outside: most Southerners do not regard the "Southern way of life" as identical with or even particularly dependent on racial oppression. (Although 21 percent of our sample agreed that "the best thing about the Southern way of life was racial segregation," 64 percent disagreed, most of them vehemently.) . . . Most people talked about manners, friendliness, morality, style and "pace" when we asked about important regional differences.

In short, although the content of Southernness is changing, it still is believed to have some content. Moreover, the other, persistent differences between Southerners and other Americans imply that regional categories will remain a useful way to organize the data of experience, not just for survey researchers (who always include region as a "face-sheet datum") but for ordinary Americans who have occasion to interact with people from different regions. Even if this were not the case, of course, regional concepts and regional stereotypes could be widely held, perpetuated by folklore, the educational system, and the mass media. As long as *non-Southerners* think of Southerners as "different"—whether because they *are* different or because non-Southerners have learned to think that way for some other reason—Southerners, our data suggest, will be pushed to think in those terms as well.

From the group's standpoint, and from my rather different one, the important differences are those (whatever they may be) that mark the group's boundaries, those that people *believe* are important. For any ethnic group, these are the critical differences. They are subject to change and some may even be fictitious, but as long as people believe that they set the group off from outsiders, the distinction between in-group and out-group will order people's thoughts, structure their behavior, and contribute to their identity.

As the anthropologist Fredrik Barth has put it, "The critical focus of investigation [in research on ethnicity is] the ethnic *boundary* that defines the group, not the cultural stuff that it encloses." He observes that "the fact of continuing dichotomization between members and outsiders" can remain even though the "cultural features that signal the boundary may change and the cultural characteristics of the members may likewise be transformed"; that boundaries can remain boundaries "despite what may figuratively be called the 'osmosis' of personnel through them"; and that "a drastic reduction of cultural differences between ethnic groups does not correlate in any simple way with a reduction in the organizational relevance of ethnic identities, or a breakdown in boundary-maintaining processes."

Barth's point of view implies that ethnic identity will be most salient at the group's boundary, recalling the paradox that underlies the confusing relationships among the variables that we have studied here. It is not those Southerners whose cognitive horizons are most constricted, not those most isolated from the American mainstream, who will find their regional identity most salient. Rather it is those who are most modern in background and experience—the increasing proportion of Southerners who live in cities, who have had a good deal of education, who travel and watch television and read, who do business with non-Southerners—who (if they are not lost to the regional group altogether) are most likely to think in regional terms, to categorize themselves and others as "Southerners" and "non-Southerners," and to believe that they know what that means.

Thus regional identification, a feeling of closeness to other Southerners and of community with them, may be threatened by the cultural changes that are making Southerners more like other Americans, but it is sustained by the fact that increasing numbers of Southerners have backgrounds and experiences that make that identification relevant to them. The fact that identification is not statistically associated to any great degree with the various "modernizing" variables we examined does not mean that these variables have nothing to do with identification; it means, rather, that they operate through two different mechanisms, both to increase it and to decrease it. Similarly, stereotyping of non-Southerners and prejudice against them are not associated because stereotyping (like regional consciousness, to which it is closely related) is increased by real or vicarious experiences with outsiders, but prejudice against them (closely linked to the traditional value orientation and its component of general ethnocentrism) is decreased by these same experiences.

Identification as a Southerner carries with it a good deal of emotional and cognitive freight, especially in the form of various grievances against the North and attachment to the historic symbols of the South, but it is more a correlate of sectional hostility than a cause of it. The latter can decrease, and it almost certainly is decreasing, without directly affecting regional identification.

So, at the end, we return to a general proposition: categories become groups, entities that enlist the loyalties and affect the self-definitions of their members, through their relations with other groups. Questions of identity are brought to consciousness for us, attributes become part of our selves, when we encounter others who are different, or who insist that we are different. Group membership is most salient at the social and cultural periphery of a group; at its core, other aspects of identity take precedence. In the United States in this century, the conditions of life increasingly put Southerners (and members of other "primordial" groups as well) "at the periphery," willy-nilly; these conditions increasingly pose the question, "Who are you?"—the answer to which, in other times and places, may have gone without saying. For some—for many, it appears—"a Southerner" is part of the answer.

This general observation is not a new one. Andrew Greeley has stated it perhaps most clearly and forcefully in an extended critique of the assimilationist assumptions that have underpinned much of American scholarship on ethnicity. He quotes Ilona Fabian: "People, while living in their own society, take their culture and identity to a great extent for granted. . . . [Q]uestions of cultural identity arise only when immigrants are asked by the host society, 'Who are you?'. . . . [T]he self-identification of the immigrant is not merely a reflection upon the old culture, [it is] also a response to a question posed by the host society in terms of its own categories." . . .

The sort of thing I am saying about Southerners is no longer particularly novel. Other people have been saying similar things about other groups in recent years. Why, then, are people reluctant to accept the logic of this argument when it is applied to American regional groups, in particular to Southerners? At the risk of sounding aggrieved, I will venture to suggest that there may be an element of wishful thinking in their unwillingness to accept this argument, an element most evident when outsiders betray their assumption that this tiresome business of Southern exceptionalism will soon be gone with the wind. And, to be fair, I should add that some natives have also looked forward with relief to the time when they could lay down the burden of Southern identity.

Apparently, however, Southernness still remains important, in some ways more important than ever. The South's "confrontation with mass society," as Alvin Bertrand called it, has indeed altered the region, in ways that were long ago predicted. But that confrontation has not reached the "final stage of more or less complete surrender" to mass society. Despite mass society, Southerners are and apparently will remain "different"; *because* of it (this analysis leads me to believe), they will remain aware of their difference. By doing so, however, they are no different—no different from the other cultural minorities that make up late twentieth-century American society.

⚓ *F U R T H E R   R E A D I N G*

Harry S. Ashmore, *An Epitaph for Dixie* (1957)
Fifteen Southerners, *Why the South Will Survive* (1981)
Joel Garreau, *The Nine Nations of North America* (1981)
Robert L. Hall and Carol B. Stack, eds., *Holding on to the Land and the Lord: Kinship, Ritual, Land Tenure, and Social Policy in the Rural South* (1982)
Florence King, *Southern Ladies and Gentlemen* (1975)
William Least Heat Moon, *Blue Highways* (1982)
John Shelton Reed, *The Enduring South* (1972)
——, *One South: An Ethnic Approach to Regional Culture* (1982)
Charles P. Roland, "The Ever-Vanishing South," *Journal of Southern History* 68 (1982), 3–20